Property, Trusts and Succession

George Gretton dedicates this book to EFG
and
Andrew Steven dedicates it to his parents

Property, Trusts and Succession

by

George L Gretton
Lord President Reid Professor of Law, University of Edinburgh

and

Andrew J M Steven
Lecturer in Law, University of Edinburgh

with a chapter on human rights by
Alison E C Struthers
Part-time Tutor, School of Law, University of Edinburgh

Tottel
publishing

Tottel Publishing Ltd
Maxwelton House
41–43 Boltro Road
Haywards Heath
West Sussex
RH16 1BJ

British Library Cataloguing-in-Publication Data
A CIP Catalogue record for this book is available from the British Library.

ISBN 978 1 84592 153 8

Preface

This book is aimed at LLB students in Scotland studying property, trusts and succession. We attempt to explain, often by use of examples, the rules of statute and common law which apply in these areas. While the book is about Scots law, we both believe firmly in the value of comparative study. We have therefore made reference in a number of places to the position in other legal systems.

In preparing the book we have benefited greatly from the course handouts used at the University of Edinburgh and in this regard we owe a particular debt to our fellow teachers, Professor Kenneth Reid and Dr Martin Hogg. The influence of Professor Reid's great contribution to Scots property law will be apparent in much of this book. The assistance of Professor Roderick Paisley (University of Aberdeen) and Scott Wortley (University of Edinburgh) has also been much appreciated. And thanks are due to John Glover and others of the Department of the Registers of Scotland for providing the sample land certificate reproduced in chapter 6.

Finally, we are very grateful to Alison Struthers for contributing the chapter on human rights.

George L Gretton

Andrew J M Steven

4 December 2008

Contents

Contents

16   Rivers, lochs and the sea

Contents

Contents

Table of statutes

Table of statutory instruments

Table of cases

C

L

M

List of abbreviations

STATUTES

AB(S)A 2004	Antisocial Behaviour etc. (Scotland) Act 2004
AFT(S)A 2000	Abolition of Feudal Tenure etc (Scotland) Act 2000
AH(S)A 1991	Agricultural Holdings (Scotland) Act 1991
AH(S)A 2003	Agricultural Holdings (Scotland) Act 2003
ALC(S)A 1991	Age of Legal Capacity (Scotland) Act 1991
A(S)A 1987	Animals (Scotland) Act 1987
B(S)A 2003	Building (Scotland) Act 2003
CFR(S)A 1970	Conveyancing and Feudal Reform (Scotland) Act 1970
CIA 1994	Coal Industry Act 1994
CPA 2004	Civil Partnership Act 2004
C(S)A 1993	Crofters (Scotland) Act 1993
CTI(S)A 2005	Charities and Trustee Investment (Scotland) Act 2005
FL(S)A 1985	Family Law (Scotland) Act 1985
FL(S)A 2006	Family Law (Scotland) Act 2006
HRA 1998	Human Rights Act 1998
H(S)A 1987	Housing (Scotland) Act 1987
H(S)A 1988	Housing (Scotland) Act 1988
H(S)A 2001	Housing (Scotland) Act 2001
H(S)A 2006	Housing (Scotland) Act 2006
LR(MP)(S)A 1985	Law Reform (Miscellaneous Provisions) (Scotland) Act 1985
LR(MP)(S)A 1990	Law Reform (Miscellaneous Provisions) (Scotland) Act 1990
LR(S)A 1979	Land Registration (Scotland) Act 1979
LR(S)A 2003	Land Reform (Scotland) Act 2003
MH(FP)(S)A 1981	Matrimonial Homes (Family Protection) (Scotland) Act 1981
PL(S)A 1973	Prescription and Limitation (Scotland) Act 1973
RoW(S)A 1995	Requirements of Writing (Scotland) Act 1995
SOGA 1979	Sale of Goods Act 1979

S(S)A 1964	Succession (Scotland) Act 1964
TC(S)A 2003	Title Conditions (Scotland) Act 2003
T(S)A 1921	Trusts (Scotland) Act 1921
T(S)A 1961	Trusts (Scotland) Act 1961
T(S)A 2004	Tenements (Scotland) Act 2004

BOOKS

Bankton	A McDouall, Lord Bankton *An Institute of the Laws of Scotland in Civil Rights* (1751–53, reprinted by the Stair Society, vols 41–43, 1993–95)
Bell *Commentaries*	G J Bell *Commentaries on the Law of Scotland and the Principles of Mercantile Jurisprudence* (7th edn by J McLaren, 1870; reprinted 1990)
Bell *Principles*	G J Bell *Principles of the Law of Scotland* (10th edn by W Guthrie, 1899, reprinted 1989)
Carey Miller with Irvine *Corporeal Moveables*	D L Carey Miller with D Irvine *Corporeal Moveables in Scots Law* (2nd edn, 2005)
Chalmers *Trusts*	J Chalmers *Trusts: Cases and Materials* (2002)
Cusine and Paisley *Servitudes*	D J Cusine and R R M Paisley *Servitudes and Rights of Way* (1998)
Erskine	J Erskine of Carnock *An Institute of the Law of Scotland* (8th edn by J B Nicholson, 1871, reprinted 1989)
Gloag and Henderson *The Law of Scotland*	W M Gloag and R C Henderson *The Law of Scotland* (12th edn by Lord Coulsfield and H L MacQueen, 2007)
Gloag and Irvine *Rights in Security*	W M Gloag and J M Irvine *Law of Rights in Security, Heritable and Moveable including Cautionary Obligations* (1897, reprinted 1987)
Gordon *Scottish Land Law*	W M Gordon *Scottish Land Law* (2nd edn, 1999)
Gretton and Reid *Conveyancing*	G L Gretton and K G C Reid *Conveyancing* (3rd edn, 2004)
Halliday *Conveyancing*	J M Halliday *Conveyancing Law and Practice in Scotland* (2nd edn by I J S Talman) vols I (1996) and II (1997)

Hiram *Succession*	H Hiram *The Scots Law of Succession* (2nd edn, 2007)
Hume *Lectures*	Baron David Hume *Lectures 1786-1822* (ed by G C H Paton, Stair Society vols. 5, 13, 15, 17– 19, 1939–58)
Johnston *Prescription*	D Johnston *Prescription and Limitation* (1999)
Macdonald *Succession*	D R Macdonald *An Introduction to the Scots Law of Succession* (3rd edn, 2001)
MacQueen and Thomson *Contract*	H L MacQueen and J Thomson *Contract Law in Scotland* (2nd edn, 2007)
McAllister *Leases*	A McAllister *Scottish Law of Leases* (3rd edn, 2002)
McBryde *Contract*	W W McBryde *The Law of Contract in Scotland* (3rd edn, 2007)
McDonald *Conveyancing Manual*	D A Brand, A J M Steven and S Wortley *Professor McDonald's Conveyancing Manual* (7th edn, 2004)
Paisley *Land Law*	R Paisley *Land Law* (2000)
Paisley and Cusine *Unreported Cases*	R R M Paisley and D J Cusine *Unreported Property Cases from the Sheriff Court* (2000)
Rankine *Landownership*	J Rankine *The Law of Landownership in Scotland* (4th edn, 1909)
Registration of Title Practice Book	I Davis and A Rennie (eds) *Registration of Title Practice Book: A guide to land registration in Scotland* (2nd edn, 2000)
Reid *Feudal Abolition*	K G C Reid, *The Abolition of Feudal Tenure in Scotland* (2003)
Reid *Property*	K G C Reid (with G L Gretton, A G M Duncan, W M Gordon and A J Gamble) *The Law of Property in Scotland* (1996), being a revised reprint of *The Laws of Scotland: Stair Memorial Encyclopaedia* vol 18
Reid and Gretton *Conveyancing*	The annual series of update volumes by K G C Reid and G L Gretton, differentiated by year, e.g. Reid and Gretton *Conveyancing 2007*

Reid and Zimmermann *History*	K Reid and R Zimmermann (eds) *A History of Private Law in Scotland*, vols 1 (Introduction and Property) and 2 (Obligations) (2000)
Rennie *Land Tenure*	R Rennie *Land Tenure in Scotland* (2004)
Stair	J Dalrymple, 1st Viscount Stair *Institutions of the Law of Scotland* (6th edn, by D M Walker, 1981)
SME	Sir Thomas Smith et al (eds) *The Laws of Scotland: Stair Memorial Encyclopaedia* (25 vols, 1987–96) with cumulative supplements and reissues
Wilson and Duncan *Trusts*	W A Wilson and A G M Duncan *Trusts, Trustees and Executors* (2nd edn, 1995)
Zimmermann, Visser and Reid *Mixed Legal Systems*	R Zimmermann, D Visser and K Reid *Mixed Legal Systems in Comparative Perspective: Property and Obligations in Scotland and South Africa* (2004)

OTHER

BGB	Bürgerliches Gesetzbuch (German Civil Code)
Cc	Code civil (French Civil Code)
ECHR	European Convention on Human Rights
ECtHR	European Court of Human Rights
OSCR	Office of the Scottish Charity Regulator
TMS	Tenement Management Scheme

Glossary

Necessarily, we have been selective. In many cases what is given is a general, imperfect definition. For the Latin terms we have sometimes preferred an explanation to a literal translation. Where a word or phrase is in **bold** it is explained elsewhere in the Glossary.

Accession (*accessio*)	The attachment of one thing to another so as to become part of it, such as paint to a wall.
A non domino	From a non-owner.
Aemulatio vicini	Spiteful acts against a neighbour.
Animus acquirendi	The intention to acquire.
Animus dominii	The intention to hold as owner.
Animus sibi habendi	The intention to hold for one's own use.
Animus transferendi	The intention to transfer.
Animus revocandi	The intention to revoke.
Assignation	Transfer of **incorporeal property**.
Assignatus utitur jure auctoris	An assignee takes the same right as the **cedent** had.
Benefited property	The land benefited by **a real burden** or **servitude**. The more traditional term is **'dominant tenement'**.
Bona fides – in bona fide	Good faith – in good faith.
Bona vacantia	Ownerless property.
Burdened property	The land burdened by a **real burden** or **servitude**. The more traditional term is **'servient tenement'**.
Cedent	Assignor.
Conditio si institutus sine liberis decesserit	Literally, the condition that the institute dies childless. For the real meaning, see ch 27.
Conditio si testator sine liberis decesserit	Literally, the condition that the testator dies childless. For the real meaning, see ch 27.
Corporeal property	Tangible property.
Crown	The monarch. In reality the state.

De cujus	The deceased person whose estate is being wound up.
Derivative acquisition	Transfer of property where the transferee acquires the transferor's title.
Disposition – dispone	Deed transferring land – to grant a disposition.
Dominant tenement	The more traditional term for **benefited property**.
Dominium	**Ownership.**
Erga omnes	With effect as against everyone; against 'the world'.
Ex lege	By force of law.
Ex voluntate	By force of will, i.e. intentional.
Feudal system	The system of tenure which existed in Scotland until 28 November 2004, under which land was not held absolutely but of **superiors** and ultimately of the **Crown**.
Floating charge	**Right in security** that can be granted only by business organisations.
Heritable property	Generally speaking, land or rights in land.
Heritable security	**Right in security** over **heritable property**.
Hypothec	**Right in security** in which the debtor retains **possession**.
Improper liferent	**Liferent** under which the thing is held by trustees and the holder of the liferent is a beneficiary under the **trust**.
Incorporeal property	Intangible property.
Intestate	Opposite of **testate**.
Intimation	Formal notification of **assignation**.
Involuntary transfer	**Derivative acquisition** which does not require the consent of the transferor.
Inter vivos	Between living persons, as opposed to *mortis causa*.
Juridical act	A voluntary and lawful act that makes a change in the legal universe, such as making a contract, granting a **disposition**, paying a debt. Also called a juristic act.
Jus in re aliena	Right in another person's property – i.e. subordinate **real right**.
Jus relictae (jus relicti)	Indefeasible succession right of widow (widower).
Keeper	The Keeper of the Registers of Scotland, who administers numerous registers including the **Land Register**.

Land Register	The newer register of land, established by the LR(S)A 1979.
Land certificate	Official copy of a **title sheet**.
Lex domicilii	The law of the place where the person in question is domiciled.
Lex situs	The law of the place where the property is situated.
Lease	Contract under which one person, the lessor, grants to another, the lessee, the right to use the property for a fixed time in return for a periodical payment known as rent. It is capable of becoming a **real right**, by **possession** or registration depending on the type of lease. A long lease (over 20 years) can be registered.
Legacy	Right to money or property given in a **testament**. Also called bequest.
Legatee	Beneficiary of a **legacy**.
Legal rights	In succession law, the indefeasible rights of spouse (*jus relictae/i*) and issue (**legitim**) to a part of the estate.
Legitim	The indefeasible succession rights of issue.
Lien	A possessory **right in security** arising by implication of law.
Liferent	The right to use a thing for life.
Mala fides – in male fide	Bad faith – in bad faith.
Missives	Letters collectively forming a contract. When the contract is formed the missives are said to be 'concluded'.
Mortis causa	On account of death.
Moveable property	All property which is not **heritable**.
Nemo dat quod non habet	Nobody transfers what he or she does not have.
Nemo plus juris ad alienum transferre potest quam ipse haberet	Nobody can transfer to another more right than he or she has.
Numerus clausus	Closed list. There is a numerus clausus of **real rights**.
Occupancy (*occupatio*)	The appropriation of something ownerless.
Original acquisition	Where an acquirer of property obtains a brand new title.
Ownership	The principal and most extensive **real right**, defined classically as the right to use, consume and destroy.
Patrimonial rights	Rights with economic value, such as **real rights** and **personal rights**.

Patrimony	The totality of a person's (a) **patrimonial rights** and (b) liabilities.
Personal right	Right enforceable only against a specific person or limited class of persons. Example: contractual right.
Pledge	**Right in security** over corporeal moveable property requiring delivery to the creditor.
Possession	The control of a thing with the intention to hold it for one's own use.
Prescription	Negative prescription is the extinction of **personal** or **real rights** by the running of time. Positive prescription is the acquisition of **real rights** by the running of time.
Prior tempore potior jure	Earlier by time, stronger by right.
Pro indiviso	Shared (title). Example: a couple buy a house together. Each has a *pro indiviso* share of the property.
Proper liferent	**Liferent** where the holder has a real right in the thing.
Real burden	An obligation affecting land, normally of a positive or negative character.
Real right	Right in a thing enforceable against the world. Two types are (i) **ownership** and (ii) **subordinate real rights**.
Right in security	A right held by a creditor against a debtor in addition to his or her personal right to recover the debt, which improves the chances of payment. Where it is a right in a piece of property it is known as a real security.
Sasine Register	The older register of land, established by the Registration Act 1617. Full name is the General Register of Sasines. Gradually being replaced by the **Land Register**.
Separate tenement	**Heritable property** owned separately from ownership of the ground.
Servient tenement	The more traditional term for **burdened property**.
Servitude	**Real right** which allows a landowner to make limited use of neighbouring land.
Specification (*specificatio*)	Creation of new thing, eg barley into ale.
Standard security	**Heritable security** regulated by the 1970 Act.
Subjects	Not the subject but the object (in the singular). A conveyancer might say 'my client bought the subjects last year', meaning the house or farm etc.

Subordinate real right	**Real right** other than **ownership**. Some examples: **servitude, right in security, liferent.**
Superior	Under the now abolished **feudal system**, a person of whom land was held.
Tantum praescriptum quantum possessum	**Prescription** is measured by **possession**.
Tenement	Building in which different parts belong to different persons.
Testament	A testament is a direction as to what is to happen after death. Also called a will.
Testate	An estate is testate if there is an operative **testament**, in which case the law of testate succession applies.
Testing clause	Clause of attestation at end of deed.
Title sheet	The **Land Register** is divided into title sheets, one for each property, giving plan of property, name of owner, subordinate **real rights**.
Traditionibus, non nudis pactis, dominia rerum, transferuntur	**Ownership** is transferred by an external act, not by mere contract.
Trust	Where property is held by a trustee or trustees for the benefit of a beneficiary or beneficiaries.
Ultimus haeres	Ultimate heir. (Failing any nearer heir, the **Crown** is the ultimate heir.)
Vassal	Under the now abolished **feudal system**, a person who held land of a **superior**.
Vigilantibus non dormientibus jura subveniunt	If you snooze you lose.
Warrandice	Guarantee.

Chapter 1

Introduction

WHAT IS PROPERTY LAW?

1.1 In its narrow sense, property law is the law of physical things, such as land and buildings, apples and bicycles. When people speak of 'property' they often mean just land or buildings, that is to say 'immoveable' property. Nevertheless, things such as apples and bicycles are also property – moveable property. Whilst there are important legal differences between moveables and immoveables,[1] both lie in the

---

[1] E.g. as to the precise rules on transfer.

field of property law. Moveables are not necessarily less valuable than immoveables: a painting by Raphael is worth much more than an average house. Property law deals with the *rights* that people can have in *things*. The most important of these rights is ownership, but there are other types of property right as well, such as servitudes[2] and leases.[3] Property law deals with the creation, transfer and extinction of such rights.

1.2 Property law also has a broader sense. Suppose that Jack borrows £1,000 from Jill, and she transfers her right to repayment to Mary. What is transferred is a contractual right, and so not a property right in the narrow sense. A contractual right is a right as between two persons. But when we look outside that person-to-person relationship, a contractual right can behave rather like a property right (narrow sense). For example, in many ways the general law about the transfer of rights is the same regardless of whether the right being transferred is a personal right (such as a contractual right) or a right of (for example) ownership of land.[4] Hence, as far as *third parties* are concerned, contractual rights are property rights. So, in its broader sense, property law includes not only rights in physical things but also other types of right – provided that they are patrimonial rights, as contractual rights are.[5]

1.3 Succession law is sometimes seen as part of property law: roughly speaking, it deals with what happens to property on death. Sometimes it is seen as part of family law or, to take the larger category, the law of persons. And sometimes it is seen as a separate branch of private law. Much the same can be said of trust law, for, however one likes to classify the law, succession and trusts are closely linked. The remainder of this chapter for the most part deals with property law in its narrower sense: trusts and succession are treated later.[6]

HISTORICAL AND COMPARATIVE

1.4 The relationship between Scots law and English law varies according to the area. Property law (other than intellectual property law) differs sharply north and south of the border. So the student must beware of the use of English sources. Though there has also been some English influence, Scots property law is based ultimately on Roman law and thus has much in common with continental systems.[7]

---

[2] A servitude is a right in favour of one property over a neighbouring property, such as a private right of way. See CHAPTER **12** below.

[3] See CHAPTER **19** below.

[4] See CHAPTER **4** below.

[5] For patrimonial rights, see PARA **1.8** below.

[6] See CHAPTERS **22** AND **25** below.

[7] We reproduce, without comment, the remarks of the English judge Lord Hobhouse of Woodborough in the Scottish case of *Burnett's Tr v Grainger* 2004 SC (HL) 19 at para 53: 'What does surprise me is that Scotland, now a highly developed economy, should have a land law which is still based on the judicial development, albeit sophisticated, of the laws of Rome … .'

As a result, Scots property lawyers tend to be less interested in English property law than in the civilian systems[8] and mixed systems[9] such as those of Louisiana, South Africa and Sri Lanka. Although the detailed rules vary considerably among such systems, the basic ideas and principles tend to be similar, because of the common origins.

> 'A lawyer trained in Scotland can without difficulty (other than linguistic difficulty) read and understand a book about the law of property in Germany … But he is likely to be perplexed and bewildered by a book on the law of property in England.'[10]

1.5   Most property law systems in Europe, including Scotland, adopted feudal law. This affected land but not moveables. Scotland was slow in removing it. It was reduced in importance by a long series of enactments starting in the fifteenth century, and by the end of the twentieth century little remained. That little was abolished, on 28 November 2004, by the Abolition of Feudal Tenure etc. (Scotland) Act 2000.[11] Feudalism played a major role not only in the history of Scots property law, but indeed in the entire history of Scots law, and accordingly even now the student needs to know something about it.[12] Finally, a word should be said about udal law. In most respects Scots law applies in Orkney and Shetland as it does elsewhere, but there are certain local rules applicable there, collectively known as 'udal law', deriving from the Norwegian law that was operative in Orkney and Shetland at the time of their annexation by Scotland in the second half of the fifteenth century.[13] Udal law is non-feudal, so one effect of feudalism's abolition has to lessen yet further the distinctiveness of the udal rules.

THE SOURCES OF PROPERTY LAW: STATUTE LAW AND COMMON LAW

1.6   Property law is a mixture of statutory law and common law. The statutory law is, unfortunately for the student, not dealt with in a single core statute. In countries where there is a civil code the main principles of property law, or most of them, are in the code,[14] with other statutes dealing with supplementary matters, such as land

---

[8]   'Civilian' systems are those in whose history the influence of Roman law has been particularly strong. Roman law has influenced English law, and the many systems rooted in English law, but only to a limited extent.

[9]   'Mixed' systems are those in which there is a mixture of civilian and English influence.

[10]   Reid *Property* para 2.

[11]   According to Lord Rodger of Earlsferry *The Courts, the Church and the Constitution: Aspects of the Disruption of 1843* (2008) 95, the feudal system was 'unceremoniously binned by the Scottish Parliament – unmourned even by its supposed acolytes, the Professors of Conveyancing'.

[12]   See the **APPENDIX** at the end of the book.

[13]   See, e.g., Gordon *Scottish Land Law* paras 3-08–3-10.

[14]   E.g. Book 3 of the BGB.

registration rules. There is nothing like that in Scotland. For example, many of the basic topics mentioned in this chapter, such as the real/personal,[15] heritable/moveable[16] and corporeal/incorporeal[17] distinctions, are largely or wholly non-statutory. Sometimes the mixture is odd. Thus the rules about the passing of ownership of, say, a bicycle, are statutory where the reason for the transfer is a contract of sale, but they are common law in other cases. Hence if Pete gives (donates) his bicycle to Rosi, ownership cannot pass without delivery[18] while if he sells it to her, ownership can pass without delivery.[19] The statutory material is scattered over numerous separate enactments, some rather old. In this book the student will encounter such still-in-force legislation as the Royal Mines Act 1424[20] and the Leases Act 1449.[21] This mixture of common law and statute, and the fact that the statutory law is scattered, make it harder to get a feel for the sources.

REFORM

1.7 Law is a ship that is being constantly reconstructed while it is afloat. That is as true of property law as it is of other topics. Law reform is not some modern enthusiasm. Anyone who reads through the statute book of the fifteenth century will see a good deal of property law reform, and the process has been going on ever since. For example, on 28 November 2004, there was major reform when three statutes came into force: the Abolition of Feudal Tenure etc. (Scotland) Act 2000 mentioned already; the Title Conditions (Scotland) Act 2003; and the Tenements (Scotland) Act 2004. The process continues, with the Scottish Law Commission tending to perform the lead role.[22] For example, there is currently a proposal for the reform of the law of land registration,[23] another for the reform of trust law[24] and another for the reform of the law of succession.[25]

PATRIMONY AND THE PATRIMONIAL RIGHTS

1.8 A patrimonial right is a right with an economic value. An obvious example is ownership of land: it is a patrimonial right. The ownership of moveable property, such as a bicycle, is equally a patrimonial right. If Alan owns land and grants to Beth

---

[15]   See PARAS **1.14–1.17** below.
[16]   See PARAS **1.20–1.21** below.
[17]   See PARA **1.19** below.
[18]   See PARA **5.17** below.
[19]   SOGA 1979. See PARA **5.21** below.
[20]   See PARA **14.17** below.
[21]   See PARA **19.11** below.
[22]   Scottish Law Commission publications are available at: http://www.scotlawcom.gov.uk/.
[23]   See PARA **6.13** below.
[24]   See PARA **22.2** below.
[25]   See PARA **25.3** below.
[26]   See CHAPTER **21** below.

the right to use it for her life (this is called a liferent[26]), that too is a patrimonial right. Contractual rights are patrimonial too. If Beth lends Alan £1,000, her right to be paid is a patrimonial right. If she writes a bestseller, her copyright is a patrimonial right. In short, a patrimonial right is what a businessperson or an accountant would call an asset. Such rights are sometimes called property rights, using 'property' in a broad sense.

1.9 Some rights are non-patrimonial. Examples are the right to vote, the right to marry, the right to make a will, the right to have a passport and the right not to be defamed. If such rights are violated, that may give rise to a right to be paid damages, and a right to damages *is* a patrimonial right. But the underlying right, the right that was violated, was non-patrimonial.[27] That is not to say that the law of delict protects only non-patrimonial rights. It equally protects patrimonial rights.

1.10 *Patrimony* is the totality of a person's assets (patrimonial rights) and liabilities. For example, a company's balance sheet sets out its patrimony. The term 'estate' is sometimes used instead.[28] A patrimony is like a suitcase with two compartments: one for assets and the other for liabilities. Every person (whether a natural person or a juristic person such as a company) has a patrimony: *personality implies patrimony*. But of course the patrimony may have little in it: a newborn baby has a patrimony, because it is a person, but the suitcase is, for the time being, an empty one.

1.11 Although every person must have a patrimony, it is not the case that every person has just one patrimony. 'One person, one patrimony' is indeed the norm, but in certain special cases a person may have more than one patrimony. That is called a trust.[29]

PRIVATE LAW AND PUBLIC LAW

General

1.12 Property law is part of private law. There are, however, public law aspects to property. For example, planning law[30] and licensing law[31] belong to public law but relate to property. Another example is capital gains tax.[32] This book does not deal

---

[27] Delict law distinguishes between (i) damages for patrimonial harm; and (ii) damages for non-patrimonial harm. For example, if a careless driver runs down a cyclist, the damages for the destruction of the bicycle are for patrimonial harm, but the damages for the cyclist's physical suffering are for non-patrimonial harm. But in each case the damages themselves constitute a patrimonial right: thus the cyclist might be entitled to £500 for each. The £1,000 claim is an asset.

[28] But 'estate' has several different meanings.

[29] See **CHAPTER 22** below.

[30] See, e.g., A McAllister *Scottish Planning Law* (3rd edn, forthcoming, 2009).

[31] See, e.g., J C Cummins *Licensing (Scotland) Act 2005* (2006).

[32] See, e.g., N Lee et al *Revenue Law – Principles and Practice* (25th edn, 2007) chs 19–27.

with the public law aspects of property, except occasionally.[33] That is not to say that those aspects are not important. They are. For example, the lawyers acting for a company that wishes to buy land and develop it for commercial purposes will have to be as much concerned with the public law aspects as with the private law ones.[34]

Location within private law

1.13 The Romans divided private law into (i) the law of persons; (ii) the law of things; and (iii) the law of actions[35] – *who* has rights, *what* rights there are and *how* rights are enforced. By 'things' they meant the whole of the law of obligations and the law of property. The Scotland Act defines 'Scots private law' as meaning:

'(a) the general principles of private law (including private international law),
(b) the law of persons (including natural persons, legal persons and unincorporated bodies),
(c) the law of obligations (including obligations arising from contract, unilateral promise, delict, unjustified enrichment and negotiorum gestio),
(d) the law of property (including heritable and moveable property, trusts and succession), and
(e) the law of actions (including jurisdiction, remedies, evidence, procedure, diligence, recognition and enforcement of court orders, limitation of actions and arbitration)'.[36]

This is the Roman classification, modified. A preliminary category (general principles) has been added, while the 'things' category has been split into two – the law of obligations and the law of property. This book is about paragraph (d). Although obligations and property fall into separate categories, it has been seen[37] that rights arising out of the law of obligations are, in relation to third parties, part of property law in its broad sense.

REAL RIGHTS AND PERSONAL RIGHTS

Personal rights

1.14 A personal right[38] is a right against a person. Contracts result in reciprocal personal rights. For example, if Fiona owns a house and enters a contract of sale with Hamish, the result is that she has a personal right against him (to be paid the

---

33   Our main departure from the general rule is public access rights. See CHAPTER **18** below.
34   For a general overview, see McDonald *Conveyancing Manual* ch 20.
35   '*Omne autem jus ... vel ad personas pertinet, vel ad res, vel ad actiones*' (Justinian *Institutes* 1, 3, 12).
36   Scotland Act 1998, s 126. It adds: ' ... and include references to judicial review of administrative action'. Many would regard that topic as belonging to public law.
37   See PARA **1.8** above.
38   *Jus personale* or *jus in personam.*

price) and he has a personal right against her (to be given possession and also a deed of transfer, called a disposition).[39] Likewise, if John is liable to Kate in the law of delict, in the sense that he must pay her damages, that is a personal right for Kate. Unlike a contract, there is no reciprocity here.

Real rights

1.15   A real right is a right directly in a thing.[40] The main example is ownership. When Fiona performs the contract of sale by transferring ownership to Hamish, he will have acquired the real right of ownership. Previously, at the contract stage, he had a personal right against Fiona, but no right in the house itself. What he had was a personal right to acquire ownership of the house.[41] Now he has the right of ownership itself. Just as there are different kinds of personal right, so there are different kinds of real right. In CHAPTER 2 these will be considered, but the right of ownership is the primary one.

Comparison

1.16   The holder of a personal right has a power – over the other person. The holder of a real right has a power – over the thing. A personal right is as good as the person against whom it is held. If Jack borrows £1,000 from Jill, and she is able and willing to repay, his claim is virtually as good as if it were cash. But if she becomes insolvent, it is of limited value. For example, if she is sequestrated[42] and her trustee pays creditors at 5%, that claim is worth only £50. A real right is as good as a thing. If Jack owns a rare book worth £1,000, and it is destroyed in a fire, Jack has nothing but ashes. So the question of whether real rights or personal rights are 'better' is an absurd one: everything depends on context. If Jill is insolvent, Jack would prefer 1,000 £1 coins to the claim against her. But coins can be stolen, which is why people commonly prefer to have personal rights against banks rather than keeping much cash. (To have money in the bank is to be owed money by the bank: it is a debtor just as much as Fiona is.)

1.17   Personal rights are sometimes called 'relative rights', and real rights are sometimes called 'absolute rights', or rights 'against the world' or *erga omnes*.[43] That is because a real right can be regarded as being a set of personal rights against

---

[39]   See PARA **4.1** below.

[40]   *Jus reale*, or *jus in rem*, or *jus in re*. The Latin word *res* means 'thing' and the adjective formed from it is *realis* (or *reale* in the neuter form), whence the word 'real'.

[41]   *Jus in personam ad rem acquirendam*.

[42]   Sequestration is what non-lawyers call bankruptcy. The insolvent debtor's assets pass to the trustee in sequestration, who realises them for the benefit of the creditors. The current statute is the Bankruptcy (Scotland) Act 1985.

[43]   *Erga omnes* – as against everyone.

everyone in the world. Hamish's right of ownership is good not just against one person (as his contractual right against Fiona was) but against everybody. Everybody has the duty not to interfere with the house. This idea that real rights are, so to speak, multiple personal rights, rights against each of the 6.7 billion inhabitants of this planet, is sometimes called the 'personalist theory', whilst the theory that real rights are rights in things is sometimes called the 'classical theory'. There are difficulties with both views. At this level it is not necessary to discuss the issue.[44]

Intellectual property

1.18 Intellectual property rights, such as copyright and patents, are sometimes regarded as real rights, because they are clearly not personal rights (there is nobody against whom they are held) and they are absolute. Others disagree, arguing that real rights can exist only in physical things, and that therefore the class of absolute rights is broader than the class of real rights. The issue will not be discussed further here, especially because intellectual property rights are not covered by the present work.[45]

CORPOREAL AND INCORPOREAL

1.19 'Corporeal' property relates to physical things such as bicycles and houses while 'incorporeal' property means everything else. If the distinction is framed in terms of rights rather than things, then real rights of ownership are corporeal property while everything else (notably personal rights, and subordinate real rights) is incorporeal property. If Jack owes Jill £1,000, that is, from Jill's point of view, an asset just as much as a bicycle is an asset and it is incorporeal moveable property. If Jill writes a book, she has copyright in it, and copyright is incorporeal moveable property. If she buys shares in a company, those shares are incorporeal moveable property. And so on.

HERITABLE AND MOVEABLE

1.20 A second distinction is between 'heritable' and 'moveable' property. 'Heritable' is perhaps a misleading term because it suggests that only heritable property can be inherited. That is not so: moveable property can be inherited as well. Heritable property means land and rights connected with land.[46] Moveable property is everything else. The heritable/moveable distinction used to be vitally important in

---

[44] See, e.g., Paisley *Land Law* para 2.1.

[45] See, e.g., H MacQueen, C Waelde and G Laurie *Contemporary Intellectual Property: Law and Policy* (2007).

[46] 'Heritable' thus more or less matches 'immoveable' and indeed that latter term is sometimes used.

the law of succession. The answer to the question of who inherited on the death of the holder of the right would often depend on whether the property in question was heritable or moveable. Today the importance of the distinction is minor, though it continues to have a limited degree of significance in succession law.[47]

1.21 A field is heritable property. So is a house.[48] Any subordinate real right in heritable property is itself heritable, with the partial exception of security rights.[49] Contractual rights about real rights in land are heritable.[50] Thus if Donna owns land and Ewan contracts to buy it, his contractual right is itself heritable. Although, in general, heritable property is connected with land, there are two exceptions. Peerages, such as the earldom of Govan, are heritable property. So is the rather obscure category of rights that 'have a tract of future time' of which the accepted definition is Erskine's: 'rights of such a nature that they cannot be at once paid or fulfilled by the debtor, but continue for a number of years … without any relation to any capital sum or stock'.[51] This includes annuities and pensions.

COMBINING THE CATEGORIES

1.22 If the corporeal/incorporeal distinction and the heritable/moveable distinction are combined, four categories emerge. The first is corporeal moveable property, such as a bicycle. The second is corporeal heritable property, such as a house. The third is incorporeal moveable property, such as most contractual rights,[52] and all rights arising in delict and in unjustified enrichment. Company shares are another example, as are intellectual property rights. Finally, there is incorporeal heritable property, the main examples being subordinate real rights in land. One misconception is that all personal rights are moveable. That is not so. A contractual right to acquire land is personal and heritable.

THREE TERMS: 'PROPERTY', 'HERITABLE PROPERTY' AND 'LAND'

1.23 'She bought property in France.' We understand the speaker to mean immoveable property: in ordinary speech, as mentioned already,[53] that is how the

---

47 See PARA **25.36** below.
48 Anything that *accedes* to a thing becomes part of it, e.g. a house accedes to the land. See PARAS **8.8–8.12** below.
49 The security in itself is heritable. The debt it secures is moveable, except for some purposes: Titles to Land Consolidation (Scotland) Act 1868, s 117. See PARAS **25.37–25.42** below.
50 So not all heritable rights are real rights, although most are. Conversely, moveable rights may be personal (e.g. a contract right) or real (e.g. ownership of a bicycle). The misconception that heritable equals real, and moveable equals personal, is, however, a common one.
51 Erskine III, 2, 6.
52 The exception has already been mentioned: contractual rights about real rights in land.
53 See PARA **1.1** above.

word 'property' is often used. Sometimes it is used in a broader sense: 'That's my property!' might be said of property other than land, and we all know that what is at a lost property office is moveable property. The legal sense of 'property' is broad: thus 'property law' is not limited to immoveable property. When lawyers speak of 'heritable property' they are almost always using it as a synonym for immoveable property, even though, strictly speaking,[54] some heritable property is not immoveable. 'Land' tends to be used to mean immoveable property. Thus a house or a flat are 'land', and thus 'land registration' includes the registration of a small top-floor flat just as much as a large estate in Argyll. For instance, the Land Registration (Scotland) Act 1979 says that '"land" includes buildings and other structures and land covered with water'.[55] That definition is just for the purposes of that Act, but nevertheless it reflects the standard language of lawyers.

TRANSFER OF RIGHTS, CONSTITUTION OF RIGHTS, EXTINCTION OF RIGHTS

1.24   Much of property law is about the transfer of rights from one person to another, in other words, from one person's patrimony to another's. Different rights are transferred in different ways. The real right of ownership of land is transferred by registration in the Land Register: the outgoing owner's name is deleted and that of the incoming owner is substituted.[56] A right to money is transferred by notice to the debtor.[57] And so on.

1.25   But transfer is not the only thing that can happen to a right. There are also birth and death or, to use legal language, constitution (also called creation) and extinction. Taken in order of time, the three events are therefore constitution, transfer and extinction.[58] An example of creation would be where Oliver, owner of Blackmains, grants to his neighbour Nigella, owner of Whitemains, a servitude of way across his land.[59] That is a new right. If, a century later, Nigella's successor as owner of Whitemains grants a 'discharge' of the servitude, then the servitude is extinguished. Another example: Kate owns Greenmains, and grants to Linda a 100-year lease.[60] That creates a new right. A few years later, Linda assigns[61] the lease to Mandy. That is a transfer: an existing right is passed from one person to another. What has changed is not the right but its holder. Later still, Mandy agrees with the current owner (who may or may not still be Kate) that the lease will come to an end: that is extinction. Extinction is not a transfer. Kate does not become tenant to herself. The lease simply

---

54   See para **1.21** above.
55   LR(S)A 1979, s 28(1).
56   See paras **6.30–6.34** below.
57   See paras **5.38–5.51** below.
58   See also para **30.4** below.
59   On servitudes, see chapter **12** below.
60   On leases, see chapter **19** below.
61   See paras **5.38–5.51** below.

ceases to exist, like a bursting soap bubble. Often the same or similar steps are required to constitute, transfer or extinguish a right. For example, with a standard security all three events require registration.[62]

1.26 A given right may not experience all three events. For instance, a right might never be transferred. Most contractual rights, or other personal rights, are not.[63] If Jack, a decorator, contracts with Jill to redecorate her flat, it is unlikely that he will transfer his right to be paid to anyone else,[64] and it is very unlikely that she will transfer her right to have the flat redecorated. In theory it could happen: for example, before the work is done she sells the flat to someone else and also transfers the right against Jack. Again, extinction may never happen. Although contract rights tend to be short-lived, real rights are often long-lived and some, such as servitudes, are potentially everlasting. Ownership is often transferred but is not normally created or extinguished.

FURTHER READING

Carey Miller with Irvine *Corporeal Moveables* ch 1.

Gloag and Henderson *The Law of Scotland* chs 31–33.

Gordon *Scottish Land Law* ch 1.

Paisley *Land Law* ch 1.

Reid *Property* paras 1–16.

Reid, K 'Property Law: Sources and Doctrine' in Reid and Zimmermann *History* vol 1 at 185–210.

Thomson, J *Scots Private Law* (2006).

See also MacCormick, D N *Institutions of Law: An Essay in Legal Theory* (2007), which helps to locate property law within law in general, as does his shorter 'General Legal Concepts' (*SME Reissue* 2008).

To a large extent the basics of property law are common to the civilian and mixed systems. Reading about such other systems can be enlightening. Excellent texts available in English include the following:

Cohn, E J *Manual of German Law* (2nd edn, 1968), about which the same remarks can be made as about Planiol's book below.

Planiol, M F *Treatise on the Civil Law* (three vols, 1959, a translation of *Traité élémentaire de droit civil*). This is about French private law in general and contains an excellent account of property law. It is now a little out of date but the basics remain relevant.

---

[62]   See below, PARAS **20.43–20.56**.
[63]   If it is transferred, this is done by assignation. See below, PARAS **5.38–5.51**.
[64]   But larger businesses often do so.

Yiannopoulos, A N *Property: The Law of Things, Real Rights, Real Actions* (4th edn, 2001), which is about Louisiana law.

See also:

Badenhorst, P J, Pienaar, J M and Mostert, H (eds) *Silberberg and Schoeman's The Law of Property* (5th edn, 2006), which is about South African law, as is:

Van der Merwe, C G 'Things', in vol 27 of Joubert, W A (ed) *Law of South Africa* (2nd edn, 2001).

Chapter 2

Real rights

THE PRINCIPAL REAL RIGHT AND THE SUBORDINATE REAL RIGHTS

Ownership: the principal real right

2.1 The principal real right is *ownership*.[1] The person who has that right is called the 'owner' or 'proprietor'. The terms mean the same. Often ownership is the only

---

[1]   The Latin term, *dominium*, is often be encountered, as is *dominus* (owner).

real right in something, and indeed that is usually true for corporeal moveables. Janet has books and clothes and furniture and a bicycle. She owns them. In practice it is unlikely that anyone else has any real right in them. If she lends a book to Fergus, she remains the owner and he has no real right. Likewise, if the book is stolen from her, she is still the owner, and no real right is held by the thief.

Subordinate real rights

2.2 A subordinate real right can also be called a 'secondary real right', 'subsidiary real right', 'limited real right',[2] 'encumbrance' or, in Latin, a *jus*[3] *in re aliena*. The Latin expression neatly stresses that a subordinate real right exists in something that is owned by *someone else*. In other words, if there is a subordinate real right in something, there must be at least two real rights in it: the real right of ownership of X and the subordinate right of Y. In the last chapter,[4] we met Oliver, the owner of Blackmains, and Nigella, the owner of neighbouring Whitemains. Oliver granted to Nigella a 'servitude' allowing her to use a track across her land, including the right to drive vehicles. (The reason why he did this does not matter. It may be because money changed hands – i.e. she bought a servitude from him.) The servitude is registered in the Land Register, appearing in both the 'title sheet' for Blackmains and in that for Whitemains.[5] There are now two real rights in Blackmains: Oliver's real right of ownership and Nigella's real right of servitude.

2.3 Is this servitude any different from a contract between Oliver and Nigella that she can cross his land? In the short term, 'no'. In the long term, 'yes'. Suppose that after a couple of years Oliver sells Blackmains to Tara. Can Nigella carry on? If her right is contractual, the answer is 'no'. A contractual right is a personal right, a right against a person. That person is Oliver. Nigella has no contract with Tara. Tara can refuse to let Nigella cross her land. That may leave Nigella with a claim against Oliver for damages for breach of contract, but even if such a claim can be enforced it still does not mean that she can use the track. By contrast, a servitude is a real right – a right in the land itself, not a right against Oliver. So it matters not whether Blackmains is still owned by Oliver. A subordinate real right is like superglue. Nothing – or almost nothing – can detach it, regardless of who owns the thing itself.[6]

ENCUMBERED OWNERSHIP IS STILL OWNERSHIP

2.4 A plot of land might be encumbered by a dozen servitudes, a liferent, a long lease, three securities and a public right of way. These might dramatically lessen the

---

2   'Limited' is the commonest term internationally.
3   The plural of *jus* (right) is *jura*.
4   See PARA **1.25** above.
5   See PARA **6.18** below.
6   Though some subordinate rights are time-limited, such as lease and liferent. See CHAPTERS **19** AND **21** below.

value of the right of ownership.[7] For example, in 1720 the owner of Greymains grants a 999-year lease over it for a rent of £5 per annum. By the 21st century, most of the economic value of the land will be held by the current tenant. The right of ownership itself may be nearly worthless. Put another way, if the landlord sells, the price will in practice be very low, while if the tenant sells (i.e. sells the lease[8]) the price will be almost as high as it would have been if the tenant had been outright owner. Yet the landlord's right remains the right of ownership no matter how encumbered it may have become. Sometimes real rights are thought of as fragments of ownership that are split off to be held by somebody else. The expression 'dismemberments of ownership' is used in some legal systems,[9] though not in Scots law. Some people find this picture a useful one, but it must not be allowed to give the false impression that what remains is anything other than the right of ownership. Ownership is a well that remains a well, no matter how many bucketfuls are drawn.

REAL RIGHTS AND INSOLVENCY

2.5 The difference between (i) a contractual right; and (ii) a real right was illustrated above by the case where the owner transfers ownership.[10] The incoming owner will be bound by the real right but will not normally be bound by a contractual right. The same point could have been illustrated by the use of insolvency law. Suppose that Nigella has a contractual right, and Oliver then becomes insolvent. His creditors use diligence to attach the land.[11] Alternatively, he is sequestrated, which works as a collective diligence in favour of all creditors.[12] Nigella will find that she cannot enforce her right.

2.6 Nigella will have a claim for damages against Oliver but since Oliver is insolvent, the full amount will not be recoverable.[13] And here we see why insolvency is so interesting as a test of real right. In the example above, if Oliver is solvent, though Nigella loses her contractual access right she can recover its monetary equivalent – damages. But if the right is lost because of Oliver's insolvency, then damages, though claimable, cannot be recovered in full, and perhaps not at all. The theory of real rights would be important even if nobody ever became insolvent, but the danger of insolvency gives to that theory a special significance. A full understanding of property law requires a basic understanding of insolvency.

---

[7]   They do not lessen the value of the land.
[8]   Such a sale is implemented by assignation. See PARA **19.33** below.
[9]   E.g. France, Louisiana, Quebec and the Netherlands.
[10] See PARA **2.3** above.
[11] On diligence, see Gloag and Henderson *The Law of Scotland* ch 49.
[12] See Gloag and Henderson *The Law of Scotland* ch 50.
[13] It may be that nothing can be recovered: in many insolvencies ordinary creditors are paid at 0%.

MULTIPLE REAL RIGHTS IN THE SAME THING

2.7   The very concept of a subordinate real right means that there is more than one real right in the same thing:

   (i) the principal real right of ownership; and

   (ii) a subordinate real right held by somebody other than the owner of the thing.

There can also be more than one subordinate real right in something – i.e. a total of three or more real rights. Suppose that after granting the servitude to Nigella, Oliver grants a proper liferent[14] of Blackmains to Tess, and this too is registered in the Land Register. A proper liferent is a subordinate real right, that gives to the holder the right to possess the thing for the holder's lifetime. There are now three real rights:

   (i)   Oliver's real right of ownership;

   (ii) Nigella's real right of servitude; and

   (iii) Tess's real right of liferent.

Each is a direct and absolute right in the land. There could easily be more than three. For example, servitudes might exist in favour of several neighbours, and there are other subordinate real rights that have not yet been mentioned.[15] Most land is subject to subordinate real rights, and most moveable property is not. That is partly because three types of subordinate real right (servitude, negative real burden and lease[16]) can exist only in land but not in moveables, and partly because of practicalities.

2.8   A given person can hold more than one real right in the same property. For example, Zara and Alan are neighbours. Zara grants to Alan a servitude over her land. She also borrows some money from him and grants him a standard security. Alan now has two real rights over Zara's land. But an owner cannot hold any other real right, any real right other than the right of ownership itself. A subordinate real right is necessarily a right over the property of *someone else*. If Alan assigned his standard security to Zara, the result would not be that Zara held a standard security over her own property. The result would be that the standard security would be extinguished, by *confusio*.[17]

WHICH ARE THE SUBORDINATE REAL RIGHTS? THE *NUMERUS CLAUSUS*

2.9   Three types of subordinate real right have already been mentioned: servitude, liferent and security. There are some others, but just a few. The law recognises only

---

14   See **CHAPTER 21** below.

15   In particular, lease (**CHAPTER 19** below) and security (**CHAPTER 20** below).

16   Moveables can be leased (hired). But whereas a lease of immoveable property has real effect, the lease of moveable property does not. See **PARA 19.1** below.

17   There may be some exceptions to what is said in the text. E.g. Jennifer grants to Kitty a 100-year lease and Kitty grants to Lisa a 50-year sublease and Lisa assigns this to Jennifer. But the property aspects of subleases have not been much explored. See also **PARA 19.35** below.

certain types of real right. A choice can be made from a short menu: people cannot create their own. There is a contrast here with contract law. The law does, it is true, recognise certain specific types of contract – the nominate contracts – but people are free to modify those standard types as they see fit[18] and, indeed, to fashion wholly new types of contract – the innominate contracts. Property law is less flexible: it offers a fixed list of nominate real rights. This is sometimes called the *numerus clausus* ('closed number').[19] Whereas innominate contracts are competent, innominate real rights are not. 'Real rights' not on the list are not available. What are these recognised types of subordinate right? They are:

(i)   servitude;
(ii) negative real burden;[20]
(ii) proper liferent;[21]
(iv) right in security;[22] and
(v)   lease of land.[23]

Some of these in turn have subdivisions: for example, there are particular types of security right, such as pledge, lien and standard security.

2.10   Sometimes other rights are included in the list. One is the set of rights over land held by the public, such as public rights of way and public rights in the foreshore.[24] Such rights certainly resemble real rights but it can be argued that since they belong to public law rather than private law they should, strictly speaking, be classified as real rights. A second is 'exclusive privilege' which in effect means intellectual property rights.[25] Such rights are certainly very like real rights: they are absolute rights, not relative (personal) rights. The counter-argument is that they do not relate to physical property in any way. Some legal systems therefore divide absolute rights into two: real rights and intellectual property rights. A third is possession. It is a complex subject and one must distinguish possession as a fact (e.g. the thief is in possession), the right to possess (which the true owner has in relation to the goods both before and after they were stolen) and rights generated by the fact of possession.

---

[18]   There are some qualifications to this statement, especially where the contract is between (i) a business party; and (ii) a consumer. See, e.g., MacQueen and Thomson *Contract* paras 7.55–7.85.

[19]   For a comprehensive comparative study, see B Akkermans *The Principle of Numerus Clausus in European Property Law* (2008).

[20]   There is also the affirmative real burden. This is not a real right, but a 'real obligation', for which see PARA **2.18** below. Real burdens have much in common with servitudes, and indeed they form the two main branches of the category of 'title conditions'. See PARA **13.3** below.

[21]   There is also something called an 'improper liferent' or 'trust liferent'. This is not a real right. See PARA **21.15** below.

[22]   Rights in security are rights to a creditor to enforce payment of a debt by selling the property. See CHAPTER **20** below.

[23]   Whether a lease of land is a real right in the full sense is arguable: see the discussion of real obligations at PARA **2.18** below.

[24]   See paras **18.25–18.28** below.

[25]   The term is slightly wider than 'intellectual property rights', because it includes non-intellectual monopoly trading rights.

To some degree the latter have a real quality and accordingly possession is sometimes classified as a real right.[26]

2.11   Legislation can create new private law rights and is not bound to fit such rights into traditional categories. A good example can be found in 'occupancy rights'. If Pat and Kim are married, or are civil partners, and the home is owned by Pat, then Kim has 'occupancy rights' in the property.[27] These rights seem to be half way between real rights and personal rights.

MULTIPLE REAL RIGHTS: LEADING SEPARATE LIVES IN THE SAME HOME

2.12   If something is subject to multiple real rights, these generally lead an independent existence. For example, suppose that Iona owns some land. She grants a servitude to her neighbour, Nick, and this is registered in the Land Register. Later, she grants a ten-year lease to Larry.[28] Later still, she borrows £125,000 from a bank (Bank A) and in security of the loan grants to the bank a security over the house, and this is registered in the Land Register. There are now four real rights in the house: Iona's right of ownership, Nick's right of servitude, Larry's right of lease and the bank's right of security. Suppose that Iona now transfers ownership to Steve. The transfer is registered in the Land Register. Steve is owner. The three subordinate real rights are unaffected. (Larry has a new landlord but that does not affect his position.)

2.13   Steve is not liable to the bank. After all, he has no contract with the bank. Iona remains liable. If she fails to pay, the bank can enforce its right by selling the house.[29] That may sound harsh on Steve but he would know about these subordinate real rights when he bought the property, because they are publicised either by registration or possession. (In practice a buyer will usually insist that any secured loans are paid off by the seller.) The sale will not affect the rights of Larry or Nick.

2.14   In this example, the various real rights co-habited reasonably happily. It can, however, be otherwise. For instance, suppose that Iona had borrowed another £125,000 from Bank B, granting a security for this new loan. This second security would have been valid but postponed to the first. Suppose that Iona became insolvent and Bank A sold the property for £200,000. Bank A would have taken the full £125,000 it was owed, and Bank B would have received the balance of £75,000. The reason is that the priority of real rights is determined by the date they become real, a principle

---

[26]   See PARA **11.18** below.

[27]   See PARAS **10.6–10.12** below.

[28]   This is not registered because only leases over 20 years can be registered. See PARAS **19.11–19.12** below. But it will nevertheless be a real right.

[29]   Suppose it sells it for £200,000. The bank pockets £125,000. The balance goes to the ex-owner, Steve. As a result of the sale the security is extinguished, so that the number of subordinate real rights falls from three to two.

summed up in the maxim *prior tempore potior jure* – earlier by time, stronger by right.[30]

2.15 In general, the only person who can grant a subordinate real right is the owner. But there are some exceptions. The holder of a registered lease can (normally) grant a security over the lease,[31] and can also grant a sub-lease. These are subordinate real rights, and they are over subordinate real rights. One can call subordinate real rights 'daughter rights' and these lower-level rights 'granddaughter rights'. They are sometimes described as 'real rights in real rights'. An alternative analysis is that they are not real rights 'in' the land but 'over' the main subordinate real right. These 'granddaughter rights' are exceptional. For example, nobody except an owner can grant a servitude or a real burden[32] or a liferent, and nobody except an owner or the holder of a registered lease can grant a standard security.[33]

SEPARATE TENEMENTS

2.16 A 'separate tenement' is a right of ownership that is held by someone other than the owner of the land itself.[34] Examples include flats,[35] mineral rights and salmon fishing rights. Thus, Kenneth owns a Perthshire estate, but the salmon fishing rights on one of his rivers belong to Donald; unworked minerals generally to Constance; unworked gold and silver to the Crown; and unworked coal to the Coal Authority. All these real rights co-exist. Functionally, such rights, except Kenneth's, can be compared to subordinate real rights, encumbering Kenneth's ownership, but in law separate tenements are themselves not subordinate real rights but ownership rights.

THE 'UNBRIDGEABLE DIVISION'? REAL OBLIGATIONS, 'OFFSIDE GOALS' ETC.

2.17 Whether the division between personal and real rights is truly 'unbridgeable'[36] can be debated. Occupancy rights[37] are statutory rights enforceable by one spouse, or civil partner, against the other, and are thus essentially personal. But in some situations, though not others, they can also be enforced against third parties. Such rights may not bridge the division, but they perhaps could be said to straddle it awkwardly.

---

[30] See **PARA 4.42** below.
[31] If there is default on the secured loan, what the creditor sells is the lease, so that the owner will have a new tenant.
[32] A partial exception to the statement is to be found in the Registration of Leases (Scotland) Act 1857, s 3, but just what that provision means is controversial.
[33] Note, however, the special rules for 'unregistered holders'. See **PARAS 4.50-4.51** below.
[34] For separate tenements in general, see **PARAS 14.13–14.18** below.
[35] See **CHAPTER 15** below.
[36] See *Burnett's Tr v Grainger* 2004 SC (HL) 19 at para 87 per Lord Rodger of Earlsferry.
[37] See **CHAPTER 10** below.

2.18 More important is the class of rights usually called 'real obligations', or *obligationes propter rem*.[38] Here, a personal right is valid against whoever is the owner of given property for the time being. Positive real burdens are examples. By contrast, negative real burdens are true real rights.[39] As for leases, at common law they are contracts and nothing more. If Candice owns land and lets it to Diana for five years, and during that period Candice dispones to Katy, Katy can require Diana to flit, leaving Diana with merely a breach of contract claim against Candice. But in most cases the common law is disapplied[40] and the contract changes from being a Diana/Candice contract into being a Diana/Katy contract, with Katy having Candice's rights and duties. Whether such leases – leases not subject to the common law rule – should be regarded as true real rights, or as real obligations, or indeed as a mixture of the two, is an unsettled point. In practice they are always called real rights.

2.19 Then there is the so-called 'offside goals' rule. This is discussed later,[41] but in brief a buyer can occasionally be subjected to the contractual obligations of the seller. There is some resemblance here to real obligations but, unlike a true real obligation, the 'offside goals' rule results in an essentially passive liability.

2.20 There are other possible cases where rights may have a real as well as a personal quality. Only one will be mentioned: trusts.[42] The rights of a beneficiary under a trust are personal rights – rights against the trustees – but they also have characteristics which make them sometimes behave like real rights. But the law is settled that such rights are personal, not real, and their seemingly semi-real effects can be explained without resorting to the theory that they are mixed in their nature.

PRESCRIPTION

General

2.21 Prescription means the alteration of rights by the running of time. There are two types of prescription: 'positive' prescription, where rights are acquired, and 'negative' prescription, where rights are extinguished. The terms 'acquisitive prescription' and 'extinctive prescription' are used in some countries and perhaps should be adopted here. The subject is regulated by the Prescription and Limitation (Scotland) Act 1973 (PL(S)A 1973).[43] Whether prescription is fair is a matter on which opinions differ. It means that if there is a split between the *de facto* position and the legal position then that split will not last indefinitely: a time comes when the

---

[38] Obligations on account of property.
[39] See PARA **13.42** below.
[40] Leases Act 1449; Registration of Leases (Scotland) Act 1857; Land Registration (Scotland) Act 1979. Almost all leases of land fall under one or other of these. Leases of moveables remain subject to the common law. See CHAPTER **19** below.
[41] See PARAS **4.45–4.48** below.
[42] See CHAPTER **22** below.
[43] The standard work is Johnston *Prescription*.

law follows the facts. It can result in unfairness in individual cases, but the argument is that it is fairer overall than a rule that allows long-forgotten rights to be resurrected at any time. In the old maxim, *vigilantibus non dormientibus jura subveniunt.*[44] Most legal systems allow for prescription to take place.

Negative prescription

2.22 Negative prescription applies mainly to personal rights. For example, a right to be paid a debt normally prescribes after five years.[45] But subordinate real rights can also be extinguished by negative prescription, by non-exercise for 20 years.[46] For example, if there is a servitude right, but it is not exercised for a period of 20 years, then, at the end of that period, it is extinguished.[47] In practice, negative prescription is more significant for title conditions, such as servitudes, than it is for other real rights.[48] The real right of ownership of land is excluded from negative prescription.[49] PL(S)A 1973 says that it is 'imprescriptible',[50] which is true but capable of being misleading. It is imprescriptible in the sense of not capable of being lost by negative prescription. It is still capable of being lost by prescription. It can be lost if someone else acquires it by positive prescription.[51]

2.23 Negative prescription should be distinguished from limitation, which is also covered by PL(S)A 1973. Whereas negative prescription extinguishes an obligation, limitation does not, but it bars the raising of an action except with the permission of the court. The limitation period is three years. It applies only to certain defined obligations, notably the obligation to pay damages for causing personal injury.[52]

Positive prescription: introduction

2.24 Positive prescription applies to real rights and is covered by PL(S)A 1973 in ss 1, 2 and 3. In practice the main cases are ownership of land, servitudes and public rights of way. For ownership of land, the core idea is that if a disposition is registered, and ten years of possession ensue, the title, if previously void or voidable, becomes absolutely good. Good faith is not a requirement. The way the system works in the Sasine Register is different from the way it works in the Land Register.[53]

---

[44]   The law protects those who are awake, not those who sleep. More pithily: 'if you snooze, you lose'.
[45]   PL(S)A 1973, s 6. This is called the short negative prescription, or the quinquennial prescription.
[46]   PL(S)A 1973, s 8.
[47]   See **PARA 12.45** below.
[48]   For the negative prescription of title conditions, see **PARAS 12.45 AND 13.67** below.
[49]   So too is a registered lease: PL(S)A 1973, Sch 3.
[50]   PL(S)A 1973, Sch 3 para (a).
[51]   See **PARAS 2.24–2.29** below.
[52]   PL(S)A 1973, s 17.
[53]   On the two registers, see **CHAPTER 6** below.

Positive prescription in the Sasine Register

2.25   Suppose that on 1 May 1991 a disposition by Zebedee is recorded in the Sasine Register in favour of Adam. Zebedee's title is void because the real owner is Yvonne.[54] In 1997 Adam grants a disposition to Eve and this is recorded in the Sasine Register. Adam and then Eve possess the property 'for a continuous period of ten years openly, peaceably and without any judicial interruption'.[55] Their possession 'was founded on, and followed the recording of, a deed', i.e. the 1991 disposition, 'which is sufficient in respect of its terms to constitute in favour of that person a title to that interest in the particular land, or in land of a description habile to include the particular land'.[56] The result is that 'from the expiration of the said period', i.e. as from 1 May 2001, 'the validity of the title so far as relating to the said interest in the particular land shall be exempt from challenge'.[57] As Zebedee was not the owner, he could not transfer ownership to Adam. So Adam was not owner when he disponed to Eve and she did not acquire ownership. This is an illustration of the *nemo plus* doctrine.[58] But on 1 May 2001 there is a flash of legal lightning and Eve becomes owner. As good faith is not a requirement, Eve becomes the owner even if she knew that the 1991 deed was invalid.

2.26   The Act adds that prescription does not operate if 'possession was founded on the recording of a deed which is invalid *ex facie* or was forged'.[59] Doris owns land. An identity thief forges her signature on a disposition to Edmund. Edmund possesses for ten years. He does not acquire ownership. The possession must, as the Act says, be 'founded on' the deed in question.[60] Suppose that Fergus owns land and Gordon holds a 50-year lease. And suppose that Hilda dispones the land to Gordon, the disposition being recorded in the Sasine Register in 1995. The fact that Gordon possesses the land from 1995 to 2005 does not give him ownership, for his possession was founded on the lease.[61] Again, suppose that Jack is owner of land, and that Kate has been in possession since 1995. In 2000 a disposition to Kate by Larry is recorded in the Sasine Register. Kate does not become owner in 2005 because only five years of the possession could be said to be founded on the disposition. Finally, the Act requires that the deed in question be 'sufficient in respect of its terms to constitute in favour of that person a title'. It has been held that prescription does not run on a deed in which the granter and grantee are the same person.[62]

---

[54]   Perhaps it is wholly void. Or perhaps it is generally valid but is void in that it includes a boundary strip that belongs to Yvonne.

[55]   PL(S)A 1973, s 1.

[56]   PL(S)A 1973, s 1.

[57]   PL(S)A 1973, s 1.

[58]   See PARA **4.39** below.

[59]   PL(S)A 1973, s 1. '*Ex facie* invalid' means that the invalidity is apparent on the face of the deed: *Cooper Scott v Gill Scott* 1924 SC 309; *Watson v Shields* 1994 SCLR 819, 1996 SCLR 81.

[60]   Some legal systems allow prescriptive acquisition of ownership of land by the simple fact of possession over a certain number of years. Scots law does not.

[61]   *Houstoun v Barr* 1911 SC 134.

[62]   *Board of Management of Aberdeen College v Youngson* 2005 SC 335.

2.27 Such examples may seem artificial. Why would an owner let someone else possess for many years without challenge? Why would a disposition by a non-owner be granted? If granted, would it be accepted for recording by the Keeper? As to the first question, the owner might be dead or not realise what was happening. Prescription often occurs in relation to small areas, particularly at boundaries. As to the second question, it might be inadvertent: a disponer might occupy more ground than is owned, and might dispone the area as occupied. Sometimes it is intentional: a deliberate attempt to get the title to reflect possession by starting the prescriptive clock running. As to the third question, this is a matter for the Keeper's practice: sometimes he will accept for recording an *a non domino* deed.[63]

2.28 In the Sasine Register, positive prescription has a role not only in mending bad titles, but also in proving to buyers that a title is good. It saves a buyer from having to check the seller's title all the way back to the beginning. Suppose that Elspeth is selling in 2009. The Sasine Register shows, among other things, these deeds: a 1987 disposition by Andrew to Ben; a 1992 disposition by Ben to Caroline; a 2001 disposition by Caroline to Desmond; and a 2003 disposition by Desmond to Elspeth. Is Elspeth the owner? Take the worst case and suppose that Andrew was not the owner. That does not now matter, because if there has been possession down the line, the title will now be good by prescription. The conveyancer who acts for the buyer goes back ten years (2009 to 1999) and then finds the first disposition before that date, which is the 1992 disposition. That is called the *foundation writ*. If there has been the necessary possession, even if the title had originally been bad it would have been validated by 2002 (1992 plus ten years). The validity of Elspeth's title depends not only on possession but on the validity of the post-1992 deeds, so these will be examined carefully. Of course, prescription may have also been running on the 1987 deed, but it is not necessary to go back that far.

Positive prescription in the Land Register

2.29 For Sasine titles, positive prescription is of great importance, not least in establishing that a granter has a good title. In the Land Register it has only a marginal role. A granter's title can be ascertained from the register itself: if the register says that X is owner, a buyer can rely on that.[64] Indeed, the general principle is that positive prescription does not apply to properties in the Land Register: it runs only on titles where indemnity has been excluded.[65]

---

63   *Registration of Title Practice Book* para 6.4.
64   See **PARAS 6.30–6.34** below.
65   1973 Act s 1.

Positive prescription: subordinate real rights

2.30   Positive prescription is also possible as a means of acquiring certain subordinate real rights, and in particular servitudes and public rights of way. The period is 20 years.[66]

Corporeal moveables

2.31   The PL(S)A 1973 does not mention corporeal moveables, either for positive or for negative prescription. For negative prescription, s 8 probably applies. Jane owns a painting. Keira steals it and hangs it in her own house. After 20 years of non-possession, it seems to be that Jane loses ownership. But that does not mean that the wicked Keira acquires it: the Crown does. This is, at any rate, the best guess as to what the law is.[67] As for positive prescription, the law is again unclear. Perhaps it does not apply at all to corporeal moveables, or perhaps there is a 40-year common law rule whereby ownership is acquired after 40 years.[68] Most corporeal moveables are of limited value and of limited lifespan, so prescription is not usually a relevant issue. But some are long-lived and of high value, as everyone in the world of antiquities and art knows. The lack of a clear rule to settle title after long possession is surprising. Most other legal systems have such a rule.

FURTHER READING

Paisley *Land Law* ch 2.

Carey Miller with Irvine *Corporeal Moveables* ch 7.

Johnston *Prescription.*

See also the reading for CHAPTER **1**.

---

[66]   1973 Act ss 2 and 3. See below, PARAS **12.27** and **18.19–18.20**.
[67]   Reid, *Property* para 675.
[68]   See generally Carey Miller with Irvine, *Corporeal Moveables* ch 7.

Chapter 3

Ownership

WHAT IS THE RIGHT OF OWNERSHIP?

3.1   Whether the right of ownership can be defined is doubtful. It can at least be described. Ownership is the most comprehensive right that can be had in an object. It is, as Stair says, 'the main real right'.[1] Erskine calls it 'the right of using and disposing of a subject as our own, except in so far as we are restrained by law or paction'.[2] Ownership has to be distinguished in particular from:

(a)   the other types of real right, i.e. the subordinate real rights, such as servitude;[3] and

(b)   possession.[4]

For example, if Kyle owns land and grants a 100-year lease to Louise, she takes possession of the land, and has a real right. But Louise is not the owner: it is still Kyle.

---

[1]   Stair II, 1, 28.
[2]   Erskine II, 1, 1.
[3]   See **CHAPTER 12** below.
[4]   See **CHAPTER 11** below.

UNLIMITED?

3.2 Ownership is seldom – perhaps never – unlimited. If there is a subordinate real right, that restricts the scope of the right of ownership and may even take away most of its economic value.[5] There are public law rules.[6] Thus, land is subject to planning law and building control law. Most land is subject to public access rights. Public rights can affect moveables too. For example, motor vehicles, aircraft, locomotives and ships are subject to a good deal of public law. If you want to sell something to a foreign buyer, the Export Control Act 2002 will not stop the sale but may prevent it from being implemented.[7] And so on.

OWNERSHIP OF WHAT?

3.3 Everyone agrees that one owns 'things' but there is some disagreement as to what this means exactly. Clearly, ownership is possible of physical things, such as fields and bicycles. (And indeed gas.[8] Electricity is less clear.[9]) But can rights be owned as well? A tenant obviously does not own the land, but might he or she be regarded as owning the tenancy? Is a money claim owned by the creditor? Is a company share owned by the shareholder? Is a patent owned by the patent holder? In ordinary speech the answer is 'yes'. for at least some types of rights: we commonly say that a person owns shares in a company, or owns a patent, though we would perhaps feel less comfortable saying that a bank lending money to a customer owns the right to be repaid, or that a tenant owns the tenancy.

3.4 On one view, rights[10] can be owned as well as things, so that 'things' means both physical things and rights. This is the predominant view. Some who hold this view make an exception for the right of ownership: that is, they say, the only right that cannot be owned.[11] The other view is that only physical things are the objects of ownership. The relationship between a person and a right is, on this view, not a right of ownership. A person has rights, but does not own them: the right of ownership is one type of right a person may have. The issues involved in this debate are complex but their practical implications are limited.[12]

---

[5] See **PARA 2.4** above.

[6] See **PARA 1.12** above.

[7] 'The Secretary of State may by order make provision for or in connection with the imposition of export controls in relation to goods of any description.' (s 1.)

[8] Paisley *Land Law* para 1.15.

[9] The criminal law classifies the unlawful abstraction of electricity as theft: G H Gordon *The Criminal Law of Scotland* (3rd edn, 2000, by M G A Christie) para 14.16. But the implications of that fact for private law are uncertain.

[10] Private law rights.

[11] This is the position taken in Reid *Property* para 16.

[12] The minority view, held by one of the authors but not the other, is set out in an unreadable article: Gretton 'Ownership and its Objects' (2007) 71 *Rabels Zeitschrift* 802.

UNOWNED THINGS AND ANIMALS

3.5 Most physical objects are owned, but not all. The air is not owned, nor is sea water or fresh running water, but these can be taken into ownership by occupancy.[13] The same is true of wild animals. As far as private law is concerned, the ownership of animals is the same as ownership of inert objects. Legislation protects them from abuse,[14] but as far as private law is concerned they are simply moveable property. German law provides that 'animals are not things'.[15] This is a statement of values but has no genuine legal effect: a horse can be owned, and bought and sold, in German law as it can in Scots law.

BONA VACANTIA – ULTIMUS HAERES – 'TREASURE TROVE'

3.6 Subject to those qualifications, physical objects cannot be ownerless. If the owner dies intestate and without traceable family, the property passes to the Crown, who is everybody's *ultimus haeres* (ultimate heir).[16] If a juristic person[17] is dissolved still holding its assets, those assets are called *bona vacantia* and likewise fall to the Crown.[18] Abandoned things are also *bona vacantia* and also pass to the Crown. In *Mackenzie v Maclean*[19] hundreds of damaged beer cans were dumped in a skip, from which locals helped themselves. The case was a theft prosecution (in the event, nobody was convicted). The sheriff noted that the cans, on being abandoned in the skip, became Crown property. Whereas property that never has been owned, such as a wild animal, can be appropriated by anyone,[20] property that has been owned is not so available. Such property cannot become ownerless, and if there is no other owner it belongs to the Crown.

3.7 Lost property is not the same as abandoned property. A person who leaves a book on a bus does not abandon it. Loss does not terminate ownership. However, the standard view is that after 20 years of being out of possession, the right of ownership is cut off by the long negative prescription whereupon ownership passes to the Crown.[21]

3.8 The English expression 'treasure trove', though commonly used, has no technical meaning in Scotland. If, say, an ancient coin hoard is discovered, it belongs

---

13   See **PARA 8.2** below.
14   Notably the Protection of Animals (Scotland) Act 1912.
15   BGB § 90a.
16   See **PARA 28.27** below.
17   Only persons can have rights and duties. Persons are divided into natural persons (human beings) and juristic persons (such as companies).
18   This is a common law rule. For companies it is statutory: Companies Act 2006, s 1012.
19   1981 SLT (Sh Ct) 40.
20   By occupancy. See **PARA 8.2** below.
21   See **PARA 2.23** above.

to the Crown, not by virtue of any special rule, but because of one of the doctrines already mentioned.[22] Thus it does not belong to the finder, nor to the owner of the land where it is found. But in practice the Crown usually gives a reward to the finder.

3.9 Procedure for handling lost and abandoned property is contained in Pt VI of the Civic Government (Scotland) Act 1982.[23] Where property falls to the Crown, whether under the *bona vacantia* rule or the *ultimus haeres* rule, the Crown is represented by the Queen's and Lord Treasurer's Remembrancer.[24]

ACQUISITION: ORIGINAL/DERIVATIVE

3.10 There is an overarching distinction between:
  (a) derivative acquisition; and, less commonly
  (b) original acquisition.

In the former the right is acquired from the previous owner. For example, if Becca goes to a baker and buys a loaf, the right of ownership of the loaf passes from the baker to Becca: derivative acquisition. This is easy to understand: the right is handed over. Original acquisition is where the right of ownership is acquired by some legal process that gives the right of ownership to the beneficiary of that process, regardless of the consent of the previous owner (if any). The main examples of original acquisition are:
  (i) occupancy: when an ownerless object is taken into possession;[25]
  (ii) accession: when one object becomes part of another, as, for instance, when a car is painted, the paint becomes part of the car and so owned by the owner of the car;[26]
  (iii) specification: when an object is so altered that it loses its identity (e.g. barley into ale), the result being that ownership vests in the person who carries out the transformation;[27]
  (iv) positive prescription: whereby ownership is acquired by long possession;[28]
  (v) registration under the Land Registration (Scotland) Act 1979: where ownership is acquired by the act of the Keeper.[29]

---

[22] *Lord Advocate v University of Aberdeen & Budge* 1963 SC 533.
[23] See Carey Miller with Irvine *Corporeal Moveables* para 2.08.
[24] See PARA **28.27** below.
[25] See PARA **8.2** below.
[26] See PARAS **8.4–8.18** below.
[27] See PARAS **8.20–8.22** below.
[28] See PARAS **2.25–2.29** above.
[29] See PARAS **6.30–6.34** below.

ACQUISITION: VOLUNTARY/INVOLUNTARY

3.11   In original acquisition, it is irrelevant whether the previous owner, if any,[30] consents: the acquisition happens anyway. In derivative acquisition, the consent of the previous owner is normally necessary: Becca's acquisition of the ownership of the loaf presupposes the baker's consent. In general, a person cannot lose ownership involuntarily. But nevertheless it can happen that derivative acquisition is involuntary – involuntary, that is, on the part of the person losing ownership. This is discussed in CHAPTER 7 below.

EVIDENCE OF OWNERSHIP

3.12   This book is generally about the substantive rules of property law, not evidential issues. But in practice these can be important. How does a person who claims to be the owner of something establish that fact? There is no short answer. But, for corporeal moveables, an important evidential rule is that possession gives rise to a presumption of ownership. Of course, it is not conclusive: if it were, every thief would be happy. But the burden of proof is thrown on to the person who, not being in possession, claims to be the owner. Thus, if goods are bought, whether from a shop or elsewhere, the fact that the seller possesses the thing raises a presumption of ownership. That is not wholly satisfactory, because the presumption is rebuttable, but it is all there is. Thus, actual proof of ownership is hardly possible. Even if it could be established that a person has possessed something for, say, 40 years, that is, strictly speaking, not enough because our law may not admit prescriptive acquisition of moveables.[31]

3.13   For land, the position is more straightforward: the person who is registered as owner of land is the owner, because title flows from the register.[32] That is on the assumption that the property is in the Land Register. If it is still in the Sasine Register the position is different, for that register is never conclusive. A person can demonstrate good title by showing possession for the prescriptive period.[33]

•

FURTHER READING

Carey Miller with Irvine *Corporeal Moveables* paras 1.12–1.17.

Reid *Property* paras 530–535 and 547–553.

---

[30]   In the case of occupancy there is no previous owner.
[31]   See PARA **2.31** above.
[32]   See PARAS **6.30–6.34** below.
[33]   See PARAS **2.26–2.28** above.

Chapter 4

Acquisition by voluntary transfer: the general principles

INTRODUCTION

4.1 Jill owns something. She contracts with Kate to sell it to her. Contractual obligations are created by agreement but, having been created, they still need to be performed. Kate's obligation is to pay. Jill's is to transfer. The right of ownership is in Jill's patrimony. The question is how to get it to Kate's. Although the mechanisms vary according to the type of property, there are certain basic ideas of general application which are covered in this chapter. CHAPTER **5** considers each of the four categories: corporeal moveable property; incorporeal moveable property; corporeal heritable property; and incorporeal heritable property.

4.2 The distinction between the constitution, transfer and extinction of rights has been discussed already.[1] This chapter and the next focus on transfer, but also cover the constitution of new rights: on the whole, the rules for constitution are the same as for transfer. For example, the transfer of ownership of land happens by registration. The same is true (with minor exceptions) for the constitution of subordinate real rights in land.

SOME TERMINOLOGY

4.3 The words 'grant', 'granter' and 'grantee' are useful terms with a broad sense. For instance, the transferor of land is a 'disponer' and the transferee a 'disponee', and the transferor of incorporeal moveable property is a 'cedent' and the transferee the 'assignee' but the broad terms 'granter' and 'grantee' can also be used. They can also be used for cases where there is not a transfer at all but the creation of a subordinate right. For example, if an owner of land creates a standard security or a servitude over the land, the words 'granter' and 'grantee' are used.

4.4 A 'successor', or 'successor in title', is anyone who subsequently acquires a given right. So if Mary transfers her bicycle to Nigel and thereafter Nigel transfers it to Olivia, Nigel is Mary's successor, and Olivia is Nigel's, and both Nigel and Olivia are Mary's successors. Successors are traditionally divided into 'singular' and 'universal'.[2] Nigel and Olivia are singular successors to Mary: they have simply acquired one particular right that she had – the right of ownership of the bicycle. Most successors are singular. A universal successor is someone who takes over the whole patrimony of someone else. An example would be an executor.[3] If X is the universal successor of Y, that means that X is bound by Y's obligations. But a singular successor is normally not so bound. Suppose that Mary was liable in delict to Larry for having knocked him down while riding too fast: that liability does not transmit to Nigel or Olivia because they are Mary's singular successors, not universal successors.

---

[1]   See PARAS **1.24–1.26** above.
[2]   See, further, Reid *Property* para 598.
[3]   See PARAS **25.46–25.47** below.

4.5 'Transfer' is self-explanatory: a right is transferred when it passes from one person's patrimony to another's. 'Alienate' and 'convey' also mean 'transfer'. Thus if Lorraine buys a cake from a baker, the baker could be said to transfer or convey or alienate the cake to her.[4]

CAPACITY AND CONSENT

4.6 Both sides must have capacity. Capacity belongs to the law of persons and so will not be discussed here,[5] except briefly. Everyone has rights capacity – the capacity to hold rights, including real rights. Thus, a baby could own land. But not all human beings have transactional capacity, such as the capacity to transfer or acquire ownership. This may sound a paradox, for if a baby cannot acquire land, how could he or she own it? The answer is given by the law of persons: human beings who lack capacity can have another person act for them. A baby's parents have the power to enter into juridical acts on the infant's behalf. If an adult suffers from mental disability, a guardian can act. So when a person is described as being an *incapax*, that refers to transactional incapacity, not to rights incapacity.

4.7 Organisations have capacity if they are juristic persons, such as registered companies. Otherwise they do not. Suppose that a university debating society buys a silver cup to be its annual prize. Unless the society is incorporated, which is most unlikely, it cannot buy the cup and cannot own it, for it lacks both transactional capacity and rights capacity. What happens in the eyes of the law is that the members buy the cup, and own it, jointly.[6]

4.8 A juristic person's capacity may be limited: this depends on the applicable legislation and on the organisation's own constitution. Most, but not all, juristic persons have the capacity to own property. When lawyers deal with organisations, they take particular care to check capacity.

4.9 As well as capacity, there must be mutual consent. The principle is the same here as for the formation of contract. No consent, no contract and, in the same way, no consent, no transfer. The transferor must have the *animus transferendi dominii* (the intention of transferring ownership) and the transferee must have the *animus acquirendi*[7] *dominii* (the intention of acquiring ownership). The consent can be through a representative, such as an agent appointed by the person in question, or through anyone else empowered to act for that person, such as, say, the guardian of an *incapax*, or a judicial factor, and so on.

---

4   Usually 'convey' is used in connection with heritable property but its meaning is in fact not so limited.
5   See, further, Gloag and Henderson *The Law of Scotland* ch 44.
6   See PARAS **9.17–9.18** below.
7   This word can also be spelled '*adquirendi*'.

TRANSFERABILITY

4.10 Private law rights are generally transferable. There are some exceptions. Whether a liferent is transferable has been debated but the better view is that it is not.[8] A servitude cannot be transferred by itself, though it can be transferred as a pertinent of the land that it benefits, and the same is true of real burdens, other than personal real burdens.[9] Some leases are transferable without the landlord's consent, but others are not.[10] Contractual rights are usually transferable.[11]

4.11 Non-transferability is not the same as a duty not to transfer. Jack owns the Old Manse and contracts to sell it to Jill. The day after the contract, Jess makes him a better offer and he transfers the property to her. The transfer to Jess was valid, and it was valid because the Jack/Jill agreement had not made the property non-transferable. Jill can claim damages from Jack. If Jess knew of the prior contract, her title may be voidable.[12] But the fact remains: the property was *capable* of being transferred by Jack to Jess – however wrongfully. Likewise, if an owner is interdicted from transfer, that does not make the property in question non-transferable. Nor does an inhibition.[13] Nor does the fact that an owner has granted a security right (or other subordinate right): transfer is still possible, though the right still encumbers the property in the hands of the transferee.

THE SPECIFICITY PRINCIPLE

4.12 Only what can be identified can be transferred: this is the *specificity principle*. It is a common law one, though there is also a statutory statement of it for the sale of goods.[14] The principle does not apply to contractual obligations. Jack can contract to sell 1,000 tonnes of mild steel to Jill. That is a valid contract even if it is not possible to point to any particular steel to which the contract relates. Indeed, the contract would be valid even if at the moment of the contract Jack does not have any steel at all. But Jill cannot acquire a real right unless it is possible to point to the steel in question. If Carl owns 50 hectares and grants to Deirdre a disposition saying 'I hereby dispone to you three hectares out of the area I hold, being the best of the arable land, the boundaries to be determined by mutual agreement which failing by a third party', that could not give her any real right.

4.13 As far as land is concerned, the common law interpretation of the principle was fairly relaxed. Thus, a disposition of 'all and whole[15] the farm of Blackmains,

---

8   See PARA **21.12** below.
9   See PARA **14.12** below.
10 See PARAS **19.33–19.34** below.
11 See PARA **5.38** below.
12 See PARAS **4.45–4.48** below.
13 See PARA **5.6** below.
14 SOGA 1979, s 16.
15 The time-honoured words used to start a description of land.

Fife' is valid, assuming that one could go there and, with the assistance of local knowledge, walk the boundaries. In the modern system of land registration, the specificity principle is applied more strictly.[16]

4.14 Certain qualifications to the specificity principle exist. (Whether these qualifications are in fact true exceptions is arguable.) One is the landlord's hypothec.[17] Another may be the floating charge, though there the charge becomes a real right only at the time when specification is possible, at the time of attachment. Another is SOGA 1979, s 20A which says that if Jack purports to transfer to Jill 5,000 tonnes of oil he has in a tanker containing 50,000 tonnes, then that operates as a transfer of a 10% *pro indiviso* share of the whole 50,000 tonnes.[18]

CONTRACT AND CONVEYANCE

4.15 An obligation to transfer is not the same as a transfer, any more than an obligation to pay is the same as a payment. Oliver owns a house. He sells it to Betty. The sale is a contract. A contract results in mutual obligations. Those obligations have to be performed. The contract binds Betty to pay. It binds Oliver to transfer possession and ownership. Thus, the sale contract creates obligations to perform: it is not itself the performance of those obligations. Betty's obligation to pay is performed by payment. Oliver's obligation to give possession is performed by moving out and handing over the keys. His obligation to transfer ownership is performed by delivering to her a paper or digital deed of transfer, known as a disposition, which she then registers in the Land Register. The contract of sale is thus the reason for, or 'cause', of the transfer. There can be other reasons for transfer, such as gift (donation) but, regardless of the reason, the transfer takes the same form. Thus, if Betty later decides to give the house to her daughter Deirdre, a disposition will again be used. The verb 'sell' and the noun 'sale' are often used to mean the whole process of contract and transfer. If someone says 'I have bought a bicycle' both the contract and the transfer can be inferred. But sale is a contract,[19] and thus a reason for a transfer, not itself a transfer. Contract and conveyance are separate juridical acts. This separation of contract and conveyance is an important aspect of property law. Some terminology: when the external act happens (registration of a deed, intimation to a third party, sometimes the taking of possession) it is said that the transferee 'completes title', and that immediately before doing so has an 'uncompleted title'. The phrase is a standard one, but potentially misleading, for it suggests that the transferee has a sort of half-real right before title is completed.

---

[16]   See **PARA 6.24** below.
[17]   See **PARA 20.65** below.
[18]   Payment by Jill is needed. See **PARAS 5.27–5.29** below.
[19]   SOGA 1979, e.g. in its definition of 'sale', departs somewhat from general property law. See **PARA 5.16** below.

4.16 Not only is conveyance *separate* from contract, but its validity does not *depend* on the contract either. As Stair wrote:

> 'We [in Scotland] follow not that subtility of annulling deeds, because they are *sine causa* … and therefore narratives expressing the cause of the disposition, are never inquired into, because, though there were no cause, the disposition is good.'

The word cause (*causa*) means the reason for the deed, such as a contract of sale. Stair is saying that the validity of the act of transfer (or constitution, or extinction) does not depend for its validity on its cause. The contract could be void, or voidable and then avoided, and the grantee's title will still be valid. This independence of title is called the principle of 'abstraction'.[20]

THE PUBLICITY PRINCIPLE: THE NEED FOR AN EXTERNAL ACT

4.17 The act of transfer is not only separate from the obligation to transfer but is carried out differently. Contract requires only mutual consent. For transfer, mutual consent is necessary, but is not sufficient.[21] An external or overt act is needed. For example, for land, the external act is a registered deed, and for corporeal moveables it is delivery. In this context the following passage from the *Codex* is often quoted: *traditionibus, non nudis pactis, dominia rerum, transferuntur* – real rights are transferred not by mere agreement but by delivery.[22] In modern law registration is sometimes an alternative, but the underlying idea – that there must be an external act – remains generally valid. Moreover, it applies not only to acts of *transfer* but also to acts of *constitution*, such as, say, the grant of a standard security.

4.18 The underlying justification for the requirement of an external act is the *publicity principle*: acts that can affect third parties should be made public, so that third parties can know of them. It is not limited to property law but is particularly important in that area.[23] It is only a broad principle, and not a firm rule. It applies especially to real rights in land – hence the Land Register. It is rather weaker for real rights in moveables[24] and for intellectual property rights.

---

[20] In other countries, such as France and the Netherlands, the conveyance is dependent on the contract being valid. This is known as a 'causal' system of transfer. See, e.g., L P W van Vliet, *Transfer of movables in German, French, English and Dutch law* (2000) ch 7.

[21] Except under SOGA 1979. See **PARA 5.21** below.

[22] This is the standard form of the maxim, though in fact the wording in the *Codex* is slightly different: *traditionibus … dominia rerum non nudis pactis transferuntur.* (C. 2, 3, 20.)

[23] See also **PARAS 22.57–22.58** below.

[24] The transfer of corporeal moveables does not need delivery if the *causa* is sale, but still needs it in other cases such as donation. See **PARAS 5.16–5.29** below.

TRANSFER IS INSTANTANEOUS

4.19 If Maria sells her house to Norman, various things will happen, notably the making of the contract of sale, the handing over of the keys to Norman, the handing over of the disposition to Norman, its registration in the Land Register, and the payment of the price to Maria. Before all these have happened, Maria is the owner, and after they have all happened, Norman is the owner. While they are happening, what is the position? Are they both owners, one being the owner for certain purposes or in certain respects, and the other the owner for other purposes or respects? Some legal systems – that in England, for example – answer that question in the affirmative. Scots law answers it in the negative. Ownership passes not like honey oozing off a spoon on to a slice of bread, but like a bullet fired from a gun. Actually, even that image is insufficient, for a measurable interval elapses between the moment of leaving the barrel and the moment of reaching the target. Transfer of a right is instantaneous. One instant the right is in Maria's patrimony and the next in Norman's. One moment the right is wholly and solely Maria's and the next it is wholly and solely Norman's. This idea is sometimes expressed by saying that Scots property law is, as civilian systems generally are, *unititular*.[25]

THE *SHARP V THOMSON* SAGA

Facts

4.20 In 1989 the Thomsons (a brother and sister) entered into a contract to buy a new flat in Aberdeen from Albyn Construction Ltd. Thus began the saga of *Sharp v Thomson*.[26] No case in Scots property law has ever generated such a volume of academic debate.[27] (Indeed, it is possible that that sentence would still be true if one changed 'property' to 'private'.) Inevitably, the account given here can only scratch the surface.

4.21 The Thomsons paid the price on 12 June 1989 and were given the keys. Normal conveyancing practice is for the disposition to be handed over at the same time and registered immediately. That did not happen. The disposition was not handed over until 9 August 1990. It was registered[28] on 21 August 1990. But on 10 August Albyn Construction Ltd went into receivership. A receivership is a means of enforcing a floating charge, a security right that extends over the whole property of the debtor

---

[25] See, e.g., *Sharp v Thomson* 1995 SC 455 at 469 per Lord President Hope, citing with approval Professor Reid's analysis.

[26] 1994 SC 503, aff'd 1995 SC 455, rev'd 1997 SC (HL) 66.

[27] Especially if one takes it, as one must, with its successor case, *Burnett's Tr v Grainger* 2004 SC (HL) 19. The literature is listed in Appendix B of Scottish Law Commission *Report on Sharp v Thomson* (2007).

[28] In the Sasine Register, because at that time the Land Register had not yet been extended to Aberdeenshire. But this point is of no significance for the dispute.

company.[29] So long as the company in question remains solvent, the floating charge is not a real right. But when the charge *attaches,* for example by receivership, it becomes a real right. So the holder of the floating charge (Bank of Scotland) obtained a real right (of security) before the Thomsons acquired their real right. That did not mean that the Thomsons did not become owners. The bank's real right was only a subordinate real right. But the Thomsons apparently acquired ownership subject to that right, so that their ownership was effectively worthless, because the receiver could sell the property from under their feet, applying the proceeds of sale for the benefit of the Bank of Scotland.

The approach of the courts

4.22　The matter was interpreted in the above way by both the Outer House[30] and the Inner House.[31] This was not as disastrous for the Thomsons as might at first appear. A conveyancer who hands over the price except in exchange for a deed is *prima facie* liable in negligence if loss results. But on a further appeal to the House of Lords the decision of the Court of Session was reversed. The grounds are unclear. One theory is that the House of Lords considered that at some stage in a transfer (perhaps the delivery of the disposition) the transferee acquires something called a 'beneficial interest'. This term is commonly used to describe the right of a beneficiary in a trust:[32] what, if anything, it could mean outside the context of trust law was unclear. Perhaps it meant that half way through the transaction ownership is somehow split, with one sort of ownership still held by the seller and another by the buyer – in short, Scots property law was not unititular. Another interpretation was that the House of Lords was not in fact saying anything much about property law, but was merely interpreting the legislation about floating charges.

Burnett's Tr v Grainger

4.23　The transaction in *Sharp v Thomson* took place in 1989–90. In 1990–91 another unhappy transaction was taking place, in Peterculter: *Burnett's Tr v Grainger*.[33] Mr and Mrs Grainger entered into a contract to buy a house from Ms Burnett. In November 1990 the buyers paid the price and were given the keys and the disposition. But their solicitors did not register the disposition. On 29 May 1991 Ms Burnett was sequestrated. Sequestration is, among other things, a conveyance to the trustee of the bankrupt's heritable property. On 10 December 1991 Ms Burnett's trustee was registered as owner of the house. When, the following month, the Graingers' solicitors finally sought registration, it was too late. Though Ms Burnett

---

29　For floating charges, see PARAS **20.37–20.40** below.
30　1994 SC 503.
31　1995 SC 455.
32　See PARA **22.55** below.
33　2002 SC 580, aff'd 2004 SC (HL) 19.

had been the owner when she delivered the disposition to the Graingers, by the time they sought registration Ms Burnett was no longer the owner and so the deed was now *a non domino*. The Graingers had lost the 'race to the register' – though, of course, they had a damages claim against their solicitors.

4.24 But the decision of the House of Lords in *Sharp v Thomson* might, on a broad interpretation, mean that the settled authorities were no longer applicable. The Graingers argued that on delivery of the disposition they had acquired the 'beneficial interest' in the property, so that a sort of ownership had already passed to them. This argument succeeded before the Sheriff Principal. On appeal the Inner House disagreed, arguing that *Sharp v Thomson* lacked a clear *ratio* and that it should be narrowly construed so as to make it fit in, as far as possible, with property law.[34] The case was appealed to the House of Lords, which upheld the decision. The trustee had won.[35]

4.25 The House of Lords did not overrule *Sharp v Thomson*, but that case must now be understood as having a narrow *ratio*, limited to the law of floating charges. The *ratio* is that property can be freed from the ambit of a floating charge even before it ceases to belong to the debtor company. When and how that happens is unclear, but as far as heritable property is concerned it is probably the time when the disposition is delivered. The 'unititularity' of property law is thus confirmed. In addition, there is no such thing as 'beneficial interest', except in the context of trust law.[36]

> 'The disponee who has not registered his title enjoys no real right in the subjects. Scots law does not recognise a right which lies between a real right and a personal right … There is no such thing as a "quasi-real right".'[37]

PAYMENT AND TRANSFER: THE STRUCTURE OF INSOLVENCY RISK

4.26 In sale, a buyer who pays before acquiring title runs the risk of the seller's insolvency – as in *Sharp v Thomson* and *Burnett's Tr*. Conversely, a seller who transfers title before receiving the price runs the risk of the buyer's insolvency. Three possibilities exist.

---

[34] 2002 SC 580. At this point Mr Grainger gave an interview to *The Scotsman* (17 May 2002):

> 'We are totally exasperated by the whole thing. The law is very strange. We paid the money in 1990, we have cleared the mortgage, we have spent another £13,000 over the years to maintain the property – yet we have nothing. Apparently, this is quite an unusual case and it is being used for teaching in law faculties. But that is little consolation.'

[35] The Graingers received damages from their solicitors.
[36] And tax law. Tax law tends to be conceptualised in English terms.
[37] *3052775 Nova Scotia Ltd v Henderson* [2006] CSOH 147 at para 11 per Lord Hodge.

(1) Ownership passes before payment. Here, the seller is at risk. This is often the position in the sale of goods, and accordingly an important theme in the property side of sale of goods has been buyer insolvency.

(2) Payment is made before ownership passes. Here, the buyer is at risk. This is the normal position in the sale of heritable property. Hence such cases as *Sharp v Thomson* and *Burnett's Tr.* If proper conveyancing practice is adopted, the buyer does not pay except in exchange for a disposition, but even so there may be a short period of risk, because ownership does not pass when the disposition is delivered but when it is registered.[38] This type of case can also happen in the sale of goods.

(3) Simultaneity: ownership passes to the buyer and payment is made by the seller at the same time. Here, neither party is at risk. That would be the ideal, but in practice it is hard to achieve.

4.27 Where there is no simultaneity, the party at risk can sometimes be protected by some sort of priority right. For example, in the sale of goods an unpaid seller may be protected by a lien or by retention of title.[39] One interpretation of *Sharp v Thomson* was that the House of Lords was creating a priority right for a buyer who has paid. Though that view of *Sharp v Thomson* cannot now be adhered to, conveyancers have developed a mechanism which, if it works, has much the same effect: the trust clause. This is a provision where the seller, after delivery of the disposition, is deemed to hold the property in trust for the buyer.[40]

4.28 From the seller's point of view, the greatest security is to be had by retaining ownership until payment: a 'suspensive condition'. In the sale of goods it is common to do that.[41] It may be wondered whether the same effect can be achieved by a 'resolutive condition': that if the buyer fails to pay, the transfer will be rescinded so that ownership reverts to the seller. The parties can indeed so agree. But the agreement works only contractually. As Bell says, 'an express paction, made by the seller when delivering property, that the property shall be reinstated in him if the price be not paid ... is ... ineffectual against the buyer's creditors'.[42] The seller cannot become owner again without a re-transfer of ownership. Unless and until the buyer does that, the property still belongs to the buyer, and so attachable by the buyer's creditors. Subject to certain qualifications, ownership cannot be subject to a resolutive condition having real effect.

---

[38] With the advent of electronic deeds, this can sometimes be done the same day. Where it cannot be done, there is a system whereby the seller's solicitors normally will guarantee their client's solvency for a period of a few days to cover the gap between the delivery of the deed and its registration. This guarantee is called a letter of obligation.

[39] See PARAS **5.24–5.26** below.

[40] See PARA **20.15** below.

[41] See PARAS **5.25–5.26** below.

[42] Bell *Commentaries* I, 260.

WARRANDICE

4.29   'Warrandice' means warranty or guarantee. In a sale, warrandice by the seller is presumed. It is also often expressly stated. There can be warrandice of the physical quality of what is sold, but from a property law standpoint the main concern is with warrandice as a guarantee of good title. In the sale of goods, warrandice is implied by SOGA 1979, s 12. In other sales it is a matter of common law.[43]

VOID, VOIDABLE AND ABSOLUTELY GOOD

General

4.30   Most titles are absolutely good. (The acquisition of an absolutely good title has already been explained in general terms, and further details are given in CHAPTER 5.[44]) Sometimes a title may be void. A third possibility is that it is voidable. A voidable title is one that exists but is precarious because it may be made void. These possibilities can be set out in a chart:

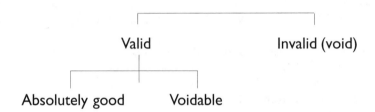

Void titles: why?

4.31   A void title happens either
   (a)   because the granter did not have the right in the first place, the granter's title was itself void, or
   (b)   though the granter had the right, there has been some fatal defect in the process of grant.

The juridical act is void and that causes the transferee's title to be void.[45] An example of (b) would be if Chris owns a bicycle and Danielle forces him to hand it over at gunpoint. The transfer has been brought about by 'force and fear' and so is void. It would be the same if Chris gave it to her when he was insane. What is lacking is

---

[43]   See PARAS **5.9–5.13, 5.33** AND **5.48** below.
[44]   See CHAPTER **5** below.
[45]   Underlying the theory of absolutely good, void and voidable titles is the theory of absolutely good, void and voidable juridical acts.

Chris's consent, the *animus transferendi dominii*. Or there might be consent, but some other fatal defect in the transfer process, such as, in the case of land, a failure to register. For examples of (a), one just has to think of examples of (b) and then add a second transfer. Thus, if Danielle transfers to Elle, Elle's title will be void.

Voidable titles: why?

4.32 A voidable title arises when someone validly acquires property, but in a way that is somehow contrary to the rights of another person. That other person then has the option of avoiding the title. For example, Oliver owns land. Fay fraudulently induces him to dispone to her. The effect of fraud is less radical than the effect of, say, force and fear: Olivia's consent is considered as being (unlike Chris's) a true consent, albeit a revocable one.[46] So Fay is now owner. But her title is voidable. That is to say, Oliver has the option to avoid it, thereby re-acquiring the property. It is only an option, and for one reason or another voidable titles are often never avoided. There are numerous grounds of voidability: the following are some examples. The first is fraud. The second is inhibition. This is discussed later,[47] but the basic idea is this: Martin is owner and Norah his creditor. She inhibits him, with the result that if he dispones any heritable property thereafter, the grantee's title will be voidable, unless she is paid when she is owed. Third, there are transfers by persons who are balance-sheet insolvent.[48] Such persons should not be giving assets away: to do so prejudices the creditors. Such transfers therefore result in a voidable title for the grantee. This area of law is divided into the law of gratuitous alienations[49] and the law of unfair preferences.[50] A fourth case is transfers in breach of a contractual obligation. This is called the 'offside goals' rule.[51] Finally, there is transfer by a person whose title is already voidable, i.e. X transfers to Y, and Y obtains a voidable title for some reason (e.g. fraud), and Y then transfers to Z. Z *may* get a voidable title.[52]

Voidable titles and voidable contracts

4.33 Voidable titles should not be confused with voidable contracts. For example, suppose that Carla, creditor of Doris, inhibits her. Doris then contracts to sell her land to Egbert. The contract is then carried out by a disposition, which Egbert registers. Egbert is now owner. His title is voidable. But the Doris/Egbert contract is not

---

[46] A distinction is sometimes drawn between 'vices of consent' which make the consent (and hence the transfer) voidable, and 'real vices' which make the consent (and hence the transfer) void.

[47] See PARAS **5.6–5.7** below.

[48] That is, total debts exceed total assets.

[49] It is partly common law and partly statutory: B(S)A 1985, s 34; IA 1986, s 242.

[50] Partly common law and partly statutory: B(S)A 1985, s 36; IA 1986, s 242.

[51] See PARAS **4.45–4.48** below.

voidable. Take another case. Fraser owns land. Gordon persuades him to swap it for shares in a non-existent South American mining company. The swap is embodied in a contract, and the contract is then implemented by a disposition to Gordon. Gordon is now owner. Both the contract and the title are voidable. But avoiding the contract will of itself not return the property to Fraser. This distinction between avoidance of contract and avoidance of title is often misunderstood.[53] The validity of a title does not depend on the validity of the contract on which that title is based.[54] The Carla/Doris case was one where the conveyance was voidable but not the contract. The Fraser/Gordon case was one where both contract and conveyance were voidable. Just to complete the picture, a contract can be voidable but not the conveyance, though that seldom happens. Harry, elderly and unworldly, owns some land worth £200,000. Ian, a con-man, produces a fake valuation saying it is worth £100,000. Ian offers Harry £120,000 and Harry accepts, on 1 May. On 2 May, due to a new 'credit crunch', property values plunge. The land is now worth £80,000. On 3 May Harry discovers the fraud. Obviously, he will not exercise his option to avoid the contract. On settlement day, say 15 June, he is delighted to receive £120,000. The disposition he hands over in exchange is not voidable.

Reduction and other remedies

4.34 If a title is voidable, what remedies are available? In the first place, if there has been a voidable transfer from X to Y, X can rescind the contract and then demand that Y re-transfer ownership.[55] In the second place, given that a voidable contract can be avoided by notice, is notice enough to avoid a voidable title? The general answer is 'no', but a possible exception exists in the case of corporeal moveables. Alfred fraudulently induces Bronwen to sell him her car. She delivers the car to him. She can rescind the contract simply by notification. But does ownership automatically pass back to her? The law is uncertain and cannot be discussed in detail here. The predominant view, with which we would agree, seems to be that it does not.[56] This follows from the fact that transfer is abstract. What Bronwen can do, having rescinded the contract, is demand a re-transfer. That needs re-delivery.[57] In the third place, there is reduction. This is available only if there is a deed of transfer to be reduced, so it is not available in sale of goods. In the case of a Sasine Register title, all that is needed is to reduce the disposition. In the case of a Land Register title, reduction of

---

52   See PARA **4.38** below.

53   E.g. *MacLeod v Kerr* 1965 SC 253. The case turned on the avoidance of the contract, when in fact the only relevant issue was avoidance of title. See further Reid *Property* paras 609 and 610.

54   This is the principle of abstraction: see PARA **4.16** above.

55   As in *Short's Tr v Chung (No 2)* 1999 SC 471. However, this remedy is not available to an inhibitor. Inhibition is enforced by reduction.

56   In *MacLeod v Kerr* 1965 SC 253 it seems to have been assumed that rescission of the contract would suffice to transfer ownership back to the seller. But the case is weak authority for that view, since it was about rescission of the contract.

the disposition is only the first step. The defender loses ownership only when the register is changed. One possibility here is to ask the Keeper to 'rectify' the Register but often this is excluded by the rules of the land registration system,[58] and if so the reduction will have to be followed up by a demand for a re-conveyance.[59] (This claim can be combined in a single action with the reduction.)

4.35 Reduction is of two types. The first is 'catholic' reduction, in which the title is simply avoided. For example, if there is a transfer of ownership from X to Y and Y's title is avoided, X becomes owner again. Or if X grants a servitude to Z and the servitude is avoided, it disappears and X's ownership is now unencumbered. The other is reduction *ad hunc effectum* which means that the title is avoided only in relation to the person who has avoided it but remains valid in relation to everyone else. That is to say, it is not absolutely invalid but only relatively invalid – void relative to the avoider. Reduction based on an inhibition is an example. Whether there are other examples is unclear. One theory[60] is that if avoidance is by one of the parties then its effect is catholic, while if it is by a third party it is *ad hunc effectum*.

TRANSFER: NATURE OF GRANTER'S TITLE

4.36 In the following paragraphs, the effect on the transferee will be considered of the three types of title the transferor may have: absolutely good, or voidable, or void. In each case it is assumed that the act of transfer itself has been validly done. Thus it is assumed, for example, that the parties are sane, that neither has acted under compulsion, and so on.

Transfer where granter's title absolutely good

4.37 If the granter's title is absolutely good then the grantee's right will likewise be absolutely good. The main exception is where the transfer breaches the right of a third party, such as where there is an inhibition[61] or where the offside goals rule applies.[62]

Transfer where granter's title voidable

4.38 First of all, if a title is voidable and has in fact been avoided, then it has become a void title.[63] Here we are considering a voidable title that has not, or not

---

[57] As will be seen in **CHAPTER 5**, ownership of corporeal moveables can pass without delivery only in a sale. But the transfer back to Bronwen is not a sale.

[58] See **PARAS 6.44–6.46** below.

[59] As in *Short's Tr v Chung (No 2)* 1999 SC 471.

[60] Professor Gretton's.

[61] See **PARA 5.6** below.

yet, been avoided, and perhaps never will be. The effect of voidability on the grantee's title depends on various factors.

(1) If the grantee knew that the granter's title was voidable (unusual in practice) then the grantee's title is also voidable.

(2) If the grant was gratuitous, then the grantee's title is also voidable, regardless of whether the grantee knew of the voidability of the granter's title. For example: Darius owns a Mercedes. When insolvent he gives it to Edwina. Under the Bankruptcy (Scotland) Act 1985 section 34 the transfer is voidable. Soon afterwards, Edwina gives the car to her daughter, Florence. Florence is now owner. Her title is voidable even though she had not known that her mother's title was voidable.

(3) In other cases, in practice the majority, the grantee's title is absolutely good.[64] For sales of corporeal moveables there is a statutory statement of the rule: 'When the seller of goods has a voidable title to them, but his title has not been avoided at the time of the sale, the buyer acquires a good title to the goods, provided he buys them in good faith and without notice of the seller's defect of title.'[65]

Timing is important: if there is a voidable transfer by X to Y, and Y later transfers to Z, a good-faith buyer, then Z is safe if but only if Y's title had not been avoided before the Y/Z transfer. By contrast, if the X/Y transfer had been void, Z's title would be void, regardless of timing.[66]

Transfer where granter's title void

4.39 If the granter's title is void, the grantee's title is void: *nemo plus juris ad alienum transferre potest quam ipse haberet*: nobody can transfer a better right than they have in the first place.[67] (There is a shorter maxim with the same substance: *nemo dat quod non habet*.) It is among the most important principles of property law. If Xerxes steals something from Yvonne, and then sells it to Zelda, ownership stays with Yvonne, even if Zelda acted in good faith. Xerxes cannot transfer a right he does not have. The principle applies to all types of right, not just ownership. Suppose that Fraser owes £10,000 to Gregory Ltd, a company wholly owned by Gregory. The right to be paid money is transferable.[68] Gregory transfers it to Henrietta. The transfer is void. The right was not Gregory's, so he could not transfer it.

---

62   See PARAS **4.45-4.48** below.

63   See PARA **4.39** below.

64   Assuming, of course, that no other grounds exist for challenging the transaction, e.g. lack of capacity etc.

65   SOGA 1979, s 23. See PARA **5.36** below.

66   This explains the difference of result between *Morrisson v Robertson* 1908 SC 332, where the X/Y transfer was void, and *MacLeod v Kerr* 1965 SC 253, where it was only voidable, and not yet avoided.

4.40   The next example is perhaps less obvious. Charles owns some land. On Monday he delivers to Doris a deed granting her a liferent of the land. On Tuesday he delivers to Euan a disposition of the land. On Wednesday Euan registers in the Land Register. On Thursday Doris applies for registration. Her application will be rejected. Why? When the deed was delivered to her, the granter, Charles, was the owner. But, real rights in land arise not when the deed is delivered but on registration.[69] At that moment Charles was not the owner: Euan was. The deed to Doris was thus *a non domino* – from a non-owner. *Nemo plus* again. Euan's title is, from Doris's point of view, a 'mid-impediment', i.e. an intervening event which prevents something from having its anticipated effect. (This example, like many in property law, raises questions about contract, delict, fraud and so on. Those questions are important, but they are not property law questions.) The result is as stated regardless of whether Euan was in good or bad faith, though if he was in bad faith his title, while not void, might be voidable.[70]

4.41   There are exceptions to the *nemo plus* principle: most of them are mentioned in the relevant place in this book.[71] But *nemo plus* is the default rule.

PRIOR TEMPORE, POTIOR JURE

4.42   *Prior tempore, potior jure*[72] means 'earlier by time, stronger by right'. The principle is closely allied with the *nemo plus* principle,[73] and indeed they may be viewed as two expressions of a single idea. Euan was earlier than Doris in obtaining his real right, and so his real right trumped hers. The expression *prior tempore, potior jure* is mainly applied to security rights. Suppose that Julius borrows £1m from Keira and £500,000 from Loretta. He owns Bluemains and he grants to each of his two creditors a standard security. He becomes bankrupt and the land is sold by his trustee in sequestration for £1,100,000. What happens to this money? The first question is whether an owner can grant two security rights, or whether the second would simply be void – as the second right was void in the case involving Doris and Euan above. The answer is that two or more securities can co-exist. That being so, one must ascertain which of the two became a real right first. That in turn depends on the order of registration. Suppose that Loretta's was registered first. In that case she would be paid £500,000 and Keira would take the balance of £600,000. Had it been the other way round, Keira would have been paid £1m and Loretta £100,000. *Prior tempore, potior jure.* Keira's security 'ranks' before Loretta's.[74]

---

[67]   D 50, 17, 54. The words are Ulpian's, and it is not wholly impossible that he wrote them in Scotland. For his visit, see T Honoré *Ulpian* (2nd edn, 2002) 21–22.

[68]   By assignation. See **PARAS 5.38–5.51** below.

[69]   The main exception is for leases of 20 years or less.

[70]   See the offside goals rule, below **PARAS 4.45–4.48**.

[71]   For the exceptions in SOGA 1979, see **PARAS 5.34–5.36** below. The modern land registration system does not fully adhere to the *nemo plus* principle: see **PARAS 6.30–6.34** below. For deeds by unregistered holders, see **PARAS 4.50–4.51** below. See also **CHAPTER 7** below.

TO WHAT IS THE GRANTEE'S RIGHT SUBJECT?

4.43 When a grantee acquires a real right, it is subject to the existing real rights of third parties. That is the principle discussed above, under the headings of *nemo plus* and *prior tempore*. So someone who acquires ownership does so subject to all existing subordinate real rights, whether he or she knows of their existence or not. (Because of the publicity principle, their existence should normally be readily discoverable. That is the point of the publicity principle.) The personal rights of third parties against the granter do not normally affect the grantee. This fact is one of the key facts of property law. Personal rights are enforceable against a given person. They are not normally enforceable against other persons. (The statement that 'personal rights are enforceable against a given person' amounts to saying that they are enforceable against the assets in the obligant's patrimony. That enforcement can be done through diligence or through a bankruptcy procedure.)

4.44 This principle – that the acquirer of a real right is unaffected by personal rights held against the granter – has certain exceptions. One is that if the granter's title is voidable (and voidability is a manifestation of a personal right held by the person entitled to avoid) then the grantee's title is also voidable, unless (as is usually the case) the grantee was unaware of the third party's right and also acted onerously.[75] Another exception comes from trust law. The common law rule was that if (i) trustees transfer trust property in breach of trust; and (ii) the transferee knows of the breach of trust or acquires gratuitously, then the transferee takes subject to the rights of the beneficiaries. The rule was modified by the Trusts (Scotland) Act 1961, s 2, which provided that when trustees sell, the buyer's title cannot be challenged: however, this modification leaves the common law intact in relation to gratuitous transferees.[76] A third exception is the 'offside goals' rule.

'OFFSIDE GOALS'

4.45

> 'The appellants assumed that their title would be safe once the goal of the Register House was reached. But in this area of the law, as in football, offside goals are disallowed.'

These were the words of Lord Justice-Clerk Thomson in *Rodger (Builders) Ltd v Fawdry*,[77] thereby giving a new name to an old rule. The facts of that case are a good illustration of the rule. The owner of land (Mark Fawdry) concluded missives to sell to Rodger (Builders) Ltd.[78] When the company failed to pay the price, he sold to

---

[72] Or, more fully, *qui prior est tempore potior est jure*.
[73] See PARA **4.39** above.
[74] See PARAS **20.22–20.23** below.
[75] See PARA **4.38** above.
[76] See PARA **23.31** below.

Marjorie Bell. A disposition was granted to her and recorded in the Sasine Register. She was now owner. But the company raised an action of reduction against her. The first argument in the case was that the first set of missives had never been validly rescinded. The court agreed. The second was that since she knew of the first set of missives, the company was entitled to reduce the disposition to her. The court agreed and the disposition was reduced. The idea behind the rule is that Marjorie Bell was considered to have acquired in bad faith – because she knew that the acquisition was in breach of the company's contractual right. This is a case of a personal right prevailing over a real right. (The term 'offside goal', though now well established, is slightly misleading. In football, offside goals are void, not voidable.)

4.46   In order to apply, certain conditions must be satisfied. In the first place, it can apply only if B2 (the second buyer) actually or constructively knew of the personal right of B1 (the first buyer). Thus in *Rodger (Builders) v Fawdry* B2's title would have been absolutely good if she had been unaware of B1's contract. It is unclear whether B2 is affected only if she knows of B1's right *before* she (B2) acquires the personal right, or if the information is received at any time before she acquires a real right – the latter being the more severe form of the rule.[79] In the second place, B2's title is not voidable unless there was a *breach* of the seller's obligation to B1. The classic case is – as in *Rodger (Builders) Ltd v Fawdry* – where the seller transfers to someone else, but the breach can be the grant of some other right, such as a standard security.[80]

4.47   In the third place, the 'offside goals' rule applies only to *voluntary* grantees. Therefore it does not apply to creditors doing diligence or to trustees in sequestration. So in *Burnett's Tr v Grainger*,[81] Mrs Burnett was contractually bound to give a good title to Mr and Mrs Grainger. She was sequestrated. Her trustee knew of the contract, but nevertheless transferred title to his own name (for the benefit of the creditors). The 'offside goals' rule could not be pled against him by Mr and Mrs Grainger. In the fourth place, the rule applies only if B1's right was capable of becoming a real right. The leading case here is *Wallace v Simmers*.[82] William Simmers agreed with his daughter, Margaret Simmers, that she could occupy a cottage on his farm indefinitely and rent-free. Later, he conveyed the farm to his son, William Simmers the younger. The latter knew of the agreement with his sister and was happy with it. Years later, he sold the farm to Robert Wallace and Douglas Wallace. They asked Margaret Simmers to leave. When she refused they sued to have her removed. She pled that they knew of her right before buying. Whether they did or not know was never established, because the court held that even if they did know, they were

---

[77]   1950 SC 483. For a good account of the offside goals rule, see McDonald, *Conveyancing Manual* ch 32.

[78]   For the transfer of heritable property, see PARAS **5.1–5.15** below.

[79]   In *Alex Brewster & Sons v Caughey* 2002 GWD-10-318, the court upheld the more severe form of the rule but the soundness of the decision may be questioned: S Wortley, 'Double Sales and the Offside Trap' 2002 *JR* 291.

not bound thereby. Margaret's right was not a lease. It was a personal right incapable of becoming a real right and so was outwith the scope of the 'offside goals' rule.[83]

4.48 Finally, something must be said of *Trade Development Bank v Warriner & Mason (Scotland) Ltd.*[84] Here, Lyon Group Ltd granted a standard security to Trade Development Bank. In doing so it agreed not to let out the property. In breach of that agreement it let the property to Warriner & Mason (Scotland) Ltd, which had actual, or at least constructive, knowledge of the agreement. When Lyon Group Ltd became insolvent, the bank sought to reduce the lease as being an 'offside goal'. It was successful. Here, the bank did not have a personal right capable of being made real, but a real right itself. That real right was earlier in time than the lease. It could be argued that the 'offside goals' rule was inapplicable, and that the bank had power to sell the property free of the lease, regardless of whether the lease was in breach of a contractual term and regardless of whether the lessees knew of that term. The issues involved are, however, too complex for discussion here.

ACCRETION OF TITLE

4.49 Suppose that the title of the granter (X) title is void, with the result that the title of the grantee (Y) is also void. And then suppose that at a later date X acquires title from the true owner, Z. Then, as soon as Z's title passes to X, Y's title is validated, without the need for any new deed. The doctrine in practice has been largely confined to heritable property, where it is called 'accretion of infeftment',[85] but it can apply to any type of property.[86] The doctrine applies not only where the X/Y transaction is a transfer, but also where it is the grant of subordinate right. Accretion presupposes that the X/Y transaction contains absolute warrandice. If it does not, it seems to be the law that accretion will not operate. (Though even in the absence of warrandice it will operate if the X/Y transaction contains a clause conveying the granter's 'whole right, title and interest present and future'.) The rules have been worked out mainly with reference to the Sasine Register, and their interaction with the Land Register is a matter of some complexity and will not be discussed here.

DEEDS BY UNREGISTERED HOLDERS

4.50 An 'unregistered holder', also called an 'uninfeft proprietor',[87] is someone who has the power to complete title but who has not yet done so. Suppose that Bill is

---

80   *Trade Development Bank v Crittall Windows Ltd* 1983 SLT 510.
81   2002 SC 580, aff'd 2004 SC (HL) 19. See paras **4.23–4.25** above.
82   1960 SC 255.
83   For another example of the application of the 'capable of being made real' requirement, see the complex case of *Advice Centre for Mortgages Ltd v McNicoll* 2006 SLT 591.
84   1980 SC 74.
85   Strictly speaking, 'infeftment', being a feudal term, should not now be used.
86   R G Anderson *Assignation* (2008) ch 11.

owner and delivers a disposition to Ben. At this stage Ben is not yet owner, for, to acquire ownership he needs to register. Someone with power to complete title is an 'unregistered holder'. If Ben had completed missives with Bill, but had not yet received a disposition, he would not have been an unregistered holder, for, without the disposition in his hands he cannot complete title. Another example of an unregistered holder is an executor who has obtained confirmation to heritable property but who has not completed title.[88]

4.51 The state of being an unregistered holder is usually short-lived. But not always. And the law allows an unregistered holder to grant certain types of deed *as if* owner. For example, Ben, instead of registering his disposition, could dispone to Betty. Betty, on registering her disposition, would become owner: in that case ownership would have passed from Bill to Betty without ever having vested in Ben. This rule can be regarded as an exception to the *nemo plus* principle: Ben, though not owner, can make Betty owner. When Betty lodges her application with the Keeper, she will of course have to submit the Bill/Ben disposition as well as the Ben/Betty disposition, in order to prove that Ben was unregistered holder. The deeds that link the currently registered owner (Bill) with the applicant (Betty) are called, in this connection, 'midcouples' or 'links in title'.[89] This example has been chosen because of its simplicity. In practice the important cases of unregistered holders occur in trust and executry conveyancing. For example, X owns land and dies. Y is confirmed as executor. Y will usually convey the land to the beneficiary, or to a purchaser, without having first completed title. There can be other examples too. For example, an Act of Parliament is passed with a section saying that the property of a given state corporation now 'vests' in another state corporation. The section operates as a conveyance. So the second corporation is now an unregistered holder.[90]

RISK

4.52 The issue of *risk* is one that applies only to sales (or other onerous transfers) of corporeal property. The question is: who bears the loss if the property is damaged without the fault of either party? At a certain point the risk is said to 'pass' but that is just a turn of phrase: risk is not an entity that can pass from one person to another. In large transactions the contract almost always has a clause about risk. But in the absence of such agreement, there are default rules. The common law rule is that risk passes when the contract of sale is made.[91] But where SOGA 1979 applies, the default rule

---

[87] 'Uninfeft proprietor' is in fact an unhappy term, in both its parts. 'Uninfeft' is a feudal term and so, strictly speaking, should not be used since feudal abolition. 'Proprietor' is wrong because an uninfeft proprietor is not a proprietor. But the term is in fact better known than 'unregistered holder' and is harmless if its defects are recognised.

[88] See PARAS **25.48–25.49** below.

is that risk passes with ownership,[92] except where the buyer is a consumer, in which case risk passes on delivery.[93]

JUDICIAL RECTIFICATION

4.53 Suppose that a conveyancing deed is bungled: it fails to reflect what the parties intended. There are numerous different possibilities but in practice the two common cases are that (a) less land or (b) more land is conveyed than provided for in the sale contract. In the first case the buyer can normally solve the problem by insisting that the contract be fully implemented. This will be done by a supplementary disposition from the seller. In the second case, the buyer is obliged to re-convey the excess land, because it was transferred *sine causa*.[94] In other words, the obligation to re-convey arises out of the law of unjustified enrichment. But in 1985 an additional remedy was introduced: 'judicial rectification of defectively expressed documents'.[95] The court is empowered to 'rectify' the deed, i.e. to rewrite it so that the new text reflects what the parties intended. Moreover, this rewriting works not *ex nunc*[96] but *ex tunc*.[97] The deed is altered retrospectively. Suppose that Alex owns 20,000 square metres and in 2009 he sells 5,000 square metres to Beth, but the disposition in fact conveys only 4,000. In 2011 the mistake comes to light and Beth successfully applies for judicial rectification. The result is that the deed is deemed *always* to have been for the full 5,000. But what about the Land Register? Changing planetary history about the *deed* does not touch the Register. So the provisions also provide that the Land Register itself is changed, and changed retrospectively.[98] It is Orwellian: the deed and the Land Register are not merely changed, but are *deemed never to have been other than they now are*. Therefore they have *not* changed. Who was the owner of the 1,000 square metres in 2010? In PastWorld 1 it was Alex. In PastWorld 2 it was Beth. It is difficult not to agree with Lord Rodger's comment that 'within a system where the register is intended to reveal the current state of the title, retrospective rectification is, almost by definition, anomalous'.[99]

---

[89]   In the case of Sasine titles it is necessary for the Ben/Betty deed to list the midcouples. This is called a clause of deduction of title. See Conveyancing (Scotland) Act 1924, s 3, and Sch A, Form 1. It is not necessary for Land Register titles: LR(S)A 1979, s 15.

[90]   E.g. Coal Industry Act 1994, s 7. The same happens when new local authorities are created, e.g. Local Government etc. (Scotland) Act 1994, s 15.

[91]   *Sloan's Dairies v Glasgow Corporation* 1977 SC 223.

[92]   SOGA 1979, s 20(1).

[93]   SOGA 1979, s 20(4).

[94]   Without legal basis.

[95]   LR(MP)(S)A 1985, ss 8 and 9. These provisions were based on English law. They are not limited to conveyancing deeds. They apply generally, though notably not to testamentary deeds: s 8(6). For an account of the provisions from a conveyancing standpoint, see Gretton and Reid, *Conveyancing* ch 17.

[96]   As from now.

[97]   As from then, i.e. from the time the deed was delivered (retrospectively).

4.54   Rather cumbersome rules protect third parties who have relied on the deed or on the Register.[100] One head-spinning remedy available to the third party is to reduce the rectification.[101] The main method of protection, however, is for the court to order that the retrospectivity does not go all the way back. For example, suppose that in 2010 Alex grants to Cherie a standard security over the 15,000 square metres he still owns. If the court considers Cherie worthy of protection,[102] it will backdate the rectification not to 2009 but to a date *immediately after* the grant of the security.

FURTHER READING

Carey Miller with Irvine *Corporeal Moveables* paras 8.01–8.11.

Reid *Property* paras 597–718.

Steven, A J M 'Transfer of Title in Scots Law' in J M Rainer and J Filip-Fröschl (eds) *Transfer in Title Concerning Movables Part 1 – Eigentumsübertragung an beweglichen Sachen in Europa* (2006) 155–172.

---

[98]   LR(S)A 1979, s 9(3A), as inserted in 1985. One must distinguish 'rectification' in the sense of the LR(MP)(S)A 1985 (judicial rectification of documents) from 'rectification of the Land Register'. The former may lead to the latter. But many judicial rectifications of documents have nothing to do with the Land Register and, conversely, the Land Register can be rectified for reasons unconnected with the judicial rectification of documents.

[99]   *Keeper of the Registers of Scotland v MRS Hamilton Ltd* 2000 SC 271 at 280.

[100]   LR(MP)(S)A 1985, s 9.

[101]   LR(MP)(S)A 1985, s 9(7)(a).

[102]   For an example where the third party failed, see *Jones v Wood* 2005 SLT 655.

Chapter 5

Acquisition by voluntary transfer: the rules for the various types of property

HERITABLE PROPERTY

Introduction

5.1 The main topic here is transfer of ownership. At the end of the section, other heritable rights will be discussed. The sale of land usually has three stages: the contract, settlement and registration. Ownership passes on registration.[1]

Contract

5.2 The first stage is the contract of sale. The subject belongs to contract law and to conveyancing practice, so little will be said here. Such a contract has to be in writing, signed by the parties or their agents.[2] It usually takes the form of *missives*. A missive is a letter, so 'missives' means an exchange of letters. The first is an offer to buy or, less commonly, an offer to sell. The reply may be a straightforward acceptance[3] or it may be what conveyancers call a 'qualified acceptance', which is, in the eyes of the law, a rejection coupled with a counter-offer. Once consensus has been reached the missives are said to be 'concluded'. The buyer does not yet have a real right. The next stage is 'settlement'. How long this happens after conclusion of missives varies: between one and two months would be fairly usual.

5.3 Contracts for the sale of land were once short. Now they typically run for several pages, covering not only the core issues of 'parties', 'property' and 'price' (the three Ps) but also other matters such as the physical condition of the property. For residential property, a standardised style is now normally used. These have evolved locally, so that there is an 'Edinburgh style', a 'Glasgow style', a 'Highland style' and so on.[4]

5.4 The core of the contract is that the seller will give possession and ownership and the buyer will pay the price. In theory, the first stage could be omitted. The parties could go straight to settlement. But that would usually be inconvenient. Each side wishes to prepare for settlement in the comforting knowledge that the other party is bound. Moreover, as mentioned, the contract usually contains provisions beyond the core ones.

5.5 In the interval between contract and settlement, the buyer's solicitor will check the title. This is usually fairly straightforward. The seller will send the land certificate[5]

---

[1]   Abolition of Feudal Tenure etc (Scotland) Act 2000 (AFT(S)A 2000), s 4. This was already the law, but the changes made by AFT(S)A 2000 made it appropriate to restate the rule in non-feudal language.

[2]   Requirements of Writing (Scotland) Act 1995 (RoW(S)A 1995) s 1(2)(a)(i): 'a contract ... for the ... transfer ... of a real right in land'. See PARA **30.3** below.

[3]   Known as a *de plano* acceptance.

[4]   These can all be found on the Law Society of Scotland website: http://www.lawscot.org.uk/ Members_Information/convey_essens/stdmissives/. For commercial properties, see http:// www.psglegal.co.uk/.

[5]   See PARA **6.19** below.

which sets out the boundaries of the property, who owns it and what the subordinate rights in it are. Assuming that it is in order, a report needs to be obtained from the Land Register to see if there have been any changes since the land certificate was issued.[6] There seldom are such changes. If, however, the title to the property is still in the Sasine Register, checking the title is more complicated.[7] The buyer's solicitor will also check in the Register of Inhibitions that the seller has not been inhibited or sequestrated. If the seller is a company, the Companies Register must also be checked. One of the risks is that what appears to be a company has never in fact been registered or, conversely, that it was validly registered but has since been struck off the Register. A search in the Companies Register will also reveal whether the company is in liquidation, and list the current directors (which enables the buyer to check that the disposition is signed by the right people).

Inhibition, sequestration and the Register of Inhibitions

5.6   An inhibition is an order from a court that affects the inhibitee's power to grant deeds affecting title to heritable property, in particular dispositions and standard securities.[8] It can be obtained by a creditor who has obtained decree for payment, and also by a pursuer during an action, as a protective measure: the latter is called inhibition on the dependence. It becomes void if the action fails and is also discharged, obviously enough, if the debtor pays the debt. The inhibition is registered in the Register of Inhibitions. This, like the Sasine Register and the Land Register, is administered by the Keeper.[9] As well as inhibitions, this register has other entries, such as sequestrations. The register is name-based, not property-based. Whenever there is a transaction affecting heritable property, the Register of Inhibitions will be checked. Obviously, if a seller turns out to be inhibited, or sequestrated, a buyer will refuse to settle, unless the disposition has the consent of the inhibitor or the trustee in sequestration. It is an implied term of the contract of sale of heritable property that the seller has an unrestricted power to dispone.

5.7   If a deed is granted notwithstanding an inhibition, it is not void, but is voidable at the inhibitor's instance – reduction *ex capite inhibitionis*. The effect is not to annul the grantee's title, except in a question with the inhibitor. The inhibitor, that is to say, can now take further steps to enforce his or her rights *as if* the offending deed had never been granted.

---

[6]   Known as a Form 12.
[7]   See PARAS **6.7–6.11** below.
[8]   See further Gretton *The Law of Inhibition and Adjudication* (2nd edn, 1996).
[9]   See PARA **6.3** below.

Settlement and registration

5.8   At the 'date of entry' what is called 'settlement'[10] takes place. The buyer pays the price. The seller gives possession and delivers the disposition, i.e. the deed of transfer, duly executed. Here is an example of a disposition:

> 'WE, JOHN POLLOCK and JANE CHRISTINE LORCA or POLLOCK, residing together formerly at Seven Mitchell Gardens, Musselburgh and now at Forty Four Portsoy Avenue there, heritable proprietors of the subjects hereinafter disponed, IN CONSIDERATION of the sum of TWO HUNDRED AND TEN THOUSAND FIVE HUNDRED POUNDS (£210,500) paid to us by CHARLOTTE DARCY ROXBURGH, residing at Fifty Ellis Road, Musselburgh, of which sum we do hereby acknowledge receipt, DO HEREBY DISPONE to the said Charlotte Darcy Roxburgh ALL and WHOLE Forty Four Portsoy Avenue, Musselburgh being the subjects registered in the Land Register of Scotland under Title Number MID 1234567; WITH ENTRY AND ACTUAL OCCUPATION as at Third July Two Thousand and Nine; And we grant warrandice: IN WITNESS WHEREOF we have subscribed these presents at Edinburgh on First July Two thousand and Nine in the presence of Fiona Cairns of Thirty Two Meadow Street Dunbar.
>
> *Fiona Cairns, witness*   *John Pollock*
>   *Jane C Pollock* '

On delivery of the disposition, the buyer does not acquire ownership, but rather the power to become owner, without any further co-operation by the granter, simply by registering the disposition in the Land Register. A person in this position is called an 'unregistered holder' of land, or a person with an 'uncompleted title', or an 'uninfeft proprietor'.[11] To 'complete a title' is to acquire a real right. So when a grantee registers a disposition he or she 'completes title'. The subject of land registration is dealt with in CHAPTER 6.

Warrandice

5.9   'Warrandice' means the guarantee given by the granter to the grantee that the title is good. In practice a deed contains an express 'grant' of warrandice but if the deed is silent, warrandice is implied by law. There are three levels of warrandice.

(1) The lowest is 'simple' warrandice. (This is what the law implies for gratuitous deeds.) The granter guarantees only that he or she will not grant any subsequent deed that could prejudice the deed now being granted. Actually, that could almost never happen anyway. Suppose that Jane owns a flat and, besotted by love, dispones it to her boyfriend, Dirk, gratuitously, and he promptly

---

[10]   The English term 'completion' is also used.
[11]   See **PARA 4.50** above.

registers. Nothing she could do thereafter could prejudice his title anyway. So it is hard to breach simple warrandice. But it could happen. For example, suppose that he delays to register the disposition. They have a row. She gives her new boyfriend, Doug, a disposition of the flat. He registers. Doug is now the owner. Jane is liable to Dirk for breach of warrandice.

(2) The middle level is 'fact and deed' warrandice. Here, the granter guarantees the grantee's title against any future *or past* act by the granter. For example, suppose that Ruth dispones to Simon and grants fact and deed warrandice. She is indeed the owner but there is a standard security over the property held by Tamsin. If that security was granted by Ruth, then she is in breach of her warrandice to Simon.

(3) The highest level is 'absolute' warrandice.[12] Deeds often say simply 'I grant warrandice' without specifying the type: in that case the meaning is absolute warrandice.[13] Absolute warrandice is the implied level in both the contract of sale (or other onerous contract) and a disposition in implement of such a contract.

5.10 Absolute warrandice is a guarantee by the granter to the grantee that:
  (i) the grantee will acquire ownership (or other right being granted) and
  (ii) the title will be unaffected by any encumbrances (notably subordinate real rights).

Title conditions[14] are a partial exception: the existence of a title condition will not amount to a breach of warrandice unless it was unknown to the grantee, was of an unusual type and causes a material loss in value to the property.[15] The special status of title conditions in relation to warrandice is because they are so common – most titles have them – and are the sort of things that buyers in general can be expected to tolerate. (By contrast, though heritable securities are common, a buyer cannot be expected to accept a property encumbered by an undischarged security. Such acceptance would require special agreement.) Another possible exception, but a controversial one, is *Lothian & Border Farmers Ltd v McCutcheon*,[16] holding that the existence of a lease does not mean breach of warrandice. The logic behind this decision is that the existence of a lease should not, in the normal case at least, mean a diminution of the value of the property, because the value of the rental stream should equate to the value of possession.[17]

5.11 The remedy for breach of warrandice in a deed is damages.[18] No claim based on the first leg of the guarantee (that the grantee will acquire ownership) can be made unless the grantee is faced with 'eviction' or 'threatened eviction'.[19] Thus, in

---

[12] See PARA **5.10** below.
[13] Titles to Land Consolidation (Scotland) Act 1868, s. 8.
[14] See PARA **13.3** below.
[15] Reid *Property* para 705.
[16] 1952 SLT 450.
[17] In practice, however, missives will normally provide for vacant possession.
[18] *Welsh v Russell* (1894) 21 R 769.
[19] *Clark v Lindale Homes Ltd* 1994 SC 210.

one case, Harold and Pamela Beck disponed to Sheila Palmer an area of land. It then turned out that the title to part of it was bad. Mrs Palmer sued them for breach of warrandice. But since no attempt had been made by the true owner to assert title to the area in question, there was no eviction and so the action failed.[20] 'Eviction', as the word is used here, does not have its ordinary meaning of physical removal. It means a successful assertion of the right of the true owner. For example, if the true owner obtains a declarator that his or her title is good, that is 'eviction'. Eviction is not a pre-requisite for a claim made under the second leg of the guarantee (no encumbrances).

5.12 As to warrandice in the contract, before settlement, the buyer is in a somewhat stronger position. Eviction is irrelevant: the buyer can simply refuse to settle until he or she is given what has been bargained for. If the defect amounts to a material breach, rescission is possible. Thus if Mrs Palmer or her solicitor identified the title defect before paying the price, she would have been in a stronger position.

5.13 The benefit of warrandice can be, and usually is, assigned. Thus X dispones to Y, and later Y dispones to Z. The warrandice that X granted to Y is assigned by Y to Z. This will give Z the benefit of two warrandices, for Y will also (in the typical case) be granting warrandice to Z.[21] Of course, there are limits to this. Suppose that the title problem is that the property is encumbered by a standard security granted by Y: clearly, X is not responsible for that. No separate process of assignation is needed: the benefit of warrandice is automatically included in what is called the 'assignation of writs' that is implied in every disposition.[22]

Letters of obligation

5.14 The reports from the registers may be a day or two old at the day of settlement, and moreover the buyer may not be able to register the disposition instantly.[23] So the buyer is at risk for a short period. To cover this risk, the practice is for the seller's solicitors to give the buyer a 'letter of obligation'. This guarantees that, provided that the buyer registers within 21 days, any unexpected entry in the registers will be cleared at the expense of the seller's solicitors. For example, suppose that the seller, a fraudster, on the day of settlement grants a standard security to a bank in exchange for a loan. The standard security happens to be registered one day before the buyer's disposition. The buyer becomes owner, but subject to the security. The seller's solicitors will have to pay to have the security lifted, assuming that they granted a letter of obligation. They can recover from their client – at least in theory.

[20] *Palmer v Beck* 1993 SLT 485.
[21] See, e.g., *Cobham v Minter* 1986 SLT 336.
[22] LR(S)A 1979, s 16.
[23] Normally because stamp duty land tax (SDLT) must be paid first. But if ATRL (see **PARA 6.26** below) is used, virtually instant registration is possible.

Subordinate real rights in land

5.15   The real right of ownership of land is transferred by disposition. Subordinate real rights in land are incorporeal property and so are transferred (assuming that they are transferable[24]) by assignation. The assignation of a registered lease is registered in the Land Register. An unregistered lease is assigned by taking possession and intimating the assignation to the landlord.[25] A standard security is transferred by registration in the Land Register, unless the property itself is still in the Sasine Register, in which case the assignation is registered in that register.[26]

CORPOREAL MOVEABLE PROPERTY

Introduction

5.16   Confusingly, two sets of rules exist for the transfer of corporeal moveable property. The Sale of Goods Act 1979 (SOGA 1979)[27] applies to all cases where the transfer is in implement of a contract of sale. Otherwise, the common law rules apply. For example, those rules apply to transfers by reason of barter, otherwise known as exchange or, to use the strictly accurate term for Scots law, 'excambion'. They also apply to transfers by way of donation (gift). If you buy a book at a bookshop, your acquisition of ownership from the shop is governed by SOGA 1979 but if a friend gives you a book as a Christmas present, your acquisition of ownership from your friend is governed by common law. Of course, in practice, sale is the most important type of case.

5.17   At common law, transfer of ownership requires delivery, i.e. the transfer of possession. This external act thus corresponds to registration in the case of heritable property. If your friend merely *tells* you that the present is yours, that is not enough:[28] no delivery, no transfer.[29] Although ownership cannot pass before delivery, it can pass after it, if the parties so agree. That follows from the fact that mutual consent is necessary for ownership to pass. So if your friend delivers the book to you subject to the condition that ownership will pass when you accept him as a friend on Facebook, ownership will pass only when you do this.

5.18   The common law rules originally applied to sales too. This was changed by the Sale of Goods Act 1893, later replaced by SOGA 1979. In contrast to the common

---

[24]   Servitudes and praedial real burdens cannot be transferred separately. They are pertinents of the benefited property. See **PARA 14.12** below. Proper liferents cannot be transferred. See **PARA 21.12** below. Some leases are non-transferable. See **PARA 19.33** below.

[25]   For the assignation of leases, see **PARAS 19.33–19.34** below.

[26]   For the assignation of standard securities, see **PARA 20.49** below.

[27]   In this chapter all references are to this Act, unless otherwise stated.

[28]   Delivery – by Santa Claus or otherwise – is required.

[29]   For the different methods of delivery, see **PARAS 11.13–11.17** below. For discussion of the common law rules of transfer, see Reid *Property* paras 619–623.

law, the statutory rules, covered in the remainder of this part of the chapter, are complex and difficult.[30]

Goods

5.19 'Goods' under SOGA 1979 essentially means corporeal moveable property,[31] though it includes heritable property that the parties agree will be 'severed', for example a contract to sell standing timber.[32] This is odd because it leads to conflicts between the law of heritable property on the one hand and the statute on the other. 'Existing' goods are those that the seller already has, while 'future' goods are those 'to be manufactured or acquired by him after the making of the contract of sale'.[33] 'Specific' goods are existing goods that are identifiable at the time of the contract.[34] For example, a contract for the sale of this bicycle, physically seen and touched by the parties, is a contract for specific goods. The contrast is with 'unascertained' goods: a contract for the sale of 1,000 tonnes of wheat would be an example. It may be that the seller has 3,000 tonnes but no particular grains of wheat can be identified as being those sold. Assuming that the contract goes ahead, the time must come when unascertained goods become ascertained. Logically, one might think that they then become 'specific' but SOGA 1979 reserves that word for goods identifiable when the contract is made.[35] Unascertained goods, on becoming separately identifiable, are said to become 'ascertained'. The same process happens to future goods, though here SOGA 1979's terminology seems to become wobbly. Unless and until goods are specific or ascertained, ownership cannot pass:[36] this is simply the specificity principle.[37]

Registered moveables: cars, ships, aircraft

5.20 In general, corporeal moveable property, unlike heritable property, is unregistered. There are some exceptions: motor vehicles, ships and aircraft. As for cars, they are, from the standpoint of property law, like other corporeal moveables. Registration with the DVLA at Swansea is not necessary for transfer. Such registration happens after the sale, and so is not a requirement of the sale, and the registration is of the 'keeper' of the car, not of its owner.[38] Ships are registered under the Merchant

---

[30]   It is not possible to go into all the difficulties here.
[31]   See **PARA 1.22** above.
[32]   SOGA 1979, s 61(1).
[33]   SOGA 1979, s 5(1).
[34]   SOGA 1979, s 61(1).
[35]   SOGA 1979, s 61(1).
[36]   SOGA 1979, s 16.
[37]   See **PARAS 4.12–4.14** above. There is, however, a qualification: the sale of quasi-specific goods. See **PARAS 5.27–5.29** below.
[38]   Cf *Central Newbury Car Auctions Ltd v Unity Finance Ltd* [1957] 1 QB 371 at 397.

Shipping Act 1995 and aircraft under the Civil Aviation Act 1982. The interaction of this body of legislation with SOGA 1979 is not wholly clear. The topic is specialised and is not examined here.

Transfer: SOGA 1979, s 17

5.21 The basic rule is given by SOGA 1979, s 17: assuming that the goods are specific, or have become ascertained, 'the property in them is transferred to the buyer at such time as the parties ... intend it to be transferred'.[39] Delivery is not necessary. No external act is needed. Hence the parties are free to agree that ownership ('property') passes before delivery, which is impossible at common law. They are equally free to agree that it passes at delivery, or after delivery. Agreement that it is to pass after delivery is common. It happens when goods are sold and delivered on credit. In such a case the seller is at risk because the buyer might become insolvent, in which case the seller is merely an ordinary unsecured creditor. Hence it is common for sellers to insist that the sale contact contain a clause providing that ownership passes on payment.[40]

Transfer: the default rules

5.22 In written contracts, it is usual to have a provision saying when ownership is to pass. But sometimes – and usually in oral contracts – there is nothing. SOGA 1979, s 18 therefore provides five default rules, i.e. rules that apply 'unless a different intention appears'.[41] Rule 1 is the most important: 'where there is an unconditional contract for the sale of specific goods in a deliverable state, ownership passes when the contract is made and it is immaterial whether the time of payment or the time of delivery, or both, be postponed'. So if Alice agrees to sell her bicycle to Boris, to be delivered next week, cash on delivery, ownership passes immediately, unless otherwise agreed. Rules 2 and 3 are about goods which, though specific, need something to be done to them by the seller. In such a case the parties are presumed to intend that ownership passes when the work has been done and the buyer informed of that fact. Rule 4 relates to goods delivered to the buyer on approval or on sale or return: here, the rule is the ownership passes when it becomes clear that the buyer means to keep the goods.[42]

5.23 Rule 5 is about contracts for the sale of unascertained or future goods by description. The rule is[43] that the parties are presumed to intend ownership to pass

---

[39] SOGA 1979, s 17(1).
[40] See **PARAS 5.25–5.26** below.
[41] All of them are subject to SOGA 1979, s 16 – the specificity principle.
[42] Rule 4 is puzzling because such contracts are probably not contracts of sale. This is one of the many puzzles in this Act.
[43] This is an approximate statement. The details are difficult.

when goods meeting the contract requirements are 'unconditionally appropriated to the contract', made identifiable. SOGA 1979, s 19 is a sixth rule: if the contract contains a 'reservation of a right of disposal' unless certain conditions are satisfied, then the parties are presumed to intend ownership not to pass until those conditions have been satisfied. For example, the contract says 'if the buyer fails to pay the price by 2 May, the seller can resell the goods'. In that case the parties are presumed to intend that ownership is not to pass before payment of the price. The same result can be obtained more directly under SOGA 1979, s 17.[44]

The seller's lien

5.24   Rule 1 of SOGA 1979, s 18 often applies in practice. It creates a risk for the seller: ownership passes immediately the parties shake hands on the deal, without payment. What if the buyer becomes insolvent? To meet this difficulty, SOGA 1979, s 41 says that the seller, on losing the real right of ownership, acquires a subordinate real right, called the seller's lien.[45] But this lien is lost as and when the goods are delivered. Hence sellers who wish to be protected even after delivery will opt for retention of title.

Retention of title

5.25   As has been seen, SOGA 1979, s 17 says that ownership passes when the parties intend it to pass. So a sale contract can say that it passes when the buyer pays. In practice most written contracts for the sale of goods have such a provision – a clause of retention of title, or reservation of title.[46] If the buyer fails to pay, the seller can rescind the contract on the ground of material breach and then demand re-delivery of the goods (assuming that they have already been delivered) on the basis that the seller is still the owner. A clause of retention of title can validly say that ownership is not to pass unless *all* sums owed by the buyer to the seller (not just the price due under this contract) have been paid.[47] Most retention of title clauses take this form.

5.26   A retention of title clause looks like a perfect protection against the risk of the seller's insolvency. And such clauses do often work. But often they do not.[48] One reason is that accession or specification may occur.[49] Goods such as, say, bricks or paint are destined to accession. Goods that are processed by the buyer may undergo

---

[44]   See PARAS **5.25–5.26** below.
[45]   For liens, see PARAS **20.58–20.64** below.
[46]   If the sale is one regulated by the Consumer Credit Act 1974, i.e. a sale on credit by a business to a consumer, it is called a 'conditional sale'.
[47]   *Armour v Thyssen Edelstahlwerke AG* 1990 SLT 891.
[48]   For what happens in practice, see S Wheeler, *Reservation of Title Clauses* (1991).
[49]   See PARAS **8.8–8.12** AND **8.20–8.22** below.

specification. In all such cases the seller's retained ownership will be defeated. Another reason is that the buyer may resell the goods to a second buyer, in which case SOGA 1979, s 25 may, depending on the circumstances, award ownership to the second buyer.[50]

SOGA 1979, ss 20A and 20B: sale of quasi-specific goods

5.27 In commercial practice it sometimes happens that a quantity is sold out of a particular and identifiable bulk, such as 200 tonnes out of 1,000 tonnes. The rules discussed so far would mean that ownership of the 200 tonnes ('quasi-specific goods', as they are sometimes called) could not pass until they had been 'appropriated to the contract'. This would involve separating them from the other 800 tonnes. Of course, this would happen on or before delivery. But in the meantime ownership would not have passed.[51]

5.28 A pre-paying buyer runs the risk of the seller's insolvency.[52] In the sale of goods the concern is usually the other way round: the concern is for the seller if ownership passes before payment. Nevertheless, pre-paying buyers are far from unknown in the sale of goods. Eventually it was decided to change the law so that a pre-paying buyer is protected from the seller's insolvency. To achieve this objective the complex set of rules in SOGA 1979, ss 20A and 20B was enacted.[53] The idea was, roughly speaking, that the pre-paying buyer would take a *pro indiviso* share[54] of the bulk. This legislative generosity applies only to quasi-specific goods. Rather than go through the rules as such, here is an example of how they work. An aspirin should be swallowed first.

STORY	ANALYSIS
1. Pete has 120,000 tonnes of oil in a ship.	Pete owns 100%.
2. He sells 40,000 tonnes to Rachel. She pays 75% of the price.	Rachel becomes owner of 75% of 40,000 tonnes = 30,000 tonnes = 25% of the whole bulk. Pete owns the other 75%.
3. Pete sells 60,000 tonnes to Sarah. The sale is on credit.	Sarah has paid nothing yet, so no property consequences.

---

50   See PARA **5.35** below.
51   SOGA 1979 s 16.
52   See PARA **4.26** above.
53   By the Sale of Goods (Amendment) Act 1995.
54   See PARA **9.2** below.

4. The 60,000 tonnes are delivered to Sarah.	60,000 tonnes remain. Rachel's ownership share increases from 25% to 50%. Pete's falls from 75% to 50%.
5. Rachel pays the balance of the price.	Rachel's ownership share increases from 50% to 66.667%. Pete's falls from 50% to 33.333%.
6. Pete sells 20,000 tonnes to Tom. Tom pays.	Tom becomes owner of 33.333%. Pete now owns nothing.
7. The 40,000 tonnes are delivered to Rachel.	Rachel becomes sole owner of what is delivered, and Tom sole owner of the rest.

5.29   In this story Pete does not become insolvent, and so the buyers had nothing to fear anyway. Had he become insolvent, then any buyer with co-ownership is protected. For example, had Pete been sequestrated after Stage 2, Rachel could still have insisted, as against his trustee in sequestration, on taking 25%.

The *nemo plus* principle

5.30   SOGA 1979, s 21 states the *nemo plus* principle:[55]

'Where goods are sold by a person who is not their owner, and who does not sell them under the authority or with the consent of the owner, the buyer acquires no better title to the goods than the seller had, unless the owner of the goods is by his conduct precluded from denying the seller's authority to sell.'

The last part of the provision is about personal bar. Whether its effect is to confer ownership is uncertain, but the balance of opinion is that it is.[56]

Example

5.31

Fiona owns a grandfather clock. It is stolen. Years later, she notices it for sale in an antique shop. She speaks to the dealer, Donald, and after extensive correspondence Donald finally agrees that the clock in his shop is the same one that was stolen from Fiona. But Donald points out that he bought the clock in good faith from the Earl of St Monans, who himself bought in good faith from a Dundee dealer, who is now dead. Further than that, the provenance of the clock cannot be traced. It is likely, however, that the thief sold direct to the Dundee dealer. The antiques dealer says he would be happy to

---

[55]   See PARA **4.39** above.
[56]   See E C Reid and J W G Blackie *Personal Bar* (2006) W Green, paras 11-16–11-25.

give the clock to Fiona, but only if she pays him what he paid to the Earl of St Monans, namely £14,550. The answer? *Nemo plus.* The thief's title was void. Hence, the Earl's title was void. Hence, Donald's title is void. The clock is Fiona's and she can insist on resuming possession of it without paying anyone anything.

5.32   This is unfair to Donald. But the opposite rule would be unfair to Fiona. Both parties are innocent, yet one must suffer. Donald is entitled to damages from the Earl for breach of warrandice,[57] which transfers the loss to another innocent party. Ultimately, the thief should make the loss good but the chances that the thief can be traced, and, if traced, made to pay, are poor. The result is that anyone who buys corporeal moveable property – as most of us do every day – takes a risk.

5.33   Most European countries tend to protect the good-faith buyer more than we do. Some, for example German law,[58] say that if the owner gives up possession *voluntarily* (e.g. Fiona had lent the clock to someone who turned out to be untrustworthy) then a good-faith buyer will obtain a good title. Others (e.g. Italian law[59]) go further and say that a good-faith buyer *always* gets good title. Our law does, however, give the buyer some protection.[60] To this protection we now turn.

The exceptions to *nemo plus*

5.34   SOGA 1979 has two exceptions to the *nemo plus* principle: ss 24 and 25.[61] Section 24[62] can be illustrated by this example.

Example

Jack sells goods to Jill and ownership has passed to Jill, but the goods have not yet been delivered to her. Jack now sells and delivers the goods to Ben, who is in good faith. The result is that Ben acquires ownership. In such a case, therefore, ownership passes from Jill to Ben and, as far as Jill is concerned, she has been deprived of ownership without her consent. Jack's sale to Ben might be a deliberate breach of his contract with Jill, or it might be mere inadvertence. (Example: Jack has an antique shop. Jill calls and buys a grandfather clock. She will collect it the next day. Jack forgets to mark it as sold. The same afternoon, while Jack is out of the shop, his assistant, unaware of the prior sale, sells it to Ben.)

---

[57]   SOGA 1979, s 12.
[58]   BGB §§ 932 and 935.
[59]   Codice civile, Art 1153.
[60]   Information about other systems of transfer of corporeal moveable property can be found in such works as J M Rainer and J Filip-Fröschl (eds) *Transfer of Title Concerning Movables Part I* (2006) and L P W van Vliet *Transfer of movables in German, French, English and Dutch law* (2000).
[61]   Or three exceptions if personal bar is included: see **PARA 5.30** above.
[62]   Inexplicably, the provision contained in SOGA 1979, s 24 is also contained in s 8 of the Factors Act 1889, extended to Scotland by the Factors (Scotland) Act 1890.

5.35   The other exception is SOGA 1979, s 25. This is textually difficult and moreover has complex exceptions. The core idea can be illustrated by an example.

Example

Beth sells and delivers a car to Clara. The contract has a clause saying that ownership passes when Clara pays. Before Clara pays, she sells and delivers the car to Dugald. He is in good faith. Dugald acquires ownership: thus ownership passes from Beth to Dugald. In keeping with its difficult wording, SOGA 1979, s 25 does not actually say this: it says that the transfer 'has the same effect as if the person making the delivery or transfer were a mercantile agent in possession of the goods or documents of title with the consent of the owner'[63] which is an oblique reference to the Factors Act 1889, s 2, as applied to Scotland by the Factors (Scotland) Act 1890. SOGA 1979, s 25 is an exception to s 21. SOGA 1979, s 25 itself has a sub-exception, stated in s 25(2), which is that if the Beth/Clara sale is a business-to-consumer credit sale (i.e. what the Consumer Credit Act 1974 calls a 'conditional sale') then Dugald is not protected. This sub-exception itself has a sub-sub-exception, which is that if the thing sold is a motor vehicle then Dugald is protected. This sub-sub-exception has a sub-sub-sub-exception, which is if Dugald is a business buyer then he is not protected. These rules are handily located in the Hire Purchase Act 1964, s 27. (Despite that Act's title, s 27 applies to sales, not just to HP.)

5.36   Finally, SOGA 1979, s 23. This is not an actual exception to *nemo plus* but can conveniently be dealt with here. It says that 'when the seller of goods has a voidable title to them, but his title has not been avoided at the time of the sale, the buyer acquires a good title to the goods, provided he buys them in good faith and without notice of the seller's defect of title'.

Example

Robert is owner. Sara, by fraud, induces Robert to sell. At this stage Sara is owner but her title is voidable. Sara now sells to Tim, who is in good faith Tim is now owner and his title is not voidable. SOGA 1979, s 23 merely restates the common law about voidable titles. It is not an exception to *nemo plus* because when Sara transferred to Tim she held the right of ownership: her title was not void but merely voidable.

---

[63]   What if something belongs to W, is sold by X to Y under retention of title, and is then sold by Y to Z? SOGA 1979, s 25 says that Z gets a good title. In *National Employers Mutual General Insurance Association Ltd v Jones* [1990] 1 AC 24 the House of Lords held that notwithstanding the wording of the statute, Z does not get good title.

INCORPOREAL MOVEABLE PROPERTY: PERSONAL RIGHTS

Introduction

5.37 Personal rights are transferred by assignation completed by intimation. Such rights can be of various types, but in practice it is usually personal rights to be paid money which are transferred. Three parties are involved. Suppose that Leonard owes £1,000 to Maria. From Maria's point of view, that is an asset. She can transfer it to Nick. The result will be that Nick will be substituted for Maria as Leonard's creditor. Maria is called the 'assignor' or (more usually) the 'cedent', and Nick is called the 'cessionary' or (more usually) the 'assignee'. The transfer is called 'assignation' (or, rarely, 'cession').[64]

Transferability

5.38 Personal rights are presumptively transferable. The consent of the debtor is not required. However, occasionally a claim (using that term in the sense of a personal right) is non-transferable. Some are unassignable by statute.[65] Where a debt arises from a contract, this may forbid assignation, and such a clause is effective.[66] This is called *delectus personae creditoris* ('choice of the person of the creditor', i.e. choice of that particular creditor) and may be an express or an implied term.

5.39 The expression 'assignation of contract' is sometimes encountered. Contracts cannot be assigned. The object of an assignation is a right. The transfer of a contract can be achieved only by a combination of assignation of the rights and delegation of the duties.[67]

Transfer by debtor?

5.40 A debtor cannot assign the obligation to pay. That would be absurd: it would mean that you could borrow money, spend it and then happily assign the debt to an undischarged bankrupt living in Outer Mongolia. However, to this general principle there exist some qualifications. The first is that such a transfer can, of course, take place if the creditor consents. So if X owes money to Y, X's obligation to pay can be transferred to Z if all three parties so agree. This is called 'delegation'. The second is that a debtor is normally[68] free to subcontract performance of the obligation. That,

---

[64] In English law, the term is 'assignment'.
[65] E.g. Social Security Administration Act 1992, s 187.
[66] *James Scott Ltd v Apollo Engineering Ltd* 2000 SLT 1262.
[67] See PARA **5.40** below.

however, does not let the debtor off the hook as far as the creditor is concerned: the debtor is still directly liable. In the third place, the contract itself may expressly or implicitly permit transfer by the debtor. Finally, it might be wondered why anyone (Z) would ever wish to take on someone else's obligation or why the creditor (Y) would ever be prepared to consent. The short answer is: commercial deals.

Assignation: how

5.41 As with other transfers, there is a distinction between contract and conveyance.[69] The contract to assign does not have to be in writing. Before the Requirements of Writing (Scotland) Act 1995, the assignation itself had to be in writing, but that requirement was abolished by that Act.[70] The Transmission of Moveable Property (Scotland) Act 1862 sets out a simple style of assignation, but it is not compulsory, and the courts have been prepared to recognise all sorts of documents as being assignations.[71]

5.42 Just as the transfer of land occurs not by delivery of the disposition but by registration, so transfer of a claim takes place not by delivery of the deed of assignation but by 'intimation' (formal notice) to the debtor – Leonard, in the example.[72] Suppose that Maria agrees to transfer to Nick, and the delivers to him a deed of assignation, but she is sequestrated before Nick intimates to Leonard. Nick is too late.

5.43 Intimation can in theory be done by the common law method, which involves a notary, but this never happens in modern practice. The Transmission of Moveable Property (Scotland) Act 1862 introduced the alternative of 'transmitting a copy [of the assignation] certified as correct by post' to the debtor. Does mere *de facto* knowledge count as intimation? 'One of the long, slow burning questions … is whether a debtor's mere knowledge of an assignation is sufficient intimation to him', writes Professor McBryde.[73] The older authorities answer this question clearly in the negative, and it does not seem that they have been overruled, so the conclusion must be that the law remains unchanged. Whether or not mere *de facto* knowledge suffices, the law recognises certain alternatives to formal intimation. One is the raising of an action by the assignee against the debtor, for the action in itself is regarded as intimation.

---

[68] But the contract may provide, expressly or by implication, that this is not permitted. This is *delectus personae debitoris*. The two types of *delectus personae* are quite different, a fact that has not prevented them from being confused: see, e.g., *Cole v Handasyde & Co* 1910 SC 68 and *Scottish Homes v Inverclyde District Council* 1997 SLT 829.

[69] See PARAS **4.15–4.16** above.

[70] RoW(S)A 1995, s 11(3)(a). (The change does not make sense because a copy of the assignation has to be sent to the debtor.)

[71] See, notably, *Carter v McIntosh* (1862) 24 D 925 and *Brownlee v Robb* 1907 SC 1302.

[72] See PARA **5.37** above.

[73] McBryde *Contract* para 12-93.

Effect

5.44 Upon intimation the personal right passes from the cedent's patrimony to the assignee's. The assignee (Nick) replaces the cedent (Maria) as creditor of the debtor (Leonard).

5.45 'All exceptions [defences] competent against the cedent before the assignation or intimation are relevant against the assignee, as payment, compensation etc.'[74] For example, suppose that Leonard had paid off £200 of the debt, so that the debt was reduced to £800. At this stage Maria assigns the claim to Nick, but purports to assign the whole original claim of £1,000. Assume that Nick was in good faith. Leonard is liable to Nick for £800, not for £1,000. This principle has a cumbersome Latin tag: *assignatus utitur jure auctoris*. The classic illustration is *Scottish Widows Fund v Buist*,[75] where Mr Moir took out a life assurance policy, assuring the company that he was in good health and of sober habits. In fact, he had a variety of health problems, including advanced syphilis, and was an alcoholic. He assigned the benefit of the policy to Mr Buist. When Mr Moir died, Mr Buist, who had acted in good faith, sought payment of the policy proceeds. The company refused to pay, citing the *assignatus utitur* principle. The defence was upheld. Suppose that Mr Moir had not assigned the policy. Then, on his death, the company could have refused to pay his executor. The assignee could not be in any better position.

5.46 The *assignatus utitur* rule applies to matters as they are at the date of intimation. A good illustration is *Macpherson's JF v Mackay*.[76] Hugh Macpherson was one of the beneficiaries of a large trust set up by his late father, Archie Macpherson. A beneficial right in a trust is incorporeal moveable property and can be assigned.[77] Hugh married Alice and a separate family trust, a marriage trust, was established. (We will call this new trust 'Trust 2', to distinguish it from his father's trust, 'Trust 1'.) Hugh assigned his share in Trust 1 to the extent of £1,000 to the trustees of Trust 2.[78] The assignation was intimated to the trustees of Trust 1. As it happened, Hugh was a trustee of Trust 1 and indeed latterly the sole trustee. Over time, Trust 1 paid out to Hugh the whole amount allocated to him under the trust. After Hugh's death, the trustees of Trust 2 claimed £1,000 from Trust 1. The trustees of Trust 1 pled *assignatus utitur*, arguing that Hugh could not have claimed that money, and so his assignees could not either. This defence failed. At the time when the assignation was intimated, the money was there.

5.47 The *assignatus utitur* principle is a shield, not a sword. In *Binstock Miller & Co Ltd v E Coya & Co Ltd*[79] there was a sale of orange juice. The buyers paid part of the price and the sellers then assigned their right to the balance. When the assignee

---

[74]   Stair II, 1, 20.
[75]   (1876) 3 R 1078.
[76]   1915 SC 1011.
[77]   It is a personal right against the trustees.
[78]   Partial assignation, though uncommon in practice, is competent.

sought payment, the buyers refused to pay, saying that the orange juice was disconform to contract and had been rejected by them. The buyers not only refused to pay the balance, but sought to claim back from the assignees the part of the price that they had already paid to the sellers. It was held that, although the buyers were entitled to refuse to pay the balance (assuming, of course, that what they said about the juice was correct), they could not recover their money from the assignees. They would have to claim from the sellers.

Warrandice

5.48   The law has some obscurities, but the basic rule is that the cedent is presumed to grant warrandice *debitum subesse* – 'that the debt subsists'. This is a guarantee that the claim being assigned does indeed exist in the form that it appears to have. Thus, if Maria assigns to Nick a claim for £1,000 and in fact £200 has already been paid off, she is in breach of her warrandice to him. This default type of warrandice is only that the claim is payable to the cedent, not that it will be paid. For example, Oliver owes money to Percy and Percy assigns the claim to Rosi. When Rosi seeks to collect from Oliver she finds that he has become bankrupt. Rosi has no remedy against Percy in terms of the warrandice *debitum subesse*. (In the law of negotiable instruments, a non-endorsing cedent warrants that the debt is payable;[80] an endorsing cedent warrants not only that the debt is payable but that it will be paid.[81])

Example

5.49

The first document is the assignation and the second is the intimation.

'I, FERGUS DUGALD STEWART of 43 Maitland Street Airdrie in consideration of the sum of Fifty-five Thousand Pounds (£55,000) paid to me by HOLSTEBRO CALEDON LIMITED, a company incorporated under the Companies Acts under number 987654321 having its registered office at 1 Vierzon Way Fraserburgh, DO HEREBY ASSIGN to the said Holstebro Caledon Limited all sums due or to become due to me by Airdrie Meteorological Consultancies Ltd, a company incorporated under the Companies Acts under number 123456789 having its registered office at 23 Calafell Road Glasgow, in terms of a contract between me and the said Airdrie Meteorological Consultancies Ltd dated 1 April 2012 and registered in the Books of Council and Session on 27 April 2012.

---

[79]   1957 SLT (Sh Ct) 47. And see *Alex Lawrie Factors Ltd v Mitchell Engineering Ltd* 2001 SLT (Sh Ct) 93.

[80]   Bills of Exchange Act 1882, s 58(3).

[81]   Bills of Exchange Act 1882, s 55(2).

IN WITNESS WHEREOF these presents are signed at Glasgow on Twenty seventh October Two thousand and twelve in the presence of Elizabeth van Groenewegen Cowper, Five Dryden Street, Glasgow.

Elizabeth Cowper (witness)   *Fergus Stewart* '

'To:
Airdrie Meteorological Consultancies Ltd,
23 Calafell Road,
Glasgow

28 October 2012

Recorded Delivery

NOTICE is hereby given that by assignation dated 27 October 2012 Fergus Dugald Stewart of 43 Maitland Street Airdrie assigned to Holstebro Caledon Ltd 1 Vierzon Way Fraserburgh all sums due or to become due to him in terms of a contract between him and yourselves dated 1 April 2012 and registered in the Books of Council and Session on 27 April 2012.

Dated at Glasgow the 28th day of October 2012.

Lorraine Woods
Member

Valeria Victrix LLP
Solicitors, 1 Meadow Lane, Glasgow.
Agents for Holstebro Caledon Ltd.'

5.50   Attached to this will be a photocopy of the assignation with 'Certified a true copy' written on it and signed on behalf of Valeria Victrix LLP. Alternatively, of course, the notice and the certification could be signed by a director of Holstebro Caledon Ltd. There will also be a covering letter, which will ask Airdrie Meteorological Consultancies Ltd to confirm receipt.

Non-standard cases

5.51   What has been described so far is the ordinary law of assignation. There are also some non-standard cases.
   (1) If the debt has been embodied in a fully negotiable instrument, special rules apply. In particular intimation is not required and the *assignatus utitur* rule does not apply. The rules are in the Bills of Exchange Act 1882, which covers almost all types of negotiable instrument. (One or two types are subject to common law, but the common law rules are the same as the 1882 Act rules.)[82]

---

[82]   The standard work is N Elliott (ed), *Byles on Bills of Exchange and Cheques* (28th edn, 2007). See also R M Goode *Commercial Law* (3rd edn, 2004) ch 19.

(2) Rights under life assurance contracts are assignable – but special legislation applies.[83] In broad terms, the rules are the same as for ordinary assignation.

(3) For company shares and bonds the Stock Transfer Act 1963 applies where there is a share certificate. The transferor signs a stock transfer form and delivers it, with the share certificate, to the transferee, who then sends them both to the company, and is issued with a new certificate in his or her name. For 'dematerialised' shares there is a dematerialised form of transfer.[84]

INCORPOREAL MOVEABLE PROPERTY: INTELLECTUAL PROPERTY RIGHTS

5.52 Intellectual property (IP) rights, such as copyright and patents, are patrimonial rights and can be sold, donated, bequeathed and so on.[85] They are transferred by assignation. Unlike ordinary incorporeal moveable property, they are not personal rights. There is no third party to whom intimation should or could be made. Some IP rights, notably copyright, exist without registration, and these are assigned by simple consent, provided that it is in writing.[86] The requirement of writing applies to the transfer of all types of IP right. Most types of IP rights are registered, and in that case so must the assignation.[87] There are uncertainties as to whether the right passes to the grantee at the time of registration (as in the case of heritable property) or whether registration has merely the effect of delivery in the sale of goods. It may be that the IP right passes on delivery of the deed of assignation, but that until it is registered a good faith buyer from the seller might obtain a good title in much the same way as is contemplated by SOGA 1979, s 24.[88]

FURTHER READING

General

See the reading for Chapter 4.

Heritable property

Gretton and Reid, *Conveyancing* ch 2.

Guthrie, T *Scottish Property Law* (2nd edn, 2005) chs 17–19.

---

[83] Policies of Assurance Act 1867, s 5. The reason for this provision is unclear. It may be that it was needed for England and was applied to Scotland without thought.

[84] Companies Act 2006, s 783 ff.

[85] See PARA **1.18** above.

[86] Copyright, Designs and Patents Act 1988, s 90.

[87] E.g. Patents Act 1977, s 33.

[88] See PARA **5.34** above.

Halliday *Conveyancing* vol 2.

McDonald *Conveyancing Manual* ch 33.

Sinclair, J H *Handbook of Conveyancing Practice in Scotland* (5th edn, 2006).

Corporeal moveable property

Atiyah, P S, Adams, J N and MacQueen, H *The Sale of Goods* (11th edn, 2005).

Carey Miller with Irvine *Corporeal Moveables* chs 8–9.

Goode, R M *Commercial Law* (3rd edn, 2004) chs 7, 8 and 16.

Incorporeal moveable property

Anderson, R G *Assignation* (2008).

McBryde *Contract* ch 12.

Chapter 6

Land registration

INTRODUCTION

6.1 The idea of land registration derives from the publicity principle.[1] If rights have to be registered, then their existence or non-existence can be known by third parties – such as someone who wishes to buy. The idea is so obvious that the question to ask is not why land rights are registered but why all rights are not registered.

(1) It is not only land rights that are registered. Most intellectual property rights are too – the main exception being copyright.[2] So too are ships, and also aircraft.[3]

(2) A registration system costs money, and so is justifiable only if the average values are high enough. Thus, registration is justifiable for rights in land but not for rights in bicycles.

(3) Land has some features that make registration easier than for some types of property: in particular, it is permanent and does not move, and so in principle is easily identifiable.

(4) More types of real right can exist in land than in moveable property. Thus, title tends to be more complex and the more complex the title, the more convenient it is for the rights to be recorded publicly.

6.2 Scotland introduced registration of land rights in 1617. This was the Sasine Register which still exists today. A replacement system was introduced in 1981,[4] the new register being called the Land Register of Scotland. Properties are being gradually transferred from the old system into the new. A terminological point is that although the Sasine Register is a register, strictly, deeds are said to be 'recorded' there, rather than 'registered', with the latter term being used for the Land Register. Thus, the expression 'first registration' means the transfer of a property out of the old register into the new. 'Unregistered property' means property that is not yet in the new register.

National registration: the Keeper

6.3 Many countries have local land registration. Scotland has a unitary, country-wide system, based in Edinburgh. That is so both for the old register and for the new. However, each register is divided into 33 areas. These are the traditional counties – not the modern local authority areas.[5] Thus, for land registration purposes Edinburgh remains in Midlothian. One exception is that Glasgow has always formed a separate registration area under the picturesque name of 'the Barony and Regality of Glasgow'. Both registers are administered by the Keeper of the Registers of Scotland – in practice called simply 'the Keeper'. Everything is done in his name, though in reality

---

[1]   See PARAS **4.17–4.18** above.

[2]   Intellectual property rights are generally outwith the scope of this book but see PARA **5.52** above.

[3]   See PARA **5.20** above.

[4]   Under Land Registration (Scotland) Act 1979 (LR(S)A 1979). The first county became operational for Land Register purposes in 1981. See PARA **6.15** below.

[5]   The old counties were abolished for local government purposes in 1974.

he is at the head of a department – the Registers of Scotland – employing more than a thousand staff.[6]

The incentive to register

6.4   A register sounds a good idea but how does one persuade people to co-operate? The answer is simple. The law makes registration a necessary part of the process of conveyancing: no registration, no real right. While the Sasine Register and the Land Register differ in many respects, both adopt that principle. Registration is compulsory in the sense that those who do not register do not acquire the right they wish to acquire. No active compulsion exists.

6.5   The rule applies only to real rights, not to personal rights. Adam owns land and enters a contract of sale with Eve. She thereby acquires a personal right – to require Adam to grant her a disposition in exchange for payment of the price. The contract creates personal rights and is thus valid without registration.

Public access

6.6   The Sasine Register and the Land Register are, like other registers, public. If Fergus grants a standard security to the bank over his house,[7] that fact can be discovered by his friends, his nosy neighbours or anyone else, for payment to the Keeper of a modest fee. Houses may have opaque walls but titles do not, and not everyone feels comfortable with living in a title glasshouse. But the public access principle is one we have had since 1617 and most other legal systems have the same principle. The digital revolution means that access is now possible online.[8]

THE SASINE REGISTER

Overview

6.7   The full name of the old register is the General Register of Sasines. In practice it is called the 'Sasine Register', the 'Sasines Register', the 'Register of Sasines' or the 'GRS'. Its existence is based on the Registration Act 1617 which remains in force, though supplemented over the centuries by piecemeal legislation. The Sasine Register is a collection of copies of deeds. Suppose that Jack dispones to Jill. She presents the deed to the Keeper. Once upon a time, a member of his staff would copy it, using quill and ink, into a large volume. Later, deeds were photocopied. Now the copying is by digital scanning. The deed is then returned, stamped with the

---

[6]   See http://www.ros.gov.uk/.
[7]   See PARAS **20.43–20.56** below.
[8]   Via a subscription service known as Registers Direct.

recording date. This is the date when Jill becomes the owner of the land. If someone loses a recorded deed, that does not matter much because an official copy can be obtained from the Keeper, i.e. a copy of the recorded copy. This is called an 'extract': an extract is an officially certified copy of a document. (The word is used not only for the Sasine Register but in other contexts too, such as an extract of a decree.)

6.8   The Sasine Register is a public warehouse of private deeds, and the Keeper's job is rather like that of a warehouse keeper. The warehouse used to be a physical one, and for the most part still is, though all new deeds are scanned and thus occupy virtual shelves, not actual ones. Like a warehouse keeper, the Keeper must keep a good inventory of his stock. Everything is indexed, by names of parties and by property.[9] Without this remarkably efficient system, the register would be unworkable because the warehouse contains millions of copy deeds, going back to 1617. Each deed, as it comes in, is assigned to whichever of the 33 areas the property is in. Apart from that, however, there is no sorting. So, for Perthshire, a disposition of a flat in Perth might be followed on the next page of the volume by a standard security over a farm near Dunkeld, and so on. If Jill wishes to buy 57 Harry Potter Loan, Auchterarder, finding the relevant deeds would be like finding a needle in a haystack, but for the indexing system. It allows the deeds to be identified quickly and reliably.

6.9   Jill could, if she wished, search[10] back to 1617 for, unlike a real warehouse, nothing that goes in the doors goes out again. And subject to one or two qualifications, she does not have to worry about unrecorded deeds because these cannot normally affect the title.[11]

6.10   Since the system is simply a collection of indexed copy deeds, there is nothing that officially says 'Jack is the owner of Redmains' or that 'Bank of Airdrie plc has a standard security over Greenmains'. Nor is there anything that officially sets out the boundaries of properties. If Jill wishes to be satisfied, before she hands over the purchase price, that the seller, Jack, is indeed the owner, and moreover that the property is free from subordinate real rights, she has to work this out for herself or, in practice, hire a solicitor to do so. Since the Sasine Register is a register of deeds, not of rights, the rights have to be inferred from the deeds. This is far from simple. If Jill locates a disposition by Alan to Tom and another from Tom to Jack, she may infer that Tom was owner and that as a result Jack is now owner. That inference is probably – but not certainly – right. Perhaps there has been a later deed by Jack in favour of someone else. Or perhaps Alan's title was bad. What Jill is interested in ascertaining is Jack's right. The Sasine Register does not offer her that, but a set of juridical acts.[12] In practice, a skilled conveyancer can check Jack's title with a high

---

9   The indexing of properties is called the system of 'search sheets' and is, for obvious reasons, a more important tool than the name indexes.

10   Checking the indexes to identify the deeds relevant to a property is called 'searching' and a report of the result of the search is itself called a 'search'. There are independent firms of searchers and, just as Jill is likely to use a firm of solicitors, the solicitors' firm is likely to use a firm of searchers.

11   For the exceptions, see PARA **6.36** below.

12   A deed is a written and signed juridical act.

degree of accuracy, partly because of the high quality of the indexing and partly because defects in title tend to be cured by prescription.[13]

6.11 If it turns out that Jack's title is defective as to part or even all of what Jill thought she was buying, she is unprotected by the system. It never promised her anything more than a set of deeds to examine. This is not quite as bad as it sounds. She will have a damages claim against Jack,[14] and she might have a negligence claim against her own solicitor. Nevertheless, as will be seen, the Land Register offers her more. It offers what people are mainly interested in: the rights themselves.

THE LAND REGISTER

Past and future

6.12 The Sasine Register is a deeds register. Many legal systems have something similar.[15] The alternative is a title register, in which what is registered is the real right itself. Title registration was an idea pioneered in Germany – a slow process that culminated in the 1890s. An earlier version of the German system influenced the Australian system, developed in the 1850s by Robert Torrens and hence often called the Torrens system. Both the modern German system and the Torrens system have been copied by many countries, with, of course, local variations.[16] In both, what is registered is primarily the right rather than the deed. There is thus an official statement that so-and-so is the owner of Blackmains or the holder of a standard security over Whitemains, and so on. Both registers are map-based. In each, a person acquiring a right in good faith from the registered owner is normally assured of a good title. A version of the Torrens system was introduced in England and Wales.[17] In the 1960s the decision was taken to introduce a similar system in Scotland,[18] and the result was the Land Registration (Scotland) Act 1979 (LR(S)A 1979) and the accompanying Land Registration Rules. LR(S)A 1979 has been amended quite often, but only in minor respects. The Rules have also been amended frequently, and the original 1980 Rules[19] were replaced in 2006.[20]

---

[13] See PARAS **2.26–2.28** above.

[14] In warrandice. See PARAS **5.9–5.13** above.

[15] For example, France and South Africa.

[16] See generally, Scottish Law Commission, *Discussion Paper on Land Registration: Void and Voidable Titles* (2004) paras 1.13–1.17.

[17] The process began with the Land Registry Act 1862. This was a failure in practice, with hardly any land being registered, and the same was true of its successor, the Land Transfer Act 1875. The third attempt, the Land Transfer Act 1897, was more successful. It was replaced by the Land Registration Act 1925, itself replaced by the Land Registration Act 2002. In England, unregistered titles were private, except in Middlesex and Yorkshire, where there were systems comparable to the Sasine Register.

[18] Registration of Title in Scotland (1963, Cmnd 2032); Scheme for the Introduction and Operation of Registration of Title in Scotland (1969, Cmnd 4137). These are known respectively as the 'Reid Report' and the 'Henry Report'.

[19] Land Registration (Scotland) Rules 1980, SI 1980/1413.

[20] Land Registration (Scotland) Rules 2006 (LR(S)R 2006), SSI 2006/485.

6.13   Experience showed that LR(S)A 1979 had certain shortcomings, and the Scottish Law Commission has been undertaking a review.[21] The Commission is expected to recommend that LR(S)A 1979 be repealed and replaced with a new statute but that the basic ideas of the new system should remain in place. The change will be evolution, not revolution, and the benefits that title registration has brought will be preserved.

Phasing in the new system

6.14   An overnight transfer of all properties from the old system to the new would have been impossible. LR(S)A 1979 provides for a phased transfer. A property switches to the new register when it is sold. That is to say, the disposition granted by the seller to the buyer cannot enter the Sasine Register but only the Land Register. Thus, if the last time Blackmains was sold was in, say, 1970, it is still in the Sasine Register. Gratuitous transfers, such as a disposition by way of donation, or a disposition by an executor to a legatee, do not trigger the switch. So, such deeds, if they deal with unregistered property,[22] still go into the Sasine Register.[23] A 'voluntary registration' is where an owner holding on a Sasine title seeks registration in the Land Register, outwith the context of any transfer. Voluntary registrations require the consent of the Keeper[24] and are in current practice uncommon.

6.15   The phasing has, however, a second dimension. The new system was not introduced in all 33 counties at once, but rather one by one. The first was Renfrewshire in 1981 and it was not until 2003 that all 33 were 'operational'. So, if, in 1999, Jack sold land in Argyll to Jill, that disposition would have entered the Sasine Register, not the Land Register, because Argyll did not become operational until 2000.

6.16   There are about 2.2 million title units in Scotland – that is, properties in separate ownership, such as a flat in Glasgow's Byres Road, or a thousand-hectare estate in Sutherland. About 52% are now in the Land Register. As larger rural properties are sold much less often than smaller urban ones, the million or so registered properties represent only about 10% of the land surface of Scotland. In the future, measures may be taken to accelerate the completion of the new register.

6.17   Once a property has switched to the new register, it stays there and so thenceforth all transactions affecting the title are registered in that register. For example, Mary owns a farm, her title being in the Sasine Register. She sells to Nick. The disposition is registered in the Land Register. This is called 'first registration'.

---

21   See the Commission's discussion papers: *Land Registration: Void and Voidable Titles* (2004); *Land Registration: Registration, Rectification and Indemnity* (2005) and *Land Registration: Miscellaneous Issues* (2005). The final report is expected shortly.

22   A slightly misleading term, for such property is in the Sasine Register.

23   For a list (a rather odd one) of the transactions that trigger the switch, see LR(S)A 1979, s 2. Sale is the main one.

24   LR(S)A 1979, s 2(1)(b).

If Nick then grants a standard security to a bank, the security is registered in the new register. If Nick donates the farm to his niece, Olivia, that too goes into the new register. The move from the old register to the new is a one-way street.

Title sheets

6.18 Each property that has entered the new system has its own 'title sheet',[25] formerly a paper document but now digital. This is the core of the system. Each has a unique number, beginning with the relevant county code. Thus, 'MID 1' was the first property registered in Midlothian – and it was Edinburgh Castle.[26] Title sheets can be split. Thus, if Tom owns land and conveys part of it to Ursula,[27] a new title sheet (with a new number) will be created for Ursula's area, and that area will be removed from Tom's. Likewise, title sheets may be merged. For instance, Vera owns Greenside. Her neighbour is Wilma. Vera dispones to Wilma. The two title sheets could now be merged into a single title sheet.[28]

Certificates of title: land certificates and charge certificates

6.19 When a person is registered as owner, the Keeper issues a document called a 'land certificate'.[29] This is an exact copy of the title sheet. An example is given at the end of the chapter. In a real land certificate, the property boundary is marked red. A land certificate thus shows what a title sheet says at the date it is issued. It does not keep itself up to date. The Keeper will issue a new land certificate with each new registration, so that when X dispones to Y, the Keeper issues a land certificate to Y; and when Y dispones to Z, the Keeper issues a new land certificate to Z. The land certificate has no value in itself: it is simply formal evidence of what the title sheet said at a given date. What ultimately matters is what the title sheet says. A land certificate is one of the two kinds of 'certificate of title'. The other is the 'charge certificate': this is issued to a standard security holder.[30]

The title sheet: the four sections

6.20 A title sheet has four sections.[31]

---

[25] LR(S)A 1979, s 6.
[26] This was a voluntary registration. Edinburgh Castle has not been sold.
[27] This is known variously as a 'break-off', 'split-off' or 'break-away' disposition. Developers typically grant break-off dispositions.
[28] LR(S)R 2006, r 8.
[29] LR(S)A 1979, s 5(2).
[30] LR(S)A 1979, s 5(3).
[31] LR(S)R 2006, rr 3–7.

(1) The Property Section (A Section) defines the property. It does so mainly by means of a detailed plan at a large scale, such as 1:2500.[32] It also contains a short verbal description – often no more than the postal address.

(2) The Proprietorship Section (B Section) identifies the owner or owners. If there is a special destination[33] it will state that too. It gives the date of registration, so that it is clear when the person in question acquired ownership of the property.[34]

(3) The Charges Section (C Section) sets out any securities that encumber the property, together with the registration date, which is important for purposes of ranking.

(4) The Burdens Section (D Section) sets out any other rights that encumber the property, such as real burdens and servitudes.[35]

Primary and secondary rights

6.21 Thus far, the title sheet has been explained as identifying a particular part of the Earth's surface and setting out the real rights in it. Actually, it is not quite as simple as that. The Land Register is defined[36] as 'a register of interests in land'. That means that there can be more than one title sheet for a given part of the Earth's surface. Although LR(S)A 1979 does not put it in this way, it divides real rights into primary real rights and secondary real rights. The primary ones have their own title sheet. The secondary rights do not, but find a home in the C or D sections of a title sheet. The primary rights are:

(a) ownership of land;

(b) separate tenements in land,[37] such as mining rights and salmon fishing rights; and

(c) long leases.[38]

Until feudal abolition,[39] there was a fourth type – superiority – and, since there could be indefinitely many superiorities in the same land, there could be indefinitely many title sheets. Indeed, this is still the case, for it is possible to have multiple long leases. Suppose that Wendy, the owner, conveys the minerals rights to Vivian. He then grants a 100-year lease to Xavier, who could grant an 80-year (sub[40])lease to Yvonne, who could grant a 50-year (sub-sub)lease to Zoe. There will then be five separate title sheets to the same part of the Earth: one for the ownership of the land,

---

[32] See PARAS **6.24–6.25** below.

[33] For special destinations, see CHAPTER **29** below.

[34] See PARA **5.8** above.

[35] See CHAPTERS **12 AND 13** below.

[36] LR(S)A 1979, s 1(1).

[37] For separate tenements, see PARAS **14.13–14.18** below.

[38] For leases, see CHAPTER **19** below.

[39] For feudal tenure, see APPENDIX.

[40] On subletting, see PARA **19.35** below.

one for the mineral rights under it, and three for each of the long leases. Of course, in practice, five would be a large number, and often there is only one.

6.22   Earlier, the phasing in of the new system was outlined.[41] In this connection, primary rights lead separate lives. Suppose that in 1970 Brian, the owner of Whitemains, Renfrewshire, conveys the mineral rights to Carla. In 1975 he grants a 100-year lease to David. Both deeds are recorded in the Sasine Register. In 1981 Renfrewshire became an operational county. In 1988 the mineral rights are sold by Carla to Ewan. The disposition in implement of the sale triggers a first registration of the mineral rights. In 1998 David sells the lease to Fiona. The assignation in implement of that sale triggers a first registration of the lease. The result is that the mineral rights and the lease are both in the Land Register, each with its own title sheet, but the land itself remains in the Sasine Register and will continue to do so until such time as it is sold.

6.23   All other rights affecting the property are secondary rights. These do not have their own title sheet but are entered on a title sheet for a primary right. For example, if a proper liferent is granted, that will be entered on the ownership title sheet. If a standard security is granted over the mineral rights, that will be entered on the minerals title sheet. No additional title sheets will be created.

Mapping

6.24   The specificity principle says that real rights must relate to identifiable property.[42] This principle applies in the Sasine Register as well as in the Land Register. Indeed, while the role of the Keeper in the Sasine Register is an essentially passive one, when it comes to the identifiability of the property, he plays an active role. He will refuse to record a deed in the Sasine Register if it relates to insufficiently identifiable property.[43] Nevertheless, the specificity principle is applied in a relaxed way. Deeds do not have to have plans. A description by postal address is valid for the Sasine Register, and not only is it valid but it is common. It is otherwise in the Land Register. LR(S)A 1979, s 6(1)(a) says that the title sheet is to include 'a description of the land which shall consist of or include a description of it based on the Ordnance Map'.[44] There are one or two qualifications. One concerns tenement flats. Here, the Keeper shows on the title sheet plan the whole 'steading', i.e. the area of ground occupied by the building. The identification of the unit within the tenement is then achieved by verbal description.[45]

---

[41]   See PARAS **6.14–6.17** above.
[42]   For the specificity principle, see PARAS **4.12–4.14** above.
[43]   *Macdonald v Keeper of the Registers* 1914 SC 854.
[44]   Produced by the Ordnance Survey, the national mapping agency: http://www.ordnancesurvey.co.uk/oswebsite/.
[45]   E.g. 'the northmost flat on the ground floor'.

6.25 The result is that the Land Register is far richer in information about title boundaries than the Sasine Register. Each title sheet plan interlocks with the neighbouring registered properties.[46] The Keeper has an 'index map'[47] which is in effect the totality of title sheet plans, so that, as the years pass, the map of Scotland is like a jigsaw that is gradually being completed. The Ordnance Map plots physical boundaries (walls, roads, burns etc.), and some legal boundaries, but only those existing in *public* law, such as local authority areas. The index map adds in the boundaries of private law.

Registration

6.26 When there is a sale of an unregistered property, the disposition cannot be recorded in the Sasine Register. Instead, there is a *first registration*. A new title sheet is opened by the Keeper.[48] Each of the four sections is filled in (though it is possible that the C or D Sections, or both, could be blank), and the disponee is entered as the first owner in the B Section. If the property is already registered, no new title sheet is needed (unless a property is being divided), and so all that happens is that the name is changed in the B Section. Transactions with registered property are usually called 'dealings'. There exist application forms both for first registrations (Form 1) and dealings (Form 2), plus a number of other forms.[49] These forms call for the applicant to confirm various items of information. Registration can be done digitally, using digital deeds and digital application forms. This is called ARTL (automated registration of title to land) and began to operate, at first on a limited scale, in 2007.[50]

6.27 One speaks of recording a 'deed' in the Sasine Register[51] and, following that usage, people speak of registering a 'deed' in the Land Register. Strictly speaking, this is not quite right. The register is a register of rights, not deeds. But the usage is a convenient one. Moreover, the Keeper retains a copy of the deed. He has to do this if the deed is referred to in the title sheet (which happens for only a small proportion of deeds, an example being a deed creating a real burden).[52] But in fact he keeps copies of all deeds, not least because the accuracy or inaccuracy of the title sheet depends on the deed. It needs to be available if a question about accuracy arises.

---

[46]   Actually, that is not always true but that complication will be ignored here.
[47]   LR(S)R 2006, r 20.
[48]   LR(S)A 1979, s 5(1)(a)(i).
[49]   LR(S)R 2006.
[50]   See S Brymer and I Davis, 'Automated Registration of Title to Land (ARTL)' in R Rennie (ed), *The Promised Land: Property Law Reform* (2008) 207–227 and R Rennie and S Brymer, *Conveyancing in the Electronic Age* (2008).
[51]   See PARA **6.2** above.
[52]   LR(S)A 1979, s 6(5).

Acceptance or rejection of applications

6.28   The Keeper should accept applications where the deed is valid and reject them if it is not. This principle is not clearly stated in LR(S)A 1979. The nearest it gets is s 4(1), which says that 'an application for registration shall be accepted by the Keeper if it is accompanied by such documents and other evidence as he may require'. The unstated idea is that the Keeper is to 'require' such evidence as is needed to show that the applicant ought to be registered. So if George grants a disposition of the Isle of Skye to Hayley, and the latter applies for registration, the Keeper should reject the application because George is not the owner of the Isle of Skye,[53] and, that being so, the applicant could not provide the 'documents and other evidence' showing that George was the owner. Another ground on which the Keeper could reject the application is LR(S)A 1979, s 4(2)(c): that the application is 'frivolous or vexatious'.[54] Thus, the *nemo plus* principle[55] is policed by refusing unjustified applications.

Transactions with subordinate real rights

6.29   If the property is still in the Sasine Register, subordinate real rights are dealt with in that register, while if the property is in the Land Register, they are dealt with in that register. For example, John owns a house, and his title is still in the Sasine Register. He grants a standard security to Kate. The standard security will be recorded in the Sasine Register. If, a year later, Kate assigns the security to Laura, the assignation is recorded in the Sasine Register. Later still, John sells to Mark. This will be a first registration. If the standard security is not discharged at this stage[56] then it will be entered in the C Section. If Laura were then to assign it to Nigel, the assignation would enter the Land Register, not the Sasine Register.

The effect of registration

The 'Midas touch'

6.30   LR(S)A 1979, s 3(1)(a) says:

'Registration shall have the effect of ... vesting in the person registered as entitled to the registered interest in land a real right in and to the interest and in and to any right, pertinent or servitude, express or implied, forming part of the interest ... '

---

[53]   Another ground on which he could reject the application is s 4(2)(c): that the application is 'frivolous or vexatious'.
[54]   See *Registration of Title Practice Book* para 6.4.
[55]   See PARA **4.39** above.
[56]   Normally it would be. But Mark is free to take the property subject to the security.

6.31 This is one of the most important provisions in LR(S)A 1979. It means that if an application for registration is accepted, then the applicant acquires the right in question. At first sight that may not seem so very remarkable. Jack sells a house to Jill. She submits the disposition, plus application form, to the Keeper and she is registered. She acquires ownership at that time. Is this not simply the same as the Sasine Register? The answer is: 'yes' and 'no'. Assuming that the disposition was in itself valid – signed by the owner, containing the right words and so on – the result is the same as in the Sasine Register: ownership passes from disponer to disponee on the day of recording, or registration.[57] For both registers the rule is that registration is a necessary condition for obtaining a real right. But suppose that the disposition is defective. Suppose, to take an extreme case, that the 'Jack' who signed it was an identity thief, and not the real Jack at all. What then?

6.32 Now, in the Sasine Register the result would have been that Jill, even though in good faith, would not acquire ownership. The *nemo plus* principle operates. But LR(S)A 1979, s 3(1)(a) means that, in the Land Register, registration is not only a *necessary* condition for acquiring a real right but it is a *sufficient* condition as well. In other words, it's not only 'if no registration, then no real right' (which is equally true of the Sasine Register) but also 'if registration, then a real right'. This is the Keeper's 'Midas touch'.[58] Everything he touches turns to 'valid'. Jill is now the owner. The effect is that the true Jack has lost ownership.

6.33 In the example, Jill was in good faith. But the result would be the same had she been Jack's partner in crime. She would still have acquired ownership. The 'Midas touch' thus can produce surprising results. In the Sasine Register, title comes from the recorded deed, and if the recorded deed is void the title is void. In the Land Register, *title flows from the register*. The deed is the reason for the registration, but it is no more than that. A void deed does not make the title void. With one or two exceptions, *there is no such thing as a void registration*.

6.34 In one sense, the 'Midas touch' means that the *nemo plus* principle does not operate. That would be true but it is really only a half-truth. First, the principle still operates at the gateway: the Keeper will reject unjustified applications – if he realises, in good time, that they are unjustified.[59] Second, although the real right is established at registration, if it was wrongfully acquired there can, in some cases at least, be rectification.[60]

---

[57] The rule, for both registers, is stated in the Abolition of Feudal Tenure etc. (Scotland) Act 2000 (AFT(S)A 2000), s 4(1).

[58] Scottish Law Commission *Discussion Paper on Void and Voidable Titles* (2004) para 5.34. In more formal language, the term 'positive' can used to describe a system that always confers the right of registration, however undeserving the applicant.

[59] See PARA **6.28** above.

[60] See PARAS **6.44–6.48** below.

The extinction of omitted encumbrances

6.35 LR(S)A 1979, s 3(1)(a) continues by providing that the vesting of the real right is 'subject only to the effect of any matter entered in the title sheet of that interest ... so far as adverse to the interest'. Suppose that the property is encumbered by a subordinate real right. The Keeper inadvertently omits it. The result is that it dies. Jill takes free from it. Once again, in some types of case, rectification may be possible, and if so, the encumbrance comes back to life.[61]

Qualifications: overriding interests

6.36 The principles just outlined are subject to one or two exceptions.[62] The main one is that the second rule (the extinction of omitted encumbrances) does not apply to encumbrances if they are what LR(S)A 1979 calls 'overriding interests'. Though the list of these[63] is long and strange, the most important in practice are servitudes and short leases.[64] The fact that an 'overriding interest' is not mentioned in the title sheet does not matter. The silence has no effect: the overriding interest is still valid, whether it is mentioned or not. Thus, someone buying land and seeing that the D Section of the title sheet mentions no servitudes cannot conclude that the land is subject to no servitude. The explanation is that 'overriding interests' are rights that can be created without registration.[65] That being so, no one has a right to expect to see them all listed on the affected title sheet. The position is in fact the same in the Sasine Register, the only difference being that the term 'overriding interest' is used only in connection with the Land Register. Of course, one might argue that all real rights *should* be registered. But that has never been the law, and in practice it would be difficult to achieve. However, if the Keeper knows about an overriding interest he can note it on the title sheet.[66]

Inaccuracy

6.37 For the most part, the Land Register is accurate. Nevertheless, inaccuracies can and do happen. At one level this is mere common sense: in the real world, things sometimes go wrong. But at another level the idea that the Land Register can be inaccurate is paradoxical, for the Keeper's 'Midas touch' means that it *is* always right: if the register says that X is owner, then X *is* owner. So, how could the register be inaccurate? LR(S)A 1979 does not explain 'inaccuracy'. The answer is that the

---

[61] See **PARAS 6.44–6.48** below.
[62] Rectification is not an exception but something that may or may not happen later.
[63] See LR(S)A 1979, s 28.
[64] A short lease is one of 20 years or under. See **PARA 19.11** below.
[65] Servitudes can be created by registration, but in some cases they can be created without. See **PARAS 12.21–12.29** below.
[66] LR(S)A 1979, s 6(4). An exception is a short lease: he is forbidden to note such leases.

register is inaccurate if an entry on a title sheet is not justified by the deed on which it is based. For example, there is a disposition by Jack to Jill, and Jill is registered as owner. Though Jill was unaware of the fact, the granter was not the real Jack but an identity thief. The deed is void, but Jill's title is not. She is the owner but the title sheet is inaccurate. When the Keeper deleted Jack's name and replaced it with Jill's, he did so on the basis of a deed that did not justify that deletion of replacement. It did not justify it because it was a nullity. Another example: Fraser is the owner of a house. He borrows from a bank and grants a standard security. This is registered. A couple of years later, when the loan has still not been repaid, he forges a deed of discharge by the bank and submits it to the Keeper for registration. The Keeper, unaware of the forgery, gives effect to the deed by deleting the standard security from the Charges Section. The property is now unencumbered by the standard security but the title sheet is inaccurate.

6.38 These are only examples. The inner logic is that to answer the question 'Is the title sheet inaccurate?' one must apply general property law. If a deed is a forgery, it cannot transfer a right held by the ostensible granter. Nor can it discharge a subordinate real right held by the ostensible granter.

6.39 In the examples above, it is easy to see that the register is inaccurate. There can be harder cases. For example, suppose that Jill dispones to Kathy. The register now shows Kathy in the B Section as owner. Is it inaccurate? One could argue this two ways.

(1) If the issue were left to general property law, Kathy would not be the owner because she is the grantee of someone (Jill) who herself would not be the owner under general property law. So the register is still inaccurate.

(2) Conversely, the register is no longer inaccurate because Kathy has acquired from a person, Jill, who was the owner.

Although LR(S)A 1979 is silent on this issue (as on so many others), there can be little doubt that the first answer is right.[67] In short, in determining the accuracy or inaccuracy of the register one has, so to speak, to apply two different systems: the LR(S)A 1979 system and general property law. If they produce the same answer then the register is accurate and if they produce different answers then it is inaccurate. This need to apply two systems of law is what the Scottish Law Commission has called bijuralism'.[68] It causes serious conceptual complexities.

6.40 If a registration takes place on the basis of a deed that is not void but voidable, that is not an inaccuracy because the registration was justified by the deed that was presented to the Keeper. For example, suppose that Ellen is owner and is induced by

---

[67]   The issue is a complex one and cannot be discussed fully here. But, in brief, if the Register were deemed to become accurate when Kathy is registered, then the real Jack would lose his right to compensation, for the right to compensation can exist only where there is an inaccuracy. That result would be an absurd one. There it follows that the Register must still be inaccurate.

[68]   Scottish Law Commission *Discussion Paper on Land Registration: Void and Voidable Titles* (2004) para 1.11.

Fraser's fraud to dispone to him. He is registered. The register is not inaccurate because fraud causes voidability, not voidness.[69] Voidability gives Ellen an option, which she may or may not decide to take up. If she does take it up, she will obtain a decree of reduction of the disposition, and that will make the Register inaccurate, but only as from the time of the reduction.

6.41 So, bijural inaccuracy is where the title sheet says something, and that something is true (because of the 'Midas touch') but, according to general property law, it should not be true.[70] There is also another type of inaccuracy: actual inaccuracy.[71] Here, the title sheet says something which is *actually* false: the 'Midas touch' has failed. For example, Sheila buys land from Tim. She decides to take title in the name of SheilaCo (No 12) Ltd. The disposition is granted to that company and the title sheet is changed by the Keeper to show it as owner. Sheila has many companies, and she thinks that one of them has this name, but in fact there is no such company. Perhaps it did exist but was struck off because of failure to lodge the right documents each year.[72] Or perhaps she meant to set it up but never did. Whatever the reason, there is no such person as SheilaCo (No 12) Ltd. A right cannot belong to a non-existent person. So, here, the Keeper's 'Midas touch' cannot work: his magic is strong, but against the force of absolute impossibility it is powerless. The result is that the right of ownership remains in Tim. The title sheet, in showing 'SheilaCo (No 12) Ltd' as owner, is *actually*, and not *bijurally*, inaccurate. Actual inaccuracy is 'an entry in, or omission from, the Land Register which is inaccurate according to both the ordinary law of property *and* the rules of registration of title'.[73]

6.42 Another example. Maria owns land and Nigel owns neighbouring land. Maria grants Nigel a servitude of way.[74] This is duly registered in both title sheets.[75] For a year or two, Nigel makes use of the way, then he stops doing so. The years pass. After 20 years of non-use, the servitude is extinguished under the law of negative prescription.[76] As a result, both title sheets become actually inaccurate.[77] In practice, most problems about inaccuracy are about bijural inaccuracy, not actual inaccuracy.

---

[69] See PARA **4.33** above.

[70] Bijural inaccuracy is 'an entry in, or omission from, the Land Register which is inaccurate according to the ordinary law of property but not according to the rules of registration of title': Scottish Law Commission *Discussion Paper on Land Registration: Miscellaneous Issues* (2005) ix.

[71] For the distinction, see Scottish Law Commission *Discussion Paper on Land Registration: Registration, Rectification and Indemnity* (2005) paras 6.2–6.5.

[72] Companies Act 2006, s 1000.

[73] Scottish Law Commission *Discussion Paper on Land Registration: Miscellaneous Issues* (2005) ix.

[74] See CHAPTER **12** below.

[75] This requirement of dual registration was introduced by TC(S)A 2003, s 75. The entry will be on the D Section of Maria's title sheet and on the A Section of Nigel's.

[76] PL(S)A 1973, s 8. See PARA **12.45** below.

[77] But there is a twist. If, with his title sheet unchanged, Nigel dispones to Olive, and the Keeper keeps the servitude on the title sheet, then it appears to be the law that the servitude pops back into existence: the 'Midas touch' again.

Disputes and 'good fairies'

6.43 An inaccuracy usually represents an underlying property conflict between two persons, often neighbours. For example, Bill and Ben are adjacent owners. Bill claims that the boundary line as set forth in their two title sheets is wrong, being too favourable to Ben. In other words, he claims that the title sheets are inaccurate. Or perhaps the Register says that Whitemains has a servitude over Blackmains, and the owner of Blackmains claims that this is an inaccuracy. Sometimes the dispute may be over the entire property – as above, where the real Jack will be arguing that the entire registration to Jill, and later to Kathy, is inaccurate. Before LR(S)A 1979, in such disputes one party would win and the other would lose. The loser might have a claim for damages against someone. For example, Kathy would have a damages claim[78] against Jill, and Jill would have a claim against the fraudster (if she could find him and, having found him, could make him pay). Sometimes there would be a negligence claim against the solicitors of the person suffering loss, and against such claims law firms have insurance. But there was no 'good fairy'. LR(S)A 1979 introduced a 'good fairy': the Keeper. Once property has shifted into the new register, the Keeper will normally compensate a loser. This is the system of *indemnity*.[79]

Rectification

6.44 There are two ways in which the Register can be changed: registration and rectification.[80] If a title sheet is discovered to be inaccurate, can it be rectified? One might think that the answer must be 'yes'. After all, for the law to say that the Register must be kept deliberately inaccurate seems strange. Yet that is indeed often the case. For, although LR(S)A 1979, s 9 says, as a basic rule, that if an inaccuracy comes to light it can be rectified, it then has an exception that is so large that in practice many inaccuracies fall under it, so that the Register remains inaccurate. An inaccuracy cannot be rectified 'if rectification … would prejudice a *proprietor in possession*'.[81] Thus, in the example above, the title sheet is inaccurate in showing Kathy as owner. But if Jack seeks rectification, he will fail if Kathy is in possession. Alternatively, take the case of the boundary dispute between Bill and Ben. Suppose that Ben is correct, and that in allocating the disputed boundary area to Bill, the Register is inaccurate. Whether rectification will now ensue depends on possession. If Bill is in possession, there will be no rectification, notwithstanding proof of the inaccuracy. If, however, Ben is in possession, there will be rectification.

6.45 LR(S)A 1979 does not elaborate on what is meant by 'proprietor in possession' and, even now, it is not wholly clear. The leading case, *Kaur v Singh*,[82] is useful but

---

[78] Based on warrandice. See PARAS **5.9–5.13** above.
[79] See PARAS **6.54–6.59** below.
[80] This statement is a slight oversimplification.
[81] LR(S)A 1979, s 9(3).
[82] 1999 SC 180.

does not give a comprehensive answer. The uncertainty that existed is illustrated by the fact that in that case a standard security holder dared to argue that it was a proprietor in possession. Believers in juridical reason will be happy to know that the argument failed, for the standard security holder was neither in possession nor a proprietor. Despite the decision, it is not wholly clear to whether both natural possession and civil possession are included and, moreover, despite LR(S)A 1979's use of the word 'proprietor', at least some subordinate real right holders may be included, such as, probably, the holders of registered leases and, possibly, the benefited owners in respect of servitudes.[83]

6.46 The rule is that an inaccuracy cannot be rectified if this would prejudice a proprietor in possession. There are certain qualifications.[84] Two are particularly important. One is that 'the inaccuracy has been caused wholly or substantially by the fraud or carelessness of the proprietor in possession'.[85] This makes common sense.[86] For example, Aunt Ada has senile dementia. Her niece, Fenella, knows that fact perfectly well and induces her aunt to sign a disposition of the property in favour of her, Fenella. This is registered. The disposition is void because Ada is *incapax*. Nevertheless, because of the 'Midas touch', ownership has passed from Ada to Fenella. Ada is in a nursing home and Fenella moves into the property. She is now a proprietor in possession. The disposition being void, the Register is inaccurate. It can be rectified[87] because Fenella's fraud caused the inaccuracy. The other qualification is that an inaccuracy can always be rectified if the Keeper has excluded indemnity.[88] For example, Leanne is registered as owner of a property extending to 10,000 square metres. There is some uncertainty as to a corner area of 100 square metres. As to that small area the Keeper excludes indemnity. If it later turns out that the inclusion of this area was an inaccuracy, and that the area ought to have been included in the neighbouring title sheet, then the inaccuracy is rectifiable, even if Leanne is in possession.

Effect of rectification

6.47 If an *actual* inaccuracy is rectified, the result is to make the Register conform to objective reality. Thus, rectification does not change anyone's legal position. No rights are changed. But if a *bijural* inaccuracy is rectified, that *does* alter the legal position. Rights are changed. Suppose that Fenella's name is deleted from the B Section and Ada's restored. The effect is to take ownership from Fenella and give it back to Ada.

---

[83] Authorities on this latter point are conflicting. See *Yaxley v Glen* 2007 SLT 756.
[84] LR(S)A 1979, s 9(3).
[85] LR(S)A 1979, s 9(3)(a)(iii).
[86] In general terms. The 'fraud or carelessness' wording can be criticised.
[87] Rectification may be sought by, for example, other members of the family or by a guardian appointed by the court to manage Ada's affairs.
[88] For indemnity, and exclusion of indemnity, see PARAS **6.54–6.59** below.

6.48 The rectification of a bijural inaccuracy is not retroactive.[89] Suppose that Fenella was registered on 1 February and rectification took place on 1 December. Ownership passes back to Ada on the latter date. In the intervening ten months it was Fenella who was owner.

Reduction and the Sasine Register

6.49 If a real right rests on a deed recorded in the Sasine Register and the deed is *voidable*, then the reduction of the deed will take away the real right. That is because the right rests on the deed. If the deed was *void*, then the reduction does not actually alter anyone's rights: its effect is declaratory. For example, Jack is owner; an identity thief, forging Jack's name, dispones to Jill, who records the disposition in the Sasine Register. Her title is void from the start. Later, the real Jack reduces the disposition. The decree of reduction *proves* the nullity but does not *create* it. Ownership does not pass back to Jack: it never left him in the first place. By contrast, suppose that Ellen is induced by Fraser's fraud to dispone to him. Fraud makes a deed voidable but not void.[90] Fraser is owner. If the disposition is later reduced, the effect will be to transfer ownership back to Ellen.

Reduction and the Land Register

6.50 In the Land Register, a real right does not rest directly on any deed but on what the Register itself says: title flows from the Register. Hence the reduction of the deed has no *direct* effect on the real right. In Jack's case, the Register was *inaccurate all along* because Jill was registered on the basis of a *void* deed. But because of the Keeper's 'Midas touch',[91] she was owner. The decree reducing the deed does not make the Register any more inaccurate than it already was but it does have evidential value, proving the inaccuracy. In Ellen's case, the Register was accurate in showing Fraser as owner. The reduction of the deed makes the Register inaccurate *as from the time of the reduction*. Thus in Jack's case the reduction did not actually change anything. In Ellen's case it did. But in neither case did it restore ownership. So Jack and Ellen are half-way there but no further. To re-acquire the ownership of the property they need to have the Register changed. How can that be done?[92] Here we come to the saga of *Short's Tr v Chung*. As we shall see, this case established that:

    (i) a decree of reduction cannot be *registered*;

    (ii) it can be used to *rectify* the register if – but only if – the defender is not protected under LR(S)A 1979, s 9; and

---

[89] *Stevenson-Hamilton's Exrs v McStay* 1999 SLT 1175; *Keeper of the Registers v MRS Hamilton Ltd* 2000 SC 271.

[90] See **PARA 4.33** above.

[91] See **PARAS 6.30–6.34** above.

[92] A title sheet itself cannot be reduced: *Foster v Keeper of the Registers* 2006 SLT 513.

(iii) if the defender is so protected the pursuer can nevertheless enforce the decree of reduction by insisting on a reconveyance.

The *Short's Tr* saga

6.51 Mr Short transferred some flats to Mr Chung, at an undervalue. There is nothing wrong with that in itself. An owner who is feeling generous can transfer at an undervalue or for no value at all. But owners who are unable to pay their creditors should not do this, for to do so is unjust to those creditors.[93] Soon after the transfer, Mr Short was sequestrated. His trustee set about recovering the properties. By then, they had been transferred by Mr Chung to Mrs Chung, for no value. The disposition by Mr Short was voidable, and since Mrs Chung was not a purchaser in good faith the disposition to her was voidable too. The titles were in the Land Register. The protracted litigation had three phases. In the first, the trustee raised an action of reduction of the dispositions and was successful.[94] Had this been a Sasine case, the decree would simply have been recorded in the Sasine Register. The trustee applied for the registration of the decree in the Land Register. The Keeper rejected that application. The trustee raised an action to compel the Keeper to accept. In this second phase of the litigation the trustee was unsuccessful.[95] It was held that a pursuer holding a decree of reduction could not seek to give effect to it in the Land Register by means of registration – but only by rectification. Otherwise, it was held, the legislation's policy of protecting registered owners would be undermined, for owners would have no protection against such a registration, whereas in the case of an application for rectification they would have the protection of LR(S)A 1979, s 9 – i.e. the protection given to proprietors in possession.[96]

6.52 After this second stage, one might perhaps have expected that the trustee would have applied for the Register to be rectified, and, if this was refused (on the ground that Mrs Chung was a proprietor in possession), he could then have sought payment of indemnity by the Keeper.[97] In fact, he took a different approach. He requested Mrs Chung to dispone the properties to him. When she refused, he raised an action against her to compel her to do so. This was the third phase of the litigation, and it ended in success for the trustee.[98]

6.53 An argument that the trustee had advanced in the second phase of the litigation was that if he could not recover the properties, then policy behind the law about gratuitous alienations would have been defeated. By contrast, the defender had argued

---

[93] This is known as the law of gratuitous alienations, and is in part common law and in part governed by B(S)A 1985 and IA 1986. See, e.g., Gloag and Henderson *The Law of Scotland* paras 50.22–50.24.

[94] *Short's Tr v Chung* 1991 SLT 472.

[95] *Short's Tr v Keeper of the Registers* 1994 SC 122, aff'd 1996 SC (HL) 14. This contains trenchant criticism of LR(S)A 1979.

[96] See PARAS **6.44–6.46** above.

[97] See PARA **6.54** below.

[98] *Short's Tr v Chung (No 2)* 1999 SC 471.

that if the trustee could recover the properties then the policy behind the law of land registration would have been defeated. At the second stage this latter argument prevailed, but the third stage turned the tables. Both arguments seem sound, but they pull in opposite directions, and the final result is seen by some as arbitrary.[99]

Indemnity: the basics

6.54 LR(S)A 1979, s 12(1) provides that:

'a person who suffers loss as a result of (a) a rectification of the register made under section 9 ... ; (b) the refusal or omission of the Keeper to make such a rectification ... shall be entitled to be indemnified by the Keeper'.

This is one of the key provisions of the legislation. If there is an inaccuracy the Keeper will either (a) rectify it or (b) not rectify it. Whichever happens, someone suffers. For example, there is a boundary dispute between Mary and her neighbour, Lucas. A boundary area is included in Mary's title sheet. Lucas establishes that that is an inaccuracy. If the Register is rectified so as to transfer the area to Lucas's title sheet, Mary suffers because she loses ownership. If it is not, Lucas suffers because he does not acquire.[100] If rectification happens, Mary is compensated under LR(S)A 1979, s 12(1)(a). If it does not, Lucas is compensated under LR(S)A 1979, s 12(1)(b). (As it is sometimes put: one party gets the mud and the other the money.[101])

Subrogation

6.55 If the Keeper pays compensation, does the loss lie with him? LR(S)A 1979, s 13(2) says that 'on settlement of any claim to indemnity ... the Keeper shall be subrogated to all rights which would have been available to the claimant to recover the loss indemnified'. Take the example of where Sarah is the owner but Tiffany forges her signature and dispones to Verity. The Keeper registers Verity as owner. Suppose that the Register is *not* rectified, i.e. that Verity keeps the property. Then Sarah is compensated under LR(S)A 1979, s 12(1)(b). The Keeper then stands in her shoes for any claim she might have had. She had a claim against Tiffany for delictual damages, so the Keeper can pursue that claim. Alternatively, suppose that the Register *is* rectified, i.e. that Sarah regains the property. Then Verity is compensated under LR(S)A 1979, s 12(1)(a), and once again the Keeper succeeds to her damages claim against Tiffany.[102] Whether, in either case, he will actually be able to recover anything

---

[99]   Scottish Law Commission *Discussion Paper on Land Registration: Void and Voidable Titles* (2004) paras 6.1–6.18.

[100]   As to whether rectification will take place, see PARAS **6.44–6.46** above.

[101]   The phrase comes from T W Mapp *Torrens' Elusive Title: Basic Legal Principles of an Efficient Torrens' System* (1978).

[102]   Here the claim will be in warrandice. See PARAS **5.9–5.13** above.

from Tiffany is another matter. The idea is similar to the principle of subrogation in insurance law. If A is insured against a loss and B wrongfully causes that loss, then, on paying A, the insurance company is subrogated to A's delictual claim against B.

Absence of indemnity and its consequences

6.56 There are two main cases where a person is barred from indemnity. The first is where the Keeper excluded indemnity at the time of registration.[103] The legislation is unclear about when he is supposed to exclude indemnity but in practice he seldom excludes it, and does so only if there is significant doubt about the title or some aspect of it. For example, he might exclude indemnity for a boundary area if he had doubts about the title: here, the indemnity would be excluded only for that area and not for the rest of the title. The second is where the inaccuracy in question is attributable to 'fraud or carelessness' of the person in question.[104] For example, that person may have induced the Keeper to effect a registration by misrepresentations on the application form.[105]

6.57 In such cases the person in question cannot claim under the Keeper's indemnity. And there is another important effect: loss of the 'proprietor in possession' defence. Thus, there is a boundary dispute between X and Y. A certain area is included in X's title sheet but Y claims that that is inaccurate. X is in possession. Under the basic rule, the fact that he is in possession means that even if it turns out that the area should have been in Y's title sheet, X keeps the area. But if either (a) the inaccuracy was caused by his fault[106] or (b) when X was registered indemnity was excluded for that area,[107] he will not be allowed to invoke the 'proprietor in possession' defence and so will lose the property – and lose it without compensation from the Keeper.

6.58 A cynical way of describing the rules would be that indemnity is available only when you do not need it. For, if it is available, you will usually be protected against rectification anyway, as a proprietor in possession. And when you do need it – because the title is rectified against you – this is precisely when you do not get it because the very factor that deprived you of your 'proprietor in possession' defence will also deprive you of the right to indemnity. There is certainly some truth in that view. But it is far from the whole truth. For example, in some types of case (e.g. a standard security) the 'proprietor in possession' defence is not available anyway.[108]

6.59 However, exclusion of indemnity does bring with it a benefit that is absent for ordinary cases. The exclusion allows positive prescription to run in favour of the

---

[103]   LR(S)A 1979, s 12(2).
[104]   LR(S)A 1979, s 12(3)(n).
[105]   As in *Stevenson-Hamilton's Exrs v McStay (No 2)* 2001 SLT 694.
[106]   LR(S)A 1979, s 9(3)(a)(iii).
[107]   LR(S)A 1979, s 9(3)(a)(iv).
[108]   *Kaur v Singh* 1999 SC 180. See para **6.45** above.

registered owner.[109] Put the other way round, positive prescription does not run on a Land Register title unless indemnity is excluded. This rule is paradoxical: it gives to worse titles a benefit it denies to better ones. (This was probably a drafting error.) It applies only where the reason for non-indemnity is specific exclusion by the Keeper. If indemnity is absent only because of the fraud or carelessness of the person in question, positive prescription does not run.[110]

FURTHER READING

Registration of Title Practice Book is the essential handbook to land registration practice, even if it is now beginning to show its age. See also:

Gretton and Reid *Conveyancing* ch 8.

McDonald *Conveyancing Manual* ch 11.

Scottish Law Commission, *Discussion Paper on Land Registration: Void and Voidable Titles* (2004).

Scottish Law Commission, *Discussion Paper on Land Registration: Miscellaneous Issues* (2005).

Scottish Law Commission, *Discussion Paper on Land Registration: Registration, Rectification and Indemnity* (2005).

---

[109]   LR(S)A 1979, s 10, amending PL(S)A 1973, s 1.
[110]   See PARA **2.29** above.

(LAND REGISTRATION (SCOTLAND) RULES 2006 Rule 15)

REGISTERS OF SCOTLAND
Executive Agency
Information about Scotland's land & property

LAND REGISTER OF SCOTLAND
LAND CERTIFICATE
VERSION 12/09/2006

TITLE NUMBER	ANG19152
SUBJECTS	79 KEPTIE ROAD, ARBROATH DD11 3EN.

THIS LAND CERTIFICATE, ISSUED PURSUANT TO SECTION 5(2) OF THE LAND REGISTRATION (SCOTLAND) ACT 1979, IS A COPY OF THE TITLE SHEET RELATING TO THE ABOVE SUBJECTS.

STATEMENT OF INDEMNITY
Subject to any specific qualifications entered in the Title Sheet of which this Land Certificate is a copy, a person who suffers loss as a result of the events specified in section 12(1) of the above Act shall be entitled to be indemnified in respect of that loss by the Keeper of the Registers of Scotland in terms of that Act.

ATTENTION IS DRAWN TO THE GENERAL INFORMATION OVERLEAF.

www.ros.gov.uk

GENERAL INFORMATION

1. OVERRIDING INTEREST

A registered interest in land is in terms of sections 3(1) of the Land Registration (Scotland) Act 1979 subject to overriding interests defined in section 28 of that Act (hereinafter referred to as "the 1979 Act") as amended by the Matrimonial Homes (Family Protection) (Scotland) Act 1981, the Telecommunications Act 1984, the Electricity Act 1989, the Coal Industry Act 1994, the Title Conditions (Scotland) Act 2003 and the Civil Partnership (Consequential Amendments) (Scotland) Order 2005 as:

in relation to any interest in land, the right or interest over it of

(a) the lessee under a lease which is not a long lease;

(b) the lessee under a long lease who, prior to the commencement of the 1979 Act, has acquired a real right to the subjects of the lease by virtue of possession of them;

(c) a crofter or cottar within the meaning of sections 3 or 28(4) respectively of the Crofters (Scotland) Act 1955, or a landholder or statutory small tenant within the meaning of section 2(2) or 32(1) respectively of the Small Landholders (Scotland) Act 1911;

(d) the proprietor of the dominant tenement in any servitude which was not created by registration in accordance with section 75(1) of the Title Conditions (Scotland) Act 2003.

(e) the Crown or any Government or other public department, or any public or local authority, under any enactment or rule of law, other than an enactment or rule of law authorising or requiring the recording of a deed in the Register of Sasines or registration in order to complete the right of interest;

(ee) the operator having a right conferred in accordance with paragraph 2, 3 or 5 of schedule 2 to the Telecommunications Act 1984 (agreements for execution of works, obstruction of access, etc.);

(ef) a licence holder within the meaning of Part 1 of the Electricity Act 1989 having such a wayleave as is mentioned in paragraph 6 of Schedule 4 to that Act (wayleaves for electric lines), whether granted under that paragraph or by agreement between the parties;

(eg) a licence holder within the meaning of Part 1 of the Electricity Act 1989 who is authorised by virtue of paragraph 1 of Schedule 5 to that Act to abstract, divert and use water for a generating station wholly or mainly driven by water;

(eh) insofar as it is an interest vesting by virtue of section 7(3) of the Coal Industry Act 1994, the Coal Authority;

(f) the holder of a floating charge whether or not the charge has attached to the interest;

(g) a member of the public in respect of any public right of way or in respect of any right held inalienably by the Crown in trust for the public;

(gg) the non-entitled spouse within the meaning of section 6 of the Matrimonial Homes (Family Protection)(Scotland) Act 1981;

(gh) The non-entitled civil partner within the meaning of section 106 of the Civil Partnership Act 2004;

(h) any person, being a right which has been made real, otherwise than by the recording of a deed in the Register of Sasines or by registration; or

(i) any other person under any rule of law relating to common interest or joint or common property, not being a right or interest constituting a real right, burden or condition entered in the title sheet of the interest in land under section 6(1)(e) of the 1979 Act or having effect by virtue of a deed recorded in the Register of Sasines,

but does not include any subsisting burden or condition enforceable against the interest in land and entered in its title sheet under section 6 (1) of the 1979 Act.

2. THE USE OF ARROWS ON TITLE PLANS

(a) Where a deed states the line of a boundary in relation to a physical object, e.g. the centre line, that line is indicated on the Title Plan, either by means of a black arrow or verbally.

(b) An arrow across the object indicates that the boundary is stated to be the centre line.

(c) An arrow pointing to the object indicates that the boundary is stated to be the face of the object to which the arrow points.

(d) The physical object presently shown on the Plan may not be the one referred to in the deed. Indemnity is therefore excluded in respect of information as to the line of the boundary.

3. Lineal measurements shown in figures on title plans are subject to the qualification "or thereby". Indemnity is excluded in respect of such measurements.

4. CAUTION

No unauthorised alteration to this Land Certificate should be made.

	Officer's ID / Date	TITLE NUMBER
LAND REGISTER OF SCOTLAND	4540 28/6/2003	**ANG19152**
	ORDNANCE SURVEY NATIONAL GRID REFERENCE	70m
	NO6241SE NO6341SW	Survey Scale 1/1250

CROWN COPYRIGHT © – This copy has been produced from the ROS Digital Mapping System on 30/04/2008 and was made with the authority of Ordnance Survey pursuant to Section 47 of the Copyright, Designs and Patents Act 1988. Unless that act provides a relevant exception to copyright, the copy must not be copied without the prior permission of the copyright owner.

THE BOUNDARIES INDICATED HEREON ARE MORE FULLY DEFINED IN THE TITLE SHEET

LAND REGISTER OF SCOTLAND

TITLE NUMBER ANG19152 A 1

A. PROPERTY SECTION

DATE OF FIRST REGISTRATION
25 MAR 2002

DATE TITLE SHEET UPDATED TO
03 APR 2007

DATE LAND CERTIFICATE UPDATED TO
03 APR 2007

INTEREST
PROPRIETOR

MAP REFERENCE
NO6341SW

DESCRIPTION
Subjects 79 KEPTIE ROAD, ARBROATH DD11 3EN edged red on the Title Plan.

Note   The boundaries between the points indicated on the Title Plan are as follows: -

        AB   North boundary Centre line
        BC   East boundary Centre line
        CD   South Boundary Centre line

See General Information, Note 2

LAND REGISTER OF SCOTLAND

TITLE NUMBER ANG19152   **B 1**

B. PROPRIETORSHIP SECTION

ENTRY NO	PROPRIETOR		
1	STEVEN MARTIN BROWN and HELEN JANE BROWN spouses, 14 Forest Park Road, Dundee DD1 5NY equally between them and the survivor of them.	**DATE OF REGISTRATION** 03 APR 2007	**CONSIDERATION** £198000
			DATE OF ENTRY 25 MAR 2007

    Note: 1   There are in respect of the subjects in
                this Title no subsisting occupancy rights
                in terms of the Matrimonial Homes (Family
                Protection)(Scotland) Act 1981 of spouses
                of persons who were formerly entitled to
                the said subjects.

    Note: 2   There are in respect of the subjects in
                this Title no subsisting occupancy rights
                in terms of the Civil Partnership Act 2004
                of partners of persons who were formerly
                entitled to the said subjects.

LAND REGISTER OF SCOTLAND

TITLE NUMBER ANG19152   C 1

C. CHARGES SECTION

ENTRY NO	SPECIFICATION	DATE OF REGISTRATION
1	Standard Security for £140000 and further sums by said STEVEN MARTIN BROWN and HELEN JANE BROWN to DUNFERMLINE BUILDING SOCIETY, registered under the Building Societies Acts, Head Office Caledonia House, Carnegie Avenue, Dunfermline.	03 APR 2007

LAND REGISTER OF SCOTLAND

D. BURDENS SECTION

ENTRY NO	SPECIFICATION
1	Feu Charter by Frederick Fothringham MacDonald to Arbroath and District Building Company Limited, recorded G.R.S. (Forfar) 12 Mar. 1935, of ground, on east side of Keptie Road, Arbroath, of which the subjects in this Title form part, contains the following burdens;

(First)

the said Arbroath and District Building Company Limited shall be bound to erect and complete on the said piece of ground hereby disponed five dwellinghouses with offices attached, and which shall be used as dwellinghouse and adjuncts conform to a Plan or Plans which have been submitted to and approved of by the Superiors and the said Arbroath and District Building company Limited shall be bound to uphold and maintain the same or similar dwellinghouses and offices of equal value on the said piece of ground in all time coming and the said disponees and their foresaids shall in all time coming be bound before erecting any buildings or structures of any kind on the said piece of ground hereby disponed to exhibit to the Superior proper Plans thereof for approval and the erection of such buildings or structures shall in no case be proceeded with until the Plans thereof be so approved;

(Second)

The said dwellinghouses shall be built of stone or brick and shall not be built nearer to Keptie Road Arbroath then the existing houses in that road and the ground in front shall not be built on, but shall be laid out as parterre or flower gardens and enclosed with a parapet wall, iron railing and suitable gates conform to a design which has been submitted and approved of by me the said Frederick Fothringham MacDonald as the Superior, and the said Arbroath and District Building Company Limited shall be bound to enclose the said piece of ground on the South with a substantial wooden fence which shall be erected wholly on the ground hereby disponed, and which fence shall be upheld and maintained by my said disponees or their foresaids in all time coming; And the said Arbroath and District Building Company Limited shall also be bound to enclose the said piece of ground on the East and North boundaries with a similar fence which shall be erected, one half on the ground hereby disponed and the other half on the adjoining

---

LAND REGISTER OF SCOTLAND

TITLE NUMBER ANG19152   **D 2**

D. BURDENS SECTION

ground, and when the adjoining ground is feued and built on the said disponees and their foresaid shall be entitled to receive from the adjoining feuars one half of the value of the said enclosing fence as the same shall be ascertained by arbiters mutually chosen or their oversman and the same shall thereafter be mutual in all time coming, and the same or a similar fence shall be mutually upheld and maintained in all time thereafter;

(Third)

No building other than a dwellinghouse or dwellinghouses and relative offices shall be erected on the said piece of ground hereby disponed nor shall the said dwellinghouses and offices, when erected, by at any time converted to any other use than as self contained dwellinghouses and no nuisance shall be created or permitted and no manufacture or trade shall be carried on, on the said piece of ground but my said disponee or their foresaids shall be entitled to erect at the side of each dwellinghouse to be erected on the said piece of ground a Garage to contain one vehicle;

(Fourth)

The feuars shall be bound to keep the said houses to be erected on the said area of ground constantly insured and in the joint names of the Superior and vassal against loss by fire with an established Insurance Company, (the said Insurance Company to be selected by the present Superior during his lifetime and the premiums to be paid by the vassals or disponees) for the full value thereof and to produce to me from time to time when required, the Polices of Insurance and the termly receipts for payment of the premiums and in the event of the said houses being destroyed or damaged by fire or from any other cause the feuars shall be bound to restore them as they stood before such destruction or damage and that within one year after such destruction or damage and in the case of fire the sum, if any, to be received from the Insurance Company shall be expended at the sight of me in re-erecting the said houses or repairing the damages done by such fire, and in any case the houses shall be re-erected or restored so as to be in all respects consistent with the conditions of this Charter.

Chapter 7

Acquisition by involuntary transfer

INTRODUCTION

7.1 In derivative acquisition the consent of both transferor and transferee is essential.[1] Therefore, if Alice is the transferor she must intend to transfer ownership and if Ben is the transferee he must intend to acquire it. If Alice does not intend a transfer to take place, there can be no transfer. She cannot be deprived of her property unless she agrees.

---

[1]   See **PARA 3.11** above.

7.2 That is the general principle. But sometimes the consent of the *transferor* is not needed. This is known as 'involuntary transfer'. It is still derivative, not original, acquisition.[2] Alice's right of ownership passes to Ben, albeit without her consent. In contrast, in original acquisition Alice's right of ownership is extinguished and a new title is created in Ben. The difference is important, because, as in other cases of derivative acquisition, the transfer is subject to the *nemo plus* rule.[3]

7.3 The main cases of involuntary transfer are the following:
- (a) compulsory purchase;[4]
- (b) sale by a secured creditor;[5]
- (c) diligence;[6]
- (d) insolvency;[7]
- (e) death;[8]
- (f) forfeiture as a criminal penalty[9] and
- (g) special statutory rules relating to sale of goods.[10]

COMPULSORY PURCHASE

General

7.4 Statutory powers authorising compulsory acquisition of land are held by certain public bodies. These include local authorities and the Scottish Government. Land might be compulsorily acquired, for example, to construct a motorway. Where the powers are exercised, the owner's consent is unnecessary. However, he or she must be compensated. This is necessary as a matter of fairness and not least to conform to Article 1 of Protocol 1 to the ECHR.[11] Where agreement cannot be reached on compensation, the matter is determined by the Lands Tribunal.[12]

7.5 The first part of a compulsory purchase is the service of a 'compulsory purchase order' (CPO). Second, there is the actual transfer of ownership, effected either by a 'schedule conveyance' or by a 'general vesting declaration' (GVD).

---

2   See **CHAPTER 8** below.
3   See **PARA 4.39** above.
4   See **PARAS 7.4–7.10** below.
5   See **PARA 7.11** below.
6   See **PARAS 7.12–7.14** below.
7   See **PARAS 7.15–7.16** below.
8   See **PARAS 7.17–7.18** below.
9   See **PARA 7.19** below.
10 See **PARA 7.20** below.
11 See **CHAPTER 31** below.
12 Land Compensation (Scotland) Act 1973, s 8.

Compulsory purchase order

7.6 The CPO is drawn up in the prescribed form.[13] It is then served on the parties affected, and also publicly advertised. There is a period for objections of at least 21 days. After that the CPO may be 'confirmed' by the 'confirming authority'. This is usually the Scottish Ministers. If objections are made, the confirming authority must either allow the objector a hearing or hold a public local inquiry. If the CPO is confirmed, this must be intimated to the affected parties. The CPO is then registered in the Land Register or the Sasine Register, depending on where the property is currently registered.[14]

Conveyancing procedures

7.7 There are two types of conveyancing procedure following the confirmation of the CPO. The transferor (the current owner) can be asked to execute a special form of disposition, known as a 'schedule conveyance', or the acquiring authority can proceed without the transferor and execute a GVD. If the transferor is unwilling to co-operate, a GVD must be used. A single GVD can be used for more than one property. This is useful if a number of different properties are to be acquired. A schedule conveyance is, however, quicker in practice than a GVD.

Schedule conveyances

7.8 The Lands Clauses Consolidation (Scotland) Act 1845 regulates schedule conveyances. There is a statutory form of disposition in a schedule to the Act – hence 'schedule conveyance'. The transfer process begins with a statutory 'notice to treat'.[15] Despite this name, the notice, when served on the transferor, may be regarded as a binding contract of sale.[16] The procedure which follows is similar to that in an ordinary transfer of land. The transferor executes and delivers the conveyance. On registration in the Land Register, ownership passes to the acquiring authority.

General vesting declarations

7.9 A transfer by schedule conveyance is not, strictly speaking, *involuntary*. The transferor does actually consent to the transfer by executing the disposition, although the reason for doing so is the CPO. A GVD is different. Here, the transferor is not involved. A GVD is drawn up in the prescribed form and executed by the acquiring

---

[13]   See the Acquisition of Land (Authorisation Procedure) (Scotland) Act 1947, Sch 1.
[14]   See CHAPTER 6 above.
[15]   See the Acquisition of Land (Authorisation Procedure) (Scotland) Act 1947, Sch 2, para 3.
[16]   For discussion, see J Rowan Robinson, *Compulsory Purchase and Compensation* (2nd edn, 2003) paras 3-08–3-09.

authority.[17] On registration of the GVD in the Land Register, ownership is transferred to the acquiring authority.

Miscellaneous compulsory purchase rights

7.10   Sometimes a right of compulsory purchase is conferred by statute, exercisable by requiring an ordinary conveyance from the owner. Examples are public-sector residential tenants,[18] crofters,[19] other tenant farmers,[20] crofting community bodies[21] and community bodies.[22] In the case of tenant farmers and non-crofting community bodies the right is only a pre-emption right – a right to buy in preference to other bidders if the owner wishes to sell. In the other cases the right to buy does not depend on the owner's willingness to sell. The price has to be fair market value, except in the first two cases. The two community body cases require ministerial approvals.

SALE BY A SECURED CREDITOR

7.11   Often rights in security give the creditor a power of sale.[23] This means that if the debtor defaults on the loan the creditor can sell the security subjects and recover the debt out of the proceeds. The balance, after deduction of expenses, then goes to the debtor. On a sale by a secured creditor the transfer following thereon is involuntary, that is to say that there is no role for the owner (the defaulting debtor). Although the debtor owns the property and the creditor does not, the act of transfer is effected by the creditor and not by the debtor. The transfer itself is carried out in the normal way for the type of property in question.[24]

DILIGENCE

General

7.12   Diligence is the process by which a creditor, typically an unsecured creditor, attaches the debtor's property to enforce payment.[25] A distinction can be drawn

---

[17]   Town and Country Planning (Scotland) Act 1997, Sch 15.
[18]   Housing (Scotland) Act 1987, s 61. This is the 'right to buy' which has had such an impact on residential property.
[19]   Crofters (Scotland) Act 1993, ss 12–19.
[20]   Agricultural Holdings (Scotland) Act 2003, Pt 2.
[21]   LR(S)A 2003, Pt 3.
[22]   LR(S)A 2003, Pt 2.
[23]   See **PARA 20.24** below.
[24]   See **CHAPTER 5** above.
[25]   See Gloag and Henderson *The Law of Scotland* ch 49.

between 'seize diligences' and 'freeze diligences'. In a 'seize' diligence the creditor seizes property belonging to the debtor; in a 'freeze' diligence he or she prevents the debtor from disposing of the property.

Seize diligences

7.13 It is seize diligences which are relevant to involuntary transfer. The main cases are attachment, adjudication, and arrestment and furthcoming. Attachment seizes corporeal moveables. Adjudication seizes land.[26] Arrestment and furthcoming seize moveable property (both corporeal and incorporeal) which is in the hands of a third party, for example a bank account.

7.14 In seize diligences the creditor probably acquires, not ownership, but a right in security over the property seized. The next step is to realise the property and thereby recover the debt: this is broadly similar to enforcement by any other secured creditor.

INSOLVENCY

Sequestration

7.15 A natural person who becomes insolvent may be sequestrated. A *trustee in sequestration* is appointed to realise the assets and distribute the proceeds rateably amongst the various creditors, who are the beneficiaries of the trust that the sequestration sets up. Sequestration is governed by the Bankruptcy (Scotland) Act 1985. The debtor's assets 'vest in', i.e. are transferred to the trustee, in trust for the creditors. The transfer is an involuntary one.[27] The trustee obtains an immediate right of possession and administration. For some types of property, such as corporeal moveable property and most incorporeal moveable property the trustee acquires title by virtue of the fact of sequestration. But for property, such as land, where title depends on registration, the sequestration functions as a delivered deed of conveyance to the trustee, conferring the power to complete title by registration. For example, Val is sequestrated, and owns a house and a bicycle. Ownership of the bicycle passes to the trustee at once, without the need for delivery. But ownership of the house does not pass until the trustee registers in the Land Register or Sasine Register. The trustee is thus an unregistered holder.[28] Registration is required before

---

26 It will be replaced by a new procedure called land attachment when and if the relevant provisions of the Bankruptcy and Diligence etc. (Scotland) Act 2007 are brought into force. See Gloag and Henderson *The Law of Scotland* paras 49.26–49.32.

27 Though the sequestration can be initiated by the debtor.

28 See PARA **5.8** above.

ownership is acquired.[29] But in practice this may not always happen, for, like any other unregistered holder, the trustee can convey to a purchaser without having first completed title in his or her own name.

Corporate insolvency

7.16 When a company goes into liquidation the position is different from sequestration. There is no vesting in the liquidator.[30] A liquidator has power of administration, and can dispose of the company's assets as its representative. However, a liquidator can obtain apply to the court for the assets to be transferred to him or her, and if that happens the position becomes the same, from the standpoint of property law, as a sequestration. Such applications are almost unknown in practice.[31] Whether liquidation is really involuntary transfer is arguable. A juristic person acts through representatives: their consent is its consent. The liquidator is the company representative. A similar point can be made about the other forms of corporate insolvency, administration and receivership.

DEATH

7.17 The property of a person who dies is administered by an executor, whose function is to gather in and then distribute the deceased's estate in accordance with the will or, where there is no will, the rules of intestate succession.[32] The executor must obtain decree of *confirmation* from the sheriff court. This operates as a judicial conveyance to the executor of the deceased's estate.[33]

7.18 Like the act and warrant of a trustee in sequestration, the grant of confirmation alone does not transfer heritable property. There must also be registration in the Land Register or Sasine Register for this to happen. In practice, executors do not usually register. Their interest in the property is temporary and as holders of an unregistered judicial conveyance (the confirmation) they are already unregistered holders, enabling them to transfer the property on by a disposition in which title is deduced through the confirmation.[34]

---

[29] *Burnett's Tr v Grainger* 2004 SC (HL) 19. The Bankruptcy and Diligence etc. (Scotland) Act 2007, s 17 prevents immediate registration.

[30] Subject to s 25 of the Titles to Land Consolidation (Scotland) Act 1868.

[31] Insolvency Act 1986, s 145(1).

[32] See **CHAPTERS 27 AND 28** below.

[33] S(S)A 1964, s 14(1).

[34] See **PARAS 4.50–4.51** above.

FORFEITURE AS A CRIMINAL PENALTY

7.19 The criminal courts have statutory powers to order forfeiture of property belonging to offenders. Some of these relate to specific offences, for example the poaching of fish.[35] In addition, the Proceeds of Crime Act 2002 has detailed general provisions allowing prosecutors to move for the confiscation of assets and, if necessary, their subsequent sale by enforcement administrators.[36]

SPECIAL STATUTORY RULES RELATING TO SALE OF GOODS

7.20 In several situations statute enables a non-owning seller of corporeal moveable property to transfer ownership to the purchaser.[37] For example, if Stephanie has agreed to buy a car from Robert and has taken delivery of it but not yet become owner, because they have agreed that this will be dependent on her paying for it next week, she has power as a 'buyer in possession' to transfer Robert's title to Tiffany.[38] If it turns out that Robert has a void title, then it is that same bad title that Tiffany, the purchaser, will receive.[39] The effect of these special statutory rules is an involuntary transfer from the third party, in our example Robert, to the purchaser (Tiffany).

FURTHER READING

Gordon, *Scottish Land Law* ch 29.

McDonald, *Conveyancing Manual* chs 29 and 30.

Reid, *Property* paras 663–668.

Rowan Robinson, J, *Compulsory Purchase and Compensation* (2nd edn, 2003).

---

[35]   Salmon and Freshwater Consolidation (Scotland) Act 2003, s 60.
[36]   Proceeds of Crime Act 2002, ss 92–155.
[37]   These provisions are discussed in more detail at PARAS **5.34–5.35** above.
[38]   SOGA 1979, s 25. See also SOGA 1979, ss 21 and 24; the Factors Act 1889, ss 8 and 9; and the Hire Purchase Act 1964, s 27.
[39]   *National Employers Mutual General Insurance Association Ltd v Jones* [1990] 1 AC 24.

Chapter 8

Original acquisition

INTRODUCTION

8.1 In 'original acquisition', the acquirer gains a brand new title to the property. This contrasts with 'derivative acquisition', where the title is only as good as that of the previous owner.[1] Instances of original acquisition can be divided into two broad categories. The first is where the property has never been owned. This category is confined to moveables, for land cannot be ownerless. (Land, unless previously

---

[1]   See **PARA 3.10** above.

acquired by someone else, belongs to the Crown.[2]) The second category is where the property has been owned. Here, the law extinguishes the existing title at the same time as it confers the new title on the acquirer. Naturally, such a serious consequence means that the operation of original acquisition is strictly limited. It is also restricted by the fact that property, if abandoned, passes to the Crown, rather than becoming ownerless.[3] For example, if a married couple separate acrimoniously and the wife throws her wedding ring away, it becomes the property of the state. Similarly, where title to moveables is lost by negative prescription, it falls to the Crown.[4] For all these reasons, derivative acquisition is far more common. A number of the original acquisition doctrines are heavily drawn from Roman law and do not always meet the needs of the modern age.[5]

PREVIOUSLY UNOWNED PROPERTY

Corporeal property: occupancy

8.2 Where something moveable is not already owned it can be acquired by occupancy (*occupatio*). This is achieved by taking possession of the property with the intention to become owner.[6] For the reasons explained in the previous paragraph, there is little ownerless property. The main examples are shells, pearls, gems and pebbles on the seashore, running water and wild animals. With an exception, occupancy can take place only once. For example, once entered into a container, running water becomes owned. It can never be ownerless again. The exception concerns wild animals. If they regain liberty, they become unowned once more.[7] Thus the mouse which escapes from its pursuer, Debbie, who managed to get hold of it temporarily under the cupboard in the kitchen, is no longer Debbie's property. The rule does not apply to farmed fish, on the basis that they are not truly wild.[8] Animals which have freedom of movement but return to a particular place, such as bees and pigeons, remain owned provided that they continue to come back. Where game is seized illegitimately by poachers on someone else's land they will acquire a title by occupancy, but this can be forfeited by a court subsequently.[9]

---

[2] Erskine II, 1, 11; Reid *Feudal Abolition* para 1.14. For positive prescription, see PARAS **2.24–2.25** above.

[3] Erskine II, 1, 12; *Lord Advocate v University of Aberdeen & Budge* 1963 SC 533; *Mackenzie v Maclean* 1981 SLT (Sh Ct) 40. A Latin maxim found in older authorities is *quod nullius est fit domini regis*: what belongs to no one becomes the property of the lord king. See also PARAS **3.6–3.8** above.

[4] PL(S)A 1973, s 8.

[5] See, e.g., N R Whitty, 'Rights of Personality, Property Rights and the Human Body in Scots Law' (2005) 9 *Edin LR* 194.

[6] In the words of the Latin maxim, *quod nullius est fit occupantis* (what belongs to no one becomes the property of the taker).

[7] Erskine II, 1, 10.

[8] *Valentine v Kennedy* 1985 SCCR 89. See C G van der Merwe and D Bain 'The Fish that Got Away: Some Reflections on *Valentine v Kennedy*' (2008) 12 *Edin LR* 418.

[9] See PARA **7.19** above.

Incorporeal property

8.3 New incorporeal property is acquired originally. Here are some examples. A company issues new shares; the shares have never had a previous owner and the purchaser therefore gains an original title. Peter invents something and applies for a patent; if the Patents Office is prepared to grant him one he acquires it by original acquisition. Hazel leases her house to Ian; he gains a new real right. Once again, this is a case of original acquisition.

PROPERTY WHICH HAS ALREADY BEEN OWNED

Accession

General

8.4 Accession takes place when two pieces of corporeal property become joined in such a way that one is considered to have become subsumed into the other. The property which is subsumed is known as the 'accessory'. The property into which it is subsumed is known as the 'principal'. For example, a house accedes to the land on which it is built. A window frame accedes to the house and so to the land. The paint accedes to the frame and so to the land. An engine accedes to the car into which it is installed. Accession is a mechanical doctrine dependent on objective factors. It follows that parties cannot contract so as to exclude its operation.[10]

Elements

8.5 Three elements of accession have been identified.[11] The first and most important is physical union. The pieces of property must be attached to each other. The greater the level of attachment, the more likely it is that accession has operated. The panelling built into a wall is a strong candidate for accession. The picture hung from a nail is not. The second element is functional subordination. The accessory must be subordinate to the principal. The entryphone system in a tenement is attached for the improvement of that building. The third element is permanency. The more permanent the attachment, the greater the likelihood there is of accession. Buildings accede: marquees do not. Similarly, cinema seats can be compared with seats fixed to the floor of a hall for one night of boxing.[12]

---

10   *Shetland Islands Council v BP Petroleum Development Ltd* 1990 SLT 82 at 94 per Lord Cullen.
11   Reid *Property* para 571.
12   T B Smith, *A Short Commentary on the Law of Scotland* (1962) 504.

Effects

8.6 Accession has three effects.[13]

(1) The accessory becomes part of the principal. This means that rights created in respect of the principal automatically affect the accessory. For example, if Penelope has a contractual right to acquire ownership of a house, she is entitled to everything that has acceded to it. The seller in such circumstances should make express provision for any accessory which is not to be included. For instance, it could be stipulated that the ornamental bird bath in the back garden is excluded from the sale and will be removed by the seller.

(2) The second effect is known as 'conversion'. This occurs when the accessory is moveable and the principal is heritable. The result of accession is to make the accessory heritable. Thus, bricks are 'born' moveable but become heritable on being used to build a house. Occasionally, moveable property which has a purpose devoted to land, for example, a house key, is deemed heritable and is known as a 'constructive fixture'.

(3) The third effect is that the existing title to the accessory is extinguished. Where it and the principal have different owners, the result is to give the owner of the principal an original title to the accessory. For example, if Bob takes Carol's slates and attaches them to his roof, he becomes their owner. Carol, if she did not consent, is left with a compensation claim.[14]

8.7 If the accessory is subsequently separated ('severed') from the principal, effects (1) and (2) are reversed, but not effect (3). If Carol removes the slates from Bob's roof, the slates no longer form part of that roof and become moveable property again. They still belong to Bob because accession operated. Effect (3) can be seen to have serious consequences. It has been suggested therefore that whether it operates depends on the parties involved. The better view, however, is that there is a unitary law and distinctions based on the circumstances are not admitted.[15]

Moveables to land

8.8 Moveable property which has acceded to land is a 'fixture'. Fixtures can be contrasted with 'fittings'. These are items found in a building, such as furniture, which do not satisfy the requirements for accession. Whether accession takes place depends on the application of the three elements discussed above. First, there must be physical union. Things which are irrevocably attached, such as buildings, are always fixtures. A heavy object may accede because of its weight alone.[16] If the accessory cannot be removed without seriously damaging it or the principal, then it will have

---

13   Reid *Property* para 574.
14   See **PARA 8.18** below.
15   Reid *Property* para 575; *Brand's Trs v Brand's Trs* (1876) 3 R (HL) 16.
16   *Christie v Smith's Exr* 1949 SC 572 (a summer house).

acceded.[17] Unless the 'physical union' test provides a decisive result, the other two elements must be considered.

8.9   As to the second element – functional subordination – the question to ask is: does the item appear to be attached for the improvement of the land or for the better enjoyment of the item itself? Sometimes the answer is clear. A heating system is clearly installed to improve a house and therefore accedes.[18] In other cases, the attachment may enhance both the moveable and the land. A picture is better viewed if hung, but it also enhances the wall. Much depends on the circumstances.[19]

8.10   Only quasi-permanency is required to satisfy the third element. In the leading case of *Brand's Trs v Brand's Trs*[20] machinery was installed by a tenant under a mining lease, with the intention of removing it at the expiry. It was held, nonetheless, to have acceded. Various factors should be considered when assessing permanency.[21] If the physical attachment used is greater than is necessary to secure the item then that points to accession.[22] So too does mutual special adaptation, as where lace looms were installed into a shed which had been adjusted to take them.[23] Also relevant is whether the item is something normally left or removed when a building changes hands. For example, industrial machinery may well be left in a factory for the new owner taking over the business. Domestic items such as a dishwasher are commonly removed. There are many borderline cases, such as fitted carpets, though perhaps these are nowadays regarded as fixtures. Finally, the length of time which the item takes to install or remove should be considered. For example, industrial machinery which needs several weeks to be fitted or removed will be regarded as an accessory.

8.11   The deemed intention of the person who installed the item (who might be a hirer) has been said to be relevant when assessing whether there has been accession.[24] This seems to be contrary to House of Lords authority.[25] The better view is that accession should be decided solely by objective factors. As one writer has put it, '[a] fixture should be a fixture if it is patent for all the world to see'.[26]

8.12   In limited circumstances, tenants have a right to sever something even if it has acceded. This is recognised for trade fixtures.[27] There is also a statutory right of

---

17   *Elitestone Ltd v Morris* [1997] 2 All ER 513. This is an English case but the law here north and south of the border is similar, following *Brand's Trs v Brand's Trs* (1876) 3 R (HL) 16. For a comparative account, see L P W van Vliet 'Accession of Movables to Land' (2002) 6 *Edin LR* 67 and 199.
18   *Assessor for Fife v Hodgson* 1966 SC 30.
19   *Cochrane v Stevenson* (1891) 18 R 1208.
20   (1876) 3 R (HL) 16.
21   Reid *Property* para 582.
22   *Leigh v Taylor* [1902] AC 157.
23   *Howie's Trs v McLay* (1902) 5 F 214.
24   *Scottish Discount Co v Blin* 1985 SC 216.
25   *Brand's Trs v Brand's Trs* (1876) 3 R (HL) 16.
26   C G van der Merwe 'Accession by Building' in Reid and Zimmermann *History* vol 1, 245 at 268.
27   *Brand's Trs v Brand's Trs* (1876) 3 R (HL) 16.

tenants to remove agricultural fixtures.[28] In English law, tenants may also remove domestic and ornamental fixtures but there is no authority on the point in Scotland.[29]

Moveables to moveables

8.13   Moveable property can accede to other moveable property, for example a button to a coat or paint to a car. In broad terms, the same rules for deciding whether accession has taken place apply as for moveables-to-land accession. As with land, there can be borderline cases. It has been held in South Africa that tyres do not accede to a car because removing them is relatively straightforward.[30] In the aviation industry there is a consensus that an aero-engine does not accede to the airframe.

8.14   In the case of fixtures, there is no difficulty in identifying the principal. It is always the land. Here, it is more complicated and the law is not settled. Bell's analysis[31] is as follows. First, if, with two substances, one can exist separately and the other cannot, then the first is the principal. An example is paint used on a car, which no longer has an independent existence.[32] Second, where both things can exist separately, the principal is the one 'which the other is taken to adorn or complete'.[33] For example, the button accedes to the coat. This might be expressed alternatively that the principal is the item which gives its name to the finished product. Bell's final rule is that if the two foregoing rules are not relevant then 'bulk prevails; next value'. In the absence of case law it is not certain that this is correct. Bulk was given some importance in the South African case of *Khan v Minister of Law and Order*.[34] There, a BMW car turned out to be the front of one car and the back of another.[35] The rear part had been stolen. It included the bodywork up to the windscreen and was held to be the principal. Hence the front acceded to it, and so belonged to the owner of the principal.

Land to land

8.15   The extent to which land is covered by water is subject to change. Any new dry land created will accede to that which exists already. This is called 'alluvion'. Alluvion also operates where the extent of the land under an area of water increases. In that case there is accession to the land already covered. There are two main conditions.

---

28   Agricultural Holdings (Scotland) Act 1991, s 18. The strict effect of this provision rather bizarrely is that such fixtures are to be treated as not having acceded in the first place.
29   Reid *Property* para 586.
30   *J L Cohen Motors v Alberts* 1985 (2) SA 427. See also Carey Miller with Irvine *Corporeal Moveables* para 3.20.
31   Bell *Principles* s 1298.
32   See Carey Miller with Irvine *Corporeal Moveables* para 3.19.
33   Bell *Principles* s 1298.
34   1991 (3) SA 439.
35   In slang terms, a 'cut and shut'.

(1) The addition must be permanent. Temporary change is insufficient, for example an inland loch that shrinks somewhat in summer.

(2) Sudden additions do not count. Such changes, for example those caused by a storm, are known as 'avulsion'.

Whilst alluvion normally happens naturally, it can happen by human intervention, such as by the building of a wall. In *Stirling v Bartlett*[36] some debris had come floating down a river, breaking it up into different channels during the 1960s. By agreement with his counterpart on the other side, one of the proprietors of land beside the river constructed a new channel. This altered the route of the river slightly. In the 1990s a successor proprietor objected. It was held that the change was permanent and the objection came too late.[37] In other circumstances, deliberate human act may be classed as avulsion.[38]

Fruits

8.16 Where the accessory is produced by the principal, this is known as 'accession by fruits'. There are three principal examples. The first is crops, trees and plants. On taking root and receiving nourishment from the ground, they accede to it. But 'industrial growing crops', such as barley, wheat and potatoes, which require 'annual seed and labour', are moveable.[39] Where a tree is on the boundary of two pieces of land, ownership will be determined by the situation of its trunk. If the trunk straddles the boundary, the tree will be common property.[40] This contrasts with the rule in Roman law, where the situation of the roots was the determining factor.[41]

8.17 The second case is the young of animals, not yet born. They accede to the mother.[42] The third is natural products of animals or plants, such as milk or raspberries. These accede to the animal or plant in question, until such time as they become separate. This is an example of the more general rule that accession ends by separation. Therefore the tree uprooted by the storm or the baby foal now born is no longer an accessory. Separation, however, in principle does not change ownership. A lamb belongs to the ewe's owner. Apples stolen from a tree still belong to the tree's owner. (Though in the case of a lease, the tenant normally acquires the fruits.)

---

[36] 1993 SLT 763.

[37] For discussion, see Gordon *Scottish Land Law* para 4.23 and D L Carey Miller, 'Alluvio, Avulsio and Fluvial Boundaries' 1994 *SLT (News)* 75.

[38] See Scottish Law Commission *Report on the Law of the Foreshore and Sea Bed* (2003) paras 6.1–6.5.

[39] Erskine II, 2, 4; *Boskabelle Ltd v Laird* 2006 SLT 1079.

[40] *Hetherington v Galt* (1905) 7 F 706.

[41] Reid *Property* para 179.

[42] *Lamb v Grant* (1874) 11 SLR 672.

Compensation

8.18   The erstwhile owner of the accessory may be entitled to compensation for loss of title on the basis of unjustified enrichment. This depends on who brought about the accession, and why. If it was the owner of the principal, then there is an enrichment claim. (Unless, of course, the accession was consensual, in which case compensation, if any, depends on the agreement.[43]) The quantum is the value of the materials but if there has been bad faith, a higher level is payable.[44] If the act was that of the accessory's owner then there is generally no enrichment claim. There is an exception, however, where that person had a reasonable belief that he or she owned the principal.

Commixtion and confusion

8.19   The mixing of solids so that it is impossible to distinguish them is 'commixtion'. For example, Janet's sheep may become mixed with John's. If the sheep have identifying marks upon them and can be separated, commixtion does not operate. The equivalent doctrine for liquids is known as 'confusion' – for instance, different whiskies being blended together.[45] The essential criterion here is mixing or fusion rather than joining. The result is common property in proportion to the value of the constituent materials. Assuming, therefore, that Janet and John had an equal number of sheep and that these had the same value, they would both now own a one-half *pro indiviso* share of each sheep. The materials must, however, be of substantially the same kind, otherwise specification (discussed below), or perhaps accession will operate. Professor Carey Miller suggests, for example, that soda water added to whisky will accede to it.[46]

Specification

8.20   Where a new kind of thing is manufactured from materials belonging wholly or partly to others, this is 'specification'. For example, Jill bakes a cake using Kirsten's butter, eggs and flour. The case always cited by the institutional writers,[47] following Roman law, is making grapes into wine. This is more apposite to the temperate climate of Italy than Scotland. Stair's example of wood being used to build a boat seems more in point.[48] It is essential that a new type of thing is created, i.e. a new species (*nova species*). It was held in one case that joining two halves of a

---

[43]   Stair II, 1, 38–39; Bankton I, 9, 43; A J M Steven, 'Recompense for Interference in Scots Law' 1996 *JR* 51 at 61.

[44]   Steven 'Recompense for Interference in Scots Law' at 61.

[45]   J Thomson *Scottish Private Law* (2006) para 3.07.

[46]   Carey Miller with Irvine *Corporeal Moveables* para 5.05.

[47]   For example, Erskine II, 1, 25.

[48]   Stair II, 1, 41.

car together met this requirement.[49] This, however, is accession, as it is merely joining and there is no *nova species*.[50] On the other hand, where a vehicle is built from scratch out of raw materials such as metal, this is truly a new species.[51] It was argued unsuccessfully in one case that where baby salmon (smolts) are industrially reared in a fish farm so as they grow to become adults, specification takes place.[52] A Dutch court in a similar case involving eggs being specially hatched to produce chickens reached the opposite result.[53] As there is no actual change of species, this seems questionable.

8.21 The issue of who owns the new species was controversial in Roman law.[54] Some jurists favoured the owner of the materials; others, the manufacturer. A middle view developed that the manufacturer acquired ownership if the work carried out was, in a practical sense, irreversible. If it was not, title was given to the owner of the materials. An example of practical irreversibility would be a boat, which in theory could be returned to planks of wood, but not in a way in which it appears that the boat was never built in the first place. This middle view has been accepted in Scotland. Of course, it may be that the manufacturer is carrying out the process as the agent of the owner of the materials. In that case the latter will naturally acquire ownership. Likewise, the matter in general can be governed by an agreement between the parties.[55]

8.22 A difficult question is whether the manufacturer needs to be in good faith in order to acquire ownership. The better view is that state of mind should be relevant only to the issue of compensation. The rules on recompensing the party who does not acquire title are similar to those for accession. Where ownership has been acquired by the manufacturer, he or she must repay the value of the materials to their erstwhile owner. In *International Banking Corporation v Ferguson Shaw & Sons*[56] oil had been used in good faith to make margarine. The value of the oil had then to be paid to the former owner. Where ownership remains with the owner of the materials the manufacturer has no claim, unless that person reasonably believed that he or she owned them.

Money and bills of exchange

8.23 For reasons of commerce, special rules enable the acquirers of money (legal tender) and of negotiable instruments to acquire an original rather than a derivative

---

[49]   *McDonald v Provan (of Scotland Street) Ltd* 1960 SLT 231.

[50]   This analysis was accepted in *Khan v Minister of Law and Order* 1991 (3) SA 439.

[51]   *Wylie & Lochhead v Mitchell* (1870) 8 M 552.

[52]   *Kinloch Damph Ltd v Nordvik Salmon Farms Ltd,* Outer House, 30 June 1999 (unreported, available at http://www.scotcourts.gov.uk/opinions/ca291499.html).

[53]   HR 24 Mar 1994, NJ 158. For discussion, see E Metzger 'Acquisition of living things by specification' (2004) 8 *Edin LR* 115.

[54]   Reid *Property* para 560.

[55]   *Wylie & Lochhead v Mitchell* (1870) 8 M 552.

[56]   1910 SC 182.

title.[57] As regards money, say that Charlie finds a £1 coin in the street and goes into a shop to buy chocolate with it. The shopkeeper acquires an original title to the coin. The fact that it does not belong to Charlie does not matter. However, good faith on the part of the shopkeeper is required.[58] Similarly, a 'holder in due course' of a bill of exchange, i.e. someone who takes it in good faith and for value, gains an original title. Therefore if the person from whom the bill was obtained had a bad title, this does not matter.[59]

Positive prescription

8.24   Where someone has possessed land openly, peaceably and continuously without being challenged in court for a period of ten years, on the basis of a conveyance which has been recorded in the Sasine Register, the title will be exempt from challenge.[60] While the matter is not certain, the better view is that in these circumstances the title acquired is an original one.[61]

Registration in the Land Register

8.25   The effect of the Keeper entering a person as proprietor of property in the Land Register is to cure any defects in that person's title.[62] Therefore if Beth dispones land to Carol and the Keeper registers Carol as owner, Carol is owner, even if Beth was not owner or that the disposition was invalid for other reasons.

FURTHER READING

Carey Miller with Irvine *Corporeal Moveables* chs 2–5.

Gordon *Scottish Land Law* ch 5.

Reid *Property* paras 539–596 and 673–676.

Thomson, J *Scots Private Law* (2006) ch 3.

C G van der Merwe, 'Accession by Building' in Reid and Zimmermann, *History* vol 1, 245-268.

L P W van Vliet, 'Accession of Movables to Land' (2002) 6 *Edin LR* 67 and 199.

---

[57]   See, for example, the discussion of money in Stair II, 1, 43 and Carey Miller with Irvine *Corporeal Moveables* para 1.19.

[58]   *Crawfurd v Royal Bank* (1749) Mor 875; *SME Reissue* 'Banking, Money and Commercial Paper' (2000) para 144.

[59]   Bills of Exchange Act 1882, s 38(2). See F Davidson and L Macgregor *Commercial Law in Scotland* (2nd edn, 2008) para 5.73.

[60]   PL(S)A 1973, s 1. Positive prescription is discussed in more detail at PARAS **2.24–2.25** above.

[61]   Reid *Property* para 674; Paisley *Land Law* para 3.13. Compare Johnston *Prescription* paras 14.01–14.15.

[62]   See PARAS **6.30–6.31** above.

Chapter 9

Co-ownership

INTRODUCTION

9.1 Two persons can own the same thing simultaneously: for example, Jack and Jill buy a house together. On the Land Register, both names will appear on the proprietorship section of the title sheet. Each owns everything. Each room is owned by both. Each wall in each room is owned by both. Each brick in each wall is owned by both. Each atom in each brick is owned by both. The same can be true of moveable property. Jack and Jill may co-own some or all of the contents of the house – each chair, each rug, each plate. Co-ownership is not limited to two people. Bashful, Doc, Dopey, Grumpy, Happy, Sleepy and Sneezy could be the co-owners of a house.

9.2 Co-ownership, also called ownership *pro indiviso*, is of two very different kinds: common ownership and joint ownership.[1] 'Common ownership' is the standard case. 'Joint ownership' is the special case, the main example being in the law of

---

[1] Formerly, landownership was divided between superior and vassal, but no longer: see **APPENDIX**. There is – or was – also something called 'commonty' but the Division of Commonties Act 1695 provided a mechanism for the termination of commonties on a case-by-case basis, and it seems that none now survive.

trusts. The property is called 'common property' or 'joint property' respectively,[2] though in practice those who are not specialists in property law often use the word 'joint' for both. The two terms are not ideal. Roman–Dutch law, which has the same distinction, uses the terms 'free' ownership for common ownership and 'bound' ownership for joint ownership.[3] Perhaps Scots law should follow suit.

9.3 It is not only ownership that can be held by two or more persons. So can other patrimonial rights. However, the law has been developed in connection with ownership, which is in practice the most important case. This is what is discussed in this chapter. For other types of right, the principles are applied by analogy, but the law is rather undeveloped.

COMMON OWNERSHIP

General

9.4 Common ownership arises in countless situations, but three represent the great majority. The first is where two people buy a home together and take the title 'in joint names' as common property. The second is where two people live together as spouses, civil partners or cohabitants, for then the moveable contents of the house are in practice usually co-owned, and indeed are presumed to be co-owned, regardless of who owns the flat or house itself.[4] The third is where there is a building development and certain parts are co-owned by the owners of the various units. An example is where a developer builds, say, 30 houses and each house has a share of the planted areas, the children's play park, shared parking areas etc. The best-known illustration is in tenements, where certain parts of the building will be co-owned by the various flat owners.[5]

9.5 The first two cases are functionally different from the third, for in the third the co-ownership is usually a permanent arrangement, and unaffected as and when individual units are sold. The common parts are shared corporeal pertinents of each unit.[6] The share in the common parts thus attaches to each flat. As a result, the law treats such cases slightly differently. Usually there are real burdens that regulate such matters as repairs, and in that case the general law of common property is to that extent displaced.[7] In the case of a tenement, there is a statutory regime and, here again, the general law of common property is to that extent displaced.[8]

---

[2] The terminology did not become settled until *Magistrates of Banff v Ruthin Castle Ltd* 1944 SC 36.
[3] D Kleyn and S Wortley 'Co-ownership' in Zimmermann, Visser and Reid *Mixed Legal Systems* 703–734.
[4] See **CHAPTER 10** below.
[5] See **PARAS 15.10–15.11** below.
[6] On pertinents, see **PARAS 14.9–14.12** below.
[7] See **CHAPTER 13** below.
[8] See **CHAPTER 15** below.

9.6   Each co-owner has a *pro indiviso* share of the property. The law presumes that the shares are equal, so that if there are two co-owners, each has a half share; if there are five, each has a fifth; and so on. This is only a presumption. The shares can be unequal. For example, two brothers buy a flat. Their contributions to the price are unequal, and so they decide that their shares should reflect their contribution, i.e. two-thirds and one-third. That will be stated on the title sheet. There is, however, no legal requirement that the size of the share and the size of the contribution match. The brothers would have been free to agree an equal share of the title or, indeed, that title would be vested in just one of them. However, if title share does not match contribution, the parties should have an agreement as to whether the amount of the mismatch is to be treated as a gift or as a loan.

Possession and use

9.7   Possession is shared. Each co-owner has a right to make use of 'every inch'[9] of the property. Jack may dislike it if Jill is in the kitchen when he is cooking but as co-owner she has the right to be there. The parties are free to agree otherwise: Jack and Jill can enter a contract whereby he is to have the exclusive right to use the ground-floor bathroom and she alone may use the first-floor bathroom. Here, the right of exclusive use is based in contract law, not in property law. Each is still co-owner of the whole house. This 'every inch' principle is the first of three principles about possession and use of common property.[10] The second is that only 'ordinary' use is permitted. In one case it was held that the owner of a flat was not entitled to use the passage of a tenement for keeping a wheelchair.[11] The third is that one co-owner cannot take 'excessive benefit' at the expense of the others. An example is where one co-owner assumes exclusive possession of part, or indeed all, of the property without the consent of the other co-owners. Whether a person who has a larger share is entitled to a greater degree of use than someone with a smaller share is uncertain.

Repairs and alterations

9.8   Repairs and alterations require unanimous agreement.[12] There is an exception for 'necessary' repairs, where any co-owner can go ahead.[13] The boundary between necessary repairs on the one hand, and unnecessary repairs and alterations on the other, is in practice often difficult to draw. Minimal alterations may be lawful without

---

[9]   Erskine II, 6, 53.
[10]   Reid *Property* para 4.
[11]   *Carmichael v Simpson* 1932 SLT (Sh Ct) 16. See also *Rafique v Amin* 1997 SLT 1385.
[12]   For an example of this rule, see *Rafique v Amin* 1997 SLT 1385.
[13]   Bell *Principles*, s 1075; *Deans v Woolfson* 1922 SC 221.

consent, for example affixing a brass name plate.[14] As mentioned above, there are special rules for common property in tenements.[15] Moreover, the unanimity requirement is subject to any real burdens.

Death and insolvency

9.9 Each share forms part of the co-owner's patrimony. If a co-owner dies, the share simply forms part of the estate and is dealt with according to succession law. For example, if Fred and Gillian are co-owners of a car, he is free to leave his share to Heidi. In that case Gillian will find that her co-owner is Heidi. Even if Fred dies intestate, that does not mean that his share passes to Gillian.[16] Likewise, if Fred, instead of dying, becomes insolvent, his share is available to his creditors. So if Jack and Jill own a house in common and he is sequestrated, his share passes to his trustee in sequestration. (In practice the trustee will sell the share to Jill, failing which raise an action of division and sale.[17])

Juridical acts

9.10 Can one co-owner, without the consent of the others, transfer his or her share, or grant a subordinate real right? The answer is 'yes' if the share can be dealt with separately from the other shares. Otherwise the answer is 'no'. A co-owner can dispone the share without the consent of the others. For example, if Jack and Jill are co-owners of a house, she can dispone her share to Julius without Jack's consent – and indeed without telling him.[18] She can even dispone her half-share to 50 different disponees, each taking a 1% share of the whole property.[19] This sort of thing could easily make co-ownership unworkable but a solution always exists: the action of division and sale.[20] Jill can also grant a standard security over her share.[21] In practice, of course, a lender will not usually be interested in taking security over less than 100% of the title because if the security has to be enforced, it would be difficult to find a buyer for a half-share. It can, however, happen that a single share is disponed, or granted in security, without the grantee so intending. This can happen if one co-owner forges the signature of another. Suppose that Jack and Jill own a house and

---

[14]   *Barkley v Scott* (1893) 10 Sh Ct Rep 23.

[15]   See **CHAPTER 15** below.

[16]   But if their shares are subject to a special destination, the position may be different. See **CHAPTER 29** below.

[17]   See **PARAS 9.10 AND 9.12** below.

[18]   But if Jack and Jill are spouses or civil partners, Julius, though acquiring Jill's share, would not be entitled to move in. See **PARA 10.9** below.

[19]   *Menzies v Macdonald* (1854) 16 D 827, affd (1856) 2 Macq 463.

[20]   See **PARA 9.13** below.

[21]   *Schaw v Black* (1889) 16 R 326. The case involved a predecessor to the standard security.

Jill grants a standard security to a bank, signing her own name and forging Jack's. The deed is valid for her share but void for his.[22]

9.11   A servitude could not exist over just a share of the property, and so has to be granted by all the owners. If Jill, acting on her own, purported to grant to Jessica a servitude it would simply be void.[23] The same is true of real burdens[24] and leases.[25] An issue that sometimes arises is whether co-owners, acting unanimously, can validly grant a lease to one of their own number. While the co-owners are free to agree, as a matter of contract, that one of them will have sole possession and will pay the others in return, that is not a lease.[26]

Ending it all

9.12   'The successful operation of a *pro indiviso* ownership of property will depend upon mutual compatibility, goodwill and understanding.'[27] So long as that sort of co-operation exists, all will be well. If one party wishes to exit, an arrangement can be come to whereby the share is bought at a fair value by the others, or the whole property is put on the market. When couples who co-own a house or flat split up, one or other of these is usually what happens because, despite the split, they can still co-operate about the property. But not always. The law is that any common owner can demand to be let out whether the others like it or not: *in communionem … nemo compellitur invitus detineri*.[28] This is particularly important because, whether the common owners are in a personal relationship or not, *communio est mater rixarum*.[29] If an action is raised the court has (subject to one exception[30]) no discretion to refuse it.[31]

9.13   The action is called an action of division or sale (also called an action of division and sale). The court will either:
  (a)   physically divide the property between the parties, so that each of the common owners will become a 100% owner of a part, the division being done by the extent of the shares, so that, for example, a 25% owner would get less than a 50% owner; or
  (b)   order that the property be sold as a unit, with the proceeds then being divided among the various (former) co-owners.

---

[22]   *McLeod v Cedar Holdings Ltd* 1989 SLT 620. But, the current law of land registration will confer a sort of validity on the transaction. See **PARAS 6.30–6.34** above.

[23]   See, e.g., *Grant v Heriot's Trust* (1906) 8 F 647 and *Fearnan Partnership v Grindlay* 1990 SLT 704. 'One out of a group of owners of a property cannot grant a servitude' (Ulpian D 8, 1, 2).

[24]   TC(S)A 2002, s 6(3).

[25]   *Bell's Exrs v Inland Revenue* 1987 SLT 625.

[26]   *Clydesdale Bank plc v Davidson* 1998 SC (HL) 51.

[27]   *Bailey's Exrs v Upper Crathes Fishing Ltd* 1987 SLT 405 at 406 per Lord Weir.

[28]   No one can be forced to remain in co-ownership: C 3, 37, 5.

[29]   Common property is the mother of quarrels.

[30]   See **PARA 9.14** below.

[31]   *Upper Crathes Fishings Ltd v Bailey's Exrs* 1991 SLT 747.

The decision between (a) and (b) is for the court. The presumption is in favour of (a), and (b) will be done only if division is not reasonably practical.[32] In reality such actions usually end in sale, not in division, because the property is in most cases a house or flat.

9.14 There are some qualifications to the right. It is excluded where the property is 'a thing of common and indispensable use as a staircase or vestibule'.[33] The words are Bell's. There is little other authority. His meaning is no doubt not merely that the thing is so used, but that it is so used as a pertinent of other properties, the owners of those other properties being the co-owners. Where the co-owners are spouses or civil partners, there are special rules.[34] Finally, if a co-owner has contracted out of the right to raise an action, that is probably effective[35] but this would not bind a successor.[36]

9.15 Can the pursuer ask the court to order, not the sale of the property on the open market, but that the defender should sell his or her share to the pursuer at market value? (Say the market value is £250,000: Jill asks the court to order Jack to transfer his share to her for £125,000.) Authority is conflicting but on the whole it supports such an argument.[37] The obvious difficulty with the 'right to buy-out' is: what should happen if both co-owners make the same demand. The answer appears to be that there is then an auction in which only the co-owners can bid.[38]

Timeshares

9.16 In a 'timeshare' the right to use something is divided between different people by time. For instance, one might buy the third week in April. Holiday properties are sometimes timeshared. So are salmon fishing rights. Timesharing is sometimes done by having the various parties as owners in common, coupled with a contract between them about time of use, maintenance and so on. But such contracts will in principle not bind successors.[39] Moreover, any successor can end the scheme by insisting on division or sale. Accordingly, it is more usual for timeshares to be done either by vesting the property in a trustee, with the timesharers having beneficial interests in the trust, or by vesting the property in a company in which the timesharers have shares.

---

[32]   *Thom v Macbeth* (1875) 3 R 161.
[33]   Bell *Principles* s 1082.
[34]   See **CHAPTER 10** below.
[35]   *Burrows v Burrows* 1996 SLT 1313; *Upper Crathes Fishings Ltd v Bailey's Exrs* 1991 SLT 747.
[36]   *Grant v Heriot's Trust* (1906) 8 F 647.
[37]   Bankton I, 8, 40; Bell *Commentaries* I, 62; *Milligan v Barnhill* (1782) Mor 2486; *Scrimgeour v Scrimgeour* 1988 SLT 590; *Berry v Berry (No 2)* 1989 SLT 292; *Gray v Kerner* 1996 SCLR 331; *Ploetner v Ploetner* 1997 SCLR 998; *Wilson v Hervey* 2004 SCLR 313.
[38]   As was observed in *Scrimgeour* 1988 SLT 590 at 593 by Lord McCluskey, referring to the Roman case of AD 214 (C 3, 37, 1) that developed this solution.
[39]   Nor can this problem be circumvented by use of real burdens: TC(S)A 2003, s 6(3).

JOINT OWNERSHIP

9.17   The only apparent cases of joint ownership are trusts and, less importantly, unincorporated associations. Joint ownership arises in a trust if there is more than one trustee. The trustees are then joint owners of the trust assets. They do not have shares.[40] The property can be dealt with only as a unit. For example, if Jack and Jill own land as trustees, and Jack purports to transfer his 'share' to Julius, this is a nullity. There is no share to be transferred. If a trustee dies, there is no 'share' to form part of the estate. The remaining trustees are the sole owners. If a trustee resigns, no conveyance to the ongoing trustees is needed of the resigning party's 'share'.[41] Likewise, there is no possibility of an action of division or sale. The trustees make decision by majority. Indeed, the law is generally the law of trusts.[42] The question of regulating possession and use as between the joint owners does not normally arise, because trustees have no right of possession or use. They hold the property for the benefit of others.

9.18   In the case of an unincorporated association, such as, say, a chess club, any assets (the chess sets, the silver championship cup etc.) are the joint property of the members. A member who leaves (or dies) automatically ceases to be a joint owner of the club's assets. Conversely, a person joining automatically becomes a joint owner. In trusts, any kind of property can be joint property. But for unincorporated associations, joint property is possible only for moveables.

FURTHER READING

Gordon *Scottish Land Law* ch 15.

Kleyn, D and Wortley, S 'Co-ownership' in Zimmermann, Visser and Reid *Mixed Legal Systems* 703–734.

MacCormack, G 'The *Actio Communi Dividundo* in Roman and Scots Law' in A D E Lewis and D J Ibbetson (eds) *The Roman Law Tradition* (1993).

Reid *Property* paras 17–36.

---

[40]   It is sometimes said that they have equal but inseparable shares. It does not matter much which formulation is adopted.

[41]   This has been confirmed by statute: T(S)A 1921, s 20.

[42]   See CHAPTERS **22–24** below.

Chapter 10

Sexual property law

INTRODUCTION

10.1 Once upon a time this was called 'matrimonial property law'.[1] Now, of course, civil partnerships are also recognised. And cohabitation, without marriage or civil partnership, is common.[2] An umbrella term is needed for the legal area dealing with the patrimonial consequences of such relationships. We offer, tastelessly, 'sexual property law'.[3]

---

[1] See, e.g., E M Clive *The Law of Husband and Wife in Scotland* (4th edn, 1997) para 14.001.

[2] The number of marriages entered into in Scotland in 2007 was 29,866, whereas in the 1970s the average number was 40,000. Source: General Register Office for Scotland. See http://www.gro-scotland.gov.uk/index.html.

[3] See also P Nicholson 'One house, many rooms' 2005 *JLSS* May 12.

10.2 Families tend to operate as economic units. If Jack and Jill are married and Jill has money problems, the family has money problems. If Jill inherits £100,000 from Uncle Albert, then the family benefits. Whether Jill owns the house or Jack does or it is co-owned, it is the family's home. Indeed, a family is usually a communist unit in which assets and obligations are pooled and in which each takes and gives according to what is fair.[4] There is some variation among families. Those embarked on second marriages are often less communistic than young lovestruck newlyweds. The overall picture, however, is usually that the patrimonies[5] of the couple, and also of any non-adult offspring, are treated more or less as a unity, as if they are a single patrimony. And so long as the family remains reasonably happy, all works reasonably well. Most legal systems in history have given some degree of recognition to the fact that the members of a family do not behave as strangers but form a patrimonial unit. Many jurisdictions have a 'community' system in which all assets, and often all liabilities too, of husband and wife are held in common, or indeed that there is only one patrimony and not two.[6] Some systems, such as the older Roman law, included the children – even adult children – in this family entity. Other systems have gone less far. Our own law has varied over the centuries. The current position is a complete separation of patrimonies, so that the spouses are treated as if they were strangers: 'Marriage shall not of itself affect the respective rights of the parties … in relation to their property.'[7] There are nevertheless numerous derogations from that principle, so that the end result actually goes some way towards a community system. When civil partnership was introduced, the legislation simply copied the existing law of marriage.[8] Cohabitation is different: here, the starting point is of course that the parties are patrimonially separate. While there are some derogations from that principle, they are much less extensive than for marriage.[9]

MARRIAGE

The basic principle: separation of patrimonies

10.3 The main patrimonial consequences of marriage come into being when the marriage ceases to be. Marriage ends by death or divorce. On death, the surviving spouse has a special position which is discussed later.[10] On divorce, the core principle is that 'the net value of the matrimonial property should be shared fairly between the

---

4   Of course, individual items may be allocated, such as clothes. A husband will not normally wear his wife's dress, although such things are not entirely unknown.
5   The words 'matrimony' and 'patrimony' carry much baggage. That baggage will not be unpacked here. But, for more on 'patrimony', see PARA **22.53** below.
6   E.g. South Africa.
7   FL(S)A 1985, s 24. 'Property' here means all patrimonial rights and not just real rights.
8   See PARA **10.12** below.
9   See PARA **10.13** below.
10   See PARAS **26.1–26.22** AND **28.7–28.19** below.

parties to the marriage'.[11] There are rules for determining 'net value' but, roughly, it means assets acquired by either, or both in common, during the marriage, less certain debts. If an asset is owned by Jill then the fact that it is matrimonial property does not give Jack any real right in it – or even any personal right. It simply goes towards calculating a figure for the divorce. The court can also make a 'property transfer order'[12] and has extensive powers to make 'incidental orders' affecting property.[13]

Derogations

10.4 During the marriage, there are some derogations from the general principle of patrimonial separation. Two will be discussed here.[14] One is about moveables and is in ss 25 and 26 of the Family Law (Scotland) Act 1985 (FL(S)A 1985). The other is about the matrimonial home and is the subject of the Matrimonial Homes (Family Protection) (Scotland) Act 1981 (MH(FP)(S)A 1981).

FAMILY LAW (SCOTLAND) ACT 1985, SS 25 AND 26

10.5 Section 25 of FL(S)A 1985 provides that household goods are presumed to be co-owned. Household goods are goods in the matrimonial home 'for the joint domestic purposes of the parties' but exclude certain things, notably cars.[15] A puzzle is that while s 25(1) is expressed merely as a presumption, not as a rule imposing co-ownership, s 25(2) says that the presumption cannot be rebutted even by proof that 'the goods ... were purchased ... by either party alone or by both in unequal shares'. This seems to make the presumption irrebuttable, i.e. not a presumption. Furthermore, the supposed presumption applies only where the 'household goods [are] obtained ... other than by gift or succession from a third party'. This is not easy to follow. A presumption applies only where actual evidence is lacking. If it is *known* that the grandfather clock was a legacy to Jill from her Uncle Walter then the presumption could not apply *anyway*. This is further support for the argument that s 25 is not a presumption but a rule of law, imposing community property for (most) household goods. It is difficult to arrive at a confident conclusion as to the section's meaning. Section 26 says that 'money derived from any allowance made by either party for their joint household expenses or for similar purposes' and 'any property acquired out of such money' is co-owned. This is a rule of law, not an evidential presumption. It too has problems. Suppose that Jill bets the money on the Lottery

---

[11] FL(S)A 1985, s 9(1)(a).
[12] FL(S)A 1985, s 8(2). For conditions, see s 15.
[13] FL(S)A 1985, s 14.
[14] In fact, a person's status as spouse (or former spouse), civil partner (or former civil partner) or cohabitant (or former cohabitant) can be relevant for many purposes including tax law, social security law and housing law and some of these special rules have patrimonial consequences. These rules are not discussed here.
[15] FL(S)A 1985, s 25(3).

and wins.[16] She uses her new wealth to buy a house, in her own name. Section 26 says that the house is co-owned. But it is not co-owned. As with s 25, it is difficult to ascertain the section's actual meaning.

MATRIMONIAL HOMES (FAMILY PROTECTION) (SCOTLAND) ACT 1981

Introduction

10.6 The main aim of this Act was, in broad terms, to ensure that each spouse would have equal rights to occupy the matrimonial home, regardless of who owns it. It applies only while the marriage exists. When it ends – by death or divorce – the provisions of MH(FP)(S)A 1981 cease to apply. In that case the parties' rights are catered for by succession law or divorce law, as the case may be.[17]

10.7 If two people own a house in common then, by general property law, each has the right to occupy.[18] Hence, MH(FP)(S)A 1981 does not need to cater for co-owning spouses, though, as will be seen,[19] it does have certain provisions which do apply to that case. Nevertheless, its main thrust concerns the case where the home is owned only by one spouse. In that case the Act confers 'occupancy rights' on the non-owning spouse.

Occupancy rights

The basic idea

10.8 MH(FP)(S)A 1981 calls the owning spouse the 'entitled spouse' and the other the 'non-entitled spouse'.[20] The non-entitled spouse has 'occupancy rights'. These are '(a) if in occupation, a right to continue to occupy the matrimonial home; (b) if not in occupation, a right to enter into and occupy the matrimonial home'.[21] So, if Jack owns a flat and then he marries Jill, who moves in with him, she acquires occupancy rights, and that means that he cannot require her to leave, even though he is the sole owner.

---

[16] As in *Pyatt v Pyatt* 1966 SLT (Notes) 73.
[17] On succession law, see CHAPTERS **25–29** below.
[18] See PARA **9.7** above.
[19] See PARA **10.11** below.
[20] MH(FP)(S)A 1981, s 1(1).
[21] MH(FP)(S)A 1981, s 1(1).

Third-party effects

10.9 Occupancy rights are not real rights. Nevertheless they sometimes have effect against third parties, and so might be called 'quasi-real'.[22] Section 6 says that no 'dealing' by the entitled spouse can affect the occupancy rights of the other spouse. Suppose that Jack dispones the property to his brother, George. Jill's occupancy rights would remain unaltered, even though the owner is not her husband. That does not mean that George does not acquire ownership: he does. But his ownership is subject to Jill's right to occupy. Nor could he even seek to occupy with her.[23] (This state of affairs cannot last forever because it ends when the occupancy rights end, which is when the marriage ends, which is likely to be soon.) Similar protection applies to other 'dealings' such as the grant of a standard security.[24] Since a third party might be unaware of the occupancy rights, there is a rather complex set of rules – which have caused conveyancers many headaches – saying, more or less, that a third party acting in good faith takes free of occupancy rights.[25] The third-party effect applies only to 'dealings'. This term is not precisely defined[26] and there are some difficulties with it, but the core idea is that the protection is against third parties who have voluntarily acquired real rights from Jack. So, if he simply becomes insolvent, his trustee in sequestration is not subject to Jill's occupancy rights.[27]

Consents, renunciations and dispensations

10.10 The non-entitled spouse is free to consent to a dealing (for example, the grant of a standard security)[28] and can also, though this seldom happens, renounce occupancy rights completely.[29] A consent to a dealing can also be given by the court: this is called a dispensation.[30] Dispensations are rare.

Where the spouses are co-owners

10.11 MH(FP)(S)A 1981 also has two provisions applying where the spouses are co-owners. One is that a dealing by one spouse cannot enable a third party to occupy.[31]

---

22 These third-party effects have, however, been reduced somewhat since MH(FP)(S)A 1981 was originally passed.
23 MH(FP)(S)A 1981, s 6(1)(b).
24 For standard securities, see PARAS **20.43–20.56** below.
25 MH(FP)(S)A 1981, ss 6(1A) and 8(2A).
26 MH(FP)(S)A 1981, s 6(2).
27 Subject to B(S)A 1985, s 41. More important than s 41 (which seldom applies) is s 40 which may give Jill at least a period of grace before Jack's trustee can force a sale.
28 MH(FP)(S)A 1981, s 6(3).
29 MH(FP)(S)A 1981, s 1(5).
30 MH(FP)(S)A 1981, s 7.
31 MH(FP)(S)A 1981, s 9. This state of affairs cannot last forever because it will end when the marriage ends.

For example, Romeo and Juliet are married and co-own the matrimonial home. Juliet dispones her half-share to her Uncle Faustus. He becomes co-owner but may not occupy. The other is a provision that says that neither of the co-owning spouses can compel a division and sale unless the court agrees.[32] There is no protection if one spouse becomes bankrupt.[33]

CIVIL PARTNERSHIP

10.12   The Civil Partnership Act 2004 (CPA 2004) closely tracks the rules for marriage. In some cases legislation dealing with married couples has been amended to add in references to civil partners. That was done, for example, in the case of the Succession (Scotland) Act 1964 (S(S)A 1964).[34] Elsewhere, the rules are left as free-standing rules within CPA 2004 itself, for instance the rules (beginning at s 101 of CPA 2004) mirroring the MH(FP)(S)A 1981.[35]

COHABITATION

10.13   At common law, cohabitation was not a legally recognised status. That gradually changed, and there is now a considerable body of law, scattered over different enactments. Particularly important is the Family Law (Scotland) Act 2006 (FL(S)A 2006). Sections 26 and 27 apply to cohabitation the same rules that are in ss 25 and 26 of FL(S)A 1985, discussed above.[36] Section 28 enables the court to order payment of financial provision if the relationship breaks up. Section 29 makes provision for claims on the estate if one party dies intestate.[37] Section 18 of MH(FP)(S)A 1981 enables the court to grant occupancy rights for up to six months. This is not very important. It needs court intervention and it is only short-term anyway. To avoid disputes over property, particularly the home, there is sense in entering into a written agreement at the time of purchase.[38]

---

[32]   MH(FP)(S)A 1981, s 19. For division and sale, see PARAS **9.12–9.15** above.
[33]   Except B(S)A 1985 s 40, already mentioned in N **27** above.
[34]   Eg as regards prior rights in intestacy. See PARAS **28.7–28.17** below.
[35]   For same-sex couples the home is called the 'family home'. This term is not used by the legislation for other-sex couples.
[36]   See PARA **10.5** above.
[37]   See PARA **28.20** below.
[38]   See Reid and Gretton *Conveyancing 2004* (2005) 63–71.

FURTHER READING

Edwards, L and Griffiths, A *Family Law* (2nd edn, 2006), especially chs 10–12.

Gretton and Reid, *Conveyancing* ch 10.

Thomson, J *Family Law in Scotland* (5th edn, 2006), especially chs 4 and 5.

Chapter 11

Possession

GENERAL

Definition

11.1 Property is 'possessed' if it is held by a person for his or her own use.[1] This means that the person must have physical control of the thing, together with the

---

[1]   Stair I, 1, 17.

intention to possess it. The nature of the control may vary depending on the circumstances of the case. As will be seen, it is possible to possess indirectly, through another person. In principle, because possession requires this control, it is limited to corporeal property.[2]

Fact or right

11.2 Possession may be said to be a fact rather than a right. On this view, it follows that it depends on certain factual criteria being satisfied. These are physical holding, which is generally easy to determine and the correct state of mind, which is less so. But the fact of possession also gives rise to certain rights, in particular the right not to be dispossessed.[3] Therefore to say that possession is merely a fact is to take too simplistic an approach. There can also be a right to possess held by a non-possessor, such as someone from whom something has been stolen.

Possession and ownership compared

11.3 The Roman jurist Ulpian said that 'ownership and possession have nothing in common'.[4] Yet, the non-lawyer will often speak of his or her 'possessions' when what is meant is actually the things that the person actually owns.[5] The reason is that despite clear theoretical differences, ownership and possession regularly coincide. For example, Alison lives in her house. Therefore she both possesses and owns that property. She also possesses and owns the contents. If, however, Barry, a burglar, were to steal Alison's television, he would gain possession of it but not ownership.

11.4 A major difference between possession and ownership is that the former involves a factual relationship to a piece of property. The latter involves a legal relationship. Whether someone is owner depends on whether that person has validly acquired the item. In contrast, a possessor may have no legal right whatsoever to it, as in the case of Barry. Ownership and possession give rise to different rights and remedies. An owner can, for example, validly transfer ownership of the property or create subordinate real rights over it. In principle, a mere possessor cannot. The remedy to protect ownership of property is vindication, whereas for possession it is spuilzie.[6]

---

[2]   But see PARA **11.8** below.
[3]   See PARA **11.21** below.
[4]   D 41, 2, 12, 1.
[5]   Indeed, Art 1 of Protocol 1 to the ECHR conflates ownership and possession. See PARA **31.11** below.
[6]   See PARA **11.21** below.

The importance of possession

11.5 Possession is important in a number of areas, such as:

(a) The acquisition of possession is necessary in order to acquire an original title by occupancy.[7]

(b) A proprietor in possession in the Land Register is normally protected from rectification.[8]

(c) A person who has possessed land for ten years on the basis of an apparently valid conveyance recorded in the Sasine Register will acquire a good title by positive prescription.[9]

(d) A tenant under a lease of 20 years or less acquires a real right by entering into possession of the property.[10]

(e) Possession is a pre-requisite of certain securities, notably pledge and lien.[11]

(f) There is an evidential presumption that a person in possession of a corporeal moveable is its owner.[12]

(g) A person who is in possession has the remedy of spuilzie if he or she is unlawfully dispossessed.[13]

REQUIREMENTS FOR POSSESSION

General

11.6 Acquisition of possession requires two things. The first is an act of the body (*corpus*). The second is an act of the mind (*animus*). Both are essential. While the distinction is clear in theory, it is less so in practice. The act of mind will often be inferred from the act of the body. For example, if Jean hands her book to Kirsty and Kirsty takes it, Kirsty's intention to take possession may be inferred. The basic rule is that possession can only be held by one person at one time. If, for instance, Bob pickpockets Colin's wallet, then Colin loses possession to Bob. But possession may be shared, as with a couple living together and possessing their flat. And as will be seen, one party (such as an owner) may be in civil possession while another (such as a tenant) has natural possession of the same property.[14]

---

[7]   See **PARA 8.2** above.

[8]   See **PARA 6.44** above.

[9]   See **PARA 2.24** above.

[10] See **PARA 19.11** below.

[11] See **PARAS 20.34 AND 20.58** below.

[12] See **PARA 11.19** below.

[13] See **PARA 11.21** below.

[14] See **PARA 11.9** below.

Act of body

11.7   For possession to be acquired, there must be an act to detain it in the first place. The fish, for example, must be hooked by the angler. The bar of chocolate requires to be lifted by the customer from the shelf. Where a piece of moveable property is too large to take hold of, the prospective possessor should enter it. Examples here are cars and tents. For land, it is not necessary to stand on every part of it. Stair states: '[H]e who possesseth a field, needs not go about it all, or touch every turf of it, by himself or his cattle, but by possessing a part, possesseth the whole, unless there were contrary possessory acts.'[15]

11.8   The requirement of an act to detain means that in principle incorporeal property cannot be possessed because one cannot acquire physical control of something which is intangible. By statute, however, it is possible to possess some incorporeal heritable rights, such as leases, for the purpose of positive prescription and registration of title.[16] This is sometimes known as quasi-possession. What is happening is that the right is being exercised. For example, a person asserting a servitude right of way walks over the land in question. Possession of incorporeal property is possible if one is willing to regard exercise as a substitute for detention.

11.9   Possession can be acquired through the physical acts of another. For example, Ulrika might purchase a flat as an investment and immediately let it to Verity and Wanda, two students, who move in. This suffices to give Ulrika possession. Her possession here is known as 'civil possession'. In contrast, Verity and Wanda are said to be in 'natural possession'. Civil possession is common. As well as the foregoing example of a landlord possessing through her tenants, pledgers possess through pledgees,[17] fiars possess through liferenters[18] and owners possess through custodiers such as warehousers and carriers.

11.10   While a physical act is necessary to *acquire* possession, it is not necessary to *maintain* it. Possession can be retained by act of mind alone. This is known as possession *animo solo*. For example, students sitting in lectures are still in possession of their flat.[19] Possession *animo solo* is lost if the possessor ceases to intend to possess, for instance by deciding to abandon the property. It also ends if a third party acquires possession without the consent of the *animo solo* possessor, for example where squatters move in to the flat.

---

[15]   Stair II, 1, 18.
[16]   In terms of PL(S)A 1973 and LR(S)A 1979. See paras **2.31** and **6.45–6.46** above.
[17]   See para **20.35** below.
[18]   See para **21.9** below.
[19]   In contrast to students who were out late the night before and who remain in direct possession of their beds.

Act of mind

11.11   Possession requires the intention, first, to exercise control of the property and, second, to do this for the benefit of oneself. In relation to the former, difficult questions arise in relation to 'container cases'. This is the situation where one piece of property is inside another, for example clothes in a wardrobe. The issue is whether possession of the container is sufficient to possess also the item within. Unusually for Scottish property law, the most influential modern authority is an English case, *Parker v British Airways Board*.[20] Someone found a bracelet in a departure lounge at Heathrow Airport. In English law, the first person to acquire possession of lost or stolen property can retain it unless the true owner vindicates the right. Here, British Airways claimed that it in fact was the first possessor because it possessed the building even although it had no knowledge of the bracelet. It was held possible to possess something without knowing, provided that there is a manifest intention to exercise control of the property it is within. Items within a house are a good example of this. As regards an airport lounge, however, where the general public has through access, there was held to be an insufficient level of control.

11.12   The second part of the act of mind – intention to hold for one's own benefit – means that those who hold solely for another party do not have possession. An example would be a warehouse storing goods. Here, the holder has *custody*. The physical requirement for possession is satisfied, but not the mental element. It is possible to have civil possession of property held by a custodier. The owner of the goods in the warehouse is one case. Equally, it is possible to have civil possession through a natural possessor, such as a landlord's possession of a shop through the tenant. The Latin tag for the relevant mental element is the *animus sibi habendi* (possession for one's own use) rather than the *animus dominii* (possession as owner). The latter, which is found in Roman law, restricts possession to those asserting ownership, as opposed to say a right under a lease.

TRANSFER OF POSSESSION

General

11.13   Where possession of a piece of property is transferred from one person to another, this is known as 'delivery'.

Transfer of natural possession: actual delivery

11.14   If a person is in natural possession of property, the possession can be transferred to another by physically handing over the property. This is 'actual delivery'. For example, Rebecca passes a book to Sara.

[20]   [1982] 1 QB 1004. See Reid *Property* para 124 and *Harris v Abbey National plc* 1997 SCLR 359.

Transfer of civil possession: constructive delivery

11.15 Where civil possession is held by the transferor, this may be transferred by 'constructive delivery'. Angela is storing her whisky in Bella's warehouse. Angela wants to make a gift of the whisky to Charles. He is willing to accept the gift. To transfer it, she instructs Bella to hold the whisky on his behalf. Charles now has civil possession. It is essential that Bella, the holder of the goods, is told.[21] If Angela merely handed over the warehouse receipt to Charles, that would not be enough.[22] Another instance of constructive delivery is where Alan's property is in Beth's natural possession, say under a contract of loan. If Alan now sells the thing to her, she acquires full possession.[23] A third example is *constitutum possessorium*: delivery by act of mind alone. For instance, Helen might transfer ownership of land to Isabel, but remain in possession as Isabel's tenant. (This is called sale and lease-back.) Helen now possesses on behalf of Isabel as well as in her own right. If *constitutum possessorium* is applied too freely, the publicity principle[24] is undermined, because a third party is unable to see any change of possession. Thus, the courts have limited its application.[25]

11.16 A final case to be mentioned is 'symbolical delivery'. Strictly speaking it is a special type of constructive delivery. It is where a symbol of the property, rather than the property itself is handed over. In practice this type of delivery is confined to the 'bill of lading'. This is the receipt handed over by the shipping company to a person who is having goods shipped. The bill of lading may be regarded in law as symbolising possession of the goods. Hence delivery of the bill amounts to delivery of the goods. Bills of lading are similar to bills of exchange in that they may be classed as either 'bearer' or 'order'. A 'bearer bill' is transferred by mere delivery. An 'order bill' requires to be both delivered and endorsed on the back in favour of the new holder. Hence if an order bill is merely delivered, the new holder may have possession of the bill, but not the goods which it represents.

Transfer of possession by means of a key

11.17 Where goods are stored under lock and key, for example in a warehouse, possession can be transferred by handing over the key.[26] This is not easily categorised as either actual or constructive delivery.

---

[21] According to SOGA 1979, s 29(4), where goods are being sold the custodier has to tell the buyer that the goods are now held for him or her.
[22] *Inglis v Robertson & Baxter* (1898) 25 R (HL) 70.
[23] Following Roman law, this is known as delivery *brevi manu*.
[24] See **PARAS 4.17–4.18** above.
[25] Reid *Property* para 623 (W M Gordon); Carey Miller with Irvine *Corporeal Moveables* para 8.24.
[26] Following Roman law, this is known as delivery *longa manu*.

THE RIGHT TO POSSESSION

Possession as of right or without right

11.18 Possessors can be divided into two categories. There are those, such as owners and tenants, who have the right to possess. They are rightful possessors. Then there are those such as thieves and squatters who do not. They are unlawful possessors. A further division can be made as regards rightful possessors. First, there are those whose possession is founded on a real right. The Latin term here is the *ius possidendi*. The right here is not an autonomous right. It depends on holding another right with an entitlement to possession, such as ownership. But it is a right enforceable against the world. Second, there are those who hold a personal right of possession. Thus if Robert lends a pen to Sally, she is a rightful possessor but she has no real right. A lease of moveable property is another example. By contrast, a lease of heritable property is usually a real right, but in some types of case it will, like a lease of moveables, be only a personal right. Therefore, with the exception of spuilzie,[27] such a person must rely on the owner or other party who granted the right to take action against any party who interferes with the possession.

Presumptions

11.19 A possessor of corporeal property is presumed both
  (i) to be in lawful possession; and
  (ii) to be the owner.[28]
The latter is important because there is no register of ownership of corporeal moveables. Nor, unlike the usual position as regards incorporeal property, where a written assignation is used, corporeal moveable property is often transferred by oral agreement. Accordingly, the presumption can be difficult to rebut. It is not necessary for the possessor to prove good faith.[29]

Possession in good faith

11.20 Someone who possesses property with no right to do so, but while reasonably believing that this right is held, is known as a *bona fide* possessor, or possessor in good faith. Such a person is entitled to harvest the fruits of the property and, on losing possession, is entitled to compensation for improvements made to it.[30] There

---

27 See **PARAS 11.21–11.22** below.
28 Stair IV, 45, 17.
29 *Chief Constable of Strathclyde Police v Sharp* 2002 SLT (Sh Ct), discussed in D L Carey Miller 'Title to moveables: Mr Sharp's Porsche' (2003) 7 *Edin LR* 221.
30 Gordon *Scottish Land Law* paras 14.47–14.59.
31 See J Wolffe 'Enrichment by improvements in Scots law' in D Johnston and R Zimmermann (eds) *Unjustified Enrichment: Key Issues in Comparative Perspective* (2002) 384–432.

is a significant body of elderly case law on the subject in relation to land.[31] Nowadays, however, land registration is map-based. Given the doctrine of constructive knowledge of what is in the Register,[32] it is increasingly difficult to establish *bona fide* possession.

POSSESSORY REMEDIES

Spuilzie

11.21   The mere fact of possession gives rise to the right not to be unlawfully dispossessed. In that event, the remedy of spuilzie (pronounced 'spooley') is available. This is a court action to compel the dispossessor to return the property. The word 'spuilzie' is used to mean the wrongful act of dispossession as well as the remedy resulting from this. In the case of land, spuilzie is also known as ejection.[33] Unlawful dispossession can be referred to as 'vitious' dispossession and happens when the possessor does not consent nor is there judicial warrant for it. The pursuer in an action of spuilzie need only prove two things:

(1) that he or she was in possession and

(2) that he or she was vitiously dispossessed.

Possession may be *animo solo* and in this case the spuilzie is known as 'intrusion'.[34] It is also possible for a civil possessor to use the remedy, but here consent to the dispossession by the natural possessor debars the claim.[35] This point was overlooked in a couple of sheriff court cases where attempts to use spuilzie were made in the context of goods on hire purchase being delivered to third parties.[36] As spuilzie depends merely on possession, it is possible for a thief to use the remedy. Indeed, a thief could in theory use it against the actual owner of the property if the requirements set out above are satisfied. This, however, would have little point, because the owner, assuming that ownership could be proven, can retort by vindicating the property i.e. demanding it back because of that ownership.

11.22   Spuilzie is a remedy which is rarely used today. Yet, in fifteenth-century Scotland it was perhaps the commonest type of legal action.[37] There are two main reasons for the change.[38] One is a less lawless society. Second, registration of land ownership commenced in 1617, with the establishment of the Sasine Register.

---

32   Cf *Trade Development Bank v Warriner and Mason (Scotland) Ltd* 1980 SC 74. But there may be room for debate about the exact scope of this doctrine.

33   See, e.g., Stair I, 9, 25–27.

34   Stair I, 9, 25.

35   Stair I, 9, 20 and IV, 28, 7.

36   *FC Finance Ltd v Brown & Son* 1969 SLT (Sh Ct) 41 and *Mercantile Credit Co Ltd v Townsley* 1971 SLT (Sh Ct) 37. See A F Rodger 'Spuilzie in the Modern World' 1970 *SLT (News)* 33.

37   J W Cairns 'Historical Introduction' in Reid and Zimmermann *History* vol 1, 14 at 73.

38   K Reid, 'Property Law: Sources and Doctrine' in Reid and Zimmermann *History* vol 1, 185 at 213–214. But see also C Anderson 'Spuilzie today' 2008 *SLT (News)* 257.

Therefore those dispossessed of land are now more likely to assert their ownership rather than rely on their prior possession.

Compensation

11.23 A person knowingly in wrongful possession is liable to compensate the rightful possessor for any income derived from the property. There are two levels of compensation. First, 'ordinary profits' may be due. This means the actual income, for example, crops growing on the land in the case of natural possession and rent in the case of civil possession. The second possible claim is for 'violent profits'. In effect these are penal damages and are quantified at the highest level of income which the property could yield. In the case of land, this will probably be double rent.[39] Violent profits are available in the case of vitious dispossession i.e. spuilzie. They are also due where a tenant will not move out at the end of the lease.[40]

Other remedies

11.24 Certain other possessory remedies are available, but they are restricted in principle to parties who can show a real right to possess i.e. the *ius possidendi*.[41] The following are the most important:
  (a) action for delivery, where the real right to possess is being asserted against another in possession of corporeal moveables;
  (b) action for removing or ejection where the real right to possess land is being asserted. In removings the defender will have had a right to possess which has ended, for example under a lease which has expired. In ejections no right will have ever been held;[42]
  (c) action for encroachment, where there is a permanent thing preventing possession of land;[43]
  (d) action for trespass, where there is temporary interference with the ability to possess land.[44]

---

[39]   Reid, *Property* para 169.
[40]   *Jute Industries Ltd v Wilson & Graham Ltd* 1955 SLT (Sh Ct) 46.
[41]   See **PARA 11.18** above.
[42]   Reid *Property* para 153.
[43]   See **PARAS 17.10–17.16** below.
[44]   See **PARAS 18.30–18.36** below.

FURTHER READING

Carey Miller with Irvine *Corporeal Moveables* paras 1.18–1.22 and 8.12–8.27.

Gordon *Scottish Land Law* ch 14.

Reid *Property* paras 114–173 and 619–623.

Reid, K, 'Property Law: Sources and Doctrine' in Reid and Zimmermann *History* vol 1, 185 at 210–216.

Chapter 12

Servitudes

ESSENTIALS

Definition

12.1 A 'servitude' is a real right that allows a landowner to enter or make limited use of neighbouring land. The classic example is a right of access. Servitudes are regulated primarily by the common law, but also by a number of important provisions in the Title Conditions (Scotland) Act 2003 (TC(S)A 2003), which came into force on 28 November 2004. Roman law has been particularly influential in the development of the law of servitudes in Scotland. Similarly, it has had a tangible effect on the English equivalent – the 'easement'. This is therefore an area of Scottish property law where it is worth having regard to English authority. The point, however, should not be pressed too far.[1]

---

[1] In the important recent House of Lords decision in *Moncrieff v Jamieson* 2008 SC (HL) 1, the English Law Lords who gave judgments seemed more inclined to use English than Scottish authority, although the case was Scottish. See Reid and Gretton *Conveyancing 2007* (2008) 108.

Two properties

12.2 Servitudes require a 'benefited property' and a 'burdened property'. More traditionally, these are referred to as the 'dominant tenement' and the 'servient tenement'.[2] The owner of the benefited property is entitled to enforce the servitude and the owner of the burdened property is obliged to accept this. For example, Neil sells a plot of land to Orla so that she can build a house on it. He grants her a servitude right of access over the retained land so that she can reach the nearest public road. Orla's plot is the benefited property and the land retained by Neil is the burdened property. The right to enforce the servitude attaches to Orla's land as a pertinent[3] and is automatically transferred if she sells her house. The servitude can be said to 'run with the land'. Similarly, if Neil sells the retained land, the new owner continues to be bound, because the servitude is a real right. For this reason too, not only Neil but any tenant of his or occupier of the burdened property must respect the servitude.[4]

12.3 Normally, the benefited and burdened properties will be contiguous – in other words, adjacent. This is not an absolute requirement. They only require to be in the same neighbourhood 'provided the distance be not so great as to obstruct all benefit from the servitude'.[5] The properties must be reasonably close or the 'praedial requirement'[6] will not be satisfied. In most cases the benefited and burdened properties will be pieces of land. It is also, however, possible for them to be an incorporeal separate tenement.[7] For example, the holder of a right of salmon fishing may need a servitude of access to get to the river.[8] In contrast, a real right of lease cannot act as a benefited or burdened property.[9] It is rights of ownership which benefit from or are burdened by servitudes. That said, as we shall see below, a tenant in the benefited property may exercise a servitude held by that property.[10]

12.4 In principle, the two properties must be in separate ownership. The Latin maxim for this is *res sua nemini servit* (no one can have a servitude over his property). It is, however, possible for a servitude to be registered by an owner of land against the one piece of property, which does not take effect until the land is subdivided.[11] For example, Beverley, a builder, may intend to develop a site for two houses. She can register a deed of conditions giving each house mutual servitude rights, such as of water supply and drainage, exercisable against the other. The servitudes, however, will not be formally created until the houses are sold separately and the title to the site is divided.

---

[2] See, e.g., Bell *Principles* s 979.
[3] For pertinents, see PARAS **14.9–14.12** below.
[4] A contrast can be made here with real burdens. Only negative real burdens are 'real' in this sense. See PARA **13.42** below.
[5] Erskine II, 9, 33.
[6] See PARAS **12.6–12.7** below.
[7] See PARA **14.17** below.
[8] E.g. *Middletweed v Murray* 1989 SLT 11.
[9] Subject to the deeply obscure Registration of Leases (Scotland) Act 1857, s 3(2).
[10] See PARA **12.31** below.
[11] TC(S)A 2003, s 75(2).

A right to enter or make limited use of the burdened property

12.5 The common law recognised two types of servitude. 'Positive' servitudes, such as access, involve a right to enter or make limited use of the burdened property. These continue to exist today. In addition, certain 'negative' servitudes were admitted. These restricted building on the burdened property. Sometimes there was a blanket ban.[12] Sometimes it was only building above a certain height which was prohibited.[13] And sometimes it was only building which interfered with light or view.[14] All of these restrictions could be performed by real burdens,[15] meaning that there was an untidy overlap in the law. Negative servitudes were also open to criticism because, unlike real burdens, registration was not a requirement for creation.[16] This meant that the servitude could be invisible to a purchaser of the land. TC(S)A 2003 addressed these issues by making it incompetent to create new negative servitudes with effect from 28 November 2004.[17] Existing negative servitudes were converted by force of statute into real burdens on that date.[18] Where, however, the right does not appear on the title to the burdened property it is necessary to register a preservation notice before 28 November 2014 or it will be extinguished on that date.[19]

Praedial benefit

12.6 A servitude must be 'praedial'. This means that it must burden the burdened property for the benefit of the benefited property and not just for the personal benefit of the latter's owner. For example, a purported servitude allowing the benefited proprietor to go on to the burdened property to sing or recite poetry is insufficiently praedial. In *Patrick v Napier*[20] a right allowing a landowner to fish for trout on a nearby river failed the test, since fishing was not to the praedial benefit of his land. Similarly, it has been held that a right of skating or curling on a loch during appropriate cold weather cannot be a servitude.[21]

12.7 Other jurisdictions, such as Louisiana and South Africa, which have been influenced by Roman law, recognise both 'praedial servitudes' and 'personal servitudes'. In a 'personal servitude' there is no benefited property. Rather, a particular person has a right of use or enjoyment of the burdened property. The only personal

---

[12] This was known as a servitude *non aedificandi*.
[13] This was known as a servitude *altius non tollendi*.
[14] This was known as a servitude *luminibus non officiendi*.
[15] See CHAPTER 13 below.
[16] *Cowan v Stewart* (1872) 10 M 735.
[17] TC(S)A 2003, s 79.
[18] TC(S)A 2003, s 80(1). They are to be known as 'converted servitudes'.
[19] TC(S)A 2003, ss 80(2)–(8) and 115.
[20] (1867) 5 M 683.
[21] *Harper v Lindsay* (1853) 15 D 768.

servitude which is recognised in Scotland is liferent.[22] In practice, the term 'personal servitude' is seldom used here.[23]

Repugnancy with ownership

12.8   Where a servitude creates a right of use it must be a *limited* one. Use which is too invasive of the burdened proprietor's right of ownership is not permitted.[24] If a comprehensive right of use is desired then a right of lease should be acquired.[25] The rule cannot be said to be applied absolutely. For example, where a servitude involves laying pipes,[26] this means making exclusive use of the stratum of ground in question.[27] The issue has exercised the courts recently in relation to car parking. In *Nationwide Building Society v Walter D Allan*[28] a purported servitude which conferred the right to park two cars on a piece of ground large enough for six was held by Lady Smith to be repugnant with ownership. The case was not discussed by the House of Lords in the landmark decision in *Moncrieff v Jamieson*,[29] but there is reason to believe that the judges there would have reached the opposite result.[30]

Known to the law

12.9   As will be seen below,[31] there are a number of ways in which servitudes can be created. Not all require an express provision to appear on the title of the burdened property. Thus, a servitude may not be obvious to a prospective purchaser. The policy of the courts has therefore been to restrict servitudes to those 'known to the law'. The idea is that a purchaser can be sure that only a limited number of types of unregistered right could affect the property. In practice there is a fixed list essentially based on Roman law, notwithstanding judicial statements that the list can be expanded.[32] Thus in *Mendelssohn v The Wee Pub Co Ltd*,[33] an attempt to establish a servitude of sign-hanging failed, because it was not a recognised servitude in Roman law. In *Neill v Scobbie*[34] the court was unwilling to extend the list to admit a servitude

---

[22]   See CHAPTER **21** below.
[23]   Rights akin to personal servitudes may be created under certain statutes. See PARA **12.51** below.
[24]   This is a common law rule, now enshrined for new express servitudes in TC(S)A 2003, s 76(2).
[25]   See CHAPTER **19** below.
[26]   See PARA **12.12** below.
[27]   See *Moncrieff v Jamieson* 2008 SC (HL) 1 at para 76 per Lord Rodger of Earlsferry.
[28]   2004 GWD 25-539.
[29]   2008 SC (HL) 1.
[30]   See Reid and Gretton *Conveyancing 2007* (2008) 109–110.
[31]   See PARAS **12.21–12.29** below.
[32]   See, e.g., *Dyce v Hay* (1852) 1 Macq 305 at 312–313 per Lord St Leonards LC and *Patrick v Napier* (1867) 5 M 683 at 709 per Lord Ardmillan.
[33]   1991 GWD 26-1518.
[34]   1993 GWD 13-887.

for overhead electricity cables.[35] Most recently, in *Romano v Standard Commercial Property Securities Ltd*[36] a servitude of 'shop front' was rejected. The list of known servitudes appears be the following.

Access

12.10 This is the most important servitude. The owner of land may need to take access over a neighbouring property. Three gradations were recognised in Roman law and still are today:

(1) *iter* (pedestrian);
(2) *actus* (right to lead cattle); and
(3) *via* (vehicular).

In general, the greater right includes the lesser. Therefore where a vehicular right of access along a road is held, the benefited proprietor may go by foot.[37] A fourth category of 'railway' has been recognised since the nineteenth century, the difference being that the access is taken along rails.[38] But it is rare in practice. Network Rail owns the ground on which its rails are laid.

Parking vehicles

12.11 It was only in 2007 that the right to park vehicles was accepted, in *Moncrieff v Jamieson*.[39] Before that, the law was unclear. Parking can be created as a stand-alone right, or one which is ancillary to a servitude of access.[40]

Service media

12.12 Buildings require to be serviced. Three types of service servitude are recognised.

(1) 'Aqueduct', also called 'watergang'[41] This is the right to lead water through the burdened property. Whether at common law this can be extended to other

---

[35] Of course, the Romans did not have electricity cables. The correctness of the decision may be doubted. See further PARA **12.18** below.

[36] 2008 SLT 859.

[37] Cusine and Paisley *Servitudes and Rights of Way* para 12.194. See, however, *Adams and Son v Cloy* (1998), reported in Paisley and Cusine *Unreported Cases* 365 (express right of vehicular access does not include the right to drive loose cattle).

[38] *North British Rly Co v Park Yard Co Ltd* (1898) 25 R (HL) 47 at 52 per Lord Watson.

[39] 2008 SC (HL) 1. See http://www.moncrieff-v-jamieson.com/.

[40] See Reid and Gretton *Conveyancing 2007* (2008) 106–117.

[41] In Latin, *aquaeductus*.

fluids, to gases and to electricity is unclear.[42] TC(S)A 2003 now does so extend it, and with retrospective effect.[43]

(2) 'Aquaehaustus', the right to take water from a river, loch or other source on the burdened property. This is more important in rural areas than urban ones where there is the mains water supply.

(3) 'Sinks', also called 'drainage' or 'outfall'. It permits the benefited proprietor to drain water to the burdened property. It can be for sewage, as where there is a septic tank on the burdened property.[44]

Support

12.13   Two forms are recognised.

(1) *Oneris ferendi*: the right to be supported by an adjacent building.[45]

(2) *Tigni immittendi*: the right to insert a beam into a neighbouring building.

Of the two, the first is the more important in practice.

Eavesdrop

12.14   'Eavesdrop', also called 'stillicide', is the right to allow water to fall off the eaves of a building on the benefited property onto the burdened property.[46] Nowadays, building regulations prevent properties from being built so close.[47]

Pasturage

12.15   This is the right to graze animals on the burdened property. Originally, the servitude was for cattle.[48] It is now accepted that sheep may also safely graze under this right.[49]

---

[42]   *Neill v Scobbie* 1993 GWD 13-887; *Ferguson v Tennant* 1978 SC (HL) 19 at 65 per Lord Fraser; *Labinski Ltd v BP Oil Development Ltd* 2002 GWD 1-46 (oil).

[43]   TC(S)A 2003, s 77. On pipeline servitudes generally, see R Paisley 'Aspects of Land Law Relative to the Transportation of Oil and Gas in Scotland' in G Gordon and J Paterson (eds) *Oil and Gas Law – Current Practice and Emerging Trends* (2007) 409.

[44]   *Todd v Scoular* 1988 GWD 24-1041.

[45]   See paras **17.17–17.20** below. Support by a subjacent building is a statutory right under T(S)A 2004, s 8. See para **15.24** below.

[46]   *Stirling v Finlayson* (1752) Mor 14526.

[47]   See generally Cusine and Paisley *Servitudes and Rights of Way* para 3.84.

[48]   See, e.g., *Fearnan Partnership v Grindlay* 1992 SC (HL) 38.

[49]   *Ferguson v Tennant* 1978 SC (HL) 19. With apologies to the well-known cantata by Bach.

Extracting materials

12.16 The right comes in two forms.
   (1) 'Fuel, feal and divot', which allows peat to be taken from the burdened property for fuel, and turf to be taken for fencing and roofing.[50] It is a right of much diminished importance today in an era of central heating and tiled roofs.
   (2) The right to take building materials, such as stone, sand and gravel.[51] Again, this is a relatively dormant area of law.
In both cases, the extracted items can only be used to service the benefited property.[52]

Bleaching and drying clothes

12.17 This right was first recognised by the House of Lords in the 1780 case of *St Clair v Dysart Magistrates*.[53] Of all the recognised servitudes, it is probably the one which is the most difficult to reconcile with the praedial rule[54] because it is people who benefit from clothes, not land. It remains of some practical importance in tenements where there is a drying green at the rear of the building but this belongs to the ground-floor proprietor, rather than being held in common.[55]

Adding to the list

12.18 As mentioned above,[56] the courts have been reluctant to extend the list. They have occasionally done so where the 'new' servitude is very similar to an existing one, for example allowing pasturage for sheep as well as for cattle.[57] This has also sometimes happened where there has been economic, social or technological development, provided that the existing criteria for servitudes are met. An example is the servitude of access for a railway line.[58] As was seen above,[59] however, as late as 1993 a servitude for electricity was denied. The most recent recognition of a servitude was that of parking.[60]

---

[50] *Watson v Sinclair* 1966 SLT (Sh Ct) 77.
[51] *Aikman v Duke of Hamilton and Brandon* (1832) 6 W and Sh 64.
[52] See **PARA 12.35** below.
[53] (1780) 2 Pat 554.
[54] See **PARA 12.6** above.
[55] This is the position unless the titles to the flats say otherwise. See **PARA 15.11** below.
[56] See **PARA 12.9** above.
[57] See **PARA 12.14** above.
[58] See **PARA 12.10** above.
[59] See **PARA 12.9** above. A servitude for electricity is now possible because of TC(S)A 2003, s 77. See **PARA 12.12** above.
[60] See **PARA 12.11** above.

Breaking the fixed list: new expressly created servitudes

12.19 The reason why the courts have been unwilling to recognise an unrestricted list of servitudes is because of the desire to protect purchasers from unregistered rights.[61] This is not an issue for servitudes created expressly since 28 November 2004 because these have to be registered on both the title of the benefited and the burdened property.[62] Therefore expressly created servitudes no longer have to be on the recognised list.[63] The general rules of servitudes, in particular lack of repugnancy with ownership,[64] nevertheless must still be obeyed. It is unlikely that there will be many new examples of servitudes. Importantly, the 'known to the law' requirement remains for servitudes which are not constituted expressly but are created impliedly or by prescription.[65]

Rural and urban servitudes

12.20 The Romans recognised a distinction between 'rural servitudes', which related to land, and 'urban servitudes', which related to buildings.[66] This classification has been used by some of the institutional writers[67] and more recent commentators.[68] There seems, however, no benefit to be had from it in modern times and it is therefore merely noted here.[69]

CREATION

Express grant

12.21 A servitude may be *expressly granted* by the owner of the burdened property. As it is a real right in land, formal writing is needed.[70] The benefited property and the burdened property must both be identified.[71] There is, however, no requirement for a detailed description of the *content* of the right because each type of servitude has recognised features. For example, the right to use a pipe for services extends to the

---

[61] See **PARA 12.9** above.
[62] TC(S)A 2003, s 75. There is an exception for cable and pipeline servitudes. See **PARA 12.21** below.
[63] TC(S)A 2003, s 75(1).
[64] TC(S)A 2003, s 75(2).
[65] See **PARAS 12.24–12.27** below.
[66] See, e.g., A Borkowski and P du Plessis *Textbook on Roman Law* (3rd edn, 2005) 171–172.
[67] E.g. Bell *Principles* ss 983 and 1001.
[68] E.g. Gordon *Scottish Land Law* paras 24-21–24-23.
[69] See further Cusine and Paisley *Servitudes and Rights of Way* paras 1.26–1.27.
[70] RoW(S)A 1995, s 1(2)(b). See **PARA 30.4** below.
[71] Cusine and Paisley *Servitudes and Rights of Way* paras 2.15–2.43.

full length of the pipe.[72] Suggested wording for a right of way might be: 'a servitude right of pedestrian access over the path coloured pink on the plan annexed and executed as relative hereto'.[73] A higher level of description may be required for servitudes which are not on the recognised list. It is not essential to use the word 'servitude',[74] but for the sake of clarity it is wise to do so.[75] The deed creating the servitude must be registered against the title of the benefited and burdened property in order to obtain a real right.[76] This rule, which was mentioned above,[77] came into force on 28 November 2004. Before that registration, creation could be by mere exercise of the servitude, or by registration against just one property. Cable and pipeline servitudes are exempt from the dual registration requirement because this would be cumbersome in the case of long-distance apparatus.[78]

12.22   Where a servitude is expressly granted, in practice one of two deeds is used. The first is a stand-alone deed, known as a 'deed of servitude'. Imagine that Alice and Benedict are neighbours. He wants to take access through her ground. She is willing to grant him a deed of servitude in return for a one-off payment. The deed is registered. Alice is now the burdened proprietor and Benedict the benefited proprietor. The second type of deed is a conveyance, typically a disposition. Michael is selling part of his large garden to Naomi, so that she may build a house on it. Naomi will need to take access through the land being retained by Michael in order to reach the closest public road. Michael will therefore grant Naomi a right of way in the disposition in her favour. Following registration, Naomi will be the benefited proprietor and Michael the burdened proprietor. It is worth remembering that where a servitude is being created by express grant in a conveyance, it is the benefited property (here, the land being sold to Naomi) which is being conveyed.

Express reservation

12.23   A servitude may be *expressly reserved*. The rules on express grant generally apply,[79] but the factual situation is different. Say that Michael, on selling the land to Naomi, needs to keep the right to have service pipes running through it. In that case, he will expressly reserve a servitude in the conveyance. This time it is Michael who is the benefited proprietor and Naomi who is the burdened proprietor. It is only possible to reserve a servitude in a conveyance. A deed of servitude cannot be used

---

[72]   *Axis West Developments Ltd v Chartwell Land Investments Ltd* 1999 SLT 1416 at 1419 per Lord Hope of Craighead.

[73]   For a more detailed example, see Halliday *Conveyancing* vol II, para 35-11.

[74]   This contrasts with the rule for real burdens. See **PARA 13.16** below.

[75]   *Moss Bros Group plc v Scottish Mutual Assurance plc* 2001 SC 779.

[76]   TC(S)A 2003, s 75(1). Registration will be in the Sasine or the Land Register depending where the title to the land is registered.

[77]   See **PARA 12.19** above.

[78]   TC(S)A 2003, s 75(3)(b).

[79]   See **PARA 12.21** above. In particular, there must be writing and dual registration.

because in that situation the properties are already separate and it is too late to reserve anything. Where a servitude is created by express reservation in a conveyance, it is the burdened property (here the land sold to Naomi) which is being conveyed. In practice, 'cross-servitudes' are common, that is to say servitudes are both granted and reserved in the same deed.

Implied grant

12.24 Unlike real burdens,[80] servitudes can be created by implication. This can only happen in a conveyance. There is no such thing as an implied stand-alone deed of servitude. The idea is that at the time the benefited and burdened properties were divided a servitude was implied. A servitude may be created by *implied grant* where the *benefited property* is conveyed. But implication is certainly not automatic. A servitude will only be impliedly granted where this is, in the words of the Lord Campbell in the leading case of *Cochrane v Ewart*,[81] 'necessary for the reasonable enjoyment of the property'. He continued: 'When I say it was necessary, I do not mean that it was so essentially necessary that the property could have no value whatsoever without this easement, but I mean that it was necessary for the convenient and comfortable enjoyment of the property as it existed before the time of the grant.' The background to the case was that a tanyard[82] and a garden were owned by the same individual. The tanyard drained into a cesspool in the garden. When the tanyard was sold separately, it was held that a servitude right of drainage had been impliedly granted in the conveyance. This demonstrates the point that in cases of implied grant a 'quasi-servitude' normally exists at the time the properties are separated. In other words, the right claimed was in effect exercised before the division.[83]

Implied reservation

12.25 Implied reservation is the factual converse of implied grant. Here it is the *burdened property* that is conveyed. There exists authority that the test here is stricter than for implied grant, that is to say it is one of 'utter necessity'. Thus in *Ferguson v Campbell*[84] a servitude of aqueduct was held to have been impliedly reserved in favour of a watermill, because the mill could not function without water. In *Murray v Medley*,[85] however, the sheriff was unwilling to accept that piped water was an utter necessity for a house. The rationale behind the strict test has been stated to be the

---

[80] See **CHAPTER 13** below.

[81] (1861) 4 Macq 117 at 123.

[82] A place where animal skins were tanned into leather. An alternative definition, suggested to one of the authors, is a place where people had their hides tanned.

[83] For another example, see *Gow's Trs v Mealls* (1875) 2 R 729.

[84] 1913 1 SLT 241.

[85] 1973 SLT (Sh Ct) 75.

principle that a granter must not derogate from the grant by impliedly reserving rights. This, however, rests principally on an English case[86] and it is open to question whether it actually represents Scots law. A less stringent test of 'necessary for comfortable enjoyment' appears to have been accepted by the sheriff in the most recent case, *McEwan's Exrs v Arnot*.[87] He also distanced himself from the decision in *Murray v Medley*. It has been argued that it is time for the law now to apply the same test to both implied grant and implied reservation.[88]

Implied servitudes and landlocked land

12.26 Imagine that Peter sells to Roger an enclave, a piece of land entirely surrounded by land, which he (Peter) is retaining. If the conveyance is silent, a servitude right of access will be impliedly granted over the retained land as this is reasonably necessary to let Roger obtain access. There is, however, an alternative approach. In *Bowers v Kennedy*,[89] the Inner House held that the right to access landlocked land was an inherent part of the ownership of that property. At a practical level it makes little difference in the beginning whether Roger is exercising his implied right of servitude or his inherent right of property. Later on, however, the importance matters, because while an implied servitude can be lost by negative prescription, the inherent right cannot.[90]

Positive prescription

12.27 A servitude may be acquired by 20 years of 'possession' i.e. exercise. This may be based on a recorded foundation writ[91] but does not require to be.[92] In practice, such rights are usually not based on a deed. The possession must be open, peaceable and without judicial interruption, the same requirements as for prescriptive acquisition of ownership.[93] The possession must be 'adverse', that is to say 'as of right', which is to say, if the servitude right were actually held.[94] The courts have had difficulty with this requirement.[95] The possession will not be adverse if it is with the tolerance of

---

[86]   *Wheeldon v Burrows* (1879) 12 Ch D 31.
[87]   7 September 2004, Perth Sheriff Court, discussed in Reid and Gretton *Conveyancing 2005* (2006) 89–92. See also *Inverness Seafield Development Co Ltd v Mackintosh* 2001 SC 46.
[88]   Reid and Gretton *Conveyancing 2005* at 92.
[89]   2000 SC 555.
[90]   See PARA **12.45** below.
[91]   PL(S)A 1973, s 3(1).
[92]   PL(S)A 1973, s 3(2).
[93]   See PARA **2.24** above.
[94]   Reid and Gretton *Conveyancing 2006* (2007) 123–124.
[95]   See *Aberdeen City Council v Wanchoo* 2007 SLT 289, aff'd [2008] CSIH 6. See also *Webster v Chadburn* 2003 GWD 18-652, where the sheriff principal seemed to say that the pursuer must normally believe that the right of servitude is held. This is not the law. See Reid and Gretton *Conveyancing 2006* (2007) 128.

the landowner. In one case the sheriff held that the party asserting prescription must prove a lack of tolerance.[96] But proving a negative is often impossible and the decision was reversed by the sheriff principal.[97] The correct rule is that a lack of tolerance can be inferred from a high volume of use of the servitude.[98] At present the Keeper is willing to enter servitudes established by prescription in the Land Register only where a declarator has been obtained confirming the right.[99]

Special statutory provisions

12.28 A servitude may be created in limited cases under special statutory provisions, for example those conferring compulsory acquisition powers.[100]

Acquiescence

12.29 According to Bell, 'although it is rightly said that mere acquiescence cannot confer a right of property, it may confer a right of use of property or servitude'.[101] But this is doubtful.[102] Rather, what can happen is that in servitudes which involve an encroachment,[103] such as laying pipes to carry water, a landowner who acquiesces in the work being carried out will be personally barred from objecting later.[104] At least this is the case if significant expenditure has been incurred.[105] Where the encroachment is obvious, successors of the landowner may be bound too.[106] While underground pipes will not generally be obvious, alterations to them may be.[107]

---

96   *Neumann v Hutchison* 2006 GWD 28-628.
97   *Neumann v Hutchison* 2008 GWD 16-297.
98   Cusine and Paisley *Servitudes and Rights of Way* para 10.19, approved in *Aberdeen City Council v Wanchoo* [2008] CSIH 6 at para 18.
99   *Registration of Title Practice Book* para 6.58. The same policy applies for implied servitudes.
100 E.g. the Communications Act 2003, Sch 4, para 4(3).
101 Bell *Principles* s 947.
102 *Moncrieff v Jamieson* 2005 SC 281 (Inner House) at para 27 per Lord Marnoch. In that case an argument of acquiescence was not pursued in the House of Lords: 2008 SC (HL) 1 at para 19 per Lord Hope of Craighead. For general discussion, see Cusine and Paisley *Servitudes and Rights of Way* paras 11.37–11.46 and E C Reid and J W G Blackie *Personal Bar* (2006) paras 6-56–6-63.
103 See **PARAS 17.10–17.16** below.
104 *Robson v Chalmers Property Investment Co Ltd* 1965 SLT 381, aff'd 2008 SLT 1068.
105 See Reid and Blackie *Personal Bar* paras 6-60–6-61.
106 *Macgregor v Balfour* (1899) 2 F 345 at 352 per Lord President Balfour. In addition, the court has a discretion not to order the removal of an encroachment. See **PARA 17.15** below.
107 See *Buchan v Hunter* (1993), reported in Paisley and Cusine *Unreported Cases* 311, and *Cheever v Jefferson Properties Ltd* (1995), reported in Paisley and Cusine *Unreported Cases* 439.

CHECKING FOR SERVITUDES

12.30 A prospective purchaser of the burdened property will want to know of any servitudes that affect it. As has been seen, servitudes created expressly since 28 November 2004 require to be registered on the titles of both properties.[108] So a search of the register will reveal them. But servitudes created in a deed before then might only appear on the title of the *benefited property*[109] or have been made real by possession without registration. Moreover, a servitude may have been created by implication or prescription. For this reason the right of a holder of a servitude is an 'overriding interest' in the Land Register.[110] The Keeper may note it if he knows of it.[111] As well as checking the register, the would-be owner can check the state of possession by going and looking at the property. But access taken at dead of night or an underground pipe may not be apparent. This ultimately may mean hoping for the best and if a servitude transpires which is a material encumbrance, pursuing a warrandice claim against the seller.[112]

RIGHTS OF THE BENEFITED PROPRIETOR

General

12.31 The benefited proprietor is entitled to enjoy the servitude to its full extent, subject to any applicable servitude conditions and to the law of nuisance.[113] As a real right, it is enforceable against third parties. The benefited proprietor is entitled to communicate the right to have any party having a direct nexus with the benefited property, such as family members or tenants.[114] In *Grant v Cameron*[115] a right of access provided in the deed to be 'for all purposes' was held exercisable by members of the public visiting a shop on the benefited property. The effect of the wording was therefore to permit a wider than usual class of people to exercise the right. Where the benefited property is divided, in principle the proprietors of each part may continue to use the servitude. But this must not lead to an unwarrantable increase in the burden on the burdened property.[116]

---

108 See PARA **12.21** above. Except for cable and pipeline servitudes.
109 *Balfour v Kinsey* 1987 SLT 144.
110 LR(S)A 1979, s 28(1). See PARA **6.36** above.
111 LR(S)A 1979, s 6(4).
112 See PARA **5.10** above.
113 On nuisance, see PARAS **17.21–17.25** below.
114 Cusine and Paisley *Servitudes and Rights of Way* paras 1.55–1.61.
115 (1991), reported in Paisley and Cusine *Unreported Cases* 264.
116 Cusine and Paisley *Servitudes and Rights of Way* paras 12.195–12.200. See paras **12.36–12.39** below.

Ancillary rights

12.32 Ancillary rights may be specified in the deed creating the servitude. In the absence of this, these will be implied if:

(a) the right is necessary for the convenient and comfortable enjoyment of the servitude; and

(b) it was within the contemplation of the parties at the time the servitude was created.[117]

In *Moncrieff v Jamieson*,[118] on the facts a right of parking was held to be ancillary to the right of access created under a deed. Two common ancillary rights may be mentioned.

(1) In the case of servitudes such as those of service media, there is the right to carry out work and to leave things such as pipes on the burdened property.

(2) There is the right to repair and, to a limited extent, improve the burdened property.

Thus in the case of a servitude of access over a road, the benefited proprietor is entitled to carry out repairs and, in some cases, upgrade work. This is provided that its nature is not materially changed and that there is not an unwarrantable increase in the burden on the burdened property.[119] The road may not be widened beyond the area which is burdened by the servitude.[120]

OBLIGATIONS OF THE BENEFITED PROPRIETOR

Express servitude conditions

12.33 Where a servitude has been created expressly the deed may impose express conditions on the benefited proprietor, for example as regards the manner in which the right is to be exercised or the purpose for which it may be used.[121]

To exercise the servitude *civiliter*

12.34 It is implied into a servitude that it must be exercised *civiliter*. This means that the right must be exercised reasonably and the minimum possible burden imposed on the burdened property consistent with full enjoyment of the right.[122] For example,

---

[117] *Moncrieff v Jamieson* 2008 SC (HL) 1. For discussion, see Reid and Gretton *Conveyancing 2007* (2008) 111–117.

[118] 2008 SC (HL) 1.

[119] Cusine and Paisley *Servitudes and Rights of Way* para 12.126.

[120] *Lord Burton v Mackay* 1995 SLT 507.

[121] Cusine and Paisley *Servitudes and Rights of Way* ch 13.

[122] Rankine *Landownership* 417.

servitude right of access is held over a yard, the benefited proprietor may not exercise it along with his dogs with the purpose of letting them defecate.[123]

To exercise the servitude for the benefit of the benefited property only

12.35   The second implied obligation is to exercise the servitude for the benefit of the benefited property alone and not for that of neighbouring property which the benefited proprietor also owns. The leading modern case is *Irvine Knitters Ltd v North Ayrshire Co-operative Society Ltd*.[124] The Co-op shop in Irvine was a building that straddled two plots. Plot 1 was the benefited property in a servitude right giving access along a lane to the rear of the building. The front was to the busy High Street. Plot 2 was not part of the benefited property. The burdened proprietors sought to interdict the Co-op from using the access to bring in goods to that part of the shop in Plot 2. They succeeded. Lord President Emslie stated:

> '[The benefited proprietors] may not use the way for the purpose of securing access for persons or goods to subjects contiguous to the dominant tenement by using the dominant tenement merely as a bridge between the end of the lane and the non-dominant subjects.'[125]

Not to increase unwarrantably the burden on the burdened property

12.36   The final implied obligation is not to cause an unwarrantable increase in the burden on the burdened property. By 'unwarrantable' is meant not permitted by the servitude in question. The baseline for increase is the extent of the servitude at the time when it is created. In the case of express servitudes the deed may provide for the extent. An example is *Grant v Cameron*[126] where the servitude was stated to be 'for all purposes'. In other cases the deed may not, or there might be no deed. Here, three general rules apply.

12.37   First, a change in the type of use made of the benefited property is not in itself an increase in the burden on the burdened property. The servitude can still be relied upon to support the new use. In *Carstairs v Spence*[127] a servitude right of access had been established by prescription. The benefited property was a market garden which subsequently became a building site. It was held that the benefited proprietor could carry building materials along the access route.

---

[123]   *Soriani v Cluckie* 2001 GWD 28-1138.
[124]   1978 SC 109.
[125]   1978 SC 109 at 117.
[126]   (1991), reported in Paisley and Cusine *Unreported Cases* 264. See PARA **12.31** above.
[127]   1924 SC 380.

12.38 Second, in passage servitudes such as access or aqueduct, a change in the type of thing passing may be an unwarrantable increase in the burden. Thus, a servitude for pedestrian access cannot be used for vehicular access. In *Kerr v Brown*[128] a servitude to carry waste water from sinks was established by prescription. It was held it could not be extended to cover sewage. This case also demonstrates the rule *tantum praescriptum quantum possessum*: prescription is measured by possession. In other words, a servitude cannot be wider than what prescription established. Nevertheless, modern versions of a previous thing are permitted. For example, cart and carriage roads may now be used for cars.[129]

12.39 Third, whether increased use is an increase in the burden is a question of scale. This is a common issue in practice in relation to access, but the law is rather obscure and each case must be assessed on its own facts.[130] The classic example is where a piece of land is developed for housing. Where, however, there has been an increase in burden for 20 years and this has not been challenged, it will be validated by positive prescription.[131]

RIGHTS OF THE BURDENED PROPRIETOR

12.40 The burdened proprietor has the right to continue to enjoy and make use of the burdened property provided that this does not interfere with the servitude.[132] In addition, the proprietor may enforce any of the express or implied obligations on the benefited proprietor mentioned above.[133]

OBLIGATIONS OF THE BURDENED PROPRIETOR

12.41 The principal obligations of the burdened proprietor are to respect the servitude and not to interfere with its exercise, such as by obstructing the benefited proprietor. Much of the case law, as may be expected, involves access rights. In *Drury v McGarvie*[134] there was a right of way over farmland from a public road to a cottage. The farmer's animals were straying off the land, so he erected stockproof gates at either end of the right of way. The owners of the cottage were elderly and disabled and struggled to open the gates. They objected. It was held that the erection of the gates was reasonable. The criterion was whether the average person could open the gates without difficulty. Where a gate is locked by the burdened proprietor, the benefited proprietor must be provided with a key.[135]

---

[128] 1939 SC 140.
[129] *Smith v Saxton* 1928 SN 59.
[130] For discussion, see Cusine and Paisley *Servitudes and Rights of Way* paras 12.186–12.201.
[131] See **para 12.27** above.
[132] Cusine and Paisley *Servitudes and Rights of Way* paras 12.12–12.22.
[133] See **paras 12.33–12.39** above.
[134] *Drury v McGarvie* 1993 SC 95.
[135] *Lee v McMurrich* Feb 5 1808, Court of Session, *Hume Session Papers*, vol 97, case 18.

12.42 Unless there is an express servitude condition requiring it, a burdened proprietor is *not* obliged to carry out repairs to an access route.[136] This may be seen as part of a general rule that servitudes must not impose positive obligations.[137] It is possible to oblige the burdened proprietor to repair by means of a real burden.[138]

EXTINCTION

Consensual

12.43 The benefited proprietor may agree to extinguish the servitude. Writing is required to constitute the agreement.[139] The servitude is then actually extinguished by a 'deed of discharge'.[140] This should be registered against the title of the burdened property.[141]

Acquiescence

12.44 Where the benefited proprietor stands by and lets the burdened proprietor carry out works which prevent the exercise of the servitude, the right to object later may be lost.[142] This will be most likely if the work involved substantial expenditure, the value of which would lost if the objection succeeded.[143] In this situation the servitude is extinguished by *acquiescence.* The acquiescence is to the extent of the breach. For example, in *Millar v Christie*[144] the building work partially blocked an access way. The result was to limit the servitude right which existed to the remaining part. Singular successors will generally be bound by the acquiescence because the building work will be obvious to them at the time of purchase.[145]

Negative prescription

12.45 Where a servitude has not been exercised for 20 years it will be lost through negative prescription.[146] In the case of a pedestrian and vehicular access right, an absence of vehicular use for the prescriptive period will reduce the servitude to foot

---

[136] *Rodgers v Harvie* (1829) 7 S 287. For the sequel, see (1830) 8 S 611.
[137] Cusine and Paisley *Servitudes and Rights of Way* para 2.85. But express servitude conditions can override the rule.
[138] See **CHAPTER 13** below.
[139] RoW(S)A 1995, s 1(2)(a)(i). See **PARA 30.3** below.
[140] Again, writing is required, this time under RoW(S)A 1995, s 1(2)(b). See **PARA 30.4** below.
[141] TC(S)A 2003, s 78.
[142] Reid and Blackie *Personal Bar* paras 6-46–6-55.
[143] *Davidson v Thomson* (1880) 17 R 287 at 290 per Lord President Inglis.
[144] 1961 SC 1.
[145] *Muirhead v Glasgow Highland Society* (1864) 2 M 420 at 426 per Lord President McNeill.
[146] PL(S)A 1973, s 8.

access only.[147] The inherent right of the proprietor of landlocked land to reach it was held to be a right exercisable as a *res merae facultatis*[148] in *Bowers v Kennedy*[149] and is therefore imprescriptible. Where a deed creating a servitude makes it clear that the right is to subsist even if it is not exercised, this may also make it as a *res merae facultatis*.[150]

Destruction

12.46 In general, land is indestructible, so extinction by destruction is rare. Where a servitude is stated to be for the benefit of a particular building and that building is demolished with no intention of rebuilding, the servitude will be lost.[151]

Confusion

12.47 A servitude will be extinguished by *confusio* where the benefited and burdened properties come into the same ownership.[152] Hence, if Alex's land has a right of servitude to lay pipes through Beth's land, the right will disappear if he buys her land. Confusion probably does not operate if the two pieces of land are held by the person in different capacities, for example as an individual and as a trustee.[153] It is unlikely that a servitude extinguished by confusion will revive on the land being subsequently separated, but new servitudes may be created by implication if the relevant tests are satisfied.[154]

Compulsory purchase

12.48 Where land is compulsorily purchased, servitudes and real burdens affecting it are normally extinguished.[155] If land is acquired consensually in a situation where compulsory purchase could have been used, these rights can be extinguished by the

---

[147] *Walker's Exrx v Carr* 1973 SLT (Sh Ct) 77.

[148] PL(S)A 1973, Sch 3, para (c). *Res merae facultatis* is 'a property right which cannot be lost by negative prescription either (1) because it is a right whose exercise implies no claim on anyone else or against their rights or (2) because it is a (normal) incident of ownership which can be lost only as a consequence of the fortification in some other person of a right inconsistent with it' (Johnston *Prescription* para 3.16). The subject is obscure.

[149] 2000 SC 555. See PARA **12.26** above.

[150] *Peart v Legge* 2007 SLT 982. But this seems similar to contracting out of prescription, which is forbidden by PL(S)A 1973, s 13. For discussion, see Reid and Gretton *Conveyancing 2007* (2008) 117–121.

[151] Cusine and Paisley *Servitudes and Rights of Way* para 17.21.

[152] Erskine II, 9, 37. Compare the rule for real burdens. See PARA **13.75** below.

[153] Cusine and Paisley *Servitudes and Rights of Way* para 17.25.

[154] See PARAS **12.24–12.25** above.

[155] TC(S)A 2003, s 106. The rights may be saved by express provision in the compulsory purchase order or the conveyance. On compulsory purchase, see PARAS **7.4–7.9** above.

acquirer giving notice to the benefited proprietor.[156] That proprietor then has the right to apply to the Lands Tribunal to have the servitude or real burden renewed.[157]

Application to the Lands Tribunal

12.49   The burdened proprietor may apply to the Lands Tribunal for the servitude to be varied or extinguished.[158] The rules are essentially the same as for real burdens and are discussed in **CHAPTER 13**.[159]

RIGHTS WHICH ARE SIMILAR TO SERVITUDES

Public rights of way

12.50   Public rights of way are covered elsewhere.[160] Two key distinctions from servitudes are that there is no benefited property and the rights are for access only. As has been seen, servitudes can be for other purposes, such as to lay pipes.

Statutory rights

12.51   Many statutes create rights that are effectively personal servitudes, that is to say there is a burdened property but no benefited property. A common example is a 'wayleave'. It is like a cable or pipeline servitude and can be created in favour of certain utility companies.[161] Access rights exist under various statutes, not least the Land Reform (Scotland) Act 2003.[162]

FURTHER READING

Cusine and Paisley *Servitudes and Rights of Way*.

Gloag and Henderson *The Law of Scotland* paras 35.34–35.41.

Gordon *Scottish Land Law* paras 24.01–24.104.

---

[156]   TC(S)A 2003, s 107(1) and (4).
[157]   TC(S)A 2003, s 107(5).
[158]   E.g. *George Wimpey East Scotland Ltd v Fleming* 2006 SLT (Lands Tr) 2 and 59.
[159]   See **PARAS 13.71–13.73** below.
[160]   See **PARAS 18.13–18.22** below.
[161]   For example, the Electricity Act 1989, Sch 4, paras 6 and 7. See further Cusine and Paisley *Servitudes and Rights of Way* para 1.04 and ch 26.
[162]   On LR(S)A 2003, see **PARAS 18.2–18.12** below. More generally, see R R M Paisley 'Personal Real Burdens' 2005 *JR* 377 at 417–420.

McDonald *Conveyancing Manual* ch 16.

Paisley *Land Law* ch 8.

Paisley, R R M 'The New Law of Servitudes' in R Rennie (ed) *The Promised Land: Property Law Reform* (2008) 91–123.

Reid *Property* paras 439–469 (A G M Duncan).

Rennie *Land Tenure* ch 11.

Chapter 13

Real burdens

ESSENTIALS

Definition

13.1 A 'real burden' is an obligation affecting land, which normally requires something to be done or not to be done. For example, it may provide for a house to be maintained or insured. In the case of property which benefits more than one owner, such as a tenement roof or a common recreational area, a contribution towards maintenance may be required. Typical examples of burdens which impose restrictions are ones which prevent trading or running a business from a residential property, or prohibit alterations. Usually, real burdens, like servitudes, involve a 'benefited property' and a 'burdened property'.[1] They are normally imposed when a piece of land is sold as a separate unit for the first time. The value of the real burdens is that they 'run with the land'. The owner[2] for the time being of a benefited property can enforce them against the owner[3] for the time being of the burdened property. The types of obligation imposed by real burdens could also be created by simple contract. But a contract would not bind successor owners.

Background

13.2   Unlike servitudes, which come from Roman law, real burdens were developed in conveyancing practice in the nineteenth century. The reason probably lay in the limited scope of servitudes: there was in effect a fixed list and positive obligations could not be imposed.[4] Real burdens were often created in feudal deeds.[5] The superiority acted as the benefited property and the vassal's interest (*dominium utile*) was the burdened property. This was convenient for developers because there was no requirement for the superior to hold neighbouring land. More than anything, this is why the feudal system survived in Scotland until 28 November 2004. Equally, however, it was possible at common law for real burdens to be imposed in non-feudal deeds, such as dispositions. In fact the 1840 House of Lords case of *Tailors of Aberdeen v Coutts*,[6] which provides the foundation of the law of real burdens involved a non-feudal deed.

Title Conditions (Scotland) Act 2003

13.3   When the Scottish Law Commission prepared the report which led to the Abolition of Feudal Tenure etc (Scotland) Act 2000 (AFT(S)A 2000),[7] it realised that separate legislation would be needed to regulate real burdens in post-feudal land law. This prompted it to issue its *Report on Real Burdens*.[8] The report led to the Title Conditions (Scotland) Act 2003 (TC(S)A 2003), most of which, like AFT(S)A 2000, came into force on 28 November 2004. Much of it is a codification of the common law, so the older case law often remains relevant. Particularly important is Pt 1 of TC(S)A 2003, which regulates creation, enforcement and extinction.[9] One might legitimately ask why the legislation is not called the 'Real Burdens (Scotland)

---

[1]   There is an exception for personal real burdens. See **PARA 13.50** below.
[2]   And certain other parties. See **PARA 13.38** below.
[3]   And in the case of negative real burdens, against everyone else too. See **PARA 13.42** below.
[4]   See **PARAS 12.9 AND 12.42** above.
[5]   See **APPENDIX** below.
[6]   (1840) 1 Robin 296.
[7]   Scottish Law Commission *Report on the Abolition of the Feudal System* (1998).
[8]   Scottish Law Commission *Report on Real Burdens* (2000).
[9]   TC(S)A 2003, ss 1–24.

Act'. The reason is that while it mainly deals with real burdens, it also deals with 'title conditions' more generally.[10] A 'title condition' is an obligation affecting land which the Lands Tribunal has power to vary or discharge.[11] TC(S)A 2003 gives an exhaustive list, but the most important are:

(a) real burdens;

(b) servitudes; and

(c) conditions in long leases.[12]

Praedial real burdens and personal real burdens

13.4   If a real burden has both a benefited and a burdened property, it is a *praedial* real burden. For example, the owner for the time being of 22 Paisley Gardens can enforce the real burdens affecting 24 Paisley Gardens. Praedial real burdens are the norm. In very limited circumstances it is possible to have real burdens which do not have a benefited property. Instead, they are enforceable by a particular person. These are *personal* real burdens.[13] For example, Scottish Natural Heritage may have title to enforce a real burden providing for the conservation of a building. Personal real burdens are rare and discussion of them is saved for later.[14] Almost all of this chapter focuses on praedial real burdens.

Subdivisions and common schemes

13.5   It was stated above that real burdens are normally imposed when land is sold as a separate unit for the first time.[15] Two factual situations can be distinguished. The first is where an owner of land sells part of it and imposes burdens on that part. For example, Jennifer has a large garden. She does not need all of it. Kurt offers to buy the part furthest from the house. He wants to build his own house on it. Jennifer is agreeable to this, but she does not want the land to be used as commercial premises at any time in the future. So in the disposition to Kurt she imposes a real burden to that effect. This can be described as a subdivision case. Typically, although not always, the burdens are non-reciprocal. This Jennifer can enforce the trading prohibition against Kurt and not vice versa. It is possible for there to be more than one benefited property. For example, in the disposition Jennifer could have given the right to enforce the burden to the immediate neighbouring properties.

---

10   Thus it provides some important rules for servitudes. See PARAS **12.1, 12.5, 12.19** and **12.21** above.

11   See PARA **13.71** below.

12   TC(S)A 2003, s 122(1).

13   The conjunction of the adjectives 'personal' and 'real' sounds odd. The 'real' refers to the burdened property. The 'personal' is because there is no benefited property.

14   See PARAS **13.50–13.58** below.

15   See PARA **13.1** above.

13.6 The second example typically involves a developer or builder. A block of flats or new housing scheme is built. Before the flats or houses are sold, real burdens are imposed on the entire site, regulating matters such as maintenance and use of the properties. These burdens are to be reciprocally enforceable by all the property owners. So James, who buys plot 31, has title to enforce against Anna, who buys plot 34, and vice versa. This is described as a 'common scheme'. Each property within the scheme is both a benefited and a burdened property. Such reciprocal burdens are called 'community burdens'.[16] There are special rules that apply only to this type of burden.[17] It is therefore important when it comes to understanding TC(S)A 2003 to differentiate subdivision cases and common scheme cases.

Affirmative and negative real burdens

13.7 Real burdens requiring something to be done are called 'affirmative burdens'.[18] Those imposing prohibitions are called 'negative burdens'.[19] In general, real burdens cannot give a right to use or enter the burdened property. That is the role of *servitudes*.[20] The distinction can be illustrated by this table.

Type of title condition	Servitude	Real burden
Positive obligation	No	Yes
Negative obligation	No	Yes
Obligation to allow use of or entry to the burdened property	Yes	No

13.8 The table is not entirely accurate. It is possible to have real burdens allowing use of or entry to the burdened property for purposes connected with another real burden. This category is known as 'ancillary burdens'.[21] For example, there might be a real burden requiring a property to be maintained and an ancillary burden allowing access onto the property to check that the maintenance obligation is being fulfilled.

13.9 Unlike servitudes,[22] there is no established list of real burdens. But in addition to the requirement that they must normally impose only positive or negative obligations, there are further rules on content. These are discussed in the following paragraphs.

---

[16]   TC(S)A 2003, s 25.
[17]   See PARAS **13.60–13.64** below.
[18]   TC(S)A 2003, s 2(1)(a) and (2)(a).
[19]   TC(S)A 2003, s 2(1)(b) and (2)(b).
[20]   See PARA **12.5** above.
[21]   TC(S)A 2003, s 2(3) and (4).
[22]   See PARA **12.9** above.

The praedial requirement

13.10   The law here is similar to that on servitudes.[23] A real burden must burden the burdened property to the benefit of the benefited property. The burden must relate to the burdened property and not simply to the person who owns that property.[24] Hence a requirement to sing a song or to support a particular football club or not to wear blue trousers would not be a valid real burden. The burden must benefit the benefit property and not merely fulfil the personal wishes of its owner.[25] Thus the examples given fail the praedial test at the benefited property end too. In the case of a *community burden*, it is permissible for the benefit to be to the community as a whole rather than to a particular benefited property.[26] Thus a requirement for a tenement to be factored would meet the test, as it is in the interests of all the owners that the building is well managed.

Restrictions on content

13.11   There are restraints on real burdens which are similar to those found in contract law.[27] They may not be contrary to public policy, such as being an unreasonable restraint on trade.[28] Nor can they be repugnant with the ownership of the burdened property: a burden can go so far but no further.[29] In a nineteenth-century case, Lord Young famously said: 'You cannot make a man proprietor and yet prohibit him from exercising his ownership.'[30] Hence a burden stating that the property cannot be sold or leased is invalid. Nor can a real burden be illegal.[31] Thus a requirement that only women may live in the property would breach sex discrimination legislation.[32] In general, a real burden must not create a monopoly, for example by requiring that a certain company always manages a development.[33] Nor is it possible to allow a person, other than a party with title to enforce the burden,[34] to give permission for the activity prohibited by the burden to take place.[35] Thus if a developer has sold all the properties

---

23   See PARAS **12.6–12.7** above.

24   TC(S)A 2003, s 3(1) and (2).

25   TC(S)A 2003, s 3(3).

26   TC(S)A 2003, s 3(4).

27   See MacQueen and Thomson *Contract* paras 7.1–7.24 and 7.30–7.47.

28   TC(S)A 2003, s 3(6). See McDonald *Conveyancing Manual* para 15.33.

29   TC(S)A 2003, s 3(6).

30   *Moir's Trs v McEwan* (1880) 7 R 1141 at 1145.

31   TC(S)A 2003, s 3(6).

32   Sex Discrimination Act 1975, ss 30 and 75.

33   TC(S)A 2003, s 3(7). This is subject to other provisions in the Act, notably those on manager burdens (ss 63–67). See PARA **13.56** below.

34   The provision refers to the 'holder' of the burden. This term is defined in TC(S)A 2003, s 122(1) and for praedial rule burdens effectively is restricted to the owner of the benefited property.

35   TC(S)A 2003, s 3(8).

in a development, a right to vary or extinguish the burdens cannot be reserved as the developer is no longer a benefited proprietor.[36]

Pre-emptions and other options

13.12 It is permissible to have a real burden allowing the owner of a benefited property to have the right to purchase the burdened property if the burdened proprietor decides to sell. This is known as a 'right of pre-emption'.[37] Often the right is to purchase at the same price as that offered by a prospective purchaser. In practice the presence of a pre-emption right may deter such purchasers and therefore it is possible to obtain a pre-sale undertaking from the holder of the pre-emption that the right will not be exercised.[38] In general, a pre-emption right constituted as a real burden will only provide one chance for it to be exercised.[39] Thus if the property is offered to the holder of the pre-emption and he or she does not wish to purchase, the right is extinguished. Where there is a pre-emption right and the property is not offered to the holder, the transfer in breach of the pre-emption may be reduced under the 'offside goals' rule.[40]

13.13 Since 28 November 2004, it has no longer been competent to create other types of option as a real burden.[41] TC(S)A 2003 mentions specifically two types, although the prohibition is a general one. A 'right of redemption' allows the granter in a conveyance to repurchase the land, normally at a fixed price and at any time. Under earlier legislation, the lifespan of a right of redemption created as a real burden is limited to 20 years.[42] This means that many such real burdens will cease to exist at latest on 26 November 2024.[43] A right of redemption is an example of a wider class of option known as 'rights of reversion'. These confer the right to re-acquire land, not necessarily in return for payment. The Scottish Law Commission

---

[36] Assuming that the developer does not hold neighbouring land which is provided to be a benefited property in the deed creating the burdens.

[37] TC(S)A 2003, s 3(5). A challenge to a pre-emption right founded on Art 1 of Protocol 1 to the ECHR failed on the basis that the existence of the pre-emption was known to the burdened proprietor at the time he acquired the land and that this may have reduced the purchase price. See *MacDonald-Haig v Gerlings,* Inverness Sheriff Court, 3 December 2001 (unreported). See Reid and Gretton *Conveyancing 2002* (2003) 63–65.

[38] TC(S)A 2003, s 83.

[39] TC(S)A 2003, ss 82 and 84. There is an exception for pre-emptions created in dispositions before 1 September 1974.

[40] *Matheson v Tinney* 1989 SLT 535; *Roebuck v Edmunds* 1992 SLT 1055. On the 'offside goals' rule, see PARAS **4.45–4.48** above.

[41] TC(S)A 2003, s 3(5).

[42] Land Tenure Reform (Scotland) Act 1974, s 12.

[43] This is because 26 November 2004 was the last date on which a right of redemption could be registered as a valid real burden. (27 November 2004 was a Saturday and the registers were closed for business. The authors remember the day well, as they were at a feudal abolition party.) Redemptions created before 1 September 1974 are unaffected.

regarded it wrong as a matter of policy that these should be capable of affecting successor landowners.[44]

13.14 It remains possible for options of any type to be created contractually, although of course successor owners of the property affected will not be bound. If, however, someone who knew about the option bought the land in breach of it, the 'offside goals' rule would apply.[45] In practice, solicitors may secure the option by means of a standard security, although the remedies available under the security for default may seem inappropriate.[46] It does mean, however, that a prospective purchaser will be put on notice about the option and allow the 'offside goals' rule to apply if the right is breached.

CREATION

A deed which is dual-registered

13.15 A real burden must be created in a *deed*, which is registered against *both* the title of the benefited property *and* that of the burdened property.[47] This is known as the 'constitutive deed'. The deed must describe both properties or, in the case of community burdens, the community.[48] Before 28 November 2004, it was only possible to create real burdens in two types of deed: conveyances and deeds of conditions. Now, there is no such restriction. Any type of deed may be used. So, for example, a new real burden could be created in a minute of waiver,[49] i.e. a deed that extinguishes a current burden. The *nemo plus* rule[50] applies. Land can be burdened only by the owner,[51] for example, a developer who has constructed houses and is about to sell them. In the example just given of a new real burden being created in a minute of waiver, the burdened property's owner would therefore need to sign the deed, whereas normally only the benefited proprietor signs a waiver. After creation, the burdens cease to have *contractual* effect between the parties.[52]

---

44 Scottish Law Commission *Report on Real Burdens* (2000) para 10.20: 'A person may lose property without his consent and, in some cases, without adequate compensation. This is private compulsory purchase.'
45 Scottish Law Commission *Report on Real Burdens* (2000) para 10.8.
46 Scottish Law Commission *Report on Real Burdens* (2000) para 10.9. On standard securities, see PARAS **20.43–20.56** below.
47 TC(S)A 2003, s 4(1) and (5). Previously, the law was that it needed to be registered only against the burdened property. Thus there exist many single-registered burdens.
48 TC(S)A 2003, s 4(2)(c) and (4).
49 On minutes of waiver, see PARA **13.59** below.
50 See PARA **4.39** above.
51 TC(S)A 2003, s 4(2)(b).
52 TC(S)A 2003, s 61.

The term 'real burden'

13.16 It is obligatory to use the term 'real burden' or an equivalent in the deed.[53] An equivalent is permitted where the real burden is of a nameable type,[54] such as a 'community burden'[55] or 'conservation burden'.[56]

The 'four corners of the deed' rule

13.17 In principle, the full terms of the real burden must be set out within the 'four corners' of the constitutive deed. For example, in *Aberdeen Varieties Ltd v James F Donald (Aberdeen Cinemas) Ltd*[57] the owner of two theatres sold one of them and imposed a real burden requiring that the property 'shall not be used in all time coming for the performance of pantomime, melodrama or comic opera or any stage play which requires to be submitted to the Lord Chamberlain under the Act for regulating Theatres 6th & 7th Vict c 68'. It was held that a valid real burden had not been created. To do so, the deed would have had to copy out the full terms of the statute.[58]

13.18 The strict common law rule has been relaxed a little by TC(S)A 2003, s 5. A real burden which requires a contribution towards or the payment of a cost can refer to a public document, without setting out the full terms of that document. By 'public document' is meant 'an enactment or a public register or some record or roll to which the public readily has access'.[59] The provision applies to all burdens, new and old, and is aimed particularly at burdens providing for the maintenance of tenements which apportion liability on the basis of rateable value or feu duty.[60]

Duration

13.19 The constitutive deed may state how long the real burden is to last, but in practice this is rare. Where, as is normally the case, the deed is silent, the real burden is perpetual,[61] subject to the rules of extinction set out at the end of this chapter.[62]

---

53 TC(S)A 2003, s 4(2)(a). Compare the position for servitudes. See PARA **12.21** above.
54 TC(S)A 2003, s 4(3).
55 See PARA **13.6** above.
56 See PARA **13.51** below.
57 1939 SC 788.
58 Actually, it would have failed even then because of other invalidities, such as restraint of trade.
59 TC(S)A 2003, s 5(2).
60 'Rateable value' refers to the local government taxation of 'rates', which was replaced for residential properties by the 'community charge' or 'poll tax' in 1989 and then by the 'council tax' in 1993. On feu duty, see the APPENDIX. Older real burdens often make flats liable for tenement repairs based on their rateable value or feu duty liability as a proportion of the total liability of the building.
61 TC(S)A 2003, s 7.
62 See PARAS **13.59–13.74** below.

THE BENEFITED PROPERTY

The common law background

13.20 Prior to 28 November 2004 the common law had strict rules that the *burdened property* must be carefully identified[63] and the real burden registered against it.[64] Unlike TC(S)A 2003, which applies these rules to *both* the burdened and the benefited properties, the common law took a lax approach when it came to the identification of the *benefited property*. Sometimes the constitutive deed would nominate this property, but usually it did not. In the latter situation, the courts developed a set of rules under which a benefited property or benefited properties would be *implied*. These rules on implied enforcement rights were complex and barely comprehensible.[65] TC(S)A 2003 for the most part abolished them.[66] In their place it provided another set of rules which are not only complex, but overlap.[67] The result is less than satisfactory.[68] The picture is also complicated by the impact of feudal abolition.

Real burdens created since 28 November 2004

13.21 The rule here is straightforward. As was seen above, the benefited property or properties must be identified in the constitutive deed and the deed registered against the title to that property.[69] There can be no implied rights of enforcement for such burdens.[70]

Real burdens created before 28 November 2004: seven rules

13.22 For real burdens created before 28 November 2004, it is possible to identify seven rules.[71] These may overlap: more than one rule may apply to the same burden. Most of these rules are in TC(S)A 2003 even though the burdens to which they apply were then already in existence: these rules thus apply retrospectively. (However, to

---

[63] *Anderson v Dickie* 1914 SC 706, aff'd 1915 SC (HL) 79.
[64] *Tailors of Aberdeen v Coutts* (1840) 1 Robin 296.
[65] See Reid *Property* paras 397–404 and McDonald *Conveyancing Manual* paras 17.8–17.31.
[66] TC(S)A 2003, s 49.
[67] TC(S)A 2003, ss 52–57.
[68] For discussion, see S Wortley 'Love Thy Neighbour: The Development of the Scottish Law of Implied Third Party Rights of Enforcement of Real Burdens' 2005 *JR* 345 and K G C Reid 'New Enforcers for Old Burdens: Sections 52 and 53 Revisited' in R Rennie (ed) *The Promised Land: Property Law Reform* (2008) 71–90.
[69] See PARA **13.15** above. Equally, there must be identification of and registration against the burdened property.
[70] There is one exception to this rule, which arises out of TC(S)A 2003, s 53. See PARA **13.26** below.
[71] Gretton and Reid *Conveyancing* para 13-15.

a considerable extent they merely restate what the common law, under which these burdens were set up, actually was.)

Rule 1: express nomination

13.23 The constitutive deed may nominate the benefited property or properties. For example, it is common to find in a deed of conditions granted by a builder over a new development a statement that each house owner has the right to enforce the burden against all the other house owners. This is sometimes stated to be an 'express *jus quaesitum tertio*'. This is an analogy with contract law.[72]

Rule 2: related properties in a common scheme

13.24 TC(S)A 2003, s 53 has caused much difficulty. It provides that where there are 'related properties' forming part of a 'common scheme' of real burdens, the burdens are mutually enforceable by the proprietors.[73] In other words, the burdens are *community burdens*[74] and can be enforced by each member of the community. The legislation does not define 'common scheme' but it seems to mean identical or similar burdens, probably imposed by the same person, for example a builder.[75] Where the same deed applies to a number of houses, for example a deed of conditions, the burdens will usually be identical. If the burdens are imposed in different deeds, for example the individual dispositions for each house, it is more likely that they vary.

13.25 Likewise, 'related properties' is not defined. The matter of whether properties are 'related' requires 'to be inferred from all the circumstances'.[76] In effect it is a subjective decision for the courts. Regard, however, must be had to a non-exhaustive list of factors, namely whether:
(a) it is convenient to manage the properties together because they have a common feature or are obliged to maintain a facility together;
(b) they share common ownership of something;
(c) they are regulated by the same burdens imposed in a deed of conditions; and
(d) they are flats in the same tenement.[77]
The Lands Tribunal has expressed the view that properties subject to the same deed creating real burdens, although this is not a deed of conditions and within (c), may be

---

[72] Under contract law, successors are not bound. Here, they are.
[73] Or tenants etc. See **PARA 13.38** below. The provision does not apply to rights of pre-emption, redemption or reversion or to maintenance obligations, for example as regards roads, which have been taken over by a public authority. See TC(S)A 2003, ss 53(2) and 122(2). A revised version of s 53 applies to sheltered or retirement housing developments by virtue of s 54.
[74] See **PARA 13.6** above.
[75] McDonald *Conveyancing Manual* para 17.33; Reid *Feudal Abolition* para 5.2.
[76] TC(S)A 2003, s 53(2).
[77] TC(S)A 2003, s 53(2).

related.[78] The Minister who introduced the provision, when the legislation was passing through the Scottish Parliament, stated that 'houses on a typical housing estate would be related properties' but not 'scattered properties in rural areas'.[79] Ultimately, each case must be decided on its facts. This is unfortunate, for TC(S)A 2003, s 53 is an important provision which can apply in many cases.

13.26 A final point about this rule is that only one of the properties requires to have been burdened before 28 November 2004. For example, where burdens are imposed in a common scheme on a housing development, TC(S)A 2003, s 53 will apply as long as ownership of one of the houses was transferred to a purchaser before that date. The later houses can still enforce and, reciprocally, have the burdens enforced against them under the rule. This is the one exception mentioned to the rule that implied enforcement rights can only arise for burdens created before 28 November 2004.[80]

Rule 3: unrelated properties in a common scheme

13.27 TC(S)A 2003, s 52 provides for implied enforcement rights for properties in a 'common scheme'. It can apply even if the properties are not 'related' within the meaning of TC(S)A 2003, s 53. In effect it is a statutory restatement of the common law rule established in *Hislop v MacRitchie's Trs*.[81] There are, however, two important pre-requisites for TC(S)A 2003, s 52 to apply.

13.28 First, for a property to be subject to implied enforcement rights under the rule, there must be *notice* of the common scheme on the title to that property.[82] Two factual situations are possible. If the deed creating the real burden applies to a wider area, this by itself is sufficient notice of the scheme. For example, the real burden may have been imposed in a disposition of a development site by a farmer in favour of a builder, with the builder subsequently subdividing the site into housing plots. If, in contrast, the deed creating the real burden applies to the burdened property alone, the situation is more complicated. There needs to be something specific in the deed to indicate a common scheme, such as an obligation by the granter to impose the same burdens on subsequently disponed houses.[83]

13.29 Second, there must be nothing in the deed creating the real burdens to negative the creation of mutual enforcement rights.[84] The classic example of this is

---

[78] *Brown v Richardson* 2007 GWD 28-490.

[79] Scottish Parliament *Official Report* Justice 1 Committee, 10 December 2002 col 4372.

[80] See PARA **13.21** above.

[81] (1881) 8 R (HL) 95. However, like TC(S)A 2003, s 53, the rule does not apply to rights of pre-emption, redemption or reversion, or to maintenance obligations taken over by a public authority. See TC(S)A 2003, ss 52(3) and 122(2).

[82] TC(S)A 2003, s 52(1).

[83] *McGibbon v Rankin* (1871) 9 M 423. See, further, Reid *Feudal Abolition* para 5.15.

[84] TC(S)A 2003, s 52(2).

the granter reserving the right to vary the burdens.[85] Where real burdens have been imposed over an area which is then subdivided, rights of enforcement in favour of the owners of the respective parts cannot arise if there was in fact a prohibition on subdivision.[86]

13.30 This rule is less important than rule 2 above. The reason is that many deeds creating burdens do not give notice of a common scheme or do have a provision allowing the granter to vary the burdens.

Rule 4: facility burdens

13.31 Where a real burden regulates the 'maintenance, management, reinstatement or use of a facility', the benefited properties are the facility itself and any property to which the facility is, and is intended to be, of benefit.[87] Examples of facilities given by the legislation are:

(a) common parts of a tenement;
(b) common recreation areas:
(c) private roads;
(d) private sewerage systems; and
(e) boundary walls.[88]

Thus, where a number of properties share a common access road and are subject to real burdens requiring it to be maintained, the burdens are mutually enforceable. The rule does not apply where the obligation to maintain the facility has been taken over by a public authority.[89] In practice, there is often an overlap between this rule and rule 2. The reason for this is that rule 2 was only conceived and introduced at a late stage during the passage of the legislation.[90]

Rule 5: service burdens

13.32 Where a real burden regulates the provision of a service, the benefited properties are the properties to which the service is to be provided.[91] For example, a burden may require the provision of water or electricity. In practice, this is rare and the rule is therefore not very important.

---

[85] *Turner v Hamilton* (1890) 17 R 494.
[86] *Girls School Co Ltd v Buchanan* 1958 SLT (Notes) 2.
[87] TC(S)A 2003, ss 56(1)(a) and 122(1).
[88] TC(S)A 2003, s 122(3).
[89] TC(S)A 2003, s 122(2).
[90] See Gretton and Reid *Conveyancing* para 13-15.
[91] TC(S)A 2003, ss 56(1)(b) and 122(1).

Rule 6: reallotted feudal burdens

13.33   Where a feudal real burden was preserved by a notice registered before 28 November 2004, the benefited property is that identified in the notice.[92] Under feudal law, burdens could be enforced by the superior, even although that person did not own any neighbouring land. Where superiors *did* own such land, the legislation that abolished the feudal system gave them a limited chance to 'reallot' burdens so that the benefited property became that land. For this option to be available the neighbouring land normally had to have on it a permanent building in use wholly or mainly as a 'place of human habitation or resort'.[93] Additionally, the building had to be within 100 metres of the burdened property.[94] The policy was that only in such circumstances did the superior have a genuine interest to enforce the burden. About 2,000 notices were registered.[95] This is a small number when set against the total number of separate titles in Scotland.[96]

Rule 7: non-feudal burdens which are not part of a common scheme

13.34   Rule 6 concerned only real burdens imposed in a feudal deed prior to 28 November 2004. In contrast, rule 7 is restricted to burdens imposed in *non-feudal deeds* such as *dispositions*. It applies in cases of subdivision, but *not* where there is a common scheme. The rule is that the benefited property is implied to be the land retained in the neighbourhood at the time that the burdens were imposed.[97] This was established in *J A Mactaggart & Co v Harrower*.[98] For example, Joelle sells a plot of her land to Keith and imposes real burdens. The benefited property is the land which she retains. Say, however, that she sold a second plot to Leah and imposed the same burdens. In principle, Leah's land would be a benefited property as regards Keith's because it was retained at the time of the grant by Joelle to Keith. But because a common scheme is capable of arising in respect of the plots of Keith and Leah, rule 7 does not confer any enforcement rights upon Leah.[99]

13.35   Rule 7 is a *temporary* one. It does not apply after 28 November 2014. Rule 7 enforcement rights die at that date unless a preservation notice has been registered

---

92   AFT(S)A 2000, s 18.
93   A building was not required in limited cases, for example for rights of pre-emption and redemption or where the nominated benefited property was to be minerals or salmon fishings. See AFT(S)A 2000, s 18(7)(b) and (c). As to whether a toilet block qualified as a building in use as a place of human habitation or resort, see *SQ1 Ltd v Earl of Hopetoun* 2 October 2007, Lands Tribunal, discussed in Reid and Gretton *Conveyancing 2007* (2008) 147–150.
94   AFT(S)A 2000, s 18(7)(a).
95   Reid and Gretton *Conveyancing 2004* (2005) 95.
96   As of June 2008, approximately 2.2 million.
97   TC(S)A 2003, ss 49(2) and 50.
98   (1906) 8 F 1101.
99   TC(S)A 2003, s 50(6).

nominating the benefited property.[100] The notice must be registered against both the benefited and the burdened properties.[101]

The Keeper's role

13.36 Where the burdened property is in the Land Register the Keeper has a statutory duty to enter on the title sheet of the burdened property a statement as to what are the benefited properties, provided that there is sufficient information to let him do this.[102] In such circumstances, he is to enter a parallel statement in the title sheet of any benefited property. Until 28 November 2004, the Keeper had a discretion over the matter. After that date he does not. The idea is that the complexity of the rules set out above will be mitigated by the Keeper stating on title sheets whether implied enforcement rights exist.

ENFORCEMENT

General

13.37 For a real burden to be enforced, both title and interest must be proven.[103]

Title to enforce

13.38 Title to enforce is tied to the benefited property and it was seen above how this property is identified.[104] The owner of it has title to enforce.[105] So too does any tenant or proper liferenter holding a real right, or non-entitled spouse or non-entitled civil partner with occupancy rights.[106] In addition, where a real burden imposes an obligation to pay a cost, the benefited property's owner at the time when the cost was occurred has title too.[107] For example, where someone bears a maintenance cost which is to be shared between a number of properties and then that person sells their property (the benefited property) they still have title to enforce.

---

[100] TC(S)A 2003, s 49(2)
[101] TC(S)A 2003, s 50(3).
[102] TC(S)A 2003, s 58.
[103] TC(S)A 2003, s 8(1).
[104] See PARAS **13.20–13.36** above.
[105] TC(S)A 2003, s 8(2).
[106] TC(S)A 2003, s 8(2)(a) and (b). But not as regards pre-emptions or other options to acquire the burdened property. See TC(S)A 2003, s 8(4). On tenants, see CHAPTER **19** below. On proper liferenters, see CHAPTER **21** below. On non-entitled spouses and partners, see CHAPTER **10** above.
[107] TC(S)A 2003, s 8(2)(c).

Interest to enforce

13.39   Interest to enforce is different from title to enforce: both are necessary for enforcement. There is interest to enforce where the breach of the real burden causes or will cause 'material detriment' to 'the value or enjoyment' of the right held in the benefited property.[108] Two factors particularly relevant are the distance between the properties and the extent of the breach. The greater the distance and the lesser the breach, the less likely it is that there is interest. For example, there is more likely to be interest to enforce a burden preventing building where the burdened proprietor has erected a block of flats as opposed to a shed.

13.40   In *Barker v Lewis*[109] the proprietor of a house in a small rural development began to run a bed-and-breakfast business, which disturbed the neighbouring householders. It breached a real burden prohibiting trading. The neighbours sought interdict, but were unsuccessful before the sheriff, who equated 'material' with 'substantial'.[110] The case was appealed to the sheriff principal. He held that the test was not so strict, but, on the facts, agreed with the sheriff's conclusion that interest had not been shown. The decision, which is controversial, underlines that many breaches of burdens will not be challengeable, because even immediate neighbours may not have interest.

13.41   There is a special rule for affirmative burdens requiring the payment of or contribution towards a cost. Here, a person who is seeking performance of the obligation, and who has grounds to do so, has interest.[111] For example, if in a common scheme, a number of proprietors must meet the repair bill for a private road, the proprietor who pays the contractor has interest to recover from the others their share.

Liability

13.42   Negative and ancillary burdens are enforceable against the owner of the burdened property and any tenant or other occupier.[112] In effect, they are real rights. The policy is that a prohibition would have little practical value if the owner could circumvent it by, say, granting a lease. In contrast, affirmative burdens, such as obligations to maintain or pay costs, are enforceable only against the owner. All that is required here is that one person performs and the law places that obligation on the party who has ownership.[113]

---

[108]   TC(S)A 2003, s 8(3)(a). For discussion, see R Rennie 'Interest to Enforce Real Burdens' in R Rennie *The Promised Land: Property Law Reform* (2008) 1–24.

[109]   2007 SLT (Sh Ct) 48, aff'd 2008 SLT (Sh Ct) 17.

[110]   For criticism, see K G C Reid 'Interest to Enforce Real Burdens: How Material is "Material"?' (2007) 11 *Edin LR* 440.

[111]   TC(S)A 2003, s 8(3)(b).

[112]   TC(S)A 2003, s 9(2).

[113]   TC(S)A 2003, s 9(1).

13.43 Where an owner is liable to perform under a real burden, for example by paying a repair bill, liability persists if the property is sold.[114] The incoming owner is in principle severally liable.[115] Where, however, the obligation is to pay for work already carried out, except where it has been carried out by the local authority, there is only liability if a 'notice of potential liability for costs' has been registered against the title to the property.[116] A similar rule for tenements is found in T(S)A 2004.[117]

Remedies

13.44 At common law it was competent to have an 'irritancy' clause in the constitutive deed.[118] This meant that the benefited proprietor in principle could go to court and have the burdened proprietor's title extinguished if a real burden was breached. The recent legislative reforms sensibly abolished this draconian remedy.[119] This leaves enforcement to be carried out by normal court remedies: action for payment; interdict; specific implement and damages. In the case of interdict, which will be the normal remedy for negative burdens, speed is of the essence. A court is unlikely to order a building which has been completed to be taken down again, even although it breaches a burden.[120] The remedy will become damages and it may be difficult for the benefited proprietor to quantify a loss.

Interpretation

13.45 In the interpretation of real burdens, there is a presumption in favour of freedom. Ambiguous terms are construed *contra proferentem*, that is against the benefited party. In one case, a restriction requiring the property to be used as 'a private dwelling house' was held not to be breached when 25 orphan girls were in residence there.[121] Similarly, piano lessons or legal consultations may be offered in properties subject to this type of burden, provided that the business use is ancillary to the residential use.[122] In another case, an obligation to build a house 'which may include a garage' did not prevent a second garage from being erected.[123]

---

[114] TC(S)A 2003, s 10(1).
[115] TC(S)A 2003, s 10(2). In other words, the benefited proprietor(s) may enforce against him or her.
[116] TC(S)A 2003, s 10(2A) and 10A.
[117] See **PARA 15.22** below.
[118] Compare irritancy clauses in leases. See **PARA 19.30** below.
[119] AFT(S)A 2000, s 53 (feudal burdens); TC(S)A 2003, s 67 (non-feudal burdens). The competency of irritancy in non-feudal cases was in fact doubtful anyway.
[120] An analogy may be made with encroachments. See **PARA 17.15** below.
[121] *Brown v Crum Ewing's Trs* 1918 1 SLT 340.
[122] *Colquhoun's Curator Bonis v Glen's Tr* 1920 SC 737; *Low v Scottish Amicable Building Society* 1940 SLT 295.
[123] *Carswell v Goldie* 1967 SLT 339.

13.46 The approach of the courts in the past to real burdens verged on the hostile.[124] This was probably because before 1970 it was not possible to go to the Lands Tribunal to seek variation or discharge. In recent times the attitude has softened somewhat.[125] Moreover, TC(S)A 2003 now says that 'real burdens shall be construed in the same manner as other provisions of deeds which relate to land and are intended for registration'.[126] The effect is that they should be interpreted reasonably, but objectively. But the presumption in favour of freedom remains, so it is not clear that any of the cases mentioned in PARA **13.45** would be decided differently today.

DIVISION

Burdened property

13.47 Where a burdened property is divided, each part remains subject to the real burden.[127] This applies whether the division took place before or after 28 November 2004. There is an exception where the burden does not relate to one of the parts. For example, a house with a large garden might be subject to a requirement to maintain the house. If part of the garden is sold, that real burden will not apply to it, because it relates to the house only.

Benefited property

13.48 If a benefited property is divided, the part transferred normally will cease to be able to enforce the real burden.[128] There are three exceptions.
  (1) The rule can be overridden by making contrary provision in the conveyance.[129]
  (2) It does not apply to real burdens imposed under a common scheme.[130] Suppose that a house is situated in a development subject to a deed of conditions creating community burdens. If part of the garden is sold, it will continue to be a benefited property in relation to the burdens.
  (3) The rule only applies to conveyances since 28 November 2004.

FEUDAL ABOLITION

13.49 Feudal abolition in principle extinguished feudal real burdens.[131] In practice, most continue to exist, non-feudally, because they were imposed as part of a common

---

[124] Reid *Property* para 415.
[125] See, for example, *Grampian Joint Police Board v Pearson* 2001 SC 772.
[126] TC(S)A 2003, s 14.
[127] TC(S)A 2003, s 13.
[128] TC(S)A 2003, s 12(1).
[129] TC(S)A 2003, s 12(1) and (3).
[130] TC(S)A 2003, s 12(4).
[131] AFT(S)A 2000, s 17. On the feudal system generally, see **APPENDIX** below.

scheme and thus remain enforceable under the rules outlined above.[132] Moreover, as has been seen, a procedure existed for superiors to reallot feudal burdens if they owned neighbouring land which satisfied certain conditions.[133] In addition, the abolition legislation allowed some feudal burdens to be converted into personal real burdens.[134] This means that essentially the only burdens which were lost were those which were not part of a common scheme and did not have a reallotment or conversion notice registered. If such burdens entered the Land Register, they will continue to be there, because the Keeper may not remove them until 28 November 2014.[135]

PERSONAL REAL BURDENS

General

13.50   As has been seen, feudal real burdens could be enforced even although the superior (the benefited proprietor) did not own any land neighbouring the burdened property.[136] Feudal abolition ended this. It was felt, however, that it was justified in a limited number of cases for there to be real burdens which do not have a benefited property. Accordingly, TC(S)A 2003 introduced the 'personal real burden'.[137] As will be seen, they are generally restricted as to content or holder or both. Apart from the absence of a benefited property, the rules are much for the same as for praedial rule burdens. Interest to enforce, however, is presumed.[138] Eight types of personal real burden are recognised.[139] They are given in the following paragraphs. In practice, all are unusual.

Conservation burdens

13.51   These can be held only by the Scottish Ministers or by bodies listed by statutory instrument.[140] This list currently includes all local authorities, Scottish Natural Heritage and the Royal Society for the Protection of Birds. Conservation burdens must be for 'preserving or protecting for the benefit of the public the architectural or historical characteristics of land' of its 'other special characteristics'

---

132   See PARAS **13.24–13.30** above.
133   See PARA **13.33** above.
134   AFT(S)A 2000, ss 18A, 18B, 18C, 27 and 27A. On personal real burdens, see paras **13.50–13.58** below. The numbers of such conversion notices were low: about 1,000 in total. See Reid and Gretton *Conveyancing 2004* (2005) 95–96.
135   AFT(S)A 2000, s 46 and Abolition of Feudal Tenure etc (Scotland) (Prescribed Periods) Order 2004 (SSI 2004/478) para 3.
136   See PARA **13.2** above.
137   See further Paisley 'Personal Real Burdens' 2005 *JR* 377.
138   TC(S)A 2003, s 47.
139   TC(S)A 2003, s 1(3).
140   TC(S)A 2003, s 38(4).

which can include nature conservation.[141] The right to a conservation burden can be assigned to another conservation body or to the Scottish Ministers.[142] If a conservation body is delisted, the burden is extinguished.[143]

Economic development burdens

13.52 Only the Scottish Ministers or local authorities may hold these burdens.[144] An economic development burden must promote economic development.[145] What is envisaged is a public body selling land, but requiring it to be used for a particular type of industry. An obligation to pay money can be constituted as an economic development burden.[146] For example, the purchaser may be required to make a payment if the land is subsequently sold. The right to an economic development burden cannot be assigned.[147]

Health care burdens

13.53 Only the Scottish Ministers can hold these burdens, which must promote the provision of health care facilities.[148] For example, land might be sold to a builder on condition that accommodation for nurses is constructed. Like the economic development burden, an obligation to pay a sum of money may be imposed and the right to the burden cannot be assigned.[149]

Maritime burdens

13.54 The Crown on behalf of the public may impose real burdens on the sea bed or foreshore.[150] These cannot be assigned.[151] For example, a section of the sea bed may be sold for the purposes of fish farming, but under certain conditions.

---

[141] TC(S)A 2003, s 38(1).
[142] TC(S)A 2003, s 39.
[143] TC(S)A 2003, s 42.
[144] TC(S)A 2003, s 45(1).
[145] TC(S)A 2003, s 45(1).
[146] TC(S)A 2003, s 45(3).
[147] TC(S)A 2003, s 45(4)(b).
[148] TC(S)A 2003, s 46(1).
[149] TC(S)A 2003, s 46(3) and (4)(b).
[150] TC(S)A 2003, s 44(1). The right is limited to territorial waters. See TC(S)A 2003, s 44(3) and see PARA **16.4** below.
[151] TC(S)A 2003, s 44(2).

Rural housing burdens

13.55   Only designated 'rural housing bodies' may hold these burdens.[152] Their content is limited to pre-emption rights.[153] The policy is to protect bodies that offer housing at a reduced price. If the purchaser wishes later to sell, a rural housing burden enables the body to buy it back and make it available to others in need of suitable accommodation, as opposed (for example) to it becoming a holiday home. Unlike ordinary pre-emption rights, they are not extinguished on first sale.[154] Like conservation burdens, rural housing burdens are assignable (but only to other rural housing bodies) and will be extinguished if the body is delisted.[155]

Manager burdens

13.56   These can be imposed by a developer. They give the sole right to appoint a manager for a development until the earlier of (a) 90 days after the last property in the development is sold and (b) the long-stop date.[156] For sheltered or retirement housing developments, the long-stop date is three years after the burden was imposed.[157] For former local authority housing, it is 30 years.[158] In all other cases, it is five years.[159] The policy is to let developers keep a measure of control over incomplete developments. A manager burden is assignable.[160]

Personal pre-emption burdens

13.57   Where a superior registered a conversion notice for a pre-emption burden before 28 November 2004, this became a personal pre-emption burden.[161] The category is thus limited to former feudal burdens which conferred a right of pre-emption. These will normally be extinguished upon the first sale of the property.[162]

Personal redemption burdens

13.58   Like personal pre-emption burdens, these are confined to former feudal burdens for which the superior has registered a conversion notice.[163] Only 642 notices

---

[152]   TC(S)A 2003, s 43(1) and (5).
[153]   TC(S)A 2003, s 43(1). On pre-emption rights, see PARA **13.12** above.
[154]   TC(S)A 2003, s 84(1).
[155]   TC(S)A 2003, s 43(10).
[156]   TC(S)A 2003, s 63(1), (2) and (4).
[157]   TC(S)A 2003, s 63(5)(b).
[158]   TC(S)A 2003, s 63(5)(a) and (6).
[159]   TC(S)A 2003, s 63(5)(c).
[160]   TC(S)A 2003, s 63(3).
[161]   AFT(S)A 2000, s 18A.
[162]   Provided that the property is offered to the holder. See TC(S)A 2003, ss 82 and 84(1).
[163]   AFT(S)A 2000, s 18A.

were registered.[164] If created in a post-1974 deed, the burden is limited to a period of 20 years from its constitution.[165]

EXTINCTION

Express discharge

Minutes of waiver

13.59   The form of deed used to extinguish a real burden is variously known as a deed of discharge, or deed or minute of waiver. Obviously, this must be granted by the holder of the burden. The price is a matter for negotiation. (If the burden is one of doubtful validity or one that the Lands Tribunal would be prepared to discharge, the price will be low.) The deed then requires to be registered against the title to the burdened property.[166] Often a minute of waiver varies a burden rather than completely discharging it. For example, a prohibition against building might be waived but only for a new garage.

Community burdens

13.60   In the case of community burdens, in principle all benefited proprietors must sign. This is often not practical, as it may involve getting many signatories. The general rule is therefore mitigated by special rules of variation and discharge which allow for minutes of waiver to bind non-signatories.

13.61   TC(S)A 2003, s 33 provides that a simple majority of the owners in the community[167] (or a manager on behalf of the majority of owners in the community) can sign a deed of variation or discharge.[168] Once signed the deed must be intimated to non-signatories. This requires a copy of the deed, and a notice to be sent to non-signatory benefited proprietors.[169] The notice must identify the affected property, the nature of the variation, and intimate that the recipient has at least eight weeks to apply to the Lands Tribunal to preserve the burden.[170]

13.62   An alternative procedure is available under TC(S)A 2003, s 35 which requires the deed to be signed only by the owners of 'adjacent units', that is those properties

---

[164]   Reid and Gretton *Conveyancing 2004* (2005) 95.
[165]   Land Tenure Reform (Scotland) Act 1974, s 12. See PARA **13.13** above.
[166]   TC(S)A 2003, ss 15 and 48.
[167]   When calculating what constitutes a majority, the property seeking the waiver is counted. See TC(S)A 2003, s 33(3). It is possible for the deed creating the burden to make special provision, e.g., require a two-thirds majority. See TC(S)A 2003, s 33(1)(a).
[168]   TC(S)A 2003, s 33.
[169]   TC(S)A 2003, s 34(1) and (2).
[170]   TC(S)A 2003, Sch 4.

within 4 metres of the burdened property excluding public roads less than 20 metres wide.[171] This is intended to mirror the neighbour notification rules in planning applications. There are generally two possible options for intimation here: a notice sent to each non-signatory benefited owner;[172] or attaching a notice to the burdened property and to lamp-posts in the vicinity of the burdened property.[173] In practice the latter is more likely because the uncertainty in relation to implied enforcement rights may make the identification of the parameters of a community difficult.[174] If there are no lamp-posts within 100 metres then an advertisement in a local newspaper is competent.[175] The notices identify the burdened property and the burdens in question and intimate to the benefited proprietors that they have eight weeks to apply to the Lands Tribunal to preserve the burden.[176]

13.63 A benefited proprietor who has not assented to the deed may object by applying to the Tribunal within eight weeks of intimation of the proposal to register it.[177] The application is then notified to the burdened proprietor.[178] If he or she does not respond the burden is preserved.[179] If the burdened proprietor objects to the application the preservation of the burden is considered by the Tribunal, but it will grant it only if the variation is not in the best interests of the proprietors of all the properties in the community; or is unfairly prejudicial to one or more of them.[180]

13.64 In order to register the deed executed under both TC(S)A 2003, ss 33 and 35, an application must be made to the Tribunal seeking a certificate that either no applications to preserve the burdens were timeously received or that applications were received but withdrawn.[181] An oath must also be sworn or affirmed by the burdened proprietor confirming compliance with the appropriate intimation procedure and the deed endorsed to this effect.[182] It is then registered and the burden is thereby varied or extinguished.

'Sunset rule'

13.65 A special termination procedure was introduced by TC(S)A 2003, known informally as the 'sunset rule'. In principle, any burden created in a deed registered

---

[171] TC(S)A 2003, ss 32 and 125. This procedure is not available for facility or service burdens, or in sheltered or retirement housing developments. See s 35(1)(a).
[172] TC(S)A 2003, s 36(2)(a) and Sch 5.
[173] TC(S)A 2003, s 36(2)(b) and Sch 6.
[174] See PARAS **13.24–13.26** above.
[175] TC(S)A 2003, s 36(2)(c).
[176] TC(S)A 2003, s 36(3) and Schs 5 and 6.
[177] TC(S)A 2003, s 34(3) and 37(1).
[178] TC(S)A 2003, s 93(1)(c).
[179] TC(S)A 2003, s 97(1)(c).
[180] For an example of an unsuccessful application, see *Sheltered Housing Management Ltd v Jack* 2007 GWD 32-533.
[181] TC(S)A 2003, ss 34(4)–(6) and 37(2).
[182] TC(S)A 2003, s 37(4).

at least 100 years ago may be discharged by the burdened owner.[183] This person is alarmingly called the 'terminator'.[184] The procedure is not available for conservation burdens, maritime burdens, facility burdens and service burdens.[185] A notice is drawn up in the required form[186] and intimated to the benefited proprietors. Those within 4 metres (discounting roads less than 20 metres wide) are sent a copy of the notice.[187] More distant neighbours are notified through posting notices on lamp-posts within the vicinity of the burdened property and by a notice placed at the property itself.[188]

13.66   After receiving notice benefited owners must then decide whether to apply to the Lands Tribunal for renewal of the burden.[189] They have eight weeks to do this.[190] If the application to preserve the burden is successful the burden survives. If unsuccessful the burdens will be varied or discharged. Where no application to preserve is made,[191] the notice of termination can be registered provided it is endorsed with a Lands Tribunal certificate confirming the lack of applications.[192] When endorsed and registered the burdens are extinguished.[193]

By breach

Negative prescription

13.67   If a real burden is contravened without challenge for five years, it is extinguished to the extent of the breach.[194] For example, if there was a general obligation not to build and a conservatory was constructed, the passing of five years would mean that this addition could not be challenged but it would not prevent a successful objection to the erection of a new house.

---

[183]   TC(S)A 2003, s 20.
[184]   TC(S)A 2003, s 20(2).
[185]   TC(S)A 2003, s 20(3).
[186]   TC(S)A 2003, s 21 and Schs 2 and 3.
[187]   TC(S)A 2003, s 21(2)(a) and (3)(b).
[188]   TC(S)A 2003, s 21(2)(b). If there are no lamp-posts, advertisement in a local newspaper is competent. See TC(S)A 2003, s 21(2)(c).
[189]   TC(S)A 2003, s 90(i)(b)(i). For an example, where the application was unsuccessful, see *Brown v Richardson* 2007 GWD 28-490.
[190]   TC(S)A 2003, s 20(5).
[191]   Or if it does not extend to all the burdens, or all the benefited properties.
[192]   TC(S)A 2003, s 23.
[193]   TC(S)A 2003, s 24. This is subject to the outcome of any Tribunal application which has been made. For example, only one of the benefited proprietors may have applied. The certificate will then disclose the lack of application from the others.
[194]   TC(S)A 2003, s 18.

Acquiescence

13.68   The idea of acquiescence is that a benefited proprietor who stands by and watches while a real burden is being breached should not be allowed to object later. The common law here, which is not entirely clear, continues to apply.[195] TC(S)A 2003, however, introduces a parallel rule.[196] The following criteria must be met:

(a) material expenditure is incurred by the burdened proprietor (or other person against whom the burden can be enforced, for example a tenant);

(b) the benefit of the expenditure would be substantially lost if the burden were now to be enforced;

(c) *either* the owner of the benefited property consented to the work, whether formally or informally; *or* (and more typically) *all* those with enforcement rights (including tenants) either consented or did not object within 12 weeks after substantial completion; and

(d) the work is sufficiently obvious that those with the right to enforce knew, or should have known, about it.

If these criteria are satisfied the burden will be extinguished to the extent of the breach. Successors of the benefited proprietor(s) will therefore be bound.

13.69   In fact, TC(S)A 2003 goes further to help a burdened proprietor. If the 12-week period has expired, there is a presumption that no objection was made and hence that acquiescence has operated.[197] The presumption is difficult to overcome, particularly where the work was completed some time ago.

No interest to enforce

13.70   A real burden which is breached at a time when there is nobody with an interest to enforce is extinguished to the extent of the breach.[198] Thus it might be the case that there is no longer interest to enforce a burden preventing trading when every other house in the street is now used as business premises.[199]

Lands Tribunal

13.71   The Lands Tribunal[200] was given jurisdiction in 1970 to vary or discharge real burdens.[201] This is now regulated by TC(S)A 2003, Pt 9. Any party who is subject

---

[195]   See Reid *Property* para 427. See also S Wortley 'Real Burdens and Personal Bar' in Rennie *The Promised Land: Property Law Reform* 25–70.

[196]   TC(S)A 2003, s 16(1). See E C Reid and J W G Blackie, *Personal Bar* (2006) paras 6-29–6-44.

[197]   TC(S)A 2003, s 16(2).

[198]   TC(S)A 2003, s 17.

[199]   *Howard de Walden Estates Ltd v Bowmaker Ltd* 1965 SC 163. But compare Reid *Property* para 430.

[200]   See http://www.lands-tribunal-scotland.org.uk/.

[201]   CFR(S)A 1970, ss 1 and 2. Application was also possible in respect of other 'land obligations' including servitudes.

to a real burden, servitude or other title condition is entitled to apply to the Tribunal for its variation or discharge.[202] When it receives an application, the Tribunal *must* intimate it to various parties, notably the benefited proprietor(s), or – in the case of a personal real burden – the holder.[203] The Tribunal *may* intimate to other parties, for example, tenants, if it thinks fit.[204] The parties to whom intimation is made are given at least 21 days to make representations.[205]

13.72   Where no benefited owner objects to the application, it is normally granted automatically and without further inquiry.[206] In this event the process is effectively an administrative one. Where, however, objection is made, the Tribunal must consider the application on its merits. It may grant the application if it is reasonable so to do.[207] But regard must be had to ten factors set out in TC(S)A 2003, s 100. Each case is therefore decided on the facts. In most cases, however, the Tribunal has granted the application.[208] The discharge or variation then takes effect on registration of the Tribunal order.[209]

13.73   The Tribunal is entitled to award compensation to the benefited proprietor but only in very limited circumstances, or to impose a replacement burden.[210] When determining the question of expenses, the Tribunal must pay particular regard to the extent of the application, or any opposition thereto.[211] Hence, an unsuccessful objector is likely to have to meet the applicant's costs.

Compulsory purchase

13.74   The rules here are the same as for servitudes.[212]

Confusion

13.75   This is not strictly a type of termination but may be dealt with conveniently here. If the benefited proprietor becomes owner of the burdened property, the doctrine of confusion naturally prevents enforcement of the real burden. In this situation,

---

[202]   TC(S)A 2003, s 90(1)(a).
[203]   TC(S)A 2003, s 93(1).
[204]   TC(S)A 2003, s 93(3).
[205]   TC(S)A 2003, ss 95 and 96.
[206]   TC(S)A 2003, s 97.
[207]   TC(S)A 2003, s 98.
[208]   See, e.g., *Ord v Mashford* 2006 SLT (Lands Tr) 15 and *Church of Scotland General Trs v McLaren* 2006 SLT (Lands Tr) 27. For a review of the case law, see Reid and Gretton *Conveyancing 2007* (2008) 83–101.
[209]   TC(S)A 2003, s 104(2).
[210]   TC(S)A 2003, s 90(6)–(11).
[211]   TC(S)A 2003, s 103.
[212]   See PARA **12.48** above.

TC(S)A 2003 provides that the burden is not extinguished.[213] In effect, it is 'suspended'. This means that if the properties come into different hands once again then it can be enforced. During the period of confusion, however, the proprietor could register a minute of waiver and this would remove the burden.

FURTHER READING

Gretton and Reid *Conveyancing* ch 13.

McDonald *Conveyancing Manual* chs 15, 17 and 18.

Rennie *Land Tenure* chs 5–9.

Reid *Feudal Abolition* chs 2–7.

Scottish Law Commission *Report on Real Burdens* (Scot Law Com No 181, 2000).

---

[213] TC(S)A 2003, s 19. Compare the rule for servitudes: see PARA **12.47** above.

Chapter 14

Landownership

INTRODUCTION

14.1   This chapter covers three aspects of landownership:
  (1) determination of horizontal and vertical boundaries;
  (2) parts and pertinents; and
  (3) separate tenements.
A number of related areas, such as boundary walls and encroachment, are treated in the chapter on neighbour law.[1]

[1]   See **CHAPTER 17** below.

HORIZONTAL BOUNDARIES

Land Register

14.2 As discussed elsewhere,[2] land may be registered either in the Sasine Register or in the Land Register. The latter is slowly but surely superseding the former because properties are transferred into the Land Register when they are sold. Ascertaining the horizontal boundaries of land differs as between the two registers. In the Land Register the title sheet for a property will always identify it by means of a plan based on the Ordnance Map.[3] In the case of flats, the title plan identifies the site of the building and any surrounding ground owned or co-owned by the flat owner. A verbal description, for example 'Flat 2/1 St Alison's Street, Edinburgh, being the northmost flat on the ground floor of the tenement known as 2 St Alison's Street, Edinburgh', is used to identify the flat itself. It follows in the Land Register that, subject to the limits of scaling on the plans used,[4] it is easy to determine the exact boundaries.

Sasine Register

14.3 In contrast to the Land Register, the Sasine Register is not map-based. Indeed, though this register was established in 1617, it only became competent to record plans attached to deeds in 1924.[5] While plans have been increasingly used, there is no requirement for this and therefore many titles to land are not based on a plan.

14.4 There is a distinction between a 'bounding' description, which states the boundaries, and a 'general' description, which does not. A bounding description can do this in various ways. It might say 'bounded on the north by the southern edge of the High Street'. It can use measurements. It can be a pictorial representation, i.e. a plan. It is common for modern Sasine deeds to use all of these methods. If there is an irreconcilable conflict between them there are rules for resolving this.[6] In particular, the plan will prevail if it is declared to be 'taxative'. It is also possible to have a bounding description by reference to an earlier recorded deed containing such a description.[7] This means that there is no need to have a long verbal description or prepare a fresh plan every time the land is transferred.

14.5 A general description is vaguer than a bounding description. It might be a postal address or the name of a farm. As the boundaries are not given, the dimensions of the title will need to be determined by extrinsic evidence. That evidence is normally the state of possession. Moreover, where there has been possession for ten years which is open, peaceable and without judicial interruption, a title to the

---

2 See **CHAPTER 6** above.
3 LR(S)A 1979, s 6(1)(a). See **PARA 6.24** above.
4 *Registration of Title Practice Book* para 4.26.
5 Conveyancing (Scotland) Act 1924, s 48.
6 Gordon *Scottish Land Law* para 4.08.
7 Conveyancing (Scotland) Act 1874, s 61.

land as possessed will be established by positive prescription.[8] This is subject to the deed containing the description being valid on the face of it and being capable of being read as covering the land as possessed.

Sasine Register to Land Register

14.6 A general description will not suffice for the Land Register. So if there is land which, in the Sasine Register, has had only a general description, or indeed a bounding description that is not precise enough, and the land is to be transferred to the Land Register, a plan will be needed so that the Keeper can plot the property on the Ordnance Map. Where boundaries are unclear it is possible for the affected parties to enter into a deed known as a s 19 agreement to clarify the position.[9]

VERTICAL BOUNDARIES

From the heavens to the centre of the earth

14.7 Ownership of land is *a coelo usque ad centrum* – 'from the heavens to the centre [of the earth]'. Thus, landownership is conical. Above the ground it includes airspace, to a ceiling of 100 kilometres,[10] and anything that has acceded, such as buildings and trees. In England, the position is different. The idea that there is ownership up to the heavens was criticised by a judge as 'leading to the absurdity of a trespass ... being committed by a satellite every time it passes over a suburban garden'.[11] So, south of the border, a landowner only has rights in the airspace 'to such height as is necessary for the ordinary use and enjoyment of his land'.[12] The ownership of airspace enables action against trespass into it, as in the situation where the jib of a crane swings across without permission.[13] In the case of aircraft, however, statute provides that there is no trespass if the flight is at a reasonable height, having regard to the wind, the weather and all the circumstances of the case.[14]

---

8   PL(S)A 1973, s 1. See **PARA 2.24** above.
9   LR(S)A 1979, s 19.
10   Art II of the Outer Space Treaty 1967 provides that 'outer space ... is not subject to national appropriation by claim of sovereignty'. Since national sovereignty ends where space begins, presumably heritable title stops there too. International law has not yet defined the start of space but it is generally regarded as being 100 km above sea level.
11   *Bernstein v Skyviews and General Ltd* [1978] QB 479 at 487 per Griffiths J.
12   *Bernstein* at 488. Professor Paisley is sympathetic to this view: 'since the advent of aviation and the use of space ... any theory asserting infinite nature of the upward boundaries is questionable' (Paisley *Land Law* para 4.22).
13   *Brown v Lee Constructions Ltd* 1977 SLT (Notes) 61.
14   Civil Aviation Act 1982, s 76.

The exception of separate tenements

14.8   Ownership from the heavens to the centre of the earth is subject to separate tenements such as minerals and flats. These are discussed below.[15]

PARTS AND PERTINENTS

General

14.9   Ownership of a piece of land carries with it ownership of the 'parts and pertinents'. These are things which are transferred to the new owner automatically, without the need for express written provision. It is nevertheless standard (albeit pointless) practice in a disposition of land in the Sasine Register to have a clause conveying the parts and pertinents. In the Land Register, this is usually omitted.[16] 'Parts' is an obscure and possibly meaningless term. It may mean things that have acceded.[17] 'Pertinents' has a fairly clear meaning: rights exercisable beyond the boundaries of the principal land. Pertinents divide into:

(1) corporeal pertinents, subdividing into:
   (a) additional land and
   (b) rights of common property, and
(2) incorporeal pertinents.

Corporeal pertinents

Additional land

14.10   There may be additional heritable property which is regarded as a pertinent of the land. Examples include lock-up garages and parking spaces serving a house or flat. Such additional land must be discontiguous to the principal land, otherwise it will simply be part of it. It will become a pertinent in one of two ways. The first is by express grant. For example, when a building company sells a new flat for the first time it conveys it together with a parking space. The second way is by positive prescription.[18] However, it is not possible to acquire title to a pertinent this way where a bounding description is used in the would-be foundation writ and the pertinent

---

15   See **PARAS 14.13–14.18** below.

16   Perhaps because LR(S)A 1979, s 3(1)(a) says that on registration 'any right, pertinent or servitude … forming part of' the land is vested in the transferee. But the same is true in the Sasine Register and indeed it is just general property law. The phrase 'pertinent or servitude' is odd because a servitude is a pertinent.

17   Reid *Property* para 200.

18   See **PARAS 2.26–2.29** above.

lies outwith the boundaries of that.[19] These rules developed for property in the Sasine Register. It is unclear what significance they have for property in the Land Register, which is map-based. A lock-up garage, for example, would be mapped.

Common property

14.11   Rights of common property may be pertinents of the principal land. The most important example is flats. It is possible to make certain parts of the tenement, such as the roof, common property by expressly granting *pro indiviso* shares of these to the flat owners. Moreover, under the Tenements (Scotland) Act 2004, s 3, a number of the parts of the building, notably the close or stair, are deemed to be owned in common and pertinents of the flats which they serve.[20] An example not involving a tenement is a common recreation area owned by the houses surrounding it. Here again, because the Land Register is map-based the significance of additional land being a pertinent is slight, though the Keeper does sometimes register common property without mapping it. Whether this is lawful is arguable.[21]

Incorporeal pertinents

14.12   The only example of any importance of an incorporeal pertinent is the benefit of a title condition,[22] such as a praedial real burden or servitude exercisable over a neighbour's land. As such, it is enforceable by the owner for the time being of the principal land against the owner of the adjacent land.

SEPARATE TENEMENTS

General

14.13   The doctrine of separate tenements is the exception to the rule, discussed above, that ownership of land is from the heavens to the centre of the earth.[23] A 'separate tenement' is a section of the land or a right to do something on the land which is capable of separate ownership. This is a different meaning to 'tenement' in the sense of a block of flats.[24] A separate tenement is transferred in its own right. It is also possible to create subordinate rights, such as a standard security over it.[25]

---

[19]   Stair II, 3, 73; Erskine II, 6, 3; Bell *Principles* s 739.
[20]   See PARAS **15.10–15.11** below.
[21]   The subject is complex. See further *PMP Plus Ltd v Keeper of the Registers of Scotland*, 20 November 2008, Lands Tribunal.
[22]   See PARA **13.3** above.
[23]   See PARAS **14.7–14.8** above.
[24]   But the individual flats are conventional separate tenements. See PARA **14.14** below.
[25]   CFR(S)A 1970, s 9(2), (8)(b).

There are two types of separate tenement: those which are 'conventional' and those which are 'legal'.

Conventional separate tenements

14.14 Where a section of land is separated from the remainder by express conveyance, this is known as a 'conventional separate tenement'. Below ground, it appears that there is no restriction on the creation of conventional separate tenements. The leading example is minerals[26] but tunnels and underground shelters may be other possibilities. Above ground, the position is rather limited. It is, of course, accepted that buildings can be divided into flats. Property such as trees or pipes which have become heritable by accession cannot be made into separate tenements. The position as regards bridges and unoccupied airspace is unclear.

14.15 With one modern exception, all conventional separate tenements must be corporeal. That exception is sporting rights reserved by superiors before 28 November 2004 under the feudal abolition legislation.[27] These are restricted to rights of fishing and game.[28] There were in fact only 65 such preservations.[29] The separate tenement created here is rather peculiar, as it can be non-exclusive.[30] Therefore the right, for example, to fish can be shared with the owner of the principal land. This is contrary to the usual notion of separate tenements.

Legal separate tenements

14.16 All land in Scotland was originally owned by the Crown. Historically, certain rights were considered so important that they were impliedly reserved when land was granted. These rights, known as the *regalia minora*, could be expressly granted to either the new landowner or another person. If they were not, they remained with the Crown. With one exception, all legal separate tenements in so far as not already granted out are Crown property. They can be either corporeal or incorporeal.

14.17 The main legal separate tenements are as follows:
(a) The right to fish for salmon. This is the most important legal separate tenement. If, for example, a section of river is sold by the Crown to Audrey, this will include the right to fish for fish other than salmon. The salmon fishing rights do not form part of this title – unless also conveyed – and may be held by someone other than the owner of the river bed or the banks.[31] If

---

[26]   But gold, silver and coal when still in the ground are legal separate tenements. On minerals generally, see R Rennie, *Minerals and the Law in Scotland* (2001).

[27]   AFT(S)A 2000, s 65A.

[28]   AFT(S)A 2000, s 65A(9).

[29]   Reid and Gretton *Conveyancing 2004* (2005) 96.

[30]   AFT(S)A 2000, s 65A(6).

[31]   Stair II, 3, 69.

Bert owns the salmon rights, both he and Audrey could fish on the same stretch of the river, but for different fish.

(b) The right to gather mussels and oysters.[32]

(c) Mines of gold and silver. Of course, such metals are rare in Scotland. Under the Royal Mines Act 1424, the oldest Scottish statute still in force, mines of these are reserved from grants of land by the Crown. There is, however, a statutory right giving landowners the right to obtain a separate grant of such mines within their land. In return they must pay the Crown one-tenth of all metal mined.[33]

(d) Petroleum and natural gas.[34]

(e) Coal. This is the exception to the rule that the legal separate tenements are part of the *regalia minora*. Coal is vested in the Coal Authority.[35]

No accession across the boundaries

14.18 Accession cannot take place across the boundaries of separate tenements. For example, a chandelier hung by Tom from the ceiling of his ground-floor flat will not accede to the flat above.

FURTHER READING

Gordon *Scottish Land Law* paras 4.01–4.16.

Paisley *Land Law* paras 1.11–1.14; 4.16–4.23.

Reid *Property* paras 193–212.

Registration of Title Practice Book ch 4.

Rennie, R *Minerals and the Law in Scotland* (2001).

[32]   Reid *Property* paras 320–330.
[33]   Mines and Metals Act 1592.
[34]   Petroleum Act 1998, Sch 3, para 3.
[35]   Coal Industry Act 1994, s 7(3).

Chapter 15

Tenements and developments

TENEMENTS: GENERAL

The Tenements (Scotland) Act 2004: a default code

15.1 The Tenements (Scotland) Act 2004 (T(S)A 2004) codified the common law of the tenement and filled gaps and clarified uncertainties. It is essential reading. The legislation is based on the Scottish Law Commission Report on the Law of the Tenement[1] to which useful reference may also be made. Like the common law, a fundamental feature of T(S)A 2004 is that it is a 'background' or 'default' law. This means that it is subject to the title of the property in question. An express term in the title, for example a statement as to ownership of a particular part of the building, will prevail over T(S)A 2004.[2] An important part of the legislation is the 'Tenement Management Scheme' which contains a set of model rules governing decision making and liability for costs relating to the building.[3] Again, as a default law, this is normally subject to any real burdens.[4]

Definitions

15.2 All tenements, old and new, are governed by the legislation, provided that they meet the definition of 'tenement'. For the purposes of T(S)A 2004, this is 'a building or a part of a building which comprises two related flats at least two of which (a) are, or are designed to be, in separate ownership; and (b) are divided from each other horizontally'.[5] Horizontal division is crucial. If properties are divided vertically, that is a terrace, not a tenement.[6] The definition is broad and is capable of embracing both a modern multi-storey apartment block and a substantial Victorian dwelling house which has been converted into an upper and a lower flat. A reference to a 'tenement' for the purposes of the legislation includes the *solum*, i.e. the ground on which the building stands and the land pertaining to the building.[7] In some cases, for example a flatted building on the corner of two roads with a shared roof but different entrances, it may be difficult to ascertain exactly what constitutes the actual tenement for the purposes of T(S)A 2004. Recourse, however, can be made to the title to the tenement and any real burdens affecting it to determine the matter.[8]

15.3 The word 'tenement' has at least two other usages in Scots law, which are different from the one which is the subject of this chapter. The first is found in the

---

[1]   Scottish Law Commission *Report on the Law of the Tenement* (1998).
[2]   T(S)A 2004, s 1(1).
[3]   See **PARA 15.12** below.
[4]   T(S)A 2004, s 4.
[5]   T(S)A 2004, s 26(1).
[6]   Although one of the authors has seen the title deeds for a terrace in which it is described as a 'tenement'.
[7]   T(S)A 2004, s 26(1).
[8]   T(S)A 2004, s 26(2).

traditional terms for 'benefited property' and 'burdened property' in relation to a servitude: the 'dominant tenement' and 'servient tenement'.[9] Here, 'tenement' simply means 'piece of heritable property'. The second is found within the expressions 'conventional separate tenement' and 'legal separate tenement', which were discussed in **Chapter 14**.[10] Again, 'tenement' here means 'a piece of property', but specifically one that can be held separately from the ground. A tenement flat is an example of a conventional separate tenement.

15.4   T(S)A 2004 defines 'flat' as including any premises. These do not require to be limited to residential use or confined to one floor.[11] This confirms that the legislation applies to tenements in which some or all of the units are commercial, for example shops. Moreover, a unit could comprise two storeys, as in the so-called 'double upper flat'.

DEFAULT RULES OF TENEMENT OWNERSHIP

General

15.5   The common law rules are codified and expanded upon by T(S)A 2004, ss 1– 3. The legislation uses common ownership very sparingly. There is good reason for this. As has been seen elsewhere, common ownership has a tendency to give rise to disputes and generally requires unanimity for decisions.[12] Where builders have disapplied the common law and used common property expansively, the result may be problematic.[13]

15.6   The starting point is that the individual owners have exclusive ownership of their flats. Rules are then provided to deal with boundaries and pertinents.

Boundaries

15.7   T(S)A 2004 divides the tenement into 'sectors'. A 'sector' is defined to mean '(a) a flat; (b) any close or lift; or (c) any other three dimensional space'[14] in the building. An example of the third category would be a cellar. The boundary between different sectors is normally 'the median of the structure that separates them'[15] – in other words, the centre line or mid-point. For example, the boundary between a flat

---

9   See, for example, Cusine and Paisley *Servitudes and Rights of Way* (1998) para 2.05.
10   See **paras 14.13–14.17** above.
11   T(S)A 2004, s 29(1). For an example, see *PS Properties (2) Ltd v Callaway Homes Ltd* 2007 GWD 31-526.
12   See **para 9.8** above.
13   See *Rafique v Amin* 1997 SLT 1385.
14   T(S)A 2004, s 29(1).
15   T(S)A 2004, s 2(1).

and the flat above will be the mid-point of the ceiling of the lower flat and the floor of the upper flat. The boundary between a flat and the close (common stair) will be the centre line of the dividing wall. There is an exception to the normal median rule for things which wholly or mainly serve one sector, for example the front door of a flat. Such things are regarded as belonging entirely to the owner of the sector.[16]

15.8 External walls are owned exclusively by the sector in question.[17] This means, for instance, that the front wall of the building is owned in sections by the owners of the front-facing flats.

15.9 Ownership of a top flat includes ownership of the roof above it.[18] If there is more than one top flat, the roof will be owned in sections. Similarly, ownership of a bottom flat carries with it the solum under the flat.[19] The 'solum' means 'the ground on which a building is erected'.[20] The close (common stair) includes the roof above it and the solum beneath it.[21] The ownership of the solum (or part of it) includes the ownership of the airspace directly above the building (or relevant part of it).[22] For example, if there is a north basement flat, it includes the north area of airspace. There is a special rule for the triangular sector of airspace above a sloping roof. It belongs to the roof's owner.[23] So a dormer window can be constructed. (Subject to building and planning consent, and assuming that it is not barred by a real burden.)

Pertinents

15.10 The close is a pertinent of all the flats which take access through it.[24] 'Close' means 'a connected passage, stairs and landings within a tenement building which together constitute a common access to two or more of the flats'.[25] A main-door flat which takes entry directly from the street and not through the close is excluded from ownership of it.[26] There is a similar rule if there is a lift. Once again, it will be co-owned by the flats using it for access, but not, in this case, a ground-floor flat which does not need it.[27]

15.11 The ground around the building, such as a back green, belongs to the flat adjacent to it.[28] If there is more than one adjacent flat then the ground is owned in

16   T(S)A 2004, s 2(2).
17   T(S)A 2004, s 2(1)(b).
18   T(S)A 2004, s 2(3).
19   T(S)A 2004, s 2(4).
20   T(S)A 2004, s 29(1).
21   T(S)A 2004, s 2(5).
22   T(S)A 2004, s 2(6).
23   T(S)A 2004, s 2(7).
24   T(S)A 2004, s 3(1).
25   T(S)A 2004, s 29(1).
26   T(S)A 2004, s 3(2).
27   T(S)A 2004, s 3(1) and (2).
28   T(S)A 2004, s 3(3).

sections. There is an exception for paths, outside stairs or other means of access to other sectors of the building. These are covered by a more general rule, namely that a part of a building serving a flat is a pertinent of it.[29] Other examples are fire escapes, rhones, pipes, flues, conduits, cables, tanks and chimney stacks. Where such parts serve more than one flat they are the common property of those flats.[30] It does not matter if one section of the thing serves one flat and another section another. For example, an entryphone system is regarded a single entity even though it has separate wires serving separate flats.[31] Normally the shares in the common property will be equal in size, but there is a special rule for chimney stacks.[32] Here, the share depends on the ratio of the number of flues serving the chimney to the total number of flues in the stack.

DEFAULT RULES OF TENEMENT MANAGEMENT

The Tenement Management Scheme

15.12   Schedule 1 to T(S)A 2004 contains the Tenement Management Scheme (TMS). This is a default set of management rules, which apply unless the Development Management Scheme (discussed below[33]) has been adopted for the building. The rules may also be disapplied by particular real burdens governing the matter in question.[34]

Scheme property

15.13   The Tenement Management Scheme applies only to the parts that fall within the definition of 'scheme property'.[35] This means, first, the strategic parts of the building. These are:
  (a) the ground on which it is built;
  (b) the foundations;
  (c) the external walls;
  (d) the roof (including supporting structures such as rafters);
  (e) any mutual gable wall shared with an adjoining building, to the centre line; and
  (f) any other wall, beam or column that is load-bearing.[36]

---

29   T(S)A 2004, s 3(4).
30   T(S)A 2004, s 3(4).
31   This is because T(S)A 2004, s 3(4) confers a right of common property 'in (and in the whole of)' the part.
32   T(S)A 2004, s 3(5).
33   See PARA **15.32** below.
34   T(S)A 2004, s 4.
35   TMS, r 1.2.
36   TMS, r 1.2(c).

These parts do not have to be co-owned (in terms of the title deeds) to be scheme property. For example, if there is one top-floor flat which has sole ownership of the roof, the roof is nonetheless scheme property. Certain things are excluded from the strategic parts mentioned, namely:

    (a) an extension forming part of only one flat;

    (b) any door, window, skylight, vent or other opening serving only one flat; and

    (c) any chimney stack or chimney flue.[37]

15.14 Second, the definition of 'scheme property' includes any part of the building that is owned in common, such as the close.[38] Third, any part of the building which is to be maintained under a real burden by two or more flats is also scheme property.[39]

Scheme decisions

Types

15.15 Some 'scheme decisions' can be made by a simple majority of the flat owners.[40] What constitutes a 'flat' is to be determined at the time the decision is taken, rather than when the building was originally constructed.[41] Of course, real burdens might provide a higher threshold, such as a two-thirds majority, which will then apply.[42] The main type of scheme decision is to carry out maintenance.[43] A decision can also be taken to arrange for an inspection to see whether maintenance is required.[44] 'Maintenance' includes 'repairs and replacement, cleaning, painting and other routine works, gardening, the day to day running of a tenement and the reinstatement of a part (but not most) of the tenement building; but does not include demolition, alteration or improvement unless reasonably incidental to the maintenance'.[45] Thus, a majority of the owners cannot make a scheme decision to demolish the tenement. Where a decision is taken to carry out maintenance, further scheme decisions can be taken to instruct the work or to appoint an owner or a firm to manage it.[46] Importantly, a scheme decision can require all the owners to deposit their estimated share of the cost of the work in advance in an interest-bearing bank or building society account.[47] This means that the owners can be sure that the money is there before the work begins.

---

[37]   TMS, r 1.3.
[38]   TMS, r 1.2(a). Except if, oddly, the title deeds provided that this was not common property.
[39]   TMS, r 1.2(b).
[40]   TMS, r 2.5.
[41]   *PS Properties (2) Ltd v Callaway Homes Ltd* 2007 GWD 31-526.
[42]   T(S)A 2004, s 4(4).
[43]   TMS, r 3.1(a).
[44]   TMS, r 3.1(b).
[45]   TMS, r 1.5.
[46]   TMS, rr 3.2(a) and (b).
[47]   TMS, r 3.2(c), 3.3 and 3.4.

15.16   Other scheme decisions include appointing a manager (factor) or dismissing a manager; delegating powers to the manager; arranging a common insurance policy; installing an entryphone system; authorising any maintenance that has already been carried out and modifying or revoking any scheme decision.[48] For common property, scheme decisions replace the rule at common law which lets any co-owner carry out necessary repairs and recover the cost from the others.[49]

Procedural requirements and voting

15.17   There is no requirement for a meeting to be held in order for a scheme decision to be made. An owner wishing a repair to be carried out can simply go round the tenement and find out if a majority agree. All the owners must be consulted.[50] Each flat has one vote.[51] If a flat is co-owned and the owners are in agreement, then any one of them can cast that flat's vote.[52] If they disagree, then the vote can be cast by co-owners in agreement who hold more than half of the shares.[53] If this is not the case – for example, there are only two owners and they disagree – no vote is cast. Where a flat is not liable for the maintenance costs in question (for example, a main-door flat would normally have no liability for the upkeep of the close) it does not get a vote about work which would incur these costs.[54]

15.18   Although the vote does not have to be in writing, it would be unwise to instruct major repairs unless the consenting owners confirm their position in writing. Should it be felt that a matter would be best discussed at a meeting, at least 48 hours' notice must be given to the other owners, including notice of the purpose of the meeting.[55] It is worth stressing that what is required to take a scheme decision is the agreement of a majority of the owners and not just a majority of those who attend.[56]

Right of appeal to the sheriff

15.19   Once a scheme decision has been made, all the owners must be notified of it.[57] The decision, unless it is one to carry out urgent work, must wait for 28 days to be implemented, because during this period an owner who opposed the decision, or an incoming owner, may challenge it in the sheriff court.[58] The sheriff can annul the

---

[48]   TMS, rr 3.1(c)–(f) and (h)–(i).
[49]   T(S)A 2004, s 16. See PARA **9.8** above.
[50]   TMS, r 2.7. Unless this is impracticable: for example, where an owner is absent.
[51]   TMS, r 2.2.
[52]   TMS, r 2.4.
[53]   TMS, r 2.4(a) and (b).
[54]   TMS, r 2.3.
[55]   TMS, r 2.6.
[56]   TMS, r 2.5.
[57]   TMS, r 2.9.
[58]   T(S)A 2004, s 5.

decision if satisfied that it is not in the best interests of all the owners or is unfairly prejudicial to one or more of the owners.[59] Where a decision is not successfully challenged it binds the owners and their successors.[60]

Scheme costs

General

15.20 The Tenement Management Scheme sets out the liability of the owners for 'scheme costs'. This means the costs arising out of a scheme decision, for example to carry out maintenance, and any other costs relating to the management of the property.[61] As with the rest of the legislation, this is subject to the titles. Where there is a real burden dealing with a scheme cost it will take precedence provided it deals with the whole bill.[62] For example, say that there are six flats in a building. The titles of four of the flats each impose a one-sixth liability for roof repairs. The titles for the other two are silent on the matter. The real burdens therefore only cover four-sixths of the bill. The result is that they do not apply. The Tenement Management Scheme does instead.

15.21 The normal rule under the scheme is that the flats are liable equally.[63] For maintenance costs, however, there are two other possibilities.

(1) If the part of the property in question is common, liability is by share of ownership.[64]

(2) If it is not owned in common but the floor area of the largest flat in the building is more than one and a half times greater than that of the smallest, liability is in proportion to floor area.[65]

There is also a special rule for the section of roof above the close.[66] If the title deeds are silent, then liability is not based on the fact that it is common property under the legislation. Rather, it is either to be equal, or calculated by means of floor area if the second possibility above applies. The idea is that the whole of the roof is to be treated together if the title deeds have nothing to say on the matter. Local authorities have the power to contribute an owner's share if that owner cannot pay or has disappeared.[67] If they do not, the other owners will have to meet that share between them.[68]

---

59 T(S)A 2004, s 5(5).
60 TMS, r 8.
61 TMS, r 4.1.
62 T(S)A 2004, s 4(6).
63 TMS, r 4.2(b)(ii).
64 TMS, r 4.2(a).
65 TMS, r 4.2(a)(i).
66 TMS, r 4.3.
67 Housing (Scotland) Act 2006, s 50.
68 TMS, r 5.

Change of ownership

15.22 Liability for costs such as maintenance arises at the time when the relevant scheme decision is made.[69] If a flat is subsequently transferred, usually because it has been sold, the liability of that owner continues.[70] Where work has been instructed but not carried out, the incoming owner is jointly and severally liable with the outgoing owner for the cost.[71] The former, however, has a right of relief against the latter, in other words a right to be reimbursed.[72] Where work has already been carried out, but not paid for, the incoming owner has no liability unless a 'notice of potential liability for costs' has been registered against the title to the flat.[73] The reason for the distinction is that a purchaser normally obtains a survey report which should flag up the need for repairs. In contrast work which has been completed may be less apparent. The effect of the notice is that the incoming owner becomes jointly and severally liable, in the same way as for work not yet carried out. The notice lasts for three years, but can be re-registered before the end of that period, making it effective for another three years.[74]

Emergency work

15.23 In the case of emergency work, any owner is entitled to instruct or carry this out.[75] 'Emergency work' is defined as 'work which, before a scheme decision can be obtained, requires to be carried out to scheme property (a) to prevent damage to any part of the tenement, or (b) in the interests of health and safety'.[76] Where such work is instructed, the owners all become liable for the cost as if the work had been authorised by a scheme decision.[77]

MANDATORY RULES FOR MAINTENANCE AND INSURANCE IN TENEMENTS

Common interest

15.24 Common law developed certain rules about support, shelter and the protection of natural light, these rules being under the umbrella of the doctrine of

---

69   T(S)A 2004, s 11.
70   T(S)A 2004, s 12(1).
71   T(S)A 2004, s 12(2).
72   T(S)A 2004, s 12(5).
73   T(S)A 2004, ss 12(3) and 13 and Sch 2.
74   T(S)A 2004, s 13(3).
75   TMS, r 7.1.
76   TMS, r 7.3.
77   TMS, r 7.2.

'common interest'.[78] They were replaced by similar statutory obligations in T(S)A 2004.[79] The owners of any part of the building providing support or shelter must maintain that part.[80] This obligation is enforceable by the other owners.[81] Such is the importance of these matters that no scheme decision is required. Provided that the part in question is scheme property (or property which must be maintained by virtue of real burdens or the Development Management Scheme[82]), a share of the cost can be recovered from the other owners as if a scheme decision had been taken.[83] The duty to maintain exists only if it is reasonable, having regard to all the circumstances, including the age and condition of the building and cost.[84] In a heavily dilapidated tenement it will not apply.

15.25   The owners or occupiers must not do anything which will, or is reasonably likely to, jeopardise support or shelter, or materially to interfere with the natural light reaching the building.[85] If loss is caused by a failure to provide support or shelter, fault needs to be shown for a damages claim to succeed. The rule is the same whether the action is based on negligence[86] or nuisance.[87]

Insurance

15.26   The flats must be insured for reinstatement value against prescribed risks.[88] These include fire, smoke, lightning, explosion, earthquake, storm, flood, theft, rioting, vandalism, subsidence and damage from certain water or oil leakage.[89] A common policy of insurance must be used if real burdens provide for this or a scheme decision is taken to that effect.[90] If not, separate policies are acceptable. Unlike motor insurance, failure to comply with the statutory requirement is not a criminal offence. Any owner, however, may enforce the obligation against another, if necessary, by going to court.[91] If there is a concern that insurance is not in place, written notice can be given to the owner in question to produce evidence that a policy is held and the premium has been paid.[92]

---

[78]   Reid *Property* paras 232–238.
[79]   T(S)A 2004, s 7.
[80]   T(S)A 2004, s 8(1).
[81]   T(S)A 2004, s 8(3).
[82]   See **PARA 15.32** below.
[83]   T(S)A 2004, s 10.
[84]   T(S)A 2004, s 8(2).
[85]   T(S)A 2004, s 9.
[86]   *Thomson v St Cuthbert's Co-operative Association Ltd* 1958 SC 380.
[87]   *Kennedy v Glenbelle Ltd* 1996 SLT 1186.
[88]   T(S)A 2004, s 18(1).
[89]   Tenements (Scotland) Act 2004 (Prescribed Risks) Order 2007 (SSI 2007/16).
[90]   TMS, r 3.1(e).
[91]   T(S)A 2004, s 18(6).
[92]   T(S)A 2004, s 18(5).

TENEMENT ACCESS RIGHTS

15.27 The owners of the flats are entitled to take access to the other flats for various purposes, including to carry out maintenance in terms of a scheme decision or other management scheme applying to the building; to carry out an inspection as to whether maintenance is required and to ensure that the duties of support and shelter are being fulfilled.[93] Reasonable notice must be given of the desire to take access, except if there is a need to carry out urgent maintenance.[94] The access rights can be delegated, for example to a contractor.[95]

DEMOLITION

15.28 A tenement may have to be demolished, for example if it has been severely damaged by fire. The cost of this in general must be shared equally by the owners.[96] Of course, a real burden may provide otherwise. Additionally, if the largest flat is more than one and a half times the size of the smallest flat then liability is based on floor area.[97] Ownership is unaffected by the demolition. This means that the owner of an upper flat continues to own the airspace where that flat once was.[98] Rebuilding is allowed only if all the owners of the former flats agree, or where there is an obligation to rebuild, normally imposed by a real burden.[99] Any owner can apply to the sheriff court for permission to have the site sold.[100] In this case the proceeds are divided in the same way as the demolition costs: either equally or by floor area, depending on the respective sizes of the former flats.[101] This is subject to any real burden regulating the matter. An application to sell can likewise be made for an abandoned tenement.[102]

STATUTORY NOTICES

15.29 Local authorities have statutory powers to require maintenance and safety work to be carried out. In practice these are used more in relation to tenements than other types of building. The typical case is where an owner cannot persuade others to agree to repairs and so contacts the council. The procedure is that the local authority, if satisfied that work is needed, serves a 'statutory notice' on the owners.

[93]   T(S)A 2004, s 17(1) and (2).
[94]   T(S)A 2004, s 17(1) and (4).
[95]   T(S)A 2004, s 17(6).
[96]   T(S)A 2004, s 21(1).
[97]   T(S)A 2004, s 21(2).
[98]   T(S)A 2004, s 20.
[99]   T(S)A 2004, s 22(2).
[100]   T(S)A 2004, s 21(3) and Sch 3.
[101]   T(S)A 2004, s 22(4) and (5).
[102]   T(S)A 2004, s 23.

Examples include defective building notices,[103] dangerous building notices[104] and work notices.[105] These require the owners to carry out remedial work within a certain period. Such a notice will appear on the 'property enquiry certificate' which a prospective buyer always requests from the local authority, and so makes the flat harder to sell unless something is done. If the owners do not carry out the work, the local authority can do it itself and bill them. In the case of tenements, this will be a 'scheme cost', so the rules on determining the respective liability of each flat will apply.[106] The local authority can if necessary secure the cost against the property by means of a charging order.[107]

DEFAULT RULES OF MANAGEMENT AND MAINTENANCE FOR OTHER DEVELOPMENTS

15.30 TC(S)A 2003 contains a set of default rules on management and maintenance. These are for property developments, other than individual tenements, for which there is the Tenement Management Scheme.[108] The legislation applies where two or more properties ('units') are regulated by burdens imposed under a common scheme and are mutually enforceable.[109] In effect it applies to properties governed by the same set of community burdens.[110] It might be a residential development, including one with a mixture of houses and tenements, or an industrial estate. The legislation refers to such properties as a 'community'.

15.31 The default rules are subject to the provisions of the community burdens in place. They are rather like a watered-down version of the Tenement Management Scheme. A majority of the owners in the community may appoint a manager and confer certain powers on that person, such as to carry out maintenance.[111] They may also revoke or vary the powers or dismiss the manager.[112] The owners are liable equally for the manager's remuneration.[113] Where there is a community burden imposing a maintenance obligation, the majority can decide to carry out work.[114] There are similar rules to those in the Tenement Management Scheme on instructing

---

[103] Building (Scotland) Act 2003 (B(S)A) 2003), s 28.
[104] B(S)A) 2003, ss 29–30.
[105] Housing (Scotland) Act 2006, s 30.
[106] TMS, r 4.1(d). See PARAS **15.20–15.21** above.
[107] See PARA **20.66** below.
[108] TC(S)A 2003, s 31A.
[109] TC(S)A 2003, ss 25 and 26(2).
[110] See PARA **13.6** above.
[111] TC(S)A 2003, s 28(1)(a), (b) and (2).
[112] TC(S)A 2003, s 28(1)(c) and (d)
[113] TC(S)A 2003, s 31.
[114] TC(S)A 2003, s 29(1) and (2).

the work and requiring all the owners to deposit their share in advance.[115] All the owners and their successors are bound by such decisions.[116]

DEVELOPMENT MANAGEMENT SCHEME

15.32 TC(S)A 2003 provides for a sophisticated management scheme for use in larger developments.[117] This is known as the Development Management Scheme. It is to be set out in a statutory instrument,[118] expected to similar to the draft in Schedule 3 to the draft Bill in the Scottish Law Commission Report on Real Burdens.[119] It will then be available for any development, for example, a single tenement, group of tenements or group of houses and tenements. Under the scheme the development is run by a manager employed by an owners' association. The association is a body corporate and so has juristic personality. The scheme has detailed rules on budgeting, services charges, meetings, maintenance and other matters. It can be applied (with or without variations) to a development by a deed of application[120] and disapplied by a deed of disapplication.[121] Where it applies to a tenement, the Tenement Management Scheme does not.[122]

FURTHER READING

Reid, D 'The Tenements (Scotland) Act 2004' in R Rennie (ed) *The Promised Land: Property Law Reform* 147–172.

Reid and Gretton *Conveyancing 2004* (2005) 121–150.

Rennie *Land Tenure in Scotland* chs 10 and 14.

Scottish Law Commission *Report on the Law of the Tenement* (Scot Law Com No 162, 1998).

Scottish Law Commission *Report on Real Burdens* (Scot Law Com No 181, 2000) Pt 8.

Van der Merwe, C G 'The Tenements (Scotland) Act 2004: A Brief Evaluation' 2004 *SLT (News)* 211.

---

[115] TC(S)A 2003, s 29(2)–(10).
[116] TC(S)A 2003, s 30.
[117] TC(S)A 2003, ss 71–74.
[118] This has to be done in London because it will provide for owners' associations, and such associations are reserved under the Scotland Act 1998. This is because 'business associations' are reserved (Sch 5, Pt II, head C1) and (oddly) even non-business associations are defined as 'business associations'.
[119] Scottish Law Commission *Report on Real Burdens* (2000).
[120] TC(S)A 2003, s 71.
[121] TC(S)A 2003, s 73.
[122] T(S)A 2004, s 4(2).

Chapter 16

Rivers, lochs and the sea

GENERAL

Water

16.1 A distinction exists between running water, such as that in a river, and standing water, i.e. water in a static state. Running water is ownerless,[1] and so it can be acquired by occupancy,[2] for example by filling a bucket. The law about standing water is less clear but, arguably, it belongs to the person on whose land it stands.[3]

---

[1] Reid *Property* para 274.
[2] See PARA **8.2** above.
[3] Reid *Property* para 274.

Alveus

16.2   Where water runs or stands in a definite channel, the bed of that channel is known as the *alveus*. The principal examples are lochs and rivers. Ownership of the *alveus* is dependent on whether the water in question is tidal or non-tidal.

TIDAL WATERS

Definition

16.3   As well as the sea itself, the category of tidal waters includes rivers and sea-lochs to the highest point reached by the flow of ordinary spring tides.[4]

Alveus

16.4   The *alveus* of tidal waters belongs to the Crown, subject to a limit of 12 nautical miles from the shore.[5] Historically, the view was taken that this ownership was as trustee for the public at large for the purpose of protecting such public rights as navigation.[6] To put it more technically, the Crown's right was regarded as part of the *regalia majora* and so incapable of transfer. This view was departed from at the end of the nineteenth century in *Lord Advocate v Clyde Navigation Trustees*[7] and it is now accepted that the Crown has absolute ownership. It has been held more recently that the ownership arises from the Royal Prerogative, rather than being an aspect of feudal law.[8] Therefore the sea bed around Orkney and Shetland, parts of Scotland which never received the feudal system, are subject to the same rule. As with other Crown property, the sea bed is managed by the Crown Estate Commissioners.[9]

Foreshore

16.5   The foreshore is that part of the shore (whether mud, sand, shingle or rock) which is covered by the sea at high tide and uncovered at the low tide. Since tides vary, the test is the ordinary spring tide.[10] Under the feudal system which persisted in Scotland until 2004, the foreshore, like any other land, was originally the property

---

[4]   J Ferguson *The Law of Water and Water Rights in Scotland* (1907) 107.

[5]   Territorial Sea Act 1987, s 1(1).

[6]   See, e.g., *Agnew v Lord Advocate* (1873) 11 M 309 at 322 per Lord Justice-Clerk Moncreiff.

[7]   (1891) 19 R 174. See N R Whitty 'Water Law Regimes' in Reid and Zimmermann *History* vol 1, 420 at 436–438.

[8]   *Shetland Salmon Farmers Association v Crown Estate Commissioners* 1991 SLT 166.

[9]   Crown Estate Act 1961.

[10]   *Fisherrow Harbour Commissioners v Musselburgh Real Estate Co Ltd* (1903) 5 F 387 at 393–394 per Lord Low.

of the Crown. It remains the rule that it belongs to the Crown in so far as the Crown has never granted ownership to any other party, nor has anyone acquired a title to it by positive prescription.[11] The position is different in Orkney and Shetland which have always been subject to udal, rather than feudal, law.[12] There, the foreshore is in private ownership – usually that of the proprietor who owns the land adjacent to it.

Public rights

16.6 A number of public rights, including navigation and recreation, exist in tidal waters and the foreshore. These are discussed elsewhere.[13]

NON-TIDAL WATERS: RIVERS

Alveus

16.7 The *alveus* of non-tidal rivers and burns is owned by the proprietors of the land through which they flow, in sections, corresponding to their ownership of the adjacent dry land. The term 'riparian proprietor' is used to denote such a person.[14] Where a river marks the boundary between two properties it is presumed that the *alveus* is owned by the respective riparian proprietor*s* to the middle line – or, in Latin, *ad medium filum*.[15]

Rights of riparian proprietors

16.8 In general, riparian proprietors are entitled to use their section of water. For example, they may sail upon it. They have the exclusive right to catch fish. Where the river is owned to the middle line, it may be permissible for the proprietors to cast their rods across this.[16] The right to fish excludes salmon, unless the proprietor also has the salmon fishing rights, which are a legal separate tenement.[17] Also included is the right to consume the water – but only for domestic purposes.[18]

---

11 On positive prescription, see PARAS **2.24–2.25** above.
12 *Smith v Lerwick Harbour Trs* (1903) 5 F 680.
13 See PARAS **18.25–18.29** below.
14 This comes from the Latin *ripa*, meaning river bank. See Whitty 'Water Law Regimes' at 448.
15 For an example of the rebuttal of the presumption, see *Safeway Stores plc v Tesco Stores Ltd* 2004 SC 29.
16 *Arthur v Aird* 1907 SC 1170.
17 See PARA **14.17** above.
18 See PARA **16.10** below.

Obligations on riparian proprietors: common interest

16.9 From the perspective of private law, the main obligations on riparian proprietors arise from common interest.[19] This doctrine recognises the fact that the *alveus*[20] is owned by several parties and that the actions of one could have adverse consequences for another. Thus it imposes restrictions which arise by operation of law. The principal obligation is not to engage in activities which materially interfere with the water or its natural flow. 'The superior heritor [i.e. a proprietor further up the river] must transmit to the inferior the water of the stream undiminished in quantity and undeteriorated in quality.'[21] Therefore if a proprietor intends to construct a building on the *alveus* which will disrupt the flow of the water, this may be interdicted.[22] Likewise, polluting the river may be a breach of common interest.

16.10 Common interest means that water must not be abstracted except for domestic purposes. That includes cooking, drinking and washing.[23] Consumption for agricultural or industrial purposes is generally impermissible, unless a servitude of *aquaehaustus* has been constituted. This might be by 20 years of use, leading to positive prescription.[24] The right to take water is nowadays less important because of the development of the public water supply system.

Other obligations on riparian proprietors

16.11 Proprietors are subject to obligations additional to those arising in common interest. Three will be mentioned here.
   (1) All proprietors must ensure that they do not do anything which amounts to a nuisance, such as polluting the water.[25]
   (2) Non-tidal rivers may be subject to a common law public right of navigation and those exercising that right must be tolerated.[26]
   (3) Statute may impose obligations. For example, the public is allowed to canoe along rivers under the Land Reform (Scotland) Act 2003.[27]
Another important piece of recent legislation is the Water Environment and Water Services (Scotland) Act 2003 which introduced a new licensing regime for the abstraction of water.[28] A final example is the statutory controls on pollution.[29]

---

[19] For common interest, see also PARA **15.24** above.
[20] The running water itself is ownerless. See PARA **16.1** above.
[21] *Hunter and Aitkenhead v Aitken* (1880) 7 R 410 at 514 per Lord President Inglis.
[22] *Morris v Bicket* (1864) 2 M 1082, aff'd (1866) 4 M (HL) 44.
[23] Bell, *Principles* s 1105.
[24] See PARA **12.27** above.
[25] *Miller v Stein* (1791) Mor 12823; *Montgomerie v Buchanan's Trs* (1853) 15 D 853.
[26] See PARA **18.29** below.
[27] See PARA **18.3** below.
[28] For discussion, see B Clark 'Water Law in Scotland: The Water Environment and Water Services (Scotland) Act 2003 and the European Convention on Human Rights' (2006) 10 *Edin LR* 60.
[29] McDonald *Conveyancing Manual* paras 20.33–20.40.

NON-TIDAL WATERS: LOCHS

Alveus

16.12   The *alveus* of a freshwater loch is the area ordinarily covered by water all year round. Seasonal variations are not counted.[30] Where the loch is surrounded by land owned by different parties, the presumption is that the *alveus* is owned in sections. An earlier view, that ownership is actually held in common, can no longer be regarded as the law.[31]

Rights of riparian proprietors

16.13   Riparian proprietors naturally have the right to use their section of the loch, for example to fish other than for salmon and to sail. There is also a right in common interest to fish and sail in other parts of the loch.[32] The court in principle may regulate matters, so as to avoid over-fishing, but will intervene only in exceptional cases.[33]

Obligations of riparian proprietors

16.14   Similar obligations exist as with rivers and burns.[34] In addition, each proprietor must permit others to fish or sail in his or her part of the loch.[35] Where a loch forms part of the same water system as a river, the common interest obligations upon the river proprietors also apply to the owners of the loch. In contrast a loch which does not fall into that category (known as a '*stagnum*') is not subject to such restrictions.

FURTHER READING

Gordon *Scottish Land Law* ch 7.

Reid *Property* paras 273–343.

Whitty, N R 'Water Law Regimes' in Reid and Zimmermann *History* vol 1, 420–479.

---

[30]   *Dick v Earl of Abercorn* (1769) Mor 12813; *Baird v Robertson* (1839) 1 D 1051.
[31]   Reid *Property* para 305.
[32]   *Mackenzie v Bankes* (1878) 5 R (HL) 192.
[33]   *Menzies v Wentworth* (1901) 3 F 941.
[34]   See PARA **16.11** above.
[35]   See PARA **16.13** above.

Chapter 17

Neighbour law

INTRODUCTION

17.1 Neighbour law is the part of property law which regulates the rights and responsibilities of a landowner in a question with neighbouring (not necessarily adjacent) owners. Two important rights – real burdens and servitudes – have their own detailed sets of rules and are treated elsewhere.[1] Moreover, they are normally[2] created expressly. The focus of this chapter is the default set of rules affecting neighbours. These are discussed under the following headings:

(a) boundary fences and walls;[3]
(b) encroachment;[4]
(c) support;[5]
(d) nuisance;[6]
(e) *aemulatio vicini* (spiteful acts);[7] and
(f) use of a neighbour's property.[8]

BOUNDARY FENCES AND WALLS

Construction

17.2 There are two types of boundary fence or wall. Type 1 is wholly on one side of the boundary. Type 2 straddles the boundary, usually with one half on each side. Subject to certain legal restraints such as planning law and real burdens, an owner is entitled to erect a Type 1 fence or wall. The expense must be borne by him or her alone, unless there is a real burden requiring a contribution from the neighbour, or the March Dykes Act 1661 applies. The 1661 Act is little used in modern times. It does not apply in towns or cities, nor to plots of land of less than 5 acres.[9] Where it does apply, the court can, on the application of one owner, order that a wall is to be constructed at joint expense.

17.3 A Type 2 fence or wall usually requires the consent of both landowners, failing which it will be an encroachment on the non-consenting owner's land. It is common for real burdens to authorise Type 2 fences or walls to be built. In other words, an owner is given power to build onto his or her neighbour's land. But there is a difficulty here. Since 28 November 2004, real burdens are only capable of imposing positive

---

1 See **CHAPTERS 12 AND 13** above.
2 Real burdens are always created expressly. Servitudes, however, can be created in other ways, for example by prescription. See **PARA 12.27** above.
3 See **PARAS 17.2–17.9** below.
4 See **PARAS 17.10–17.16** below.
5 See **PARAS 17.17–17.20** below.
6 See **PARAS 17.21–17.25** below.
7 See **PARAS 17.26–17.27** below.
8 See **PARAS 17.28–17.30** below.
9 *Penman v Douglas and Cochrane* (1739) Mor 10481.

(affirmative) or negative obligations.[10] Existing real burdens allowing use of a neighbour's land were converted by force of law on that date into servitudes.[11] There is, however, authority to the effect that a reserved right to build on another's land cannot be a servitude.[12] It is, arguably, repugnant with the ownership of the burdened property.[13] In view of this, new real burdens should be drafted to require both neighbours to co-operate in the building of the fence or wall. A time limit should also be imposed for completion or the burden will be invalid.[14]

17.4   There is a special rule for common gables. A 'common gable' is an end wall shared by two buildings, for example terraced houses or adjacent tenements. In towns and cities it is sometimes permissible for a builder to construct a straddling gable.[15] When the adjacent plot is developed, the gable can be used, but only on payment of half the cost of erecting it.[16] This rule was important in nineteenth-century building practice when adjacent plots were normally granted to different builders. Nowadays, the one builder normally builds a whole development. So the rule is now of little importance.

Ownership

17.5   Ownership of a boundary fence or wall is in principle governed by the law of accession.[17] Graeme and Harvey are neighbours and a wall separates their gardens. If the wall is built wholly on Graeme's side of the boundary, it belongs to Graeme. If it is built entirely on Harvey's side, it belongs to Harvey. If it is a straddling wall then each owns it to the middle line.[18] In neither case is the wall common property. (Some older authorities suggesting that it is common property must now be regarded as wrong.[19]) But each party has a right of common interest in the other's part of the wall.

17.6   It is unclear whether the title deeds can alter the rule and make a boundary fence or wall the common property of the neighbours. There is authority that it is impossible to contract out of accession.[20] But the position might be different here because of an express statement in the title deeds. This effectively would treat the wall or fence as a conventional separate tenement.[21]

---

[10]   See **PARA 13.7** above.
[11]   TC(S)A 2003, s 81.
[12]   *Campbell's Trs v Glasgow Corporation* (1902) 4 F 752.
[13]   Compare TC(S)A 2003, s 76(2).
[14]   *Gammell's Trs v The Land Commission* 1970 SLT 254.
[15]   Reid *Property*, para 218.
[16]   *Law v Monteith* (1855) 18 D 125; *Sanderson v Geddes* (1874) 1 R 1198; *Robertson v Scott* (1886) 13 R 1127.
[17]   See **PARAS 8.4–8.12** above.
[18]   The Latin expression '*ad medium filum*' is often used to mean 'to the mid-point'.
[19]   Reid *Property* para 223. And see Scottish Law Commission *Report on Boundary Walls* (1998).
[20]   See **PARA 8.4** above.
[21]   See **PARA 14.14** above. But the law generally does not admit separate tenements above ground.

Maintenance

17.7 The neighbours are free to agree between themselves as to maintenance and paying for the cost thereof. The position is commonly dealt with by means of a real burden, perhaps stating that each neighbour is liable to pay a half-share of the expense of maintenance. In the case of a Type 2 fence or well which traverses the boundary, each neighbour is under a duty in common interest to maintain the stability of a wall as a whole. This is a *positive* obligation. If it is not complied with, the other neighbour can carry out the work and recover the cost.[22] In the case of a wall or fence owned in common,[23] either neighbour may carry out necessary repairs and recover a proportion from the other based on the size of the other's share.

17.8 Where the March Dykes Act 1661 applies, it enables an owner to ask the court to require the neighbour to pay half the cost of repairing or rebuilding the fence or wall. The 1661 Act applies where the fence or wall was originally erected by court order under the Act,[24] where it was erected by agreement where a court order could have been so sought; or where it has been always regarded as governed by the legislation.[25] Local authorities also have a battery of powers to deal with defective and dangerous buildings, including to repair the property and to bill the owner(s).[26] The definition of 'building' includes wall and fences.[27]

Alterations

17.9 Subject to any agreement or real burden to the contrary, the owner is free to alter, extend or demolish a Type 1 fence or wall. In the case of a straddling wall, a common interest obligation prevents each neighbour from carrying out any acts which would adversely affect the structure as a whole. The rule here is stated by Lord Jauncey in *Thom v Hetherington*,[28] where one of the neighbours had erected a new fence along the existing wall:

> 'The presence of the fence up against the wall would only have been actionable if such presence impaired the strength or interfered with the stability of the wall … Such impairment or interference must in my view be measurable and note merely negligible. It is beyond dispute that the owner of one side of a garden wall would be entitled to insert nails or rose ties into the mortar for the purpose of training roses up it. Theoretically every intrusion into the mortar

---

[22]   *Newton v Godfrey,* Stranraer Sheriff Court, 19 June 2000, Paisley and Cusine, *Unreported Cases* 86.
[23]   If this is possible. See PARA **17.6** above.
[24]   See PARA **17.2** above.
[25]   *Strang v Steuart* (1864) 2 M 1015, aff'd (1866) 4 M (HL) 5.
[26]   Building (Scotland) Act 2003 (B(S)A 2003), ss 28–30.
[27]   B(S)A 2003, s 55. Subject to some exceptions, the definition covers 'any structure or erection, whether temporary or permanent'.
[28]   1988 SLT 724.

must weaken the bond which it creates between the bricks, but it is equally clear that the court would not restrain an owner from so acting.'[29]

In principle, the party carrying out the alteration must pay for it.[30]

ENCROACHMENT

General

17.10   Where something permanently or quasi-permanently invades a person's land without consent or lawful authority this is known as 'encroachment'. The effect is to interfere with the right of possession of the owner or other occupier of the land and thereby commit a delict. Encroachment, unlike trespass,[31] is always by things. The typical example is a person building beyond his or her boundaries. An example is the pillars on the front of the Assembly Rooms in George Street in Edinburgh, which were built onto a neighbouring proprietor's land.[32] A number of other cases can be given.

(a) Where a signpost or other object is affixed to a building. The leading modern case involved an Edinburgh chip shop placing a flue on the side of someone else's wall.[33]

(b) Where pipes are laid.[34]

(c) Where a tree's roots spread under or its branches overhang the land.[35]

(d) Where rubbish or other moveable property is left.[36]

Encroachment, even if trivial, is a delict: 'a proprietor is not entitled to encroach upon his neighbour's property even to the extent of driving a nail into it'.[37] Nevertheless, the extent of the encroachment is relevant to the remedies available.[38]

---

[29]   1988 SLT 724 at 728.

[30]   But the parts, of course, are free to agree otherwise; there might be a real burden governing the position or the March Dykes Act 1661, if applicable, might allow the cost to be halved with the neighbour.

[31]   See PARAS **18.30–18.36** below.

[32]   *Duke of Buccleuch v Magistrates of Edinburgh* (1865) 3 M 528. For a more recent example, see *Young v West,* Elgin Sheriff Court, 3 September 2003, unreported, discussed in Reid and Gretton, *Conveyancing 2003* (2004) 83–85.

[33]   *Anderson v Brattissani's* 1978 SLT (Notes) 42.

[34]   *Cheever v Jefferson Properties Ltd,* Dumfries Sheriff Court, 26 May 1995, Paisley and Cusine, *Unreported Cases* 439.

[35]   *Halkerston v Wedderburn* (1781) Mor 10495; Bell *Principles* s 942.

[36]   Hume, *Lectures* III, 204–205; *Scott v Law,* Cupar Sheriff Court, 20 May 1987, Paisley and Cusine, *Unreported Cases* 21.

[37]   *Leonard v Lindsay & Benzie* (1886) 13 R 958 at 964 per Lord Young.

[38]   See PARA **17.15** below.

Defences: consent and acquiescence

17.11   There is no encroachment where the owner or lawful possessor of the property expressly agrees to the invasion. The party who has title to the land may also acquiesce in the encroachment. For example, Keith and Leila are neighbours. There is no boundary fence separating their back gardens. Leila builds a summer house, part of which is within Keith's boundaries. Keith makes no objection and lets her complete the work and use the summer house. Only much later does he complain. In these circumstances, he may well be personally barred from having the summer house removed.[39] In the case involving the Assembly Rooms, mentioned in PARAGRAPH **17.10**, objection was not made for over 30 years. This was held to be too late.

17.12   In principle, consent and acquiescence do not bind successors. However, where the successor has notice of the encroachment or it is obvious, then that person may be bound.[40] The preferable analysis is that the successor is barred here because of his or her own conduct rather than that the bar itself transmits.[41] Where a predecessor has given consent to the encroachment, the court will take this into account if the successor objects.[42] This may lead to an award of damages rather than removal.[43]

17.13   While consent and acquiescence mean that the encroachment stays in place, in the normal case[44] it will accede to the neighbour's land and fall into his or her ownership. This is likely to cause problems if either piece of land is sold. The way to resolve the matter is a conveyance of the relevant section of land to the encroacher, but this will require the neighbour's agreement.

Other defences

17.14   Only two possible defences will be mentioned. The first is that the encroachment is lawful. The encroacher may actually own the land, so in fact the encroachment is not an encroachment at all. Rather, there is a dispute over the boundary and the neighbour is mistaken. The encroachment might also be permissible under some special statutory rule. For example, in one case it was submitted that the erection of a tent on the foreshore was justified by the White Herring Fisheries Act 1771.[45] Second, the failure to object for a period of 20 years may lead to this right

---

[39]   On personal bar more generally, see E Reid 'Personal Bar: Case-Law in Search of Principle' (2003) 7 *Edin LR* 340 and E C Reid and J W G Blackie *Personal Bar* (2006).

[40]   Gloag *Contract* 170–171.

[41]   Reid 'Personal Bar: Case-Law in Search of Principle' at 347–348.

[42]   *Anderson v Brattissani's* 1978 SLT (Notes) 42.

[43]   See PARA **17.15** below.

[44]   There are exceptions. For example, overhanging branches and dumped rubbish.

[45]   *Montgomerie v Mearns*, Kilmarnock Sheriff Court, 9 January 1976, Paisley and Cusine, *Unreported Cases* 467.

being lost by negative prescription.[46] This is questionable, however, because the right may fall within the definition of a *res merae facultatis*.[47]

Judicial remedies

17.15   Three court remedies are available. The first is interdict. Speed is of the essence here, because this is a preventative remedy. If the encroachment is a building and it is complete, or at least substantially complete, it is too late to interdict. The appropriate remedy then becomes an order for removal. However, the court has a discretion not to make such an order. It will do so where the removal 'would be attended with unreasonable loss and expense, quite disproportionate to the advantage it would give to the successful party'.[48] Thus in one case buttresses supporting a gable wall encroached on neighbouring land.[49] The neighbour made no attempt to stop their construction. The level of encroachment was minimal and did not cause the neighbour any cost or inconvenience. It was also in the interests of the neighbour's land that the wall did not collapse. The court accordingly exercised its discretion. The third remedy is damages. It is available both in cases where the court has exercised its discretion and those where it has not.[50]

Self-help

17.16   A party whose land is subject to an encroachment can take matters into his or her own hands. However, careful thought should be given to whether to engage in self-help as, in Professor Paisley's words, 'unilateral action may lead to fights on site'.[51] Where the encroachment by accession has become solely the property of the person encroached upon, then that person has power over it and may destroy it. In the case of a building which crosses the boundary the part encroaching can be demolished.[52] With trees, it has been held that if the trunk is on the boundary then the tree is the common property of the neighbours.[53] Therefore it cannot be felled without both agreeing. Where the branches of a neighbour's tree overhang, they may be cut off and returned to the neighbour. The same goes for roots. It is also possible to obtain a court order for removal in such circumstances.[54] Where a building over-

---

[46]   PL(S)A 1973, s 7.
[47]   PL(S)A 1973, Sch 3(c). On the meaning of '*res merae facultatis*', see PARA **12.45** above.
[48]   *Jack v Begg* (1875) 3 R 35 at 43 per Lord Gifford.
[49]   *Scott v Law,* Cupar Sheriff Court, 20 May 1987, Paisley and Cusine *Unreported Cases* 21.
[50]   For an example of the way damages are assessed, see *Craig v Powrie,* Perth Sheriff Court, 18 September 1985, Paisley and Cusine, *Unreported Cases* 17.
[51]   Paisley *Land Law* para 4.30.
[52]   This sits uneasily with the fact that if a court order were sought, the court could exercise its discretion to refuse. See Reid *Property* para 179.
[53]   *Hetherington v Galt* (1905) 7 F 706.
[54]   *Halkerston v Wedderburn* (1781) Mor 10495.

hangs, self-help is not available.[55] Finally, rubbish and other moveables may simply be returned to the encroacher with or without the neighbour's compliments.

SUPPORT

Land to land

17.17 There is an obligation upon landowners to support the land above and beside their own land. In other words, there is a duty of both *subjacent* and *adjacent* support. (In practice, subjacent support is more important, particularly where minerals have been worked.) More exactly, the obligation is a negative one: not to withdraw support. Consequently, if Jean owns the minerals under Katie's land, Jean must be careful when working the minerals not to cause subsidence. Otherwise, she will be liable to Katie in damages for the loss suffered. Katie is also entitled to interdict works which endanger support. The extent to which the duty to support includes support for buildings is not clear. On one view, it always does.[56] Others contend that the duty does not apply where there is excessive building on the surface, unless that level of building was contemplated at the time that the strata of land were separated.[57] Where support is withdrawn, there is strict liability. Negligence need not be proven.[58] It is possible for the title deeds to exclude the duty to support, or the right to damages if support is withdrawn. An exclusion of the latter may, depending on the wording, impliedly include the former.[59] Where there has been exclusion, it is possible under statute to make application for restrictions to be imposed on the working of minerals in order to protect support.[60]

Coal specialities

17.18 Formerly, coal was one of the most important industries in Scotland, but no more. Nevertheless, there are many old coal mines which may give rise to support issues. Following privatisation in the 1990s, the Coal Authority has ownership of unworked coal and the power to grant licences to work this.[61] An operator to whom a licence is given can in principle withdraw support in order to work the coal on three months' notice.[62] This, however, leads to a duty to compensate the surface

---

55 Bankton II, 7, 8.
56 Reid *Property* para 260.
57 Gordon *Scottish Land Law* paras 6.90–6.92; R Rennie *Minerals and the Law of Scotland* (2001) paras 4.3–4.6.
58 *Dryburgh v Fife Coal Co Ltd* (1905) 7 F 1083; *Angus v National Coal Board* 1955 SC 175. Compare PARA **17.23** below with the rule for nuisance.
59 *Buchanan v Andrew* (1873) 11 M (HL) 13.
60 Mines (Working Facilities and Support) Act 1966, s 7.
61 Coal Industry Act 1994 (CIA 1994), ss 7(3) and 25–36.
62 CIA 1994, ss 38 and 39.

owner or to carry out remedial works.[63] There is also liability for damage caused by workings which pre-date the licence.[64] Where there is no licensed operator, liability rests with the Coal Authority.[65]

Buildings to buildings

17.19 Subjacent building-to-building support is regulated by the Tenements (Scotland) Act 2004 (T(S)A 2004) under which the lower part or parts of a building must support the upper part or parts.[66] Adjacently, where two buildings share a common gable, each owning it to the mid-point, there is a duty in common interest to support the other half, just like the position for boundary walls discussed above.[67] There is no such obligation if the wall is wholly within the boundaries of one of the properties, unless there is a servitude of support.[68] Similarly, a servitude is needed for there to be a duty to support the separate wall of an adjacent building.

Servitude of support

17.20 The title to a property may provide for an express servitude of support which goes beyond or limits what the law would imply, for example by being restricted to a certain weight or size of building.[69] A servitude of support may also possibly arise by prescription, but there may be difficulties establishing the requisite 'open' possession required.[70]

NUISANCE

General

17.21 Nuisance[71] is a delict. Owners and other lawful occupiers of land are protected from interference with their use and enjoyment of that land. Members of the public have similar rights in relation to public places.[72] A nuisance will be actionable where what the would-be pursuer is exposed to is *'plus quam tolerabile*[73] when due weight

---

63   Coal Mining Subsidence Act 1991, ss 2, 7, 8 and 9.

64   CIA 1994, s 43(4)–(6). See *British Coal Corporation v Netherlee Trust Trs* 1995 SLT 1038.

65   CIA 1994, s 43(3)(b).

66   T(S)A 2004, s 11. See **PARAS 15.24–15.25** above.

67   See **PARA 17.7** above.

68   See **PARA 12.13** above.

69   Paisley *Land Law* para 8.9. See **PARA 12.13** above.

70   PL(S)A 1973, s 3. See Cusine and Paisley *Servitudes and Rights of Way* para 3.73.

71   The classic modern treatment is N R Whitty 'Nuisance' in *SME* (Reissue, 2001). See also Gordon *Scottish Land Law* paras 26.21–26.35.

72   Whitty 'Nuisance' para 2.

73   'More than tolerable.'

has been given to all the surrounding circumstances of the offensive conduct and its effects'.[74] This must be determined objectively. In other words, it is not whether the particular pursuer feels that the interference is more than reasonably tolerable, but whether a reasonable person placed in that situation would be of that view.[75]

Examples

17.22   There is an open-ended list of types of conduct which can be classed as a nuisance, but the case law can be broadly divided into instances of:
(1) physical damage; and
(2) interference with the use and enjoyment of land.[76]
Examples of the former are:
(a) Vibrations which cause structural damage to buildings.[77]
(b) Removing a load-bearing wall, causing damage to a flat above.[78]
(c) Attracting pigeons by frequently putting out feed, the consequence being that the birds' droppings choked pipes and polluted the water in them.[79]
Examples of the latter are:
(a) Noise. In one of the most famous modern cases, an unsuccessful attempt was made to interdict the Edinburgh Military Tattoo on the basis that it was a nuisance.[80]
(b) Disagreeable smells, for example sewage.[81]
(c) Excessive electric light.[82]

Assessment of nuisance

17.23   In assessing whether conduct is more than reasonably tolerable, the courts take an account of various factors including the nature of the harm, the social value of the use or enjoyment invaded, the sensitivity to harm of the persons and property affected.[83] They also consider in relation to the defender the primary purpose of the conduct, the suitability of the conduct to the character of the local and how practicable

---

[74]   *Watt v Jamieson* 1954 SC 56 at 57 per Lord President Cooper (Outer House).
[75]   *Maguire v Charles McNeil Ltd* 1922 SC 174 at 191 per Lord Skerrington; Whitty, 'Nuisance' para 41.
[76]   Whitty 'Nuisance' paras 45–46.
[77]   *Lord Advocate v Reo Stakis Organisation Ltd* 1981 SC 104.
[78]   *Kennedy v Glenbelle* 1996 SC 95. This may also be actionable under T(S)A 2004, s 11. See **PARA 15.25** above.
[79]   *Allison v Stevenson* (1908) 24 Sh Ct Rep 214.
[80]   *Webster v Lord Advocate* 1984 SLT 13, aff'd 1985 SLT 361.
[81]   *Houldsworth v Wishaw Magistrates* (1887) 14 R 920.
[82]   *Summers v Crichton* 2000 GWD 40-1495.
[83]   Whitty 'Nuisance' paras 43–66.

it is for the defender to remedy the conduct.[84] Fundamentally, for the defender to be liable, fault (*culpa*) must be proven.[85] For example, referring to one of the cases mentioned above, a party who removes a wall which they know to be load-bearing, causing damage to the property above, is at fault and therefore liable.[86]

Defences

17.24   There are a number of available defences. These include:
  (1) negative prescription of the right to object (20 years);[87]
  (2) acquiescence by the pursuer;[88] and
  (3) statutory authorisation.[89]

In an English action against a water company for damage caused by sewers flooding, reliance on the relevant statutory regime was a successful defence to a claim based on both nuisance and ECHR, Art 8 and Protocol 1, Art 1.[90] In contrast, it is no defence that the nuisance was going on before the pursuer arrived at the property, nor that it is in the public interest.[91]

Remedies

17.25   The usual court remedies apply. Interdict is possible. An order *ad factum praestandum* can be sought to make the defender carry out remedial works.[92] Damages are available for the loss suffered.[93]

AEMULATIO VICINI (SPITEFUL ACTS)

General

17.26   Where an owner does something that is in itself lawful but does it merely out of *aemulatio vicini* (spite towards a neighbour), the act is unlawful. (This idea of 'abuse of right' has been developed in many legal systems, but not much in Scotland, other than in property law.) The doctrine may also be applicable in circumstances where the respective proprietary rights of the parties have not been established, for

---

84   Whitty 'Nuisance' paras 67–77.
85   *RHM Bakeries (Scotland) Ltd v Strathclyde Regional Council* 1985 SC (HL) 17.
86   *Kennedy v Glenbelle* 1996 SC 95.
87   PL(S)A 1973, s 7.
88   E.g. *Colville v Middleton,* 27 May 1817 FC.
89   E.g. under the Civil Aviation Act 1982, ss 76 and 77.
90   *Marcic v Thames Water Utilities Ltd* [2004] 2 AC 42.
91   *Webster v Lord Advocate* 1984 SLT 13, aff'd 1985 SLT 361.
92   E.g. *Adam v Alloa Police Commissioners* (1874) 2 R 143.
93   E.g. *Stevenson v Pontifex and Wood* (1887) 15 R 125.

example where there is a boundary dispute.[94] One example is interference with underground water which would normally percolate to the complainer's property.[95] Another is building fences or growing hedges which block out the complainer's light.[96] The remedies for *aemulatio vicini*, like nuisance, are the usual court remedies.

USE OF A NEIGHBOUR'S PROPERTY

General

17.27   Clearly, there are many grounds upon which a landowner may make limited use of a neighbour's property. Servitudes and public rights of way are obvious examples.[97] The concern here is merely with two residual rights:

   (a) drainage and

   (b) access for repairs.

Drainage

17.28   A landowner is entitled to let water lying outside a definite channel, such as a river, drain onto lower-lying neighbouring land.[98] The right applies to both surface and underground water. The owner is entitled to carry out works which alter the route of the drainage, but there are certain limitations. Only water naturally arising on the property, for example by rain, may be drained. The drainage must follow the natural lie of the land. Moreover, regard must be had to not damaging the inferior land by overstretching the right,[99] for example by carrying out building works on the superior land which cause an excessive amount of water to come down. In particular, unless there is a servitude of eavesdrop there is no right to collect rainwater on a roof and let it fall onto a neighbouring property.[100]

Access for repairs

17.29   In an important passage which does not seem to have been founded on in court, Hume states:

'I think it may be maintained with respect to conterminous proprietors in a Burgh, which in many instances, owing to the crowded situation of the building,

---

[94]   Whitty 'Nuisance' para 34.
[95]   *Milton v Glen-Moray Glenlivet Distillery Co Ltd* (1898) 1 F 135. See also *More v Boyle* 1967 SLT (Sh Ct) 38.
[96]   *Dunlop v Robertson* (1803) Hume 515; *Glassford v Astley* (1808) Mor 'Property', App, No 7, Hume 516.
[97]   See **CHAPTER 12** above and **PARAS 18.13–18.22** below.
[98]   *Campbell v Bryson* (1864) 3 M 254.
[99]   *Logan v Wang (UK) Ltd* 1991 SLT 580.
[100]   On eavesdrop, see **PARA 12.14** above.

cannot be repaired without some temporary interference, as by resting ladders on the next area, or suspending a scaffold over the next area, that this slight and temporary inconvenience must be put up with, from the necessity of the case.'[101]

FURTHER READING

Gordon *Scottish Land Law* paras 4.01–4.16; 4.37–4.51; 7.61–7.63; 13.07–13.09; 26.20–26.35.

Paisley *Land Law* paras 4.13–4.15; 4.24–4.27; 4.30.

Reid *Property* paras 175–180, 193–226; 252–272; 337–343; 359.

Whitty, N R 'Nuisance' in *SME* (Reissue, 2001).

---

[101]   Hume *Lectures* III, 207.

Chapter 18

Public access rights

INTRODUCTION

18.1 Private ownership of land is subject to certain rights in favour of the public. At common law the most important is the public right of way. Also significant are the rights to use public roads and rights over water and the foreshore. The common law however, is of less importance given the wide-ranging nature of the recent Land Reform (Scotland) Act 2003 (LR(S)A 2003) which gives access rights over private land for recreation and other purposes. If there is no right to be on someone else's land whether at common law or under statute, the landowner or other lawful possessor will have the remedy of trespass against those who come onto the land without permission. This is the subject of the final section of this chapter.[1] We begin with statutory access rights.

LAND REFORM (SCOTLAND) ACT 2003

The right to roam

18.2 Part 1 of LR(S)A 2003 was passed to improve access to land. A statutory 'right to roam' (an expression not used in the Act itself) was introduced. The legislation makes it clear that the rights under it are distinct from and do not affect other access rights, for example a servitude or public right of way allowing vehicular traffic.[2] This leads to a rather awkward overlap between LR(S)A 2003 and the common law.

Content of the access rights

18.3 LR(S)A 2003, s 1 confers on everyone statutory *access rights* to land. These rights are:
  (a) the right to be, for specified purposes, on land; and
  (b) the right to cross land.

The specified purposes in relation to (a) are set out in LR(S)A 2003, s 1(3). There are three. The first is 'recreational purposes'. This is not further defined, but the

---

[1] See PARAS **18.30–18.36** below.
[2] LR(S)A 2003, s 5(3).

Scottish Outdoor Access Code,[3] introduced under the legislation, gives examples: pastimes such as watching wildlife, sightseeing and photography; family and social activities, such as walks, picnics and kite flying; active pursuits, such as canoeing, horse riding,[4] mountaineering, sailing and wild camping; and participation in events such as marathons and mountain biking competitions.[5]

18.4 The second specified purpose for exercising access rights is 'carrying on a relevant educational activity'. This is defined as relating to furthering the understanding of natural or cultural heritage.[6] It allows access rights to be exercised by a leader and his or her students and support staff on a trip to learn about wildlife or landscapes or geological features.[7] The third purpose is 'carrying on, commercially or for profit, an activity which the person exercising the right could carry on otherwise than commercially or for profit'. This is a rather unclear provision, but it would seem to authorise the activities of paid mountain guides and the like. Therefore John is entitled to charge for a walking tour of hills belonging to Kaira, without Kaira having to be paid. Specific activities are not permitted, in particular hunting, shooting or fishing and using a motorised vehicle or vessel.[8] The right to roam may not be exercised by car or motorbike.

Excluded land

General

18.5 Access rights can be exercised above and below, as well as on, the surface of land,[9] with 'land' including bridges, inland waters, canals and the foreshore.[10] But the rights may not be exercised over the land listed in LR(S)A 2003, s 6. The list is a long one but, significantly, includes:
  (a) buildings;
  (b) caravans, tents or other places providing people with privacy or shelter;
  (c) school grounds;
  (d) sports or other playing fields;
  (e) land to which access is prohibited by other legislation;
  (f) land set out for a particular recreational purpose;

---

3   Scottish Outdoor Access Code para 2.7 (available at http://www.outdooraccess-scotland.com/default.asp).
4   On which see *Tuley v Highland Council* 2007 SLT (Sh Ct) 97, where an attempt to exclude horse riders from a particular path failed. At the time of writing, the case is under appeal.
5   Scottish Outdoor Access Code para 2.7.
6   LR(S)A 2003, s 1(5).
7   Scottish Outdoor Access Code para 2.8.
8   LR(S)A 2003, s 9.
9   LR(S)A 2003, s 1(6).
10   LR(S)A 2003, s 32.

> (g)   land on which building, civil engineering or demolition works are being carried out; and
>
> (h)   land in which crops have been sown or are growing.[11]

Three important cases

18.6   Three further types of land on the list require more detailed mention. First, the access rights do not extend to 'sufficient adjacent land' to allow person living in houses or the places mentioned in (b) above 'to have reasonable measures of privacy in that house or place to ensure that their enjoyment [thereof] is not unreasonably disturbed'.[12] The Scottish Outdoor Access Code attempts to provide some guidance.[13] 'Sufficient adjacent land' is normally to mean an individual's garden. In relation to larger houses with what may be termed 'policies', the Code says that access rights do not apply to those parts 'intensively managed for the domestic enjoyment of the house'. Examples given are lawns, flower beds, paths, seats, sheds, water features and summer houses. But 'less intensively managed' parts such as grasslands and woodlands are to be subject to access rights. The Code's approach was criticised by the sheriff in *Gloag v Perth and Kinross Council*[14] because LR(S)A 2003 does not make the *use* of the land the test. Otherwise, large landowners might be tempted to turn their whole estate into a lawn.[15] More fundamentally, LR(S)A 2003, s 10 says that the Code is about the *how* of access, not the *where*. In the *Gloag* case, well-known businesswoman Ann Gloag obtained declarator that 11 acres of her estate at Kinfauns Castle in Perthshire were exempt from access rights under this ground, by reason of the need to protect her privacy. In *Snowie v Stirling Council*[16] the owners of Boquhan House, Kippen sought to have all 70 acres of their estate declared exempt. This failed except for a relatively small area.

18.7   Second, land open to the public in return for payment for at least 90 days in the year ending 31 January 2001, and which has continued since then to be open upon payment, is not subject to access rights.[17] The date relates to when the draft Land Reform Bill was first published. It means that an established tourist attraction such as Blair Drummond Safari Park can continue to charge an admission fee but, in principle, someone opening a new safari park cannot restrict access by fee-charging. Such a person should therefore ask the local authority to exempt the land from LR(S)A 2003.

---

[11]   Woodland and orchards are in principle excluded from (h). See LR(S)A 2003, s 7(10)(c)(i).
[12]   LR(S)A 2003, s 6(1)(b)(iv).
[13]   Scottish Outdoor Access Code paras 3.13–3.17.
[14]   2007 SCLR 530 at para 36.
[15]   Reid and Gretton *Conveyancing 2007* (2008) 131.
[16]   2008 GWD 13-244.
[17]   LR(S)A 2003, s 6(1)(f).

18.8   This is the third type of excepted land referred to above.[18] There are detailed rules on how the local authority can make an exemption order.[19] In particular, the order must be confirmed by the Scottish Ministers if it is to last for six or more days. Ministers also have power to exempt land.[20]

Responsible conduct

18.9   Both those exercising access rights and the owner of the land in question must act responsibly.[21] The exercise of access rights is presumed to be responsible if it does not 'cause unreasonable interference' to the rights of others, for example the rights of the landowner or others taking advantage of their access rights.[22] Landowners are prohibited from taking action which has 'the main purpose of preventing or deterring' the exercise of access rights.[23] This expressly includes putting up signs and fences. Local authorities have enforcement powers.[24]

Duty of care of landowners

18.10   The duty of care owed by landowners to individuals present on their land is not altered by LR(S)A 2003.[25] Nevertheless, it is not unreasonable to suppose that more people may exercise access as a result of the legislation. Therefore, the risk in practice of a civil action may increase.[26]

The role of Scottish Natural Heritage

18.11   LR(S)A 2003 imposes certain responsibilities on Scottish Natural Heritage, most notably the creation and issue of the Scottish Outdoor Access Code.[27] The Code contains much detail about how access rights should be exercised. Its legal status is not entirely clear. A comparison could be made with the Highway Code.

---

[18]   LR(S)A 2003, s 6(1)(j).
[19]   LR(S)A 2003, s 11.
[20]   LR(S)A 2003, s 8.
[21]   LR(S)A 2003, ss 2 and 3.
[22]   LR(S)A 2003, s 2(2).
[23]   LR(S)A 2003, s 14(1).
[24]   LR(S)A 2003, ss 13 and 14. See *Caledonian Heritable Ltd v East Lothian Council* 2006 GWD 22-487 and *Tuley v Highland Council* 2007 SLT (Sh Ct) 97.
[25]   LR(S)A 2003, s 5(2).
[26]   For discussion, see D Mackenzie Skene and A M Slater 'Liability and Access to the Countryside: The Impact of Part 1 of the Land Reform (Scotland) Act 2003' 2004 *JR* 353.
[27]   LR(S)A 2003, s 10.

The role of local authorities

18.12   Local authorities are given a wide-ranging regulatory role in relation to the legislation. They have a general duty to uphold access rights.[28] More particularly, they have the power to make byelaws[29] and can install notices and fences, as well as 'means of contributing to the comfort and convenience' of those exercising access rights.[30] Lavatories are expressly mentioned. Local authorities are also tasked with establishing a 'core path' plan, to facilitate the public in gaining reasonable access to land in their area.[31]

PUBLIC RIGHTS OF WAY

General

18.13   At common law, a public right of way can be created giving members of the public a right of access over land in order to travel from one public place to another. There are over 7,000 such rights recorded in the National Catalogue of Rights of Way maintained by the Scottish Rights of Way and Access Society in association with Scottish Natural Heritage.[32] Public rights of way remain important notwithstanding the new access rights under LR(S)A 2003. For example, they may have a route over land excluded from those rights, or may be vehicular.

18.14   A public right of way is similar to a servitude.[33] But there are some key differences.[34] First, with a servitude there is not only a burdened property but also a benefited property. With a public right of way, there is *only* a burdened property. Second, a servitude can facilitate access to private land. A public right of way must connect two public places. Third, servitudes allow use of land for various purposes, such as to lay pipes and take building materials. Public rights of way give access rights only. These features are discussed further in the following paragraphs.

A burdened property

18.15   Land burdened by a public right of way may be in either private or public ownership. The right may be across open ground or through a structure that has acceded, such as a covered walkway over a road.[35] It is an essential requirement,

---

[28]   LR(S)A 2003, s 13.
[29]   LR(S)A 2003, s 12.
[30]   LR(S)A 2003, s 15.
[31]   LR(S)A 2003, ss 17–22.
[32]   See http://www.scotways.com/.
[33]   On servitudes, see CHAPTER 12 above.
[34]   See also *Thomson v Murdoch* (1862) 24 D 975 at 982 per Lord Deas; and Cusine and Paisley *Servitudes and Rights of Way* paras 1.12 and 18.11.
[35]   *Cumbernauld and Kilsyth District Council v Dollar Land (Cumbernauld) Ltd* 1993 SC (HL) 44.

however, that there is a fixed route. A public right of way has the purpose of allowing access from A to B. It cannot permit general wandering.[36] In the words of Lord Sands in one of the leading cases:

> '[T]he right of way claimed must be by a definite path. I do not think that this necessarily requires that under all circumstances that there should be a visible path.'[37]

Where, however, there is not an actual path it may be more difficult to establish the existence of the right.

Two public places

18.16   The requirement that a public right of way requires to connect two public places requires a definition of what is a 'public place'. The courts have approached this question on a case-by-case basis but, in summary, it is a place to which the public has resort for a lawful purpose.[38] The following have been held to be public places:

(a) a public road;[39]
(b) Portobello beach, being an example of a beach used by the public regularly for recreation;[40]
(c) a town;[41] and
(d) a harbour.[42]

The following have been held not to be public places:

(a) a market open for four days a week only;[43]
(b) a sub-post office in a private house;[44]
(c) a curious natural object such as a large rock;[45] and
(d) Prestwick Airport, on the basis that the public does not have a right to access it at all times.[46]

---

[36]   *Mackintosh v Moir* (1871) 9 M 574 at 575 per Lord President Inglis and at 579 per Lord Ardmillan.
[37]   *Rhins District Committee of Wigtownshire County Council v Cuninghame* 1917 2 SLT 169 at 171.
[38]   Cusine and Paisley *Servitudes and Rights of Way* paras 20.03–20.22.
[39]   *Jenkins v Murray* (1866) 4 M 1046 at 1052 per Lord Deas.
[40]   *Darrie v Drummond* (1865) 3 M 496 at 501 per Lord Deas. See also *Richardson v Cromarty Petroleum* 1982 SLT 237 and *Lauder v MacColl* 1993 SCLR 753.
[41]   *Duncan v Lees* (1871) 9 M 855 at 856 per Lord President Inglis.
[42]   *Moncreiffe v Lord Provost of Perth* (1842) 5 D 298. But, depending on the facts, a harbour could be private.
[43]   *Ayr Burgh Council v British Transport Commission* 1955 SLT 219.
[44]   *Love-Lee v Cameron* 1991 SCLR 61.
[45]   *Duncan v Lees* (1870) 9 M 274.
[46]   *PIK Facilities Ltd v Watson's Ayr Park Ltd* 2005 SLT 1041.

Access only

18.17   A public right of way permits access across the burdened property only. It does not authorise other rights such as pasturage or the laying of pipes. There is an argument that the public may have certain rights ancillary to that of access, such as the placing of signs to indicate the way.[47] Local authorities have a statutory right to install and maintain facilities 'contributing to the comfort and convenience' of those exercising a public right of way such as gates, stiles, seats and lavatories.[48] The extent of the access, for example, whether it is confined to passage on foot will be determined by what type of right has been created.

Creation

18.18   In principle, a public right of way may be created expressly in a deed granted by a landowner.[49] A grant cannot be made in favour of the public as such; rather, it should be favour of a representative body such as a local authority or the Scottish Rights of Way and Access Society.[50] The relevant deed may state how the right may be exercised, for example by means of non-commercial vehicles. It is thought that the deed does not have to be registered, but it can be.[51] If it is not, it is unclear whether possession is required to constitute the right. It might that a right of way does not actually require a deed it to be voluntarily granted by the landowner. This is discussed below.[52]

18.19   Creation by deed is rare. Constitution by positive prescription is far more common. This requires possession by members of the public for a period of 20 years.[53] No foundation writ or other former of registration is required. Therefore public rights of way are overriding interests in the Land Register.[54] The possession must meet a number of requirements.
  (1) It must be along the *entire* length of the route.[55]
  (2) It must be continuous and uninterrupted.[56]
  (3) The use must be *substantial*. This depends on the facts of the case, in particular whether the route is located in a remote or populous area. Generally, a greater level of use must be made in an urban situation.[57]
  (4) Finally, the possession must be 'adverse' and not by tolerance.

---

[47]   Cusine and Paisley *Servitudes and Rights of Way* para 2.18.
[48]   LR(S)A 2003, s 15(4) applied by s 31.
[49]   *Marquis of Bute v McKirdy & McMillan* 1937 SC 93 at 131 per Lord Moncreiff.
[50]   *Marquis of Bute* at 131 per Lord Moncreiff.
[51]   Cusine and Paisley *Servitudes and Rights of Way* para 19.11.
[52]   See PARA **18.23** below.
[53]   PL(S)A 1973, s 3(3).
[54]   LR(S)A 1979, s 28. See PARA **6.36** above.
[55]   *Rhins District Committee of Wigtownshire County Council v Cuninghame* 1917 2 SLT 169.
[56]   *Mann v Brodie* (1885) 11 R (HL) 52.
[57]   *Cumbernauld and Kilsyth District Council v Dollar Land (Cumbernauld) Ltd* 1993 SC (HL) 44.

This means that if, for example, John, a landowner, explicitly gives permission for a group of local walkers to cross his land then their doing so will not amount to adverse possession. John might, however, not have given permission but not objected either. In that case, 'the law will assume a public right rather than an easy-going proprietor'.[58] Ironically, the introduction of the statutory access rights under LR(S)A 2003 may make it more difficult to establish a public right of way by prescription. This is because a court may attribute the exercise to those rights and this of itself cannot found a prescriptive right of way.[59]

18.20   The extent of a right of way created by prescription is the extent of the possession: *tantum praescriptum tantum possessum.* This means, for example, if access has only been taken on foot, a car may not be used. But the greater right includes the lesser. Hence a right for vehicles will mean that pedestrians and horse riders can use the way.[60] It has been held that bicycles may be ridden where the right was created by pedestrian use, on the perhaps challenging ground that 'the pedal cycle is only an aid to pedestrianism'.[61]

Exercise

18.21   Like a servitude, a public right of way must be exercised in a manner which is least burdensome to the landowner.[62] Exercise must not interfere with the rights of other members of the public wishing to take advantage of it either. The landowner is not entitled to obstruct the way.[63] Gates are permissible, if erected for good reason, such as to confine animals.[64] They must not be locked, however, unless a stile or other method of passing the gate is provided.[65] Local authorities have the same powers to deal with obstructions to rights of way as for access rights under LR(S)A 2003.[66] There is similar power available to planning authorities, i.e. local authorities under separate legislation.[67] The landowner is not under a duty to repair the route,[68] but should consider this matter carefully, given the Occupiers' Liability (Scotland) Act

---

[58]   *Marquis of Bute v McKirdy & McMillan* 1937 SC 93 at 120–121 per Lord President Normand.
[59]   LR(S)A 2003, s 5(5). See R R M Paisley *Access Rights and Rights of Way: A Guide to the Law in Scotland* (2006) 9.
[60]   *Mackenzie v Bankes* (1868) 6 M 936.
[61]   *Aberdeenshire County Council v Lord Glentanar* 1999 SLT 1456. This case was actually decided in 1931.
[62]   *Lord Burton v Mackay* 1995 SLT 507.
[63]   *Lord Donington v Mair* (1894) 21 R 829.
[64]   *Hay v Earl of Morton's Trs* (1861) 24 D 116.
[65]   *Kirkpatrick v Murray* (1856) 19 D 91.
[66]   LR(S)A 2003, s 14, as applied by s 31.
[67]   Countryside (Scotland) Act 1967, s 46(1).
[68]   *Allan v MacLachlan* (1900) 2 F 699.

1960.[69] In principle, members of the public may do so,[70] but in practice this is likely to fall to the local authority under statute.[71]

Extinction

18.22   A public right of way is extinguished by 20 years of non-use.[72] It will also cease to exist if either or both the places at the ends of the way are no longer public places. There are also various statutory powers in favour of public bodies such as local authorities which can be used to bring about the demise of the right.[73] Where a public right of way is extinguished intermediate proprietors may nonetheless take access along the route to reach their properties.[74]

PUBLIC ROADS

General

18.23   There exists a complex set of common law and statutory rules on public roads. This whole area of law is under-researched and difficult. A local authority may 'adopt' a road.[75] It may do so in relation to roads over which there is a public right of passage.[76] It has been held that a road does not need to be the subject of an established right of way to meet this requirement; acquiescence by the landowner in use by the public will do.[77] Adoption means that the authority becomes responsible for the maintenance of the road. Ownership is unaffected. It has been stated that adoption does not mean that there is a public right to use the road.[78] But, even if this is correct it would be a very unusual situation. For roads older than 20 years, positive prescription may have operated.[79] But there is a difficulty with this. Where a developer builds a road for a new development or the Scottish Government constructs a new motorway on land which it has compulsorily acquired, the subsequent use of the road or motorway will be with the consent of the developer or Government. Thus it will not be 'adverse' possession, as required for positive prescription.[80] It may be

---

[69]   *Johnstone v Sweeney* 1985 SLT (Sh Ct) 2. See also J W G Blackie 'Liability as Occupier to User of a Right of Way' 1994 *SLT (News)* 349.

[70]   *Rodgers v Harvie* (1830) 8 S 611.

[71]   Countryside (Scotland) Act 1967, s 46(2).

[72]   PL(S)A 1973, s 8.

[73]   Cusine and Paisley *Servitudes and Rights of Way* paras 24.08–24.13.

[74]   *Lord Burton v Mackay* 1995 SLT 507.

[75]   Roads (Scotland) Act 1984, ss 1 and 16.

[76]   Roads (Scotland) Act 1984, s 15(1).

[77]   *MacKinnon v Argyll and Bute Council* 2001 SLT 1275. But compare *Hamilton v Dumfries and Galloway Council* 2008 SLT 531.

[78]   A Faulds, T Craggs and J Saunders, *Scottish Roads Law* (2nd edn, 2008) 52. Compare Paisley *Land Law* para 10.12 and Reid and Gretton *Conveyancing 2000* (2001) para 50-51.

[79]   See PARA **18.19** above.

[80]   See PARA **18.19** above.

that in such circumstances our law permits the creation of a public right of way, or more narrowly, a public road, voluntarily without the need for a deed. This is speculative. The essential point is that our law is obscure. A further argument is that there exists a common law right of highway which may be invoked, although the applicable rules are not certain.[81] Finally, where land is acquired by a public authority in order for a road to be constructed, it can be argued that such a road is irrevocably dedicated to public use.[82] Whether this amounts to the establishment of a public right of way is again uncertain.

Public roads and public rights of way compared

18.24   The inter-relationship between public roads and public rights of way is also unclear. It may be that a public road is a specific sub-type of public right of way. This is arguably presupposed by PL(S)A 1973, which refers to the prescriptive creation of 'public rights of way'[83] but not of 'roads'. Professor Paisley has identified certain differences, between public roads and (other?) public rights of way, some of which may be mentioned.[84] In general, it would seem that a right over a public road is imprescriptible.[85] While public rights of way may be limited to pedestrian use, public roads can always be used by vehicles. Moreover, they may be used to convey services, but this latter right is now under the control of the roads authority.[86] Finally, while limited obstructions such as unlocked gates can be erected on (non-road) public rights of way, there is, subject to statutory exceptions,[87] a prohibition on obstructions across public roads.[88]

RIGHTS OVER WATER AND THE FORESHORE

General

18.25   At common law the public have certain rights over tidal and non-tidal waters, as well as the foreshore.[89] As with public rights of way, there is a rather awkward overlap with the new statutory access rights under LR(S)A 2003. The common law rights are held in trust by the Crown for the benefit of the public under the doctrine of the *regalia majora*.[90] Thus the Crown is entitled to enforce these rights.[91] But so

---

[81]   Cusine and Paisley *Servitudes and Rights of Way* paras 18.03–18.10.

[82]   *Elmford v City of Glasgow Council (No 2)* 2001 SC 267.

[83]   PL(S)A 1973, s 3(3).

[84]   Paisley, *Land Law* para 10.12.

[85]   *Waddell v Earl of Buchan* (1868) 6 M 690.

[86]   Roads (Scotland) Act 1984, ss 61 and 90–93.

[87]   For example, for certain bridge tolls, prior to the Abolition of Bridge Tolls (Scotland) Act 2008.

[88]   *Sutherland v Thomson* (1876) 3 R 485 and Roads (Scotland) Act 1984, s 59.

[89]   For definitions of these terms, see **PARAS 16.3 AND 16.5** above.

[90]   See Gordon *Scottish Land Law* para 27.06.

[91]   *Crown Estate Commissioners v Fairlie Yacht Slip Ltd* 1979 SC 156 at 178 per Lord President Emslie.

too are members of the public, by means of an action known as the *actio popularis*.[92] The Scottish Law Commission has proposed that the common law rights be replaced by a set of statutory rights directly enforceable by the public.[93] If these proposals are implemented, the Crown's enforcement role would cease. Instead, local authorities would be charged with this.[94]

18.26 With one important exception, the rights arise automatically. That exception is the right to navigate non-tidal waters, which is constituted by 40 years of use.[95] It follows that none of the rights require registration for their constitution and that therefore they are overriding interests for the purposes of land registration.[96]

Tidal waters

18.27 There are two rights over tidal waters. The first is *navigation*. This is confined to waters which are 'navigable', that is waters which in their usual state are capable of navigation.[97] By 'navigation' is meant travelling by boat or equivalent vessel on the water. It does not include propelling a canoe by wading along the sea or river bed.[98] Certain rights ancillary to navigation are permitted, such as dropping anchor. The attaching of fixed moorings to the sea bed is not.[99] The second right is that of *white fishing* and *fishing for shellfish*. By 'white fishing' is meant the right to take all swimming fish other than salmon. By 'shellfish' are meant all shellfish on the sea bed, apart from mussels and oysters. The rights to salmon, mussels and oysters are legal separate tenements and are thus excluded from the public rights.[100]

Foreshore

18.28 Various rights exist over the foreshore. Akin to the rights relating to tidal waters, there are rights ancillary to navigation, such as fishing for whitefish and shellfish, embarkation, shooting wildfowl[101] and recreation.[102] The latter does not include selling refreshments.[103] The Scottish Law Commission has recommended

---

92   See, e.g., *Walford v David* 1989 SLT 876.

93   Scottish Law Commission *Report on Law of the Foreshore and Sea Bed* (2003) paras 3.1–3.8.

94   *Report on Law of the Foreshore and Sea Bed* paras 3.31–3.35.

95   See PARA **18.29** below.

96   LR(S)A 1979, s 28(1). See PARA **6.36** above.

97   *Will's Trs v Cairngorm Canoeing and Sailing School Ltd* 1976 SC (HL) 30 at 165 per Lord Fraser.

98   *Scammell v Scottish Sports Council* 1983 SLT 462.

99   *Crown Estate Commissioners v Fairlie Yacht Slip Ltd* 1979 SC 156.

100 See PARA **14.17** above. But the Scottish Law Commission has proposed that there should be a public right to take mussels and oysters except where the right to these has been specifically granted by the Crown. See *Report on Law of the Foreshore and Sea Bed* (2003) para 3.19.

101 *Hope v Bennewith* (1904) 6 F 1004.

102 *Nicol v Blaikie* (1859) 22 D 335.

103 *Marquess of Ailsa v Monteforte* 1937 SC 805.

the enactment of a non-exhaustive list of recreational activities, including picnicking, sunbathing and making sandcastles.[104]

Non-tidal waters

18.29   At common law there are no public rights in non-tidal waters, except that the right of navigation can be acquired by 40 years of use.[105] In that case the rule *tantum praescriptum quantum possessum*[106] does not apply: the water can be navigated to its full extent.[107] The importance of the common law in this area has been much diminished by LR(S)A 2003, under which non-motorised passage along rivers is permitted.[108] But the common law right can still apply where the statutory rights cannot, for example where the river is near a house and is excluded by the legislation on the ground of privacy.[109]

TRESPASS

Introduction

18.30   It is sometimes said that there is no law of trespass in Scotland. This, however, is to be 'loose and inaccurate'.[110] Were it to be otherwise, there would be no need for the common law public rights over land and water, nor the new statutory rights under LR(S)A 2003. *Trespass* is the temporary intrusion into the land of another. It is a delict. For example, Ann might take a short-cut through Bob's garden. Someone may trespass by means of an animal (Carol's dog runs about on Donald's lawn) or of a thing (Elspeth's crane swings across Fred's airspace).[111] Trespass is a *transient* interference with someone's right of possession of his or her land exclusively. By contrast, in the case of *encroachment* the interference is more than transient.[112]

Defences

18.31   If a trespass action were to be raised, two main defences are available to the defender.

---

[104]   Report on Law of the Foreshore and Sea Bed para 3.14.
[105]   *Will's Trustees v Cairngorm Canoeing and Sailing School Ltd* 1979 SC (HL) 30, about canoeing on the Spey.
[106]   See PARA **18.20** above.
[107]   1979 SC (HL) 30 at 169 per Lord Fraser.
[108]   See PARA **18.3** above.
[109]   LR(S)A 2003, s 6(1)(b)(iv). See PARA **18.6** above.
[110]   *Wood v North British Railway* (1899) 2 F 1 at 2 per Lord Trayner.
[111]   *Brown v Lee Constructions Ltd* 1977 SLT (Notes) 61.
[112]   See PARAS **17.10–17.16** above.

(1) That the owner or other lawful possessor has either expressly or impliedly *consented* to the intrusion. For example, a university agrees to the use of its library by its students.[113]

(2) That the intrusion is permitted by law. For example, Grace may be entitled to cross Herbert's field because of a servitude or a public right of way or the access rights in LR(S)A 2003.[114] The intrusion might also be justified by judicial warrant. An example is where a judicial officer executes diligence.[115]

A further instance is *emergency*. On this basis, escape from a fire, or the chasing of a criminal through the property of another, is justified.[116]

Criminal liability

18.32   In general, trespass is not a crime. There are, however, a number of statutes making it illegal in particular circumstances. These include the Trespass (Scotland) Act 1865 which makes it an offence to lodge or encamp on private property except where exercising access rights under LR(S)A 2003;[117] the Game (Scotland) Act 1832 and the Night Poaching Act 1828 which are aimed at poachers;[118] and the Criminal Justice and Public Order Act 1994, aimed at New Age travellers.[119]

Civil remedies

18.33   Trespass may be interdicted. In practice, the remedy can be difficult to obtain. The name(s) of the trespasser(s) must be known. It is impossible to interdict the public at large. The courts will not grant interdict unless there is a reasonable likelihood of trespass.[120] Proof of past trespass is the best evidence.[121] The pursuer is expected to have warned the trespasser off before seeking an interdict.[122] Interdict will not be awarded if the trespass is trivial. In *Winans v Macrae*[123] the pursuer sought an interdicting preventing the defender 'from putting any lamb, lambs, sheep, cattle, or other bestial' on his 200,000 acres of unfenced rough grazing. The defender, who lived in an adjacent cottage, had only a pet lamb. The action failed.

---

[113]   Reid *Property* para 181.
[114]   See LR(S)A 2003, s 5(1).
[115]   Debtors (Scotland) Act 1987, s 87.
[116]   Hume *Lectures* III, 205–206.
[117]   Trespass (Scotland) Act 1865, s 3.
[118]   Game (Scotland) Act 1832, s 1; and Night Poaching Act 1828, s 1.
[119]   Criminal Justice and Public Order Act 1994, ss 61, 62, 68 and 69.
[120]   *Inverurie Magistrates v Sorrie* 1956 SC 175.
[121]   *Warrand v Watson* (1905) 8 F 253.
[122]   *Paterson v McPherson* (1916) 33 Sh Ct Rep 237.
[123]   (1885) 12 R 1051.

18.34   A trespasser who causes damage is liable for it. But liability is not strict. There must be *culpa* i.e. fault.[124] There is an exception for damage caused by certain animals.[125]

Self-help

18.35   Rather than going to court, the landowner or lawful possessor may seek to deal with the trespasser directly. Steps may be taken to stop trespass happening in the first place such as locking gates and erecting high walls. Premises may also be protected by guard dogs, but here there is specific legislation. The dog must be under the control of a person or tied up and there must be notices at the entrances warning of the animal's presence.[126] Where the trespass is taking place, the trespasser may be asked to leave. If he or she does not do so, force may be used but this must be kept to the absolute minimum required in the circumstances. In *Bell v Shand*,[127] a late nineteenth-century case, a landowner was held to be justified in dragging a 15-year-old poacher for some distance by the scruff of the neck. Whether this is good law today is open to question. Force is more justifiable where the trespass is into a private house for the purpose is to commit theft, but it requires to be proportionate. For example, shooting a burglar might lead to criminal charges.[128]

Straying animals

18.36   Trespass by straying animals deserves particular comment. The courts are reluctant to grant interdict here unless the animal is of the type whose movements can be easily restricted, for example chickens. In the case of cattle and sheep and the like, the onus is more likely to be placed on the owner of the land which is being trespassed upon to enclose it by fencing rather than upon the owner of the animal to prevent the intrusion.[129]

18.37   The provisions of the Animals (Scotland) Act 1987 are also relevant. Under that legislation, the occupier of land may detain a straying animal which is not under any person's control in order to prevent injury or damage by it.[130] There is immunity from civil liability where such an animal is killed or injured by the occupier in self-defence or in order to protect another person or livestock.[131] This, however, only

---

[124]   *Harvie v Turner* (1910) 32 Sh Ct Rep 267.
[125]   See **PARA 18.36** below.
[126]   Guard Dogs Act 1975, s 1.
[127]   (1870) 7 SLR 267.
[128]   Cf the headline-hitting English case, *R v Martin* [2003] QB 1. For Scots law, see G H Gordon *The Criminal Law of Scotland* (3rd edn by M G A Christie, 2001) vol 2, paras 24-16 and 24-17.
[129]   *Winans v Macrae* (1885) 12 R 1051 at 1064 per Lord Young; *Forest Property Trust v Lindsay* 1998 GWD 31-1581.
[130]   Animals (Scotland) Act 1987 (A(S)A 1987), s 3(1).

applies if the occupier acted in the reasonable belief that there was no other way of preventing or dealing with the attack and where the police are notified within 48 hours.[132] Where damage has been caused, in certain circumstances strict liability is placed upon the 'keeper' of the animal, i.e. its owner or possessor.[133] An example is where the land or its produce is materially damaged by the foraging of particular animals including cattle, goats, horses, pigs and sheep.[134]

FURTHER READING

Cusine and Paisley *Servitudes and Rights of Way* chs 18–24.

Gordon *Scottish Land Law* paras 7.06; 7.18–7.20; 13.10; 24.105–24.154.

Paisley, R R M *Access Rights and Rights of Way: A Guide to the Law in Scotland* (2006).

Paisley *Land Law* ch 10.

Reid *Property* paras 180–190; 494–528.

Rennie *Land Tenure* ch 15.

Scottish Law Commission *Report on Law of the Foreshore* (Scot Law Com No 190, 2003).

---

[131]   A(S)A 1987, s 4(1)(a) and (3).
[132]   A(S)A 1987, s 4(1)(b) and (4).
[133]   A(S)A 1987, ss 1(1)(a), (b), (3) and 5(1)(a). For a recent case involving a labrador, see *Welsh v Brady* 2008 SLT 363.
[134]   A(S)A 1987, s 1(1)(b) and (3)(b).

Chapter 19

Leases

INTRODUCTION

19.1 A lease is a contract in which one person (the lessor) grants to another (the lessee) the right to use the property for a fixed time in return for a periodical payment known as rent. Leases are common: many students will be a party to one in relation to the flat in which they live. Leases can also be granted over other types of property, such as agricultural and commercial property. It is also competent to lease moveable property. Such a lease is normally referred to as 'hire'. For example, a couple on holiday from abroad might hire a car for a week to drive around Scotland. In the business world, machines are frequently hired. Only leases of land are capable of becoming real rights and for that reason this chapter will be confined to that type of lease. Leases of heritable property divide into three main types:

(1) commercial property;
(2) agricultural property; and
(3) residential property.

The latter two are subject to special statutory regimes – several different ones in each case. This chapter concentrates on the general law of leases, because an account of all the special statutory regimes would be impossible, though a brief overview of these is given. The special regimes often derogate from the general law, and within the framework of a brief account it is not possible to note all these derogations.

Terminology

19.2   The lessor is commonly called the 'landlord', and the lessee the 'tenant'. 'Tenancy' is often used as an equivalent term for lease, particular for residential property. 'Tack' is the traditional Scottish word, now seldom encountered. 'Location' is a term which comes from the Roman *locatio*. Its use is now confined to the expression 'tacit relocation' which, as will be seen, means an implied renewal of a lease.[1] 'Mail' is an old Scottish term for rent. As well as having to pay rent, tenants sometimes have to pay a 'grassum', which is a capital payment due at the commencement of the lease, also sometimes called a 'premium'. The duration of a lease is traditionally called the 'term' and the end of the lease the 'ish'.

THE FOUR CARDINAL ELEMENTS

19.3   Four cardinal elements must be present in order for there to be a valid contract of lease. These are:
  (a) the parties;
  (b) the property;
  (c) the rent; and
  (d) the duration.

(a) Parties

19.4   There must be agreement as to who the lessor and the lessee are. It is permissible for either to be joint parties. For example, a husband and wife might rent out their house or four students might take a lease of a flat. Both natural and juristic persons are capable of being parties to a lease. In the case of partnerships, however, it is common for the partners act as trustees for the firm and to contract on that basis.[2]

(b) Property

19.5   The property can be land or buildings. In these cases, the lessee must be given exclusive possession. In other words, the landlord is not entitled to retain natural possession of the land. Fishing rights, mineral rights and shooting rights can also be leased. In these cases, the landlord may continue to use the land over which the lease is granted for purposes other than those which are the subject of the lease. Under the general principle of specificity, the subjects of a lease must be identified.[3]

---

[1]   See **PARA 19.38** below.
[2]   This is also the practice when a partnership buys land, notwithstanding the Abolition of Feudal Tenure etc (Scotland) Act 2000 (AFT(S)A 2000), s 70.
[3]   E.g. *Conway v Glasgow City Council* 1999 SCLR 248.

If the tenant has already entered into possession it may be possible to refer to that possession to determine the extent of the lease.[4]

(c) Rent

19.6   The rent is usually payable on a monthly basis in residential cases and quarterly in commercial ones. But it is also permissible for rent to be paid in kind, for example by handing over a certain amount of fish or performing certain services.[5] If the other three cardinal elements are in place and the lessee has already taken possession, then the court may be willing to hold that a lease exists, and to fix a market rent.[6] The requirement for rent is for a periodical payment. A grassum on its own at the start of a lease is insufficient.[7] Older leases often contain provisions whereby a payment to the landlord known as a 'casualty' was triggered on the happening of a specified event. It became incompetent to impose such casualties in 1974[8] and existing ones in leases with a duration of more than 175 years have been abolished.[9]

(d) Duration

19.7   The only requirement about duration at common law is that there is one. A lease for 'as long as the grass growth up and the water runneth down' is valid.[10] So, too, is a lease for an ultra-long period such as 999 years.[11] There are now statutory restrictions. Leases of dwellinghouses created since 1974 cannot have a duration over 20 years.[12] Leases of other types of property created since 2000 cannot have a duration over 175 years.[13] These rules are not retrospective: for instance, a 999-year lease of a dwellinghouse created in 1821 would still be valid. The rules were introduced to prevent leases being used to mimic feudal tenure, which was being dismantled and has now been abolished. Where no duration has been agreed, but the other cardinal elements are present and the lessee has taken possession, the court will imply a duration of one year.[14]

---

[4]   *Andert Ltd v J & J Johnston* 1987 SLT 268.

[5]   Paisley *Land Law* para 7.9.

[6]   *Glen v Roy* (1882) 10 R 239; *Shetland Islands Council v BP Petroleum Development Ltd* 1990 SLT 82.

[7]   *Mann v Houston* 1957 SLT 89.

[8]   Land Tenure Reform (Scotland) Act 1974, s 16.

[9]   Leasehold Casualties (Scotland) Act 2001.

[10]   *Carruthers v Irvine* (1717) Mor 15195.

[11]   *Welwood v Husband* (1874) 1 R 507.

[12]   Land Tenure Reform (Scotland) Act 1974, ss 8–9.

[13]   AFT(S)A 2000, s 67. The Scottish Law Commission has also published proposals to convert existing 'ultra-long' leases into ownership rights: see *Report on Conversion of Long Leases* (2006).

[14]   *Gray v University of Edinburgh* 1962 SC 157.

CONSTITUTION

Formalities

19.8 Leases of one year or less do not require writing.[15] Those that exceed that period must be subscribed by both parties.[16] Equivalent rules apply to any prior missives of let (a contract preceding the actual lease[17]), or any transfer, variation or extinction of the lease. If the lease or deed relating to it is to be registered in the Land Register or Books of Council and Session, then attestation by a witness will be required.[18]

Leases and other rights of use

19.9 Merely because someone has the right to use the property of another does not mean that there is a contract of lease. It might be some other type of contract. For example, suppose that the possession of land is given for a period in exchange for a grassum but no rent. Lack of *exclusive* possession will again mean that the agreement is not a lease.[19] The possibilities of rights of use not being leases are endless. For example, in *Scottish Residential Estates Development Co v Henderson*[20] the owner of a cottage wrote to a lady, stating that 'you and your sons may have the use of the cottage until we require possession of it'. It was held that there was no intention to create a lease. Co-owners cannot grant a lease to one co-owner.[21]

Lease as a real right?

19.10 If the contractual essentials are satisfied and writing has been used if required, the tenant will have a valid contract of lease. This, however, is only a personal right. As such, it will not bind a successor owner if the landlord sells the property. For example, Kirsteen owns land and grants to Louise a twenty-five-year lease. A year later, she dispones to Matthew. Unless the lease has been made real, Matthew can require Louise to leave. She may protest: 'But I have a contract allowing me to remain another nine years!' But Matthew can reply: 'You may have a contract, but not with me. Get off my land.' Off Louise must go – though she will have a claim against

---

[15] RoW(S)A 1995, s 1(7). The rule likewise applies to assignations and renunciations of such leases.
[16] RoW(S)A 1995, s 1(2)(b).
[17] These are sometimes encountered in practice but their status is unclear. A lease is itself a contract, so such missives are contracts to contract – something that is highly problematic in contract law.
[18] RoW(S)A 1995, s 6. While s 6 mentions the Sasine Register, the same rule is applied for the Land Register – where all new long leases must go now.
[19] *Magistrates of Perth v Assessor for Perth & Kinross* 1937 SC 549.
[20] 1991 SLT 490.
[21] *Clydesdale Bank plc v Davidson* 1998 SC(HL) 51.

Kirsteen for breach of contract. Nor would the contract bind the owner's trustee in sequestration. For these parties to be bound, the lease needs to be *also* a real right. At common law this was not possible. A lease was a contract and nothing more, and this remains the position for leases of moveables. For land the law was changed by the Leases Act 1449, since when most leases of heritable property have been contracts *with real effect*. The way in which this happens depends on whether the lease is a short lease (20 years or under) or a long lease. (As with all real rights, the *nemo plus* rule[22] applies: the lease must be granted by the right person.) Although a lease can be a real right, i.e. a subordinate real right, it is unlike other subordinate real rights. In the first place, it is, unlike them, an ongoing contract, though one that has acquired real effect. A real lease straddles rather awkwardly the law of contract and the law of real rights. In the second place, other subordinate real rights detract from the value of the property: they are pure encumbrances. By contrast, a lease is an encumbrance but it is also a pertinent: it is an asset for the owner. In business terms, it represents an income stream. Indeed, property, especially commercial property, may be more valuable let than unlet, in which case the pertinent aspect of the lease outweighs its encumbrance aspect.[23]

Short leases: possession under the Leases Act 1449

19.11 The Leases Act 1449 (LA 1449) is the second oldest statute still in force[24] and was passed by the old Scottish Parliament to protect rural tenants from being evicted from the land which they were leasing if the landlord sold. Nevertheless, it is of general application. The property can be any heritable property which is capable of being held as a separate tenement,[25] as well as freshwater fishing rights.[26] Whether LA 1449 applies to shooting rights is uncertain[27] as these cannot normally be a separate tenement.[28] As regards rent, this must not be 'illusory' – in other words, effectively non-existent.[29] In relation to duration, there must be a definite ish. A lease with the duration mentioned above – 'so long as the grass growth up and the water runneth down' – would not be protected by LA 1449.[30] If these requirements are satisfied, the tenant can obtain a real right by entering into possession. This may be natural possession, by himself or herself, or civil possession by a representative, such as a sub-tenant. In one case, the carrying out of preliminary agricultural

---

22   See PARA **4.39** above.
23   See further PARA **2.4** above.
24   The oldest is the Royal Mines Act 1424. See PARA **14.16** above.
25   See PARAS **14.13–14.18** above.
26   Salmon and Freshwater Fisheries (Consolidation) (Scotland) Act 2003, s 66.
27   *Pollock, Gilmour & Co v Harvey* (1828) 6 S 913; *Palmer's Trs v Brown* 1989 SLT 128. Such rights cannot be separate tenements except under AFT(S)A 2000, s 65A.
28   Except under AFT(S)A 2000, s 65A.
29   For example, a penny a year. See *Alison v Ritchie* (1730) Mor 15196.
30   Such wording points to a period longer than a short lease, in any case.

operations before the entry date was held not to amount to possession.[31] But even if it did so amount, it would have been irrelevant as it was before the entry date.

Long leases: registration

19.12 Originally LA 1449 applied to leases of any duration, and it was the only way of conferring real effect on a lease. Then the Registration of Leases (Scotland) Act 1857 allowed long leases to be recorded in the Sasine Register, thereby acquiring real effect. But this was optional: real effect could still be obtained under LA 1449 without recording. Then LR(S)A 1979 provided that registration in the Land Register is now the *only* way of obtaining a real right.[32] Hence LA 1449 now applies only to short leases. If a long lease is not registered it is not a real right. That does not mean it is not a valid lease, but the common law applies, so that it lacks real effect.

'Offside goals' and leases

19.13 If the owner of land agrees to grant a lease, but then sells the land before the tenant has gained a real right, the tenant may seek to invoke the offside goals rule if the new owner knew about the grant of the lease.[33] The balance of authority is against the applicability of the rule here. But the law cannot be regarded as certain.[34] Where the tenant has agreed to assign the lease, but then grants a standard security over it which is made real before the assignation, the assignee may have the security reduced under the 'offside goals' rule if the creditor is in bad faith.[35]

Personal and real conditions

19.14 If the landlord transfers the property, the successor will be bound by the lease. But not by *all* the terms of the lease. Only those conditions which can be regarded as real or – to use the standard expression used in this context – *inter naturalia* of the lease are binding. In essence these are the fundamental conditions, such as the duty to let the tenant occupy the property. It is difficult to give a more precise definition as the case law lacks coherence. For example, in a modern case it was held that an 'exclusivity clause' providing that the tenant was to be the only optician in a shopping centre was not *inter naturalia*.[36] An earlier case in relation to

---

[31] *Millar v McRobbie* 1949 SC 1.

[32] LR(S)A 1979, s 3(3). The registration of leases is now governed partly by the Registration of Leases (Scotland) Act 1857 and partly by LR(S)A 1979.

[33] McDonald *Conveyancing Manual* para 32.60. See also *Rodger v Paton* 2004 GWD 19-425.

[34] *Jacobs v Anderson* (1898) 6 SLT 234; *Millar v McRobbie* 1949 SC 1. Compare *Greig v Brown & Nicolson* (1829) 7 S 274 (a servitude case). But note *Advice Centre for Mortgages Ltd v McNicoll* 2006 SLT 591.

[35] *Trade Development Bank v Crittall Windows* 1983 SLT 510.

[36] *Optical Express (Gyle) Ltd v Marks and Spencers plc* 2000 SLT 644.

a similar clause reached the opposite conclusion.[37] So too did a subsequent case, where there was no argument over the matter.[38] A provision for a reduction in rent in return for services performed by the tenant will not bind a successor landlord.[39] Neither, it seems, will an option to purchase.[40] Since the question of what is *inter naturalia* is important in practice, it is unfortunate that the law is so unclear.

Leases and standard securities

19.15 Once a lease becomes a real right, the subsequent grant of a standard security by the landlord cannot affect it. The rule *prior tempore potior jure* applies: the lease is the prior real right.[41] If the creditor has to enforce the security by selling the property, the lease remains in place. The tenant merely has a different landlord. If the landlord grants a lease *after* granting a standard security, then it is the standard security that is the prior real right. It is one of the standard conditions of a standard security that a lease will not be granted without the creditor's consent.[42] If this is not obtained, the creditor can have the lease set aside.[43] Finally, a standard security can be granted over a registered lease itself. If the creditor has to enforce the security by selling the lease, the landlord will have a new tenant. A lease is only of value as a security if it has some capital value, for otherwise a sale would realise little or nothing.[44]

RIGHTS AND OBLIGATIONS OF THE PARTIES

19.16 Most leases will carefully set out the rights and obligations of the landlord and tenant in detail. In the absence of specific terms, the common law implies certain things. Lease is one of the 'nominate contracts' recognised by the law and thus comes with its own set of implied-in-law terms. To exclude the application of the implied terms, there must be clear contrary provision in the lease.[45] In the following paragraphs, the main implied terms are set out.

---

[37] *Davie v Stark* (1876) 3 R 111. See McAllister *Leases* paras 2.34–2.37. *Davie* was not cited in the later case.

[38] *Warren James (Jewellers) Ltd v Overgate GP Ltd* 2006 GWD 12–235, aff'd 2007 GWD 6–94.

[39] *Ross v Duchess of Sutherland* (1838) 16 S 1179.

[40] *Bisset v Magistrates of Aberdeen* (1898) 1 F 87. In *Davidson v Zani* 1992 SCLR 1001, a successor landlord was held bound on the basis of the 'offside goals' rule. But that case has now been disapproved: *Advice Centre for Mortgages Ltd v McNicoll* 2006 SLT 591.

[41] See **PARA 4.42** above.

[42] CFR(S)A 1970, Sch 3, Standard Condition 6.

[43] *Trade Development Bank v Warriner & Mason* 1980 SC 74; *Trade Development Bank v David Haig (Bellshill) Ltd* 1983 SLT 510. See also **PARA 4.48** above.

[44] See **PARA 19.34** below.

[45] *Mars Pension Trs Ltd v County Properties & Developments* 2000 SLT 581.

(a) Possession

19.17   The landlord is bound to give the tenant natural possession[46] and not interfere with that possession. In turn, the tenant must enter into possession and use the property. Failure to do so is material breach.[47] Short periods of absence may be permissible. In one case, the absence of the tenant due to detention in Saughton Prison for more than a year meant that the landlord could bring the lease to an end on the ground of material breach.[48]

(b) Plenishing

19.18   If the landlord's hypothec is available to the landlord,[49] the tenant must plenish the property sufficiently to provide security for payment of the annual rent.[50] Interdict may be obtained to prevent displenishment.[51]

(c) Rent

19.19   The tenant is obliged to pay the rent at the due dates. It is normally paid in advance. Because of inflation, leases for more than about five years usually provide for review of the rent at the end of a certain period, for example, after every five years in a 25-year lease. The lease says that if the parties cannot agree on the new rent, a third party will set it in line with market rates. This is standard practice in commercial leases and there is a constant stream of case law on the interpretation of rent review clauses.[52] But rent review clauses are not implied by law. Such clauses began to be used only in the 1960s. The result is that there are some ultra-long (e.g. 999-year) leases created before that time (e.g. in the eighteenth and nineteenth centuries) where the rent has been rendered nominal by inflation.

(d) Purposes of let

19.20   The landlord is obliged to ensure that the property is reasonably fit for the purposes of let. The standard is not one of perfection, but assumes reasonable use by the tenant.[53] For example, in *North British Storage and Transit Co v Steele's Trs*[54] it was held that while a drainage system could have been upgraded to a higher

---

[46]   Unless the lease is an interposed lease. See **PARA 19.32** below.
[47]   *Graham v Black & Stevenson* (1792) Hume 781.
[48]   *Blair Trust Co v Gilbert* 1940 SLT 322.
[49]   See **PARA 19.29** below.
[50]   *Wright v Wightman* (1875) 3 R 68.
[51]   *Co-operative Insurance Society Ltd v Halfords Ltd* 1998 SLT 90.
[52]   See McAllister *Leases* ch 11.
[53]   *Glebe Sugar Refining Co v Paterson* (1902) 2 F 615.
[54]   1920 SC 194.

standard, it was adequate as it stood for the purposes of the lease. In urban leases, where the property is a building, the landlord has a duty to ensure that it is wind and watertight.[55] In rural leases, the tenant is liable for repairs.[56] But, as with the other implied obligations, the parties may contract out of the common law.[57] The tenant must only use the property for the purposes of the let. This is called the 'use clause' or 'permitted user clause'. Breach is known as 'inverting the possession'. Unauthorised alterations also fall under this heading.[58]

(e) State of property

19.21   It is implied in leases of buildings that the landlord must maintain the property in a tenantable condition. For example, in *Gunn v National Coal Board*,[59] a landlord who failed to deal with rising damp was held in breach. The obligation is to carry out appropriate repairs once the matter is highlighted by the tenant. It is not a warranty as such, because the landlord is only liable if he or she fails to take action within a reasonable time once notified.[60] The landlord is not required to carry out repairs to damage caused by an act of God (*damnum fatale*) such as lightning.[61] Similarly, where a third party has caused the damage it is that party who is liable and not the landlord. Finally, the landlord is not liable where the damage has been caused by the negligence of the tenant. In that case, the tenant is liable, as well as being in breach of the obligation implied by law to take reasonable care of the property.[62] Of course, most leases have express provisions about repairing obligations, and if so the common law is to that extent excluded.[63]

REMEDIES AVAILABLE TO BOTH PARTIES

19.22   The lease may provide for particular remedies for either party. In addition, general remedies are available.

(a) Specific implement and interdict

19.23   In the case of positive obligations (obligations *ad factum praestandum*) such as the landlord's obligation to carry out repairs, specific implement is the

---

[55]   *Wolfson v Forrester* 1910 SC 675.
[56]   *Little Cumbrae Estates Ltd v Island of Little Cumbrae Ltd* 2007 SC 525.
[57]   *Mars Pension Trs Ltd v County Properties & Developments* 2000 SLT 581.
[58]   Cf *British Linen Bank v Purdie* (1905) 7 F 923.
[59]   1982 SLT 526.
[60]   *Wolfson v Forrester* 1910 SC 675.
[61]   Nor is the tenant: *Little Cumbrae Estates Ltd v Island of Little Cumbrae Ltd* 2007 SC 525.
[62]   *Mickel v McCoard* 1913 SC 896.
[63]   But the common law rules still apply as to any matters not covered: *Little Cumbrae Estates Ltd v Island of Little Cumbrae Ltd* 2007 SC 525.

appropriate remedy. The courts, however, only award this is if the obligation is sufficiently clear or precise. There has been a stream of cases in recent years seeking to enforce so called 'keep open' clauses. These are common in retail unit leases and require the tenant not merely to possess but to trade from the premises on specified days during specified hours. The Scottish courts are willing to enforce such clauses by implement provided that they are clearly drafted.[64] In contrast, their English counterparts have refused to award the equivalent remedy of specific performance, instead awarding damages.[65] Interdict may be used to prevent the other party from doing something, for example unauthorised use.[66]

(b) Damages

19.24   This is a standard remedy. For example, the landlord has failed to carry out repairs, and the tenant has suffered loss as a result.[67] Sometimes quantification is problematic, as in the case of breach of a 'keep open' clause.[68]

(c) Action for payment

19.25   Where one party is obliged to make a monetary payment, the appropriate action is simply one for payment. Typically, it will be used by the landlord to compel payment of rent. Leases often have a clause saying: 'The parties hereto consent to registration of this lease for preservation and execution.' The lease is then registered in the Books of Council and Session.[69] Registration for execution enables a judicial officer to carry out diligence based on an extract copy of the lease. This is known as 'summary diligence' and can take place without a court action.

(d) Rescission

19.26   In the case of a material breach by one party, the other party is in principle entitled to rescind the lease. For example, the tenant may do so if the landlord does

---

[64]   See, in particular, *Retail Parks Investments Ltd v The Royal Bank of Scotland plc (No 2)* 1996 SC 227; *Highland and Universal Properties Ltd v Safeway Properties Ltd* 2000 SLT 414 and *Oak Mall Greenock Ltd v McDonald's Restaurants Ltd* 2003 GWD 17-540. See also A Smith 'Keep on Keeping Open: *Highland and Universal Properties Ltd v Safeway Properties Ltd*' (2000) 4 *Edin LR* 336.

[65]   *Co-operative Insurance Society Ltd v Argyll Stores (Holdings) Ltd* [1998] AC 1.

[66]   *Leckie v Merryflats Patent Brick Co* (1868) 5 SLR 619.

[67]   *Gunn v National Coal Board* 1982 SLT 526.

[68]   *Douglas Shelf Seven Ltd v Co-operative Wholesale Society Ltd* [2007] CSOH 53. See M Hogg 'Damages for breach of a keep-open clause' (2007) 11 *Edin LR* 416.

[69]   Leases are often registered in this register. But such registration does not promote the validity of a lease. For example, if a lease is a short lease, and so needs possession to make it real, registration in the

not provide subjects which are reasonably fit for the purposes of the let.[70] Statute, however, provides that a landlord may not terminate the lease in a case of material breach of a monetary obligation without first serving a written notice giving 14 days to pay.[71] In the case of non-monetary obligations, it must be fair and reasonable to rescind.[72] For breaches which it is possible for the tenant to remedy within a reasonable time, it is a relevant consideration in determining whether the termination is fair and reasonable whether the tenant has been given a reasonable opportunity to remedy the defect.[73]

(e) Retention

19.27 This is a self-help remedy arising out of the doctrine of mutuality of contract. If one party is in breach, the other party may suspend performance of any counter-obligation. Retention of rent is the typical example. For example, the tenant can do this if the landlord is failing to fulfil the obligation to keep the premises wind and watertight. It is competent, however, to contract out of the right to retain.[74] Further, tenants who continue to pay rent during the period in which the landlords are failing in their obligations may be barred from exercising the right of retention later for that breach.[75]

REMEDIES AVAILABLE ONLY TO THE LANDLORD

19.28 In addition to the remedies available to both parties, there are three remedies available only to the landlord.

(a) Landlord's hypothec

19.29 The landlord has a right in security over the goods brought into the property by the tenant – known as the *invecta et illata* – for the rent. This right is unavailable in agricultural and residential leases and essentially is confined to commercial lettings.[76] It cannot be used against property which is exempt from diligence.[77] Curiously, at common law the hypothec could apply to goods which do not belong to the tenant.[78] This probably contravened ECHR, Protocol 1, Art

---

Books of Council and Session is no substitute. The same is true if the lease is a long one, in which to become real registration in the Land Register is necessary.

[70] *Kippen v Oppenheim* (1847) 10 D 242.
[71] Law Reform (Miscellaneous Provisions) (Scotland) Act 1985 (LR(MP)(S)A 1985), s 4(1).
[72] LR(MP)(S)A 1985, s 5(1).
[73] LR(MP)(S)A 1985, s 5(3). The Scottish Law Commission has recommended reforms: *Report on Irritancy in Leases of Land* (2003).
[74] *Skene v Cameron* 1942 SC 393.
[75] *British Railways Board v Roccio* 1979 SLT (Sh Ct) 11.
[76] Bankruptcy and Diligence etc (Scotland) Act 2007 (BD(S)A 2007), s 208(3). See also PARA **20.65** below.
[77] Debt Arrangement and Attachment (Scotland) Act 2002, s 60(2).

1[79] and recent legislation has now restricted the remedy to the tenant's goods.[80] The hypothec was enforced at common law by a diligence known as sequestration for rent, which was confined to the sheriff court. It is now a preference in the tenant's insolvency which is also capable of enforcement by attachment.[81]

(b) Irritancy

19.30   Irritancy is the right of the landlord to bring the lease to an end prematurely. The result is to extinguish the lease and any rights in it, such as subleases. The effect is equivalent to the landlord rescinding the lease, but, unlike rescission, which is available in principle for any material breach by the tenant, irritancy has a more defined scope.[82] There is only one type of 'legal irritancy' – in other words, where the right to irritate arises by operation of law. This is where the rent has been unpaid for two years.[83] The tenant is entitled to stop the irritancy – known as 'purging' it – by making payment at any time before decree is extracted. The Scottish Law Commission has proposed that legal irritancy be replaced with an implied option to terminate if rent has not been paid for six months.[84] The lease can also provide *express* grounds upon which the landlord can irritate. This is known as 'conventional irritancy' and most leases have a conventional irritancy clause. Typical examples in commercial leases are the tenant being more than 21 days late paying the rent, or going into receivership or liquidation. If the landlord subsequently accepts payment once irritancy proceedings have begun, this may waive the breach.[85] At common law, it was not possible to purge a conventional irritancy.[86] This was felt to be unfair and the statutory rules described above in relation to rescission were introduced to apply to situations where the landlord was seeking to irritate.[87]

(c) Action for recovery of heritable property

19.31   If the tenant fails to leave the property when bound to do so at the ish,[88] the landlord can raise an action to compel this. The common law action is one of

---

[78]   See, for example, *Dundee Corporation v Marr* 1971 SC 96 and *Scottish & Newcastle Brewers Ltd v Edinburgh District Council* 1979 SLT (Notes) 11.

[79]   See **CHAPTER 31** below and A J M Steven 'Goodbye to the Landlord's Hypothec?' 2002 *SLT (News)* 177.

[80]   BD(S)A 2007, s 208(4).

[81]   BD(S)A 2007, s 208(2).

[82]   The exact relationship of irritancy and rescission is arguable.

[83]   In agricultural leases, the period is six months: AH(S)A 1991, s 20.

[84]   Scottish Law Commission *Report on Irritancy in Leases of Land* (2003) para 3.15.

[85]   *HMV Fields Properties Ltd v Bracken Self Selection Fabrics Ltd* 1991 SLT 31; *Aubrey Investments Ltd v D S Crawford Ltd* 1998 SLT 628.

[86]   *Dorchester Studios (Glasgow) Ltd v Stone* 1975 SC (HL) 56.

[87]   See **PARA 19.26** above.

'removing', but in modern times the procedure is regulated by statute.[89] If the tenant fails to flit voluntarily, it is unlawful for the landlord to compel, or seek to compel, removal without a court order. To do so is a delict, giving rise to a damages claim, and, in the case of residential tenancies, is also a criminal offence.[90] But a tenant who stays on without agreement after the ish is liable for 'violent profits' – a form of penal damages.[91]

TRANSFER

Alienation by landlord

19.32   The landlord does not require the tenant's permission to transfer the property. The new owner simply becomes the new landlord. It is also competent for the landlord to create an 'interposed lease' between itself and the tenant.[92] In that event, the original tenant becomes the owner's subtenant.

Alienation by tenant

19.33   It may be possible for the tenant to assign the lease. Say that Rebecca is the landlord and Sara the tenant. If Sara assigns to Tracey, then Sara steps entirely out the picture. Tracey is now the tenant. In deciding whether assignation is permissible, the first thing is to consider the terms of the lease. The lease may expressly authorise assignation, or may expressly forbid it. This is called the 'alienation clause'. A common provision is a half-way house, saying that assignation is forbidden without the landlord's permission, but with a qualification that this permission must not be 'unreasonably withheld in the case of a respectable and responsible assignee of sound financial standing' or words to similar effect. Unsurprisingly, such clauses often give rise to disputes. In one case it was held unreasonable for the landlord to insist on new conditions being written into the lease in return for permission.[93] In another, the landlord was held to have acted reasonably in withholding permission until an outstanding rent review was concluded.[94] If the lease is silent on the question of assignation, then the rule is that permission is required if *delectus personae* exists in the lease. This is the doctrine of whether or not the choice of the other party to the contract was crucial to the contract being concluded.[95] It is presumed in agricultural leases of 'ordinary duration' and furnished house lets. It is not presumed

---

88   Where tacit relocation has operated, the tenant may stay put. See **PARA 19.38** below.
89   Sheriff Courts (Scotland) Act 1971, s 35(1)(c), as amended by the Sheriff Courts (Scotland) Act 1971 (Privative Jurisdiction and Summary Cause) Order 2007 SSI 2007/507. The statutory action proceeds by way of summary cause, unless a claim is being made for a sum exceeding £5,000.
90   Rent (Scotland) Act 1984, s 22.
91   *Jute Industries Ltd v Wilson & Graham Ltd* 1955 SLT (Sh Ct) 46.
92   Land Tenure Reform (Scotland) Act 1974, s 17.
93   *Renfrew District Council v AB Leisure (Renfrew) Ltd (In Liquidation)* 1988 SLT 635.

in agricultural leases of 'extraordinary duration' and unfurnished urban lettings, for example shops. The length at which an agricultural lease moves from being ordinary to extraordinary seems to be 21 years.[96]

19.34 An assignation has to be completed by the act which is necessary to create the lease in the first place. For an unregistered lease, this means the assignee taking possession. For a registered lease, this means registration in the Land Register.[97] In practice an assignation will also be formally intimated to the landlord, but the taking of possession or registration may amount to deemed intimation.[98] The effect of an assignation has been described judicially as follows: 'The assignation of his lease by a tenant who has power to assign has the effect of making the assignee sole tenant from the time he obtains possession of the subject of the lease, and of discharging the cedent from future liability to the landlord.'[99] The cedent will, however, remain liable for any rent arrears, though the assignee also becomes liable for these.[100] So much for *whether* a lease can be assigned, and, if so, *how* it is assigned. A few words need to be said about *why* it might be assigned. The reasons for the transfer of a lease are as various as the reasons for the transfer of anything else. If a lease has a capital value it may be sold. Whether a lease has a capital value depends on the circumstances. A 999-year lease created in 1720 for a fixed rent of £5 per annum will now have a value virtually the same as that of unencumbered ownership.[101] A 25-year lease created seven years ago at full market rent and with a five-yearly rent review provision has little or no capital value, because the transferee will be taking over liability for the rent, and the rent represents the value. Indeed, if property values (and hence rental values) have fallen,[102] a lease may have a negative capital value and the transferor will have to pay the transferee a lump sum to take the lease off its hands.

Subletting

19.35 If Sara sublets to Tracey, Sara remains the tenant. Tracey becomes the subtenant and is entitled to enter into possession. The Rebecca/Sara lease is the 'head lease' and the Sara/Tracey lease is the 'sublease', also known as an 'under-lease'. If that head lease is terminated, whether prematurely or at the ish, the tenant's right under the sublease to possess will also end. As with assignation, there may be express provision in the lease as to whether subletting is permissible. In the event of silence, the same presumptions in relation to *delectus personae* apply as with

94   *Lousada & Co v J E Lesser (Properties) Ltd* 1990 SLT 823.
95   See MacQueen and Thomson, *Contract* para 2.87.
96   McAllister *Leases* paras 6.17–6.18.
97   For long leases, see LR(S)A 1979, s 3(1)(a), (3) and (4)(a).
98   McAllister *Leases* para 6.27.
99   *Lord Elphinstone v Monkland Iron & Coal Co* (1886) 13 R (HL) 98 at 102 per Lord Watson.
100 McAllister *Leases* para 6.30.
101 Cf PARA **2.4** above.

assignation and to the same effect. Likewise, a subtenant needs to take the same steps as any lessee to obtain a real right, possession or registration. Whether the sublet can be registered will depend on its length rather than that of the head lease. In a sublet, the liability of the tenant under the original lease remains unaffected. Thus suppose that the rent under the head lease is £100,000 per annum and under the sublease is £105,000, there are two entirely separate payments, one by Sara to Rebecca and one by Tracey to Sara. If Tracey fails to pay Sara that does not affect Sara's continuing obligation to pay Rebecca.

Succession

19.36 In general, the tenant's death does not end the lease. The question of who then takes the lease is complex and the following is a mere outline. Where a lease is freely assignable, the tenant can bequeath it in his or her will. If no such bequest is made, the executor may transfer it to any party who would have been entitled to succeed to the tenant's estate had he or she died intestate, including a spouse or civil partner in respect of their prior rights, or to any party entitled to legal rights.[103] If there is an implied prohibition on alienation, such as if *delectus personae* is presumed, the tenant is entitled to bequeath the lease to any party who could be entitled to succeed to his estate if it was intestate.[104] This could mean any member of the family. Where there is an express prohibition on assignation, the landlord will require to consent before a bequest can take effect. There exist special rules on succession to agricultural and residential tenancies.[105]

TERMINATION

Termination at ish

19.37 A lease normally provides a fixed date at which it ends.[106] Nevertheless, if the contracted date arrives without either party having given due notice, the lease will not finish. In other words, a fixed date of termination is regarded as being merely a mutual *option* to terminate at that date. The option is, like any option, exercised by notice. The notice is traditionally called a 'warning to remove' when served by the landlord. But the English term 'notice to quit' is now generally used. When given by the tenant, the notice is called a 'letter of removal'. At common law, notice of not

---

[102] Perhaps because of a general turndown. Or it may be that property values fall in a particular location. See, e.g., *Burgerking Ltd v Rachel Charitable Trust* 2006 SLT 224.

[103] S(S)A 1964, s 16(2). On the meaning of 'prior rights' and 'legal rights', see **PARAS 28.5–28.21** below.

[104] S(S)A 1964, s 29(1).

[105] S(S)A 1964, s 16(2)–(9); AH(S)A 1991, s 11; AH(S)A 2003, ss 21–23; Crofters Holdings (Scotland) Act 1886, s 16; Small Land Holders (Scotland) Act 1911, s 21; Crofters (Scotland) Act 1993, s 10; Rent

less than 40 days before the ish must be given. For example, the lease between Ulrika and Valerie is stated to end on 30 June. If Ulrika gives Valerie notice on 31 May, that is too late.

The common law period is varied for certain leases by statute. The rules are complex. For agricultural holdings, the period is not less than one year and not more than two years before the ish.[107] The same period applies for leases of land exceeding 2 acres which are not agricultural holdings, but where such a lease is for less than three years, the minimum notice period is six months.[108] For all other leases of four months or less, notice of one-third of the length of the lease is required, subject to a minimum period of four weeks.[109] Notices to quit have to be in the right form, and this can vary according to the type of tenancy.[110] Finally, under the Removal Terms (Scotland) Act 1886, if a lease is due to end at Whitsunday or Martinmas and notice of 40 days is required, this period is (confusingly) calculated back from 15 May or 11 November respectively.[111] This legislation applies to a lease of a 'dwelling house, shop or other building and their appurtenances' or a house let with agricultural land. While 15 May and 11 November were recognised as Whitsunday and Martinmas at common law, by statute they have been replaced by 28 May and 28 November.[112] The continued application of the 1886 Act thus leads to a longer notice period.

Tacit relocation

19.38 If proper notice is not given, the lease continues by 'tacit relocation' (Latin *relocatio tacita*), that is to say, by implied re-lease.[113] If the original lease was for a year or more, tacit relocation is for a further year. If it was for less than a year, tacit relocation is for the period of the lease. The doctrine can operate any number of times and it is quite common for a lease to continue long after the agreed length on this basis. The rule applies equally to both parties, but in practice it is more often pled by tenants against landlords than vice versa. But this is not always so. For example, in *Signet Group plc v C & J Clark Retail Properties Ltd*,[114] the tenants served an invalid notice, and also shut down their business and vacated the premises well before

---

(Scotland) Act 1984, ss 3 and 3A and Schs 1, 1A and 1B; Housing (Scotland) Act 1988, s 31; and Housing (Scotland) Act 2001, s 22 and Sch 3.

[106] But it is competent for it to provide that it will continue from month to month (or other period) until notice by either party. This might, but does not have to, follow an initial fixed period.

[107] AH(S)A 1991, s 21.

[108] Sheriff Courts (Scotland) Act 1907, s 34. Rather oddly, this Act contains much of the law about the termination of leases.

[109] Sheriff Courts (Scotland) Act 1907, s 38. For dwellinghouses, see also the Rent (Scotland) Act 1984, s 112.

[110] See Sheriff Courts (Scotland) Act 1907, Sch 1, para 34.6 and 34.7. For residential tenancies, see also Rent (Scotland) Act 1984, s 112, and Assured Tenancies (Notice to Quit Prescribed Information) (Scotland) Regulations 1988 (SI 1988/2067). There are also special rules for the various types of

the ish. It was held that the lease continued. An example of the doctrine not applying because of the parties' actions is where they enter into a new lease. It is a difficult question whether the parties can contract out of tacit relocation – to contract out of the need to send notice to quit – in the lease itself. According to one sheriff court case, it can.[115] But the position cannot be regarded as settled, except for agricultural holdings where statute prohibits contracting out of the doctrine.[116]

Termination before the ish

19.39   There are various reasons why a lease may not last its full course. Rescission and irritancy have already been considered.[117] At the outset of the lease, the parties may decide that either or both has the right to terminate the lease early. This is known as a 'break clause'. If there is no such clause, it is of course nonetheless open to the parties to agree on premature termination later. In that case, that agreement is given effect to by a 'deed of renunciation'. (The name makes it sound as if it is a unilateral act by the tenant. But a tenant cannot unilaterally renounce a lease.) The lease may also be brought to an early end by frustration, a general doctrine of contract law.[118] Three cases of this can be given.

(1) The subjects of the lease may be entirely destroyed, for example a shop razed by a fire. This is known as *rei interitus*.[119]

(2) There may be constructive destruction. This is where there is not total destruction, but the lease can no longer subsist, for example where a house has been damaged to the extent that it is uninhabitable.[120]

(3) The lease may be unable to continue for other reasons. For example, in *Tay Salmon Fisheries Co v Speedie*[121] a lease of salmon fishings was frustrated by impossibility because the Ministry of Defence designated the area as a firing range.

Finally, the death of the tenant will bring the lease to an end in situations where it cannot be transferred.[122]

---

agricultural tenancy. In practice, notices to quit often fail to comply with the applicable rules and so are invalid.

[111]   Removal Terms (Scotland) Act 1886, s 4.
[112]   Term and Quarter Days (Scotland) Act 1990, s 1(1) and (2)(a).
[113]   For a detailed treatment, see S Halliday, 'Tacit Relocation' 2002 *JR* 201.
[114]   1996 SLT 1325.
[115]   *Macdougall v Guidi* 1992 SCLR 167.
[116]   AH(S)A 1991, s 3.
[117]   See PARAS **19.26** and **19.30** above.
[118]   See McBryde *Contract* ch 21; MacQueen and Thomson *Contract* paras 4.91–4.113.

TYPES OF LEASE

19.40   Specialities apply to different types of leases. A short overview will be given of these as they apply to commercial, residential and agricultural properties.

Commercial leases

19.41   Many Scottish solicitors specialise in this area. It is little regulated by statute and the terms of the lease are eventually determined by the relative negotiating strength of the parties. That strength will depend on a number of factors, such as the state of the property market and the demand for the type of premises in question. Heads of terms in commercial leases, such as duration and rent, will normally be agreed by surveyors, before the lawyers draw up the lease. Shopping centres such as the Buchanan Galleries in Glasgow or the Gyle Centre in Edinburgh are usually owned by institutional investors who use the rents from the units as a reliable income stream.[123] Here, the leases will contain a service charge provision, whereby the tenant is liable for a proportion of the cost of cleaning, heating and lighting the common parts of the centre, refuse collection, security provision and the like.[124] Commercial leases are usually entered into on an FRI ('full repairing and insuring') basis. The tenant will be solely liable for all repairs, in contrast to the common law position. He or she will also be responsible for the payment of insurance premiums. A key feature of commercial leases is detailed rent review clauses, typically providing for the rent to be reassessed on an upward-only basis, every five years.[125] A rare example of statutory intervention in the area of commercial leases is the Tenancy of Shops (Scotland) Act 1949. It enables shop tenants who receive a notice to quit in the run-up to the ish to apply to the sheriff court for renewal of their lease.[126] The sheriff can extend it for a period of a year. The tenant is free to make a repeat application when the extension comes to an end and the lease in theory could continue indefinitely on the basis of annual applications.

Residential leases

Private sector

19.42   Detailed regulation of this type of lease began in the early twentieth century, the main original purposes being to keep rental levels below what they would be on a free-market basis and to limit the power of landlords to terminate tenancies. Frequent

---

[119]   It is possible to contract out of *rei interitus*: see *Cantors Properties (Scotland) Ltd v Swears and Wells Ltd* 1980 SLT 165. This is standard practice in commercial leases where landlords do not wish to lose the income stream from rent: insurance should pay for reconstruction: see D Cockburn *Commercial Leases* (2002) paras 5.6 and 7.7.1.

[120]   *Duff v Fleming* (1870) 8 M 769.

[121]   1929 SC 593.

legislation, reflecting changing political agendas, made the subject fiendishly complex. The current regime is found in the Housing (Scotland) Act 1988 (H(S)A 1988), which introduced 'assured tenancies' and 'short assured tenancies'. Leases created under the prior regime are known as 'regulated tenancies' and although these can still exist, they will not be discussed here.[127] For there to be an assured tenancy, a house must be leased as a separate dwelling and be occupied by the tenant as his or her only or principal home.[128] 'House' can mean a flat or, exceptionally, a hotel room occupied by a long-term resident.[129] There is a list of cases where an assured tenancy cannot arise, including leases to students by educational institutions, situations where the landlord is resident and tenancies in favour of asylum seekers.[130]

19.43 The lease starts life as a 'contractual assured tenancy'. It becomes a 'statutory assured tenancy' if the contractual assured tenancy ends by a valid notice to quit – unless, of course, the tenant chooses to remove. A statutory assured tenancy can be ended by the landlord only by persuading the sheriff that one of the specified *statutory grounds* applies. Some of the grounds for recovering natural possession are mandatory. In other words, the sheriff must grant the order if satisfied that the ground exists. Examples include where there has been default on a standard security created before the tenancy and where there are rent arrears of at least three months.[131] The remaining grounds are a matter for the sheriff's discretion. Examples include where the rent is persistently paid late and where the condition of the house has deteriorated because of the tenant's negligence.[132] The landlord can avoid the difficulty of recovering the property by creating the lease at the outset as a 'short assured tenancy'.[133] Such a tenancy must have a minimum length of six months. Advance written notice (Form AT5) must be given to the tenant that this type of lease is being granted. The effect is that when the tenancy comes to an end it comes to an end: there is no security of tenure beyond the ish. Short assured tenancies are popular with landlords. Under the previous regime of 'regulated' tenancies, the tenant was entitled to pay a 'fair' rent, which was in most cases a rent below market rates. The tenant under an assured tenancy (including a short assured tenancy) merely has the right not to pay above market rent. Hence if the landlord proposes a new rent[134] to

---

[122] See **PARA 19.36** above.
[123] E.g. the Clyde Shopping Centre in Clydebank is owned by Co-operative Insurance Society Ltd.
[124] See *Marfield Properties Ltd v Secretary of State for the Environment* 1996 SLT 1244 and *Mars Pension Trs Ltd v County Properties & Developments Ltd* 2000 SLT 581.
[125] See McAllister *Leases* ch 11 and M J Ross and D J McKichan *Drafting and Negotiating Commercial Leases in Scotland* (2nd edn, 1993) ch 6.
[126] Tenancy of Shops (Scotland) Act 1949, s 1(1) and (2). See McAllister *Leases* ch 13.
[127] See McAllister *Leases* paras 15.65–15.106.
[128] H(S)A 1988, s 12(1).
[129] *Uratemp Ventures Ltd v Collins* [2001] 3 WLR 806, a case under the equivalent English legislation.
[130] H(S)A 1988, Sch 4.
[131] H(S)A 1988, Sch 5, Pt 1.
[132] H(S)A 1988, Sch 5, Pt 2.

which the tenant objects, he or she can apply to the local Rent Assessment Committee to fix a market rent.[135]

Private landlord licensing

19.44 Though it might not be guessed from the title, the Antisocial Behaviour etc (Scotland) Act 2004 (AB(S)A 2004) introduced a licensing system for private sector landlords.[136] The licensing body is the local authority and so a landlord with several properties may need several licences. To let out residential property without a licence is a criminal offence.[137] Moreover, in such circumstances the local authority can serve a notice ending the landlord's right to collect rent.[138] Only a person regarded by the local authority as a 'fit and proper person to act as landlord' will be licensed. The legislation also contains provisions enabling local authorities to serve an 'antisocial behaviour notice' on the landlord of a tenant who appears to them to be 'engaging in antisocial behaviour'.[139] The notice requires the landlord to deal with the behaviour. Failure to comply can lead to a number of sanctions being imposed. These include the rent no longer being payable, if the local authority successfully applies to the court to that effect, and criminal liability.[140] It remains to be seen how these rules will operate in practice. There exist other statutory obligations on private sector landlords. For example, they must ensure that any gas pipes and appliances are in a safe condition. Annual safety checks should be made. Failure to comply is an offence.[141] Finally, landlords who intend to lease houses for multiple occupancy, for example to a group of students, must – in addition to the licence mentioned above – obtain a multiple occupancy licence from the local authority.[142]

Public sector

19.45 Since 30 September 2002, public-sector tenancies have been regulated by the Housing (Scotland) Act 2001 (H(S)A 2001). The landlord has to be a local authority, water or sewerage authority, or a registered social landlord.[143] The property must be a house let as a separate dwelling and the tenant must be an individual whose

---

[133]   H(S)A 1988, ss 32–35.

[134]   Of course, a landlord cannot unilaterally increase the rent. One party to a contract cannot unilaterally change its terms. But a landlord can, at common law, decline to renew the tenancy at its ish except at a higher rent. The tenant then must choose to renew or not to renew. The same can work the other way round: a tenant can decide not to renew at the ish unless the landlord agrees a lower rent. At common law all this is simply a matter of bargaining. But once a tenant has a statutory right to ignore the common law ish, the law has to provide a mechanism for determining the rent after the ish.

[135]   H(S)A 1988, s 25.

[136]   To check if your landlord has registered, see https://www.landlordregistrationscotland.gov.uk/Pages/Process.aspx?Command=ShowHomePage.

[137]   Antisocial Behaviour etc (Scotland) Act 2004 (AB(S)A 2004), s 93(1). The offender is the landlord, not the tenant.

[138]   AB(S)A 2004, s 94.

only or principal home is that house.[144] There are two types of tenancy: the 'Scottish secure tenancy' and the short 'Scottish secure tenancy'. These are modelled on the assured and short assured tenancies described above. Once again there is a list of excepted categories, including certain leases of police and fire service accommodation and leases to students where the landlord is the student's educational institution.[145] There is also security of tenure, like the assured tenancy.[146] Repairing obligations are imposed on the landlord.[147] An important feature is the right to buy the property in certain circumstances.[148] There is a discount below market value. The discount is determined by the length of time that the tenant has been in occupation.[149] If the tenant resells the property within three years then the landlord can claw back the discount or part of it.[150] The short Scottish secure tenancy requires a minimum duration of six months and advance notice to the tenant that such a lease is being granted.[151] Its use is limited to a small number of cases, including where the tenant has been guilty of anti-social behaviour or is a homeless person.[152] There is no extended security of tenure, nor right to buy for tenants.[153]

Agricultural leases: general

19.46   Many farms in Scotland are farmed by tenant farmers. There are five special statutory regimes. Taking them by the name of the tenant, they are:

(a) tenants of an agricultural holding;[154]

(b) crofters;

(c) cottars;

(d) small landholders; and

(e) statutory small tenants.

Of these, the first two are the most important. The law is complex and only the briefest outline is possible here.

---

[139]   AB(S)A 2004, s 68.

[140]   AB(S)A 2004, ss 71, 74, 78 and 79.

[141]   Gas Safety (Installation and Use) Regulations 1994 (SI 1994/1886). See *Mackenzie v Aberdeen City Council* 2002 Hous LR 88.

[142]   Civic Government (Scotland) Act 1982 (Licensing of Houses in Multiple Occupation) Order 2000 (SSI 2000/177).

[143]   H(S)A 2001, s 11(1)(b).

[144]   H(S)A 2001, s 11(1)(a) and (c). 'House' is defined in s 111 and includes flats and yards, gardens, outhouses and pertinents pertaining to a house.

[145]   H(S)A 2001, Sch 1. Many of the public bodies who may grant Scottish secure tenancies are clearly not educational institutions.

[146]   H(S)A 2001, s 14 and Sch 2, Pt 1.

[147]   H(S)A 2001, Sch 4.

[148]   Housing (Scotland) Act 1987 (H(S)A 1987), ss 61–84.

Agricultural holdings

19.47 The relevant statutes are the Agricultural Holdings (Scotland) Acts 1991 (AH(S)A 1991) and 2003 (AH(S)A 2003). Broadly speaking, an 'agricultural holding' is a lease of land used for agriculture as part of a trade or business.[155] The general principle is that the tenant has security of tenure. Usually, where the landlord has served a notice to quit, the tenant can serve a counter-notice.[156] The effect of the counter-notice is that the landlord can only remove the tenant by applying to the Land Court and proving that one of the limited number of statutory grounds applies.[157] The security of tenure rules were unpopular with most landlords and so avoidance measures developed.[158] AH(S)A 2003 blocked the main avoidance device, which involved the use of a limited partnership. At the same time it introduced two new types of lease, in parallel with the ordinary statutory agricultural holding. These are the 'Short Limited Duration Tenancy' (SLDT) which cannot exceed five years and the 'Limited Duration Tenancy' (LDT) which must be not less than 15 years in length.[159] Tenants under such leases do not have security of tenure after the ish. Certain other rights are conferred on tenants of agricultural holdings. Where they have security of tenure, they are entitled to have the rent set by an arbiter, normally on an open market basis.[160] At the termination of the lease there are rights to compensation for improvements and to remove fixtures.[161] In leases which are not SLDTs or LDTs, tenants are given a pre-emptive right to purchase the farm.[162] In order to do so, they must first register a notice in the Register of Community Interests in Land.[163]

Crofts

19.48 Crofting tenure has its origins in the Highland Clearances. Resistance led eventually to the Napier Commission (1884) and the first statute to give some protection to the remaining crofters (Crofters Holdings (Scotland) Act 1886). A croft is a piece of leased land of normally not more than thirty hectares with a maximum annual rent of £100.[164] The land will usually be in one of the six crofting counties: Argyll; Caithness; Inverness; Ross and Cromarty; Sutherland; and Orkney

---

149 H(S)A 1987, s 62.
150 H(S)A 1987, s 72. For sales within one year, 100% of the discount is returnable; for sales within two years, 66% and for those within three years, 33%.
151 H(S)A 2001, s 34 and the Short Scottish Secure Tenancies (Notices) Regulations 2002 (SSI 2002/315).
152 H(S)A 2001, Sch 6.
153 H(S)A 2001, s 36; and H(S)A 1987, s 61(2).
154 This category itself has subdivisions: see para **19.47**.
155 AH(S)A 1991, ss 1(1) and 2; AH(S)A 2003, s 93.
156 AH(S)A 2003, s 22. In certain cases, for example, where the tenant is apparently insolvent, a counter-notice may not be served.
157 AH(S)A 2003, s 24.
158 See McDonald *Conveyancing Manual* para 26.10.

and Shetland.[165] The Land Court has jurisdiction over crofting matters and there is also the Crofters Commission, in Inverness,[166] which has significant administrative powers. Crofters have the right to a 'fair' rent,[167] security of tenure[168] and compensation for improvements.[169] In addition, they have the right to buy the land.[170] Recently, crofting communities have been given the right to form a 'crofting community body'. It can seek the approval of the Scottish Ministers to acquire ownership of the land where the community is situated.[171]

Cottars

19.49 A cottar is a tenant who occupies a house, with or without garden ground, either rent-free or on the basis of an annual lease with a maximum rent of £6 per year.[172] The land must be in one of the crofting counties. Like crofters, cottars have the right to compensation for improvements on their occupation terminating and a statutory right to buy.[173]

Small landholders

19.50 For an agricultural tenant to be a small landholder and be protected by the Small Landholders (Scotland) Act 1911, a number of criteria must be satisfied.[174]

(1) The holding must have had a rent of not more than £50 a year in April 1912 or be not more than 20 hectares in extent.

(2) The tenancy must have been in existence when the 1911 legislation was passed or the tenant has been registered with the Land Court since then as a new holder.

(3) The tenant must cultivate the land by himself or herself, with or without hired labour.

(4) Finally, he or she or a predecessor in the same family, must have provided or paid for all or the greater part of the buildings and permanent improvements on the land.

---

[159] AH(S)A 2003, ss 4 and 5.
[160] Agricultural Holdings (Scotland) Act 1991, s 13.
[161] AH(S)A 1991, ss 33–36 and 18; AH(S)A 2003, ss 43–49.
[162] AH(S)A 2003, ss 24–38.
[163] AH(S)A 2003, s 25.
[164] Crofters (Scotland) Act 1993 (C(S)A 1993), ss 1–4. The 1993 Act has been the subject of recent amendment by the Crofting Reform etc Act 2007.
[165] But under C(S)A 1993, s 3A, the Scottish Ministers have power to designate land outwith these counties as croft land.
[166] http://www.crofterscommission.org.uk/.
[167] C(S)A 1993, s 6.

Like a crofter, a small landholder has the right to a fair rent,[175] security of tenure[176] and compensation for improvements.[177] Once again the Land Court has jurisdiction over such holdings.

Statutory small tenants

19.51 This type of tenant in principle would be eligible to be a small landholder. But, because neither he nor she nor a predecessor in the same family provided the greater part of the buildings and permanent improvements on the land, he or she is not.[178] Statutory small tenants have far less rights. They may, however, apply to the Land Court for renewal of their lease at the ish, as well as for an *equitable rent*.[179] A process exists whereby statutory small tenants can convert their status to that of small landholder.[180]

FURTHER READING

Cockburn, D *Commercial Leases* (2002).

Gill, Rt Hon Lord *Law of Agricultural Holdings in Scotland* (3rd edn, 1997).

McAllister *Leases*.

McDonald *Conveyancing Manual* chs 24–27.

Paisley *Land Law* ch 7.

Paton, G C H and Cameron, J G S *The Law of Landlord and Tenant in Scotland* (1967).

Rankine, J *The Law of Leases in Scotland* (3rd edn 1916, reprinted 1986).

Robson, P *Residential Tenancies* (2nd edn, 1998).

SME, vol 13 (landlord and tenant) and vol 14 (location: leasing and hiring of moveables).

168   C(S)A 1993, s 5.
169   C(S)A 1993, ss 30–35.
170   C(S)A 1993, ss 12–19.
171   LR(S)A 2003, ss 68–97A.
172   C(S)A 1993, s 12(5).
173   C(S)A 1993, ss 36 and 12.
174   Small Landholders (Scotland) Act 1911, ss 2(1), 7, 10(1) and 26.
175   Crofters Holdings (Scotland) Act 1886, s 6.
176   Crofters Holdings (Scotland) Act 1886, s 1 (as amended by the Small Landholders (Scotland) Act 1911, s 10).
177   Crofters Holdings (Scotland) Act 1886, s 8 (as amended by the Small Landholders and Agricultural Holdings (Scotland) Act 1931, s 12).
178   Small Landholders (Scotland) Act 1911, ss 2(1)(iii) and 32.
179   Small Landholders (Scotland) Act 1911, s 32.
180   Small Landholders (Scotland) Act 1931, s 14.

Chapter 20

Rights in security

GENERAL PRINCIPLES

The purpose of security

20.1   John and Karen wish to buy a house together. Like most couples, they have insufficient savings to meet the purchase price. Their solution is to borrow from a lender, in their case Banff Bank plc, the loan being secured on the property. This means that if John and Karen do not keep up the repayments then Banff Bank can sell the house. Thus, home loan advertisements state:

> 'YOUR HOME IS AT RISK IF YOU DO NOT KEEP UP REPAYMENTS ON A MORTGAGE OR OTHER LOANS SECURED ON IT.'[1]

As a matter of law, however, the 'mortgage' is not the loan that the bank gives to John and Karen, but rather the security right which they will give to the bank over the house. (John and Karen may tell their friends that 'the Banff gave us a mortgage'. In fact, it was they who gave the Banff the mortgage.) 'Mortgage' is a term of English law, but is now used commonly north of the border in everyday language. It is even to be found in a statute passed by the Scottish Parliament.[2] The legal name for the security right which John and Karen grant to Banff Bank plc is a 'standard security'.[3]

20.2   The reason why the bank will insist on a security is to improve its chances of being paid. Before John and Karen receive the money, they will have to enter into a contract of loan with Banff Bank. This might be thought sufficient to protect the bank's interests, because if the couple fail to repay, it can raise an action for payment. In other words, the bank can enforce its *personal right* under the loan contract. A personal right, as we have seen elsewhere,[4] can, however, be a weak right. If John and Karen have become insolvent, that means they cannot pay their creditors in full. In fact this is probably the very reason why they have not been keeping up the repayments. If the bank obtains decree for payment it may seek to carry out diligence against the couple's assets. Once again, however, there may be a shortage and there may be other creditors trying to do exactly the same thing. In contrast, if the bank obtains a standard security, this means that it has a *real right* over the property. That right will prevail over the other creditors and will protect them in the event of John and Karen's insolvency.

Definition

20.3   The accepted definition of a right of security is that of Gloag and Irvine: 'any right which a creditor may hold for ensuring payment or satisfaction of his debt, in

---

[1]   In fact, the debtor's home is at risk if any loan is not repaid because a creditor can carry out diligence against it or have the debtor sequestrated. These may result in the house being sold to pay the debt.

[2]   See the Mortgage Rights (Scotland) Act 2001, discussed at PARA **20.52** below.

[3]   See PARA **20.44** below.

[4]   See PARA **1.16** above.

distinction from and in addition to his right of action and execution against the debtor'.[5] Thus in our example, the right of action and execution is the right to raise an action of payment and carry out diligence against John and Karen in terms of the contract of loan. The additional right is the standard security which has been granted in favour of the bank.

Benefits of security

20.4   In his sixth-century account of Roman law, Justinian wrote that 'A security is given for the benefit of both parties: of the debtor in that he can borrow money more readily, and of the creditor in that his loan is safer'.[6] We have already seen how the loan is made safer for the creditor. As for debtors, first, it allows them to obtain credit which otherwise would have not been available. Second, a secured loan normally attracts a lower rate of interest than an unsecured loan. Security, however, is not an entirely 'win–win' situation because it means that other creditors who are unsecured lose out if the debtor becomes insolvent. Secured creditors may exhaust the assets leaving nothing for the unsecured creditors. One American scholar has written that 'security is an agreement between A and B that C takes nothing'.[7] It may also be argued that even without security rights banks would have to lend. Otherwise they would not obtain income (from interest charges) and would go out of business. Despite such arguments, security rights have been with us since at least the time of Genesis[8] and their position, for want of another word, is secure.

Personal security and real security

20.5   Rights in security can be divided into 'personal security' (caution) and 'real security' (security over assets). Personal security is a guarantee from another person. For example, Anna, a student, seeks a £7,000 loan from a bank. It agrees but, because Anna has a limited income, it insists that her mother guarantees the repayments. Anna's mother then acts as 'guarantor' (or, to use the correct Scottish legal term, 'cautioner'). If Anna fails to repay, the bank can enforce the guarantee against her mother. No more needs to be said on this subject, as it is not a matter of property law.[9] The rest of this chapter covers real security.

A subordinate real right

20.6   A right in security gives the creditor a subordinate real right in the property in question. To return to the earlier example, the result of John and Karen granting

5   Gloag and Irvine *Rights in Security* 2.
6   Justinian, *Institutes* 3, 14, 4. Of course, this was not written by the Emperor personally.
7   L LoPucki 'The Unsecured Creditor's Bargain' (1994) 80 *Virginia Law Rev* 1887 at 1899.
8   Genesis 38:18.
9   See further Gloag and Henderson *The Law of Scotland* ch 17.

Banff Bank a standard security is that the bank obtains a subordinate real right in the house. This means that there are (at least) two real rights in the house:

(1) the right of ownership of John and Karen;

(2) the bank's standard security.

20.7 The bank's security, being a real right, is good against the world. Most importantly, it is good against *creditors* and *singular successors*.[10] We have already seen how the security is good against creditors. If John and Karen become insolvent, the bank has a right to be paid out of the proceeds of sale of the house, which has priority over the rights of other creditors. Say, however, that the couple, in a bid to escape their creditors, sell the house to Leslie for £300,000 and depart for Penang. This does not affect the bank's right of security. It can still be enforced by selling the house. In practice, Leslie would not buy without the assistance of a solicitor, who would check for any standard securities by means of a search of the register.

Making a security real

20.8 As the law confers an advantage on secured creditors, it usually insists that there is compliance with the *publicity principle*,[11] so that third parties are warned. In general a security right cannot be created by mere agreement, for agreements are usually private. Thus an obligation to grant a security is not a good security.[12] In fact, such an obligation has no practical value because if existing obligations are already being performed by the debtor there is no need for a security. It is only where there is default, for example on a loan contract, that a security is beneficial.

20.9 The publicity principle is satisfied for standard securities by the requirement for registration in the Land Register or Sasine Register to make the security real. The appropriate register is determined by where the property is registered.[13] For floating charges there must be registration in the Companies Register. This requirement will be replaced by registration in the new Register of Floating Charges when new legislation is brought into force.[14] For corporeal moveables, the creditor generally has to be placed in possession of the property, but there are some exceptions to this rule.[15]

Registration of securities granted by companies

20.10 There are additional rules to publicise securities granted by companies and limited liability partnerships. Generally, these must be registered at Companies

---

[10] See **PARA 4.4** above.
[11] See **PARA 4.17** above.
[12] *Bank of Scotland v Liquidators of Hutchison Main & Co Ltd* 1914 SC (HL) 1.
[13] See **PARA 20.44** below.
[14] See **PARA 20.39** below.
[15] See **PARAS 20.35, 20.41** and **20.65** below.

House in the relevant part of the company's file, known as the 'Charges Register'.[16] This must be done within 21 days of the security being created as a real right. Failure to do so means effectively that the security cannot be enforced.[17] These rules for registration of company securities apply *only* where the company is the debtor, *not* the creditor. As we have just seen, a standard security becomes real by registration in the Land Register or Sasine Register. It may be questioned what the point is in requiring a second registration in the Companies Register. This has been recognised by the legislature and the Companies Act 2006, in an important provision, gives Ministers the power to dispense with the second registration.[18] What will then happen is that the Keeper will transmit the details of the standard security to Companies House. The same procedure will eventually be applied to other registrable security rights. Another example is the floating charge, which under the new rules, will be registered in the new Register of Floating Charges.[19]

True securities and functional securities

20.11 It has been mentioned that a right in security gives the creditor a subordinate real right in the property.[20] The debtor retains the real right of ownership. Strictly, however, this is only the position for 'true securities'. In a number of cases, the right of ownership itself acts as the security right. The cases of this are known as 'functional securities'. True securities are sometimes also called 'proper securities' and functional securities 'improper securities'. In a true security, both the debtor and the creditor have real rights. In a functional security, only one of them has a real right and that is ownership. The other has only a personal right. Usually, it is the creditor who has ownership, and the security is sometimes known as a 'right of retention' because it is a right to retain ownership until the debt has been paid. In cases where trusts act as functional securities, it is the debtor who has ownership. Here are some examples of functional securities.

Retention of title in the sale of goods

20.12 As mentioned elsewhere,[21] it is common, especially in commercial cases, for contracts for the sale of goods to have a retention of title clause. The seller retains ownership until the price, or even *all* sums owed by the buyer to the seller,

---

[16] See Companies Act 1985, s 410, to be replaced by the Companies Act 2006, s 878. The terminology is messy: 'Charges Register' sounds as though there is such a register but there is not. It is just a part of a file, so every company's file has its 'Charges Register'.

[17] The actual position is more complex. See Gretton 'Registration of Company Charges' (2002) 6 *Edin LR* 146.

[18] Companies Act 2006, s 893.

[19] See PARA **20.39** below.

[20] See PARA **20.6** above.

[21] See PARAS **5.25–5.26** above.

are paid. Here ownership acts in the same way as a security right. But, strictly, it is not a security right: it is ownership.

Hire purchase

20.13 Where a purchaser cannot pay for goods outright, a hire purchase contract might be used. Here ownership of the property is typically transferred by the dealer to a financial institution. The price is paid by the institution and the purchaser agrees to repay it in monthly instalments. The purchaser, however, has the immediate use of the goods. Ownership is not acquired until the last instalment is paid. The effect of the contract is that if the purchaser does not keep up the repayments the institution can take back the goods. Its right of ownership functions as a security right.

Assignation in security

20.14 It does not seem to be possible in Scotland to create a subordinate real right over an incorporeal personal right, such as a debt or a life assurance policy. Therefore if the right is to be used for security, it must be assigned to the creditor.[22] The holder of the right (the cedent) assigns to the creditor. The creditor therefore becomes the new holder of the right. For the security to be extinguished the right will have to be retrocessed.

Trusts

20.15 Trusts are sometimes used as securities. The idea is that the property is placed into a special trust patrimony and therefore becomes unavailable to the debtor's ordinary creditors.[23] For example, in an attempt to protect against the risk of the seller's insolvency, a disposition of land may be drafted to include a clause stating that the seller will hold the land in trust for the buyer pending registration.[24] It may be questioned if such clauses should be enforceable as a matter of policy because they do not satisfy the publicity requirements for the creation of securities. The attitude of the courts has varied and it is impossible to be sure that the trust would be upheld.[25]

---

[22]   On assignation, see PARAS **5.37–5.50** above.

[23]   See PARAS **22.57** AND **22.58** below.

[24]   For discussion, see A J M Steven and S Wortley 'The Perils of a Trusting Disposition' 1996 *SLT (News)* 365 and J Chalmers 'In Defence of the Trusting Conveyancer' 2002 *SLT (News)* 231.

[25]   Compare *Clark Taylor & Co Ltd v Quality Site Development (Edinburgh) Ltd* 1981 SC 111 with *Tay Valley Joinery Ltd v CF Financial Services Ltd* 1987 SLT 207.

Restricted and unrestricted securities

20.16 A security can be for a fixed debt. For example, Banff Bank lends £100,000 to John and Karen. In turn, they grant the bank a standard security to secure that amount. This is the limit of the bank's security. In such circumstances the security can be referred to as 'restricted' or 'special'. If the bank were to make a further advance[26] of £20,000 so that John and Karen could add a conservatory to their house, that amount would be *unsecured*. The bank, however, in practice would want security and that is why standard securities are normally granted for 'all sums due and to become due'. If the security granted by John and Karen were in these terms, then not only would the £100,000 be secured, but also the £20,000 and indeed any sums due to the bank. (Of course, the bank would require to have in mind the value of the house). Such a security is known as 'unrestricted' or 'general' and can cover both existing and future debts.

Accessory nature of security

20.17 As the purpose of security is to ensure payment of a debt (or debts), in principle there can be no security without a debt. The real right of security is *accessory* or parasitic upon the debt. No debt: no security. Thus if the debt is paid off the security is extinguished.[27] Similarly, if the debt is invalid, so too is the security. In *Nisbet's Creditors v Robertson*[28] a heritable security had been granted by a merchant in Scotland to his supplier in Holland for the price of smuggled goods. The contract was illegal and so the security failed too.

20.18 The accessoriness principle is not absolute because of the competence of securities for future and unrestricted sums. For example, a standard security may be created in security of a future advance. The security will come into effect upon registration but cannot be enforced until the advance is made and the debt is actually due. Similarly, a standard security can secure a bank overdraft. If the bank account goes into credit the security will continue, but cannot be enforced unless and until the account goes back into overdraft. In effect the security is suspended.

Third-party security

20.19 It is competent to grant a security for another person's debt. For example, John sets up a small business. The bank offers him a loan, but on condition that a standard security is granted over the house he owns with Karen. The result is that both the *pro indiviso* shares of the house secure the loan. In doing this, Karen does not become personally liable – though if the debt is not paid, she will lose her share

---

26   Loan. Loans are often called 'advances'.
27   *Rankin v Arnot* (1680) Mor 572.
28   (1791) Mor 9554.

of the house. (Of course, she could alternatively, or additionally, give a personal guarantee for the debt.) In such situations it is important that the bank ensures that Karen is offered independent legal advice on the implications of the security.[29]

Transfer of securities

20.20 *Accessorium sequitur principale*: the accessory follows the principal.[30] The assignation of a debt carries with it all accessories of the debt, including in principle any security.[31] For real securities, however, further action may be required. A standard security requires to be specifically assigned and that assignation registered.[32] This is part of a more general rule that the same steps required to create a real right are normally needed to transfer it.[33] It is crucial that if a security is to be transferred that the debt is assigned. Otherwise, the security being an accessory right, will be unenforceable.[34]

Transfer of the security subjects

20.21 The existence of the security does not prevent the property being transferred.[35] This is simply an aspect of the wider principle that a subordinate real right does not prevent transfer of the encumbered property. We saw above that John and Karen could transfer their house to Leslie notwithstanding the standard security.[36] The effect of this now needs to be more carefully considered. A distinction can be drawn between 'personal liability' (liability of a person) and 'real liability' (liability of a thing). Neither is affected by the transfer. The personal liability of John and Karen to the bank under the contract of loan remains. The bank cannot sue Leslie directly for payment of the debt as he was not a party to the loan contract. But the real liability, the liability of the house also continues. As the security is a real right, it is not affected by the transfer and therefore the bank can enforce it. The practical result is that Leslie loses the house. As was seen above, in practice this does not happen because his solicitor will have checked the register before the transfer.

---

[29] *Smith v Bank of Scotland* 1997 SC (HL) 111. See Gretton and Reid *Conveyancing* para 1-11.

[30] See *Trayner's Latin Maxims* (4th edn, reprinted with an introduction by A G M Duncan, 1993) 8.

[31] Stair III, 1, 17; Bankton III, 1, 7; Erskine III, 5, 8.

[32] CFR(S)A 1970, s 14.

[33] See **PARA 1.25** above.

[34] *Watson v Bogue (No 1)* 2000 SLT (Sh Ct) 125.

[35] The terms of the security may in practice prohibit this. Such a prohibition has, however, contractual, not real, effect. Transfer without consent would be breach of contract, but the transfer would still take effect.

[36] See **PARA 20.7** above.

Ranking

20.22 It is usually competent for more than one security to be granted over the same property. Thus one hears of people 'taking out second mortgages'. John and Karen, having granted a standard security to Banff Bank plc for the £100,000 they needed to buy the house, may then grant a second standard security to Alvah Bank plc for the £20,000 required to add a conservatory. If the couple default and the securities have to be enforced, then the issue of ranking must be considered. The rule is that the earlier the security, the higher the rank: *prior tempore potior jure* (earlier by time, stronger by right). Thus if the house, after the expenses of the sale, is worth £115,000, Banff Bank will receive its £100,000 in full but there will only be £15,000 left for Alvah Bank. It will be an unsecured creditor for the shortfall of £5,000.

20.23 A first-ranked security is known as a security *primo loco* (in the first place). A second-ranked security is known as *secundo loco* and so on and so forth, using Latin. A bottom-ranked security is referred to as *ultimo loco*. Securities ranking equally are referred to as ranking *pari passu*. This will happen if the securities were created at the same time, or (more commonly) because a ranking agreement between the creditors so provides. Clearly the lower the ranking the more the creditor is at risk. This is particularly the case where house prices fall. If the house is worth less than the value of the security or securities this is known as 'negative equity'. This tends to happen on a substantial scale every time there is a property market downturn.[37]

Enforcement

20.24 Historically, securities were enforced by the property being forfeited to the creditor.[38] This was not fair to the debtor, because the property might be worth several times the debt. Forfeiture was replaced by sale,[39] with any surplus having to be returned to the debtor. If the sale does not meet the debt entirely, then the creditor is left with a personal (unsecured) right against the debtor for the deficit. This right may be worth little if the debtor is insolvent. (And the debtor usually is insolvent, because were it otherwise the enforcement would probably not have happened.) The fact that the debtor is always personally liable is not always understood. For example, some debtors with negative equity think that they can simply 'hand the keys to the bank' and walk away from the loan when they walk away from the property. Not so.

20.25 The creditor is under a duty to sell for the best price which can be reasonably obtained.[40] The reason for this is best explained by an example. Say that a house is

---

[37] Of course, it depends on the percentage of value that has been lent. If a property is worth £200,000 and there is a secured loan of £150,000, a market downturn that reduces the property's value to £170,000 does not result in negative equity. But if the bank's loan had been 95% of value, £190,000, there is now negative equity.

[38] See A J M Steven *Pledge and Lien* (2008) para 8-14.

[39] It is doubtful nowadays that even an express forfeiture clause in the contract would be enforceable. See Steven *Pledge and Lien* para 8-17.

[40] This is a common law duty. For standard securities it is stated expressly in CFR(S)A 1970, s 25.

worth £300,000 and there is a standard security over it for £100,000. The debtor defaults. All the creditor is interested in obtaining is the £100,000 plus the expenses of the sale. It would be unfair to the debtor if the creditor could sell for this amount. The house is worth almost £200,000 more and the debtor is entitled to that surplus. Hence the law imposes this duty, which also protects any lower-ranked creditors.

Extinction

20.26 Securities can be extinguished in a number of ways. These include the following.

Discharge of the debt

20.27 As a security is an accessory right, the discharge of the debt ends the security. No further action is needed, but for registered security rights such as standard securities a discharge will be registered to publicise the extinction.[41] As was seen above,[42] in the case of unrestricted securities, repayment of the present debt suspends rather than discharges the security, because if there is future indebtedness it would be secured. But in this case the owner can require the creditor to sign a discharge, and will in practice do so if there is no intention to borrow in future. In such a case the deed of discharge does not merely *evidence* the fact of a discharge that has already happened (as above), but is itself the discharge.

Property no longer exists

20.28 If the property over which the security exists is destroyed or otherwise ceases to exist, so too does the security. For example, a security over a gold bar will disappear if the bar is melted down and the gold used to make other things. Heritable property is of course generally indestructible. Where a tenement is destroyed and the site is sold the proceeds must be used first to pay the debts due under any standard securities over the former flats.[43]

Renunciation

20.29 The creditor may decide to give up the security voluntarily, even though the debt has not been paid. This of course is rare. However, not so rare is a *partial renunciation* – this is called a restriction[44] – in which the creditor releases part of the property from the security.

[41] See PARA **20.56** below.
[42] See PARA **20.18** above.
[43] T(S)A 2004, Sch 3, para 5(2)(a).
[44] See PARA **20.55** below.

Enforcement

20.30 Once enforced and the property sold, the security ceases to affect the property.

Confusion

20.31 If the creditor acquires ownership of the security subjects the security will be extinguished by confusion.[45]

TYPES OF SECURITY

20.32 Real securities can be divided into two main categories: those which are 'voluntary' and those which are 'involuntary'. A voluntary security requires the consent of the owner of the property, normally the debtor. An involuntary security does not.

VOLUNTARY SECURITIES

General

20.33 The main examples of voluntary securities are:
  (1) pledge (for corporeal moveable property);[46]
  (2) floating charge (for the property of companies and limited liability partnerships);[47]
  (3) mortgage (for ships and aircraft);[48]
  (4) securities over intellectual property;[49] and
  (5) standard security (for heritable property).[50]

Pledge

Definition and use

20.34 A pledge is a real right in security over corporeal moveable property, created by the delivery of the property from its owner to another, in terms of an agreement for the property to secure an obligation owed to the other. The agreement normally

---

[45] Cusine and Rennie *Standard Securities* para 10.11.
[46] See PARAS **20.34–20.36** below.
[47] See PARAS **20.37–20.40** below.
[48] See PARA **20.41** below.
[49] See PARA **20.42** below.
[50] See PARAS **20.43–20.56** below.

does not need to be in writing.[51] The granter of the security is the 'pledger' or 'pledgor'. The party receiving the security is the 'pledgee'. Pawnbrokers are professional pledge takers and the website of the National Pawnbrokers Association of the UK reveals that the most commonly pawned items are things made of gold, watches and jewellery.[52]

Delivery

20.35 It is essential for the creation of a pledge that the creditor is placed in possession. Moreover, possession must be maintained or the security will be lost. This makes pledge commercially inconvenient because it is not feasible for a company to run its business if it has handed over key assets to a creditor. (Equally, the creditor may not wish to store goods.) There exists authority that pledge can only be constituted by *actual* delivery, that is physically handing over the property.[53] This is probably wrong.[54] Rather, pledge can also be established by constructive delivery where the goods are in the possession of a third party such as a warehouse company by instructing the third party to hold them for the pledgee. In the case of goods being shipped, these can be pledged by delivering the bill of lading to the creditor. This is the special document issued by the shipping company to the person who is having the goods transported. In such cases pledge is perfectly convenient since the debtor is not losing natural possession.

Enforcement

20.36 If the debtor defaults, the creditor's remedy is to apply to the sheriff for authority to sell. But this is not necessary where the contract between the parties authorises sale, and of course in practice contracts do so provide.[55] Moreover, licensed pawnbrokers have a statutory power to sell where the property is not redeemed within six months or such longer period that has been agreed.[56] Where the debt does not exceed £75, there is no sale. Instead, the property is forfeited to the pawnbroker.[57]

---

[51] But pledge to a licensed pawnbroker requires writing: Consumer Credit Act 1974 s 115.

[52] http://www.thenpa.com/pawnbroking.htm.

[53] *Hamilton v Western Bank* (1856) 19 D 152. On delivery more generally, see PARAS **11.13–11.17** above.

[54] See Steven *Pledge and Lien* paras 6-21–6-34.

[55] *Murray of Philiphauch v Cuninghame* (1668) 1 Br Sup 575.

[56] Consumer Credit Act 1974, ss 116(1)–(3) and 121(1); Consumer Credit (Realisation of Pawn) Regulations 1983 (SI 1983/1568).

[57] Consumer Credit Act 1974, s 120(1)(a), read with SI 1998/997, Sch 1, para 1. This is so even if the thing is worth more than the debt. Tom borrows £70 from Sue, pledging a painting worth £1,000. He fails to redeem within the redemption period. The painting has been forfeited. Does she now owe him £930? That would be fair, but the 1974 Act does not say so. Moreover, it says that forfeiture operates 'notwithstanding anything in s 113'. The meaning of s 113 is obscure but it is probably declaratory of the common law rule that a creditor cannot obtain a windfall gain from security. Seemingly she gets a

Floating charge

General

20.37   The floating charge was not recognised at common law. In the well-known words of Lord President Cooper, 'It is clear in principle and amply supported by authority that a floating charge is utterly repugnant to the principles of Scots law'.[58] It is in fact a creature of English equity, which was introduced to Scotland by statute in 1961.[59] It was felt then that the common law of security was too restrictive, in particular in relation to the delivery requirement for the pledge of corporeal movables.[60] As a non-possessory security, the floating charge solved this problem. In 1972, receivership, the special procedure by which a floating charge is enforced, was imported too,[61] although the reforms of the Enterprise Act 2002 mean that (with certain exceptions) it only now applies to those charges granted before 15 September 2003.

20.38   The floating charge was introduced with insufficient consideration of how its English equitable features would fit with civilian Scottish property law. This is compounded by the deficient drafting of the legislation, which has led to many difficulties, most notably as regards the relationship between the floating charge and diligence.[62] Some improvements have been made by the new provisions in the Bankruptcy and Diligence etc (Scotland) Act 2007 (BD(S)A 2007), which are not yet in force.[63]

Creation

20.39   Floating charges may only be granted by companies, limited liability partnerships and a few other commercial entities.[64] Writing is required.[65] The security

---

windfall profit of £930. Indeed, it has been so held: *Henderson v Wilson* (1834) 12 S 313, construing the similar provisions of the Pawnbrokers Act 1800. (And see *McMillan v Conrad* (1914) 30 Sh Ct Rep 275.)

[58]   *Carse v Coppen* 1951 SC 233 at 239.

[59]   Companies (Floating Charges) (Scotland) Act 1961.

[60]   *Eighth Report of the Law Reform Committee for Scotland* (1960, Cmnd 1017) para 2.

[61]   Companies (Floating Charges and Receivers) (Scotland) Act 1972. The current legislation is CA 1985, ss 462–487 and the Insolvency Act 1986, ss 50–71. Future regulation will be by the Bankruptcy and Diligence etc (Scotland) Act 2007, ss 37–49, which provisions are not yet in force.

[62]   The leading case is *Lord Advocate v Royal Bank of Scotland* 1977 SC 155. See S Wortley 'Squaring the Circle: Revisiting the Receiver and "Effectually Executed Diligence"' 2000 *Juridical Review* 325.

[63]   BD(S)A 2007, ss 37–49.

[64]   CA 1985, s 462(1); Limited Liability Partnerships (Scotland) Regulations 2001 (SSI 2001/128), para 3. See Gordon *Scottish Land Law* para 20-205.

[65]   Not by RoW(S)A 1995, but by the fact that the particulars of the charge must be registered within 21 days of its signature. See CA 1985, s 410.

is created[66] merely by signature of the debtor and delivery of the constitutive deed to the creditor. Registration in the Companies Register must follow within 21 days on pain of nullity.[67] Under BD(S)A 2007, registration in the new Register of Floating Charges will be required to create the security.[68] Usually a floating charge extends to all the company's assets, or, to use the words in the statute, the company's entire 'property and undertaking'.[69] Therefore, both immoveable and moveable property and corporeal and incorporeal property may be encumbered. The fact that a creditor has a security over the entirety of the company's assets makes the floating charge popular with lending institutions.

Nature and enforcement

20.40 The idea of the security is that it 'floats' over the company's assets in the company's patrimony. When an asset leaves the patrimony, for example as a result of sale, it automatically escapes the charge: no act of discharge by the creditor is needed. When an asset enters the patrimony, for example as a result of purchase, it automatically comes under the charge. Only when (and if) the debtor defaults on the obligation, and the chargeholder enforces the security by appointing an administrator (or in some cases a receiver), or where the company goes into liquidation, does the charge *attach*[70] to the assets.[71] Attachment means that the creditor obtains a limited real right or, in the legislative terminology, the floating charge becomes a 'fixed security'.[72] An attached charge has ceased to float.

Aircraft and ship mortgages

20.41 At common law the captain of a ship had the power to grant a non-possessory security over the ship itself, known as a 'bond of bottomry', and over the cargo, known as a 'bond of respondentia'. Both these securities are *hypothecs*. A hypothec is a security where the creditor does not have possession. Hypothecs can be granted only if funds are needed to continue the journey and the captain is unable to contact the ship's owner. Due to modern global communication technology these securities are obsolete in modern practice. What continues to be important is the 'ship mortgage'. This requires registration in the Register of Ships in order to be a real

---

66   The security is not, however, a real right unless or until it attaches on receivership or liquidation. See **PARA 20.40** below.
67   CA 1985, s 410.
68   BD(S)A 2007, s 38.
69   CA 1985, s 462(1).
70   The term used in England, 'crystallise', is often used here. (One might think, of course, that a charge that ceases to float should 'sink'.)
71   CA 1985, s 463(1); Insolvency Act 1986, s 53(7). Enterprise Act 2002, s 250 limits severely the power of a floating charge holder to appoint a receiver, and in most cases an administrator must be appointed.
72   *National Commercial Bank of Scotland Ltd v Telford, Grier Mackay & Co Ltd* 1969 SC 181.

right.[73] Much the same applies to aircraft. Aircraft mortgages must be registered in the Register of Aircraft.[74]

Securities over intellectual property

20.42 Security rights can be granted over intellectual property rights, though the subject is not well developed. A security over a patent can be created by a security registered in the Patents Register.[75] The same rule applies to registered trademarks.[76] There is no special statutory security for copyright, so it if it is used for security it must be assigned to the creditor. There is no requirement for the assignation to be registered.[77] Upon repayment of the debt, the right will be retrocessed to the debtor.

Standard securities

General

20.43 *Standard securities* were introduced by the Conveyancing and Feudal Reform (Scotland) Act 1970 (CFR(S)A 1970), which provided that grants of security over heritable property must be in the form of a standard security.[78] The result is that the types of heritable security which existed before CFR(S)A 1970 can no longer be competently granted.[79] A standard security is a very common type of security. When people talk about 'getting a mortgage from the bank', they are in reality granting a standard security to the bank over the house in security of a loan. (The loan is usually to buy the house in the first place.[80] In this case, the security is usually created at once upon the acquisition of the property. Thus in the Land Register the conveyance to the buyer and the security by the buyer to the lender will normally be registered on the same date.)

---

[73] Merchant Shipping Act 1995, s 16 and Sch 1. For a recent case, see *Air and General Finance Ltd v RYB Marine Ltd* 2007 GWD 35-589.
[74] Civil Aviation Act 1982, s 86.
[75] Patents Act 1977, ss 31(3) and 33. See further D P Sellar 'Rights in Security over Scottish Patents' (1996) 1 *SLPQ* 137 and T Guthrie and A Orr 'Fixed Security Rights over Intellectual Property Rights in Scotland' (1996) 18 *EIPR* 597. See also *Buchanan v Alba Diagnostics Ltd* 2004 SC (HL) 9.
[76] Trade Marks Act 1994, ss 24(5) and 25.
[77] Copyright Designs and Patents Act 1988, s 90.
[78] CFR(S)A 1970, s 9(3). Terminology: heritable security is security over heritable property. A standard security is thus a species of heritable security – the only species now competent. The creditor in a heritable security is often called the 'heritable creditor'.
[79] On the older forms of heritable security, see Gordon *Scottish Land Law* paras 20-04–20-102.
[80] See PARA **20.1** above.

Creation

20.44   A standard security must be writing[81] and must be registered in either the Land Register, or Sasine Register, in order to become a real right.[82] The appropriate register depends on where the right over which the security is being granted is itself registered. If the property is on the Land Register then the standard security must be registered there and the Keeper will enter it into Section C of the title sheet.[83] If the property is still in the Sasine Register that is where the security must be recorded. No security is created by merely handing over the title deeds to the creditor.[84]

Security subjects

20.45   The usual object of a standard security is land itself. For example, John and Karen grant a standard security to the bank over their house. It is also competent, but uncommon, for the right to be granted over a registered lease.[85] A standard security can in principle be granted over a standard security. This mind-boggling arrangement happens, but only very rarely.

Forms

20.46   CFR(S)A 1970 provides two forms of standard security: Form A and Form B.[86] Either can be used. In Form A both the loan contract and the standard security are set out. This is the form commonly used for security over residential property. Unless otherwise stated, the loan is repayable on demand.[87] Form B is a pure grant of security. The loan contract is found in an entirely separate document. Form B is typically used in commercial cases.

Style standard security

20.47   Here is an example of a simple Form A standard security:

'WE, JOHN LITTLE AND KAREN RAE or LITTLE, residing at Twenty Seven Cornwall Road, Aberdeen undertake to pay to BANFF BANK PUBLIC LIMITED COMPANY a company registered under the Companies Acts in Scotland under number SC634637 and having its registered office at 5 Trinity Street, Banff the sum of ONE HUNDRED THOUSAND POUNDS (£100,000) which capital sum shall be repayable on the eleventh day of November in the year two thousand and twenty nine (11 November 2029); With interest on the amount from time to time

---

[81]   RoW(S)A 1995, s 1(2)(b).
[82]   CFR(S)A 1970, s 11(1).
[83]   LR(S)A 1979, s 2(3)(i). See PARA **6.20** above.
[84]   Bell *Commentaries* II, 24.
[85]   CFR(S)A 1970, s 9(2) and (8)(b).
[86]   CFR(S)A 1970, Sch 2. The schedules to the Act are full of over-fussy forms.
[87]   CFR(S)A 1970, s 10(1).

outstanding from the date hereof at the rate of four and a quarter per centum per annum (4.25%) payable twice yearly on eleventh November and fifteenth May, commencing on fifteenth May two thousand and ten; And we agree that should any sum due hereunder not be fully paid timeously as aforesaid the amount unpaid shall be added to and compounded with the outstanding capital as at the missed payment date so that subsequent amounts payable shall be increased accordingly; And we further agree that notwithstanding the foregoing provision should any sum due hereunder remain unpaid in whole or in part more than twenty one days after the due date of payment thereof then in that case the whole moneys hereby secured shall in the option of the said Banff Bank plc (which option must be intimated in writing to us not later than thirty days after the missed payment date) become instantly due and payable; And we also bind ourselves to pay to the said Banff Bank plc all other sums due or to become due by us; For which we GRANT A STANDARD SECURITY in favour of the said Banff Bank plc over ALL AND WHOLE the subjects at Twenty Seven Cornwall Road Aberdeen registered under Title Number ABN 7654321; The Standard Conditions specified in Schedule 3 to the Conveyancing and Feudal Reform (Scotland) Act 1970 and any lawful variation thereof operative for the time being shall apply; And we grant warrandice; And we consent to registration for execution: IN WITNESS WHEREOF we have subscribed these presents at Aberdeen on First November Two thousand and Nine in the presence of Jennifer Sharp of Thirty Golf Crescent, Kirkcaldy.

Jennifer Sharp, witness   *John Little*

Karen Little ˈ

The standard conditions

20.48 Towards the end of this standard security there is a reference to the 'standard conditions'. These are a set of default terms, set out in CFR(S)A 1970, Sch 3.[88] In practice, lending institutions generally have their own set of 'mortgage conditions', and in that case the standard conditions apply only to the extent that they are consistent with the 'mortgage conditions'. The standard conditions can be divided into two categories.

(1) Those that protect the creditor's interests by requiring the debtor, for example, to maintain and insure the property.[89] The creditor's consent is required if the property is leased.[90]

[88] A limited number of the conditions, in particular those relating to enforcement of the security, cannot be varied. See CFR(S)A 1970, s 11(3). And see A J M Steven and D A Massaro 'Standard Securities and Variation to the Standard Conditions' *2008 SLT (News)* 271.

[89] CFR(S)A 1970, Sch 3, standard conditions 1 and 5.

[90] CFR(S)A 1970, Sch 3, standard condition 6. In the event of this not being obtained, the creditor may reduce the lease: *Trade Development Bank v Warriner and Mason (Scotland) Ltd* 1980 SC 74.

(2) Those that protect the debtor's interests by regulating enforcement and redemption procedures.[91]

Assignation

20.49 Standard securities can be assigned. The assignation must be registered in the Land Register or the Sasine Register, depending on where the security itself is registered.[92] As was seen above,[93] it is essential to assign the secured debt too.

Ranking

20.50 Standard securities follow the *prior tempore potior jure* principle discussed above, and so rank by order of registration.[94] However, there is a special rule affecting those granted for 'all sums'. It is best explained by an example.

EXAMPLE

Suppose that John and Karen have granted a standard security to Banff Bank for £100,000 and 'all sums due and to become due'. They wish to add a conservatory. Alvah Bank plc is prepared to lend them £20,000 for this purpose but insists on a standard security. This will rank below Banff Bank's security since it will be registered later. The house is worth £150,000 so there is £50,000 of so-called 'free equity' to reassure Alvah Bank. So far, so good. But suppose that John and Karen subsequently borrow another £50,000 from Banff Bank. As its security is for 'all sums', it prevails. The further advance effectively wipes out the equity on which Alvah Bank was relying. CFR(S)A 1970, s 13 deals with this problem by allowing the postponed creditor (Alvah Bank) to send a notice to the prior creditor (Banff Bank). The effect of the notice is that any further advances made by the prior creditor will not prevail over the postponed creditor. In practice a postponed creditor will always send such a notice. The earlier creditor will still, however, have priority for:

(1) the interest due on the earlier advance(s); and
(2) any subsequent sums lent which have been already contracted.

Thus if Banff Bank had contracted with John and Karen, before the security to Alvah Bank, to make a subsequent advance two years later, then this would have priority over the later security.

---

[91]   CFR(S)A 1970, Sch 3, standard conditions 7–11. 'Redemption' is where the debtor wishes to repay the debt and so get rid of the security.

[92]   CFR(S)A 1970, s 14 and Sch 4, Forms A and B.

[93]   See PARA **20.20** above.

[94]   See PARAS **20.22–20.23** above.

Enforcement

20.51 The enforcement rules in CFR(S)A 1970 are complex and would benefit from reform, although they work in practice. The principal remedy is sale and there are three roads to get there.

(1) The 'calling-up notice'.[95] This provides that the entire debt must be repaid within *two months*, failing which the creditor may sell.

(2) The 'notice of default'.[96] The default may relate to being in arrears with repayment of the debt or failure to comply with other terms of the security, for example the duty to insure the property. The notice gives the debtor *one month* to remedy the default, failing which the creditor may sell.

(3) The creditor can apply to the sheriff for authority to sell. This is known as a 's 24 order'.[97]

The first and second options do not require a court order. In practice, however, lenders do go to court because the debtor can only be evicted from the property (if he or she does not leave voluntarily) by court order.[98]

20.52 Under the Mortgage Rights (Scotland) Act 2001, the debtor (and certain other parties, such as the debtor's spouse or civil partner) can apply to the sheriff for suspension of the enforcement proceedings. This legislation is limited to residential properties.[99] The sheriff may grant the order if it is reasonable to do so in all the circumstances of the case. Regard must be had to certain specified factors including the nature and reasons for the default and the ability of the applicant and those living at the security subjects to find reasonable alternative accommodation.[100]

20.53 The sale of the property is carried out by the creditor rather than the court or a judicial officer, unlike the position in many other countries. There is a specific statutory duty to obtain the best price.[101] The distribution of the proceeds is governed by CFR(S)A 1970, s 27. First come the expenses of the sale. Next is any amount owed to a creditor with a higher ranking standard security than the selling creditor. (This is seldom relevant because if there is more than one security it is usually the first-ranked that carries out the sale.) Then comes the amount due to the selling creditor. Next comes the amount due to the holders of any lower-ranked standard security. Finally, if there is anything left, this must be returned to the debtor, or those representing the debtor. (For instance, it is not unlikely in such a case that the debtor has been sequestrated, and in that case payment is made to the trustee.) The

---

[95] CFR(S)A 1970, s 19.
[96] CFR(S)A 1970, s 21.
[97] CFR(S)A 1970, s 24.
[98] See the Heritable Securities (Scotland) Act 1894, s 5 for the relevant procedure.
[99] Mortgage Rights (Scotland) Act 2001, s 1(1).
[100] Mortgage Rights (Scotland) Act 2001, s 2(2).
[101] CFR(S)A 1970, s 25. See further PARA **20.25** above.

real rights of the selling creditor, and of any postponed standard security holders, are extinguished.[102] The result is that the buyer receives an unencumbered title.[103]

Foreclosure

20.54 'Foreclosure' can be used colloquially to mean enforcement of a security. Its legal meaning is narrow: the creditor acquires ownership.[104] The creditor can seek a decree of foreclosure from the court, but only if it has not proved possible to find a buyer for the property. This would be very unusual.

Restriction

20.55 It is possible for the creditor to reduce the physical coverage of the security by granting a deed of restriction, which then must be registered.[105] For example, a developer grants a bank a standard security over a site in order to receive funding to build houses. When each house is built and sold the buyer will require an unencumbered title. The bank will therefore in return for some of the sale proceeds grant a deed of restriction releasing the house from the scope of the security.

Discharge

20.56 CFR(S)A 1970 provides for a form of deed known as a 'discharge', which is granted by the creditor and then registered in the appropriate register.[106] It extinguishes the security. If the security is restricted to a specific sum, the accessoriness principle means that it is automatically extinguished upon repayment, without the need for a deed of discharge.[107] But the discharge is needed for evidential purposes: for example a prospective purchaser of the land will insist that the register is clear. If the security is for 'all sums' then repayment of the original debt will not extinguish the security, because any subsequent advances will be secured. In this case it is essential to register a discharge to end the security.

---

[102] CFR(S)A 1970, s 26.
[103] Unless, of course, there is a prior ranked standard security. This is very unlikely.
[104] CFR(S)A 1970, s 28.
[105] CFR(S)A 1970, s 15 and Sch 4, Form C.
[106] CFR(S)A 1970, s 17 and Sch 4, Form F.
[107] See **PARA 20.17** above.

INVOLUNTARY SECURITIES

Categories

20.57 Involuntary securities can be subdivided into three groups.

(1) 'Tacit securities' – in other words, those arising by operation of law. The main examples are lien and the landlord's hypothec, discussed below.[108]

(2) 'Judicial securities', comprising rights of security granted by the court – in other words, diligences. The law of diligence is outwith the scope of this book.[109]

(3) Securities which can be constituted by public bodies over the heritable property of a person who owes them money. These are known as 'charging orders' and are discussed below.[110]

Lien

Introduction

20.58 A lien is a real right to retain property until the discharge of an obligation or certain obligations, the property not having been delivered to the retaining party for the purpose of security. A typical example is a jeweller holding on to a watch until the repair bill is paid. Where the property may be lawfully retained until the performance of a single obligation the right is known as 'special lien'. If the law permits retention for more than one obligation the right is known as 'general lien'.

Possession

20.59 A lien depends on the creditor having possession on the property. If that possession is lost, so too normally is the lien.[111] In this way, lien is very similar to pledge.[112]

Types of property

20.60 In modern times lien has been viewed as a security over corporeal moveable property. It is possible to assert a lien over land too,[113] assuming that the requisite possession is held, but such claims seem unknown in current practice.

---

[108] See PARAS **20.58–20.65** below.
[109] See Gloag and Henderson *The Law of Scotland* ch 49.
[110] See PARA **20.66** below.
[111] For an exception, see *Goudie v Mulholland* 2000 SC 61.
[112] See PARA **20.35** above.
[113] *Binning v Brotherstones* (1676) Mor 13401.

Lien as an equitable remedy

20.61   The courts can control the exercise of lien and, if the circumstances justify it, order the release of the property. In *Onyvax Ltd v Endpoint Research (UK) Ltd*[114] a company asserting a lien over a document containing the results of the trial of a new cancer drug was ordered to hand it over to the company developing the drug on condition of the disputed debt being consigned (paid to the court) until the matter was resolved. It was in the public interest that the information was made available.

Enforcement of lien

20.62   To enforce the lien by sale the authority of the court is necessary, unless of course the debtor consents. Sale is only possible where the property is marketable. This is usually not the case for documents, for example where a law firm, whose fee is unpaid, asserts a lien over the client's papers and deeds held by the firm.

Special lien

20.63   A special lien arises through the doctrine of mutuality of contractual obligations.[115] For example, in a contract for the sale of goods the seller's duty to deliver and the buyer's duty to pay are regarded as reciprocal. The seller therefore has a lien over the goods until paid.[116] Likewise, a warehouse may hold on to goods until the storage charges are met, as can a carrier until the carriage account is settled. Hoteliers (or 'innkeepers', as they are still often called in this context) have a lien over a guest's goods for their bill. In *McKichen v Muir*[117] the Muir family had booked into an inn in order to attend a local ball. On returning from the event, Mr Muir argued about the bill with the innkeeper, who then detained the family's clothes.[118] This meant that they had to walk 8 or 9 miles home on a rainy night, with the ladies wearing only 'thin shoes and light muslin dresses, and without bonnets'.[119] As well as arising in a contractual context, a special lien may be available in situations of unjustified enrichment and – less commonly – delict. For example, where there has been benevolent intervention (*negotiorum gestio*) the intervening party may hold onto the property until compensation is received from the owner.[120]

---

[114]   2008 GWD 1-3.
[115]   But it is a real right.
[116]   SOGA 1979, ss 39 and 41.
[117]   (1849) J Shaw 223. See McBryde *Contract* para 20-87.
[118]   It is arguable that the right is a hypothec rather than a lien as it depends on the property being brought into the hotel, rather than the hotelier having possession. See Steven *Pledge and Lien* paras 16-86–16-92.
[119]   (1849) J Shaw 223 at 224.
[120]   Steven *Pledge and Lien* paras 11-12–11-34.

General lien

20.64 A general lien secures a general balance, for example all the sums owed to a solicitor by the client or to a commercial agent (factor) by that agent's principal. The other main instances of general lien are those of the banker and the broker. A general lien is not an entirely unrestricted security, because it does not secure *all* sums – rather, only those owed to the creditor in the particular capacity of solicitor or banker or agent or broker.[121] Only a limited number of general liens are recognised because of the potential prejudice to other creditors by what is a powerful security.

Landlord's hypothec

20.65 The landlord's hypothec gives the landlord a security over the corporeal moveables in the leased premises – the *invecta et illata* – in respect of the rent. Like so much else in property law its basis is Roman,[122] but it has been curtailed by statute. The Hypothec Abolition (Scotland) Act 1880, as its name suggests, abolished it, but only for agricultural leases of more than two acres.[123] BD(S)A 2007 abolished it for all other agricultural leases as well as for residential ones.[124] The effect is that it is restricted to commercial leases. The hypothec used to be enforceable by a special diligence known as 'sequestration for rent' but the 2007 Act abolished this too.[125] Ordinary diligence has to be used instead. A remarkable feature of the hypothec at common law was its ability to cover goods which were not the tenant's.[126] This rule was removed by BD(S)A 2007, principally because it may have been an unlawful interference with the third party's right to the property in terms of ECHR, Protocol 1, Art 1.[127]

Charging orders

20.66 A 'charging order' can be registered by a local authority and certain other public bodies against the title to a heritable property for certain sums owed by the owner.[128] A typical example is where a building is found to be dangerous. The local authority can instruct the owner to repair it or demolish it.[129] If this is not done, the authority can carry out the work itself and bill the owner.[130] If the owner fails to pay, the authority can register a charging order – known in this case as a 'repayment

---

[121]   *McCall & Co v James Black & Co* (1824) 2 Sh App 188; *Largue v Urquhart* (1883) 10 R 1229.
[122]   See A J M Steven 'The Landlord's Hypothec in Comparative Perspective' 2008 *Stell LR* 278.
[123]   Hypothec Abolition (Scotland) Act 1880, s 1.
[124]   BD(S)A 2007, s 208(3). See also PARA **19.29** above.
[125]   BD(S)A 2007, s 208(1).
[126]   See, e.g., *Scottish and Newcastle Breweries Ltd v Edinburgh District Council* 1979 SLT (Notes) 11.
[127]   BD(S)A 2007, s 208(4).
[128]   See Paisley *Land Law* para 11-32.
[129]   Building (Scotland) Act 2003, ss 28 and 30; Housing (Scotland) Act 2006 (H(S)A 2006), ss 30 and 33.
[130]   H(S)A 2006, s 35.

charge' – over the land.[131] The effect is that the land is encumbered by a security. In practice, the owner will unable to sell the property without paying the debt and having the order discharged.

FUTURE REFORM

20.67   There have been periodic proposals to reform the law on security over corporeal moveables.[132] In a consultation paper published in 1994, the Department of Trade and Industry proposed an extension to the current law in respect of non-possessory security.[133] It wished to see all businesses being able to create floating charges over their property.[134] Further, it proposed the introduction of a new registered hypothec over moveables, to be known as the 'moveable security'.[135] The consultation paper did not suggest making any alterations to the existing common law securities.[136] Its proposals have not been implemented. Later research commissioned by the Scottish Executive concluded that there was no evidence that the reforms were needed, at least for small and medium sized businesses.[137]

20.68   Assignation of, and security over, incorporeal moveable property is a subject which is being currently examined by the Scottish Law Commission.[138]

20.69   At present there are no plans to reform the law of security over land. At European Union level, there have been proposals to harmonise the law and create a 'Euromortgage'.[139] A compelling case, however, has yet to be made. The different laws in England and Scotland have never been a bar to financial institutions in England lending in Scotland and vice versa.[140]

---

[131]   H(S)A 2006, ss 172 and 173.
[132]   D O'Donnell and D L Carey Miller 'Security over Moveables: A Longstanding Reform Agenda in Scots Law' (1997) 5 *ZEuP* 807.
[133]   Department of Trade and Industry Consultation Paper *Security over Moveable Property in Scotland* (1994).
[134]   Consultation Paper, para 2.10.
[135]   Consultation Paper, para 2.11.
[136]   Consultation Paper, para 2.9.
[137]   Scottish Executive Central Research Unit *Business Finance and Security over Moveable Property* (2002) 99-100.
[138]   Scottish Law Commission *Annual Report 2007* (2008) 13.
[139]   S Nasarre-Aznar 'The Eurohypothec: A Common Mortgage for Europe' [2005] 69 *The Conveyancer and Property Lawyer* 32.
[140]   C von Bar and U Drobnig *The Interaction of Contract Law and Tort and Property Law in Europe: A Comparative Study* (2004) 361.

FURTHER READING

Gloag & Henderson, *The Law of Scotland* ch 37.

Paisley, *Land Law* ch 11.

Gretton & Reid, *Conveyancing* chs 18–19.

McDonald, *Conveyancing Manual* chs 21–23.

A J M Steven, *Pledge and Lien* (2008).

Gordon, *Scottish Land Law* ch 20.

D J Cusine and R Rennie, *Standard Securities* (2nd edn, 2002).

Gloag & Irvine, *Rights in Security*.

Chapter 21

Liferent

INTRODUCTION

21.1 *Liferent*, also occasionally called 'usufruct' – from the Latin term for this right, *ususfructus* – is the right to use someone else's property for life.[1] It is a subordinate real right, encumbering the other party's ownership. While the word 'liferent' might suggest that some sort of rent is paid, that is not so. The holder of the right is called the 'liferenter' or, less often, the 'usufructuary'.[2] The owner is

[1] As the Roman jurist Paulus put it, 'usufruct is the right of using and enjoying the things of another person, but without prejudice to the substance of the thing': D 7, 1, 1. See also Justinian's *Institutes* 2, 4.

[2] 'Liferentrix' is normally used where the liferenter is a woman. In this chapter 'liferenter' will be used as a gender-neutral term.

called the 'fiar' and the ownership that is encumbered is called the 'fee'. The fact that a special term (fee) is used does not mean that this is a special sort of right. It is simply ownership, but subject to this particular subordinate real right. One may use the terms 'owner' and 'ownership' instead of 'fiar' and 'fee'. Sometimes the English terms 'reversion' or 'reversionary interest' are used instead of 'fee'.

WHY ARE LIFERENTS USED?

21.2   The creation of a liferent can be a commercial arrangement, with money changing hands. For instance, an owner might sell the property, reserving a liferent. Obviously, the buyer would not be prepared to pay the full market value. The amount would depend on the owner's life expectancy. If the owner is 100 years old, the price might be near full market value, whereas if he or she is 25 years old and in excellent health, it would be low. Conversely, an owner might sell a liferent and reserve the fee, although this would be unusual. In fact, most liferents are not created for commercial reasons but as family arrangements. Vera might transfer ownership of her house to her two children, reserving to herself a liferent. Liferents are often testamentary. Thus Tom might leave his house in liferent to his widow and to his children in fee.

CREATION

21.3   A liferent is created as a real right by a deed[3] registered in the Land Register or Sasine Register.[4] It can be created either by *grant* or by *reservation.* A liferent by grant is where the owner confers a liferent on someone else. For instance, Olivia owns land and grants to Luke a liferent of it. The alternative to a liferent by grant is a liferent by reservation. That happens when the owner, Oliver, transfers ownership to Georgina, reserving to himself a liferent. Liferents created *inter vivos* can be either by grant or by reservation. Obviously, testamentary liferents cannot be created by reservation.

21.4   In modern law, liferents come into existence only by the owner's voluntary act. Previously, two sorts of liferent could arise *ex lege* (by law). They were 'terce' and 'courtesy'. These sometimes came into being on the death of the owner, in favour of the widow (terce) or widower (courtesy). They were abolished by the Succession (Scotland) Act 1964.

---

[3]   Writing is required under the Requirements of Writing (Scotland) Act (RoW(S)A 1995), s 1(2)(b). See **PARA 30.4** below.
[4]   AFT(S)A 2000, s 65.

WHO CAN BE A LIFERENTER?

21.5 Since a liferent is a right that lasts for the holder's life, only a natural person can hold a liferent. It is the only real right that cannot be held by a juristic person. Some legal systems, but not Scotland, allow juristic persons to be usufructuaries, with the period of the usufruct defined as a certain number of years.

THE LEGAL NATURE OF LIFERENT

Subordinate real right – or temporary ownership?

21.6

'By the institutional writers a liferent was regarded as a mere burden on the fee ... the more modern view is to treat the rights of liferent and fee as forming two separate and co-existent estates ... the liferenter being no longer regarded as a mere burdener but as interim proprietor.'

wrote Dobie in 1941.[5] This 'more modern' view did not establish itself and the traditional conception of liferent as a subordinate real right remains intact today. What a liferenter has is not interim ownership but a subordinate real right. Ownership is vested exclusively in the fiar.

Personal servitudes

21.7 In Roman law liferent was classified as a 'personal servitude'. The contrast was with the praedial servitudes,[6] where the relationship is between two properties (one piece of land 'serves' another), and the benefited party is the owner of one of them, whereas with personal servitudes there is only one property, the encumbered property. The term 'personal servitude' is not now much used. The same parallel exists with real burdens, which may be either praedial or personal.[7] In Roman law there were three personal servitudes, namely *ususfructus*, *usus* and *habitatio*, but only the first of these was received into Scots law.

WHAT SORT OF PROPERTY?

21.8 Liferent is competent for corporeal property, though for moveables it is rare. (Example: liferent of a house *plus contents*.) Whether there can be a liferent of

---

[5]   W J Dobie *Manual of the Law of Liferent and Fee in Scotland* (1941).
[6]   See **CHAPTER 12** above.
[7]   See **PARA 13.4** above.

incorporeal property is not wholly clear, though the answer is probably negative. But this fact does not cause practical problems, because an improper liferent can be used.[8]

POSSESSION AND UPKEEP

21.9 The liferenter has possession of the property. A liferented house can be lived in, a liferented farm can be farmed, and so on. The liferenter's possession may be either natural or civil.[9] For example, a liferent could be granted of leased property. The liferenter's possession would then be civil, not natural. The lessee would pay the rent to the liferenter rather than to the owner. As for upkeep, the liferenter must not harm what is called the 'substance' of the property. For instance, the liferenter is not free to demolish. Moreover, the property must be maintained by the liferenter in a reasonable condition. But there are complexities and difficulties about how the fiar can enforce this obligation.[10]

DEATH

21.10 When the liferenter dies, the liferent ends, and so the fiar's ownership ceases to be encumbered. If the fiar dies, there are no special rules: the property is like any other property subject to a subordinate real right. The owner could bequeath the property, for instance. Since liferent is a real right, the liferenter is unaffected, whatever happens.

INSOLVENCY

21.11 If the liferenter becomes insolvent, the creditors can attach the liferent; and likewise if the liferenter is sequestrated the liferent becomes an asset in the sequestration. But the liferent cannot be realised by sale. The way its value is realised is by letting the property out, though any leases will end with the termination of the liferent itself. Alternatively, the trustee in sequestration could seek to do a deal with the fiar whereby the liferent would be renounced in exchange for payment. If the fiar becomes insolvent, there are no special rules: the property is like any other property subject to a subordinate real right. The fiar's creditors can attach the property, while, if the fiar is sequestrated the fee will simply become one of the assets in the sequestration. Since liferent is a real right, none of this affects the liferenter.

---

[8] See **PARA 21.15** below.
[9] See **PARA 11.9** above.
[10] *Stronach's Exrs v Robertson* 2002 SLT 1044.

JURIDICAL ACTS

21.12   A liferenter can use the property, but in general cannot grant real rights over it. Obviously, the liferenter cannot leave a legacy of the liferent. A liferenter can grant a lease but such a lease will end when the liferent ends. A liferent cannot be transferred. It can be sold, in the sense that the liferenter can enter a contract with a buyer whereby the buyer exercises the liferenter's possessory rights: the buyer's right will end with the liferenter's death. Here, the buyer's right is not real, but only personal, being a right against the liferenter.[11] A liferenter can also sell the liferent to the fiar: the effect is that the liferent vanishes and the fiar's ownership becomes unencumbered.

21.13   The fiar, by contrast, is free to deal with the property in any way, subject only to the liferent. For instance, the property can be sold, or a standard security granted over it. But whatever the fiar does, it cannot affect the liferenter's rights. For example, suppose that the fiar, Fraser, grants a standard security to Selma. Fraser defaults on the loan. Selma enforces the security and sells the property to Bertha. Bertha is the new fiar. None of these events affects the liferenter.

TERMINATION

21.14   Liferent ends with the liferenter's death. The liferenter can also 'renounce' the liferent. Renunciation (also called 'discharge') may be either for payment or not. When a liferent ends, no real right passes to the fiar. The effect is simply that the fiar's ownership is no longer encumbered with the liferent. The same is, of course, true of the effect of the discharge of other subordinate real rights.

PROPER LIFERENT AND IMPROPER LIFERENT

21.15   Proper liferent is what has been described above. There is also something else, known interchangeably as 'improper liferent', 'trust liferent' and 'beneficiary liferent'. This is, in functional terms, very similar to the liferent (i.e. to the proper liferent). The inner legal nature, however, is different.[12] It is simply a trust[13] which is used in a certain way. Ownership is vested in Teresa (trustee), while Laura and Fraser have personal rights against her. Laura's personal right is that she is allowed to use the property *as if* she were the liferentrix of the property. Fraser's right is that when Laura dies Teresa must transfer ownership to him. Whereas in a true liferent there are two persons involved (owner and liferenter), in a trust liferent there are three

---

[11]   Different views have been expressed on whether a liferent can be assigned. The position adopted in the text is believed to be correct. See, e.g., Stair II, 6, 7.

[12]   Most books deal with proper and improper liferents together. This is convenient but can be confusing.

[13]   See **CHAPTER 22** below.

(the trustee, the improper liferenter and the improper fiar).[14] And whereas in a true liferent both liferenter and fiar have real rights, in a trust liferent neither the improper liferenter nor the improper fiar has a real right: their rights are only personal. The only person in a trust liferent who has a real right is the trustee, who has ownership.[15]

	Proper	**Improper**
Number of parties	Two (liferenter, fiar)	Three (trustee/s, beneficial liferenter, beneficial fiar)
Number of real rights	Two	One (trustee/s)
Nature of liferenter's right	Real (subordinate)	Personal
Nature of fiar's right	Real (ownership)	Personal

LIFERENTS AND DESTINATIONS

21.16   There exists a legal institution called the 'special destination', which is a little like a liferent.[16] There, a provision inserted in the title to property, whereby on the owner's death the property will pass to a defined person (the 'substitute') rather than to whoever would otherwise inherit it. Here, the similarity between the two institutions ends. In a liferent, the person who 'gets the property next' is already the owner, whereas in a special destination the substitute has (while the previous party is still alive) no real right at all. In other words, the substitute takes by succession, but the fiar does not: strictly he or she does not 'take' at all, being already owner. Moreover, whereas there is nothing a liferenter can do to prevent the fiar becoming unencumbered owner in due course, a person who is the owner of a property that is subject to a special destination can sometimes divert the succession away from the substitute. This is called 'evacuating' the destination.[17]

21.17   An example is *Cochrane's Exr v Cochrane*.[18] Here, a testament said: 'I William Gilchrist Cochrane … bequeath all I possess[19] to my sister Mary Jane Slight Cochrane. Anything she may desire to dispose of or realise after my decease … may be done. On her decease everything of mine to be sold and the proceeds divided' among certain named charities. Did Mr Cochrane intend to give a liferent to Mary (with power to sell) and the fee to the charities? Or did he mean Mary to become the owner but subject to a destination to the charities?[20] Or was Mary to have a right intermediate between ownership and liferent? The court rejected this last argument.

---

[14]   Of course, there may be more than one trustee and more than one beneficiary with the right to use and more than one beneficiary who is eventually to be given ownership.

[15]   See also PARAS **22.21** and **22.31–22.34** below.

[16]   See PARAS **29.5–29.24** below.

[17]   See PARAS **29.11–29.18** below.

[18]   1947 SC 134.

[19]   He did not mean 'possess' in its legal sense. He meant everything that belonged to him, all his assets. Obviously, this was a home-made will.

[20]   For destinations, see CHAPTER **29** below.

A person either has the real right of ownership or some subordinate real right: there is no real right of semi-ownership. The court also held that Mary was meant to receive ownership as opposed to a liferent.[21]

STATUTORY RESTRICTIONS ON LIFERENTS

21.18   By the Law Reform (Miscellaneous Provisions) (Scotland) Act 1968, s 18,[22] a liferent in favour of a person not yet alive will normally give that person a right to the fee, notwithstanding the original grantor's intentions. This policy is to prevent property being tied up for unreasonably long periods.[23] The provisions apply to both proper and improper liferents, but it is doubtful whether a proper liferent could ever trigger the Act's provisions.

FURTHER READING

Dobie, W J *Manual of the Law of Liferent and Fee in Scotland* (1941).

Gloag and Henderson *The Law of Scotland* ch 42.

Gordon *Scottish Land Law* ch 17.

SME vol 13 (S C Styles).

---

[21]   The way the case was pled meant that the court did not have to decide whether or not there was a valid special destination to the charities. However, Lords Cooper and Jamieson said that 'our preference is for the view that the testator intended that the charities should take in succession to the sister as substitutes or quasi-substitutes'.

[22]   Re-enacting earlier statutory provisions which remain in force for older cases. See, e.g., *Earl of Balfour, Petitioner* 2002 SLT 981, 2002 SLT 1385.

[23]   The same policy which led to the abolition of tailzies (entails). See PARA **23.15** below.

Chapter 22

Trusts: what they are and how they are created

INTRODUCTION

Overview

22.1 Trust law is huge. (As are many other topics in this book.) We sketch it here in three chapters, the first (this one) dealing with what trusts are, the different kinds of trusts, and how they are set up. **CHAPTERS 23** and **24** deal with the way trusts are run, and with their variation and termination.

Sources – reform – comparative

22.2 Although the core of the law of trusts remains common law, there are some important statutes, notably the Trusts (Scotland) Act 1921 (T(S)A 1921), the Trusts (Scotland) Act 1961 (T(S)A 1961),[1] and the Charities and Trustee Investment (Scotland) Act 2005 (CTI(S)A 2005). More legislation is likely.[2] The area has been much influenced by English law. Though trust law is often the same, or at least similar, in the two jurisdictions, there are also important differences. (English authorities are often relevant, but are sometimes used uncritically.) In particular, in England trusts form a branch of the law known as 'equity'. There is no such thing in Scots law. English trust law and Scottish trust law achieve fairly similar practical objectives, but using somewhat different underlying conceptions. One might say that what they produce on screen is similar but the software is not the same. Still, the similarities with English law are striking if one compares our law with civilian systems. Few such systems have anything fully equivalent to the trust, though most do have trust-

---

[1] This has been repealed for England and Wales.

[2] The Scottish Law Commission has published six discussion papers, namely *Breach of Trust* (2003), *Apportionment of Trust Receipts and Outgoings* (2003), *Trustees and Trust Administration* (2004), *Variation and Termination of Trusts* (2005), *The Nature and the Constitution of Trusts* (2006) and *Liability of Trustees to Third Parties* (2008). There has been one report: *Variation and Termination of Trusts* (2007).

like institutions of one sort or another, such as the French *fiducie* and the German *Treuhand*.

WHAT IS A TRUST? THE BASICS[3]

What is a trust?

22.3   The question of what a trust is cannot be answered in a simple way, and perhaps not even in a complex way. The trust is conceptually problematic. But the basic idea is not difficult. Normally if an asset belongs to someone, that person has the benefit of that asset. If Tom owns a house he can live in it. He can also sell it, and if he does so the price is his to spend or save as he wishes. If he has investments he can spend the income that they produce on whatever he likes. Title and benefit coincide. In a trust, title and benefit are divided. Tom owns the house, but he cannot live there. He has investments, but cannot use the income for himself. He must use his rights (to the house, the shares and so on) not for his own benefit, but for the benefit of someone else, or a set of other persons. Tom is the 'trustee' and the others are the 'beneficiaries'.

22.4   A trustee is an example of a 'fiduciary', someone who must act in the interests of someone else. Other examples are agents for their principals, company directors for their companies, guardians for their wards and parents for their under-age children. What distinguishes trustees from other fiduciaries is that the assets that they administer actually belong to them. By contrast, company directors (for example) have no title to the company's assets. These are vested in the company itself, as a juristic person. Thus company directors are fiduciaries, but are not trustees.[4] Trustees are fiduciaries in whom title is vested.

22.5   Something like a trust can be created simply under the law of contract. Tom is the owner of a house. He contracts with Beatrice to the effect that he will exercise his right of ownership for her benefit. She can live in it. When it is sold she will receive the price, and so on. This comes close to a trust. But trust has additional features that cannot be explained on the basis of contract law. The most important is the 'insolvency effect'. This is the rule that trust property cannot be touched by the trustee's creditors. Since Beatrice's right as a beneficiary defeats the rights of Tom's creditors, it looks as if Beatrice has some sort of real right. Indeed, in some countries, such as England, she is considered a sort of owner. She is the owner 'in equity' while Tom is the owner 'in law'. But in Scots law the beneficiary's right is personal, not real.[5]

---

[3]   The difficult question of the nature of the trust is resumed later in this chapter. See PARAS **22.53–22.58** below.

[4]   In England the word 'trustee' is often used not only in the narrow sense but also as a synonym for 'fiduciary'. In Scotland the word is generally used only in its narrow meaning, as explained above, but there are exceptions. For instance, T(S)A 1921, s 2 defines 'trustee', for the purposes of the Act, to include some non-trustee fiduciaries.

[5]   See PARA **22.55** below.

Real subrogation

22.6   Tom owns some land in trust for Beatrice. He sells it. The money he receives itself becomes trust money. Suppose that he uses this money to buy UK Government stock. The stock is a trust asset, just as the money was. Tom's duties and Beatrice's rights remain the same, but now relate to the stock instead of the land. (And, in the middle, related to the money.) Thus the trust assets form a 'fund' or 'estate' or 'special patrimony' – in this context these terms are interchangeable – the elements of which may change over time, without affecting the fund's identity. The traditional term to describe this replacement, or substitution, of one asset with another, is 'real subrogation'.[6] The word 'real' does not imply that the assets in question are necessarily real rights. They may be personal rights. Indeed, in the example, UK Government stock is simply a personal right against the UK Government. The contrast is with the doctrine of 'personal subrogation', where, instead of one asset being substituted for another, one person is substituted for another.[7]

Definitions of 'trust'

22.7   While no one has produced a definition that perfectly captures the essence of the trust, the following, by Wilson and Duncan, is good:

'A trust then is a legal relationship in which property is vested in one person, the trustee, who is under a fiduciary obligation to apply the property to some extent for another person's benefit, the obligation being a qualification of the trustee's proprietary right and preferable to all claims of the trustee or his creditors.'[8]

A longer definition, from an international standpoint, is given in the *Principles of European Trust Law*:

'(1) In a trust, a person called the "trustee" owns assets segregated from his private patrimony and must deal with those assets (the "trust fund") for the benefit of another person called the "beneficiary" or for the furtherance of a purpose. (2) There can be more than one trustee and more than one beneficiary; a trustee may himself be one of the beneficiaries. (3) The separate existence of the trust fund entails its immunity from claims by the trustee's spouse, heirs and personal creditors. (4) In respect of the separate trust fund a beneficiary has personal rights and may also have proprietary rights against

---

[6]   *In universalibus pretium succedit in locum rei, res in locum pretii.* (In a universality the price stands in the place of the thing [that has been sold] and the thing stands in the place of the price [where something has been bought]. A trust estate is a universality.

[7]   For example, motorist Adam negligently collides with Eve, injuring her. Eve claims on her insurance policy with Z plc. Z pays her. Z can now enforce against Adam Eve's delictual claim against him. One person (Z) stands in the shoes of another (Eve).

[8]   Wilson and Duncan *Trusts* para 1-63.

the trustee and against third parties to whom any part of the fund has been wrongfully transferred.'[9]

Finally, the definition in the Hague Convention on the Recognition of Trusts, given effect to in the UK by the Recognition of Trusts Act 1987, is:

'The term "trust" refers to the legal relationship created – *inter vivos* or on death – by a person, the settlor,[10] when assets have been placed under the control of a trustee for the benefit of a beneficiary or for a specified purpose. A trust has the following characteristics: (a) The assets constitute a separate fund and are not part of the trustee's own estate. (b) Title to the trust assets stands in the name of the trustee or in the name of another person on behalf of the trustee. … '[11]

Trusts that are not trusts and trustees who are not trustees

22.8 The words 'trust' and 'trustee' are sometimes used where there is no trust. For instance, company directors are sometimes called 'trustees'. What is meant is that they are fiduciaries.[12] The charities legislation uses the term 'charity trustees' to mean 'the persons having the general control and management of the administration of a charity' whether or not the charity is in fact a trust.[13] Perhaps more confusingly, some juristic persons are called trusts, for instance the National Trust for Scotland. Investment trusts are not trusts either. They are ordinary companies, the business of which is investing in other companies. Functionally, they are like unit trusts.[14]

Are trusts part of property law, the law of obligations or the law of persons?

22.9 Trusts can be regarded as part of the law of obligations, or as part of the law of property, or as part of the law of persons. Each viewpoint is valid.[15] First, a trust is to a large extent a set of obligations owed by trustee to beneficiary. Second, trust property can be regarded as a special form of property, and the right of beneficiaries being rights which, though personal, behave rather like real rights. Third, a trust is like a person in its own right, like a juristic person, with the trustees its directors.

---

9   D J Hayton, S C J J Kortmann and H L E Verhagen, *Principles of European Trust Law* (1999) 13.
10   This is the English term for a truster.
11   Recognition of Trusts Act 1987, Sch 1, Art 2.
12   See **PARA 22.4** above.
13   Charities and Trustee Investment (Scotland) Act 2005 (CTI(S)A 2005), s 106.
14   See **PARA 22.25** below.
15   Scotland Act 1998, s 126, in defining 'private law', places trusts as part of the law of property.

has sometimes been suggested that trusts should be formally classified as juristic persons.[16] But under current law they are not persons, merely person-ish.

What are trusts used for?

22.10 The French comparative lawyer, Pierre Lepaulle, wrote:

'Si l'on demande à quoi sert le trust, on peut presque répondre "à tout".'[17]

The trust is perhaps private law's strangest institution. It is protean.

DIFFERENT TYPES OF TRUSTS

Ways of classifying

22.11 Trusts can be classified in different ways for different purposes. In the following paragraphs some of these are mentioned. The classifications are not necessarily mutually exclusive. For instance, trusts are divided into *inter vivos* trusts and *mortis causa* trusts, and also into private trusts and public trusts, but any given trust might be both *inter vivos* and public, or *inter vivos* and private, and so on.

Inter vivos trusts and *mortis causa* trusts

22.12 An *inter vivos*[18] trust is set up by a living truster. A *mortis causa*[19] trust arises on death and is set up by the truster's testament. It is also called a testamentary trust.[20] In such cases the executor may be the trustee, or may be directed to make over money or property to someone else, who is to be the trustee.

Voluntary trusts and involuntary trusts

22.13 Most trusts are created deliberately, whether *inter vivos* or *mortis causa*. These are voluntary trusts. Occasionally, trusts arise involuntarily (see below). Finally, there are one or two types of trust which arise judicially, and which are hard to classify. One is sequestration. Another is confirmation of executors.[21]

[16] For discussion, see Scottish Law Commission *Discussion Paper on the Nature and Constitution of Trusts* (2006) paras 2.39–2.45.

[17] P Lepaulle *Traité Theorique et Pratique des Trusts* (1932) 12. ('If someone asks what trusts are used for, one could almost answer: "for everything".')

[18] 'Between the living.'

[19] 'By reason of death.'

[20] Every intestacy also seems to create a trust, at least in modern law. So, strictly speaking, testamentary trusts are only one kind of *mortis causa* trust.

[21] See **PARAS 25.48–25.49** below.

22.14 An example of a trust imposed by law is the Conveyancing and Feudal Reform (Scotland) Act 1970 (CFR(S)A 1970), s 27. This says that when a standard security holder sells, the proceeds of sale are held on trust for defined purposes. Another example of a statutory trust occurs in the sale of dematerialised company shares.[22] When an involuntary trust arises not by statute but by common law it is called a constructive trust. Whereas English law readily recognises constructive trusts, it is uncertain to what extent, if at all, our law does so. 'I confess an almost instinctive abhorrence of the notion of constructive trusts in the law of Scotland' remarked one judge.[23] Many of the cases commonly cited as being examples of constructive trust are doubtful examples, or are English. The strongest candidate for constructive trust is where a fiduciary, other than a trustee, comes to hold assets which he or she ought to hand over to the principal. (If a trustee has assets which ought to be trust assets then they *are* trust assets, and so there is no constructive trust.[24])

Public trusts and private trusts

22.15 Public trusts are for the benefit of the public or some section of the public. Examples: a trust for helping the long-term unemployed get back into work, or for providing support for elderly people in Fife on low incomes, or for supporting cancer research, or for preserving the historic buildings of Moray, or for providing education for children with special needs. As can be seen, the public benefit may be indirect and selective. The cancer research might never produce useful results. The preservation of the historic buildings of Moray benefits that part of the public that has an interest in such buildings. Charitable trusts are a sub-class of public trusts. Most public trusts are charitable.[25] Private trusts are for the benefit of particular persons, either named ('my son Dennis McFee') or unnamed but capable of identification either immediately or in due course ('Donna Norman's children'). Sometimes it is difficult to determine whether a trust is public or private. Thus in *Salvesen's Trs v Wye*[26] a truster directed that a part of the trust estate was to be distributed 'among any poor relations, friends or acquaintances of mine'. This could plausibly have been classified as private or public.[27]

Private trusts: examples

22.16 Here are some examples of private trusts.

---

[22]   Uncertificated Securities Regulations 2001 (SI 2001/3755), reg 31(4)(b).

[23]   *Mortgage Corporation v Mitchells Roberton* 1997 SLT 1305 at 1310 per Lord Johnston.

[24]   See generally Gretton 'Constructive Trusts' (1997) 1 *Edin LR* 281 and 408.

[25]   See PARA **22.35** below.

[26]   1954 SC 440.

[27]   In fact, it was held to be private. For another borderline case, see *Lord Glentanar v Scottish Industrial Musical Association Ltd* 1925 SC 226.

Example 1

22.17

John is a successful businessman. He wants to benefit his grandchildren. He could give them money now, but they are young and cannot be trusted with capital until they are older, by which time he may no longer be alive. He does not necessarily want them all to take the same amount either by way of income or by way of capital. He sets up a trust. They are the beneficiaries but their beneficial entitlements depend on the discretion of the trustees. Over the years, payments from the trust can be used for their 'education, maintenance and benefit'. Eventually, the capital will be paid out.

Example 2

22.18

Trusts for those unable to manage their own affairs, because they are children, or suffer from mental health problems, are common. In such cases the persons in question will have parents or guardians to manage their affairs so that a trust is not actually necessary. Nevertheless it can be an attractive way of handling matters, especially from the standpoint of the person giving the money. Moreover, suppose someone wants to make provision for a person who, though not under any legal incapacity, lacks the practical ability to manage substantial assets. Here, a trust can be the sensible solution.

Example 3

22.19

Donald wants to take time out because of illness, or to travel. He appoints his sister, Lucinda, to manage his affairs. He could do this by a power of attorney, or he could transfer his assets to her in trust. This is called a 'trust for administration'. It could also be called a 'bare' (or 'simple') trust. A bare trust is where there are no trust purposes except to hold for the benefit of one beneficiary, or more than one in common. The beneficiary can at any time insist that the trustee make over the estate to him.[28]

Example 4

22.20

Shona is a rising politician. She wants to ensure that no one can criticise her for failing to act impartially in cases where political decisions might have an impact – whether positive

---

[28] There may be logical difficulties in distinguishing bare trusts from other private trusts since in all private trusts the beneficiaries can jointly insist that the trust be wound up. See PARAS **24.6–24.9** below.

or negative – on companies she has interests in. So she transfers her investments into a trust for administration, with this speciality: it is a 'blind' trust. In a blind trust the beneficiaries do not know how the fund is invested.

Example 5

22.21

Julia owns a house. After she dies she wants it to go to her only child, Davinia. She expects to die before her second husband, Oliver, who is not Davinia's father, and she wishes to ensure that Oliver has a home in his declining years. She could leave the house to Oliver in liferent and to Davinia in fee.[29] But she decides to leave the house to trustees, to hold for Oliver in liferent and Davinia in fee. This is an 'improper' or 'trust' liferent.[30]

Example 6

22.22

A company wants to set up a pension scheme for its employees, funded by regular contributions partly from the employees and partly from the company. The fund will be vested in trustees. The beneficiaries will be the past and present employees. Only the retired employees will receive pensions, but the pre-retired ones nevertheless count as beneficiaries. One does not have to be in current receipt of money to be a beneficiary.

Example 7

22.23

Olga wants to sell something to Peter but they do not want to have to transfer title, at least for some time, perhaps to save the expenses of transfer, or to keep the sale secret. So she declares that she holds it in trust for him.

Example 8

22.24

Some friends set up a chess club. They subscribe money. There is a bank account into which the subscriptions are paid. Money is spent on chess sets, chess clocks, tea, travel to tournaments and so on. The club is an 'unincorporated voluntary association'. The

---

[29] See **CHAPTER 21** above.
[30] See further, **PARAS 21.14–21.15** above.

assets, including the bank account, will belong to the members jointly.[31] But it would also be possible to vest the assets in the committee as trustees for the members (whose beneficial interests in that case would be joint). Heritable property belonging to unincorporated voluntary associations has to be held through a trust.

Example 9

22.25

A group of small investors wish to pool their savings so as to achieve efficiency. They pay their money to a trustee who invests the money on the London Stock Exchange. The legal holder of the investments is the trustee. The investors are beneficiaries. This is a 'unit trust'.

Example 10

22.26

Iona has become insolvent. A creditor petitions for her sequestration. The petition is successful and James is appointed as her trustee in sequestration. Her assets pass to James, in trust for the creditors.[32]

Example 11

22.27

Sam has become insolvent. He appoints Tara, a chartered accountant, to be his trustee and he conveys his assets to her, 'for behoof of' his creditors.[33] This is like a sequestration but is extra-judicial.

22.28 Whether an executor is a trustee in the fullest sense of the term is a point that can be debated.[34] But, for most purposes, at least, an executor is a trustee and those who are to succeed to the deceased are the beneficiaries.

Discretionary trusts

22.29 Discretionary trusts have already been mentioned.[35] Confusingly, this expression has two meanings. It has a meaning in general trust law and it has a second,

---

[31] See **PARAS 9.17–9.18** above.
[32] Bankruptcy (Scotland) Act 1985.
[33] This expression means 'in trust for'. For discussion, see *Leitch v Leitch* 1927 SLT 575.
[34] See **PARA 25.50** below.
[35] See **PARA 22.17** above.

narrower, meaning in tax law. Under the general law, a trust is a discretionary one if the trustees are given an element of discretion as to the extent to which given beneficiaries will benefit.[36] Suppose that there are three beneficiaries, Mary, Nigel and Olga. The trust deed might authorise the trustees to give more to one and less to the others.[37] A trust may be wholly or partially discretionary. For instance the trust deed might say that the income is to go for ten years to Mary, Nigel and Olga, in such proportions as the trustees choose, and after ten years the capital is to be paid to Paul. This trust is discretionary as to Mary, Nigel and Olga but not as to Paul. The discretion cannot be too broad. In *Anderson v Smoke*[38] the trustees were directed to 'dispose of the balance in any way they should think proper'. This was invalid. But a discretionary trust is valid if the trust deed sets out a defined class of persons, such as 'my children'.

Taxation and tax-based classifications

22.30   Trust law itself recognises certain different categories of trust: for instance, there are private trusts and public trusts, *inter vivos* trusts and *mortis causa* trusts. But tax law also has its own classifications, the point being that the applicable tax regime depends on which tax slot a given trust is deemed to fit into. A given trust may not fit into any slot very comfortably, but into one or other it must go, even if shoving is necessary. Like most things in tax law, these classifications are devised with English law mainly in mind. They are important in practice, and indeed the initial decision whether or not to set up a trust is often heavily influenced by tax considerations. The classifications are liable to change: for instance the Finance Act 2006 made major changes. This book does not cover tax law and so nothing more will be said.

Liferent trusts (improper liferents)

22.31   Improper liferents (liferent trusts) were explained briefly above,[39] as one example of why trusts are used. Such liferents are commoner than proper ones, and their importance in practice justifies a few more words.

22.32   One reason why they are more popular than proper liferents is their flexibility. In a proper liferent, if the property is to be sold free of the liferent, that will need the agreement of both parties. But in an improper liferent the trustee can sell, and unless

---

[36]   'There is little Scottish authority on the subject of the discretionary trust', comment Wilson and Duncan *Trusts* para 2-22. Despite this, such trusts are common in practice.

[37]   This sort of discretion ('distributive' discretion) must be distinguished from 'administrative' discretion. Almost all trusts involve administrative discretion. For instance, trustees almost always have a discretion whether or not to sell the shares in one company and use the money to invest in another. The existence of administrative discretion does not make a trust discretionary: what makes it discretionary is that the rights of the beneficiaries depend on the discretion of the trustees.

[38]   (1898) 25 R 493.

[39]   See PARA **22.21** above.

the trust deed says otherwise, the trustee does not need anyone's consent to do this. Suppose that Oliver one day wishes to move to sheltered accommodation. The trustees could sell the house. The money received would be trust money, and so the interests of Oliver and Davinia would be unaltered. So the trustees could buy a flat for him in a sheltered accommodation development. Any surplus funds they could invest. The income would be paid over to him, and the capital retained. When Oliver dies, the flat would be sold, and the proceeds, plus the investments, would be made over to Davinia. The trustees in such a case would have the power to sell the house without the consent of the beneficiaries.[40] To achieve a similar result with a proper liferent would need not only Oliver's co-operation but also Davinia's.

22.33 A second reason is that proper liferents of investments are not possible. Yet in practice people often wish to create liferents over investments, or at least, as in the previous paragraph, have the possibility that investments will be part of the liferent. The solution is a 'trust liferent'. The investments are held by the trustees. In the case of company shares, the trustees are the shareholders, with all the rights of shareholders. The same is true, *mutatis mutandis*, for company bonds and public bonds, for bank deposits and so on. The income received (dividends, interest etc.) is received by the trustees and then paid over to the beneficial liferenter. The trustees can change the portfolio, selling some shares and buying others, for example. When the liferent ends, the investments are made over to the fiar.

22.34 Another reason why trust liferents are usually preferred to proper ones is that the trustees can function as neutral intermediaries between liferenter and fiar. If liferenter and fiar have friendly relations, that does not matter. If not, it does.

Charities

22.35 Just as not all trusts are charities,[41] so not all charities are trusts.[42] A charity can take the form of a trust, but it can also take other forms. A common form is that of a non-profit company under the Companies Acts: this is known as a 'company limited by guarantee'.[43] The Scottish universities are all educational charities and are all bodies corporate. A new form of entity, which, unlike the other forms, is available only for charities, is the Scottish Charitable Incorporated Organisation (SCIO). How many charities will opt for this form remains to be seen. Each type of charity is governed by the law applicable to the type of organisation in question (trusts, companies limited by guarantee etc) but in addition they are all subject to the law of charities. 'Charity' is a classification based on an organisation's purpose, not its form.[44] Charities are supervised by the Office of the Scottish Charity Regulator

---

[40] T(S)A 1921, s 4; *Mauchline, Petitioner* 1992 SLT 421.

[41] In fact, most are not.

[42] The traditional technical term for a charity was a 'mortification'. This word has been displaced by the English term 'charity'. Many older charities still have 'mortification' as part of their name.

[43] Not all such companies are charities.

(OSCR).[45] This maintains the Scottish Charity Register.[46] Confusingly, some charities are not registered with OSCR, but that is a complication that will not be entered into here.

22.36   Just as a charity may take the form of a trust, so there can also be a trust for the benefit of another charity. Suppose that Tom leaves a legacy of £100,000 to Oxfam. Oxfam is a company limited by guarantee. Tom's executor holds the money on trust for Oxfam, because all executors are trustees. This trust is short-lived. Within a few months of Tom's death, his executor will pay the money to Oxfam. The trust ends. The same analysis would apply if Oxfam had itself been a trust. Then Tom would have created a testamentary trust in which the beneficiary was itself a trust: a trust for a trust. The first trust would, as in the previous case, be short-lived.

BIRTH

How trusts are created

General

22.37   A *mortis causa* trust is created simply by the deceased's testament, which will nominate trustees and identify the assets that are to be trust assets. *Inter vivos* trusts are not quite so simple, and indeed some uncertainty exists as to the law about creation, though in practice there are seldom problems.

22.38   The creation of *inter vivos* trusts is usually analysed into two elements:
  (a) the 'declaration of trust'; and
  (b) the vesting of property in the trustee.[47]
In the typical case, the declaration of trust takes the form of a deed of trust signed by the truster and delivered to the trustee. The deed contains details about the beneficiaries and the trust purposes. It will usually be registered in the Books of Council and Session, although this is not a legal requirement. The deed will identify some trust property, but often it is nominal, such as £10. What happens is that once the trust has been established, the substantial assets can be transferred afterwards, such as land, or stock market investments, or whatever. The reason it is usually done this way is that it is convenient to establish the trust before transferring the assets to it, but there is authority that a trust cannot exist unless it has *some* assets.[48] Thus the truster can add the main assets to the trust after it has been set up with nominal assets.

[44]   See P Ford 'Supervising Charities: A Scottish-Civilian Alternative' (2006) 10 *Edin LR* 352.
[45]   CTI(S)A 2005, ss 1–2.
[46]   CTI(S)A 2005, ss 3–6.
[47]   Often called 'delivery' to the trustee – but this is a muddle. Delivery is the transfer of possession, and so only physical things can be delivered. (See **PARAS 11.13–11.17** above.) The issue is not one of delivery but of vesting of rights, which may or may not require delivery.
[48]   But this authority is of doubtful soundness. See K G C Reid 'Constitution of Trust' 1986 *SLT (News)* 177; Scottish Law Commission *The Nature and the Constitution of Trusts* (2006) part 3.

Indeed, other people can also contribute, and in the case of charitable trusts that is normal. Sometimes the truster wishes to be one of the trustees. That makes little difference. Thus if Tom owns land and wants to establish a trust of that land, with himself and Ulrica as trustees, he will sign a deed of trust naming himself and Ulrica, with an initial fund of, say, £1. He then dispones the land to himself and Ulrica 'as trustees acting under the Thomas Tomkins Family Trust established by Deed of Trust by the said Thomas Tomkins dated ... and registered in the Books of Council and Session on ... '.

Truster-as-trustee trusts

22.39   Occasionally it happens that a person wishes to make himself or herself the sole trustee of certain assets that he or she already has. This is sometimes called a 'truster/trustee' or 'truster-as-trustee' trust. The rules on how such a trust is created are 'uncertain and contentious'.[49] In so far as there can be said to be a conventional view it is that such a trust can be created by a declaration of trust intimated to at least one beneficiary.[50] No transfer is possible since the transferee would be the same person as the transferor. (A transfer involves *two* people.)

Magic words?

22.40   No special words are needed to create a trust. Usually the word 'trust' is used, but it is not necessary. Occasionally, and especially in home-made testaments, the intention is unclear. It sometimes happens, for instance, that the testator says that something is to be done with some asset, but the words are words of request[51] rather than of instruction. If the words of request are directed to the executor, they will normally be regarded as binding, but if they are directed to a legatee they usually will not be.[52] For instance, in *Garden's Exr v More*[53] the testator directed his trustees to convey certain assets to his wife, adding: 'I should like not less than £50 sterling left to the widow of my brother, Alexander Garden, New Elgin, or her family, if she predeceases my wife, and I desire that my wife may make a settlement providing for this.' The wife inherited but herself later died without making any provision for Alexander's widow. It was held that the quoted words created no trust. Cases of this sort turn on their own particular facts.

---

[49]   Scottish Law Commission *Discussion Paper on the Nature and the Constitution of Trusts* (2006) para 4.16.

[50]   This is based on the case which first recognised truster-as-trustee trusts as lawful (*Allan's Trs v Lord Advocate* 1971 SC (HL) 45) but the decision could be criticised.

[51]   Such words are known in this context as 'precatory'.

[52]   Wilson and Duncan *Trusts* para 2-13.

[53]   1913 SC 285.

22.41 Just as the word 'trust' is not necessary, so, conversely, 'Scots law does not recognise the validity of a trust simply on the basis that those responsible for the constituent documents use the language of trust as a matter of drafting'.[54]

22.42 In a *mortis causa* trust writing is necessary, for testaments must be in writing.[55] *Inter vivos* truster/trustee trusts must also be in writing.[56] Other trusts do not have to be in writing, but in practice they are.

Registration?

22.43 There is no requirement that the trust deed be registered. If registered property is involved, such as shares or land, the transfer to the trustee will require registration, but the title need not be taken expressly in trust. Thus for instance land may be conveyed to Tom as trustee but that fact may or may not be discoverable from the Land Register. Although trust deeds need not be registered, in practice most are. Testamentary trusts are registered because testaments are registered in the Sheriff Court Books in the sheriffdom where confirmation is granted. *Inter vivos* trusts are usually registered in the Books of Council and Session.

TRUSTEES AND BENEFICIARIES

Who may be a trustee?

22.44 Both natural and juristic persons can be trustees. There are restrictions on who can be the trustee of a charitable trust: for instance those with convictions for dishonesty are barred.[57] It is not uncommon for a trustee to be a body corporate (juristic person). For instance, many law firms have a special corporate entity ('Sue Grabbit and Runne Trustee Company Ltd') the sole function of which is to act as a trustee,[58] and which will be at any one time the trustee of numerous different trusts.

---

[54] *Balfour Beatty Ltd v Britannia Life Ltd* 1997 SLT 10 at 18 per Lord Penrose. For another case on whether the use of the word 'trust' was not enough, see *Clark Taylor & Co Ltd v Quality Site Development (Edinburgh) Ltd* 1981 SC 111.

[55] See **PARA 30.6** below.

[56] RoW(S)A 1995, s 1(2)(a)(iii).

[57] CTI(S)A 2005, s 69.

[58] In *Ommanney, Petitioner* 1966 SLT (Notes) 13 the court said that 'an impersonal body such as a bank or a trust corporation is not a suitable party to exercise … a discretion involving personal and family considerations'. But the facts of the case were special. A truster can appoint a corporate trustee even where the trust is discretionary.

Who may be a beneficiary?

22.45 Anyone may be a beneficiary, including juristic persons, though beneficiaries are usually natural persons. Acceptance is unnecessary. Indeed, someone may be a beneficiary without even knowing it. Trusts can exist in favour of persons who are, at the time that the trust is set up, indeterminate and even unborn. (For instance, a trust for the truster's grandchildren, born or to be born.)

The three parties: role-sharing

22.46 At the outset a trust normally involves three parties. There is:
 (a) the truster[59] who sets up the trust;
 (b) the trustee or trustees (for it is common to have more than one trustee); and
 (c) the beneficiary or beneficiaries.
Once the trust has been set up, however, the truster drops out of the picture, and the relationship is between the trustees and the beneficiaries. But it may be that the trust deed reserves some ongoing role for the truster. In a private trust (but not a public one) the truster has two implied rights. The first is a right to appoint new trustees in the event that the trust becomes a lapsed trust.[60] The second is that if there is a failure of trust purposes, the assets are held in trust for the truster. This is called a 'resulting' trust.

22.47 In certain special cases there is no truster. One example is a sequestration. Here, there is a trustee (the trustee in sequestration) and beneficiaries (the creditors) but there is no truster.

22.48 Although in a normal trust there are the three parties – truster, trustees and beneficiaries – some role-sharing is possible. The truster can be a trustee. The truster can be a beneficiary. A beneficiary can be a trustee.

Appointment of trustees

22.49 The first trustees are appointed in the trust deed. There may, however, be a need for future appointments, especially if some trustees have disappeared by death or resignation. The trust deed may make provision about how new trustees can be chosen. But there is a default rule that the trustees in office from time to time can 'assume' (appoint) new trustees.[61] Another default rule is that if the trust is a private

---

[59] The English term 'settlor' is also sometimes encountered.

[60] See, e.g., *Glentanar v Scottish Industrial Musical Association* 1925 SC 226. For lapsed trusts, see PARA **23.4** below.

[61] T(S)A 1921, s 3(b). For deeds of assumption, see T(S)A 1921, s 21. Deeds of assumption are usually registered in the Books of Council and Session.

one and all the trustees have left office the truster can appoint new ones. Finally, the court can in case of need appoint new trustees.[62]

22.50 On appointment, the new trustee joins the others in the administration of the trust. But appointment does not give a title.[63] To become joint owner of the trust assets, a conveyance is needed to the new trustee. Hence in practice a deed of assumption contains words conveying the whole trust estate, and is thus what is called a 'deed of assumption and conveyance'. The usual way of doing it is for the existing trustees to be not only the granters but also the grantees. Thus suppose that Bella and Carl assume Dugald. The deed would convey the trust estate from Bella and Carla to Bella and Carl and Dugald. For most types of property (for example land or shares) the deed in itself will not give a title to the new trustee. Some further step, such as registration, is needed.

22.51 Nobody can be compelled to be a trustee. Acceptance does not have to be in writing, though it commonly is. The mere fact of taking on the administration of the trust constitutes acceptance.[64]

Ex officio trustees

22.52 An *ex officio* trustee is someone who is a trustee of a particular trust simply by virtue of holding a certain 'office'. Thus suppose that someone establishes a trust for the benefit of poor elderly people in a certain area. The deed might nominate the parish minister as a trustee *ex officio*. That would mean that when one minister retired, or died, he or she would automatically cease to be a trustee and the new minister would become one. The subject is full of difficulty.

WHAT IS A TRUST? FURTHER DISCUSSION

The special patrimony

22.53 The patrimony is the totality of a person's assets and liabilities. The general principle is: one person, one patrimony. But in a trust, the trustee has two patrimonies. There is the ordinary, or general, patrimony. And there is the special patrimony of the trust. Each has its own assets and liabilities. A patrimony is like a suitcase, with two compartments, one for assets and the other for liabilities. A trustee has two suitcases. If an asset is sold, the asset leaves the suitcase but the price replaces it. The same happens in reverse if an asset is purchased. Again, if an asset generates

---

[62] T(S)A 1921, s 22. One of the many striking features of trust law is the extensive role of the court. All trusts are subject to all sorts of intervention by the court.

[63] Is this rule is perfectly consistent with the rule that on death or resignation a trustee's title passes to the ongoing trustees without conveyance?

[64] *Ker v City of Glasgow Bank* (1879) 6 R (HL) 52 is an example.

income (for example rent from land, or dividends from shares, or interest from a loan) the income forms part of the same patrimony. The trustee is under a duty of segregation, to ensure that the two patrimonies remain distinct, so that there can never be any question to which patrimony an asset belongs. If, as commonly happens, there are two or more trustees, they hold the suitcase together. Figures 22.1, 22.2 and 22.3 give the idea.[65]

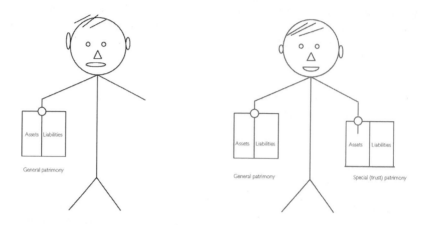

Figure 22.1   **Figure 22.2**

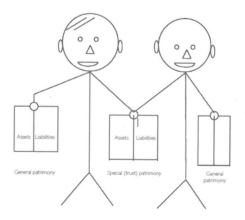

Figure 22.3

---

[65]   From Gretton 'Trusts without Equity' (2000) 49 *International and Comparative Law Quarterly* 599.

Varying theories of the trust

22.54 'The property of the thing intrusted, be it land or moveables, is in the person of the intrusted, else it is not a proper trust', wrote Stair.[66] This traditional view is also the modern view, but in between there has been some wobbling, especially during the second half of the nineteenth century. According to one theory, the truster remained owner.[67] According to another, ownership was vested in the beneficiary or beneficiaries.[68] Neither theory succeeded in establishing itself, and today Stair's view is almost unquestioned.[69]

The nature of the beneficiary's right

22.55 The right of a beneficiary – the 'beneficial interest' as it is often called – is a personal right against the trustee. It thus part of the beneficiary's patrimony. Like most other rights it can be transferred. This is done by assignation plus intimation.[70] If the beneficiary dies, it will form part of the estate and will be dealt with by the executor according to the law of succession. If the beneficiary becomes insolvent, the beneficial interest is available to the creditors, whether through diligence or an insolvency process.

22.56 This is the normal picture, but there can be exceptions. Everything depends on the trust's terms. For instance a beneficial interest that ends on death will clearly not pass to the beneficiary's estate. Again, in a discretionary trust the beneficiary's rights depend on the trustees' choices. Such a beneficiary might end up receiving little or even nothing.

Trusts and the publicity principle

22.57 One of the most important features of the trust is the 'insolvency effect', the fact that the trustee's ordinary creditors (the liabilities in the general patrimony) cannot attach the assets in the special patrimony. The trust estate is a ring-fenced fund. This principle applies both to diligence and to insolvency processes (sequestration and liquidation). The fact that the beneficiaries' rights survive the trustee's insolvency means that they behave rather like real rights. But they are not. They are personal rights in relation to the special patrimony, while the trustee's

---

[66] Stair I, 13, 7.

[67] For this theory, see Gretton 'Radical Rights and Radical Wrongs' 1986 *JR* 51 and 192.

[68] This was the theory advanced by Lord Watson in *Heritable Reversionary Co v Millar* (1892) 19 R (HL) 43.

[69] *Inland Revenue v Clark's Trs* 1939 SC 11 was a significant milestone. The European Court of Justice has held that for the purposes of EU private international law the beneficiary's right is personal not real – an approach which fits in with Scots law neatly, though not with English law. See *Webb v Webb* 1984 ECR 1-1717.

[70] See PARAS **5.37–5.50** above.

personal rights in relation to the general patrimony. Thus in principle the two sorts of claims do not conflict.

22.58   In general, transactions that have third-party effect (for example against creditors) are subject to the publicity principle.[71] In general, third parties should not be prejudiced by secret transactions. That is why the law requires, for instance, the registration of standard securities. The law also requires publicity for certain other things. With one exception, juristic persons cannot be created without publicity, such as the registration at Companies House. The exception is partnership, and the reason why publicity is not required is that there is little effect against third parties.[72] In particular, creditors can hold either the firm itself or any partner liable.[73] The trust is a virtual juristic person that can be created secretly. Tom owns Blackmains. He signs a deed saying he holds it in bare trust for Barbara. This deed is delivered to Barbara but is otherwise secret. Ten years later Tom becomes insolvent. His creditors find that they cannot touch the land. Had he disponed the land to Barbara, registration would have been needed. Yet by secret deed a similar effect has been achieved. Not surprisingly, bare trusts are often used when, for one reason or another, an actual transfer (disposition of land, assignation of a money claim or whatever[74]) is inconvenient to the parties. There is some concern that the policy of the law can thus be circumvented. As well as using trusts as virtual transfers they can also be used as virtual securities, and the same issues arise.[75] There is a case for saying that all such trusts are invalid as being contrary to public policy, but the whole subject remains undeveloped.[76] Such devices are commonly used.

VESTING

Introduction

22.59   Back in 1905, an anonymous writer commented:

'The subject of vesting has long been regarded by Scots lawyers with a sort of gloomy despair as a mere chaotic mass of conflicting decisions; one has even heard proposed as the only possible improvement the destruction of all reports

---

[71]   See PARAS **4.17–4.18** above.

[72]   The governing legislation is the Partnership Act 1890.

[73]   This is not so for limited partnerships or for limited liability partnerships. Unsurprisingly, such partnerships need registration: Limited Partnerships Act 1907; Limited Liability Partnerships Act 2000.

[74]   See *Tay Valley Joinery Ltd v CF Financial Services Ltd* 1987 SLT 207. The soundness of the decision is open to question.

[75]   Gretton 'Using Trusts as Commercial Securities' (1988) 33 JLSS 53.

[76]   *Clark Taylor & Co Ltd v Quality Site Development (Edinburgh) Ltd* 1981 SC 111 is one of the few cases to have raised this issue. In some cases the courts have upheld trusts which were arguably contrary to public policy: a noteworthy example is *Tay Valley Joinery Ltd v CF Financial Services Ltd* 1987 SLT 207, though that case has complicating factors, including cross-border issues.

dealing with the subject, and the prohibition under severe penalties of reporting any more.'[77]

He was right and matters have not improved – perhaps the opposite – since 1905. The concept of vesting is itself somewhat elusive, while the detailed rules about vesting are complex and perhaps inconsistent.

22.60 Once a beneficial right has 'vested' it is like any other patrimonial right. For instance, Alan dies, leaving his house to Barbara. Barbara dies the next day. Her right to the house is part of her patrimony. The right that she had, when she died, was not ownership, because there would have been no time for ownership to be transferred to her. But it was a right to become owner.[78] Suppose that her testament leaves everything to Carl. Consider the structure of rights at this moment. Barbara had, when died, a personal right against Alan's executor.[79] Barbara's right passes to her executor, so that Barbara's executor has a personal right against Alan's executor. And Carl has a personal right against Barbara's executor. So Alan's executor will convey to Barbara's executor, who will then convey to Carl. Alternatively and more simply, Alan's executor will convey to Carl at the request of Barbara's executor.

22.61 We have just considered a vested legacy. Now an unvested one. Donna leaves her house to Euan, but only if he survives her by thirty clear days.[80] Donna dies on 1 May and Euan dies on 20 May, leaving everything to his children. Will they take the house? That depends on a prior question: is the right to the house part of Euan's estate? No. The legacy was subject to a 'suspensive condition'. That condition was never satisfied. The legacy was not vested and has now lapsed.[81] Who takes the house? That depends. Assuming that the testament had a list of special and pecuniary legacies, and then a legacy of residue, the house would form part of the residue of Donna's estate, and pass to the residuary legatees.

22.62

'Probably in no other department of law is less influence allowed to precedent. A question of vesting is always decided with reference to the character and phraseology of the particular deed.'[82]

'When the question arises under a *mortis causa* settlement, whether a benefit given is or has become a vested right, the intentions of the testator, in so far as they can be discovered or reasonably inferred from the deed taken as a whole,

---

[77]   (1905) 21 Sc Law Rev 234. This was a review of the first edition of R Candlish Henderson *Principles of Vesting in the Law of Succession*. The second, and last, edition appeared in 1938.

[78]   But a qualified one. For instance, it might have been necessary for Alan's executor to sell the house to pay Alan's debt.

[79]   There are problems here, because the confirmation of an executor takes some weeks. So Barbara has, in the hours between Alan's death and her own, a personal right against ... whom?

[80]   Such provisions are common.

[81]   For lapse of legacies, see PARA **27.44** below.

[82]   R Candlish Henderson *Principles of Vesting in the Law of Succession* Preface.

and from the circumstances, legitimately collected under which the deed was made, should have effect given to them. It is *quaestio voluntatis*.[83] That is the cardinal rule and guide.'[84]

But in reality the task of ascertaining the testator's intention is to a considerable extent artificial, because of the default rules that have developed out of the plentiful case law. Nevertheless, the default rules are complex and probably incoherent and no attempt will be made here to summarise them.

A footnote on the word 'vesting'

22.63 It is sometimes said that when a legacy or other beneficial right vests it becomes the 'property' of the legatee. That is true in the broad sense of 'property' – i.e. patrimonial rights – but it should not be understood to mean that the beneficiary acquires ownership at that moment. In a trust the beneficiaries do not have *ownership*, for their right is personal, not real. They may have a personal right to acquire ownership.

22.64 A related sense of 'vesting' is that in which the estate is said to 'vest' in the executor on confirmation. An executor has two patrimonies: his or her own ordinary, general, patrimony, and the executry patrimony. Suppose that Alfred owes Beata money. Beata dies, bequeathing the debt to Charles. Donna is confirmed as Beata's executor. The debt owed by Alfred now apparently vests in two different people: Charles and Donna. In fact, it is not. The debt itself is vested in Donna, as executor. What is vested in Charles is not a right against Alfred, but a right against Donna that she should either (i) collect the debt from Alfred and pay the proceeds to Charles; or (ii) assign the debt to Charles. Likewise, if Beata owned a house and left it to Charles, the house would be vested in Donna,[85] and what would be vested in Charles would be a right to have ownership of the house transferred to him by Donna.

22.65 A terminological note. The word 'vest' is sometimes used in other senses too. When conveyancers say that 'title to Blackmains is vested in Abracadabra Ltd' they mean that Abracadabra Ltd has the real right of ownership. If they say that title 'was last vested' in Donald Cook, they imply that he has died but that ownership has not, up to now, been transferred to anyone else.[86] The word is also used in this sense about subordinate real rights. Finally, Parliamentary drafters often use the word, but often vaguely, so that the precise meaning has to be guessed.

---

[83] Latin: 'question of intention'.
[84] *Carleton v Thomson* (1867) 5 M (HL) 151 at 153 per Lord Colonsay.
[85] There are a number of problems in this area. Is Donna's right real? Not unless she completes title in the Land Register or Sasine Register. So is it personal? But against whom?
[86] Which raises the question of who does own the land. One view is that death ends active personality, but that a dead person still has a passive juridical personality, and thus can still be an owner. On this view, the Land Register does not suddenly become inaccurate when an owner dies. But the precise legal effect of death remains mired in difficulties.

FURTHER READING

Chalmers *Trusts* chs 1–5.

Gloag and Henderson *The Law of Scotland* ch 42.

Hayton, D J (ed) *Modern International Developments in Trust Law* (1999).

Hayton, D J, Kortmann, S C J J and Verhagen, H L E *Principles of European Trust Law* (1999).

Hayton, D J and Underhill, A *Law Relating to Trusts and Trustees* (17th edn, 2007) (on English law).

Lupoi, M *Trusts: A Comparative Study* (2000).

Mowbray, J (ed) *Lewin on Trusts* (18th edn, 2008).

Norrie, K and Scobbie, E *Trusts* (1991) chs 1–5.

Paisley, R *Trusts* (1999) chs 1–5.

Wilson and Duncan *Trusts* chs 1–4, 6 and 18.

Chapter 23

Trusts: their life in health and in sickness

TRUSTEES: GENERAL

Must the trustees act gratuitously?

23.1 To be a trustee means to accept the onerous responsibility of administering a fund. This is time-consuming and responsible work. Trustees are entitled to be reimbursed for reasonable *expenses*, so that they do not end up out of pocket but the default rule is that they are not entitled to be paid for their *time*.[1] The trust deed may nevertheless provide for payment. In practice it might be supposed that, without payment, nobody would agree to be a trustee. That is sometimes true, but usually not. In public trusts people will usually be happy to act gratuitously, because they are public-spirited and believe in the cause. In private trusts family members will usually agree to act gratuitously out of family solidarity. But if a client wishes to appoint a solicitor as a trustee, the latter will usually insist on the right to remuneration. Likewise, the trustees of a unit trust will insist on payment, and so on. A special case is the trustee in sequestration, who is entitled to remuneration by statute.[2]

Cessation of office: (1) death, (2) resignation and (3) removal by the court

23.2 A trustee loses office by death, by resignation or by removal by the court. The trust deed can prohibit resignation, but that is rare. The default rule, which usually applies, is that a trustee is free to resign, unless he or she is the sole trustee (in which case the solution is to assume new trustees first, and then resign) or unless he or she is remunerated.[3] Even then the court can authorise resignation. Whether resignation has to be in writing is uncertain. In practice it is assumed that it is. The deed is called a 'minute of resignation'.[4] Unless the trust deed otherwise provides, there is no power for a trustee to be expelled by fellow trustees. But the court can remove a trustee, under a statutory power that covers certain defined circumstances,

---

[1]   There was one exception to this at common law but in *Home v Pringle* (1841) 2 Rob App 384 it was abrogated and English law extended.

[2]   Bankruptcy (Scotland) Act 1985 (B(S)A 1985), s 51.

[3]   T(S)A 1921, s 3(a).

[4]   T(S)A 1921, s 19 and Sch A.

notably absence and insanity.[5] There is a concurrent common law power which is used where there is 'malversation of office', i.e. serious breach of trust.[6] The bankruptcy of a trustee, and conviction for an offence, are irrelevant (unless the trust deed so provides) in private trusts. But they disqualify a person from being a trustee of a charity.[7]

23.3 When a trustee demits office, no conveyance to the remaining trustees is necessary. The reason is that the title of trustees is not common but joint, and when a trustee leaves the stage the remaining trustees are the sole owners.[8]

Lapsed trusts

23.4 A trust is said to lapse if no trustee remains in office. This can happen if the sole trustee (or the sole surviving trustee) dies. (The word 'lapsed' suggests that the trust thereby comes to an end, but that is not so.[9]) It will be necessary for one or more new trustees to be appointed so that the trust administration can be continued. The court can appoint a new trustee.[10]

23.5 The common law rule is that if a trustee dies in office, no rights pass to his or her executor. In general that is still the law. But if a sole trustee dies, there exists a limited statutory power in favour of the executor to take up the office.[11]

Deciding and doing

General

23.6 The trust deed is the constitutive document and it can lay down the rules for the trust's administration. The general law applies only in so far as the trust deed is silent. In practice, trust deeds are often silent. The default rules are as follows. A meeting of trustees must be quorate, and a quorum is a majority of trustees.[12] Decisions can be made by a majority. But the majority must be a majority of the trustees, not merely a majority of those trustees at the meeting. Suppose that there are six trustees. Four turn up to a particular meeting. A decision is taken by a three-to-one majority. The decision is invalid because three is not a majority of six. Hence if there are two trustees they will both have to agree. Deadlocks, though possible,

---

[5]   T(S)A 1921, s 23.

[6]   For this power, see *Gilchrist's Trs v Dick* (1883) 11R 22; *MacGilchrist's Trs v MacGilchrist* 1930 SC 635 and *Shariff v Hamid* 2000 SLT 294.

[7]   Charities and Trustee Investment (Scotland) Act 2005, s 69.

[8]   See PARAS **9.17–9.18** above.

[9]   A lapsed legacy is indeed void: see PARA **27.44** below.

[10]   T(S)A 1921, s 22.

[11]   Executors (Scotland) Act 1900, s 6. This is quite commonly used.

[12]   For the quorum, see T(S)A 1921, s 3(c).

are rare: in most trusts the trustees succeed in making decisions unanimously. Occasionally a breakdown of relations produces total deadlock: the ultimate remedy is for the court to appoint a judicial factor.

Consultation

23.7 All trustees must be 'consulted': in the absence of consultation any decision reached is invalid. In the leading case, *Wyse v Abbott*,[13] there were three trustees. Two of them appointed additional trustees, but they had not consulted the third. Even though a majority decision was in itself sufficient, the lack of consultation made the appointment invalid. Although the principle is clear, its application in practice is less so. At a minimum it means that every trustee must be notified of forthcoming meetings. But 'consultation' is unnecessary where it would be pointless or impossible, such as where the trustee in question is uncontactable.[14]

Execution of documents

23.8 Suppose that the trustees decide to sell a plot of land. Must all sign the disposition? This question really has two aspects.
   (1) Whether any trustee who dissented from the decision has a duty, as a matter of trust law, to sign. The answer is affirmative.
   (2) Whether, as a matter of conveyancing law, signature by a majority suffices. The law is unclear. In *Harland Engineering*[15] the Outer House held that majority signature was sufficient. The case was appealed to the Inner House on another point, and there some doubt was expressed as to whether the decision on signatures had been correct. There is no other authority. The Trusts (Scotland) Act 1921 (T(S)A 1921), s 7 says that in *some* cases majority signature suffices, but the section's exact meaning is obscure. In practice all trustees sign.

TRUST PURPOSES

General

23.9 Every trust has its 'purposes'. If these were simply to hold for the beneficiary or beneficiaries, then every trust would be a 'bare' trust.[16] Some trusts are bare, but in most the purposes are rather more complicated, such as to hold for Laura in liferent

---

[13]   (1881) 8 R 983.
[14]   *Malcolm v Goldie* (1895) 22 R 968.
[15]   1914 2 SLT 292.
[16]   See PARA **22.19** above.

and for Fiona in fee. It is competent to identify certain beneficiaries and then give
the trustees a discretion as to what each is to take. Where that happens, it is common
for the truster to give them a non-binding 'letter of wishes' indicating how he or she
would like to discretion to be exercised.

Failure

23.10　If the purposes are too indeterminate or too obscure to be interpreted, the
trust will be void 'by reason of uncertainty'.[17] A 'secret' trust is a trust where the
trust purposes are known only to the trustee. Such trusts are also invalid.[18] There is
some tension between that rule and the fact that a 'discretionary trust' is lawful.[19] In
a discretionary trust there is an ascertained or ascertainable class of beneficiaries,
and the trustees can choose which of them to benefit and to what extent. If that is the
case then the trust is not invalid. The trust is void if its purposes are contrary to
public policy. There is also what is sometimes called the 'rule against perpetuities',
which places time-limits on private trusts.[20]

23.11　Another way in which a trust may be void is if it confers no substantial human
benefit.[21]This is probably a sub-type of the 'contrary to public policy' rule. The cases
all deal with testamentary trusts but the principles presumably apply to all trusts. In
McCaig v University of Glasgow[22] John Stuart McCaig left a testamentary trust,
which is, alas, too long to quote here, except for a few words:

> 'The purpose of the trust is that my heritable property be not sold, but let to
> tenants, and the clear revenue or income be used for the purpose of erecting
> monuments and statues for myself, brothers, and sisters on the tower or circular
> building called the Stuart McCaig Tower, situated on the Battery Hill above
> Oban, the making of these statues to be given to Scotch sculptors … '

23.12　The Court of Session declined office but the University ('College') of
Glasgow accepted. The truster's sister, Catherine McCaig, sought reduction of the
trust. (She would benefit if it were held invalid.) She was successful. It was held that
a trust must have beneficiaries, and this trust had none. Actually, that is debatable: it
could be argued that there was human benefit in promoting the arts. Many public
trusts are regarded as valid even though they confer only remote benefits on living

---

[17]　E.g. *Hardie v Morison* (1899) 7 SLT 42.
[18]　*Sutherland's Trs v Sutherland's Tr* (1893) 20 R 925; *Shaw's Trs v Greenock Medical Aid Society* 1930
　　 SLT 39; Wilson and Duncan *Trusts* para 2-30. What is secret is not the trust but its purposes. There
　　 have been one or two decisions to the opposite effect, such as *Warrender v Anderson* (1893) 1 SLT 304
　　 but they seem erroneous.
[19]　*Crichton v Grierson* (1828) 3 W & S 329. For a borderline case where the trust was upheld, see
　　 Smellie's Trs v Glasgow Royal Infirmary (1905) 13 SLT 450.
[20]　See PARA **23.15** below.
[21]　For the special case of trusts for animals, see K McK Norrie 'Trusts for Animals' (1987) 32 *JLSS* 386.
[22]　1907 SC 231. For McCaig's Folly see the cover of this book.

persons. At all events, the case is a leading one. Lord Kyllachy gave the following as examples of purposes contrary to public policy:

' ... to lay the truster's estate waste, and to keep it so; or to turn the income of the estate into money, and throw the money yearly into the sea; or to expend the income in annual or monthly funeral services in the testator's memory; or to expend it in discharging from prominent points upon the estate, salvoes of artillery upon the birthdays of the testator, and his brothers and sisters ...'[23]

Catherine McCaig died soon afterwards, setting up a testamentary trust with similar purposes. This too was struck down.[24] There have been similar cases, such as *Aitken's Trs v Aitken*.[25] George Aitken set up a testamentary trust:

'In respect of the ancient connexion of my family ... with the town of Musselburgh, extending over several centuries, and seeing that I am the last of the male line ... I wish to be erected on the site of the property at the corner of High Street, Fisherrow, and South Street ... a massive equestrian bronze statue of artistic merit, representing me as Champion at the Riding of the Towns Marches; for this purpose the present building will be removed and the site enclosed in an artistic manner and laid out with shrubs or otherwise; the whole work is to be done unsparing of expense ... '

23.13 This too was held invalid. Lord Sands commented that 'if the testamentary directions are unreasonable as conferring neither a patrimonial benefit on anybody nor a benefit upon the public or any section thereof, the directions are invalid',[26] and this is perhaps the best attempt that has been made to state the law succinctly. However, it must be conceded that the authorities in this area are 'confused'.[27] The 'no human benefit' rule is applied in *mortis causa* trusts more readily than in *inter vivos* ones.

23.14 If a trust is invalid then it becomes a 'resulting' trust, which is to say that the trustees hold on bare trust for the truster, or, if he is dead, for his estate. Battles about the validity of trusts usually arise when the truster is dead, and are between those who would benefit if the trust is upheld and the truster's heirs.

THE RULE AGAINST PERPETUITIES

23.15 The rule against perpetuities[28] is a statutory one rather than a common law one. People have a natural wish to control assets into the future. Some people desire

---

23   1907 SC 231 at 242.
24   *McCaig's Trs v Kirk Session of United Free Church of Lismore* 1915 SC 426.
25   1927 SC 374. And see *Macintosh's JF v Lord Advocate* 1935 SC 406 and *Sutherland's Tr v Verschoyle* 1968 SLT 43.
26   1927 SC 374 at 380.
27   Wilson and Duncan *Trusts* para 14-10.
28   See Wilson and Duncan *Trusts* ch 8. For the history, see R Burgess *Perpetuities in Scots Law* (1979). The rule does not apply to public trusts and is in many respects obscure.

to do so – especially in relation to land – for ever. The law's attitude has varied on whether such desires are socially acceptable or not. The Entail Act 1685 actually assisted such desires. It allowed an owner of land to create a 'tailzie'[29] whereby the land would pass down the generations in the family until Doomsday. Each successive owner lacked power of sale. This sort of thing is nowadays regarded as unacceptable. The dead should not rule from their graves – or at least only for a reasonable period. The 1685 Act has been repealed.[30] Similar arrangements could, unless prohibited, be achieved by means of trusts. For instance, land could be conveyed to trustees to hold for a successive series of family members until Doomsday. Rules against such devices were first introduced by the Entail Amendment (Scotland) Act 1848 and are now contained in the Law Reform (Miscellaneous Provisions) (Scotland) Act 1968, s 18. As soon as the beneficiary is someone who was unborn when the trust was set up, the trust becomes a bare trust for that beneficiary. Thus, suppose that in 1980 Eustace conveys his land in trust to hold for his heirs-male successively in perpetuity. At this time his eldest son Foster is alive and also Foster's eldest son, Gregor. In 2000 Gregor has a son, Horatio. Eustace dies in 1990, Foster dies in 2010 and Gregor dies in 2030. In 2030 the trust becomes a bare trust for Horatio.[31]

POWERS

General

23.16 *Powers* are different from *purposes*. Purposes are about ends; powers are about means. The distinction is actually somewhat fuzzy but it is a traditional one. Take a trust for Laura in liferent and Fiona in fee. The trust assets are stock market investments. The trustee, Tara, is thinking of selling the shares and using the money to buy, and then let out, heritable property, so that the trust income would be rents rather than dividends. This would be within the purposes of the trust. But it might or might not be within the powers. The trust provisions might not allow investment in land.

23.17 The trustees' powers are determined by the trust deed. In practice trust deeds usually say that the trustees can do virtually anything. The law also has a set of default powers, i.e. powers that exist unless the trust deed excludes them. Some are implied by common law, some by legislation. There is a good deal of overlap between the common law powers and the statutory powers. The latter are in T(S)A 1921, s 4. Over time it has been much amended,[32] resulting in a higgledy-piggledy list of powers

---

[29]   The Scots word. More recently, the English word 'entail' has come to be used. Entails are a blessing for novelists: see, e.g., Jane Austen's *Pride and Prejudice*.

[30]   AFT(S)A 2000, s 50. But tailzies had already been virtually destroyed by a series of statutes culminating in the Entail (Scotland) Act 1914.

[31]   An illustration is *Earl of Balfour Petitioner* 2002 SLT 1385.

[32]   Most recently by the Charities and Trustee Investment (Scotland) Act 2005. As well as extending the implied powers, this Act also made a technical simplification, in that previously trustees' powers were dealt with both by T(S)A 1921 and by the Trustee Investments Act 1961. The latter is now for the most part repealed.

that is almost unreadable. The amendments have been expansions, and the law has now reached the point where trustees have implied powers to do almost anything.[33] T(S)A 1921, s 5 provides that even if the trust deed actually excludes any of the s 4 powers (unlikely in practice) the court may grant such powers. Trustees sometimes wish to employ a professional to manage the investment portfolio, and T(S)A 1921, s 4B empowers them to do this.

Sale by trustees

23.18 A common misconception is that a sale by trustees will be a breach of trust. In fact, trustees presumptively have the right to sell any trust asset.[34] The proceeds will of course themselves be trust property. For example, if a house that is subject to an improper liferent is sold[35] the proceeds of sale would be invested, and the improper liferenter would receive the income. Because the law implies a power to sell, sale would be in breach of trust only if the trust deed were to limit the power, but in practice that seldom happens.

DUTIES

Investment duties

23.19 Trustees have duties to invest the trust funds in a reasonable manner. The investments must be both 'authorised' (i.e. within their powers) and 'proper'. This common law duty is given greater specification by T(S)A 1921, s 4A.[36] One requirement is that the trustee must 'have regard' to the possibility that 'diversification' of investments may be in the best interests of the beneficiaries. In other words, a reasonable trustee will not normally put all the eggs into one basket.

23.20 An example of an investment that, though authorised, was improper, is *Melville v Noble's Trs*.[37] Here, trustees left money on deposit receipt for 19 years. A deposit receipt is a reasonable way of 'parking' money on a short-term basis, but in the longer term it is likely to prove a poor investment. Although there was no doubt that the trustees had the *power* to put money on deposit receipt, they were held liable for having failed to invest reasonably. In *Clarke v Clarke's Trs*[38] the trustees held certain shares for many years which steadily declined in value, eventually

---

[33] The list of powers in T(S)A 1921, s 4 is not complete, so one still has to reply on the common law for some powers, e.g. the power to open a bank account.

[34] T(S)A 1921, s 4(1)(a).

[35] *Mauchline, Petitioner* 1992 SLT 421.

[36] As inserted by the Charities and Trustee Investment (Scotland) Act 2005 (CTI(S)A 2005), and replacing the now-repealed Trustee Investments Act 1961, s 6.

[37] (1896) 24 R 243.

[38] 1925 SC 693.

reaching zero. They were held liable to make good the loss. Though this is often regarded as a leading case, the logic is less than clear. They had not reviewed this investment, but there seems to have been no evidence that, if they had done so, they would have acted differently.

23.21　The case perhaps illustrates the economic naïveté common among lawyers: the fact that the value of the shares eventually fell to zero does *not* mean that it was unreasonable to hold on to them. It merely shows that the investment turned out to be a bad one. (In principle, it can never be obvious *now* that a share, or other investment asset, *will* lose value, for if it *were* obvious then market forces would mean that that fact would be reflected in its *present* value. Thus it can be reasonable to retain an investment asset the value of which in fact declines steadily every year. Equally, it can be unreasonable to retain an investment asset that gains value steadily every year. The rationality of investment decisions can be assessed only on the basis of the information available at the relevant time. *Clarke's Trs* also illustrates another danger for trustees. In their administration, the trustees had been very successful, achieving rich profits for the beneficiaries. But none of this was relevant: the ungrateful beneficiaries were entitled not only to those profits but also to help themselves to even more out of the personal resources of the trustees, because one particular investment had proved unlucky. The trustees could not set off the losses against the gains.

23.22　One could express the matter thus: trustees have two types of investment duty. The first is not to invest in a way that is outwith their powers, even if the investment promises to be a good one. The second is to choose wisely between the various possible investments that are within their powers. Trustees actually are faced with a problem. It is a law of economics that the higher the yield, the higher the risk; and the lower the risk, the lower the yield.[39] In *Melville v Noble's Trs* the trustees chose low risk, low yield. They were held personally liable. In *Raes v Meek*[40] the trustees chose high yield, high risk. They were held personally liable. So trustees are between the devil and the deep. In practice they tend to go for a diversified portfolio producing moderate yield and moderate risk, and the courts seem happy with that.

The rule against accumulation

23.23　The rule against accumulation is a rule limiting the powers of trustees to 'accumulate', i.e. to reinvest income so as to build up capital. In 1797 an English

---

[39]　In principle the two yields should be the same once the risk has been multiplied into the equation. In practice it is not always quite like that: thus, a deposit receipt gives a lower return than certain other investments with an equally low risk. With a deposit receipt the investor is buying the convenience of quick and easy realisation in exchange for a lower return.

[40]　(1889) 16 R (HL) 31.

banker named Peter Thellusson died.[41] His testament left various large bequests. Even after those bequests the residue was about £600,000.[42] This he left to trustees. They were to re-invest the income until his great-grandchildren had all died, and then they were to distribute the capital to certain defined descendants. The lawfulness of the trust was litigated but upheld. The case attracted much attention, and it was felt that such long-term accumulation was against the public interest. Three years after his death, an Act was passed, limiting the period during which a trust could accumulate income.[43] The rules are now contained in the Trusts (Scotland) Act 1961 (T(S)A 1961), s 5 and the Law Reform (Miscellaneous Provisions) (Scotland) Act 1966, s 6. The rules are complex and obscure.[44] The basic rule is that income may be accumulated only for the first 21 years of a trust's life. Once the period during which accumulation has elapsed, income has to be distributed to the beneficiaries. Of course, in many trusts there never is any accumulation. An example is a liferent trust. And many trusts do not last long enough for accumulation to be an issue.

Duty to keep accounts and to give information to beneficiaries

23.24   Trustees must keep accounts and must retain the 'vouchers': relevant documents such as receipts. Whereas the form of accounts that companies must keep is highly regulated, there is little authority on the form in which trustees must keep their accounts.[45] It is also unclear how long they have to keep records. They must provide information (including the accounts) to the beneficiaries.[46] But, again, it is unclear how much information, and it is unclear to what extent the duty is an active one or whether it is merely that they must produce information if asked. Trust deeds sometimes restrict the rights of beneficiaries to information,[47] and occasionally provide that a beneficiary is not even to be told that he or she is a beneficiary until a certain time has come.[48] The validity of such provisions is untested. But it is generally assumed that such provisions are valid.

---

[41]   For the full story, see P Polden *Peter Thellusson's Will* (2002).
[42]   A fortune in modern money. And there was no inheritance tax.
[43]   39 & 40 Geo III c 98, commonly called the Thellusson Act.
[44]   See Wilson and Duncan *Trusts* ch 9. A leading case is *Elder's Trs v Free Church of Scotland* (1892) 20 R 2.
[45]   Except for charitable trusts: CTI(S)A 2005, s 44. There are, however, well-established ways of doing things: see, e.g., M F Morley *Accounting for Scottish Executries and Trusts* (1984).
[46]   Authority is sparse but see *Nouillan v Nouillan's Exrs* 1991 SLT 270. A leading English case is *O'Rourke v Darbishire* [1920] AC 581 but it gives little detail.
[47]   E.g. the 'blind trust' used by politicians.
[48]   Wealthy people often fear that their children or grandchildren will become idlers or spendthrifts if they learn too early that they are to come into money.

Fiduciary duties of trustees

23.25   To state the obvious: trustees must adhere to the terms of the trust deed and to general trust law. Investment duties have just been mentioned. Trustees, being fiduciaries, are subject to fiduciary duties.[49] A trustee must not, as it is often put, be an *auctor in rem suam*.[50]A trustee must not buy from the trust,[51] or sell to the trust,[52] or borrow from the trust,[53] or lend to the trust[54] or in any other way deal with the trust in his or her personal capacity, except in so far as the trust deed so allows. The justification is this: the trustee's interest as an individual would be in conflict with his or her duty as a trustee. For instance, if the trustee were to buy an asset from the trust, his or her economic interest as a buyer would be to obtain a low price, but the duty as seller would be to obtain a high price. Trustees must not put themselves in such a position where their interest conflicts with their duty. The fact, if it is a fact, that the price was a fair market price is irrelevant. In *University of Aberdeen v Magistrates of Aberdeen*[55] Aberdeen Council owned some land in trust. It then bought the land from itself. The price became part of the trust fund. Many years later some of the beneficiaries sought to reduce the sale. One defence to the action was that the price had been the full market value. This defence was held irrelevant and reduction was granted.[56]

23.26   Trust deeds can derogate from the 'no conflict' principle, and they often do so, especially as to charging for time. The reason is that whilst sometimes trustees are happy to give their time for nothing, sometimes they are not. If a client wishes his or her solicitor to be a trustee, the solicitor will usually agree to do so only if the trust deed allows him or her to charge. Likewise, in unit trusts the trustee will be authorised to charge. The trust deed's authorisation can be implicit as well as express.[57] As with other duties, the duty not to be an *auctor in rem suam* can be waived by the beneficiaries. The same principles apply equally to executors[58] but in practice executors often transact with themselves and their actions are seldom challenged.

---

[49]   This principle has its origin in Roman law: 'a tutor cannot buy a thing belonging to his ward; this rule extends to other persons with similar responsibilities, that is curators, procurators and those who conduct another's affairs': D 18, 1, 34, 7 (Translation A Watson et al).

[50]   'Give authority for a transaction in his own interests.'

[51]   E.g. *University of Aberdeen v Magistrates of Aberdeen* (1877) 4 R (HL) 48; *Johnston v Macfarlane* 1987 SLT 593.

[52]   E.g. *Cherry's Trs v Patrick* (1911) 2 SLT 313.

[53]   E.g. *Perston v Perston's Trs* (1863) 1 M 245.

[54]   E.g. *Wilson v Smith's Trs* 1939 SLT 120. Here, the rule seems to be applied more strictly than to other sorts of fiduciaries. For instance, while company directors cannot borrow from their company, they can lend to it.

[55]   (1877) 4 R (HL) 48.

[56]   If the land had been sold to a third party at the same price, the sale would have been valid.

[57]   *Sarris v Clark* 1995 SLT 44.

[58]   For examples involving executors, see *Inglis v Inglis* 1983 SC 8; *Johnston v Macfarlane* 1987 SLT 593 and *Sarris v Clark* 1995 SLT 44.

23.27   The trustees must (unless the trust deed says otherwise) consider only the beneficiaries' interests. In *Martin v City of Edinburgh*[59] the defenders were trustees who allowed their political outlook to influence their investment decisions. It was held that they were acting in breach of trust: there was a conflict between their duty as trustees and their political agenda. One may suspect that the motivation for the litigation – by a politician of one party against a Council controlled by a different one – was itself primarily political. In the English case of *Cowan v Scargill*[60] where the facts were rather similar the same result was reached. The court commented that 'trustees may even have to act dishonourably (though not illegally) if the interests of their beneficiaries require it', citing examples from earlier English case law. It is uncertain whether our law goes as far as that. One hopes not.

BREACH OF TRUST

Types

23.28   'Not every breach of duty by a fiduciary is a breach of fiduciary duty.'[61] Breach of trust can be divided into:

   (a) *ultra vires* breach;
   (b) *intra vires* breach; and
   (c) breach of fiduciary duty.[62]

Ultra vires breach is where the trustees do something that is outwith their powers, such as making an unauthorised investment or paying the wrong beneficiary. *Intra vires* breach is where they do something that is within their powers but do it badly, such as making an unwise investment decision. Breach of fiduciary duty speaks for itself. The classification is, however, not free from difficulty. One could argue that trustees have no power to act in breach of their fiduciary duties, so that (c) is really an aspect of (a). The distinction between *intra vires* and *ultra vires* breach is said to be important because liability for *ultra vires* breach is strict, whereas liability for *intra vires* breach is fault-based. The authorities are, however, less than clear on this point.[63] A case could be made for the view that there is no liability without fault.

---

[59]   1988 SLT 329.
[60]   [1985] Ch 270.
[61]   *Bristol and West Building Society v Mothew* [1998] Ch 1 at 16 per Millett LJ. The same is true in Scots law.
[62]   See Scottish Law Commission *Discussion Paper on Breach of Trust* (2003) parts 2–4.
[63]   For instance it is said that trustees are strictly liable if they pay out too much or to the wrong person. But has this ever been so held where there was no fault? For instance in *Corbridge v Fraser* (1915) 1 SLT 67 trustees were held personally liable for paying the wrong beneficiary, but it seems part of the *ratio* that they were aware that there was doubt as to whether they were paying the right person. In *Warren's JF v Warren's Exr* (1903) 5 F 890 it was held that there was no liability for any loss on an *ultra vires* investment, because the trustee had acted reasonably.

Some consequences of breach of trust

23.29 If trustees are personally liable, they must to restore to the trust the lost value.[64] Breach may not cause loss, and in that case there is no liability. Take the following examples. First, suppose that the trust forbids investment in land. The trustees nevertheless invest £200,000 in land. The land's value falls and a year later it is worth only £150,000. The trustees are personally liable to make good the loss. Second, suppose that the land proved a good investment, and that a year later it is worth £300,000. There is no loss to the trust. Indeed, there has been a handsome gain. So the trustees have no liability.

23.30 If an unauthorised investment is made, the trustees are bound to realise the investment and reinvest appropriately, and that is so even if the unauthorised investment has proved profitable.

23.31 A transaction with a third party that is in breach of trust will not be void and will not normally be voidable either. At common law such a transaction was voidable, at the instance of the beneficiaries, unless the counterparty gave value and was in good faith. (Which in practice was almost always the case.) The common law was modified by T(S)A 1961, s 2, so that even if the counterparty is in bad faith the transaction is not normally voidable. This provision has raised many eyebrows over the years. Whether a buyer in bad faith might be open to attack in some other way, such as a delictual claim, is unclear. The provision applies only to a sale to a *third party*, and thus not to trustees themselves. As for donations, trustees have no right to give away trust assets (except, of course, to beneficiaries in pursuance of the trust provisions) and if they do it appears that the donation is voidable.

23.32 What has just been said applies to transactions with third parties. If a trustee acts as *auctor in rem suam*, then not only is the trustee personally liable for the loss (if any) so caused, but the transaction is either void or voidable.[65]

23.33 A trustee who is involved in serious breach of trust can be removed by the court on the petition of the beneficiaries or co-trustees.[66] If there are no trustees (for example because the court has removed them all) the court can appoint new ones.[67] Where there has been serious breach of trust this can be particularly useful, for the new trustees can, for instance, sue the former trustees for any losses they have caused.

23.34 The same applies to public trusts, but in addition because public trusts exist in the public interest the Lord Advocate has a common law power to enforce. If the

---

[64] Trustees can insure against liability, and it is possible for the premiums to be charged to the trust estate, provided the trust deed so provides or the court so permits: *Governors of Dollar Academy v Lord Advocate* 1995 SLT 596.

[65] Which of these is applicable is a question of some difficulty.

[66] *Gilchrist's Trs v Dick* (1883) 11 R 22; *MacGilchrist's Trs v MacGilchrist* 1930 SC 635 and *Shariff v Hamid* 2000 SLT 294.

[67] T(S)A 1921, s 22.

trust is a charitable one, the Office of the Scottish Charity Regulator has extensive statutory powers of supervision, intervention and enforcement.[68]

Remedies for breach of trust

23.35   The beneficiaries have the usual remedies of civil law, such as actions of declarator and interdict and payment. Another such remedy which can be of particular value is an action of 'count, reckoning and payment'. This is an action for payment which requires the trustees to produce their accounts to the court so as to enable the pursuer to determine how much is due.[69]

Judicial relief

23.36   The T(S)A 1921, s 32 provides that if a trustee has incurred personal liability, the court can discharge that liability if the trustee acted 'honestly and reasonably'. This is a strange provision: in what other area of law can a debt that has come into existence be nullified at discretion? Like much trust law, this comes from England, where it is common for rights to be variable by judicial discretion. It would seem more sensible, in the context of Scots law, to say that a trustee who has acted honestly and reasonably has no liability. Indeed, that may well be what the law is. If so, that would perhaps explain why T(S)A 1921, s 32 has, it seems, never been applied.

Immunity clauses

23.37   Due to the high standards that the law demands of trustees, trust deeds sometimes seek to modify those standards by what is called an 'immunity clause'. The effect of such clauses has been controversial.[70] The standard view is that they protect trustees from liability arising out of ordinary negligence, but not out of gross negligence or fraud.[71] The distinction between ordinary and gross negligence is not without its problems.

---

[68]   CTI(S)A 2005, especially s 34.

[69]   See, e.g., *Cunningham-Jardine v Cunningham-Jardine's Trs* 1979 SLT 298 and *Nouillan v Nouillan's Executors* 1991 SLT 270.

[70]   And not only in Scotland. The leading English case is *Armitage v Nurse* [1998] Ch 241. For a comparative study, see the Scottish Law Commission *Discussion Paper on Breach of Trust* (2003), Appendix A.

[71]   *Lutea Trs Ltd v Orbis Trs Guernsey Ltd* 1998 SLT 471.

Prescription

23.38   Most obligations can be extinguished by negative prescription.[72] The obligations of trustees are an exception.[73] Whether this exception is justifiable is perhaps debatable.

RUNNING FOR COVER

23.39   It sometimes happens that the trustees are uncertain what they should do, for example about the meaning of a provision in the trust deed. There are several ways of bringing the issue before the court. One is a declarator. Another is a special case.[74] Another (though useful only if the issue is about paying or transferring assets to beneficiaries) is multiplepoinding. All those procedures can also be used outwith the field of trust law. Trustees can also 'petition for directions'[75] and seek a 'superintendence order'.[76]

LIABILITY OF TRUSTEES TO THIRD PARTIES

23.40   If trustees incur liability to third parties, the question of whether they are *personally* liable is generally of little significance, for even if they are, they are entitled to be reimbursed from the trust estate.[77] The question becomes important in the unusual case where the trust becomes insolvent. In such a case the creditors will wish, if possible, to hold the trustees personally liable. It is commonly said that if trustees enter a contract, they are personally liable on it unless the contract expressly states that they are contracting only as trustees. The alternative view is that no such express declaration is necessary: if they contracted as trustees and the other party knew that, then they are not personally liable.[78]

INSOLVENCY

Four cases

23.41   Four different cases of insolvency must be considered:

[72]   See PARAS **2.22–2.23** above.
[73]   PL(S)A 1973, Sch 3. These provisions are not free from obscurity. See, e.g., *Hobday v Kirkpatrick's Trs* 1985 SLT 197 and *Ross v Davy* 1996 SCLR 369.
[74]   Court of Session Act 1988, s 27.
[75]   Court of Session Act 1988, s 6. See *Peel's Trs v Drummond* 1936 SC 786 and *Taylor, Petitioner* 2000 SLT 1223.
[76]   T(S)A 1921, s 17.
[77]   Unless the liability was incurred in the course of breach of trust.
[78]   See R G Anderson 'Contractual Liability of Trustees to Third Parties' 2003 *JR* 45 and Scottish Law Commission *Discussion Paper on Contractual Liability of Trustees to Third Parties* (2008).

(1) that of a beneficiary;
(2) that of a truster;
(3) that of a trustee as an individual; and
(4) that of the trust.

'Insolvency' here is used in a broad sense to cover sequestration, liquidation and also the diligence of creditors.

(1) Beneficiaries

23.42   If a beneficiary becomes insolvent, the beneficial interest is part of his or her patrimony and so is in principle available to the creditors. Suppose, for instance, that John is entitled to £5,000 each quarter from a trust. His creditors could arrest in the hands of the trustees. Or suppose that trustees hold a house in beneficial liferent for Laura and in beneficial fee for Fiona. Fiona is sequestrated. The beneficial fee passes to her trustee in sequestration for the benefit of her creditors. This does not affect Laura's rights.

(2) Truster

23.43   The insolvency of the truster after the trust has been established is normally irrelevant. But there is a qualification. Insolvency law says that a person who is factually insolvent must conserve his or her assets for the creditors' benefit, and not transfer assets gratuitously. If there is such a transfer – what is called a 'gratuitous alienation' – the creditors can insist that the assets be re-transferred. Usually the claim is made after the transferor has been sequestrated, or gone into liquidation, and the claim is made by the trustee in sequestration or the liquidator. This general principle applies as much to transfers to a trust as it does to other transfers.[79]

(3) Trustee as individual

23.44   The insolvency of a trustee as an individual has no effect on the trust. The rule is a common law one, and remains so as far as diligence and liquidation are concerned. For sequestration, the rule has been put on a statutory footing.[80] The common law rule is often traced to the late nineteenth-century case of *Heritable Reversionary Co Ltd v Millar*.[81] In fact, it goes back to the seventeenth century, but at common law there was an exception in relation to heritable property where the fact of the trust was kept secret, i.e. not disclosed on the register. In *Heritable Reversionary Co Ltd v Millar* the House of Lords changed the law so as to remove the exception.

---

[79]   For the law of gratuitous alienations, see W W McBryde *Bankruptcy* (2nd edn, 1995) ch 12.
[80]   Bankruptcy (Scotland) Act 1985, s 33(1).
[81]   (1891) 19 R (HL) 43.

(4) Trust

23.45   In the unusual situation where a trust itself becomes insolvent, it can be sequestrated.[82]

FURTHER READING

Chalmers *Trusts* chs 6–10.

Norrie, K and Scobbie, E *Trusts* (1991) chs 7–11.

Paisley, R *Trusts* (1999) chs 7–11.

Wilson and Duncan *Trusts* chs 23–30.

---

[82]   Bankruptcy (Scotland) Act 1985, s 6(1)(a).

Chapter 24

Trusts: variation and termination

INTRODUCTION

24.1 'Variation' means the varying of the terms of trust: this is unusual but by no means rare. 'Termination', or 'extinction', is when a trust comes to an end. The two are connected because a trust may be varied so as to terminate it.

24.2 Most trusts run their course and come to a natural termination without ever having been varied. For instance, in a trust for Letitia in liferent and Malcolm in fee, when Letitia dies the trustees will make over the trust estate to Malcolm, and the trust will be ended. When a private trust is finally wound up so that nothing is left in the trustees' hands, the trustees are said to 'denude'. Much the same is true of public trusts. For example, there is a natural disaster and a relief fund is set up with generous people giving it money. The money is expended fairly quickly and the trust will then come to an end.[1]

---

[1] Although permanent public trusts are also possible.

VARIATION AND EARLY TERMINATION OF PRIVATE TRUSTS

24.3 The court can vary public trusts.[2] Subject to two qualifications,[3] it cannot vary private trusts. The sole, but also the sufficient, means of variation (including early termination) of private trusts is unanimous agreement among the beneficiaries. That is to say, the beneficiaries collectively may not only *consent* to a variation, but can *compel* a variation: their wishes, if unanimous, override the terms of the trust deed and the views of the trustees. Actually, solid authority for this is not easy to find,[4] but the point is never doubted and indeed it is presupposed by the Trusts (Scotland) Act 1961 (T(S)A 1961), s 1. This was enacted to allow variations to go ahead even without the consent of certain beneficiaries. In practice the commonest reason for a variation is tax planning.

24.4 The first of the two qualifications mentioned above is that T(S)A 1961 allows the court to vary the trust terms in two respects, namely to enlarge the administrative powers of the trustees[5] and to permit the trustees to make an advance of capital.[6] In practice neither is common. If it is simply a question of enlarging the powers of the trustees, that can be done by a court order under T(S)A 1961, s 5.

24.5 The other qualification is T(S)A 1961, s 1. The rule that all the beneficiaries can opt for a variation sounds straightforward, but there are two catches. The first is that a beneficiary who is under age[7] cannot consent, and, moreover, it seems that nobody can consent for them.[8] The second is that one or more beneficiaries may be as yet non-existent. (An example would be a trust for X in liferent and in fee for those children of Y as are alive when X dies.) The court can consent on behalf of such beneficiaries.[9]

---

[2] See PARAS **24.11–24.15** below.

[3] See PARAS **24.4–24.5** below.

[4] The case usually cited is *Gray v Gray's Trs* (1877) 4 R 378. See generally Wilson and Duncan *Trusts* para 12-02.

[5] Trusts (Scotland) Act 1921 (T(S)A 1921), s 5.

[6] T(S)A 1921, s 16.

[7] Whether this means – for this purpose – 16 or 18 is a complex issue. The Age of Legal Capacity (Scotland) Act 1991 (ALC(S)A 1991) says that the age of capacity for juridical acts in private law is 16, but this rule must be read in the light of T(S)A 1961, s 1(2), as substituted by ALC(S)A 1991, Sch 1. T(S)A 1961, s 1(2) is less than clear. The practical position is that for those aged 16 or 17 the court's consent is needed as it is for those under 16.

[8] There is an argument that consent can be given by the parent or guardian, but the general view is that consent to a termination or variation on behalf of someone under 18 can only be given by the court. For discussion, see A B Wilkinson and K McK Norrie *The Law Relating to Parent and Child in Scotland* (2nd edn, 1999) paras 15.57–15.58.

[9] T(S)A 1961. The leading case on the interpretation of the section is *Phillips, Petr* 1964 SC 141.

PRIVATE TRUSTS: THE RULE IN *MILLER'S TRS*

24.6   The rule in *Miller's Trs v Miller*,[10] confirmed by the Whole Court in *Yuill's Trs v Thomson*[11] allows the partial or complete termination of a trust at the request of a single beneficiary, where that beneficiary is the only person with an interest. It is thus closely related to the 'all beneficiaries' rule given above. Arguably they are both aspects of some super-rule which has yet to be articulated. The 'all beneficiaries' rule, however, is about any sort of variation, including termination, where the rule in *Miller's Trs* is only about termination.

24.7   The rule is as follows: if a beneficial interest is vested in a given person, and there is no reason for the trustees not to pay or transfer to that person, except for a direction in the trust deed that they must not do so until that person has reached a specified age, then that person, if he or she has reached the age of 16, can demand that the trustees pay, or transfer, to him or her, notwithstanding that the trust deed forbids them to do so.[12] If the beneficiary is the sole beneficiary then the trust is terminated.

24.8   The rule is well illustrated by *Miller's Trs* itself. Sir William Miller set up a trust for his son John. The trust deed provided that the trustees were not to transfer the trust estate to John until he was 25. This was, therefore, a bare trust, with the speciality that beneficiary could not demand that the trustees denude until a stated time.[13] Before he was 25, John sued the trustees to have the property made over to him. He was successful.

24.9   If the trust had provided, for example, that if he died before 25 the property would go to someone else then his action would have failed. But there was no reason for the trustees to withhold, apart from the direction to do so. Despite the rule in *Miller's Trs v Miller*, trusters often do provide that assets be withheld from a beneficiary until a certain age – 25 is the typical age chosen – is reached. The reason is obvious: many trusters do not think young adults should be given substantial capital. In practice beneficiaries often do not assert their right under *Miller's Trs v Miller*, and so the truster's wishes prevail.

---

[10]   (1890) 18 R 301. The rule is the same in England: *Saunders v Vautier* (1841) 4 Beav 115, 49 ER 282, aff'd (1841) Cr & Ph 240, 41 ER 482. But in some other countries the rule is different. Scotland should perhaps be among them: the dissenting opinion of Lord Young is powerful. However, *Miller's Trs* must now be accepted as settled law.

[11]   (1902) 4 F 815.

[12]   Actually, a precise statement of the rule is problematic, partly because in both cases the judges explain the rule by the inappropriate use of the word 'fee'. The text is an attempt to state the rule without using that word.

[13]   Actually, the trust did not start off as a bare trust. But that complication can be omitted. It had become a bare trust by the time that John sued the trustees.

TERMINATION OF A PRIVATE TRUST BY FAILURE OF PURPOSES: RESULTING TRUSTS

24.10   In a private trust it can occasionally happen that after the purposes have been fulfilled there is still trust property left, or that the trust purposes cannot be fulfilled at all. In these cases the remaining trust property is deemed to be held on a bare trust for the truster. This is called a 'resulting trust'. This is not, as the name suggests, a distinct species of trust. It is simply that in every private trust the truster is himself or herself the implied longstop beneficiary. If the truster is dead – which is necessarily the position for *mortis causa* trusts – the trustee holds in trust for the truster's estate.

VARIATION AND EARLY TERMINATION OF PUBLIC TRUSTS

Variation of public trusts

24.11   In a public trust, consent to a variation cannot be given by the beneficiaries because it is the nature of a public trust that there does not exist a finite set of beneficiaries. Variation is nevertheless possible. In some cases it can be done by the trustees themselves. In others the court must be involved, and in some cases the regulatory body for charities, OSCR.[14]

Variation of non-charitable public trusts

24.12   Non-charitable public trusts can be varied under the Law Reform (Miscellaneous Provisions) (Scotland) Act 1990 (LR(MP)(S)A 1990), ss 9–11. The main provision is LR(MP)(S)A 1990, s 9. Several grounds exist for variation, such as if the purposes of the trust 'have been fulfilled as far as it is possible to do so'. The court can vary the trust purposes, or provide for the trust assets to be transferred to another trust. Any variation must have regard to the 'spirit' of the trust deed: the new scheme 'must enable the resources of the trust to be applied to better effect consistently with the spirit of the trust's constitutive document, having regard to changes in social and economic conditions since the time when the trust was constituted'.[15] LR(MP)(S)A 1990, ss 10 and 11 provide simplified machinery for the variation of smaller trusts. As well as the statutory rules, the court has a common law power to vary public trusts: this goes by the curious name of the '*cy près* procedure'.[16]

---

[14]   For OSCR, see PARA **22.35** above.

[15]   Charities and Trustee Investment (Scotland) Act 2005 (CTI(S)A 2005), s 9(2).

[16]   For this procedure, see PARAS **24.14–24.15** below.

Variation ('reorganisation') of charitable trusts

24.13   The provisions just mentioned used to include charitable trusts. But today LR(MP)(S)A 1990 covers only non-charitable public trusts.[17] Charitable trusts (and indeed charities that are not trusts) are now 'reorganised' under the Charities and Trustee Investment (Scotland) Act 2005 (CTI(S)A 2005).[18] This can be done in two ways. The first is for the trustees to propose a variation to OSCR, which can then if it sees fit approve the proposal. In this case the court does not have to be involved. Alternatively, OSCR can petition the court to approve a variation. Such a petition does not require the trustees' consent. The conditions for such a reorganisation (for example about the 'spirit' of the trust) are similar to those in LR(MP)(S)A 1990.

Cy près

24.14   If a charitable trust is unworkable, the court has power to modify its provisions to make it workable. This is called a '*cy près*'[19] scheme. There are two types of case. The first is 'initial failure', where the trust cannot be put into operation, and the other is 'supervening failure', where the charitable trust is up and running but later becomes unworkable. In either case the court makes a *cy près* scheme, which is supposed to be as near to the original intention of the truster as possible, consistent with workability. Nowadays the 'supervening failure' cases are usually handled through the statutory system already mentioned. For 'initial failure' cases *cy près* remains the only route.

24.15   There can be many reasons for unworkability, such as changes in the law,[20] or changes in social or economic conditions.[21] One type of initial failure is a testamentary trust in favour of a named charity that in fact does not exist – something that happens surprisingly often. In such a case, if it can be established that the testator had a 'general charitable intention' the court will approve a *cy près* scheme.[22] Otherwise the legacy will be void. A *cy près* scheme can take the form of simply directing that the funds be made over to an existing charity.

---

[17]   Law Reform (Miscellaneous Provisions) (Scotland) Act 1990, s 15(9) as amended by CTI(S)A 2005, Sch 4, para 7(e). The terms 'charity' and 'charitable' are rather slippery, and here we use them to mean charities that are registered is the Register of Charities.

[18]   CTI(S)A 2005, ss 39–43. Three minor points: (a) These provisions do not apply to chartered or statutory charities: CTI(S)A 2005, s 42(5). (b) The *cy près* procedure is competent for charitable trusts as it is for other public trusts: CTI(S)A 2005, s 42(4). (c) 'Educational endowments' are governed, in part, by the Education (Scotland) Act 1980, though the scope of this Act has been reduced by CTI(S)A 2005, ss 42(6) and 43. Some educational endowments are centuries old. The local authority is often the trustee.

[19]   Pronounced 'see-pray'. The expression comes from English law but is neither good English nor good French but rather what is called in England 'law French'.

[20]   See, e.g., *Burgess's Trs v Crawford* 1912 SC 387.

[21]   See, e.g., *Trs of the Domestic Training School etc, Glasgow, Petrs* 1923 SLT 603.

[22]   See, e.g., *Pomphrey's Trs v Royal Naval Benevolent Trust* 1967 SLT 61.

Alimentary trusts

24.16 An alimentary trust is one expressly established for the alimentary support of the beneficiary. Though nowadays unusual, they are not unknown. They have a number of special features, one of which is that the rule in *Miller's Trs*[23] does not apply. Another is that the beneficiary's rights are unassignable. A third is that the beneficial interest is, to a limited degree, protected from the beneficiary's creditors.

FURTHER READING

Chalmers *Trusts* (2002) chs 12–13.

Norrie, K and Scobbie, E *Trusts* (1991) chs 12–14.

Paisley, R *Trusts* (1999) chs 13–14.

Wilson and Duncan *Trusts* chs 11–16.

[23]   (1890) 18 R 301. See PARAS **24.6–24.9** above.

Chapter 25

Succession: general issues

INTRODUCTION

Location of succession within private law

25.1   The law of succession is the law regulating what happens to a person's assets and liabilities on death. It can be considered as part of property law, in the sense that it deals with the effect of death on property.[1] It can also be regarded as part of family law.[2] Many legal systems regard it as a separate subject in its own right.

Succession law and trust law

25.2   The relationship of the law of succession and the law of trusts is close. Indeed, it is arguable that the former has, over the centuries, been absorbed into the latter, in the sense that every executry is now a trust.[3] Whatever the theoretical position, in practice succession and trusts still tend to be thought of as being separate from each other.

Sources of the law: past and future

25.3   Our succession law differs from English succession law in many ways: so different are they that English authorities are seldom cited. The law is in part statutory and in part common law, the latter being a mix of Roman law, canon law and customary law. The main statute is the much-amended Succession (Scotland) Act 1964 (S(S)A 1964).[4] In 1990 the Scottish Law Commission produced a report recommending major changes.[5] It has not so far been implemented, but legislation in the near future is not unlikely.[6]

---

[1]   The Scotland Act 1998, s 126 assigns succession to property law.
[2]   Particularly as regards intestate succession. See, e.g., K McK Norrie 'Three proposals' 2007 *JLSS* Oct/ 20 at 21.
[3]   See **PARA 25.50** below.
[4]   This implemented the Mackintosh Report of 1951 (Cmnd 8144).
[5]   Scottish Law Commission *Report on Succession* (1990).
[6]   The Scottish Law Commission is working again in this area: see its *Discussion Paper on Succession* (2007). For a vigorous critique, see D Reid 'From the Cradle to the Grave' (2008) 12 *Edin LR* 391.

Different approaches to succession

25.4   When someone dies, what should happen to the estate? The answer depends, in part at least, on basic ideas about the nature of property.[7]

   (1)   There are those who have an individualistic idea of property. They argue that people should be free to decide what happens to their assets when they die. If Adam wants to disinherit his wife and children, he should be free to do so. People should be guided by conscience, but not coerced by law. This approach is that of 'freedom of testation'.

   (2)   Some people have a family-based idea of property. They argue that family members have rights that are indefeasible in conscience and ought to be indefeasible in law. While there may be scope of debate as to how 'family' should be defined, people should be unable to disinherit their families completely.[8]

   (3)   Others have a 'socialistic' idea of property. Property ultimately belongs to society. When a member of society dies, the property should revert to society, either in whole or at least in part.[9]

25.5   If there is an intestacy, the first approach is irrelevant. The owner has not expressed any wishes as to what should happen, and so the conflict is only between the second and third approaches. But in a testate case the conflict becomes a three-cornered one.

25.6   Each approach has sub-approaches, and the second has three in particular.

   (a)   There should be no right of testation at all. Everyone would die intestate, so that the rules of intestacy, which give the estate to the family, would always apply.

   (b)   There should be a right of testation, but not for the whole estate: a minimum slice should be set aside for the benefit of the family.

   (c)   Since circumstances vary (one child might be poor and another rich, so why should they receive the same?), the system should be discretionary, with the discretion being vested in a determined person or body, such as a judge.

25.7   The first approach (freedom of testation) has tended to be favoured by the Anglo–American legal systems, while the second, in its (b) version, has tended to be favoured in the civilian tradition.[10] Almost all systems have an element of the third approach by way of death tax – in the UK called inheritance tax.[11] In some Anglo–American legal systems there has been a recent tendency to move towards a mixture of the first approach and the second approach in its (c) version. England is an example,

---

[7]   The following discussion is a brief one and so cannot do full justice to the issues.

[8]   The system of indefeasible inheritance rights for the family is known among comparative lawyers by the rather odd name of 'forced heirship'. The idea behind the phrase is not that heirship is forced on the family but that it is forced on the testator.

[9]   Perhaps this is just a variant of the 'family' philosophy, with the whole of society being the family.

[10]   E.g. the French Cc, art 913, and German BGB, § 2303.

[11]   Inheritance Tax Act 1984.

where succession rights are subject to the court's discretion.[12] But such discretion applies only if it is invoked: if no one seeks to invoke it then the estate is distributed according to determinate rules. Moreover, only certain defined persons can seek to invoke the discretion: for instance, suppose that someone dies unmarried and childless and with no dependants, then the court's discretion could not be invoked. The third approach in its pure form (everything to the state) was applied for a few years in the former Soviet Union, but was quickly abandoned.

25.8 Like most legal systems, Scots law is a compromise. Inheritance tax takes away part of the estate, at a rate of 40%, though there are various exemptions, and smaller estates, in particular, are exempt. The second of the three approaches is adopted in its (b) variant – which puts us in the 'civilian' camp. Our law has an institution called (oddly) 'legal rights', whereby the spouse (or civil partner) and children (and sometimes grandchildren) have certain rights that cannot be excluded by the testament of the deceased.[13] But *other* family members have no such protection. Thus those who leave behind them neither spouse (or civil partner) nor issue[14] can write their testaments without concerning themselves about possible rights. As for the first of the three views, people can do what they like with such part of their estates as will be net of taxes and legal rights.

Moral claims

25.9 Succession rights are legal entitlements. Merely moral claims, however strong, have no legal status. Neither need nor merit enter the calculation. The courts have no discretion to depart from the legal rules in favour of a claimant with a strong moral case. Thus suppose that Rosie has two daughters, Shilpa and Tara. Rosie is aged and infirm and is looked after for many years by Shilpa. Tara lives in Australia and never even sends her mother a Christmas card. Shilpa is poor. Tara is rich. If Rosie dies intestate, Shilpa has no greater right than does Tara, and even if Rosie leaves everything to Shilpa, Tara can still claim legal rights. In this approach Scotland is in line with most, but not all, countries. There are strong arguments for the discretionary approach, as the example shows, but there are also strong arguments the other way.

Death

25.10 The Registration of Births, Marriages and Deaths (Scotland) Act 1965 is the governing statute for the registration of deaths. Section 23 provides that

---

[12] Inheritance (Provision for Family and Dependants) Act 1975, s 2. Both testate *and* intestate succession are subject to the discretionary rights.

[13] See CHAPTER 26 below.

[14] 'Issue' means children or remoter descendants.

'it shall be the duty of

(a) any relation of the deceased,[15]

(b) any person present at the death,

(c) the deceased's executor or other legal representative,

(d) the occupier, at the time of death, of the premises where the death took place,

(e) if there is no such person as is mentioned in the foregoing paragraphs, any other person having knowledge of the particulars to be registered'

to register the death. The person registering the death submits a certificate of cause of death signed by a physician.[16] The Registrar can issue extracts from the Register, and the term 'death certificate' means such an extract, rather than the physician's certificate.[17]

25.11 Sometimes a formal inquiry before the sheriff will be conducted by the procurator fiscal, in order to determine the circumstances of the death: this is regulated by the Fatal Accidents and Sudden Deaths Inquiry (Scotland) Act 1976.[18] Such inquiries happen in three types of case:

(a) accidents at work;

(b) deaths in custody; and

(c) in cases where it is 'expedient in the public interest'.[19]

25.12 If a person simply disappears, so that there is no body, a declarator of death can be obtained.[20] If it is unclear whether the person is still alive or not, but seven years have passed since he or she was last known to be alive, then the court can deem him or her to have died at the end of the seven-year period.[21] This opens the way to rights of succession to the estate.[22]

The body

25.13 Bodies are disposed of either by burial or by cremation. The latter requires official permission because it destroys evidence. There is therefore a rather bureaucratic procedure whereby two physicians must certify the cause of death and a third person, the 'medical referee', certifies that cremation may proceed.[23]

---

[15] Since everyone is, ultimately, a relation of everyone else, this means that the duty is imposed on the whole planetary population.

[16] Registration of Births, Marriages and Deaths (Scotland) Act 1965, s 24.

[17] Registration of Births, Marriages and Deaths (Scotland) Act 1965, s 27.

[18] On which see I H B Carmichael *Sudden Deaths and Fatal Accident Inquires* (3rd edn, 2005).

[19] Fatal Accidents and Sudden Deaths Inquiry (Scotland) Act 1976, s 1(1)(b).

[20] Presumption of Death (Scotland) Act 1977.

[21] Before that period has elapsed, the estate can, if necessary, be administered by a judicial factor.

[22] The Presumption of Death (Scotland) Act 1977 has provisions about what is to happen if the person later turns up.

[23] Cremation Acts 1902 and 1952.

25.14 Is a dead body owned? If so, by whom? This has never been absolutely settled but it appears that 'there is no right of property in a dead body'.[24] Presumably, however, it is unlike other ownerless property, for it would be absurd to suggest that ownership could be acquired by occupation. If it has no owner, the question of who is entitled to possession has to be determined without reference to ownership.[25] If no one takes any steps to dispose of a body, the local authority has power to do so.[26] The procurator fiscal is entitled to take temporary possession of dead bodies to the extent that the public interest so requires: an example would be the body of a murder victim.

WHO MAY INHERIT? THE LIVING AND THE DEAD

General

25.15 There are three principal ways in which one person may inherit from another.
(1) By legacy (also called bequest). This can happen only in a testate case.[27]
(2) By intestate succession.[28]
(3) By legal rights.[29]
Legal rights can operate in both testate and intestate cases. In all three cases there are certain general issues which can arise, and they are discussed below.

25.16 The living can inherit. The dead cannot. These two principles are obvious but it is easy to lose sight of them. Alice's testament gives a legacy of a house to Brian. She dies on Monday and Brian dies on Tuesday. When she dies, Brian is still alive, and the legacy 'vests' in him.[30] That is to say, he acquires a personal right to it. The fact that from a practical point of view Brian does not live long enough to receive the legacy makes no difference. Personal rights form a part of a person's patrimony just as much as real rights. Suppose that Brian had lived long enough for ownership of the house to be transferred to him. Then when he died the ownership of the house would have been in his estate. Since he died the day after the testator, what was in his estate was a personal right to have ownership of the house conveyed to him. But the financial value of that right is the same as that of ownership itself.[31] What will happen is that Alice's executor will transfer the legacy to Brian's executor. (It is then up to

---

24   *Robson v Robson* (1898) 5 SLT 351 at 352. See also *McGruer, Petitioner* (1899) 15 Sh Ct Rep 38.
25   The problems in this area are considerable. See further N R Whitty 'Rights of Personality, Property Rights and the Human Body in Scots Law' (2005) 9 *Edin LR* 194.
26   Public Health (Scotland) Act 1897, s 69. See generally *SME* vol 3, 'Burial and Cremation' (1994).
27   See CHAPTER 27 below.
28   See CHAPTER 28 below.
29   See CHAPTER 26 below.
30   It would be otherwise if Alice's testament had made the legacy conditional on Brian's surviving her for a stated period, such as one month. Such conditions are sometimes found. On vesting, see PARAS 22.59–22.65 above.
31   Assuming that Alice's estate is solvent etc.

the latter to determine what is to happen to the property as far as Brian's estate is concerned. It would be quite wrong for Alice's executor to make that determination.)

25.17 Now, reverse the order of deaths. Brian dies on Monday and Alice on Tuesday. The legacy to Brian cannot take effect. The legacy has lapsed.[32] The dead cannot inherit. Thus suppose that Brian's testament left everything to his widow, Clara. All Brian's estate would then pass to Clara[33] but his estate would not include the legacy from Alice.

25.18 Hence small differences in the timing of deaths can make big differences in the effects of the deaths. For example, Deirdre and Ewan are married but have no children. Deirdre's nearest relative is her brother, Fraser. Ewan's nearest relation is his sister, Gina. Deirdre's testament leaves everything to Ewan. Ewan's leaves everything to Deirdre. Deirdre dies on Monday and Ewan dies on Tuesday. The whole of both Deirdre's and Ewan's estates end up with Gina, to the exclusion of Fraser. Why? Because Ewan's testament is without effect, since when he dies, Deirdre, his sole legatee, is already dead – she has predeceased. (The verbs 'to survive' and 'to predecease' are commonly used in succession law. If X 'predeceases', Y that means that X dies before Y. If X 'survives' Y, that means that Y dies before X.) Hence Ewan dies intestate. So everything of Ewan's, which by now includes a personal right to the whole of Deirdre's estate, passes to his next of kin, his sister Gina. Had the dates of death been reversed, everything would have ended up in the hands of Fraser, for the same reasons.

Common calamity

25.19 'Common calamity' is the name given to the situation where two or more people die in the same incident, such as a road accident or a house fire. This is, alas, common. If those who die[34] have no potential succession rights to the estates of the others, there is no problem. But what if they have? Sometimes the evidence will show that one died before the other. If it can be shown, on balance of probabilities, that Deirdre died one minute after Ewan, then she survived him, and so inherited. The same is true, the other way round, if he lived for one minute after her.

25.20 If they died at the exactly the same moment, then neither survives the other. To inherit from someone you must survive them, so neither inherits from the other. However, that conclusion, however reasonable, it not what the law says. If they die at precisely the same moment, S(S)A 1964, s 31 sets out certain rules. If the parties are spouses or civil partners, then neither is regarded as surviving the other.[35] Otherwise, the rule is that – contrary to the actual fact of simultaneous death – the

---

[32] For lapse of legacies, see **PARA 27.44** below.
[33] Subject to debts and legal rights.
[34] The Latin term *commorientes* ('those who die together') is sometimes used.
[35] S(S)A 1964, s 31(1)(a).

younger person survives the elder.[36] But there is an exception – a somewhat convoluted one – to this latter rule. It is that if:

(a) the elder has left a legacy to the younger; and

(b) there is a destination-over to somebody else;[37] and

(c) the younger is intestate,

then the rule is that the elder survives the younger.[38]

25.21 These rules apply not only (a) in the case where the evidence shows that they died at the same moment but also (b) in the case where the evidence is simply unclear, so that it cannot be shown that either survived the other. So, for example, two people die in a house fire. That they perished at exactly the same moment is highly unlikely. But unless evidence can be led to show that one died after the other,[39] the S(S)A 1964, s 31 rules apply.

25.22 Incidentally, the rules may be inconsistent. Here is an example. Three people die together. The dates of birth are: A 1980; B 1981; and C 1982. A and C are married to each other. B is presumed to die before C, because B is older than C. But equally C is presumed to die before B. Why? A and C presumptively die at the same moment. Since A presumptively dies before B (because A is older than B), it follows that C must also die before B.

WHO MAY INHERIT? SOME PARTICULAR TYPES OF PERSON

General

25.23 This section deals with particular types of potential claimant, such as adopted children, cohabitants and so on. All such persons may inherit to the extent that a legacy has been left to them by the deceased.[40] So this section is concerned with whether they have inheritance rights *independently* of any legacy.

Children out of wedlock

25.24 The common law rule was that children born out of wedlock were not treated, for succession purposes, as the child of either parent. This rule was gradually eroded by legislation, and eventually disappeared.[41] William, a widower, dies intestate at the

---

[36] S(S)A 1964, s 31(1)(b). For the background to s 31, see *Ross's JF v Martin* 1955 SC (HL) 56.

[37] For destinations-over, see **PARAS 29.3–29.4** below.

[38] S(S)A 1964, s 31(2).

[39] As in *Lamb v Lord Advocate* 1976 SC 110, where the standard of proof about the order of deaths was held to be the ordinary one of balance of probabilities.

[40] The deceased is sometimes also called the defunct, and also the *de cuius* (also spelled *de cujus*), meaning the 'of whom', i.e. the person whose estate is to be wound up.

[41] Law Reform (Parent and Child) (Scotland) Act 1986, s 1. And see Family Law (Scotland) Act 2007, s 21.

age of 75. He has one child, Mary, by his late wife, Wendy. At the funeral appears a man, Michael, who can show that Mary's father was his genetic father. Mary and Michael have equal rights to the estate.

Adopted children

25.25   An adopted child is treated, for succession purposes, as a child of the adoptive parent(s), and not as the child of the actual parents.[42] Tom, the child of Ursula and Vernon, is adopted by Wilma and Xerxes, who also have a child of their own, Yolanda. If Ursula dies, Tom receives nothing (unless it happens that she left him a legacy). If Xerxes dies, Tom has the same position as Yolanda. If Tom dies, his birth parents are not treated as being his parents for succession purposes. His adoptive family is treated as being his family.

Stepchildren

25.26   A stepchild is not the child of the stepparent. Iona and James marry and have one child, Kate. James dies and Iona marries Louis. Kate is Louis's stepdaughter. If he dies, she has no succession rights in his estate. (Unless, of course, he left her a legacy.) Were it otherwise, Kate would in effect inherit from *three* parents.

Posthumous children

25.27   A baby born after its father's death has the same succession rights as if it had already been born at the time of the death. This rule is usually expressed in Latin as *nasciturus pro jam natus habetur, si de ejus commodo agitur* (an unborn child is to be considered already born if to do so is in its interests).

Cohabitants

25.28   Until 2006, cohabitants had no succession rights, unless they left legacies in each other's favour, which, of course, was and is common. The rule now is that in intestate cases the court may, on a discretionary basis, make a cohabitant an award.[43] This is the only case where judicial discretion can be an element in our succession law. In a testate case a cohabitant may receive a legacy, but otherwise has no claim.

---

[42]   Adoption and Children (Scotland) Act 2007, s 40.
[43]   Family Law (Scotland) Act 2006, s 29. See PARA **28.20** below.

Spouses and civil partners: current, former and separated

25.29 Spouses and civil partners have the same rights in succession.[44] Divorce dissolves marriage. The same is true of civil partnerships, though the word 'divorce' is not used. If Jack and Jill marry and later divorce, and Jack then dies, Jill has no succession rights. A fair settlement between them should have been achieved at the time of the divorce. Of course, Jill's children by Jack will have succession rights in his estate. You can divorce your spouse, but relationship by blood is indissoluble.[45]

25.30 If a married couple separate but do not divorce, they are, to state the obvious, still married, and so have succession rights in each other's estate. That is true even if they have agreed that they will divorce. What dissolves the marriage is not the decision to divorce, but the divorce itself. There are two qualifications. One is that when spouses part they sometimes sign a separation agreement, and such agreements typically contain a clause of mutual renunciation of all succession rights.[46] The other is that non-cohabitation of spouses can affect intestate succession rights.[47]

Juristic persons and trusts

25.31 Juristic persons and trusts obviously are not family members and so have no inheritance rights independently of any legacy. But it is competent to leave a legacy to them, and indeed it is common to do so, since people often leave legacies to charities, and charities are organised either as juristic persons or as trusts.[48]

The unworthy heir

25.32 An 'unworthy heir'[49] is someone barred from inheriting because he or she unlawfully killed the deceased.[50] The typical example is where one spouse kills the other. The result of being an unworthy heir is that all rights are lost, where by way of legacy, or legal rights, or intestate rights, or rights under special destination.[51] Whether the unworthy heir is considered as having predeceased is a difficult

---

[44] S(S)A 1964, ss 2, 8 and 9; Civil Partnership Act 2004, s 131.

[45] Except by adoption.

[46] Formerly, judicial separation barred the husband's rights against the wife's estate but did not bar the wife's rights against the husband's estate: Conjugal Rights (Scotland) Amendment Act 1861. This was repealed by the Family Law (Scotland) Act 2006. Judicial separation now has no effect on succession rights.

[47] See PARA **28.12** below.

[48] See PARAS **22.35–22.36** above.

[49] Or, in Latin, the *haeres indignus*.

[50] Whether a person might be an unworthy heir on other grounds as well is uncertain. For instance, in many legal systems a person who forges a testament is an unworthy heir.

[51] And see *Burns v Secretary of State for Social Services* 1985 SLT 351 (woman who killed husband barred from claiming widow's allowance).

question.[52] The law was modified by the Forfeiture Act 1982 which provides that the court has a discretionary power to 'modify' the common law rule.[53] But the power exists only if the killer is convicted of culpable homicide rather than murder. It has been held that the word 'modify' means that the court cannot waive the rule completely.[54]

NO OBLIGATION TO ACCEPT

25.33 No one is obliged to accept anything by way of succession. Succession rights are occasionally refused. Sometimes the family gets together after the death and agrees a division that is different from what the applicable law (of testate or intestate succession) provides. Such an agreement is usually called a 'deed of variation'. If it is entered into within two years of the death, it is treated, for tax purposes, as if it had effect as from the moment of death.[55] Indeed, deeds of variation are often done purely for reasons of tax planning.

THE ESTATE

Active and passive transmissibility

25.34 The 'estate' is a person's patrimony upon death – the collection of assets and liabilities of the deceased that must be 'wound up' by the executor.[56] 'Winding up' means that the executor pays the debts, pays any tax due, and distributes the balance – in kind or in money – to the beneficiaries. In general, all the deceased's assets form part of the estate: this is sometimes known as the principle of 'active transmissibility'. Assets include personal as well as real rights. Suppose that Monica borrows £50 from Lucretius. He dies. The right to repayment forms part of his estate: she must pay his executor. In some special types of case, however, an asset does die with its holder. An example is a liferent.[57] But such exceptions are rare. Solatium claims have proved difficult, and the law has changed more than once. The current position is that such claims are actively transmissible.[58]

---

[52]　According to *Hunter's Exrs, Ptnrs* 1992 SLT 1141 the answer is negative.

[53]　This Act also applies in England and Wales, and its approach is arguably more English than Scottish. For an example of the way the Act works, see *Paterson, Petitioner* 1986 SLT 121.

[54]　*Cross, Petitioner* 1987 SLT 384. Here, the court thought that complete waiver would have been desirable, and so waived the forfeiture to the extent of 99%.

[55]　Inheritance Tax Act 1984, s 142.

[56]　The word 'estate' is likewise used for the patrimony of a person upon sequestration. This too must be 'wound up', in this case by the trustee in sequestration.

[57]　See CHAPTER 21 above.

[58]　See the Damages (Scotland) Act 1976.

25.35   Side by side with the principle of active transmissibility is the principle of 'passive transmissibility'.[59] This means that the liabilities of the deceased continue as liabilities of the estate. *Death does not dissolve obligations.* If the deceased owed money, that obligation remains payable: 'It is a general rule that a personal obligation transmits against the personal representatives of the obliger.'[60] (As with active transmissibility, there are one or two exceptions.) It is for the executor to discharge the obligations. This is done by means of the assets. In other words, the executor pays debts by realising assets. It may be that there are sufficient assets in money form (for example, a bank account) to do this without having to sell anything. But the executor has power to sell assets, and must do so if necessary, because debts come first. The rights of the beneficiaries are to be satisfied only out of the *net* estate. The greater the debts, the less the beneficiaries take.[61] If the deceased died with more debts than assets – that is died insolvent – then the beneficiaries take nothing. But that is the worst that can happen. Neither the executor nor the beneficiaries have any *personal* obligation to pay the deceased's debts. If the value of the assets is insufficient to meet the claims of the creditors, then the creditors must grin and bear it.

Heritable and moveable

25.36   Whether an asset is heritable or moveable may make a difference. There are three ways this happens.
   (1) Legal rights are calculated on the net value of the moveable estate.[62]
   (2) Whether an asset is heritable or moveable can make a difference where cross-border issues are concerned.[63]
   (3) It makes a difference to which part of the estate pays off the debts.

Incidence of debts

25.37   As far as the creditors are concerned, it makes no difference which part of the estate is to be realised to meet their claims. No asset is exempt from the possibility that it must be realised to pay creditors. But for the beneficiaries, the issue can be important. Suppose that the estate consists of a house, which is bequeathed to Ivan, and a car, which is bequeathed to Jade. There are debts. Who suffers? Ivan, or Jade, or both? S(S)A 1964 is silent, leaving the topic to the common law.[64] The case law is

---

[59]   The 'active' and 'passive' sides of a patrimony are the assets and liabilities respectively: hence active and passive transmissibility.
[60]   *Morton's Trs v Aged Christian Friend Society* (1899) 2 F 82 at 87 per Lord Kinnear.
[61]   On larger estates inheritance tax is payable. But this book does not cover tax issues.
[62]   See PARA **26.4** below.
[63]   See PARAS **25.56–25.58** below.
[64]   S(S)A 1964, s 14(3).

mostly old and there has not been much academic discussion. The topic is underdeveloped and probably has lurking problems. The account below, taken with the discussion of the sub-topic of abatement in **CHAPTER 27**,[65] must be taken with that warning.

25.38 If a debt is secured against a particular asset, for instance a debt secured by standard security over a house, that asset is regarded as the fund out of which that debt is to be paid.[66] In the example just given, suppose that the house is worth £300,000; the car £30,000; and the debts are £290,000, all secured over the house. The house would have to be sold, and Ivan would receive the free proceeds – £10,000. Jade would get the car. (Alternatively, Ivan could choose to pay off the debt, and take the house.) Vary the example by increasing the debts to £310,000, all secured over the house. Both house and car would have to be sold. Jade would receive £20,000 and Ivan nothing. (If the debts amounted to £330,000 or more, neither Ivan or Jade would get a penny.)

25.39 Sometimes a debt is secured over two assets. In that case, both are burdened, in the ratio of their values.[67] Suppose that Alan has a debt of £72,000 which is secured both against his house, worth £160,000, and against a life assurance policy, worth £80,000. Then £48,000 of debt is ascribed to the house and £24,000 to the policy.

25.40 In calculating legal rights, all the debts, except those secured against heritable property, are notionally deducted from the moveable part of the estate. For example, Robert dies with moveables worth £200,000 and a house worth £200,000. He owes Sarah £30,000, secured on the house, £30,000 to Tom, secured on certain moveable assets and £40,000 to Una, unsecured. The net moveable estate for the purposes of calculating legal rights is not £170,000 (as one might expect) but £130,000. That is because legal rights are calculated on the basis of the moveable estate minus the 'moveable debts' and the 'moveable debts' are, roughly speaking, all debts except those secured over heritable property. Although this is how the value of legal rights is calculated, legal rights are not necessarily paid out of the moveable estate.[68]

25.41 In a testate case, debts reduce the value of the residuary legacy. Thus Jane leaves her house to Kate and the residue of her estate to Luke. The debts must be paid out of the residue. The only exception to that is if the debts, or part of them, are secured over the house. For example, suppose that the house is worth £300,000 and the residue of the estate is worth £200,000. There are two debts. The first, £100,000, is secured over the house. The second, £50,000 is not. Then Kate could choose to pay off the £100,000 and take the house, or she could choose that the house be sold, in which case she will receive £200,000. The other debt, £50,000, comes out of the residue. By contrast, if neither debt had been secured, both would have been charged against the residue.

---

[65]   See **PARAS 27.35–27.40** below.
[66]   See, e.g., *Stewart v Stewart* (1891) 19 R 310.
[67]   *Graham v Graham* (1898) 5 SLT 319.
[68]   See **PARA 26.8** below.

25.42 In some cases the debts may be so large, or the residue so small, that other legacies (over and above the legacy of residue) will be affected. In that case the other legacies are 'abated', which is to say scaled down so as to make it possible to pay the debts. The details of abatement are looked at elsewhere.[69]

Executory contracts to buy or sell: 'conversion'

25.43 John owns land. On Monday he contracts to sell it to Kate. On Tuesday he dies. At this stage his estate has two assets and one liability. They are:

(a) ownership of the land;

(b) the contractual right to be paid the price by Kate; and

(c) an obligation to convey the land to Kate, an obligation his executor must perform.[70]

It is usually said that the land is 'converted' into moveable property (i.e. the price). But the land does not become moveable. But the second asset, the right to the money, *is* moveable, and it is that asset, and not the land, that will be subject to the rights of John's beneficiaries.

25.44 Reverse the facts. John owns land. On Monday he contracts to sell it to Kate. On Tuesday she dies. Her estate has:

(a) a contractual right to acquire the land; and

(b) an obligation to pay the price.[71]

(It may also have the money for the purchase.) Her contractual right to the land is itself a heritable right, and will be treated as such for the purposes of her estate. However, since she has died the land is probably now not wanted, so her executor may try to negotiate with John to be released from the contract.

EXECUTRY

Introduction

25.45 The law of succession must deal not only with the question 'Who gets what?' but also with that of 'How do they get it?'. Assets have to move from the patrimony of the person who has died into the patrimonies of the living. The 'how' question is thus in a sense one of conveyancing. This is a large subject and only a brief account is given here.

---

[69] See PARAS **27.35–27.40** below.

[70] See, e.g., *Chiesley v His Sisters* (1704) Mor 5531.

[71] See, e.g., *Ramsay v Ramsay* (1887) 15 R 25.

Executors

25.46 In some legal systems death itself operates as an immediate and complete transfer to those entitled to succeed.[72] The 'how' question is thus easy to answer in theory, though in practice there are evidential problems and also complications caused by the need to pay creditors. In some other systems the transfer is direct but not immediate. Historically, Scotland has experimented with both systems, but nowadays we route everything through the executor.[73] Thus whereas in many legal systems an executor is an optional extra, in Scots law the executor is, in most cases at least, essential. We use an executor even in an intestate case.

25.47 There are two sorts of executor.
(1) An 'executor-nominate' is appointed by the deceased in the testament.
(2) An 'executor-dative' is appointed by the sheriff.
The sheriff has administrative oversight of all executors. Strictly, he or she is acting not as sheriff but as commissary; however, the post of commissary is nowadays always held by the sheriff, and commissary courts are physically the same as sheriff courts, and the administration of them is almost completed fused. If more than one person seeks appointment as executor-dative, there is an order of priority.[74] An executor-dative is needed if there is no testament, or if there is one but it does not make an effective appointment. As with trustees, a person nominated as executor is free to decline the office. The order of the sheriff appointing someone as executor-dative is called 'decerniture'. An executor-dative, unlike an executor-nominate, must *find caution*, obtain a guarantee from someone acceptable to the court (in practice an insurance company) that if he or she embezzles the estate then the cautioner will make good the loss.

Confirmation

25.48 The executor now prepares an inventory of the estate. All heritable properties, investments and bank accounts will be separately listed but furnishings can normally be lumped together. Each item must be given an estimated value. The executor then petitions the sheriff to be 'confirmed'. The inventory is submitted as part of the petition. The 'confirmation' is a decree authorising the executor to administer the estate: the right of administration does not exist before confirmation.[75] For example, a debtor of the deceased cannot be required to pay, except by the confirmed executor. Thus without confirmation the estate cannot be 'ingathered' i.e. brought under the executor's control.

---

[72] E.g. Germany.
[73] There are one or two qualifications to this remark. The only important one concerns survivorship special destinations, for which see PARAS **29.8–29.10** below.
[74] See, e.g., *Russo v Russo* 1998 SLT (Sh Ct) 32.
[75] That is at least the basic rule.

25.49 The executor's authority only extends to the inventoried assets. An executor who later discovers other assets must petition for the wonderfully named 'eik', whereby the sheriff authorises the executor to administer the additional assets. There can be many eiks as are necessary. (But in most cases no eik is needed.) The inventory must also be submitted to HM Revenue and Customs for inheritance tax purposes. Once confirmed, the executor can sue for debts owing to the deceased, can convey specific assets to beneficiaries, can pay beneficiaries, and can sell. Sale may be necessary to raise money to pay debts, to pay inheritance tax and to pay legal rights claimants or pecuniary legatees.[76] An executor can also complete title to registered property (land, company shares etc) in his or her own name, *qua* executor, but this would be unusual.

The executor as a trustee

25.50 An executor is in a sense the heir of the whole estate but not for his or her own benefit.[77] In practice, however, the executor may be and almost always is, one of the beneficiaries, and sometimes is the sole beneficiary. An executor is thus like a trustee. Whether an executry is in truth a trust is a point of some difficulty. For most purposes it is, both at common law[78] and under the Trusts (Scotland) Acts, which define 'trustee' to include executors.[79]

Insolvency

25.51 Occasionally, the debts are so great that they exceed the value of the estate. There are two ways of handling an insolvent estate. One is for a creditor to be appointed as executor-creditor.[80] This tends to be quick and cheap. The other is for the estate to be sequestrated, and a trustee in sequestration appointed.[81] If an executor is confirmed in the ordinary way and later realises that the estate is insolvent, he or she must have the estate sequestrated.[82]

Personal liability of the executor?

25.52 The general principle is that neither the executor nor the beneficiaries have any personal liability for the debts of the deceased. The creditors can sue the executor,

---

[76] For legal rights and pecuniary legacies, see **CHAPTER 26**.
[77] The executor has sometimes been called a fideicommissary heir (*haeres fideicommissarius*). The term is accurate.
[78] See, e.g., Erskine III, 9, 42; Bell *Commentaries* II, 80; *Taylor v Ferguson* 1912 SC 165.
[79] T(S)A 1921, s 2, read with S(S)A 1964, s 20.
[80] *Smith's Trs v Grant* (1862) 24 D 1142 is the leading case.
[81] Bankruptcy (Scotland) Act 1985, s 5(3).
[82] Bankruptcy (Scotland) Act 1985, s 8.

but their claims are against the executor only as such. The executor has two patrimonies: his or her own general patrimony, and the executry estate, and it is only against the latter that creditors of the deceased can enforce their claims. The executor can incur personal liability only through fault.

The six-months rule

25.53 Since creditors have priority over beneficiaries, there is a practical problem. It might take years before all creditors came forward, and it would be unfair to the beneficiaries if they had to wait for years before the distribution was made. But equally it would be unfair to the creditors if the executor could wind up the estate more or less immediately, without waiting to see the full extent of the debts.

25.54 So the law sets a period of six months, starting from the day of death.[83] Once the six months are up, the executor is free to wind up the estate on the basis of the debts as known at that time. If the executor distributes the estate within the six-month period, this is done at his or her own risk, in the sense that if new debts come to light the executor may be personally liable for them. Once the six-month period has elapsed, the executor can wind up the estate without having to worry about unknown creditors. Suppose that after seven months the estate appears to be solvent, and the executor at that stage distributes the estate. A week afterwards, another creditor turns up. The executor has no personal liability to that creditor. The six-month rule thus means that:

    (a) no creditor can insist on payment within the period; and

    (b) no beneficiary can force the executor to pay, or convey, within the period.

Personal liability of others?

25.55 Non-lawyers often suppose that a deceased person's family is responsible for ensuring that the debts are paid. That is not the law. If a person dies with debts, no one has any personal liability to pay those debts. The executor is liable, but only as executor, for the executry assets. Of course, a family member might be liable for some special reason. For instance, he or she might have been a cautioner for a loan to the deceased. Married couples often take out loans on the basis of solidary (joint and several) liability. But, apart from such special cases, there is no liability. There are two qualifications to the foregoing.

    (1) If the executor distributes the estate to the beneficiaries and it later turns out that a creditor has not been paid, the creditor can recover from the beneficiaries, but no beneficiary can be made to pay more than he or she received.

---

[83]   Act of Sederunt of 28 February 1662 anent Executors-creditors.

(2) The other is the quaintly named doctrine of vitious intromission. If someone other than the executor 'intromits' with the deceased's property, that person thereby is deemed to become a sort of cautioner for the debts. This can be seen as a penalty, deterring people from unlawful intromission.

INTERNATIONAL PRIVATE LAW

25.56 Scottish international private law says that moveables devolve according to the *lex domicilii* and immoveables according to the *lex situs*.[84] So if Lucy, who is Scottish, dies with a house in France, its furnishings, a bank account in Italy, a house in Scotland, its furnishings, and investments and moveables in Scotland and England, Scottish international private law would say that the house in France devolves according to French law but that everything else devolves according to Scots law.

25.57 This split approach is known as 'scission'. Some other countries have a similar approach, while others adopt the 'unitary' approach, meaning that one and the same succession law applies to the whole estate. The unitary approach is simpler. Countries that adopt it usually make the nationality of the deceased the test.

25.58 Because different countries have different approaches, conflicts can arise. Our approach can easily lead to conflicts. Hamish is a UK citizen of Scottish domicile. He dies. He has some moveables and land in Scotland, and some in Italy. Scots international private law says that the land in Scotland, and all the moveables, are subject to Scots succession law, but that the land in Italy is subject to Italian succession law. Italian international private law says that the whole estate, including the land in Italy, is subject to Scots succession law. So for the land in Italy, each system points to the other. Take another case. Francesca is an Italian citizen of Italian domicile. She dies. She has some moveables and land in Italy, and some land in Scotland. Scots international private law says that the land in Italy, and all the moveables, are subject to Italian succession law, but that the land in Scotland is subject to Scots succession law. Italian international private law says that the whole estate is subject to Italian succession law. So for the land in Scotland, each system points to itself. All this is incoherent.

FURTHER READING

Currie, J G *Confirmation of Executors* (8th edn, by E M Scobbie, 1995).

Gordon, A *Succession* (2nd edn, 2007).

Hayton, D J *European Succession Laws* (3rd edn, 2002).

Hiram *Succession* chs 1–2.

---

[84] See further E B Crawford and J M Carruthers *International Private Law in Scotland* (2nd edn, 2006) ch 18.

Macdonald *Succession* chs 1–3 and 13–14.

McLaren, J *The Law of Wills and Succession* (3rd edn, 1894), with supplementary volume by D Oswald Dykes (1934).

Meston, M C *The Succession (Scotland) Act 1964* (5th edn, 2002).

O'Donnell, D (ed) *Meston's Succession Opinions* (2000).

Reid, K G C, De Waal, M J and Zimmermann, R (eds) *Exploring the Law of Succession* (2007).

Chapter 26

Legal rights

INTRODUCTION

General

26.1 The relict[1] (if any) and the children (if any) have indefeasible rights, called, rather oddly, legal rights. Civil partners have the same rights as spouses: the term 'relict' is here used to cover them too. Legal rights are common law rights, though somewhat modified by statute. They are indefeasible in the sense that they cannot be defeated by testament. So if Norma has a husband and three children, and she leaves

---

[1]   A gender-neutral term meaning 'widow or widower'.

everything to charity, the charity will not take everything. It will take everything that remains after the legal rights of her husband and children have been satisfied. Other relatives do not have this protection from disinheritance. Had Norma been single and childless, the charity would have received everything, and her relatives nothing. Those without spouse (or civil partner) or issue have complete testamentary freedom.

26.2 Legal rights, in one form or another, are common round the world, but in Scots law there is one particularly unusual feature, which is that legal rights are based on the moveable part of the estate only. By contrast almost all other countries that have legal rights make no such distinction.[2] It is difficult to defend the Scottish system, which makes legal rights depend on the lottery of the respective sizes of the two parts of the estate at death. Xerxes and Yvonne each have money to invest. Xerxes invests on the stock exchange and Yvonne invests by buying a flat to let out. It is hard to see why this choice should affect the rights of their respective families. Indeed, if Yvonne decides to buy the flat via a company she sets up, Yvonne Residential Investments (Lanark) Ltd, a company with one shareholder (her) and one asset (the flat), when she dies the investment is, like Xerxes's, moveable, because company shares are moveable. (As for the flat, she did not own it: her company did.) So her decision to take title through the company has arbitrary effects on succession rights.

Jus relictae, jus relicti and legitim

26.3 The legal right of the relict is called the relict's right or, more commonly, *jus relictae* for a widow or *jus relicti* for a widower. It is a right to the value of a fixed fraction of the moveable part of the estate. If the deceased left issue[3] then the fraction is one-third. If the deceased left no issue, the fraction is one-half. The legal right of the children is called bairns' part or, more commonly, legitim.[4] Legitim is the same in amount as relict's right: one-third of the value of the moveables if there is a relict, or one-half if there is no relict.

Example

26.4 Suppose that Donald dies, estranged from his second wife, Eva, by whom he had no children, and from his two children, Flora and Gordon, by his divorced first wife. His testament leaves everything to his brother, Harry. Donald's net estate consists of a house worth £200,000, contents worth £50,000 and investments worth £100,000.[5] Despite being disinherited, Eva will receive £50,000 and Flora and Gordon will receive £25,000 each. This is because the value of the moveable estate is

---

[2] Jersey, like Scotland, applies legal rights only to moveables.
[3] 'Issue' means children or remoter descendants.
[4] From *legitima portio*.
[5] 'Net estate' means the estate net of debts and taxes.

£150,000. Eva is entitled to the value of one-third of that. A further third (called the 'legitim fund') goes to the children. Harry will take the rest. Donald's first wife, assuming that she is alive, has no claim. Divorce, like death, dissolves marriage. Moreover, the fact that the children are not children of Donald's marriage with Eva is irrelevant. The calculation of legal rights is the same whether or not Eva is the mother of Flora and Gordon.

26.5 Suppose that Eva had died shortly before her husband. In that case neither she nor her estate would take anything, for the dead cannot inherit.[6] Flora and Gordon would have received £37,500 each. Harry would have taken the rest. Thus legal rights are calculated, like other succession rights, on the state of affairs at the moment of death. For example, suppose that Jill has a husband and a daughter. If she dies when they are alive, they have their legal rights. But if they were to die before her, she would have complete testamentary freedom.

The dead's part

26.6 The expression 'dead's part' is often encountered. This term means that part of the estate which the deceased was able to dispose of by testament. So the dead's part is the net estate minus the legal rights claims, if any.

Applicability

26.7 Legal rights operate in both testate and intestate succession. The latter fact is perhaps illogical since in intestate succession the estate goes to the family anyway. It is thus in the context of testate succession that legal rights are important, and this chapter concentrates on that situation.

LEGAL RIGHTS ARE A CLAIM FOR MONEY

26.8 In some countries legal rights give a co-ownership share. This can be rather awkward in practice. In other countries, including Scotland, legal rights are rights to receive money. Thus the moveables merely form the basis for calculating how much money is due.[7] Take the following case. Mary is unmarried. She has one child, Norman. Her estate consists of shares in Royal Bank of Scotland plc (worth £80,000) and some land (worth £200,000).[8] Her testament says: 'I leave my shares to Oliver and the residue of my estate to Paula.' The legitim fund is £40,000. Oliver receives the shares. The legitim fund is £40,000, which goes to Norman. To find the money to pay him, the executor will have to sell the land. Paula will receive a cheque for

---

[6] See PARAS **25.15–25.18** above.

[7] See, e.g., *Cameron's Trs v McLean* 1917 SC 416.

[8] In practice there would probably be other property, but the example is for the sake of illustration.

£160,000. Thus *immoveable* property has borne the burden of the legal rights. This is because residue is what (if anything) is left over *after* all other claims on the estate have been met.[9] Put another way, residue must abate before special legacies.[10]

PRIORITY

26.9 Legal rights claimants are thus, from one point of view, creditors. Indeed, there is a traditional maxim that 'the relict and the bairn are heirs among creditors, and creditors among heirs'.[11] That means that (a) as between them and actual creditors, they are treated as beneficiaries, so that their claims are postponed to the claims of creditors but (b) as between them and other beneficiaries they are treated as creditors, in that they have claims for money that must be met before other beneficiaries can receive anything.[12]

26.10 This priority operates in an unqualified manner in testate succession, which is the main focus of this chapter. In testate succession the order is:
- (i) debts and taxes;
- (ii) legal rights; and
- (iii) legacies.

In intestate succession the position is more complicated. There, the order of priority is:
- (i) debts and taxes;
- (ii) prior rights;
- (iii) relict's right;
- (iv) cohabitant's right;
- (v) legitim; and
- (vi) free estate.

It will be seen that in intestate succession legitim is not only postponed to prior rights (which are in favour of the relict), but is even postponed to the cohabitant's right. In intestate succession it is common for the amount available for legitim to be zero. That leads to a paradox. In testate succession the idea of disinheriting one's children is regarded as so shocking that the law forbids it. But in intestate succession such disinheritance is (except in larger estates) not only permitted but indeed compulsory – by force of the law itself.[13]

---

9   For legacies of residue, see PARA **27.27** below.
10   For abatement, see PARAS **27.35–27.40** below.
11   *MacGregor's Exrx v MacGregor's Trs* 1935 SC 13 at 18 per Lord President Clyde.
12   'Before' here does not refer to time of payment but to priority of right.
13   Because a relict may be better off in intestacy (because of the priority that prior rights have over legitim), if a spouse is able to convert a testate estate into an intestate one, he or she may wish to do so. For this odd idea of 'artificial intestacy', see *Kerr* 1968 SLT (Sh Ct) 61 and PARA **29.28** below.

RENUNCIATION

26.11 Rights of succession can, like other rights in private law, be renounced. Legal rights are, in fact, often declined. There are two main reasons. The first is altruism, the second is the opposite. First, altruism. Suppose that Jack is married to Jill. They have two children, Dick and Jane. Jack's testament leaves everything to Jill. Indeed, it is common for one spouse to bequeath everything, or almost everything, to the other. It is very likely that Jack and Jill both made testaments at the same time, in mirror terms. Dick and Jane could claim legitim. But that would mean claiming against their own mother. In most cases they would not do this, but would, instead, renounce their legitim. But suppose that Jill was not their mother but their stepmother. In that case they might feel differently.

26.12 The other main reason for renunciation is the doctrine of approbate and reprobate, which is discussed below.[14]

26.13 If a person who is entitled to legal rights renounces them, this does not benefit anyone who does opt to claim. Alan and Beth are married. They have two children, Carla and Donald. Alan dies. His net moveable estate is £120,000. Beth renounces her relict's right. Carla renounces legitim. Donald claims legitim. How much does he receive? £20,000, that is, one-half of one-third of the value of the net moveable estate. It is the same sum as he would have received if both Beth and Carla had claimed legal rights. Or suppose that Beth and Donald claim legal rights, but Carla does not. Then Beth would receive £40,000 and Donald would receive £20,000.

26.14 What has just been said is true if the renunciation happens *after* the death. It is also competent to renounce legal rights before the death, although in practice this seldom happens. But if it does happen the rule is different. In that case the renunciation *does* benefit those persons who do claim legal rights. Suppose that Carla renounces before Alan's death. Beth and Donald both claim legal rights. Beth receives £40,000 and Donald also receives £40,000. Or suppose that Beth and Donald both renounce before Alan's death, but Carla claims. Carla then receives £60,000.

APPROBATE AND REPROBATE

26.15 People who die testate usually leave much or all of their estate to their family. So in testate cases it is common to find that those with legal rights are also legatees. For instance, Claire's testament leaves £10,000 to each of her children, David, Eilidh and Frank, and the rest to her husband Greg. Each of those four persons also has legal rights. Can they take both? Or must they take one or the other? Can they perhaps choose? The law is that they can choose, but they cannot take both. If David takes the legacy he must renounce his legitim. If he decides to take his legitim he must give reject the legacy. This rule – that they can choose one or the other but

---

[14] See PARAS **26.15–26.19** below.

not both – is known by the curious name of 'approbate and reprobate'. To accept the legacy is to 'approbate' the testament and to take legal rights instead is to 'reprobate' the testament. The rule is that you can approbate or you can reprobate but you cannot do both. It is a common law one. There existed certain qualifications to the doctrine, but S(S)A 1964, s 13 now puts the rule into statutory form, without exceptions.

26.16 Usually it will be obvious whether the legacy or legal rights will be worth more. However, occasionally it is not so clear. Suppose that the testator, Tom, provides that his second wife, Wendy, is to have a liferent of the house and his daughter Diana the fee. Diana may hesitate between accepting the fee or claiming legitim. If her stepmother, Wendy, is old and in poor health it may be better to take the fee. If Wendy is young and healthy it may be better to take the legitim. The beneficiary is allowed time to decide.[15] Of course, it must not be assumed that people will necessarily decide to maximise what they take.

26.17 Sarah's testament gives a trust liferent to her elder daughter, Tara, and the fee to her younger daughter Ursula. Tara claims legal rights. The law is complex in relation to what happens to the liferent. In some cases the fiar simply takes the liferent fund, as if the liferenter had died. But in others the liferent continues without a liferenter, as a 'shadow liferent', and the proceeds are used to make 'equitable compensation' to compensate those who have suffered by Tara's claiming of legitim.[16]

26.18 Claiming legal rights means forfeiture of any legacy. But it does not mean the loss of other rights. Nicholas's estate is £240,000, all moveable. He has two children, Oliver and Prunella. He is single. His testament leaves a legacy of £80,000 to Oliver, £80,000 to charity and the residue to Quinten, Nicholas's brother. Prunella is not mentioned in the testament. Quinten predeceases Nicholas. Prunella claims legitim. The legitim fund is £120,000.[17] Prunella takes half of this, i.e. £60,000. Oliver accepts the legacy. The residue is worth £20,000. As the residuary legatee (Quinten) predeceased the testator, this legacy fails to take effect, and so the residue falls into intestacy.[18]

26.19 *Naismith v Boyes*[19] held that if X accepts a legacy, and if the estate is partially intestate, the doctrine of approbate and reprobate does not bar X from claiming legal rights in relation to the intestate estate. How much? Neither *Naismith* nor later cases entirely clarify this issue, but it seems that Oliver takes half (because he is one of two siblings) of a half (because no relict), i.e. £5,000. Prunella does not put

---

[15] *Stewart v Bruce's Trs* (1898) 25 R 965.

[16] See, e.g., *Macfarlane's Trs v Oliver* (1882) 9 R 1138 and *Munro's Trs, Petitioners* 1971 SLT 313. See J Murray 'Some of the Problems of Equitable Compensation' 1995 *SLT (News)* 59.

[17] As there is no relict.

[18] This is called the lapse of a legacy. In certain special cases the predecease of the legatee does not result in lapse: see paras **27.44–27.51** below.

[19] (1899) 1 F (HL) 79.

her scoop in again at this stage, because she has already taken all her *legitim*. What is left is £15,000. That goes equally to the two heirs in intestacy, Oliver and Prunella, under S(S)A 1964, s 2.[20]

THREE MISCONCEPTIONS ABOUT LEGAL RIGHTS

26.20   There are three common misconceptions about legal rights. The first is that claiming legal rights means a court action. It does not. Of course, any estate could end up in litigation. But it seldom happens, and there is no more reason why claiming legal rights should mean litigation than any other claim on an estate. The second misconception is that claiming legal rights will convert the estate from a testate one to an intestate one. It does not. The third is that legitim can be claimed only by younger children, such as those under 16, or that it is in some way a dependency-based right. Legitim exists in favour of adult children just as much as young children. If Mark dies at the age of 95, leaving one child, Naomi, aged 70, Naomi is entitled to legitim.

MORE EXAMPLES

Example 1

26.21

Jane, who is single, dies leaving heritage worth £100,000 and moveables worth £300,000. She is single and has one son, Kevin. Jane's testament leaves the house to Kevin and the residue to Jane's lover, Larry. Kevin claims legitim (£150,000). That means he must renounce the legacy of the house. Larry gets the whole estate, minus £150,000.

Example 2

26.22

Walter dies. He is single and has two daughters, Alice and Beth. He had heritage worth £100,000, and moveables worth £300,000. His testament leaves the heritage to Alice and Beth equally and also leaves £100,000 to Alice. The residue is left to Walter's brother, Charles. Beth claims legitim, and thus renounces the legacy. Alice claims the legacy, and thus renounces legitim. The legitim fund is £150,000. Beth gets half of this, £75,000. Alice gets half of the heritage plus £100,000. Charles gets the rest.

---

[20]   See PARAS **28.22–28.26** below.

REPRESENTATION IN LEGITIM: *PER STIRPES* AND *PER CAPITA* DIVISION

26.23 If a child has predeceased, leaving children (i.e. grandchildren of the *de cujus*), then those children step into their parent's shoes.[21] Suppose that Alice has two children, Brenda and Charles. Brenda has two children, David and Ellen. Charles has one, Fraser. Brenda dies on 1 March. Alice dies on 3 March. The legitim fund is £60,000. Charles takes £30,000 and David and Ellen take £15,000 each. (Assuming that all claim legitim.) David and Ellen are said to *represent* their mother.

26.24 Why is the legitim fund divided in this way, and not £20,000 to each of the three people entitled? Well, it does not have to be done that way. It depends. The type of division just illustrated is a division *per stirpes*.[22] The opposite method would be a division *per capita*.[23] The rule is this: if all the claimants are of equal propinquity (nearness of kinship) to the deceased then the division is *per capita*, but if of unequal propinquity the division is *per stirpes*. In the example just given, the claimants were of unequal propinquity, because Charles was the child of the deceased, but David and Ellen were the grandchildren. Change the facts a little and suppose that Charles, as well as Brenda, had died before Alice. Then there would have been three legitim claimants: David, Ellen and Fraser. The division would have been *per capita* and so each would have received £20,000. (These rules about representation also apply to intestate succession rights.[24])

26.25 There is representation in *legitim* but not in the relict's right. Arthur and Guinevere are married. Guinevere dies on Monday, leaving one child, Henry, from a previous relationship. On Tuesday, Arthur dies. Henry cannot claim the relict's right that his mother would have had if the dates of death had been reversed.

COLLATIO INTER LIBEROS

26.26 Sometimes a potential legitim claimant will have been given a substantial gift by the deceased during the latter's life. The law may regard this as a 'collatable advance', a sort of pre-payment of legitim, and if so it must be brought into account, to achieve fairness as between the various legitim claimants. This is the doctrine of *collatio inter liberos*.[25] Suppose that Jack dies, leaving a relict, Rebecca, and three sons, Tom Dick and Harry. There is heritable property of £300,000 and moveable property of £180,000. He leaves the heritable property to Rebecca and everything else to charity. The sons claim legitim. Tom had a collatable advance of £12,000. To claim legitim Tom must notionally add this to the legitim fund. The notional legitim

---

[21]   S(S)A 1964, s 11.
[22]   The Latin word *stirps* (plural *stirpes*) means a stock, or family.
[23]   The Latin word *caput* (plural *capita*) means a head.
[24]   See PARA **28.26** below.
[25]   Latin, meaning 'collation between the children'.

fund is therefore £60,000 + £12,000 = £72,000. Thus, Dick and Harry take £24,000 each, and Tom takes £24,000 less £12,000 = £12,000. The charity receives the rest of Jack's estate.

26.27 One difficulty with applying the doctrine is knowing what counts as a collatable advance. The typical case in the earlier authorities was the 'tocher' – a settlement given on marriage. Only gifts of moveables count[26] and, according to Stair, only money gifts count.[27] Any provision made by virtue of the parent's alimentary obligations is excluded from collation.

26.28 If we change the figures in the example, Tom could end up worse off. For example, suppose that the collatable advance was not £12,000 but £60,000. If that is added to the legitim fund, the result is £120,000. Divided three ways, each brother would be due £40,000. But since Tom would have paid in £60,000, he would suffer a net loss of £20,000. But that does not happen, because there is an additional rule that *a person who opts not to claim legitim does not have to collate*. So Tom would be free to refuse legitim. In that case he would not collate. The legitim fund would remain £60,000. Dick and Harry would each take a third = £20,000 each. (Only a third: as was seen above, if someone rejects legal rights, that does not benefit other legal rights claimants.) Tom will receive nothing from his father's estate – but he will keep the £60,000 that his father gave him.

26.29 If there is only one legitim claimant, there is no collation. Take this case. Maud's estate is £120,000, all moveable. She is single and has two children, Natasha and Olivia. Maud's testament leaves £20,000 to Natasha and £60,000 to Olivia, and the residue to charity. Natasha renounces the legacy and claims legitim. Olivia renounces legitim and claims the legacy. The legitim fund is £60,000, so Natasha takes £30,000. Now, suppose that she had had a collatable advance of £12,000. Does this mean that the legitim fund is £72,000, so that Natasha receives half of that (£36,000) minus the advance = only £24,000? The answer is 'no': being the sole legitim claimant, she does not collate. (She is the sole claimant because it is in Olivia's interests to accept the legacy.) Natasha receives £30,000 legitim and keeps the £12,000 that she received earlier.[28]

CIRCUMVENTING LEGAL RIGHTS

26.30 It may be possible to defeat legal rights. Sheila has a husband. Tom, and two daughters, Una and Vera. She wishes to disinherit Tom and Vera and to leave everything to Una. Because of legal rights, she cannot do this absolutely. Is there any way round legal rights? One way is to divest herself of assets while she is still alive. For instance,

---

[26] *Duke of Buccleugh v Earl of Tweeddale* (1677) Mor 2369.
[27] Stair III, 8, 45.
[28] *Coat's Trs v Coats* 1914 SC 744.

she could transfer assets into a trust, with the trustees holding for her in liferent and for Una in fee. Another possibility is that she could buy an annuity.

26.31   An alternative way is to minimise her moveable estate and to maximise her heritable estate. For instance, suppose that she has stock market investments worth £500,000. She could sell those and use the proceeds to buy flats as an investment. The flats, unlike the stock market investments, would not be subject to legal rights. (But if she bought the flats in the name of a company, the trick would not work, because what would be in her patrimony would not be the flats themselves but her shares in her company, and shares are moveable.)

26.32   Yet another method which, however, is possible only in certain types of case, is 'artificial intestacy'.[29]

FURTHER READING

Hiram *Succession* ch 3.

Macdonald *Succession* paras 4.34–4.69.

---

[29]   See PARA **26.10** above and PARAS **28.28–28.29** below.

Chapter 27

Testate succession

TESTAMENTS

Introduction

27.1   A will or testament[1] is a document saying what is to happen to the granter's estate on death.[2] Here is an example.

'I ALEXANDER ROBERTSON GILLIES residing at fifty-four Middleton Street Jedburgh being desirous of settling the succession to my means and estate after my decease[3] HEREBY NOMINATE and APPOINT[4] my son THOMAS WOODHEAD GILLIES, residing at 50 Macaulay Place, Berwick-upon-Tweed, and HUGO PONTIFEX SAGAMORE, Writer to the Signet, 88 Scotland Street, Edinburgh, and the survivor and acceptor of them, to be my executors and trustees; and I ASSIGN DISPONE AND CONVEY[5] to them my whole means and estate heritable and moveable real and personal of whatever nature and wherever situated which shall belong to me at the time of my death including without prejudice to the foregoing generality all means and estate held or which may then be held by me under special destinations and all means and estate of which I may have or may then have power of disposal or appointment; But these presents are granted for the following purposes only, namely:– (In the first place) for payment of my debts and funeral expenses and the expenses of administering the executry hereby created; (In the second place) for payment or making over of the following legacies, that is to say (primo) to the Scottish Association for the Deaf, Moray House, 31 Holyrood Road, Edinburgh, the sum of four thousand pounds; (secundo) to the Scottish Musicians Benevolent Fund, 9 Branziert Road, Glasgow, three thousand pounds; (tertio) to the Royal National Mission to Deep Sea Fishermen, 3 Queen Margaret Road, Glasgow, one thousand five hundred pounds; (quarto) to my nephew Oliver St John of 1 Hope

---

[1]   The traditional Scottish term is 'testament' but 'will' is now the word used by non-lawyers and generally by lawyers too, though some – especially some judges – are conservative. In English law there is a distinction (not always observed in practice) between testaments and wills: a 'testament' deals with personal property and a 'will' with real property. Hence a document dealing with both is a 'will and testament'. This expression is sometimes copied in Scotland. 'Last will' comes from Latin *ultima voluntas*.

[2]   A 'trust disposition and settlement' is a testament that contains a clause conveying the estate to the executors as trustees for the beneficiaries. There is in modern law no difference between this and an ordinary testament.

[3]   The dozen or so preceding words demonstrate 'testamentary intent'. Such intent can be inferred from a document as a whole but it is usual to have express words.

[4]   The nomination of an executor (or joint executors) is normal. But a testament can be valid without such a nomination.

[5]   This conveyance of the estate to the executors is not necessary but it is common, and for certain purposes can be useful.

[6]   This legacy of books is a special legacy, i.e. a legacy of identifiable assets. The legacies of money are general legacies.

Street, Durham, all my books;[6] (quinto) to my god-daughter Eleanor Duplessis of 22 Pym Street, Brechin, ten thousand pounds; (In the third place)[7] to pay and make over the whole residue of my estate to my daughter Janet Mary Gillies or Godwin of 21 St Andrew Square, Peebles, and to my said son Thomas Woodhead Gillies equally between them; DECLARING that should any of the beneficiaries hereunder predecease me leaving lawful issue I direct my executors to pay and make over to such issue *per stirpes* the legacy or share of my estate which his her or parent would have taken; FURTHER DECLARING that in the event of any beneficiary hereunder being under legal incapacity by means of non-age or by law otherwise incapacitated my executors shall pay and make over the legacy or share of my estate to which such beneficiary is entitled to his or her legal representative or guardian or guardians or to any other person who may be willing to act as guardian although not legally appointed, the receipt and discharge of such legal representative or guardian or guardians (legal or otherwise) being a full and sufficient discharge to my executors; WITH POWER to my executors to appoint one of their number to act as solicitors in the executry hereby created at the usual professional remuneration; And I desire that my body may be cremated;[8] And I revoke all former testamentary writings executed by me:[9] IN WITNESS WHEREOF I have subscribed these presents typewritten on this and the preceding page at Edinburgh on the twenty-fourth day of January in the year two thousand and ten in the presence of Suzanne Elvenstone of 88 Scotland Street, Edinburgh.

S Elvenstone, witness   *Alex. R. Gillies*

Testamentary capacity

27.2 At common law girls attained testamentary capacity at 12 and boys at 14. This has been changed to 12 for both girls and boys.[10] Of course, few people of that age make wills. Recent research shows the percentage of those in each age group who have made a will:[11]

18-24	25-34	35-44	45-54	55-64	65+
4%	14%	30%	40%	52%	69%

27.3 Loss of general capacity, for instance by reason of senility, will mean loss of testamentary capacity. This can be unfortunate. Mary makes a will when she is 70. When she is 80 she becomes senile. She dies when she is 90. By that time the

---

7 Here we come to the legacy of the residue.

8 A testator cannot insist on cremation, though, conversely, cannot veto it.

9 The revocatory clause. It is not essential, but its absence can occasionally cause difficulties.

10 Age of Legal Capacity (Scotland) Act 1991, s 2(2).

11 S O'Neill *Wills and Awareness of Inheritance Rights in Scotland* (Scottish Consumer Council, 2006).

provisions of her testament may have become inappropriate. But they cannot now be changed.

Execution

27.4   The law on execution is dealt with elsewhere.[12] The one speciality for testaments is that while signature at the end is sufficient for *validity*, for *probativity* the granter (but not the witness) must sign each sheet.[13] Forgery is a particular danger because the main potential challenger is dead when the document comes to light. If a testament is improbative, there is a special affidavit procedure for establishing that it was validly executed.[14] In practice courts are lenient towards the home-made testaments. Thus 'Connie' and 'Mum' have both been upheld as valid subscriptions.[15] But there are limits to this lenience. In *McLay v Farrell*,[16] Jane McLay left this:

> 'I leave to
> Lizzie McLay Farrell £50
> C Herken £50
> Robert Farrell £20
> *Jane McLay*
> All to Anne McLay'

27.5   Then, as now, the granter's signature had to be at the end. So the last line (which perhaps meant that the residue[17] was to go to Anne McLay) could not be given effect.

27.6   The international private law is regulated by the Wills Act 1963, which says that 'a will shall be treated as properly executed if its execution conformed to the internal law in force in the territory where it was executed, or in the territory where, at the time of its execution or of the testator's death, he was domiciled or had his habitual residence, or in a state of which, at either of those times, he was a national'.[18]

Codicils, adoption and execution on the testator's behalf

27.7   A codicil is a later document that varies a testament. The rules for execution are the same. In practice it can be difficult working out what the combined effect is

---

[12]   See **CHAPTER 30** below.
[13]   RoW(S)A 1995, s 3(2).
[14]   RoW(S)A 1995, s 4. In practice this is simply done as part of the application for confirmation: see RoW(S)A 1995, s 4(4).
[15]   *Draper v Thomason* 1954 SC 136; *Rhodes v Peterson* 1972 SLT 98. These cases pre-date RoW(S)A 1995 but would have been decided the same way under the current law. See RoW(S)A 1995, s 7. See also below **PARA 27.10** below
[16]   1950 SC 149.
[17]   The residue means the rest of the estate. A legacy of residue may, according to circumstances, be very little, or be the bulk of the estate.
[18]   Wills Act 1963, s 1. See also the Administration of Justice Act 1982, ss 27–28.

supposed to be, and so solicitors usually recommend making a new will rather than using a codicil.[19]

27.8   The concept of adoption is a general one in the law of execution of deeds.[20] A striking example from the law of succession is *Davidson v Convy*,[21] where the deceased left an envelope with 'My will: Agnes Bess Sim' on it. Inside there was a sheet of paper of a testamentary nature but it was unsigned. It was held, perhaps a little generously, that the envelope was a validly executed testament which adopted the sheet of paper.

27.9   Finally, mention should be made of the testament being executed on behalf of the testator.[22] This is discussed elsewhere[23] but is worth mentioning here because testaments are often made by the dying, and the dying are sometimes unable to use a pen.

Concluded testamentary intent

27.10   To be valid, a juridical act needs to be based on intention. In most areas of law, juridical acts involve some overt action involving at least one other person, such as the communication of a contractual offer, or getting married, or registering a title in the Land Register. The overt action is powerful (albeit not conclusive) evidence of intention. But a testament is not effected by communication or delivery or registration. It can sit in the testator's desk until he or she dies. So the question of intention needs to be discovered from the four corners of the document itself. How does one distinguish a true testament from mere musings or provisional thoughts? (Testamentary musings are very common.) Usually it is obvious.[24] Signature is a strong indicator of intent. But sometimes there can be doubt. The document must exhibit 'concluded testamentary intent' if it is to receive effect, but judging this is not an exact science. In *Draper v Thomason*[25] Constance Tupper wrote a letter to her sister, with the following in it:

> ' ... By the way, while I'm speaking of dying! should anything happen to me (which it will one day) I haven't made a will but everything I have is for Billy, knowing he will do the right thing. Connie.'

It was held that this exhibited concluded testamentary effect, so that the letter was a valid testament. In another case[26] Evelyn Peterson wrote a letter to her daughter:

---

19   In *Burns' Trs v McKenna* 1940 SC 489 the trustee left a testament followed by 49 codicils.
20   Another example is under the pre-RoW(S)A 1995 law, when documents were 'adopted as holograph'. See **PARA 30.51** below.
21   2003 SLT 650.
22   RoW(S)A 1995, s 9.
23   See **PARA 30.16** below.
24   See, for instance, the formal testament given in **PARA 27.1** above.
25   1954 SC 136.
26   *Rhodes v Peterson* 1972 SLT 98.

> 'Dearest Dorothy ... I have been thinking a lot about you recently and I am concerned about your future ... As the boys have their own houses ... I want you to have 63 Merchieston and all the contents ... when I am gone so that I can rest in peace in the knowledge that you are not homeless ... I am not going to say anything to John or Angus about this ... I feel better having at least got this down on paper. Do not lose this letter ... lots of love, Mum.'

It was held that the letter exhibited concluded testamentary intent. Letters to friends or relations are one common type of case. Another is the letter to the solicitor asking that a testament be drawn up in certain terms, with the client dying before this is done. Here is an example, where the client is asking for the existing testament to be changed in certain ways:[27]

> 'I should like if the sum of money left to St Mary's on the Rock was doubled – also that left to Mr David Alexander to be doubled. If the residue of my estate to be divided between my four cousins exceed 5000 pounds I should like that excess amount to be divided between the two charities in my will. I do hope that this can be done. I have been having some pain of late and I just wanted to note this down. E R Jamieson 22.3.80.'

It was held that a letter to a solicitor is from its nature provisional: it looks forward to a formal deed. Accordingly, it cannot itself have testamentary effect.[28]

Where is the testament?

27.11 Usually testaments are left with the law firm that drafted them, in a fireproof safe. The client has a photocopy. But sometimes testators keep the document themselves, and this is usually the case for 'home-made' wills. The family or friends will – hopefully – find it after the death.[29] If a will cannot be found, and its terms are known – typically because there is a photocopy – then the deed can be established by an action of 'proving the tenor'. This action is available to establish any type of lost document. But the reason the will cannot be found may be that it was deliberately destroyed by the testator. In that case it can never take effect.

Revocation

27.12 'All is ambulatory during the defunct's life, and may be taken away expressly or implicitly, by posterior or derogatory deeds, unless the defunct by obliged by contract inter vivos, not to alter the same'

---

[27] *Jamieson's Exrs* 1982 SC 1.

[28] There have been a number of such cases. *Munro v Coutts* (1813) 1 Dow 437 is still perhaps the leading one. A decision that went the other way is *Barker's Exrs v Scottish Rights of Way Society Ltd* 1996 SC 396.

[29] And if they don't like what they read, there is the possibility that they may quietly destroy it.

as Stair puts it.[30] A testament does not become live until the granter ceases to be so, so that alteration or complete revocation is always competent. (The exception – as Stair says – is if the testator has promised to someone to give them a legacy.[31]) If the testator wishes to alter the will it is usual to revoke it and replace it by a new one. The alternative is a codicil. This refers to the existing testament and modifies it in certain respects but in other respects leaves it in force. Or a testator could simply revoke a will without replacing it. If death then happens, the result is intestacy.

27.13 The usual method of revocation is destruction, that is by physically destroying the testament. Suppose that when a person dies no testament can be found, even though it is known that there was one. Does that mean that it was destroyed with the intention of revocation,[32] or might it be that the document has simply been lost? This is an evidential question. But if the testament was in the possession of the testator at the time of death, but cannot be found, the presumption is that it was destroyed deliberately.[33]

27.14 If a testament is drawn up by a solicitor it will invariably contain a clause revoking any previous testament, so that any earlier one will be revoked even if it is not destroyed. In *Bruce's JF v Lord Advocate*[34] Mr Bruce made a will in 1945, and another in 1949. The second revoked the first. At his death the first one could be found (his solicitors held it) but the second could not, though its terms were known. It had been in his possession and so was presumed to have been deliberately destroyed by the testator. It was held that the first testament took effect. This shows that revocation by destruction is in a sense stronger than revocation by a revocatory clause in a later deed.[35]

27.15 Although testaments drawn by solicitors contain a revocatory clause, home-made ones seldom do so. If there exists an earlier unrevoked testament, both deeds take effect, but in so far as there is inconsistency the later one prevails. For instance, in *Duthie's Trs v Taylor*[36] the first testament contained various pecuniary and special legacies[37] and a legacy of the residue. The later one, which contained no clause of revocation, contained various other pecuniary and special legacies, to some extent inconsistent with the earlier ones, but no legacy of residue. It was held that the later testament had priority, but the earlier remained in force except in so far as there was an inconsistency, so that the legacy of residue in the earlier one was still effective.

---

[30] Stair III, 8, 33.
[31] See, e.g., *Paterson v Paterson* (1893) 20 R 484.
[32] *Animo revocandi* – with the intention of revoking.
[33] *Clyde v Clyde* 1958 SC 343.
[34] 1969 SC 296.
[35] See also *Elder's Trs v Elder* (1894) 21 R 704. For a case where destruction did not revoke the testament, see *Cullen's Trs v Elphinstone* 1948 SC 662.
[36] 1986 SLT 142.
[37] A pecuniary legacy is a legacy of a sum of money and a special legacy is a legacy of a thing, such as a house.

27.16 Under the doctrine of *conditio si testator sine liberis decesserit*,[38] if a child is born to the testator after the testament has been made, the testament is voidable at the instance of that child.[39] The doctrine is subject to certain qualifications and exceptions.[40] In practice it is often overlooked.

Reduction

27.17 Sometimes suspicion surrounds a testament. It may be challenged by an action of reduction. As with other deeds, the action may be based on the assertion that the testament is an absolute nullity (for instance because of forgery[41] or lack of capacity[42]), or on the assertion that it is valid but voidable (for instance because of facility and circumvention[43] or undue influence).

Solicitor's duty of care to potential legatees?

27.18 In *Holmes v Bank of Scotland*[44] Mary Davidson wrote to her bank to ask them to prepare a new testament in favour of her nephew and niece. About two weeks later, she died. The new testament was not ready by then. The nephew and niece sued the bank for the amount they would have received if the new testament had been prepared and signed, averring that the bank owed them a duty of care which they had breached by their delay. The action was held relevant.[45] It may be wondered whether the law is coherent. Either (a) the letter to the bank disclosed concluded testamentary intent or (b) it did not. If it did (a), then the letter should have been accorded testamentary effect, so that the whole basis of the claim against the bank would disappear, because the pursuers would have inherited as the letter directed. But if it did not (b), then the bank could not be charged with having failed to give effect to the deceased's wishes, because the deceased had not finally decided what she wished to happen.

---

[38] The Latin means 'the condition that the testator dies without children'. This is hard to connect with the doctrine. The Latin is especially unfortunate because there exists another doctrine, quite unconnected, but with a similar name: the *conditio si institutus sine liberis decesserit*. See PARA **27.49** below. (The substance of that doctrine is likewise not reflected by the Latin.)

[39] The *post natus* (the 'after-born').

[40] *Stuart Gordon v Stuart Gordon* (1899) 1 F 1005; *Milligan's JF v Milligan* 1910 SC 5; *Stevenson's Trs v Stevenson* 1932 SC 657; *Elder's Trs v Elder* (1894) 21 R 704, (1895) 22 R 505; *Nicolson v Nicolson's Tutrix* 1922 SC 649; *Greenan v Courtney* 2007 SLT 355.

[41] Forgery is far from unknown. It was the forgery of a patient's will and testament that led to the downfall of multiple murderer Harold Shipman.

[42] See, e.g., *Boyle v Boyle's Exr* 1999 SC 479.

[43] See, e.g., *McDougal v McDougal's Trs* 1931 SC 102; *West's Trs v West* 1980 SLT 6; *Pascoe-Watson v Brock's Executor* 1998 SLT 40.

[44] 2002 SLT 544.

[45] Following English law: *White v Jones* [1995] 1 AC 207.

Quasi-testaments

27.19   There are various alternatives to a testament for ensuring that on X's death Y will have some asset. Julius owns a house and wishes Olivia to have it when he dies. He could dispone it to her with a reservation of a liferent.[46] Of course, the effect is not precisely the same as a legacy to Olivia. In the case of a legacy Julius would still be the owner when he dies, and moreover a legacy is revocable. The same idea could be effected through a trust: Julius dispones to a trustee, who holds for Julius while he lives and then for Olivia. Indeed, in wealthier families assets are often held in trust. Another possibility is the *donatio mortis causa*. Here, an asset is transferred by X to Y, subject to the condition that if at any time X so wishes, Y will transfer it back, and that if X dies without having demanded it back, Y will keep it.[47] Yet another possibility is the special destination.[48]

TESTATE SUCCESSION

Introduction

27.20   If there is a valid testament, the estate is distributed according to its provisions,[49] subject always to (a) debts[50] and (b) legal rights.[51] The general idea of testate succession is thus straightforward. But there are many detailed points of difficulty.

Interpretation

27.21   As with other documents, testaments may be unclear, ambiguous or simply muddled. This is often, but by no means always, true of home-made wills. But it can also be true of those drawn by solicitors. Many of the reported cases on the law of succession are cases in which the court has to interpret a testament. In doing so, it may take into account the whole circumstances, but not direct evidence as to the testator's intention. The following passage sums up the law:

> 'The difference between saying that the Court does not allow parole evidence to show what the testator intended, but that it does allow, in suitable cases, investigation by parole into what the words used by the testator were intended to mean, although fine, is a very real one … There is no doubt that certain

---

[46]   See **CHAPTER 21** above.
[47]   The leading case is *Morris v Riddick* (1867) 5 M 1036.
[48]   See **CHAPTER 29** below.
[49]   Assuming that the legatees wish to accept. No legatee can be compelled to accept a legacy, and occasionally legacies are indeed rejected.
[50]   See **PARAS 25.37–25.42** above.
[51]   See **CHAPTER 26** above.

investigations are usually allowable, as to the state of the testator's family and the surrounding circumstances of the making of the will. This is often absolutely necessary for the proper understanding of the will, and it has been for generations accepted that the proper exposition of a testament requires that the interpreting court should be put, as it were, into the testator's chair and given an outlook based on the testator's knowledge.'[52]

27.22   The Law Reform (Miscellaneous Provisions) (Scotland) Act 1985, s 8 allows a court to alter the wording of a document to bring it into line with what was truly intended.[53] But testaments are excluded from the scope of this provision.[54] Thus if the wording of a testament is clear, it is incompetent to lead evidence that the testator really meant something different.

Types of legacy

27.23   A legacy – also called a bequest – is a provision in a testament conferring some benefit on the beneficiary (the legatee). How many kinds of legacy there are depends on how they are classified.

(a) General legacies

27.24   A 'general legacy' is a legacy of a certain quantity of a certain type of thing. For example, a legacy of 'one hundred grammes of pure gold' would be a general legacy. A 'pecuniary legacy' is a sub-type of general legacy. It is a legacy of money, such as a legacy of £10,000. The pecuniary legacy is the only type of general legacy that is ever encountered in practice. A pecuniary legacy's validity does not depend on the testator having liquid funds. Suppose that a testator leaves £15,000 to Ann and everything else to Bob. His estate consists of a house, contents and a bank account with £10,000 in it. Ann will be paid the full £15,000. The executor will have to sell assets to raise the money.

(b) Special legacies

27.25   A 'special legacy' is a legacy of a particular asset, or an identifiable set of assets, such as a house, or a car, or all the testator's books, or the testator's shares in Royal Bank of Scotland plc. A special legacy can be of a share of an asset: thus a special legacy might leave a half-share of a house to one person and the other half to another. Suppose that Ant owes Bee £10,000. Bee could leave this as a legacy to

---

[52]   *Hay v Duthie* 1956 SC 511 at 528–529 per Lord Carmont.
[53]   See **PARA 4.53** above.
[54]   Law Reform (Miscellaneous Provisions) (Scotland) Act 1985, s 8(6).

Ladybird, so that Ant would have to pay the debt to Ladybird. This is not a pecuniary legacy but a special legacy.

(c) Universal legacies

27.26 A 'universal legacy' is where the testator leaves his or her entire estate in a single legacy, such as 'everything to my daughter Jane'.

(d) Residuary legacies

27.27 A 'residuary legacy' is a legacy of everything that remains (if anything *does* remain) after all other claims on the estate have been met. Any testament, other than one with a universal legacy, should have a residuary legacy. Home-made wills often lack one.

27.28 Thus Tom leaves his house to his daughter Ursula, £50,000 to his son Vernon, and everything else to his daughters Wendy and Yvonne equally. The first legacy is a special legacy, the second legacy is a general (and pecuniary) legacy and the third legacy is a residuary legacy. Sometimes the residuary legacy will take the lion's share of the estate, and sometimes little or even nothing.

(e) Demonstrative legacies

27.29 Last, and least important, is the 'demonstrative legacy', which is perhaps best classified as a sub-type of pecuniary legacy. It is a legacy of a certain amount of money to be taken from a particular source, such as '£2,000 to be taken from my account with the Bank of Scotland'. If the identified source turns out to be insufficient, the question is then whether it should be topped up from other assets.[55]

Conditions in legacies

27.30 Legacies may be conditional. If a condition is contrary to good morals (*contra bonos mores*) it is void.[56] Only the condition is void, not the legacy.[57] For example, in *Fraser v Rose*[58] a legacy was left on condition that the legatee did not live with

[55] *Reid's Trs v Dawson* 1915 (HL) 47.
[56] See J Chalmers 'Testamentary Conditions and Public Policy' in K G C Reid, M J de Waal and R Zimmermann (eds) *Exploring the Law of Succession* (2007) 99–113.
[57] See, e.g., *Fraser v Rose* (1849) 11 D 1466; *Grant's Trs v Grant* (1898) 25 R 929; *Balfour's Trs v Johnston* 1936 SC 137. The law is the same as for conditions relating to beneficial interests in trusts. See Wilson and Duncan *Trusts* paras 7-22–7-26.
[58] (1849) 11 D 1466. See also *Grant's Trs v Grant* (1898) 25 R. 929 and *Balfour's Trs v Johnston* 1936 SC 137. The law is the same as for conditions relating to beneficial interests in trusts. See Wilson and Duncan *Trusts* paras 7-22–7-26.

her mother. The condition was held to be *pro non scripto*,[59] so the legatee took the legacy free of the condition.

Invalid legacies

27.31 Occasionally a legacy is held invalid because of uncertainty or because it confers no human benefit. This issue is discussed in **CHAPTER 23**.[60]

27.32 As Erskine says,

'A legacy is valid though there should be an error in the name of the legatee ... provided his description distinguishes him sufficiently from all others'.[61]

In case of doubt, extrinsic evidence is competent as to which person the testator had in mind. Thus in *Cathcart's Trs v Bruce*[62] there was a legacy to 'the children of General Alexander Fairlie Bruce'. This was claimed by (i) the children of General Alexander James Bruce and (ii) the children of Alexander Fairlie Bruce. Evidence showed that the testator had meant the former. In this case it will be noted that the verbal description did not exactly match either set of claimants. What would happen if it did exactly match, but evidence was available indicating that in reality someone different was intended? This situation arose in *Nasmyth's Trs v NSPCC*.[63] Here, there was a legacy to the 'National Society for the Prevention of Cruelty to Children'. There was an English society of that name, and also a Scottish society called the Scottish National Society for the Prevention of Cruelty to Children. Both claimed the legacy, the Scottish society offering to adduce evidence that it was the intended beneficiary. The Court of Session held that evidence should be heard. The English society appealed to the House of Lords, which held that since the wording of the legacy was unambiguous, evidence as to the testator's real intention could not be adduced.

27.33 Sometimes the description of the legatee may mention some position or relationship, such as 'my daughter-in-law, Jane Black' or 'my butler, Alan White'. What if, by the time of the testator's death, that relationship, or position, has ceased? The presumption is that it was not a condition of the legacy. For instance, in *Couper's JF v Valentine*[64] the testament gave a legacy to 'my wife Mrs Dorothy Couper'. Later, the Coupers were divorced. A few months after the divorce, he died, without having changed the testament. It was held that the legacy took effect.[65]

---

[59] 'As if not written.'
[60] See PARAS **23.11–23.13** above.
[61] Erskine III, 9, 8.
[62] 1923 SLT 722. A similar case is *Keiller v Thomson's Trs* (1826) 4 S 724.
[63] 1914 SC (HL) 76.
[64] 1976 SC 63.
[65] For a remarkable case, see *Ormiston's Exr v Laws* 1966 SC 47.

27.34 A legacy to a 'class' is a legacy to a set of people who are described but not identified, such as a legacy to 'my sister Fiona's children'. Suppose that at the date of the testament Fiona had four children, A, B, C and D. Later, D died. Then the testator died. A year after the death of the testator, Fiona had another child, E. Who receives the legacy? The answer is: A, B and C. A class is normally to be ascertained at the date of the testator's death.

Abatement

27.35 It may be impossible to pay, or make over, all legacies in full. Thus if Tim leaves a million pounds each to ten different people, but dies with assets worth only a few thousand pounds, the legacies cannot be paid in full. The legacies must be scaled down. This is known as abatement. When abatement is needed, it is usually not because the gross estate was inadequate, as in Tim's case. Usually it is because, whilst the gross estate is adequate, the net estate is not, i.e. the debts – which always have priority over legacies or other succession rights – are such that the legacies cannot be met in full.[66] Legal rights can have the same effect.

27.36 There are three rules.[67]
   (1) The residue abates first. In fact, this is not an independent rule because, by definition, 'residue' is what is left after other claims – debts, legal rights and other legacies – have been met.
   (2) General legacies abate before special legacies.
   (3) Legatees in a particular class suffer *pro rata* abatement – i.e. equal suffering.

27.37 For instance, Fiona leaves £100,000 to Gregory, £200,000 to Heather and the rest to Ian. Her estate is a house worth £200,000, a painting worth £100,000 and other moveables worth £100,000. There are £160,000 of debts, all unsecured. The net estate is thus £400,000 minus £160,000 = £240,000. Ian would take nothing, and the £240,000 has to be divided between Gregory and Heather. Gregory would take £80,000 and Heather would take £160,000. (The house and painting would have to be sold by the executor.) What has happened is that the two legacies have abated equally. Gregory's legacy was half of Heather's and what he actually receives is also half.

27.38 Suppose that the legacy to Gregory had not been a pecuniary legacy of £100,000, but had been a special legacy of the painting. In that case he would have received the painting, and Heather would have received £140,000. Ian, as before, would have received nothing. The reason is that pecuniary legacies abate before special ones.

27.39 If an asset that is subject to a special legacy has to be sold by the executor, the rights of the legatee are transferred to net proceeds of sale. Suppose that Euan

---

66   For incidence of debts in general, see PARAS **25.37–25.42** above.
67   These are only default rules: the testator could make other provision.

his house to Fraser and everything else to Hilda. The house is worth £200,000 and the rest of the estate is worth £100,000. There are £150,000 of unsecured debts. The house must be sold. Euan will be paid £150,000. Hilda receives nothing.

27.40 Abatement may also be necessary to make it possible to pay out legal rights claimants.[68] Janette is married to Keith. They have no children. She leaves her house to Luke, £100,000 to Martin and the residue to Norah. The house is worth £200,000, and the rest of the estate, all moveable, is worth £150,000. There are no debts. If it were not for legal rights, Luke would take the house, Martin would be paid £100,000 and Norah would receive the balance, worth £50,000. But Keith's *jus relicti* is a claim for £75,000 (half the value of the moveable estate). So Luke takes the house, Keith takes £75,000, Martin takes £75,000 and Norah takes nothing. Martin's legacy suffers rather than Luke's, because pecuniary legacies abate before special ones.

Ademption

27.41 It sometimes happens that the object of a legacy no longer belongs to the testator at the time of death. For instance, Edward leaves his house at 22 Privet Avenue to Finola. Later he sells that house and with the money he buys another, at 11 Acacia Drive. He then dies, without having changed his testament. The legacy is void because it has been 'adeemed'. Sometimes a legacy is so worded as to prevent ademption. For instance: 'I bequeath to Janet Smith my house at 57 Corra Linn Road, Turriff, or such other house which I may own at my death as my principal residence.'

27.42 Sometimes the asset in question has been converted into some other asset. As in the example just given, the asset is sold and the proceeds are used to buy another, similar, asset. Attempts are sometimes made to argue that the real intention of the testator must have been that the legatee was to receive the substituted asset. But 'it is settled (for better or worse) that ademption is a question of fact, and not of intention'.[69] The test for ademption is simply whether the asset is still in the testator's patrimony or not. If it is not, the legacy is adeemed. For instance, in *Ogilvie-Forbes' Tr v Ogilvie-Forbes' Tr*[70] there was a legacy of some land. When the testator died, it was found that he had transferred title to the land to a company of which he was effectively the sole shareholder. It was held that the legacy had been adeemed. Conversely, if it is still within the patrimony, the legacy is not adeemed. Thus in *Tennant's Tr v Tennant*[71] there was a legacy of some company shares. At the time of the testator's death he had signed and delivered a share transfer document. But the transfer had not been registered with the company. So the legacy had not been adeemed.

---

[68]　*Tait's Tr v Lees* (1886) 13 R 1104.
[69]　*Cobban's Exrs v Cobban* 1915 SC 82 at 89–90 per Lord Dundas.
[70]　1955 SC 405.
[71]　1946 SC 420.

Legatum rei alienae

27.43   *Legatum rei alienae* is a Latin expression meaning 'legacy of someone else's property'. Obviously, this seldom happens. An example would be where the testator possesses something and mistakenly believes it to his/hers. Very occasionally, the testator knows that the property is someone else's. The law is succinctly stated by Erskine:

> 'By the Roman law, if one bequeathed a subject which he knew did not belong to himself, the legacy had this effect, that the heir must either have purchased it for the legatee, or paid its value to him if it could not be purchased ... Where the testator ... believed the subject to be his own, which *in dubio* is to be inferred from his act of bequeathing, neither the thing itself, nor its value, could have been claimed from the heir ... These rules... hold also by the usage of Scotland.'[72]

Death of legatee: lapse of legacies

27.44   A legatee who has died before the testator cannot take the legacy. The dead cannot inherit.[73] Nor does the legacy pass to his or her estate. Thus suppose that Fraser leaves his house to Georgiana, and Georgiana leaves everything to Harry. Fraser dies one hour after Georgiana. The house does not go to Georgiana or to Harry. So what does happen to it? The basic rule is that the legacy 'lapses', which is to say, it is void.[74] Suppose that the testament said 'my house to Georgiana and the residue of my estate to Ian'. Ian would take the house. Suppose, alternatively, that Charlotte's testament says 'my house to David and the residue to Eliza'. David survives her but Eliza does not. The legacy of the residue lapses. Thus Charlotte dies partly testate (as to the house) and partly intestate (as to the residue).

27.45   As mentioned, the basic rule about the effect of predecease is that the legacy lapses. But there are important qualifications. To these we turn.

Express destinations-over[75]

27.46   A 'destination-over' is a provision in a legacy which provides that if the legatee predeceases then the legacy is to go to someone else. Thus Fraser might leave his house 'to Georgiana whom failing to Jessica'. If, when he dies, both Georgiana and Jessica are alive, Georgiana takes the house. If Georgiana is alive, but

---

[72]   Erskine III, 9, 10. See, generally, *Meeres v Dowell's Exr* 1923 SLT 184.
[73]   See PARAS **25.15–25.18** above.
[74]   Lapsed legacies should not be confused with lapsed trusts. If a legacy lapses, it is void. If a trust lapses, it is not. For lapsed trusts, see PARA **23.4** above.
[75]   See further CHAPTER **29** below.

not Jessica, then once again Georgiana takes the house. But if Georgiana is dead while Jessica is alive, Jessica takes the house.

27.47 A 'survivorship destination-over' is of this form: 'I leave my house to Alice and Boris equally between them and to the survivor.' If you unpack that, what it means is: 'I leave a one-half share of my house to Alice, whom failing to Boris, and I leave the other one-half share to Boris, whom failing to Alice.' If both Alice and Boris survive, each takes a half. If Alice survives but Boris predeceases, Alice takes the whole. And if Boris survives but Alice predeceases, Boris takes the whole.

Implied destinations-over – accretion and the *conditio si institutus*

27.48 As well as the express destination-over, the law in two types of case will imply a destination-over. The first case is 'accretion'. Suppose that there is a legacy of £20,000 'to Anne and Brian'. If both survive, each receives £10,000. But what if Anne predeceases while Brian survives? Does the legacy lapse to the extent of £10,000, with Brian receiving £10,000? Or does Brian take £20,000? The law presumes that in a joint legacy of this sort the testator meant 'Anne and Brian and the survivor'. This is called 'accretion' and it is said that Anne's share 'accresces' to Brian. But it is only a presumption and so is rebuttable by evidence of contrary intention. The simplest way to avoid accretion is to make the legacies separate, for instance '£10,000 to Anne and £10,000 to Brian'. Alternatively, what are called 'words of severance' can be used. Thus if the legacy is 'to Anne and Brian equally between them', the effect of the words 'equally between them' is to exclude accretion.[76]

27.49 The other implied destination-over is the doctrine of *conditio si institutus sine liberis decesserit*.[77] The rule is that if a legacy is given to the testator's child, there is an implied destination-over to the children of that child. Ingrid leaves her house to her son Julius. He predeceases his mother, leaving three children. Those three children will take the legacy equally between them. The doctrine has also been occasionally applied where the legacy was to some other family member, but the case law here is unclear. The doctrine can apply only to relatives. If Kate leaves a legacy to her friend Linda, and Linda predeceases, leaving issue, the legacy lapses, and does not pass to Linda's issue. (Unless, of course, there is an express destination-over to that effect.)

27.50 The doctrine is in substance much the same as the doctrine of representation. But representation applies to (a) *legitim*[78] and (b) intestate succession rights,[79] whereas the *conditio* applies to legacies.

---

[76]   *Paxton's Trs v Cowie* (1886) 13 R 1191.
[77]   See D R Macdonald 'Lapse of Legacies' in E Cooke (ed) *Modern Studies in Property Law: Volume 1: Property 2000* (2001) 275–289.
[78]   See PARAS **26.23–26.25** above.
[79]   See PARA **28.26** below.

27.51 The *conditio*, where it applies, receives special favour from the law, in that it will prevail over accretion, and will even prevail over an express destination-over unless the testator indicates otherwise.

  (1) Accretion. Suppose that a legacy is left to Oliver and Peter. Oliver predeceases. There are no words of severance, so the whole legacy should go to Peter. But if Oliver was the testator's son, and left issue, then the issue take Oliver's half of the legacy, not Peter. So there is a conflict between the *conditio* and accretion. In this situation, the *conditio* prevails. But the *conditio* carries only the original and not any accretion share. Suppose that a legacy is given 'to my children Alice and Beth and Chris'. Alice and Beth predecease. Alice leaves a daughter, Doris. Doris takes one-third. Chris takes two-thirds.

  (2) An express destination-over. In *Devlin's Trs v Breen*[80] the testator left the residue of her estate to 'my two children the said Elizabeth Darney Devlin or Breen and Thomas Leishman Devlin or the survivor'. Elizabeth survived, but Thomas predeceased, leaving five children (Thomas, Adair, Margaret, Patricia and Robert). The question was whether Thomas's half-share of the residue should go to his children or to their aunt. The aunt litigated against her nephews and nieces unsuccessfully all the way up to the House of Lords.

VESTING

27.52 A succession right is said to 'vest' when the beneficiary acquires a right to it. In almost all cases that is at the moment of the death of the *de cujus*. But occasionally vesting is postponed. Vesting is a subject that belongs to the law of trusts.[81]

FURTHER READING

Barr, A, et al *Drafting Wills in Scotland* (1994).

Hiram *Succession* chs 5–9.

Kerrigan, J *Drafting for Succession* (2004).

Macdonald *Succession* chs 6–8 and 11.

---

[80] 1943 SC 556, aff'd 1945 SC (HL) 27.
[81] See PARAS **22.59–22.65** above.

Chapter 28

Intestate succession

INTRODUCTION

28.1 Although intestacy is common, it is less important in practice than testacy, for a simple reason: the larger the estate, the more likely it is that there is a testament.

28.2 Occasionally there can be intestacy even if there is a valid testament. For example, Ursula's testament says 'I leave everything to Vernon'. By the time that Ursula dies, Vernon is already dead. The universal legacy lapses, and as a result there is an intestacy. Even if Vernon were alive, he could renounce the legacy, and then the result would, again, be intestacy. It might seem improbable that he would do that, but, surprisingly, there can be circumstances in which it would be in his interests to do so.[1] Sometimes there can be partial intestacy. For instance, suppose that Henry's

---

[1]   See PARAS **28.28–28.29** below.

testament says 'I leave my house to Iona and everything else to James' and suppose that Henry is survived by Iona but not by James. Iona will take the house, but the bequest of residue lapses. The residue falls into intestacy. It would have been different if it had been the other way round, and Iona had predeceased Henry while James had survived him. In that case James would have taken everything, including the house, and there would have been no partial intestacy.

28.3 The law on intestacy is partly to be found in the Succession (Scotland) Act 1964 (S(S)A 1964), and partly in common law.

POLICY?

28.4 S(S)A 1964 was based on the Mackintosh Report of 1951.[2] This said that 'we have throughout kept in view that when a man dies without a will the law should try to provide as far as possible for the distribution of his estate in the manner he would most likely have given effect to himself if he had made a will'.[3] If this approach were to be taken seriously, it would be necessary to have an enquiry after each intestate death, to find out, as nearly as possible, what the deceased would have wanted to happen. But such an approach would be slow and expensive, and in any case would in most cases be little more than guesswork. The Mackintosh Committee never even contemplated such a possibility. Instead it laid down a single system of fixed rules, with, however, different sub-rules according to whether or not the deceased left a relict or issue.

FIVE STAGES

28.5 In an intestacy one begins, as always, with paying the debts, including taxes. After that, there are up to five stages to go through. These are:
  (1) prior rights;
  (2) relict's right (including civil partner's right);
  (3) cohabitant's right;
  (4) legitim; and
  (5) free estate.
The prior rights stage itself has three elements. A chart may be useful (see Figure 28.1):

28.6 But it must not be supposed that in every intestacy all stages are relevant. If the deceased was single and childless, for example, only the fifth stage would be applicable. Nevertheless, overall it cannot be denied that the scheme is a complex one.

---

[2]   Cmnd 8144.
[3]   At 8.

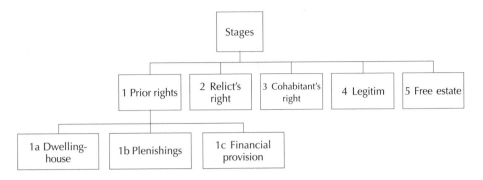

Figure 28.1

Stage 1: Prior rights

(a) Dwellinghouse right[4]

28.7 If the deceased had a 'relevant interest'[5] in a dwellinghouse in which the relict was 'ordinarily resident' at the date of death then that 'interest' passes to the relict. Jack and Jill are married. Their home is owned by Jill and is worth £200,000. Jill dies intestate.[6] Jack inherits the house. If the value of the deceased's 'relevant interest' exceeds a set figure (currently £300,000[7]) then the relict does not inherit the property, but is entitled to be paid the sum in question. For instance, suppose that the house is worth £400,000. Jack does not inherit it. Instead he is entitled to be paid £300,000. The same rules apply if the home is co-owned. Suppose that Jack and Jill co-own their home and it is worth £500,000. Jack dies intestate. His share is worth £250,000. Jill inherits it.

28.8 In calculating the value, debt secured on the property is deducted. Suppose that Jill is the sole owner of the house, and it is worth £400,000, but £150,000 is secured by standard security. The value, for the purposes of prior rights, is £250,000. Jack inherits.

28.9 Often the house is co-owned. One deducts from the value of the share of the deceased the amount that is secured over that share. Bob and Elle are co-owners of

---

4   S(S)A 1964, s 8.
5   S(S)A 1964, s 8(6)(d). For almost all practical purposes this means ownership or co-ownership.
6   Jill is said to be the 'intestate' – i.e. the intestate person. This is an odd usage, because a person who is testate is not called the 'testate'.
7   This and the other figures in S(S)A 1964, are changed from time to time by statutory instrument. The latest is the Prior Rights of Surviving Spouse (Scotland) Order 2005 (SSI 2005/252).

a house worth £200,000. Bob borrows £10,000 from Bank of Scotland, secured over his share, and Elle borrows £20,000 from Clydesdale Bank, secured over her share. Bob dies. The net value of his share is £90,000. That sort of arrangement would be highly unlikely in practice. Usually there is a joint loan that is secured over both shares. But the same principles apply.

28.10   Suppose that the house is co-owned by Jack and Jill and is worth £700,000. There is a secured loan of £80,000. The security is over both his share and her share. Assuming that their liability on the loan is equal, the net value of his share is £310,000.

28.11   In the typical case their liability will be solidary (joint and several), so that the whole £80,000 is secured over both shares. So one might seek to argue, on the basis of a literal reading of S(S)A 1964, s 8(6)(d), that the whole amount should be deducted, so that the net value of his share is £270,000. But the more commonsense approach, and the one adopted in practice, is to deduct from the gross value of his share the amount that he is liable as between himself and his wife, i.e. £40,000.

28.12   The dwellinghouse right exists only if the relict was ordinarily resident there. Thus, a house owned as an investment and let out would not count. Or suppose that Jack and Jill are co-owners but have separated. Jill lives in the house, and Jack lives elsewhere. If he dies, Jill has the dwellinghouse right. But if she dies, he does not.[8] The rule thus can produce arbitrary effects.

(b) Plenishings right

28.13   The relict has right to 'furniture and plenishings' within the dwellinghouse, up to a set figure (currently £24,000). If the value is less than that figure, the relict takes it all. If the value is higher, the relict chooses items up to the value. (Note that this rule is different from the rule for the dwellinghouse. In that case, if the value is over the limit, the relict takes money in lieu.) In practice most or all of the furniture and plenishings will be co-owned.[9] Thus, suppose that their value is £40,000. The relict will typically take all, because if she co-owns each item, the value of the deceased's share is only £20,000. To have this right the relict must be 'ordinarily resident'. Thus, as in the previous example, if Jack and Jill are separated, with Jill living in the house, Jack would not have this prior right if she dies but she has it if he dies.

(c) Financial provision

28.14   The third prior right is a right to money. The amount depends on whether the deceased left issue. In the absence of issue the figure is £75,000. Otherwise it is

---

8   But there may have been a separation agreement: see PARA **25.30** above.
9   Co-ownership is presumed by the Family Law (Scotland) Act 1985, s 25.

£42,000. Suppose that Iain dies intestate, survived by his second wife, Jenny, from whom he was separated but not divorced, and by one son from first marriage, Karl. Jenny is entitled to £42,000. (The marriage of Iain and Jenny was childless, but that is not the point. The deceased had issue.) Naturally, financial provision is payable only if the estate can pay. Thus suppose that Iain's estate consists of a half-share of a house that he co-owned with Jenny (value of the share being £100,000) and a half-share of the contents (the value of the share being £20,000) and a bank deposit of £5,000. He dies intestate. Jenny takes the whole estate. She receives only £5,000 of the financial provision. She will not receive the rest, since there is no estate out of which it could be paid. In this example there was a handy £5,000 bank deposit. But financial provision does not depend on the existence of a fund of that sort. Suppose that instead of the bank deposit Iain had owned a field worth £5,000. Jenny could still claim her financial provision. Note that Karl takes nothing and that his stepmother takes everything. In smaller intestate estates, the relict (if there is one) tends to take everything. Whether that is fair is arguable. It is curious that in testate succession Karl would receive something because in testate succession legal rights come first, but in intestate succession prior rights come before legal rights.

28.15 This point leads on to the next. In calculating legal rights (see below), it is necessary to know how much moveable estate is left after prior rights have been satisfied, because legal rights are calculated on the value of the moveables. Hence there has to be a rule about how the financial provision is to be taken out of the estate, in cases where both heritable and moveable property are available. Actually, in most cases the problem does not arise, because in most cases there is only one piece of heritable property, the dwellinghouse. But sometimes there is other heritable property too. The rule is this: financial provision must be deducted *rateably* from the heritable and the moveable estate.[10] The following is an example.

28.16 Paul dies intestate survived by his widow, Rachel, and their two children, Sandra and Tim. The dwellinghouse is worth £170,000 and is owned in common with Rachel. There is a secured loan of £40,000. The contents are worth £40,000 and are co-owned. There is also a holiday cottage owned by Paul alone, worth £80,000. There are sundry moveables, mainly stock market investments, worth £200,000.

28.17 The first prior right gives Rachel the house. The second prior right gives her the contents. What is left is heritage worth £80,000 and moveables worth £200,000. The third prior right is financial provision of £42,000. This comes rateably from the remaining heritage and the remaining moveables. The ratio of 200,000 to 80,000 is 5:2. So the moveables must contribute 5/7 and heritage 2/7. Thus the heritage contributes £12,000 and the moveables £30,000 = £42,000. What is left at the end of the prior rights stage is £68,000 of heritage and £170,000 of moveables.

---

[10]   S(S)A 1964, s 9(3).

Stage 2: Relict's right

28.18 There are two kinds of legal rights: relict's right (including civil partner's right) and legitim.[11] In testate succession, the two have the same priority: they come first, subject only to the rights of creditors. In intestate succession legal rights also apply, but not in the same way. Both legal rights are postponed to prior rights. And legitim, but not relict's right, is postponed to cohabitant's right.

28.19 The previous example can be continued. Legal rights are exigible only from net moveable estate. After prior rights, the value of the moveable estate is £170,000. The relict's right is one-third. So Rachel takes £56,666.

Stage 3: Cohabitant's right

28.20 Next: cohabitant's right. The existence of a cohabitant does not exclude the existence of a spouse: there could be both. Actually, to speak of the cohabitant's 'right' is slightly misleading. The court has a power to make an award to the cohabitant, but the power is discretionary. The Family Law (Scotland) Act 2006[12] sets out a list of factors which the court should take into account. The award is made out of the 'net intestate estate'. The way that is defined means that the award comes *after* prior rights and relict's right have been satisfied, but *before* legitim or free estate. There is a maximum:

> 'An order ... shall not have the effect of awarding to the survivor [= cohabitant] an amount which would exceed the amount to which the survivor would have been entitled had the survivor been the spouse or civil partner of the deceased.'

That maximum does not, however, necessarily mean that the children will receive anything. For instance, Sarah has two children by her former husband. She dies intestate, with a cohabitant, Brad. The award to Brad might be such as to mean that the two children receive nothing.

Stage 4: Legitim

28.21 If there is no cohabitant, the legitim is a third of the net value of the moveables. So Sandra and Tim take £56,666 between them, i.e. £28,333 each.

Stage 5: Free estate

28.22 'Free estate' means anything left of an intestate estate after satisfaction of prior rights, legal rights and cohabitant's right. In some cases there may be no free

---

[11] See **CHAPTER 26** above.
[12] Family Law (Scotland) Act 2006, s 29.

estate. The example above,[13] where Iain died and Jenny took the whole estate by prior rights, shows why this may happen. At the other extreme, if there are no prior rights, legal rights or cohabitant's right the whole estate is free estate. For example, Natasha dies intestate without spouse, civil partner, cohabitant or issue. Everything is free estate.

28.23 S(S)A 1964, s 2 lists those entitled to inherit the free estate, starting with the children, if any. Confusingly, it says that the persons in question inherit *the whole of the intestate estate*. But in fact s 2 is subject to prior and legal rights.[14] The s 2 list is a modern statutory form of the common law conception of 'next of kin'. Thus at common law if Mary dies survived by her three children, Norman, Olivia and Perpetua, those three children are the next of kin. ('Next of kin' means 'nearest by blood'.) At common law the spouse is never the next of kin. (Unless cousins marry and with no nearer relatives.) The s 2 list departs somewhat from the common law conception, one of the departures being that the spouse does appear in the s 2 list, though only a long way down. It is unusual for a relict to inherit under s 2. So while relicts do well under prior rights and legal rights, they do less well at this third stage. Suppose that Aileen has a civil partner and two children. If she dies intestate with an estate worth £40,000, the civil partner takes everything and the children nothing. If she dies intestate with an estate worth £4,000,000, her partner does quite well, but the children and the taxman take the lion's share.

28.24 If we continue the previous example,[15] the estate left after the first two prior rights is £56,666 of moveables and £68,000 of heritage. This goes to Sandra and Tim.

28.25 All the possibilities inherent in S(S)A 1964, s 2 will not be discussed here. Only a few examples will be given.
(1) Brian has no issue. He is an only child. Both his parents survive him. His estate goes to them, equally.
(2) The same, but only one parent is alive. That parent takes all.
(3) Carla has no issue. She has two brothers. Her parents are dead. Her two brothers take her estate, equally.
(4) Deirdre has no issue. Her parents, Ewan and Faye, are dead. Deirdre has one sibling, Genevieve. Genevieve is from Faye's first marriage, and thus Deirdre's half-sister. Genevieve takes all.
(5) The same, but with one difference, namely that Ewan and Faye had another child, Hilda. Thus Hilda, unlike Genevieve, is Deirdre's sister of the full blood. Hilda takes everything.[16]

---

13   See PARA **28.14** above.
14   The explanation is to be found in S(S)A 1964, s 1(2) which says that 'nothing in this part of this Act shall affect legal rights or the prior rights of a surviving spouse'.
15   See PARAS **28.16–28.17, 28.19** AND **28.21** above.
16   S(S)A 1964, s 2(2) admits siblings of the half blood, but s 3 gives priority to siblings of the whole blood.

In these examples it would make no difference, as far as the free estate (if any) is concerned, if the deceased (Brian or Carla or Deirdre) had been married. Their spouses would have the benefit of prior rights and legal rights, but they would not be the section 2 heirs.

28.26 The rules about representation are substantially the same as for legitim.[17] Kate and John have three children, Laura, Marie and Nigel. Kate and Nigel died some years ago. Nigel was married to Ottalie. They had two children, Paula and Rosi. Marie now dies, childless, single and intestate. Prior rights and legal rights are inapplicable. So everything is free estate. Under the S(S)A 1964, s 2 rules, a half goes to her father, John, a quarter to her sister Laura and an eighth each to her nieces Paula and Rosi. (The division as between Laura on the one hand and the two nieces on the other is a division *per stirpes*, since the heirs are of unequal propinquity. Had Laura predeceased leaving one child, Robert, then Robert, Paula and Rosi would have taken one-sixth each.)

ULTIMUS HAERES

28.27 In some legal systems only relatives within a certain degree can be intestate heirs. Thus if someone dies and the nearest relative is a fifth cousin, that cousin does not inherit. In our law there is no limit. Since everyone is related to everyone else, it follows that nobody can die heirless. But in practice it occasionally happens that someone dies intestate and no relative can be traced. The Crown is the *ultimus haeres*.[18] Hence if nobody else can be traced, the Crown takes. The splendidly named Queen's and Lord Treasurer's Remembrancer (QLTR) administers such inheritances for the Crown.[19] The beneficiary is not the UK Treasury but the Scottish Consolidated Fund.

ARTIFICIAL INTESTACY

28.28 David and Evelina are married. They have one child, Fraser. David dies. He leaves everything to Evelina. She is thus the universal legatee. The estate is worth £45,000. It is all moveable. Fraser can claim legitim, and will receive £15,000. Evelina takes the rest. Now, suppose that Evelina rejects her legacy. The estate is now intestate. She claims prior rights. There is no house. There are no plenishings. She takes financial provision of £42,000, leaving £3,000. She takes one-third of this under her relict's right = £1,000. Fraser takes £1,000 by way of legitim, and the remaining £1,000 under S(S)A 1964, s 2. Thus, by renouncing her legacy Evelina is

---

[17] For which see PARAS **26.23–26.25** above. But whereas the representation rules for legitim are in S(S)A 1964, s 11, the representation rules for s 2 rights are in S(S)A 1964, ss 5 and 6.

[18] Latin, meaning 'last heir'.

[19] http://www.copfs.gov.uk/About/roles/qltr/qltr-overview.

better off than she would have been had she accepted it: £43,000 as opposed to £30,000. This curious result, which is known as 'artificial intestacy', follows from the logic of S(S)A 1964.[20]

28.29 Artificial intestacy makes sense for the relict only if she would get more in that way than by accepting the legacy. If the estate is a large one, artificial intestacy would not make sense for her. Nor would artificial intestacy make sense if the legacy says, for example, 'all to Evelina whom failing to Oxfam'.

PARTIAL INTESTACY

28.30 Partial intestacy happens when the testament (combined with legal rights and cohabitant's right, if applicable) fails to dispose of the whole estate. An example was given at the beginning of this chapter: Henry's testament says 'I leave my house to Iona and everything else to James'. He is survived by Iona but not by James. Iona takes the house, but the bequest of residue lapses. It falls into intestacy, and is distributed under S(S)A 1964, s 2.

28.31 Partial intestacy becomes difficult where there is a relict. This is because prior rights rank before legal rights. Legal rights rank before legacies. Legacies rank before prior rights. Thus there is a circle of priority. The problems seem to be insoluble.[21]

FURTHER READING

Hiram *Succession* ch 4.

Macdonald *Succession* ch 4.

---

[20] For an example, see *Kerr* 1968 SLT (Sh Ct) 61.
[21] Gretton 'Partial intestacy' 1986 *SLT (News)* 201.

Chapter 29

Destinations

INTRODUCTION

29.1 In **Chapter 27** above something was said about destinations-over.[1] Here, a more detailed treatment of destinations is given. There are two kinds:

(a) destinations-over; and

(b) special destinations.

A destination-over is found in a testament, or trust, as part of the terms of a legacy or beneficial right. Any type of property may be involved. A special destination is found in a disposition, and enters the Land Register, or the Sasine Register.[2]

---

[1] See **paras 27.46–27.51** above.

[2] It is also possible to have a special destination of moveable property but they are rare, and nothing will be said about them here.

29.2   In both types of destination, a transferor (testator, truster, disponer) is saying that property is to go to X but that that if X dies, the property is then to pass to Y. Sometimes a destination-over can convert itself into a special destination. While some special destinations are thus born out of destinations-over, most are not.

DESTINATIONS-OVER: THE BASICS

29.3   If in a testament there is a legacy to Jack, and Jack predeceases the testator, the legacy normally lapses.[3] But if the testament says 'to Jack *whom failing to Jill*', then the result is different. If Jack predeceases the testator, then Jill, if she is alive, takes the legacy. An important sub-type of destination-over is the survivorship destination-over. Here, Tara leaves a legacy to 'Jack and Jill and the survivor'. That is really two legacies: (1) half to Jack whom failing to Jill; and (2) half to Jill whom failing to Jack. Thus suppose that when Tara dies, Jill is alive but Jack is not. Then Jill takes both halves.

29.4   In a destination-over the primary legatee (Jack) is the 'institute'. The secondary legatee (Jill) is either (1) the 'conditional institute' or (2) the 'substitute'. Those latter two terms do not mean quite the same thing. How they differ, and how to determine which Jill is, will be discussed below.

SPECIAL DESTINATIONS

The basics

29.5   Alan owns a house. He dispones it to 'Beth whom failing to Clara'. The disposition is registered. The owner is Beth. Clara is not a co-owner and indeed has no real right. Beth is the institute and Clara is the substitute.

Effect

29.6   If both (a) when Beth dies Clara is still alive and (b) the property is then still owned by Beth, Clara takes the property.[4] In other words, the property does not form part of Beth's estate for succession purposes. For example, suppose that Beth was married to Duncan. She dies intestate. Duncan claims prior rights, including the dwellinghouse right.[5] He will fail. The house goes to Clara. The destination thus prevails if Beth dies *intestate*. But what if she dies *testate*? What if her testament says 'I leave my house to my darling husband Duncan'? The answer is: usually the

---

[3]   See **PARA 27.44** above.
[4]   Normally. For the exception, see **PARA 29.13** below.
[5]   For prior rights, see **PARAS 28.7–28.17** above.

destination defeats the legacy. Occasionally the legacy can defeat the destination. The rules are given below.[6]

29.7 While the destination may work in favour of Clara on Beth's death, it does *not* prevent Beth from transferring the property while she (Beth) is still alive.[7] If Beth does that, Clara takes nothing.

Survivorship

29.8 The sort of special destination mentioned above (to Beth whom failing to Clara) is nowadays rare. Special destinations are indeed common, but almost all of them are survivorship special destinations. Archie and Barbara are married, or perhaps just living together. They buy a house. They are likely to want to be co-owners, even if their contributions to the price are unequal. So the disposition will, in the typical case, be to both of them, as common property. This can be done in two ways: first, 'to Archie and Barbara' and second 'to Archie and Barbara and the survivor'.

29.9 In both cases they become co-owners. Nevertheless, the effect of the two is different. In the first, if Archie dies, his half share will form part of his estate. It may then go to Barbara. But it may not. The second is equivalent to: 'half to Archie whom failing to Barbara and half to Barbara whom failing to Archie'. If Archie dies, his share will normally go to Barbara, even if Archie's will leaves it to someone else. Although one speaks of a 'survivorship destination' in the singular, the reality is plural, for there are two destinations – one for one half-share and another for the other.[8]

29.10 Most people who buy a property together opt for one of these survivorship special destinations. It is the seller who signs the disposition but the terms of the disposition in such matters are chosen by the buyers.

Evacuation

29.11 To remove the effect of a destination is called 'evacuating' the destination. That is what Beth sought to do by leaving the house to Duncan. How can this be done?[9]

---

[6]   See PARAS **29.13–29.15** below.
[7]   *Steele v Caldwell* 1979 SLT 228; *Smith v Mackintosh* 1989 SLT 148.
[8]   So the evacuation of the one leaves the other intact, with consequences that can be unexpected: see *Gardner's Exrs v Raeburn* 1996 SLT 745.
[9]   For a fuller account, see Reid and Gretton *Conveyancing 2005* (2006) 72 ff.

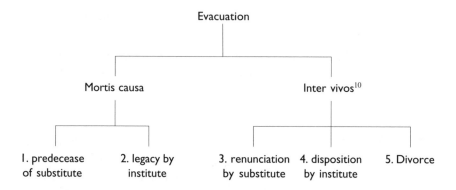

29.12 First, a destination is evacuated by the death of the substitute. Suppose that there is a special destination 'to Charlotte whom failing Fergus'. Fergus dies on Monday and Charlotte dies on Tuesday. Neither Fergus nor his estate takes the property. Fergus was the substitute, and he prececeased the institute (Charlotte). The destination died with him. Or suppose that Beth and Duncan are co-owners with a survivorship destination. Beth dies on Monday and Duncan dies on Tuesday. When she dies, her share passes to him. But when he dies, his initial half-share does not pass to her estate.

29.13 Second, a destination is *sometimes* validly evacuated by a legacy by the institute. For such a legacy to succeed, two conditions must *both* be satisfied:
  (a) a power to evacuate must exist; and
  (b) the evacuating legacy must conform to the requirements of the law, currently contained in S(S)A 1964, s 30.

29.14 To ascertain if there is a power to evacuate, the first step is to look at the title. This may say expressly that there is, or is not, power to evacuate. If so, well and good. Usually it is silent. In that case certain presumptions apply. The most important is that laid down in *Perrett's Trs v Perrett*.[11] This is that if the destination is a survivorship destination, and if both parties contributed to the price, as is almost always the case, then there is no power of evacuation by either co-owner. Since most married and co-habiting homeowners are co-owners, and since most of them opt for a survivorship destination in the title, and since in practice both will have contributed to the price, it will be seen that survivorship destinations are very common and that they are usually non-evacuable.

29.15 The issue of power to evacuate arises only in a testate case. In an intestate case there is no testament, and so obviously no attempt at evacuation has been made.

---

[10] Sometimes the term 'evacuation' is used only for *mortis causa* evacuation. Here we use the term in its broader sense.
[11] 1909 SC 522. See further M Morton 'Special Destinations as Testamentary Instructions' 1984 *SLT (News)* 133.

29.16   In the third place, the substitute can renounce the benefit of the destination.

29.17   In the fourth place, the institute can divest himself of the property before his death, i.e. dispone to someone else. A special destination takes effect only if the institute still owns the property at death. An institute is free to dispone. For example, go back to Beth and Duncan. While they are both alive, she dispones her half-share to Ethel. If Beth dies the next day, Duncan does not take her share, for Ethel has it. But had it been Duncan who had died, Beth would still have taken his share. Parties who co-own with a survivorship destination can thus cheat.

29.18   The four ways of evacuation are all common law ways. A fifth – statutory – way also exists. If a married couple are co-owners with a survivorship destination, divorce will automatically evacuate the destination.[12] The same applies to civil partners.

Practical significance of special destinations

29.19   Often, a special destination transfers the property to the person who would have received it anyway. Suppose that in the case of Archie and Barbara there had been no special destination. Then (a) if he had died *testate* he would probably have bequeathed his half-share to her anyway, and (b) if he had died *intestate* then it is likely that she would have taken his half share anyway by virtue of the first prior right – assuming that they were married. But sometimes special destinations do work to take property off in a different direction from the direction that it would otherwise have taken.

29.20   Special destinations are rather weak. They can be defeated by an *inter vivos* transfer or, to say the same thing, they operate only if the person who dies still owned the property at that time. Additionally, a special destination only operates if the substitute is still alive.

Special destinations: transferring to the substitute

29.21   If the institute dies, the *method* of transfer of ownership to the substitute depends on whether it is a *survivorship* destination. In a survivorship special destination, the share of the institute passes to the substitute without any act of conveyance and without any entry in the Land Register or Sasine Register. For other destinations, it is necessary to have a conveyance from the institute's executor.[13]

---

12   Family Law (Scotland) Act 2006, s 19.
13   S(S)A 1964, s 18. The distinction was introduced by a mistaken decision, *Bisset v Walker* 26 Nov 1799, FC. But mistakes can become law.

Special destinations and insolvency

29.22   If the institute dies insolvent, does the substitute take free of the creditors' rights? For example, title is held by Archie and Barbara and the survivor. Barbara dies insolvent. Archie can be required to pay the value of the half-share that he took from Barbara.[14]

Special destinations, joint property and liferents

29.23   Common ownership of X and Y with a survivorship destination is like joint property, in that if X dies, Y will normally be then the sole owner.[15] In fact, one decision held that they were the same.[16] But the two are in fact different.[17] For example a joint owner, unlike an owner in common, cannot grant a disposition of his or her share, and cannot raise an action of division and sale.

29.24   Common ownership of X and Y with a survivorship destination is also rather like a proper liferent.[18] If property is conveyed to X whom failing Y, that is a bit like a liferent to X and fee to Y. But in fact liferent is very different. In a proper liferent Y is the owner. By contrast, in the destination, Y is not only not the owner, but in fact has no real right at all. X is the owner, and is free to sell the property (thereby ending Y's hope of succession), or to grant subordinate real rights in it.

BACK TO DESTINATIONS-OVER

29.25   Tom leaves a house to Dick whom failing Harry. Take the following possibilities. When Tom dies:
   (a) Dick is alive but Harry is not. In that case Dick takes the house. End of story.
   (b) Harry is alive but Dick is not. In that case Harry takes the house. End of story.
   (c) Both are alive. Then Dick takes the house. *But the story may not end here.*

29.26   If the destination-over was a *conditional institution* then the story *does* end here. Dick takes the house and that is that. But if the destination-over was a *substitution* then the story does *not* end here. The destination-over is converted into a special destination. In other words, Tom's executor dispones 'to Dick whom failing to Harry'.

29.27   How does one know whether there is a conditional institution or a substitution? First, look at the wording of the testament. This may make it clear. If it does not, then one applies the legal presumptions. If the legacy is of heritage, the destination-over is

---

14   *Fleming's Tr v Fleming* 2000 SC 206.
15   See CHAPTER **9** above.
16   *Munro v Munro* 1972 SLT (Sh Ct) 6.
17   *Steele v Caldwell* 1979 SLT 228; *Smith v Mackintosh* 1989 SLT 148.
18   See PARA **21.16** above.

a substitution. If it is of moveables, or partly of heritage and partly of moveables, then it is a conditional institution.

29.28 Suppose that William leaves his house to 'Beth and Nicola and the survivor'. Beth and Nicola survive William. His executor dispones the house not to 'Beth and Nicola' but to 'Beth and Nicola and the survivor'. But if the legacy was of the house *and contents*, that would be a conditional institution (mixed heritable and moveable) so the disposition by the executor would be to 'Beth and Nicola'.

JUS AND *SPES*

29.29 The substitute is said to have a *spes successionis* (hope of succession) rather than a *jus* (right). If the substitute dies before the institute then the *spes* vanishes. It does not form part of the substitute's estate. It is said to 'fly off'.

TAILZIES (ENTAILS)

29.30 Scots law used to have a type of special destination called the 'tailzie' (also called the 'entail'). Here, the destination (a) operated perpetually and (b) prevented alienation *inter vivos*. It was thus much stronger than the ordinary special destination. For example, land could be tailzied to 'X and the heirs-male of his body'. That would mean that the land would descend to a chain of heirs until Doomsday. Each current owner's ownership would be so limited that it was, functionally speaking, rather like a liferent, for he could not alienate, so on his death the land would pass to the next heir as defined in the original deed of tailzie. Tailzies had to be registered in the Register of Tailzies.[19] The Entail Amendment Act 1848 made disentailment possible. After the Entail (Scotland) Act 1914 no new tailzies could be created. The Abolition of Feudal Tenure etc (Scotland) Act 2000 abolished the few remaining tailzies.[20] What was once an important aspect of property law has thus now disappeared.

NON-DESTINATIONS: BANK ACCOUNTS

29.31 Lastly, it is common for two people to have a joint bank account. Such accounts can take various forms, depending on the terms of the contract. But a common one is the 'either and survivor' account. Here, the bank pays out on the signature of either party. That continues to be so if one dies. Suppose that Darby and Joan have such an account. Darby dies. Joan can draw out from the account on her sole signature, just as she could when her husband was still alive. This looks like a survivorship destination. But it is not. The rule is that when he dies, she can withdraw all the money, but she cannot necessarily keep it. That depends on to what extent, as between her and her

---

19   Entail Act 1685.
20   AFT(S)A 2000, s 50.

husband, the money was his or hers. To the extent it was not, she must pay it to her husband's executor. On that issue the law is, unfortunately, not wholly clear, but it is probably (a) that if there was an agreement, that has effect; (b) if there was no agreement, then the money is divided accordingly to which party was the source;[21] (c) if neither (a) nor (b) can be established, the division is equal. (In practice she may end up getting the money anyway, as beneficiary of the estate.)

FURTHER READING

Gretton and Reid *Conveyancing* ch 23.

Hiram *Succession* paras 9.13–9.16 and 11.12–11.15.

Macdonald *Succession* paras 5.02–5.27 and 11.26–11.37.

---

[21]   *Cuthill v Burns* (1862) 24 D 849; *Dinwoodie's Exr v Carruther's Exr* (1895) 23 R 234; *Forrest-Hamilton's Tr v Forrest-Hamilton* 1970 SLT 338.

Chapter 30

Execution of documents

THE NEED FOR WRITING

Requirements of Writing (Scotland) Act 1995

30.1   In general, the law does not insist that transactions are set out in writing. For example, Penelope can buy groceries without entering into a written agreement for the transfer of the goods. Roger can hire Simona to mow his lawn without drawing up a contract of employment. Tamsyn can pledge her watch to Ulrika in security of a loan, once again without writing anything down.[1] In a limited number of cases, however, the law regards the transaction as significant enough to insist on writing. This has always been so. The current rules are in the Requirements of Writing (Scotland) Act 1995 (RoW(S)A 1995). (Although this changed the law in many ways, much of it is similar to or the same as the pre-1995 law.) As well as setting out the categories where a written document is mandatory, it also provides a set of rules stating how parties are to sign and, importantly, on what is required for a document to be *presumed* to be valid.

---

[1]   See **PARA 20.34** above.

The five categories where writing is required

30.2 RoW(S)A 1995 Act lists five categories where writing is mandatory. In all other situations, it is not.[2] But, of course, even in such cases the parties may *choose* to use writing, and usually will do so in important transactions. A £1m machine can be sold without writing, just as much as a £1 screwdriver. But in practice the contract would be in writing. The five categories are:

(a) A contract or unilateral obligation for the creation, transfer, variation or extinction of a real right in land[3]

30.3 This deals with documents which create personal rights, either under a contract or a promise (unilateral obligation), relating to real rights in land. The commonest example is a contract for the sale of land, i.e. 'missives'.[4] Missives are an agreement for the transfer of the real right of ownership in land in return for payment. A second example is an option. Bob Ltd grants Colin plc the option of buying a development site at any time within the next ten years. A third example is an agreement by a landowner to lease land to a prospective tenant. But writing is not needed if the real right to which the personal right relates is a lease of a year or less.[5]

(b) The creation, transfer, variation or extinction of a real right in land[6]

30.4 This provision deals with documents relating directly to the real right in question. A document that *creates* a real right is a 'deed of constitution'. Examples include a lease[7] and a standard security.[8] A document that *transfers* a real right is a 'deed of transmission'. Examples include a disposition,[9] which transfers ownership of land, and an assignation,[10] which transfers incorporeal property. Then there are deeds of 'variation', which neither transfer nor create a real right, but alter one, such as a minute of waiver,[11] under which a benefited proprietor varies the terms of a real burden. Finally there are 'deeds of extinction' such as a renunciation[12] of a lease or a discharge[13] of a standard security.

---

2   RoW(S)A 1995 s 1(1). But other legislation may require writing in specific cases.
3   RoW(S)A 1995, s 1(2)(a)(i).
4   See **PARA 5.2** above.
5   RoW(S)A 1995, s 1(7). See **PARA 19.8** above.
6   RoW(S)A 1995, s 1(2)(b).
7   See **CHAPTER 19** above.
8   See **PARAS 20.43–20.56** above.
9   See **PARA 5.8** above.
10   See **PARA 5.41** above.
11   See **PARA 13.59** above.
12   See **PARA 19.39** above.
13   See **PARA 20.56** above.

30.5   All the deeds just mentioned are *inter vivos*. This Latin term means 'between living persons'. Most of the deeds are unilateral, in the sense that *only* the granter has to sign. For example, in a disposition the seller signs, but the buyer does not have to and normally does not. The reason is that the deed places obligations on the granter not the grantee. This, however, is not entirely accurate. Unilateral deeds can place obligations on the grantee, for example a standard security places obligations on the creditor although he or she does not sign it.[14] In such cases, the grantee becomes bound by the obligations by accepting delivery of the deed.[15] Deeds which are signed by both parties are known as 'bilateral'. The most common example is a lease, which will be signed by both the landlord and the tenant.

(c)   Wills, testamentary trust dispositions and settlements, and codicils[16]

30.6   These documents provide how a person's estate is to be distributed on death. A 'testamentary trust disposition and settlement' is a sophisticated version of a will, requiring some or all of the estate to be held in trust for a certain period.[17] A 'codicil' is a document amending an existing will or testamentary trust disposition and settlement.[18] All of these can be described as *mortis causa* (on the occasion of death) deeds. This means that they take effect on the granter's death.

(d)   Gratuitous unilateral obligations, except in the course of a business[19]

30.7   Gratuitous unilateral obligations must be in writing. There is an exception where the promise is made in the course of a business. Thus if a bank's customer owes an obligation to a third party and the bank gives to that third party a guarantee that the obligation will be performed, no writing is required by RoW(S)A 1995. In practice, however, banks never grant guarantees gratuitously. The customer pays them a premium to do so. But as Professor MacQueen has said, 'a voluntary obligation is gratuitous when its beneficiary comes under no counterpart obligation'.[20] So if customer A asks bank B to give a guarantee to A's creditor C, the guarantee is gratuitous *in relation to* C. Writing is therefore still not needed. (In practice, however, writing would be used.) In contrast, if a wife guarantees her husband's business debts a document *is* required, because *she* is not acting in the course of a business.

---

[14]   In particular in relation to enforcement of the security. See paras **20.51–20.53** above.
[15]   See para **30.52** below.
[16]   RoW(S)A 1995, s 1(2)(c).
[17]   See para **27.1** above.
[18]   See para **27.7** above.
[19]   RoW(S)A 1995, s 1(2)(a)(ii).
[20]   H L MacQueen 'Constitution and Proof of Gratuitous Obligations' 1986 *SLT (News)* 1 at 2.

(e) Truster-as-trustee trusts[21]

30.8 Where persons declare themselves to be sole trustee of their own property or property to be subsequently acquired, the declaration must be in writing.[22] The policy is to protect third parties, in particular the person's creditors. In practice, almost all trusts are constituted in writing by means of a trust deed.[23]

Failure to use writing

30.9 Where writing is required but is not used, the basic rule is that the purported transaction is void. For example, an oral agreement to buy land is unenforceable. There is an exception, which applies to contracts, promises and trusts but not to deeds dealing with real rights.[24] The person who wants to deny that the obligation in question has been created may be *personally barred* from doing so as a result of the actings of the other party.[25] For the provisions to apply the other party must as a result of these actings have been affected to a material extent and if the obligation were not now to be enforced would be adversely affected, once again to a material extent.[26] The idea is that it would be unfair for the obligation not to be enforceable.[27]

FORMAL VALIDITY

Reasons for requiring writing

30.10 Why does the law insist on writing for certain significant transactions?
(1) The first reason is to provide evidence. The parties to the transfer of a piece of land which imposed real burdens in 1890 are no longer alive but the disposition which gave effect to it can still be examined. This leads to the second reason.
(2) Writing facilitates registration. The reason that the 1890 disposition can be inspected is that it is in the Sasine Register.
(3) The requirement for writing communicates to the parties the seriousness of the transaction being carried out. This is important for juridical acts such as creating or transferring real rights in land.
(4) Writing reduces the risk of fraud.

---

21   RoW(S)A 1995, s 1(2)(a)(iii).
22   See **PARA 22.42** above.
23   See **PARA 22.42** above.
24   For the exception see *Advice Centre for Mortgages Ltd v McNicoll* 2006 SLT 591, discussed by E Reid 'Personal Bar: Three Cases' (2006) 10 *Edin LR* 437 at 437–440.
25   RoW(S)A 1995, s 1(3)–(6). See generally, E C Reid and J W G Blackie *Personal Bar* (2006) ch 7.
26   RoW(S)A 1995, s 1(4). See *Caterline Ltd v Glasgow International Prestwick Airport Ltd* 2005 SLT 1083.
27   Reid and Blackie *Personal Bar* paras 7-21–7.33.

The role of notaries

30.11   In Scotland, the role of notaries public is more limited than in most other European countries. A notary acts as a state official[28] who supervises the execution of a deed and keeps a copy of it. In most European countries the conveyancing deeds require a notary. Here, few deeds require to be notarised.[29] The Scottish rules about execution of deeds are undemanding; some would say not demanding enough.[30]

The Books of Council and Session

30.12   In practice deeds that are not registered in the Land Register or Sasine Register are often registered in the Books of Council and Session or the sheriff court books. As with the notarial system, that ensures that an official copy can always be obtained, so accidental loss is not a concern, and like the notarial system, registration makes possible proof that a document existed by a certain date. Any probative deed can be registered, whether or not it contains a clause consenting to registration,[31] but such clauses are commonly found, and are necessary if the registration is not only for 'preservation' – which is what has just been described – but also for 'execution'. For example, at the end of most commercial leases the tenant consents to 'registration for preservation and execution'. If a deed is registered for execution that means that summary diligence can be carried, for example for unpaid rent, in other words diligence without the need for a court order.[32] It is good practice to register a will in the Books of Council and Session after the testator's death.

Formal validity: the one requirement

30.13   There is only one requirement for formal validity. The granter must subscribe the document.[33] In the case of contracts constituted by separate offer and acceptance documents, both must be subscribed.[34]

---

28   In Scotland, only solicitors may be notaries. The system is administered by the Law Society of Scotland, and notaries must holding a practising certificate. See the Legal Profession and Legal Aid (Scotland) Act 2007, s 62.

29   An example is a notice to preserve a real burden under TC(S)A 2003, s 50 and Sch 7. See **PARA 13.35** above.

30   See Gretton and Reid *Conveyancing* para 14-25.

31   RoW(S)A 1995, s 6(4).

32   See Gloag and Henderson *The Law of Scotland* para 49.01.

33   RoW(S)A 1995, s 2(1).

34   RoW(S)A 1995, s 2(2).

Meaning of 'subscription'

30.14   RoW(S)A 1995 defines 'subscription' as signing at the end of the last page of the document, excluding any annexations.[35] There is an exception for Her Majesty the Queen. She is entitled to 'superscribe' documents, that is to say, sign at the top.[36] Where there is more than one granter, only one of them needs to to sign at the foot of the final page. The other or others may sign on an additional blank sheet of paper.[37] The signature does not have to be legible.[38] But legibility will be needed for the document to be probative.[39]

Execution on behalf of someone else

30.15   A document can be signed on behalf of the granter by a mandatory or agent. In principle, the mandate or agency does not need to be constituted in writing. In practice, it is normally created by a probative deed called a 'power of attorney'.[40] For example, John, who works abroad, might appoint Kirsten, his solicitor, as his 'attorney'.

30.16   There is a special procedure for execution of documents where a person is blind or unable to write. It is sometimes called 'notarial execution'. This is misleading because there is no requirement for a notary. The document may be signed on the person's behalf by a solicitor who holds a practising certificate, an advocate, a justice of the peace or a sheriff clerk.[41] The granter must declare orally that he or she is blind or unable to write and the signatory must read out the document before signature, unless the granter states that this need not be done.[42] The document must be signed in the granter's presence.[43] Blind people are not obliged to use the procedure and can sign the document themselves.[44]

30.17   Where a granter is mentally incapable, an application will have to be made to the sheriff court for an intervention order or guardianship order under the Adults with Incapacity (Scotland) Act 2000.[45] The guardian or intervener may be given power to execute. Where, however, a continuing power of attorney was executed by the

---

[35]   RoW(S)A 1995, s 7(1). For annexations, see **PARA 30.46** below.

[36]   RoW(S)A 1995, s 13(1)(a)(i). Her Majesty's formal signature is 'Elizabeth R'. The 'R' stands for '*Regina*', the Latin for 'Queen'.

[37]   RoW(S)A 1995, s 7(3).

[38]   *Stirling Stuart v Stirling Crawfurd's Trs* (1885) 12 R 660.

[39]   On probativity, see **PARAS 30.25–30.44** below.

[40]   RoW(S)A 1995, s 12(2).

[41]   RoW(S)A 1995, s 9(1) and (6) and Sch 3.

[42]   RoW(S)A 1995, s 9(1).

[43]   RoW(S)A 1995, s 9(2).

[44]   RoW(S)A 1995, s 9(7).

[45]   Adults with Incapacity (Scotland) Act 2000, ss 53–79. Note also the Adult Support and Protection (Scotland) Act 2007. See A Ward *Adult Incapacity* (2003) ch 10 and Reid and Gretton *Conveyancing 2002* (2003) 100–111 (A J M Steven and A Barr).

granter under this legislation – that is a power of attorney which continues to have effect despite the granter's subsequent mental incapacity – the attorney may execute, assuming of the course that this power has been given.[46]

Methods of signing

Natural persons

30.18   There are three ways in which natural persons can subscribe.
(1) The first is to sign their surname and a forename (or initial or abbreviation or familiar form of forename).[47] This can be described as the 'standard method'. Examples are 'Thomas N Johnston', 'T N Johnston', 'T Johnston' and 'Tom Johnston'. The flexibility applies only to the forename.
(2) The second possibility is to sign the full name by which the granter is identified in the document.[48] This can be described as the 'longstop method'. An example would be 'Thomas Nelson Johnston'.
(3) The third and final possibility is to sign by means of any other name or description or initial or mark.[49] This can be described as the 'informal method'. Examples are 'Thomas', 'Tom', 'Johnston', 'T' or 'Dad'. In this case, however, the signature must either be the granter's normal method of signing the type of document in question, or be intended by the granter to be his or her signature.[50] Importantly, a deed *cannot* be probative if this method is used.[51]

Juristic persons

30.19   Juristic persons, of course, cannot write. Someone has to sign on their behalf. RoW(S)A 1995 sets out special rules in Schedule 2.

(A) PARTNERSHIPS

30.20   A signature of a partner or a person authorised to sign on behalf of the partnership is required.[52] Signatories can use their own name or that of the partnership itself.[53]

---

[46] For continuing powers of attorney, see the Adults with Incapacity (Scotland) Act 2000 ss 15–24.
[47] RoW(S)A 1995, s 7(2)(b).
[48] RoW(S)A 1995, s 7(2)(a).
[49] RoW(S)A 1995, s 7(2)(c).
[50] RoW(S)A 1995, s 7(2)(c)(i) and (ii).
[51] On probativity, see PARAS **30.25–30.44** below.
[52] RoW(S)A 1995, Sch 2, para 2(1).
[53] RoW(S)A 1995, Sch 2, para 2(2).

(B) COMPANIES

30.21 Either a director or the secretary or an authorised person may sign on behalf of the company.[54]

(C) LIMITED LIABILITY PARTNERSHIPS

30.22 Documents must be signed by a member of the LLP.[55] There is no provision for authorised persons, but there would nothing to stop the partnership granting a power of attorney in favour of such a person.

(D) LOCAL AUTHORITIES

30.23 The signature of the proper officer of the authority is needed.[56] This will be a person designated to carry out this function.

(E) OTHER BODIES CORPORATE

30.24 This is a residuary category and includes building societies, industrial and provident societies, trade unions, universities and foreign companies. The signature of a member of the governing board of the body (or a member of the body itself if there is no board), or the secretary, or an authorised person is required.[57]

PROBATIVITY

Definition

30.25 'Probative' is a word which has been given different meanings over the years and is in fact not used by RoW(S)A 1995. It is, nevertheless, a useful term to describe a document which complies with s 3 of the legislation. In other words, a 'probative' document is one which is *presumed to be validly executed.*

Probative versus improbative

30.26 The presumption of validity is one conferred by the law of evidence. It is particularly important where the document is the subject of litigation. Suppose that Cathy sues David on the basis of a probative document. She does not have to prove that the document was validly executed. The law presumes this. The onus is on David

---

[54] RoW(S)A 1995, Sch 2, para 3(1).
[55] RoW(S)A 1995, Sch 2, para 3A(1).
[56] RoW(S)A 1995, Sch 2, para 4(1).
[57] RoW(S)A 1995, Sch 2, paras 5(1) and (2).

if he claims that it is not validly executed. In contrast, if Martin sues Nicola on the basis of an improbative document, and she denies that the deed was validly executed, the onus falls on him. This may be an uphill or impossible task, particularly where the document is old. If Martin is unable to prove the matter, his case will fail.

Achieving probativity

30.27 A document that is subscribed under RoW(S)A 1995, s 2 is valid but not necessarily probative. To achieve probativity, more is required. Normally, the document must be witnessed. This is 'probativity by attestation'.[58] For certain juristic persons, there are other possibilities, involving additional signatures.[59]

Probativity by attestation

30.28 Under this rule, a document is made probative by obtaining a witness to the granter's subscription. There are three requirements. The first is that the document bears to have been subscribed by the granter.[60] However, only the standard or the longstop methods of signature may be used.[61] And because the document must *bear* to have been subscribed by the individual in question an illegible signature will not do either.

30.29 The second requirement is that the document bears to have been signed by a witness to the granter's signature and the name and address of the witness are given.[62] The legislation requires the witness to 'sign' rather than 'subscribe' but in practice the witness's signature is always added at the end of the document, beside that of the granter. The witness must sign using either the standard or longstop methods, just like the granter.[63] The same person may witness the signatures of more than one granter and if that is the case requires only to sign once.[64] It is crucial that the witness is designed by name and address. RoW(S)A 1995 allows this to be done in the deed itself or in the testing clause.[65] A 'testing clause' is a standard addition to most deeds following signing. It will usually give the date and place of execution, although this is not mandatory.[66] Indeed the testing clause itself is not compulsory, because the witness details could be given in the deed.

---

[58] See, PARAS **30.28–30.31** below.
[59] See PARAS **30.35–30.39** below.
[60] RoW(S)A 1995, s 3(1)(a).
[61] See PARA **30.18** above and RoW(S)A 1995, s 7(2)(c).
[62] RoW(S)A 1995, s 3(1)(b).
[63] RoW(S)A 1995, s 7(5).
[64] RoW(S)A 1995, s 7(5).
[65] RoW(S)A 1995, s 3(1)(b) and (4)(f).
[66] However, if given, this information will be presumed to be correct. See PARA **30.40** below.

30.30   Here is an example of a testing clause:

'IN WITNESS WHEREOF these presents typewritten on this and the preceding page are subscribed by me, the said Sydney John Legge at Aberdeen on Fifth July Two Thousand and Eight before this witness, Margaret Dutch of Two High Street, Elgin.'

The expression 'these presents' simply means 'this document'. The testing clause will be added after execution. A space is left for it, normally marked out in pencil. This means that, strictly speaking, the testing clause is not part of the deed itself.

30.31   The third requirement is a negative one. There must be nothing in the document or the testing clause which indicates that the document was not subscribed in the way which it bears to have been, nor anything to indicate that it was not validly witnessed.[67] RoW(S)A 1995 gives a list of requirements for the witnessing to be valid.

(1) The witness's signature must not be forged.[68]
(2) A granter of the deed cannot be a witness.[69] So, if there are two granters they cannot each witness the other's signature.
(3) The witness must know the granter, be 16 years old or over and be mentally capable of acting as a witness.[70] The legislation defines 'know' for these purposes as having 'credible information' as to the identity of the granter.[71] The granter and the witness can be acquaintances rather than close friends.
(4) The person who signed as witness must actually have witnessed the granter's subscription.[72] The legislation permits the witness either to be there as the granter subscribes or to have the subscription acknowledged to him or her at a later time.[73]
(5) The witness must sign after the granter has signed, or after the granter has acknowledged his or her signature and this must be 'one continuous process'.[74] RoW(S)A 1995 does not define 'one continuous process' but, in a case under earlier legislation, the court reluctantly said that a gap of 45 minutes was not too long.[75] The witness therefore should sign straight away. In acknowledgement cases, however, the witness could sign months or years after the granter's subscription provided that this was immediately after the acknowledgment of that subscription.

---

[67]   RoW(S)A 1995, s 3(1)(c).
[68]   RoW(S)A 1995, s 3(4)(a).
[69]   RoW(S)A 1995, s 3(4)(b).
[70]   RoW(S)A 1995, s 3(4)(c).
[71]   RoW(S)A 1995, s 3(5).
[72]   RoW(S)A 1995, s 3(4)(d).
[73]   Acknowledgement in principle should be by the granter saying 'this is my signature' or words to this effect but something less express may do. See *Lindsay v Milne* 1995 SLT 487 and *McLure v McLure's Exr* 1997 SLT 127.
[74]   RoW(S)A 1995, s 3(1)(e).
[75]   *Thomson v Clarkson's Trs* (1892) 20 R 59.

(6) The designation of the witness must be added before the document is founded on in court, or registered, and must not in any material respect have errors in it.[76]

Probativity is all about appearance

30.32   Probativity may be compared to the WAGs (wives and girlfriends) of some of our famous footballers – it is all about appearance. Whether a document is probative is determined by visual inspection. Either it looks valid or does not. For probativity, looks are everything. Recourse to extrinsic evidence is not permitted.[77] The judgment must be made by looking at the deed alone. And the judgment must be made. No sitting on the fence is permissible. There is no such thing as (as is often suggested in exam answers) a document which is presumed to be probative. Either it is probative or not. Of course if it is probative, it is presumed to be valid.

30.33   This means that if a fault in executing or witnessing cannot be determined by visual inspection, the document is still probative. A forged deed will be probative, unless the forgery is apparent, which is unlikely. A document that has been witnessed by a four year old is probative, unless the child's signature reveals that he or she is underage. This will be more likely the younger the child is. If the subscription and witnessing are not one continuous process, the document will still be probative, unless the gap in time is revealed on the face of the deed. This follows from the wording of RoW(S)A 1995, s 3(1): the document is probative if it *bears* to have been validly subscribed and witnessed.

Special rule for wills

30.34   There is an additional requirement to make testamentary documents such as wills probative. They must be signed on every sheet of paper comprising the document.[78] While what is strictly required is *signature* on *each sheet* rather than subscription, in practice the granter will sign at the bottom of *each page*. Therefore if both sides of the paper are used the granter will subscribe twice.

Probativity by other methods: juristic persons

30.35   Attestation is the only method of achieving probativity where the granter is a natural person or partnership.[79] In other cases, there is an alternative method.

---

[76]   RoW(S)A 1995, s 3(4)(f).
[77]   Extrinsic evidence can be used to challenge probativity but not to support it.
[78]   RoW(S)A 1995, s 3(2).
[79]   Except by making an application to the court. See PARA **30.44** below.

(a) Companies

30.36 The document may be subscribed by a second signatory. The three permitted combinations are:

(1) two directors;

(2) a director and the company secretary; or

(3) two authorised signatories.[80]

'Mixed doubles' – such as a director and an authorised signatory – are not allowed. This means that in total there are six ways in which a company can execute a document in a probative manner: the three mentioned already, as well as (4) a director plus a witness; (5) the secretary plus a witness; and (6) an authorised signatory plus a witness.

(b) Limited liability partnerships

30.37 The document may be subscribed by two members of the LLP.[81]

(c) Local authorities and other bodies corporate

30.38 Once the document is subscribed in accordance with the relevant requirements of RoW(S)A 1995,[82] it is sealed with the body's *common seal*.[83] This must be done by a person with authority on the same day as subscription.[84]

(d) Appearance again

30.39 Once again, with these alternative methods it is appearance that matters. Thus, for example, if it cannot be seen from the face of the document that the common seal was not attached by an authorised person then, even if this was the case, the document is probative.

Three presumptions

30.40 The probativity of a document generates three presumptions. The first and most important is that it is presumed to have been validly executed.[85] The idea is to give some protection against forgery. The point of requiring a witness etc is to make it harder for a fraudster to impersonate the granter. Compared with other countries which insist on notarial execution,[86] the level of protection is low, because the witness

---

[80]   RoW(S)A 1995, Sch 2, para 3(5).

[81]   RoW(S)A 1995, Sch 2, para 3A(5).

[82]   See PARAS **30.23** and **30.24** above.

[83]   RoW(S)A 1995, Sch 2, paras 4(5) and 5(5).

[84]   RoW(S)A 1995, Sch 2, paras 4(6) and 5(6).

[85]   RoW(S)A 1995, s 3(1).

[86]   See PARA **30.11** above.

can be complicit in the fraud, and indeed the fraudster can simply forge the signature of the 'witness' as well. Happily, such criminality is uncommon but certainly not unknown.[87] The second presumption is that the document was subscribed on the *date* stated in the document or testing clause.[88] It is not compulsory to give the date, but if this is done then this presumption applies. The third presumption is that it was subscribed at the *place* stated in the document or testing clause.[89] Again, it is not mandatory to state the place, but the presumption applies where this is done.

30.41   As evidential presumptions, they may be rebutted by evidence to the contrary. A probative document can be challenged in two ways.[90] The first ('direct attack') is to prove that the granter did not subscribe. A successful challenge will result in the document being declared void. The second way ('indirect attack') is to show that the attestation or equivalent was not properly carried out, for example because the witness was under age or the granter and witness did not subscribe in one continuous process.[91] A successful result is that the document is declared to be improbative and then the onus of proving valid execution is now on the person seeking to rely on it. That person may or may not be able to do so.

30.42   Probativity *only* concerns execution. The document may be invalid for other reasons, for example, it may be void from uncertainty or because the granter lacks legal capacity, or lacks title to grant it. Thus if John grants a deed transferring Jane's property it will be void because of the *nemo plus* rule.[92] Just because a deed is probative does not mean it is valid.

The benefits of probativity

30.43   A document may be subscribed under RoW(S)A 1995, s 2 or made probative by attestation (or the equivalents for juristic persons) under s 3. Making a document probative has the obvious benefit of presumed validity, which as mentioned previously, is particular important for older documents.[93] Documents prepared by solicitors will normally be in probative form. There are two further benefits to probativity. The first is that, subject to minor exceptions, only probative documents can be recorded in the Sasine Register or in the Books of Council and Session or sheriff court books.[94] In practice the same rule is applied in the Land Register.[95] The second benefit relates solely to testamentary documents. An executor is only able to obtain confirmation under a will or other testamentary document if it is probative.[96]

[87]   For an example, see *Kaur v Singh* 1999 SC 180.
[88]   RoW(S)A 1995, s 3(8).
[89]   RoW(S)A 1995, s 3(8).
[90]   See Gretton and Reid *Conveyancing* para 14-13.
[91]   See PARA **30.31** above.
[92]   See PARA **1.27** above. Of course, there are qualifications: for instance, John might be Jane's agent.
[93]   See PARA **30.10** above.
[94]   RoW(S)A 1995, s 6.
[95]   Gretton and Reid *Conveyancing* para 14-02.
[96]   S(S)A 1964, s 21A. See PARA **27.4** above.

Converting improbative documents into probative documents

30.44 It may be wished, or indeed required, for a document to be made probative some time after subscription. For example, registration or confirmation is sought. Here there are two possibilities.

(1) The granter is alive and available. In that case the granter may be asked to acknowledge his or her signature to a witness who then signs, thus achieving probativity by attestation.

(2) The granter is dead or otherwise unavailable, for example no longer has mental capacity. Here, an application can be made to the sheriff court to have the document endorsed by a certificate stating that it was subscribed by the granter.[97] It is necessary to provide evidence of valid subscription, but this may be done by means of an uncorroborated affidavit by someone who knows the granter's handwriting.[98]

ADDING TO THE DOCUMENT

Incorporation of earlier documents

30.45 Under the common law a document can incorporate by reference some or all of an earlier document. This is done to save repeating the terms of the earlier document in full. For example, in dispositions recorded in the Sasine Register the practice is to refer to the detailed description of the land in the break-off disposition.[99] There is in fact a statutory procedure for descriptions by reference.[100] The general common law procedure for incorporation has two requirements.

(1) The document must contain words of incorporation, for example 'but always with and under the burdens set out in [reference to deed imposing real burdens]'.

(2) The earlier document must be described in such a way that it can be identified. Therefore, if it has been registered the registration details should be given. The earlier document does not need to be signed or marked.

Annexations

30.46 It is common in practice to incorporate an annexation into a document, for example a plan describing land, or a schedule setting out a service charge provision in a lease.[101] Usually such annexations are physically attached, typically by a staple

---

[97] RoW(S)A 1995, s 4(1). For procedure, see Act of Sederunt (Requirements of Writing) 1996 (SI 1996/1534).

[98] RoW(S)A 1995, s 4(3).

[99] For break-off dispositions, see PARA **6.18** above.

[100] See the Conveyancing (Scotland) Act 1874, s 61.

[101] See PARA **19.41** above.

in the case of relatively brief documents. This, however, is not mandatory. It is competent to incorporate annexations at common law, but in practice the provisions in RoW(S)A 1995, s 8 are relied upon. The first requirement is that the document contain words of incorporation,[102] for example 'which subjects are shaded pink in the plan annexed and executed as relative hereto'. The second is that the annexation is identified on its face as being the annexation referred to in the document,[103] for example 'This is the plan referred to in the foregoing Disposition by Isabel Cook in favour of Alice Hay dated 22 June 2008'. The third and final requirement only applies where the annexation describes land. Here, if it is pictorial, that is to say 'a plan, drawing, photograph or other representation',[104] it must be signed on each page. If it merely describes the land in writing, it only needs to be signed on the last page.[105]

Alterations

30.47   After the document is completed, a mistake may be noticed that needs correction. This is less common nowadays with word processing, but still possible. RoW(S)A 1995,s 5 regulates alterations. An 'alteration' is defined as including 'interlineations, marginal addition, deletion, substitution, erasure or anything written on erasure'.[106] It is necessary to distinguish 'pre-subscription' and 'post-subscription' alterations. A pre-subscription alteration, that is one made before subscription, does form part of the document.[107] A post-subscription alteration, that is one made after subscription, does not unless the granter signs it.[108] Of course, it is usually impossible to tell when the alteration was made simply by looking at the document. Evidence may have to be led. But if the document is probative and there is a statement in the testing clause or the document itself that the alteration was added before subscription, that statement is *presumed* to be correct.[109] The onus then falls on the person asserting that the alteration was added later to prove this.

ELECTRONIC DOCUMENTS

30.48   Where the law requires formal writing,[110] this means a physical document (paper, parchment …) with a handwritten subscription by the granter. This may be changed in future to allow e-deeds that are e-signed. That change has indeed been

---

[102]   RoW(S)A 1995, s 8(1)(a).
[103]   RoW(S)A 1995, s 8(1)(b).
[104]   RoW(S)A 1995, s 8(1)(c)(i).
[105]   RoW(S)A 1995, s 8(1)(c)(ii).
[106]   RoW(S)A 1995, s 12(1).
[107]   RoW(S)A 1995, s 5(1)(a).
[108]   RoW(S)A 1995, s 5(1)(b).
[109]   RoW(S)A 1995, s 5(4) and (5).
[110]   See PARAS **30.2–30.8** above.

made but *only* for some conveyancing deeds, as part of the ARTL (Automated Registration of Title to Land) system. ARTL allows certain Land Register transactions to be carried out electronically.[111] (A deed is still needed, but it is an e-deed.) For formal validity of an ARTL deed there must be both a digital signature and the certification of that signature.[112] In practice most granters do not have the high-level security type of digital signature that is required, and so must sign through an agent, normally their solicitor, who acts for them under a probative mandate.[113] There are no further requirements to achieve probativity: the deed does not have to be witnessed[114]

EXECUTION UNDER THE PREVIOUS LAW

General

30.49   As mentioned,[115] probativity enables reliance on older documents. RoW(S)A 1995 is relatively new. It is therefore necessary to say a little about the previous law which applied before 1 August 1995. It distinguishes between 'attested' and 'holograph' documents.[116]

Attested documents

30.50   These are the broad equivalent of probative documents under RoW(S)A 1995, s 3. The law was regulated by a number of statutes of the old Scottish Parliament.[117] Prior to 29 November 1970, the granter had to subscribe the document on every sheet and after then only at the end of the last sheet, except for wills where the requirement to subscribe on every sheet continued.[118] There had to be *two* witnesses. The rules of attestation were almost the same as those under RoW(S)A 1995. A document which appears to be properly attested is probative. A crucial difference with the current law is that attestation confers not just probativity but also validity. For example, a disposition executed in 1990 with only witness is not only improbative but also invalidly executed. There was, however, a procedure by which minor errors, such as failure to sign on every sheet, could be cured by means of a court petition.[119] The result was to render the document valid but improbative.

---

[111]   See **PARA 6.26** above.
[112]   RoW(S)A 1995, s 2A. See R Rennie and S Brymer, *Conveyancing in the Electronic Age* (2008) ch 8.
[113]   RoW(S)A 1995, s 12(3).
[114]   RoW(S)A 1995, s 3A.
[115]   See **PARA 30.10** above.
[116]   See generally G L Gretton and K G C Reid *Conveyancing* (1993) ch 15.
[117]   The Subscription of Deeds Acts 1540, 1579 and 1681, and the Deeds Act 1696.
[118]   CFR(S)A 1970, s 44.
[119]   See the Conveyancing (Scotland) Act 1874, s 39.

Holograph documents

30.51 The broad equivalent of a document which has merely been subscribed under RoW(S)A 1995, s 2 is one which is 'holograph'. The common law governed such documents and required these to be subscribed by the granter. There were then two possibilities. They had either to be substantially in his or her own handwriting (for example an informal will) or executed with a handwritten docket comprising the words 'adopted as holograph'. Before 1995, missives would be signed by law firms using such a docket. Holograph documents are improbative.

DELIVERY OF DOCUMENTS

30.52 In general, a document is not effective unless it is delivered to the grantee. There may be some exceptions to this rule, such as deeds granted by parents in favour of their children, but they are open to question.[120]

FURTHER READING

Gretton and Reid *Conveyancing* ch 14.

McDonald *Conveyancing Manual* ch 2.

Reid, K G C *Requirements of Writing (Scotland) Act 1995* (Greens Annotated Statutes).

Rennie, R and Brymer, S *Conveyancing in the Electronic Age* (2008).

Rennie, R and Cusine, D J *The Requirements of Writing* (1995).

Scottish Law Commission *Report on Requirements of Writing* (Scot Law Com No 112, 1988).

---

[120] See McBryde *Contract* paras 4-44–4-69.

Chapter 31

Human rights

THE LEGISLATION

European Convention on Human Rights

31.1   In the aftermath of the Second World War, the Council of Europe was founded in 1949 by ten of the continent's nations as a means of preserving peace. Upholding human rights was a high priority for the new organisation. The European Convention for the Protection of Human Rights and Fundamental Freedoms (ECHR) was drawn up by the Council and entered into force in September 1953. It sets out a number of specific guaranteed rights. At the same time the European Court of Human Rights (ECtHR) in Strasbourg was established to hear and determine disputes about the application of the ECHR. A number of 'protocols' (add-on provisions) have since been added to the ECHR, adding further guaranteed rights. Since 1949, many countries have acceded to the ECHR.[1] Originally, the ECHR was binding on the United Kingdom simply as an international treaty. Indeed, it still is. Later, those who considered that their Convention rights had been breached could take a case against the United Kingdom to the ECtHR.[2] Such a case was not an appeal from the decisions of the domestic courts, but an entirely distinct action. And such cases are still competent.

Human Rights Act 1998

31.2   In 1998 the position changed: the ECHR was incorporated into domestic law by the Human Rights Act 1998 (HRA 1998), in force from 2000.[3] Convention rights can now be enforced in domestic courts, without the delay and expense of an application to Strasbourg. A court or tribunal is obliged to 'take into account' any relevant case law of the ECtHR when determining questions involving Convention rights.[4] Primary and subordinate Westminster legislation must be read and given effect to in a way which is compatible with Convention rights, but only 'so far as it is possible to do so'.[5] Where a court determines that such legislation is not capable of such interpretation, a 'declaration of incompatibility' may be made.[6] Public authorities, such as the Scottish Government, local authorities, courts and tribunals, must not act in a way which is incompatible with Convention rights.[7] Where there is a breach of Convention rights, the court 'may grant such relief or remedy, or make such order, within its powers as it considers just and appropriate'[8] including damages.

31.3   It is clear that Convention rights may be invoked against the state and other public authorities. This is known as 'vertical effect'. It is less certain whether they can be invoked in cases between private individuals, or other non-public persons, such as companies, in other words, whether there is 'horizontal effect'. This is important for property lawyers because many property disputes are between non-public parties. It appears that certain provisions of HRA 1998 have some horizontal effect. The requirement on the courts to interpret legislation in a Convention-compliant manner, as far as it is possible to do so, applies irrespective of whether a party to the case is a public body. Further, because a court is a 'public body' in terms of HRA 1998 it must act in a way which is Convention-compliant. This opens up the

---

[1]   See, generally, Lord Reed and J Murdoch *A Guide to Human Rights Law in Scotland* (2nd edn, 2008) ch 2. As of 2008, the ECHR applies in 47 states.

[2]   See *James v UK* (1986) 8 EHRR 123 for an example of a pre HRA 1998 case.

[3]   And also, in another way, by the Scotland Act 1998 (in force from 1999).

[4]   HRA 1998, s 2. Case law includes any judgments, decisions, declarations or advisory opinions of the ECtHR, as well as advisory opinions and decisions of the former European Commission on Human Rights and decisions of the Committee of Ministers of the Council of Europe.

[5]   HRA 1998, s 3(1).

[6]   HRA 1998, s 4.

[7]   HRA 1998, s 6.

[8]   HRA 1998, s 8.

possibility for parties to claim that a court failing to uphold a claim for a breach of a Convention right by one party against another would itself be acting in a manner incompatible with the Convention.[9]

Scotland Act 1998

31.4

'An Act of the Scottish Parliament is not law so far as any provision of the Act is outside the legislative competence of the Parliament. A provision is outside that competence so far as … it is incompatible with any of the Convention rights.'[10]

If successfully challenged, it is void.[11] The consequences of breaching Convention rights are thus more radical for the legislation of the Scottish Parliament than they are for that of the United Kingdom Parliament.

THE ECHR AND PROPERTY RIGHTS: PROTOCOL 1, ART 1

General

31.5 The ECHR as originally drafted did not protect property rights. This was added later as Art 1 of Protocol 1 to the Convention, which provides:

'Every natural or legal person is entitled to the peaceful enjoyment of his possessions. No one shall be deprived of his possessions except in the public interest and subject to the conditions provided for by law and by the general principles of international law.

The preceding provisions shall not, however, in any way impair the right of a State to enforce such laws as it deems necessary to control the use of property in accordance with the general interest or to secure the payment of taxes or other contributions or penalties.'

31.6 It is generally accepted that the article comprises three distinct rules.[12] The second sentence, on *deprivation,* and the third, on *control,* represent particular examples of state interference with the right enunciated in the first sentence. Thus if state action does not constitute deprivation or control, it may nevertheless violate the right to the peaceful enjoyment of possessions.[13]

---

[9]   See Lord Reed and J Murdoch *A Guide to Human Rights Law in Scotland* para 1.62 and A J M Steven 'Property Law and Human Rights' 2005 *JR* 293 at 295–297.

[10]   Scotland Act 1998, s 29(1).

[11]   Subject to s 102. For an example of an unsuccessful challenge, see *Adams v Advocate General* 2003 SC 171.

[12]   *Sporrong and Lönnroth v Sweden* (1983) 5 EHRR 35 at para 61.

[13]   See, e.g., *Loizidou v Turkey* (1996) 23 EHRR 513.

State deprivation of property

31.7 The second sentence of Protocol 1, Art 1 strikes principally at actions which result in extinction of a person's title to property.[14] Only formal and permanent deprivation by the state is therefore likely to be considered a violation. However, *de facto* appropriation is also within the ambit of Protocol 1, Art 1. This occurs where ownership remains with the affected party although the practical reality is that the retained title is rendered worthless.[15]

31.8 The protection afforded is not absolute. Deprivations are permissible in the 'public interest' but any state action must be in accordance with law.[16] States are also granted a 'margin of appreciation', i.e. a degree of flexibility, thus allowing divergence on issues where national authorities are deemed better placed to assess the requirements of their societies.[17] Although not expressed in Protocol 1, Art 1, proportionality has been added as an additional criterion, requiring a fair balance between the means employed and the result sought by any state action.[18] Finally, there is a presumption of a right to compensation for deprivation in all but exceptional circumstances.[19] In other words, if compensation is not paid there is likely to be a breach of Convention rights.

State control of property

31.9 The third sentence of Protocol 1, Art 1 deals with the situation where there is state interference with a person's right to property but no expropriation. Examples of state control include restricting the purposes for which land may be used,[20] imposing positive obligations on land owners[21] and restricting who may live in a particular property.[22]

31.10 Like deprivation, control is permissible only if certain requirements are met. There will be no violation of Protocol 1, Art 1 where the control is deemed necessary in accordance with the general interest or is required to secure the payment of taxes or other contributions or penalties.[23] States rarely have trouble convincing the Strasbourg Court that measures are in the general interest. It is considered not

---

[14] See, e.g., *James v UK* (1986) 8 EHRR 123 and *Lithgow v UK* (1986) 8 EHRR 329.
[15] See *Papamichalopoulos v Greece* (1993) 16 EHRR 440, where the inability of the applicants to sell, bequeath, grant security over, make a gift of, make use of or even obtain access to their properties was held to be a *de facto* expropriation.
[16] See Reed and Murdoch *A Guide to Human Rights Law in Scotland* paras 8.14–8.15.
[17] See Reed and Murdoch *A Guide to Human Rights Law in Scotland* paras 3.83–3.88.
[18] *James v UK* (1986) 8 EHRR 123 at para 50.
[19] See, e.g., *Pinnacle Meat Processors v UK* (Application 33298/96), 21 October 1998.
[20] *Pine Valley Developments v Ireland* (1991) 14 EHRR 319.
[21] *Denev v Sweden* (Application 12570/86) (1989) 59 DR 127.
[22] *Gillow v UK* (1989) 11 EHRR 335.
[23] 'General interest' for state control has been interpreted as akin to 'public interest' for state deprivation. See *James v UK* (1986) 8 EHRR 123 at para 43.

for European judges to determine the best solutions to national problems.[24] Again, there is a requirement that any state control must be in accordance with law. Greater leeway is given for margins of appreciation in control cases than for deprivations.[25] Proportionality is a factor that will be considered in determining the legitimacy of state control, though, in contrast to state deprivation, there is no presumption of compensation for control of property.[26]

What sort of property?

31.11   Protocol 1, Art 1 speaks vaguely of 'possessions' and 'property'. The ECtHR has construed the provisions broadly, to include, for example, money claims,[27] leases,[28] intellectual property rights,[29] liquor licences[30] and social security benefits.[31]

IMPACT OF PROTOCOL 1, ART 1 ON SCOTTISH PROPERTY LAW

General

31.12   The incorporation of the ECHR into national law under HRA 1998 has had a noticeable effect upon Scottish property law and will continue to do so.[32] Some areas where Convention rights have been considered are:

(1) real burdens;
(2) positive prescription; and
(3) diligence on the dependence.

(1) Real burdens

31.13   *Strathclyde Joint Police Board v The Elderslie Estates Ltd*[33] concerned the Lands Tribunal's powers of variation and extinction of real burdens.[34] The

24   Wide-ranging general interest justifications have been accepted: e.g. environmental protection in *Pine Valley Developments v Ireland* (1991) 14 EHRR 319 and combating alcohol abuse in *Tre Traktörer Aktiebolag v Sweden* (1989) 13 EHRR 309.
25   *Handyside v UK* (1976) 1 EHRR 737.
26   See D Anderson 'Compensation for Interference with Property' [1999] EHRLR 543 at 550.
27   *Stran Greek Refiners v Greece* (1994) 19 EHRR 293; *Pressos Campania Navra v Belgium* (1995) 21 EHRR 301.
28   *Mellacher v Austria* (1989) 12 EHRR 391.
29   *Lenzing v UK* (1999) EHRLR 132.
30   *Tre Traktörer Aktiebolag v Sweden* (1989) 13 EHRR 483.
31   *Gaygusuz v Austria* (1996) 23 EHRR 365; *Szrabjer v UK* (1998) EHRLR 230.
32   See generally A J M Steven 'Property Law and Human Rights' 2005 *JR* 293.
33   2002 SLT (Lands Tr) 2.
34   Now governed by TC(S)A 2003, ss 90–104. See **PARAS 13.71–13.73** above.

applicants in the case claimed that the right to extract a fee for a minute of waiver was a 'possession' in terms of Protocol 1, Art 1 and refusal by the Lands Tribunal to allow compensation[35] was therefore a 'deprivation' of that possession.[36] While the Lands Tribunal was willing to accept that the right to extract a fee for waiver was indeed a possession,[37] there was found to be no violation of the Convention. The statutory provisions at issue were deemed to pursue a legitimate aim in the public interest, namely removing the ability of a benefited proprietor to demand unreasonable sums from a burdened proprietor in exchange for discharging a burden.

(2) Positive prescription

31.14 *J A Pye (Oxford) Ltd v UK*[38] involved a challenge to the English law on adverse possession.[39] This is the broad equivalent of positive prescription under the Prescription and Limitation (Scotland) Act 1973 (PL(S)A 1973).[40] The European Court found the rules on adverse possession to contravene Protocol 1, Art 1. Parallels between the Scottish and English rules cast doubt upon whether positive prescription would stand up to similar challenge. The legislation both north and south of the border effectively extinguished the owner's title to the property, without compensation.

31.15 The case was subsequently heard by the Grand Chamber and the decision overturned.[41] The Grand Chamber considered that limitation periods pursue a legitimate aim in the general interest. Extinction of the owner's title following expiry of a relatively lengthy limitation period was deemed to be a proportionate measure and one that fell within the United Kingdom's margin of appreciation.[42]

(3) Diligence on the dependence

31.16 *Karl Construction Ltd v Palisade Properties plc*[43] concerned a challenge to the ECHR-compatibility of inhibition on the dependence. The law permitted this diligence to be carried out more or less automatically in favour of a creditor upon

---

[35] CFR(S)A 1970, s 1(4)(i).

[36] Before feudal abolition, the jurisdiction of the Lands Tribunal was governed by CFR(S)A 1970, ss 1 and 2.

[37] This decision is itself questionable in the light of *S v UK* (Application 10741/84) (1984) 41 DR 226.

[38] (2006) 43 EHRR 3. See also *Beaulane Properties Ltd v Palmer* [2006] Ch 79.

[39] The law has now been reformed by the Land Registration Act 2002, Sch 6, para 2. See Law Commission *Report on the Limitation of Actions* (2001) paras 4.126–4.135.

[40] See **PARAS 2.24–2.25** above.

[41] (2008) 46 EHRR 45.

[42] Due to the absence of compensation, the Grand Chamber also reclassified the case as one of state control rather than state deprivation. See Gretton 'Private Law and Human Rights' (2008) 12 *Edin LR* 109.

[43] 2002 SC 270.

raising an action for payment of a debt. The effect was to prevent the debtor disposing of land. Lord Drummond Young found that the automatic entitlement to this remedy violated Protocol 1, Art 1. The requirement for a judicial hearing before diligence on the dependence was introduced.[44] The later case of *Advocate General for Scotland v Taylor*[45] restricted the impact of *Karl Construction* by removing the need for an actual hearing. The law has since these cases undergone statutory reform, the new provisions ensuring, among other things, that the procedure should be ECHR-compatible.[46]

THE ECHR AND PROPERTY RIGHTS: OTHER RELEVANT ARTICLES

31.17 While Protocol 1, Art 1 deals specifically with property law, a number of other ECHR articles are relevant. Three are worth mentioning.

(1) Art 6, on the right to a fair trial in the determination of civil rights and obligations. The current land registration rules permitting the Keeper to alter title to land with no notice to the owner have come under scrutiny regarding compliance with Art 6.[47]

(2) Art 8 ensures respect for family and private life. The new access rights regime under the Land Reform (Scotland) Act 2003 was a likely candidate for Art 8 disputes but specific protection for the privacy of householders has helped to avert a challenge thus far.[48]

(3) Art 14, which ensures that Convention rights are enjoyed without discrimination, is relevant to all Convention rights.[49]

TRUSTS AND SUCCESSION

31.18 Little consideration appears to have been given to the issue of human rights within trusts and succession law. A couple of English cases concerning succession rights under the Housing Act 1980 have made their way to Strasbourg.[50] An

---

[44]   *Karl Construction* dealt with inhibition on the dependence. It was applied to arrestment on the dependence by *Fab-Tek Engineering Ltd v Carillion Construction Ltd* 2002 SLT (Sh Ct) 113.

[45]   2003 SLT 1340.

[46]   Bankruptcy and Diligence etc. (Scotland) Act 2007, Pt 6.

[47]   See Gretton 'Property Rights' in A Boyle, C Himsworth, H MacQueen and A Loux (eds) *Human Rights and Scots Law* (2002) 275 at 288–291 and Scottish Law Commission *Discussion Paper on Land Registration: Void and Voidable Titles* (2004) para 5.33. See also *Foster v Keeper of the Registers of Scotland* 2006 SLT 513.

[48]   Land Reform (Scotland) Act 2003, s 6(1)(b)(iv). See *Gloag v Perth and Kinross Council* 2007 SCLR 530 at paras 61–65. See PARA **18.6** above.

[49]   For discussion of Art 14 in the context of property law, see D Rook *Property Law and Human Rights* (2001) ch 6.

[50]   See *S v UK* (Application 11716/85) (1986) 47 DR 274 and *Fitzpatrick v Sterling Housing Association Ltd* [1999] 4 All ER 705.

unsuccessful challenge was made under Protocol 1, Art 1 and ECHR, Art 14 to the rules on inheritance tax which provide tax exemptions for spouses and civil partners, but not to cohabiting family members.[51] Human rights have been a concern in the reform of Scottish trust law, with certain proposals being dismissed due to their potential for challenge under Protocol 1, Art 1.[52] As yet, however, there appears to have been no Scottish case law on trusts or succession in which Convention rights have been invoked.

FURTHER READING

Gretton 'Property Rights' in A Boyle, C Himsworth, H MacQueen and A Loux (eds) *Human Rights and Scots Law* (2002) 275–292.

Reed, Lord and Murdoch, J *A Guide to Human Rights Law in Scotland* (2nd edn, 2008).

Rennie *Land Tenure* ch 16.

Rook, D *Property Law and Human Rights* (2001).

Springham, K 'Property Law' in Lord Reed (ed) *A Practical Guide to Human Rights Law in Scotland* (2001) 235–276.

Steven, A J M 'Property Law and Human Rights' 2005 *JR* 293.

---

[51] *Burden v UK* (Application 13378/05), 29 April 2008.
[52] For example, Scottish Law Commission *Report on Variation and Termination of Trusts* (2007) paras 5.12–5.15.

Appendix

The feudal system

FULL CIRCLE

A.1   There has been a full circle: from civilian ideas to feudal ideas, and from feudal ideas back to civilian ones. The Roman law distinguished private law from public law. Roman property law recognised no fundamental difference between moveables and immoveables. Where Roman lawyers saw distinction, medieval lawyers saw unity, and where Roman lawyers saw unity, medieval lawyers saw distinction. In the medieval worldview, public law and private law were merged. And immoveables were utterly different from moveables. Not only this, but the law of immoveable property was itself public law. In modern law we distinguish ownership (*dominium*) from sovereignty (*imperium*). So did Roman law. But in the medieval worldview, to have land was to have sovereignty, and to have sovereignty was to have land. This was the feudal vision.

HISTORY OF FEUDALISM: A ONE-MINUTE SUMMARY

A.2   Feudalism, in its earliest forms, originated in the Frankish empire and eventually spread over most of western Europe. (One exception was Scandinavia. This is why feudal law never fully extended to Orkney and Shetland, which until 1468 belonged to Norway.) Land was not owned. It was held by one person 'of' another person. Land law was relationship law. The 'vassal' held land of the 'superior' or 'lord'. They owed each other reciprocal duties. In some ways (not in all ways) it was like a mafia boss and his followers. Each owed the other loyalty, including a duty to fight. In giving land to his vassal, the lord increased his own power. The relation just described could be more than dyadic. The superior had an over-superior. There could be many links in the chain. At the top was the king, or, in the Holy Roman Empire, the Emperor. But the top was not the top. For king and Emperor were alike vassals of God. Each person in the chain was, to that extent, sovereign. He could and did hold courts in both civil and criminal matters. Indeed, the right of a feudal superior to hold courts was not finally abolished until feudalism itself was abolished in 2004. For *dominium* and *imperium* were one, and land was a relational concept: those on the land were the lord's subjects.

A.3   The decline of feudalism happened in different ways and at different speeds in different countries. Much had already faded by the end of the eighteenth century, when the hurricane of the French Revolution blew down the remains of feudal law over much of Europe. It survived in several parts of Germany till the 1850s, and in one or two until 1919. In England the decline began the earliest but dragged on the longest. There feudalism went into sharp decline as a result of the statute Quia Emptores (1290), which prohibited subinfeudation. Cromwell abolished most of what remained. A fragment called copyhold survived until 1925. Since then English law has no feudal characteristics left. But the Crown superiority, though now empty of content, has never been abolished there.

A.4   In Scotland the decline of feudalism was also prolonged. It was cut back little by little by a series of statutes beginning in the 15th century and continuing until recent times. By the late 20th century little was left, but the concept was by no means vacuous, as it was in England. The final abolition of feudalism on 28 November 2004, by virtue of the Abolition of Feudal Tenure etc (Scotland) Act 2000 was thus by no means a mere gesture. It genuinely changed the law.

THE FEUDAL CHAIN

A.5   The feudal system was, at least in its latter days, like a system of leases, sub-leases and sub-subleases. At the top was the Crown. Below the Crown were the Crown vassals, those holding directly of the Crown. Typically, these were peers. Then there were those at the next stage down, and so on. As one went down the chain, the units tended to become smaller. Thus the Earl of Cumbernauld might hold 10,000 hectares of the Crown. Under him might be three sub-vassals each holding 1,000 hectares. (The remaining 7,000 hectares here were held by the Earl without any sub-vassal.) These sub-vassals might have sub-sub-vassals for all or parts of their land, and so on. One might easily have a chain of half a dozen or even more. Figure A.1 gives the idea of the holding for a single plot of land of, say, a hectare.

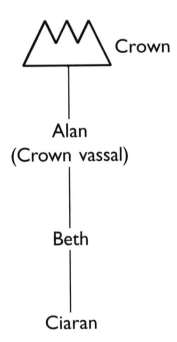

Ciaran is the Crown's sub-sub-vassal. But he is also Alan's sub-vassal and Beth's vassal. It is rather like child, grandchild, great-grandchild. Conversely, Beth is Ciaran's superior. Alan is Beth's superior, and is also Ciaran's over-superior. Ciaran's over-over-superior is the Crown. Each superior may have more than one vassal, rather as any parent may have more than one child. Thus while Ciaran holds one hectare of Beth, Donald might hold a neighbouring plot from her as well. In that case they are co-vassals.

THE TYPES OF TENURE

General

A.6 In a lease there is an annual payment due to the landlord. Likewise the vassal had obligations to the superior. This was called the 'reddendo'. It varied according to the type of 'tenure'. The following kinds existed.

(1) Wardholding

A.7 This was the pure ancient feudal tenure, because what the vassal had to give was, literally, military service. Since it was thought that women should not fight, a woman could not hold land on this tenure. It was abolished (and converted into feufarm) by the legislation passed following the 1745 Jacobite Rebellion.

(2) Mortification

A.8 Here, the vassal was the church and the service due was prayer, and especially prayer for the superior's soul. It disappeared as a result of the Reformation.[1]

(3) Burgage tenure

A.9 This was the tenure in burghs. It was feudal in name only. The land was held of the Crown, and only two links in the chain were possible: the Crown and the vassal. It was eventually merged into feufarm.

(4) Blench

A.10 Here, the reddendo was nominal, typically 'one penny Scots but only if asked for'.

(5) Feufarm

A.11 By the time that feudalism was finally abolished, this was the main tenure. Originally the reddendo could be money or goods, typically agricultural produce. This was the 'feuduty', for 'reddendo' was a general word and the reddendo for each tenure had its own terminology. Over time non-money feuduty was 'commuted' into money. Feuduty was payable twice a year, at the term-days of Whitsunday and Martinmas. Each reddendo was separate. Thus the reddendo due by Ciaran to Beth

---

[1] But the word lived on, with the meaning of 'charitable foundation'.

was quite independent of the reddendo due by Beth to Alan. Feuduty is sometimes regarded as an imposition by evil superiors. In reality it was a way that people could buy land even if they could not afford the full price. Nowadays such a buyer will typically borrow the amount needed from a financial institution. In the past such loans were harder to come by. Instead, the buyer and seller would agree that only part of the value of the property would be paid, and the balance would be represented by feuduty. For example, land worth £1,000 might be sold for £700 plus £15 per annum feuduty. The sale would be done by way of feu, making the seller the buyer's superior. The seller could then turn the feuduty into a lump sum by selling the superiority to someone else for a price of around £300.

DOMINIUM DIRECTUM, DOMINIUM UTILE, DOMINIUM EMINENS

A.12   Once upon a time, the words 'ownership' and 'feudal' could hardly occur in the same sentence. The system of real rights, revolving round the real right of ownership, applied to moveable property. But it did not apply to land. In the second half of the eleventh century, the study of Roman law began to revive, first of all in Italy. Lawyers were unhappy that feudal tenure did not fit in with civilian law. So they began to civilianise it. (Since feudalism did not arrive in Scotland until rather late, namely the twelfth century, this process was in fact already just beginning by the time that feudalism arrived here.) These new thinkers decided that there had to be ownership of land as well as of moveables, and they decided that ownership was shared between the various people in the feudal chain. The Latin word for ownership is *dominium*.[2] The new lawyers decided to call the ownership at the foot of the feudal chain (Ciaran) *dominium utile*. Each superiority was called, without distinction, a *dominium directum*.[3] Thus the Crown, Alan and Beth all have a *dominium directum* – but not the same *dominium directum*. The highest one was also called the *dominium eminens*.

A.13   This idea of shared ownership did not work well at the conceptual level: it was simply not possible for feudalism and civilian property law to be happy bedfellows. Some theorists argued that the system should be made coherent (i.e. coherent in civilian terms) by saying that only the person at the top had ownership, while everyone else had some sort of subordinate real right. But this view did not make much progress anywhere and was not accepted in Scotland. From a purely practical point of view, it would have been nearer the truth to say that the person at the foot of the chain – Ciaran – had ownership and that all the superiorities were mere subordinate real rights of some sort. Certainly, as time went on, superiorities

---

[2]   There is also another Latin word with the same meaning: *proprietas*.

[3]   Literally, these expressions mean 'useful ownership' and 'direct ownership' but that does not help much. Actually, the *utile/directum* distinction had its origins in procedural law, not in substantive property law.

slight significance, and in practice the person at the foot of the chain was simply called 'the owner'. But in theory shared ownership remained.

A.14   This initial civilianisation of feudal law led to further civilianisation. As feudalism declined, civilian ideas naturally came in to fill the gaps. By the time of the final abolition of the remains of the feudal system, land law was already predominantly civilian.

CASUALTIES AND IRRITANCIES

A.15   A casualty was a payment due to the superior on either the death of the vassal or on a transfer by the vassal. The abolition of casualties was begun by the Conveyancing (Scotland) Act 1874 and completed by the Feudal Casualties (Scotland) Act 1914. An irritancy was the forfeiture of a feu because of breach of the feudal terms, such as failure to pay feuduty. The idea is similar to the irritancy of a lease. Irritancy cut the chain. Suppose that Alan irritated because of Beth's breach. That would not only terminate Beth's right but Ciaran's too. Since the *dominium utile* is definitionally the foot of the chain, Alan would now have held the *dominium utile*. No compensation was due, so irritancy could mean a windfall gain.

A ME AND *DE ME*

A.16   Suppose that Ciaran wanted to transfer his right to Fiona. He could do this in either of two ways.
  (1) In the first place he could simply have disponed it to her. The result would be that Fiona would then be substituted for Ciaran as Beth's vassal. Ciaran would disappear from the feudal chain.
  (2) The alternative was that he could feu the land to her. He would remain Beth's vassal, and he would now be Fiona's superior. Fiona would be Beth's sub-vassal. This was called subinfeudation.
In the first case the deed used was the disposition. In the second case it was a feu disposition.[4] In a disposition the magic words were, then as now, 'do hereby dispone'. In the case of a feu disposition (etc.) the magic words were 'do hereby dispone in feufarm fee and heritage forever'.[5] Feu dispositions were much less common than dispositions. They were used only for special reasons. In particular, if the parties had agreed that real burdens were to be imposed, in general a feu disposition was used. More terminology: a feu disposition was a conveyance *de me*, meaning 'of me' because Fiona would hold 'of' Ciaran, he would be her superior. A disposition, by contrast, was a conveyance *a me*, meaning 'from me' or 'away from me'. That meant that Ciaran was divesting himself wholly.

---

[4]   Or feu charter, or feu contract: the three terms were, in substance, interchangeable.
[5]   It is being assumed that the tenure was feufarm. For other tenures, details would differ.

A.17   Just as Ciaran could dispone, or grant a security, so could Beth or Alan. Thus if Beth disponed her superiority to Peter, Peter would be Alan's vassal, and also the superior of Ciaran. This conveyance would necessarily be an *a me* conveyance, for only the person at the foot of the chain had the option of conveying either *a me* or *de me*.

At common law a conveyance *a me* required the superior's consent. Before 1500, means had been developed whereby the superior could be, so to speak, compelled to consent. But a deed from the superior remained necessary until 1874.

REAL BURDENS

A.18   Real burdens were perhaps the main reason why feudalism lasted so long. Although real burdens could be created non-feudally, over one property in favour of a neighbouring property, as in modern law, that fact was not well known and in any case there were technical drawbacks in doing it that way. If one wished to create a real burden the normal method was to feu. After the creation of feuduties was prohibited in 1974 (see below), the creation of real burdens was really the only reason for a seller to feu rather than to dispone. Moreover, the vast mass of existing feudal real burdens presented a hurdle for the final abolition of feudalism: if all superiorities were to be abolished, what would happen to all the existing feudal burdens? For the way in which the formidable technical problems were eventually overcome, see CHAPTER **13**.

'THE FEUDAL SYSTEM OF LAND TENURE ... IS ... ABOLISHED'

A.19   By the 1960s, feudalism was a mere shadow. A consensus emerged that what remained should be done away with. One obstacle was feuduty. In 1974 a statute was passed prohibiting the creation of new feuduties and providing a mechanism for the gradual redemption of existing ones.[6] But redemption did not extinguish the superiority. Moreover, land could still be feued, albeit without feuduty, and this continued to happen. It was not until 30 years later that the final step was taken. 'The feudal system of land tenure, that is to say the entire system whereby land is held by a vassal on perpetual tenure from a superior is, on the appointed day, abolished.'[7] The appointed day was 28 November 2004. All superiorities, including the ultimate superiority of the Crown, were extinguished, and so every *dominium utile* became simple ownership. Ownership of land is now like the ownership of moveables: ownership in the Roman sense.

---

[6]   Land Tenure Reform (Scotland) Act 1974.
[7]   AFT(S)A 2000, s 1.

FURTHER READING

Reid *Feudal Abolition* ch 1.
Reid *Property* paras 41–113 (Gretton).

INDEX